FUNDAMENTALS

OF

DATA STRUCTURES

IN C

SECOND EDITION

ELLIS HOROWITZ
University of Southern California

SARTAJ SAHNI
University of Florida

SUSAN ANDERSON-FREED
Illinois Wesleyan University

Universities Press

Fundamentals of Data Structures in C

Universities Press (India) Private Limited

Registered Office
3-6-747/1/A & 3-6-754/1, Himayatnagar, Hyderabad 500 029 (A.P.), India
Email: info@universitiespress.com

© 2008 Silicon Press
Published under licence from Silicon Press, Summit, NJ 07901 USA

First published in India by
Universities Press (India) Private Limited 2008
Reprinted 2008

ISBN 13: 978 81 7371 605 8
ISBN 10: 81 7371 605 6

Printed at
Orion Printers Private Limited
Hyderabad 500 004

Published by
Universities Press (India) Private Limited
3-6-747/1/A & 3-6-754/1, Himayatnagar, Hyderabad 500 029 (A.P.), India

PREFACE

Why *Fundamentals of Data Structures in C?* There are several answers. The first, and most important, is that C has become the main development language both on personal computers (PCs and Macs) as well as on UNIX-based workstations. Another reason is that the quality of C compilers and C programming development environments has improved to the point where it makes sense to provide instruction to beginners in a C environment. Finally, many of the concepts that need to be taught in the programming systems areas of computer science, such as virtual memory, file systems, automatic parser generators, lexical analyzers, networking, etc. are implemented in C. Thus, instructors are now teaching students C early in their academic life so that these concepts can be fully explored later on.

We have chosen to present our programs using ANSI C. ANSI C, adopted in 1983, has attempted to strengthen the C programming language by permitting a variety of features not allowed in earlier versions. Some of these features, such as typing information in the function header, improve readability as well as reliablity of programs.

For those instructors who have used other versions of the book *Fundamentals of Data Structures*, you will find that this book retains the in-depth discussion of the algorithms and computing time analyses. In addition we have attempted to preserve the chapter organization and the presentation style of the earlier book whenever it was desirable. But this has not kept us from making improvements. For example, pointers and dynamic memory allocation are introduced in Chapter 1 as these concepts are quite common in C. Error messages are written to *stderr*. Programs that use system function calls, such as *malloc*, check that they return successfully. However, to enhance program readability, we define macros such as *MALLOC* that both invoke *malloc* and do the checking. We use *exit(EXIT_FAILURE)* and *exit(EXIT_SUCCESS)* for normal and abnormal program termination. The discussion of strings is now found in the chapter on arrays.

Non-C related changes include the placement of exercises immediately after the relevant section. Exercises which have a section marker, §, next to the exercise number denote difficult exercises. Exercises which are suitable for programming projects are labeled as such. In addition, we have rearranged the sections in each chapter so that the basic material appears early in the chapter and the difficult or optional material appears at the end of the chapter.

One of the major new features in this book, compared to its earlier version, is the inclusion of abstract data types. The major idea is to separate out the issue of data type specification from implementation. Languages such as C++ and Java provide direct support for such a split, but in C there is no equivalent construct. Therefore, we have devised a straightforward notation in which we express an abstract data type. Basically, we provide a description of the objects of the type followed by the names and arguments of the functions of the type. Instructors can discuss with the students the specification of the data type before moving on to implementation issues and concerns for efficiency of the algorithms.

Over the past decade the field of data structures has not stood still, but has matured significantly. New and useful data structures have been devised and new forms of complexity measures have been introduced. In this new edition we attempt to keep up with these developments. For example, the implementation of polynomials, matrices, stacks, and queues using dynamic arrays and array doubling is discussed in Chapters 2 and 3 and the Bellman-Ford shortest paths algorithm has been added to Chapter 6. In Chapter 9, which is devoted to the study of priority queues, the sections on min-max heaps and deaps have been removed and new sections on pairing heaps, symmetric min-max heaps, and interval heaps added.

Chapter 10 of the first edition focused on search structures. This chapter has been replaced by 3 chapters. The new Chapter 10 is devoted solely to binary search structures and red-black trees now are introduced independent of 2-3 and 2-3-4 trees. Also, we have added a discussion on top-down spay trees, which perform better than bottom-up splay trees. In Chapter 11, which focuses on multiway search trees, we have added a section on B^+-trees. Chapter 12 includes the material on tries that used to be in Chapter 10. Because of the growing applications for tries, the discussion on tries has been enhanced significantly. Chapter 12 includes a new section on suffix trees and another on applications of tries to Internet packet forwarding.

Another issue treated more thoroughly in this edition is amortized complexity.

Most of the algorithms have their best, worst, and occasionally their average computing time analyzed. Amortized complexity considers how efficiently a sequence of operations is carried out. This form of complexity measure was popularized by R. Tarjan and in many cases it is a more accurate measure of a data structure's performance than the more traditional ones.

The URL http://www.cise.ufl.edu/~sahni/fdsc2ed contains useful material related to the content of this book.

USING THIS TEXT FOR A COURSE

For the instructor who intends to use this book and is teaching on a semester basis we present the following two possibilities, a medium pace and a rigorous pace. The medium pace is recommended when the course is for begining computer science majors, possibly their second or third course of the curriculum. Most people, including the authors, have taught according to the medium pace. The outline below corresponds to the curriculum recommended by the ACM.

SEMESTER SCHEDULE - MEDIUM PACE

Week	Subject	Reading Assignment
1	Intro. to Algorithms and Data Organization	Chapter 1
2	Arrays	Chapter 2
3	Arrays (strings)	First program due
4	Stacks and Queues	Chapter 3
5	Linked Lists (singly and doubly linked)	Chapter 4
6	Linked Lists	Second program due
7	Trees (basic facts, binary trees)	Chapter 5
8	Trees (search, heap)	
9	Mid Term	
10	Graphs (basic facts, representations)	Chapter 6
11	Graphs (shortest paths, spanning trees, topological sorting)	Third program due
12	Internal Sorting (insertion, quick, and merge)	Chapter 7
13	Internal Sorting (heap, radix)	Fourth program due
14	Hashing	Chapter 8
15	Selected Advanced Topics	Chapters 9-12
16	Selected Advanced Topics	Chapters 9-12

We recommend that several programming assignments be given, spaced somewhat evenly thoughout the semester. The aim of the first program is primarily to get the students familiar with the computing environment. The second program should emphasize list structures, as discussed in Chapter 4. There are several suggestions for projects at the end of the exercises of Chapter 4. One topic we have chosen to skip is external sorting. This leaves time to cover one of the most important of techniques, hashing. This topic is used in several courses later on in the curriculum, so it is important to cover it this semester. After hashing, we recommend that selected topics from Chapters 9-12 be covered.

The more rigorous pace would be appropriate when the book is used for a first year graduate course, or for an advanced undergraduate course. Our suggested outline follows.

SEMESTER SCHEDULE - RIGOROUS PACE

Week	Subject	Reading Assignment
1	Intro. to Algorithms and Data Organization	Chapter 1
2	Arrays	Chapter 2
3	Stacks and Queues	Chapter 3
		First program due
4	Linked Lists	Chapter 4
5	Trees	Chapter 5
6	Trees continued	Second program due
7	Mid Term	
8	Graphs	Chapter 6
9	Graphs continued	Third program due
10	Internal Sorting	Chapter 7
11	External Sorting	Chapter 7
12	Hashing	Chapter 8
13	Priority Queues (selected topics)	Chapter 9
		Fourth program due
14	Efficient Binary Search Trees (selected topics)	Chapter 10
15	Multiway Search Trees (selected topics)	Chapter 11
16	Digital Search Structures (selected topics)	Chapter 12

The programming assignments and midterm exam are paced exactly as in the medium case. However, the lectures proceed at a faster rate. For the rigorous pace, four weeks are allotted for Chapters 9-12. This allows the coverage of only a few topics selected from each chapter.

Finally we present a curriculum for an advanced Data Structures course. This presupposes that the student has already encountered the basic material, in particular the material on lists, trees, and graphs.

SEMESTER SCHEDULE - ADVANCED DATA STRUCTURES COURSE

Week	Subject	Reading Assignment
1	Review of Trees	Chapter 5
2	Review of Graphs	Chapter 6
3	External Sorting	Chapter 7
4	External Sorting (continued)	
5	Hashing (review basic hashing, Bloom filters, dynamic hashing)	Chapter 8 First program due
6	Priority Queues (leftist trees symmetric min-max heaps, interval heaps)	Chapter 9
7	Priority Queues (amortized complexity, binomial heaps)	Chapter 9
8	Priority Queues (Fibonacci heaps, pairing heaps)	Second program due
9	Efficient Binary Search Trees (optimal BSTs, AVL Trees)	Chapter 10
10	Mid Term	
11	Efficient Binary Search Trees (red-black trees, splay trees)	
12	Multiway Search Trees (B-trees, B+ trees)	Chapter 11
13	Digital Search Structures (digital search trees, binary tries, Patricia)	Chapter 12 Third program due
14	Multiway Tries	
15	Suffix Trees	Fourth program due
16	Tries and Internet Packet Forwarding	

For schools on the quarter system, the following two quarter sequence is possible. It assumes prior exposure to algorithm analysis and elementary data structures at the level obtained from an advanced programming course.

QUARTER 1

Week	Subject	Reading Assignment
1	Review of algorithms and arrays	Chapters 1-2
2	Stacks and Queues	Chapter 3
3	Linked Lists (stacks, queues, polynomials)	Chapter 4
4	Linked Lists	
5	Trees (traversal, set representation)	Chapter 5
		First program due
6	Trees (heaps, search)	
	Mid Term	
7	Graphs (traversal, components)	Chapter 6
8	Graphs (minimum spanning trees)	
9	Graphs (shortest paths)	Second program due
10	Graphs (activity networks)	

QUARTER 2

Week	Subject	Reading Assignment
1	Internal Sorting (insertion, quick, bound, $O(1)$ space merging, merge sort)	Chapter 7
2	Sorting (heap, radix, list, table)	
3	External Sorting	Chapter 7
4	Hashing	Chapter 8
5	Mid Term	First program due
6	Priority Queues (Leftist Trees, Symmetric Min-Max heaps, Interval Heaps)	Chapter 9
7	Priority Queues (Amortized Complexity, Binomial and Fibonacci Heaps)	Chapter 9
8	Efficient Binary Search Trees (AVL or Red-black trees, Splay trees)	Chapter 10
9	Multiway Search Trees (B-Trees, B+ Trees)	Second program due
		Chapter 11
10	Digital Search structures (Tries, Suffix Trees)	Chapter 12

Once again we would like to thank the people who assisted us in preparing the first edition of this book. Thanks go to Professor Lisa Brown, Illinois Wesleyan University, and the students in her Programming III class, as well as to Dr. Dinesh Mehta, Colorado School of Mines, for their assistance in the debugging of the first edition of this book, and to Trey Short and Curtis Kelch of the Computer Services staff at Illinois Wesleyan

University for providing technical assistance. Thanks also to Narain Gehani, AT&T Bell Laboratories, Tomasz Müldner, Arcadia University, and Ronald Prather, Trinity University, who reviewed early drafts of the manuscript. Special thanks go to Barbara and Art Friedman, our first publishers who nurtured the book through its early years.

Ellis Horowitz
Sartaj Sahni
Susan Anderson-Freed
June 2007

Contents

CHAPTER 1

BASIC CONCEPTS

1.1 OVERVIEW: SYSTEM LIFE CYCLE

We assume that our readers have a strong background in structured programming, typically attained through the completion of an elementary programming course. Such an initial course usually emphasizes mastering a programming language's syntax (its grammar rules) and applying this language to the solution of several relatively small problems. These problems are frequently chosen so that they use a particular language construct. For example, the programming problem might require the use of arrays or **while** loops.

In this text we want to move you beyond these rudiments by providing you with the tools and techniques necessary to design and implement large-scale computer systems. We believe that a solid foundation in data abstraction, algorithm specification, and performance analysis and measurement provides the necessary methodology. In this chapter, we will discuss each of these areas in detail. We also will briefly discuss recursive programming because many of you probably have only a fleeting acquaintance with this important technique. However, before we begin we want to place these tools in a context that views programming as more than writing code. Good programmers regard

1

large-scale computer programs as systems that contain many complex interacting parts. As systems, these programs undergo a development process called the system life cycle. We consider this cycle as consisting of requirements, analysis, design, coding, and verification phases. Although we will consider them separately, these phases are highly interrelated and follow only a very crude sequential time frame. The Selected Readings and References section lists several sources on the system life cycle and its various phases that will provide you with additional information.

(1) Requirements. All large programming projects begin with a set of specifications that define the purpose of the project. These requirements describe the information that we, the programmers, are given (input) and the results that we must produce (output). Frequently the initial specifications are defined vaguely, and we must develop rigorous input and output descriptions that include all cases.

(2) Analysis. After we have delineated carefully the system's requirements, the analysis phase begins in earnest. In this phase, we begin to break the problem down into manageable pieces. There are two approaches to analysis: bottom-up and top-down. The bottom-up approach is an older, unstructured strategy that places an early emphasis on the coding fine points. Since the programmer does not have a master plan for the project, the resulting program frequently has many loosely connected, error-ridden segments. Bottom-up analysis is akin to constructing a building from a generic blueprint. That is, we view all buildings identically; they must have walls, a roof, plumbing, and heating. The specific purpose to which the building will be put is irrelevant from this perspective. Although few of us would want to live in a home constructed using this technique, many programmers, particularly beginning ones, believe that they can create good, error-free programs without prior planning.

In contrast, the top-down approach begins with the purpose that the program will serve and uses this end product to divide the program into manageable segments. This technique generates diagrams that are used to design the system. Frequently, several alternate solutions to the programming problem are developed and compared during this phase.

(3) Design. This phase continues the work done in the analysis phase. The designer approaches the system from the perspectives of both the data objects that the program needs and the operations performed on them. The first perspective leads to the creation of abstract data types, while the second requires the specification of algorithms and a consideration of algorithm design strategies. For example, suppose that we are designing a scheduling system for a university. Typical data objects might include students, courses, and professors. Typical operations might include inserting, removing, and searching within each object or between them. That is, we might want to add a course to the list of university courses, or search for the courses taught by some professor.

Since the abstract data types and the algorithm specifications are language-independent, we postpone implementation decisions. Although we must specify the information required for each data object, we ignore coding details. For example, we might decide that the student data object should include name, social security number, major, and phone number. However, we would not yet pick a specific implementation for the list of students. As we will see in later chapters, there are several possibilities including arrays, linked lists, or trees. By deferring implementation issues as long as possible, we not only create a system that could be written in several programming languages, but we also have time to pick the most efficient implementations within our chosen language.

(4) Refinement and coding. In this phase, we choose representations for our data objects and write algorithms for each operation on them. The order in which we do this is crucial because a data object's representation can determine the efficiency of the algorithms related to it. Typically this means that we should write those algorithms that are independent of the data objects first.

Frequently at this point we realize that we could have created a much better system. Perhaps we have spoken with a friend who has worked on a similar project, or we realize that one of our alternate designs is superior. If our original design is good, it can absorb changes easily. In fact, this is a reason for avoiding an early commitment to coding details. If we must scrap our work entirely, we can take comfort in the fact that we will be able to write the new system more quickly and with fewer errors.

(5) Verification. This phase consists of developing correctness proofs for the program, testing the program with a variety of input data, and removing errors. Each of these areas has been researched extensively, and a complete discussion is beyond the scope of this text. However, we want to summarize briefly the important aspects of each area.

Correctness proofs: Programs can be proven correct using the same techniques that abound in mathematics. Unfortunately, these proofs are very time-consuming, and difficult to develop for large projects. Frequently scheduling constraints prevent the development of a complete set of proofs for a large system. However, selecting algorithms that have been proven correct can reduce the number of errors. In this text, we will provide you with an arsenal of algorithms, some of which have been proven correct using formal techniques, that you may apply to many programming problems.

Testing: We can construct our correctness proofs before and during the coding phase since our algorithms need not be written in a specific programming language. Testing, however, requires the working code and sets of test data. This data should be developed carefully so that it includes all possible scenarios. Frequently beginning programmers assume that if their program ran without producing a syntax error, it must be correct. Little thought is given to the input data, and usually only one set of data is used. Good test data should verify that every piece of code runs correctly. For example, if our program contains a **switch** statement, our test data should be chosen so that we can check each **case** within the **switch** statement.

Initial system tests focus on verifying that a program runs correctly. While this is a crucial concern, a program's running time is also important. An error-free program that runs slowly is of little value. Theoretical estimates of running time exist for many algorithms and we will derive these estimates as we introduce new algorithms. In addition, we may want to gather performance estimates for portions of our code. Constructing these timing tests is also a topic that we pursue later in this chapter.

Error removal. If done properly, the correctness proofs and system tests will indicate erroneous code. The ease with which we can remove these errors depends on the design and coding decisions made earlier. A large undocumented program written in "spaghetti" code is a programmer's nightmare. When debugging such programs, each corrected error possibly generates several new errors. On the other hand, debugging a well-documented program that is divided into autonomous units that interact through parameters is far easier. This is especially true if each unit is tested separately and then integrated into the system.

1.2   POINTERS AND DYNAMIC MEMORY ALLOCATION

1.2.1   Pointers

Pointers are fundamental to C and C provides extensive support for them. Actually, for any type T in C there is a corresponding type pointer-to-T. The actual value of a pointer type is an address of memory. The two most important operators used with the pointer type are:

- & the address operator
- * the dereferencing (or indirection) operator

If we have the declaration:

```
int i, *pi;
```

then *i* is an integer variable and *pi* is a pointer to an integer. If we say:

```
pi = &i;
```

then &*i* returns the address of *i* and assigns it as the value of *pi*. To assign a value to *i* we can say:

or
```
                    i = 10;

                    *pi = 10;
```

In both cases the integer 10 is stored as the value of *i*. In the second case, the * in front of the pointer *pi* causes it to be dereferenced, by which we mean that instead of storing 10 into the pointer, 10 is stored into the location pointed at by the pointer *pi*.

There are other operations we can do on pointers. We may assign a pointer to a variable of type pointer. Since a pointer is just a nonnegative integer number, C allows us to perform arithmetic operations such as addition, subtraction, multiplication, and division, on pointers. We also can determine if one pointer is greater than, less than, or equal to another, and we can convert pointers explicitly to integers.

The size of a pointer can be different on different computers. In some cases the size of a pointer on a computer can vary. For example, the size of a pointer to a **char** can be longer than a pointer to a **float**. C has a special value that it treats as a null pointer. The null pointer points to no object or function. Typically the null pointer is represented by the integer 0. The C macro *NULL* is defined to be this constant. The null pointer can be used in relational expressions, where it is interpreted as false. Therefore, to test for the null pointer in C we can say:

```
                    if (pi == NULL)
```
or more simply:
```
                    if (!pi)
```

1.2.2   Dynamic Memory Allocation

In your program you may wish to acquire space in which you will store information. When you write your program you may not know how much space you will need (for example, the size of an array may depend on an input to the program), nor do you wish to allocate some very large area that may never be required. To solve this problem C provides a mechanism, called a *heap*, for allocating storage at run-time. Whenever you need a new area of memory, you may call a function, *malloc*, and request the amount you need. If the memory is available, a pointer to the start of an area of memory of the required size is returned. When the requested memory is not available, the pointer *NULL* is returned. At a later time when you no longer need an area of memory, you may free it by calling another function, *free*, and return the area of memory to the system. Once an area of memory is freed, it is improper to use it. Program 1.1 shows how we might allocate and deallocate storage to pointer variables.

The call to *malloc* includes a parameter that determines the size of storage required to hold the **int** or the **float**. The result is a pointer to the first byte of a storage area of the proper size. The type of the result can vary. On some systems the result of *malloc* is a **char ***, a pointer to a **char**. However, those who use ANSI C will find that

```
int i, *pi;
float f, *pf;
pi = (int *) malloc(sizeof(int));
pf = (float *) malloc(sizeof(float));
*pi = 1024;
*pf = 3.14;
printf("an integer = %d, a float = %f\n", *pi, *pf);
free(pi);
free(pf);
```

Program 1.1: Allocation and deallocation of memory

the result is **void ***. The notation (*int **) and (*float **) are *type cast* expressions, which may be omitted in Program 1.1. They transform the resulting pointer into a pointer to the correct type. The pointer is then assigned to the proper pointer variable. The *free* function deallocates an area of memory previously allocated by *malloc*. In some versions of C, *free* expects an argument that is a **char ***, while ANSI C expects **void ***. However, the casting of the argument is generally omitted in the call to *free*.

Since there is the possibilty that a call to *malloc* may fail for lack of sufficient memory, we can write a more robust version of Program Program 1.1 by replacing the lines of code that invoke *malloc* by the code

```
if ((pi = (int *) malloc(sizeof(int))) == NULL ||
    (pf = (float *) malloc(sizeof(float))) == NULL)
{fprintf(stderr, "Insufficient memory");
 exit(EXIT_FAILURE);
}
```

or by the equivalent code

```
if (!(pi = malloc(sizeof(int))) ||
    !(pf = malloc(sizeof(float))))
{fprintf(stderr, "Insufficient memory");
 exit(EXIT_FAILURE);
}
```

Since *malloc* may be invoked from several places in your program, it is often convenient to define a macro that invokes *malloc* and exits when *malloc* fails. A possible macro definition is:

```
#define MALLOC(p,s) \
   if (!((p) = malloc(s))) {\
      fprintf(stderr, "Insufficient memory"); \
      exit(EXIT_FAILURE);\
   }
```

Now, the two lines of Program 1.1 that invoke *malloc* may be replaced by the code

```
MALLOC(pi, sizeof(int));
MALLOC(pf, sizeof(float));
```

In Program 1.1 if we insert the line:

```
pf = (float *) malloc(sizeof(float));
```

immediately after the *printf* statement, then the pointer to the storage used to hold the value 3.14 has disappeared. Now there is no way to retrieve this storage. This is an example of a *dangling reference*. Whenever all pointers to a dynamically allocated area of storage are lost, the storage is lost to the program. As we examine programs that make use of pointers and dynamic storage, we will make it a point to always return storage after we no longer need it.

1.2.3   Pointers Can Be Dangerous

When programming in C, it is a wise practice to set all pointers to *NULL* when they are not actually pointing to an object. This makes it less likely that you will attempt to access an area of memory that is either out of range of your program or that does not contain a pointer reference to a legitimate object. On some computers, it is possible to dereference the null pointer and the result is *NULL*, permitting execution to continue. On other computers, the result is whatever the bits are in location zero, often producing a serious error.

Another wise programming tactic is to use explicit **type casts** when converting between pointer types. For example:

```
pi = malloc(sizeof(int));
    /* assign to pi a pointer to int */
pf = (float *) pi;
    /* casts an int pointer to a float pointer */
```

Another area of concern is that in many systems, pointers have the same size as type **int**. Since **int** is the default type specifier, some programmers omit the return type when defining a function. The return type defaults to **int** which can later be interpreted as a pointer. This has proven to be a dangerous practice on some computers and the programmer is urged to define explicit return types for functions.

1.3   ALGORITHM SPECIFICATION

1.3.1   Introduction

The concept of an algorithm is fundamental to computer science. Algorithms exist for many common problems, and designing efficient algorithms plays a crucial role in developing large-scale computer systems. Therefore, before we proceed further we need to discuss this concept more fully. We begin with a definition.

Definition: An *algorithm* is a finite set of instructions that, if followed, accomplishes a particular task. In addition, all algorithms must satisfy the following criteria:

(1)   **Input.** There are zero or more quantities that are externally supplied.

(2)   **Output.** At least one quantity is produced.

(3)   **Definiteness.** Each instruction is clear and unambiguous.

(4)   **Finiteness.** If we trace out the instructions of an algorithm, then for all cases, the algorithm terminates after a finite number of steps.

(5)   **Effectiveness.** Every instruction must be basic enough to be carried out, in principle, by a person using only pencil and paper. It is not enough that each operation be definite as in (3); it also must be feasible. □

In computational theory, one distinguishes between an algorithm and a program, the latter of which does not have to satisfy the fourth condition. For example, we can think of an operating system that continues in a *wait* loop until more jobs are entered. Such a program does not terminate unless the system crashes. Since our programs will always terminate, we will use algorithm and program interchangeably in this text.

We can describe an algorithm in many ways. We can use a natural language like English, although, if we select this option, we must make sure that the resulting instructions are definite. Graphic representations called flowcharts are another possibility, but they work well only if the algorithm is small and simple. In this text we will present most of our algorithms in C, occasionally resorting to a combination of English and C for our specifications. Two examples should help to illustrate the process of translating a problem into an algorithm.

Example 1.1 [*Selection sort*]: Suppose we must devise a program that sorts a set of $n \geq 1$ integers. A simple solution is given by the following:

From those integers that are currently unsorted, find the smallest and place it next in the sorted list.

Although this statement adequately describes the sorting problem, it is not an algorithm since it leaves several unanswered questions. For example, it does not tell us where and how the integers are initially stored, or where we should place the result. We assume that the integers are stored in an array, *list*, such that the ith integer is stored in the ith position, *list* [i], $0 \leq i < n$. Program 1.2 is our first attempt at deriving a solution. Notice that it is written partially in C and partially in English.

```
for (i = 0; i < n; i++) {
  Examine list[i] to list[n-1] and suppose that the
  smallest integer is  at list[min];

  Interchange list[i] and list[min];
}
```

Program 1.2: Selection sort algorithm

To turn Program 1.2 into a real C program, two clearly defined subtasks remain: finding the smallest integer and interchanging it with *list* [i]. We can solve the latter problem using either a function (Program 1.3) or a macro.

```
void swap(int *x, int *y)
{/* both parameters are pointers to ints */
    int temp = *x;   /* declares temp as an int and assigns
                to it the contents of what x points to */
    *x = *y; /* stores what y points to into the location
                where x points */
    *y = temp; /* places the contents of temp in location
                pointed to by y */
}
```

Program 1.3: Swap function

Using the function, suppose *a* and *b* are declared as **int**s. To swap their values one would say:

```
swap(&a, &b);
```

passing to *swap* the addresses of *a* and *b*. The macro version of swap is:

```
#define SWAP(x,y,t) ((t) = (x), (x) = (y), (y) = (t))
```

The function's code is easier to read than that of the macro but the macro works with any data type.

We can solve the first subtask by assuming that the minimum is *list*[i], checking *list*[i] with *list*[$i+1$], *list*[$i+2$], $\cdots$, *list*[$n-1$]. Whenever we find a smaller number we make it the new minimum. When we reach *list*[$n-1$] we are finished. Putting all these observations together gives us *sort* (Program 1.4). Program 1.4 contains a complete program which you may run on your computer. The program uses the *rand* function defined in *math.h* to randomly generate a list of numbers which are then passed into *sort*. At this point, we should ask if this function works correctly.

Theorem 1.1: Function *sort*(*list*,*n*) correctly sorts a set of $n \geq 1$ integers. The result remains in *list*[0], $\cdots$, *list*[$n-1$] such that *list*[0] $\leq$ *list*[1] $\leq \cdots \leq$ *list*[$n-1$].

Proof: When the outer **for** loop completes its iteration for $i = q$, we have *list*[q] $\leq$ *list*[r], $q < r < n$. Further, on subsequent iterations, $i > q$ and *list*[0] through *list*[q] are unchanged. Hence following the last iteration of the outer **for** loop (i.e., $i = n - 2$), we have *list*[0] $\leq$ *list*[1] $\leq \cdots \leq$ *list*[$n-1$]. $\square$

Example 1.2 [*Binary search*]: Assume that we have $n \geq 1$ distinct integers that are already sorted and stored in the array *list*. That is, *list*[0] $\leq$ *list*[1] $\leq \cdots \leq$ *list*[$n-1$]. We must figure out if an integer *searchnum* is in this list. If it is we should return an index, i, such that *list*[i] = *searchnum*. If *searchnum* is not present, we should return -1. Since the list is sorted we may use the following method to search for the value.

Let *left* and *right*, respectively, denote the left and right ends of the list to be searched. Initially, *left* = 0 and *right* = $n-1$. Let *middle* = (*left*+*right*)/2 be the middle position in the list. If we compare *list*[*middle*] with *searchnum*, we obtain one of three results:

(1) **searchnum < list[middle].** In this case, if *searchnum* is present, it must be in the positions between 0 and *middle* $- 1$. Therefore, we set *right* to *middle* $- 1$.

(2) **searchnum = list[middle].** In this case, we return *middle*.

(3) **searchnum > list[middle].** In this case, if *searchnum* is present, it must be in the positions between *middle* $+ 1$ and $n - 1$. So, we set *left* to *middle* $+ 1$.

```
#include <stdio.h>
#include <math.h>
#define MAX_SIZE 101
#define SWAP(x,y,t) ((t) = (x), (x)= (y), (y) = (t))
void sort(int [],int); /*selection sort */
void main(void)
{
   int i,n;
   int list[MAX_SIZE];
   printf("Enter the number of numbers to generate: ");
   scanf("%d",&n);
   if( n < 1 || n > MAX_SIZE) {
     fprintf(stderr, "Improper value of n\n");
     exit(EXIT_FAILURE);
   }
   for (i = 0; i < n; i++) {/*randomly generate numbers*/
     list[i] = rand() % 1000;
     printf("%d  ",list[i]);
   }
   sort(list,n);
   printf("\n Sorted array:\n ");
   for (i = 0; i < n; i++) /* print out sorted numbers */
     printf("%d  ",list[i]);
   printf("\n");
}
void sort(int list[],int n)
{
   int i, j, min, temp;
   for (i = 0; i < n-1; i++)   {
     min = i;
     for (j = i+1; j < n; j++)
        if (list[j] < list[min])
           min = j;
     SWAP(list[i],list[min],temp);
   }
}
```

Program 1.4: Selection sort

If *searchnum* has not been found and there are still integers to check, we recalculate *middle* and continue the search. Program 1.5 implements this searching strategy. The algorithm contains two subtasks: (1) determining if there are any integers left to check, and (2) comparing *searchnum* to *list*[*middle*].

```
while (there are more integers to check ) {
   middle = (left + right) / 2;
   if (searchnum < list[middle])
      right = middle - 1;
   else if (searchnum == list[middle])
         return middle;
      else left = middle + 1;
}
```

Program 1.5: Searching a sorted list

We can handle the comparisons through either a function or a macro. In either case, we must specify values to signify less than, equal, or greater than. We will use the strategy followed in C's library functions:

* We return a negative number (−1) if the first number is less than the second.

* We return a 0 if the two numbers are equal.

* We return a positive number (1) if the first number is greater than the second.

Although we present both a function (Program 1.6) and a macro, we will use the macro throughout the text since it works with any data type.

```
int compare(int x, int y)
{/* compare x and y, return -1 for less than, 0 for equal,
   1 for greater */
   if (x < y) return -1;
   else if (x == y) return 0;
      else return 1;
}
```

Program 1.6: Comparison of two integers

The macro version is:

```
#define COMPARE(x,y) (((x) < (y)) ? -1: ((x) == (y))? 0: 1)
```

We are now ready to tackle the first subtask: determining if there are any elements left to check. You will recall that our initial algorithm indicated that a comparison could cause us to move either our left or right index. Assuming we keep moving these indices, we will eventually find the element, or the indices will cross, that is, the left index will have a higher value than the right index. Since these indices delineate the search boundaries, once they cross, we have nothing left to check. Putting all this information together gives us *binsearch* (Program 1.7).

```
int binsearch(int list[], int searchnum, int left,
                                          int right)
{/* search list[0] <= list[1] <=  · · ·  <= list[n-1] for
 searchnum. Return its position if found. Otherwise
 return -1 */
   int  middle;
   while (left <= right)  {
     middle = (left + right)/2;
     switch (COMPARE(list[middle], searchnum)) {
        case -1: left = middle + 1;
                 break;
        case 0 : return middle;
        case 1 : right = middle - 1;
     }
   }
   return -1;
}
```

Program 1.7: Searching an ordered list

The search strategy just outlined is called *binary search*. □

The previous examples have shown that algorithms are implemented as functions in C. Indeed functions are the primary vehicle used to divide a large program into manageable pieces. They make the program easier to read, and, because the functions can be tested separately, increase the probability that it will run correctly. Often we will declare a function first and provide its definition later. In this way the compiler is made aware that a name refers to a legal function that will be defined later. In C, groups of functions can be compiled separately, thereby establishing libraries containing groups of logically related algorithms.

1.3.2 Recursive Algorithms

Typically, beginning programmers view a function as something that is invoked (called) by another function. It executes its code and then returns control to the calling function. This perspective ignores the fact that functions can call themselves (*direct recursion*) or they may call other functions that invoke the calling function again (*indirect recursion*). These recursive mechanisms are not only extremely powerful, but they also frequently allow us to express an otherwise complex process in very clear terms. It is for these reasons that we introduce recursion here.

Frequently computer science students regard recursion as a mystical technique that is useful for only a few special problems such as computing factorials or Ackermann's function. This is unfortunate because any function that we can write using assignment, **if-else**, and **while** statements can be written recursively. Often this recursive function is easier to understand than its iterative counterpart.

How do we determine when we should express an algorithm recursively? One instance is when the problem itself is defined recursively. Factorials and Fibonacci numbers fit into this category as do binomial coefficients where:

$$\begin{bmatrix} n \\ m \end{bmatrix} = \frac{n!}{m!(n-m)!}$$

can be recursively computed by the formula:

$$\begin{bmatrix} n \\ m \end{bmatrix} = \begin{bmatrix} n-1 \\ m \end{bmatrix} + \begin{bmatrix} n-1 \\ m-1 \end{bmatrix}$$

We would like to use two examples to show you how to develop a recursive algorithm. In the first example, we take the binary search function that we created in Example 1.2 and transform it into a recursive function. In the second example, we recursively generate all possible permutations of a list of characters.

Example 1.3 [*Binary search*]: Program 1.7 gave the iterative version of a binary search. To transform this function into a recursive one, we must (1) establish boundary conditions that terminate the recursive calls, and (2) implement the recursive calls so that each call brings us one step closer to a solution. If we examine Program 1.7 carefully we can see that there are two ways to terminate the search: one signaling a success (*list*[*middle*] = *searchnum*), the other signaling a failure (the left and right indices cross). We do not need to change the code when the function terminates successfully. However, the **while** statement that is used to trigger the unsuccessful search needs to be replaced with an equivalent **if** statement whose **then** clause invokes the function recursively.

Creating recursive calls that move us closer to a solution is also simple since it requires only passing the new *left* or *right* index as a parameter in the next recursive call. Program 1.8 implements the recursive binary search. Notice that although the code has changed, the recursive function call is identical to that of the iterative function. □

```
int binsearch(int list[], int searchnum, int left,
                                          int right)
{/* search list[0] <= list[1] <= ... <= list[n-1] for
    searchnum. Return its position if found. Otherwise
    return -1 */
    int middle;
    if (left <= right) {
        middle = (left + right)/2;
        switch (COMPARE(list[middle], searchnum)) {
            case -1: return
                binsearch(list, searchnum, middle + 1, right);
            case 0 : return middle;
            case 1 : return
                binsearch(list, searchnum, left, middle - 1);
        }
    }
    return -1;
}
```

Program 1.8: Recursive implementation of binary search

Example 1.4 [*Permutations*]: Given a set of $n \geq 1$ elements, print out all possible permutations of this set. For example, if the set is $\{a, b, c\}$, then the set of permutations is $\{(a, b, c), (a, c, b), (b, a, c), (b, c, a), (c, a, b), (c, b, a)\}$. It is easy to see that, given n elements, there are $n!$ permutations. We can obtain a simple algorithm for generating the permutations if we look at the set $\{a, b, c, d\}$. We can construct the set of permutations by printing:

(1) a followed by all permutations of (b, c, d)

(2) b followed by all permutations of (a, c, d)

(3) c followed by all permutations of (a, b, d)

(4) d followed by all permutations of (a, b, c)

The clue to the recursive solution is the phrase "followed by all permutations." It implies that we can solve the problem for a set with n elements if we have an algorithm that works on $n - 1$ elements. These considerations lead to the development of Program 1.9. We assume that *list* is a character array. Notice that it recursively generates permutations until $i = n$. The initial function call is *perm* (*list*, 0, $n - 1$).

Try to simulate Program 1.9 on the three-element set $\{a, b, c\}$. Each recursive call

```
void perm(char *list, int i, int n)
{/* generate all the permutations of list[i] to list[n] */
   int j, temp;
   if (i == n) {
      for (j = 0; j <= n; j++)
         printf("%c", list[j]);
      printf("    ");
   }
   else {
   /* list[i] to list[n] has more than one permutation,
     generate these recursively */
      for (j = i; j <= n; j++) {
         SWAP(list[i],list[j],temp);
         perm(list,i+1,n);
         SWAP(list[i],list[j],temp);
      }
   }
}
```

Program 1.9: Recursive permutation generator

of *perm* produces new local copies of the parameters *list*, *i*, and *n*. The value of *i* will differ from invocation to invocation, but *n* will not. The parameter *list* is an array pointer and its value also will not vary from call to call. □

We will encounter recursion several more times since many of the algorithms that appear in subsequent chapters are recursively defined. This is particularly true of algorithms that operate on lists (Chapter 4) and binary trees (Chapter 5).

EXERCISES

In the last several examples, we showed you how to translate a problem into a program. We have avoided the issues of data abstraction and algorithm design strategies, choosing to focus on developing a function from an English description, or transforming an iterative algorithm into a recursive one. In the exercises that follow, we want you to use the same approach. For each programming problem, try to develop an algorithm, translate it into a function, and show that it works correctly. Your correctness "proof" can employ an analysis of the algorithm or a suitable set of test runs.

1. Consider the two statements:

   (a) Is $n = 2$ the largest value of n for which there exist positive integers x, y, and z such that $x^n + y^n = z^n$ has a solution?

(b) Store 5 divided by zero into x and go to statement 10.

Both fail to satisfy one of the five criteria of an algorithm. Which criterion do they violate?

2. Horner's rule is a strategy for evaluating a polynomial $A(x) =$

$$a_n x^n + a_{n-1} x^{n-1} + \cdots + a_1 + a_0$$

at point x_0 using a minimum number of multiplications. This rule is:

$$A(x_0) = (\cdots ((a_n x_0 + a_{n-1}) x_0 + \cdots + a_1) x_0 + a_0)$$

Write a C program to evaluate a polynomial using Horner's rule.

3. Given n Boolean variables $x_1, \cdots, x_n$, we wish to print all possible combinations of truth values they can assume. For instance, if $n = 2$, there are four possibilities: <*true, true*>, <*false, true*>, <*true, false*>, and <*false, false*>. Write a C program to do this.

4. Write a C program that prints out the integer values of x, y, z in ascending order.

5. The pigeon hole principle states that if a function f has n distinct inputs but less than n distinct outputs then there are two inputs a and b such that $a \neq b$ and $f(a) = f(b)$. Write a C program to find the values a and b for which the range values are equal.

6. Given n, a positive integer, determine if n is the sum its divisors, that is, if n is the sum of all t such that $1 \leq t < n$ and t divides n.

7. The factorial function $n!$ has value 1 when $n \leq 1$ and value $n*(n-1)!$ when $n > 1$. Write both a recursive and an iterative C function to compute $n!$.

8. The Fibonacci numbers are defined as: $f_0 = 0$, $f_1 = 1$, and $f_i = f_{i-1} + f_{i-2}$ for $i > 1$. Write both a recursive and an iterative C function to compute f_i.

9. Write an iterative function to compute a binomial coefficient, then transform it into an equivalent recursive function.

10. Ackerman's function $A(m, n)$ is defined as:

$$A(m, n) = \begin{cases} n + 1 & , \text{if } m = 0 \\ A(m - 1, 1) & , \text{if } n = 0 \\ A(m - 1, A(m, n - 1)) & , \text{otherwise} \end{cases}$$

This function is studied because it grows very quickly for small values of m and n. Write recursive and iterative versions of this function.

11. [*Towers of Hanoi*] There are three towers and 64 disks of different diameters placed on the first tower. The disks are in order of decreasing diameter as one scans up the tower. Monks were reputedly supposed to move the disk from tower

1 to tower 3 obeying the rules:

(a)   Only one disk can be moved at any time.

(b)   No disk can be placed on top of a disk with a smaller diameter.
Write a recursive function that prints out the sequence of moves needed to accomplish this task.

12.   If S is a set of n elements the power set of S is the set of all possible subsets of S. For example, if $S = \{a, b, c\}$, then *powerset* $(S) = \{ \{\}, \{a\}, \{b\}, \{c\}, \{a, b\}, \{a, c\}, \{b, c\}, \{a, b, c\}\}$. Write a recursive function to compute *powerset(S)*.

1.4   DATA ABSTRACTION

The reader is no doubt familiar with the basic data types of C. These include **char**, **int**, **float**, and **double**. Some of these data types may be modified by the keywords **short**, **long**, and **unsigned**. Ultimately, the real world abstractions we wish to deal with must be represented in terms of these data types. In addition to these basic types, C helps us by providing two mechanisms for grouping data together. These are the array and the structure. *Arrays* are collections of elements of the same basic data type. They are declared implicitly, for example, *int list*[5] defines a five-element array of integers whose legitimate subscripts are in the range 0 $\cdots$ 4. *Structs* are collections of elements whose data types need not be the same. They are explicitly defined. For example,

```
struct {
        char lastName;
        int studentId;
        char grade;
        } student;
```

defines a structure with three fields, two of type character and one of type integer. The structure name is *student*. Details of C structures are provided in Chapter 2.

All programming languages provide at least a minimal set of predefined data types, plus the ability to construct new, or *user-defined types*. It is appropriate to ask the question, "What is a data type?"

Definition: A *data type* is a collection of *objects* and a set of *operations* that act on those objects. □

Whether your program is dealing with predefined data types or user-defined data types, these two aspects must be considered: objects and operations. For example, the data type **int** consists of the objects $\{0, +1, -1, +2, -2, \cdots, \text{INT\_MAX}, \text{INT\_MIN}\}$, where INT_MAX and INT_MIN are the largest and smallest integers that can be represented on your machine. (They are defined in *limits.h*.) The operations on integers are many, and would certainly include the arithmetic operators +, −, *, /, and %. There is also testing for equality/inequality and the operation that assigns an integer to a variable. In all of these cases, there is the name of the operation, which may be a prefix operator, such as *atoi*, or an infix operator, such as +. Whether an operation is defined in the language or in a library, its name, possible arguments and results must be specified.

In addition to knowing all of the facts about the operations on a data type, we might also want to know about how the objects of the data type are represented. For example on most computers a **char** is represented as a bit string occupying 1 byte of memory, whereas an **int** might occupy 2 or possibly 4 bytes of memory. If 2 eight-bit bytes are used, then INT_MAX is $2^{15} - 1 = 32,767$.

Knowing the representation of the objects of a data type can be useful and dangerous. By knowing the representation we can often write algorithms that make use of it. However, if we ever want to change the representation of these objects, we also must change the routines that make use of it. It has been observed by many software designers that hiding the representation of objects of a data type from its users is a good design strategy. In that case, the user is constrained to manipulate the objects solely through the functions that are provided. The designer may still alter the representation as long as the new implementations of the operations do not change the user interface. This means that users will not have to recode their algorithms.

Definition: An *abstract data type (ADT)* is a data type that is organized in such a way that the specification of the objects and the specification of the operations on the objects is separated from the representation of the objects and the implementation of the operations. □

Some programming languages provide explicit mechanisms to support the distinction between specification and implementation. For example, Ada has a concept called a *package*, and C++ has a concept called a *class*. Both of these assist the programmer in implementing abstract data types. Although C does not have an explicit mechanism for implementing ADTs, it is still possible and desirable to design your data types using the same notion.

How does the specification of the operations of an ADT differ from the implementation of the operations? The specification consists of the names of every function, the type of its arguments, and the type of its result. There should also be a description of what the function does, but without appealing to internal representation or implementation details. This requirement is quite important, and it implies that an abstract data type is *implementation-independent*. Furthermore, it is possible to classify the functions of a data type into several categories:

(1) **Creator/constructor**: These functions create a new instance of the designated type.

(2) **Transformers**: These functions also create an instance of the designated type, generally by using one or more other instances. The difference between

constructors and transformers will become more clear with some examples.

(3) **Observers/reporters**: These functions provide information about an instance of the type, but they do not change the instance.

Typically, an ADT definition will include at least one function from each of these three categories.

Throughout this text, we will emphasize the distinction between specification and implementation. In order to help us do this, we will typically begin with an ADT definition of the object that we intend to study. This will permit the reader to grasp the essential elements of the object, without having the discussion complicated by the representation of the objects or by the actual implementation of the operations. Once the ADT definition is fully explained we will move on to discussions of representation and implementation. These are quite important in the study of data structures. In order to help us accomplish this goal, we introduce a notation for expressing an ADT.

Example 1.5 [*Abstract data type NaturalNumber*]: As this is the first example of an ADT, we will spend some time explaining the notation. ADT 1.1 contains the ADT definition of *NaturalNumber*.

ADT *NaturalNumber* is

    objects: an ordered subrange of the integers starting at zero and ending at the maximum integer (*INT_MAX*) on the computer

    functions:

        for all $x, y \in$ *NaturalNumber*; *TRUE, FALSE* $\in$ *Boolean*
        and where $+, -, <$, and $==$ are the usual integer operations

NaturalNumber Zero( )	::=	0
Boolean IsZero(x)	::=	**if** (x) **return** *FALSE*
		else return *TRUE*
Boolean Equal(x, y)	::=	**if** ($x == y$) **return** *TRUE*
		else return *FALSE*
NaturalNumber Successor(x)	::=	**if** ($x == INT\_MAX$) **return** x
		else return $x + 1$
NaturalNumber Add(x, y)	::=	**if** (($x + y$) $<= INT\_MAX$) **return** $x + y$
		else return *INT_MAX*
NaturalNumber Subtract(x, y)	::=	**if** ($x < y$) **return** 0
		else return $x - y$

end *NaturalNumber*

ADT 1.1: Abstract data type *NaturalNumber*

The ADT definition begins with the name of the ADT. There are two main sections in the definition: the objects and the functions. The objects are defined in terms of the integers, but we make no explicit reference to their representation. The function definitions are a bit more complicated. First, the definitions use the symbols x and y to denote two elements of the data type *NaturalNumber*, while *TRUE* and *FALSE* are elements of the data type *Boolean*. In addition, the definition makes use of functions that are defined on the set of integers, namely, plus, minus, equals, and less than. This is an indication that in order to define one data type, we may need to use operations from another data type. For each function, we place the result type to the left of the function name and a definition of the function to the right. The symbols "::=" should be read as "is defined as."

The first function, *Zero*, has no arguments and returns the natural number zero. This is a constructor function. The function *Successor(x)* returns the next natural number in sequence. This is an example of a transformer function. Notice that if there is no next number in sequence, that is, if the value of x is already *INT_MAX*, then we define the action of *Successor* to return *INT_MAX*. Some programmers might prefer that in such a case *Successor* return an error flag. This is also perfectly permissible. Other transformer functions are *Add* and *Subtract*. They might also return an error condition, although here we decided to return an element of the set *NaturalNumber*. □

ADT 1.1 shows you the general form that all ADT definitions will follow. However, in most of our further examples, the function definitions will not be so close to C functions. In fact, the nature of an ADT argues that we avoid implementation details. Therefore, we will usually use a form of structured English to explain the meaning of the functions. Often, there will be a discrepency even between the number of parameters used in the ADT definition of a function and its C implementation. To avoid confusion between the ADT definition of a function and its C implementation, ADT names begin with an upper case letter while C names begin with a lower case letter.

EXERCISES

For each of these exercises, provide a definition of the abstract data type using the form illustrated in ADT 1.1.

1. Add the following operations to the *NaturalNumber* ADT: *Predecessor*, *IsGreater*, *Multiply*, *Divide*.

2. Create an ADT, *Set*. Use the standard mathematics definition and include the following operations: *Create*, *Insert*, *Remove*, *IsIn*, *Union*, *Intersection*, *Difference*.

3. Create an ADT, *Bag*. In mathematics a *bag* is similar to a *set* except that a *bag* may contain duplicate elements. The minimal operations should include: *Create*, *Insert*, *Remove*, and *IsIn*.

4. Create an ADT, *Boolean*. The minimal operations are *And*, *Or*, *Not*, *Xor* (Exclusive or), *Equivalent*, and *Implies*.

1.5 PERFORMANCE ANALYSIS

One of the goals of this book is to develop your skills for making evaluative judgments about programs. There are many criteria upon which we can judge a program, including:

(1)   Does the program meet the original specifications of the task?

(2)   Does it work correctly?

(3)   Does the program contain documentation that shows how to use it and how it works?

(4)   Does the program effectively use functions to create logical units?

(5)   Is the program's code readable?

Although the above criteria are vitally important, particularly in the development of large systems, it is difficult to explain how to achieve them. The criteria are associated with the development of a good programming style and this takes experience and practice. We hope that the examples used throughout this text will help you improve your programming style. However, we also can judge a program on more concrete criteria, and so we add two more criteria to our list.

(6)   Does the program efficiently use primary and secondary storage?

(7)   Is the program's running time acceptable for the task?

These criteria focus on performance evaluation, which we can loosely divide into two distinct fields. The first field focuses on obtaining estimates of time and space that are machine independent. We call this field *performance analysis*, but its subject matter is the heart of an important branch of computer science known as *complexity theory*. The second field, which we call *performance measurement*, obtains machine-dependent running times. These times are used to identify inefficient code segments. In this section we discuss performance analysis, and in the next we discuss performance measurement. We begin our discussion with definitions of the space and time complexity of a program.

Definition: The *space complexity* of a program is the amount of memory that it needs to run to completion. The *time complexity* of a program is the amount of computer time that it needs to run to completion. □

1.5.1 Space Complexity

The space needed by a program is the sum of the following components:

(1) **Fixed space requirements:** This component refers to space requirements that do not depend on the number and size of the program's inputs and outputs. The fixed requirements include the instruction space (space needed to store the code), space for simple variables, fixed-size structured variables (such as **structs**), and constants.

(2) **Variable space requirements:** This component consists of the space needed by structured variables whose size depends on the particular instance, I, of the problem being solved. It also includes the additional space required when a function uses recursion. The variable space requirement of a program P working on an instance I is denoted $S_P(I)$. $S_P(I)$ is usually given as a function of some *characteristics* of the instance I. Commonly used characteristics include the number, size, and values of the inputs and outputs associated with I. For example, if our input is an array containing n numbers then n is an instance characteristic. If n is the only instance charcteristic we wish to use when computing $S_P(I)$, we will use $S_P(n)$ to represent $S_P(I)$.

We can express the total space requirement $S(P)$ of any program as:

$$S(P) = c + S_P(I)$$

where c is a constant representing the fixed space requirements. When analyzing the space complexity of a program we are usually concerned with only the variable space requirements. This is particularly true when we want to compare the space complexity of several programs. Let us look at a few examples.

Example 1.6: We have a function, *abc* (Program 1.10), which accepts three simple variables as input and returns a simple value as output. According to the classification given, this function has only fixed space requirements. Therefore, $S_{abc}(I) = 0$. □

```
float abc(float a, float b, float c)
{
    return a+b+b*c+(a+b-c)/(a+b)+4.00;
}
```

Program 1.10: Simple arithmetic function

Example 1.7: We want to add a list of numbers (Program 1.11). Although the output is a simple value, the input includes an array. Therefore, the variable space requirement depends on how the array is passed into the function. Programming languages like Pascal may pass arrays by value. This means that the entire array is copied into temporary storage before the function is executed. In these languages the variable space requirement for this program is $S_{sum}(I) = S_{sum}(n) = n$, where n is the size of the array. C passes all parameters by value. When an array is passed as an argument to a function, C interprets it as passing the address of the first element of the array. C does not copy the array. Therefore, $S_{sum}(n) = 0$. □

```
float sum(float list[], int n)
{
   float tempsum = 0;
   int i;
   for (i = 0; i < n; i++)
      tempsum += list[i];
   return tempsum;
}
```

Program 1.11: Iterative function for summing a list of numbers

Example 1.8: Program 1.12 also adds a list of numbers, but this time the summation is handled recursively. This means that the compiler must save the parameters, the local variables, and the return address for each recursive call.

```
float rsum(float list[], int n)
{
   if (n) return rsum(list,n-1) + list[n-1];
   return 0;
}
```

Program 1.12: Recursive function for summing a list of numbers

In this example, the space needed for one recursive call is the number of bytes required for the two parameters and the return address. We can use the *sizeof* function to find the number of bytes required by each type. Figure 1.1 shows the number of bytes required for one recursive call under the assumption that an integer and a pointer each require 4 bytes.

If the array has $n = MAX\_SIZE$ numbers, the total variable space needed for the recursive version is $S_{rsum}(MAX\_SIZE) = 12*MAX\_SIZE$. If $MAX\_SIZE = 1000$, the variable space needed by the recursive version is $12*1000 = 12,000$ bytes. The iterative version has no variable space requirement. As you can see, the recursive version has a far greater overhead than its iterative counterpart. □

Type	Name	Number of bytes
parameter: array pointer	*list*[]	4
parameter: integer	*n*	4
return address: (used internally)		4
TOTAL per recursive call		12

Figure 1.1: Space needed for one recursive call of Program 1.12

EXERCISES

1. Determine the space complexity of the iterative and recursive factorial functions created in Exercise 7, Section 1.3.

2. Determine the space complexity of the iterative and recursive Fibonacci number functions created in Exercise 8, Section 1.3.

3. Determine the space complexity of the iterative and recursive binomial coefficient functions created in Exercise 9, Section 1.3.

4. Determine the space complexity of the function created in Exercise 5, Section 1.3 (pigeon hole principle).

5. Determine the space complexity of the function created in Exercise 12, Section 1.3 (powerset problem).

1.5.2 Time Complexity

The time, $T(P)$, taken by a program, P, is the sum of its *compile time* and its *run* (or *execution*) *time*. The compile time is similar to the fixed space component since it does not depend on the instance characteristics. In addition, once we have verified that the program runs correctly, we may run it many times without recompilation. Consequently, we are really concerned only with the program's execution time, T_P.

Determining T_P is not an easy task because it requires a detailed knowledge of the compiler's attributes. That is, we must know how the compiler translates our source program into object code. For example, suppose we have a simple program that adds and subtracts numbers. Letting n denote the instance characteristic, we might express $T_P(n)$ as:

$$T_P(n) = c_a ADD(n) + c_s SUB(n) + c_l LDA(n) + c_{st} STA(n)$$

where c_a, c_s, c_l, c_{st} are constants that refer to the time needed to perform each operation, and *ADD*, *SUB*, *LDA*, *STA* are the number of additions, subtractions, loads, and stores that are performed when the program is run with instance characteristic *n*.

Obtaining such a detailed estimate of running time is rarely worth the effort. If we must know the running time, the best approach is to use the system clock to time the program. We will do this later in the chapter. Alternately, we could count the number of operations the program performs. This gives us a machine-independent estimate, but we must know how to divide the program into distinct steps.

Definition: A *program step* is a syntactically or semantically meaningful program segment whose execution time is independent of the instance characteristics. □

Note that the amount of computing represented by one program step may be different from that represented by another step. So, for example, we may count a simple assignment statement of the form $a = 2$ as one step and also count a more complex statement such as $a = 2*b+3*c/d-e+f/g/a/b/c$ as one step. The only requirement is that the time required to execute each statement that is counted as one step be independent of the instance characteristics.

We can determine the number of steps that a program or a function needs to solve a particular problem instance by creating a global variable, *count*, which has an initial value of 0 and then inserting statements that increment count by the number of program steps required by each executable statement.

Example 1.9 [*Iterative summing of a list of numbers*]: We want to obtain the step count for the sum function discussed earlier (Program 1.11). Program 1.13 shows where to place the *count* statements. Notice that we only need to worry about the executable statements, which automatically eliminates the function header, and the second variable declaration from consideration.

```
float sum(float list[], int n)
{
   float tempsum = 0;  count++; /* for assignment */
   int i;
   for (i = 0; i < n; i++)  {
      count++;                     /* for the for loop */
      tempsum += list[i]; count++;  /* for assignment */
   }
   count++; /* last execution of for */
   count++; /* for return */  return tempsum;
}
```

Program 1.13: Program 1.11 with count statements

Since our chief concern is determining the final count, we can eliminate most of the program statements from Program 1.13 to obtain a simpler program Program 1.14 that computes the same value for *count*. This simplification makes it easier to express the count arithmetically. Examining Program 1.14, we can see that if *count*'s initial value is 0, its final value will be $2n + 3$. Thus, each invocation of *sum* executes a total of $2n + 3$ steps. □

```
float sum(float list[], int n)
{
   float tempsum = 0;
   int i;
   for (i = 0; i < n; i++)
      count += 2;
   count +=3;
   return 0;
}
```

Program 1.14: Simplified version of Program 1.13

Example 1.10 [*Recursive summing of a list of numbers*]: We want to obtain the step count for recursive version of the summing function. Program 1.15 contains the original function (Program 1.12) with the step counts added.

```
float rsum(float list[], int n)
{
   count++;      /* for if conditional */
   if (n) {
      count++;   /* for return and rsum invocation */
      return rsum(list,n-1) + list[n-1];
   }
   count++;
   return list[0];
}
```

Program 1.15: Program 1.12 with count statements added

To determine the step count for this function, we first need to figure out the step count for the boundary condition of $n = 0$. Looking at Program 1.15, we can see that when $n = 0$ only the **if** conditional and the second **return** statement are executed. So, the total step count for $n = 0$ is 2. For $n > 0$, the **if** conditional and the first **return** statement are executed. So each recursive call with $n > 0$ adds two to the step count. Since there are n such function calls and these are followed by one with $n = 0$, the step count for the function is $2n + 2$.

Surprisingly, the recursive function actually has a lower step count than its iterative counterpart. However, we must remember that the step count only tells us how many steps are executed, it does not tell us how much time each step takes. Thus, although the recursive function has fewer steps, it typically runs more slowly than the iterative version as its steps, on average, take more time than those of the iterative version. □

Example 1.11 [*Matrix addition*]: We want to determine the step count for a function that adds two-dimensional arrays (Program 1.16). The arrays a and b are added and the result is returned in array c. All of the arrays are of size $rows \times cols$. Program 1.17 shows the *add* function with the step counts introduced. As in the previous examples, we want to express the total count in terms of the size of the inputs, in this case *rows* and *cols*. To make the count easier to decipher, we can combine counts that appear within a single loop. This operation gives us Program 1.18.

```
void add(int a[][MAX_SIZE], int b[][MAX_SIZE],
                int c[][MAX_SIZE], int rows, int cols)
{
    int i, j;
    for (i = 0; i < rows; i++)
        for (j = 0; j < cols; j++)
            c[i][j] = a[i][j] + b[i][j];
}
```

Program 1.16: Matrix addition

For Program 1.18, we can see that if *count* is initially 0, it will be $2rows \cdot cols + 2rows + 1$ on termination. This analysis suggests that we should interchange the matrices if the number of rows is significantly larger than the number of columns. □

By physically placing count statements within our functions we can run the functions and obtain precise counts for various instance characteristics. Another way to obtain step counts is to use a tabular method. To construct a step count table we first determine the step count for each statement. We call this the *steps/execution*, or *s/e* for short. Next we figure out the number of times that each statement is executed. We call this the *frequency*. The frequency of a nonexecutable statement is zero. Multiplying s/e

```
void add(int a[][MAX_SIZE], int b[][MAX_SIZE],
                int c[][MAX_SIZE], int rows, int cols)
{
    int i, j;
    for (i = 0; i < rows; i++) {
        count++;  /* for i for loop */
        for (j = 0; j < cols; j++) {
            count++; /* for j for loop */
            c[i][j] = a[i][j] + b[i][j];
            count++; /*  for assignment statement */
        }
        count++; /* last time of j for loop */
    }
    count++; /* last time of i for loop */
}
```

Program 1.17: Matrix addition with count statements

```
void add(int a[][MAX_SIZE], int b[][MAX_SIZE],
                int c[][MAX_SIZE], int rows, int cols)
{
    int i, j;
    for (i = 0; i < rows; i++) {
        for (j = 0; j < cols; j++)
            count += 2;
        count += 2;
    }
    count++;
}
```

Program 1.18: Simplification of Program 1.17

by the frequency, gives us the *total steps* for each statement. Summing these totals, gives us the step count for the entire function. Although this seems like a very complicated process, in fact, it is quite easy. Let us redo our three previous examples using the tabular approach.

Example 1.12 [*Iterative function to sum a list of numbers*]: Figure 1.2 contains the step count table for Program 1.11. To construct the table, we first entered the steps/execution for each statement. Next, we figured out the frequency column. The **for** loop at line 5 complicated matters slightly. However, since the loop starts at 0 and terminates when i is equal to n, its frequency is $n + 1$. The body of the loop (line 6) only executes n times since it is not executed when $i = n$. We then obtained the total steps for each statement and the final step count. □

Statement	s/e	Frequency	Total steps
float sum(float list[], int n)	0	0	0
{	0	0	0
float tempsum = 0;	1	1	1
int i;	0	0	0
for (i = 0; i < n; i++)	1	$n+1$	$n+1$
tempsum += list[i];	1	n	n
return tempsum;	1	1	1
}	0	0	0
Total			$2n+3$

Figure 1.2: Step count table for Program 1.11

Example 1.13 [*Recursive function to sum a list of numbers*]: Figure 1.3 shows the step count table for Program 1.13. □

Example 1.14 [*Matrix addition*]: Figure 1.4 contains the step count table for the matrix addition function. □

Summary

The time complexity of a program is given by the number of steps taken by the program to compute the function it was written for. The number of steps is itself a function of the instance characteristics. While any specific instance may have several characteristics (e.g., the number of inputs, the number of outputs, the magnitudes of the inputs and outputs, etc.), the number of steps is computed as a function of some subset of these. Usually, we choose those characteristics that are of importance to us. For example, we might wish to know how the computing (or run) time (i.e., time complexity) increases as the number of inputs increase. In this case the number of steps will be computed as a function of the number of inputs alone. For a different program, we might be interested in

Statement	s/e	Frequency	Total steps
float rsum(float list[], int n)	0	0	0
{	0	0	0
if (n)	1	$n+1$	$n+1$
return rsum(list,n−1) + list[n−1];	1	n	n
return list[0];	1	1	1
}	0	0	0
Total			$2n+2$

Figure 1.3: Step count table for recursive summing function

Statement	s/e	Frequency	Total Steps
void add(int a[][MAX−SIZE] $\cdots$)	0	0	0
{	0	0	0
int i, j;	0	0	0
for (i=0; i<rows; i++)	1	$rows+1$	$rows+1$
for (j = 0; j < cols; j++)	1	$rows \cdot (cols+1)$	$rows \cdot cols + rows$
c[i][j] = a[i][j] + b[i][j];	1	$rows \cdot cols$	$rows \cdot cols$
}	0	0	0
Total			$2rows \cdot cols + 2rows+1$

Figure 1.4: Step count table for matrix addition

determining how the computing time increases as the magnitude of one of the inputs increases. In this case the number of steps will be computed as a function of the magnitude of this input alone. Thus, before the step count of a program can be determined, we need to know exactly which characteristics of the problem instance are to be used. These define the variables in the expression for the step count. In the case of *sum*, we chose to measure the time complexity as a function of the number, n, of elements being added. For function *add* the choice of characteristics was the number of rows and the number of columns in the matrices being added.

Once the relevant characteristics $(n, m, p, q, r, \ldots)$ have been selected, we can define what a step is. A step is any computation unit that is independent of the characteristics $(n, m, p, q, r, \ldots)$. Thus, 10 additions can be one step; 100 multiplications can also be one step; but n additions cannot. Nor can $m/2$ additions, $p+q$ subtractions, etc., be counted as one step.

The examples we have looked at so far were sufficiently simple that the time complexities were nice functions of fairly simple characteristics like the number of elements, and the number of rows and columns. For many programs, the time complexity is not dependent solely on the number of inputs or outputs or some other easily specified characteristic. Consider the function *binsearch* (Program 1.7). This function searches an ordered list. A natural parameter with respect to which you might wish to determine the step count is the number, n, of elements in the list. That is, we would like to know how the computing time changes as we change the number of elements n. The parameter n is inadequate. For the same n, the step count varies with the position of the element *searchnum* that is being searched for. We can extricate ourselves from the difficulties resulting from situations when the chosen parameters are not adequate to determine the step count uniquely by defining three kinds of steps counts: best case, worst case and average.

The *best case step count* is the minimum number of steps that can be executed for the given paramenters. The *worst-case step count* is the maximum number of steps that can be executed for the given paramenters. The *average step count* is the average number of steps executed on instances with the given parameters.

EXERCISES

1. Redo Exercise 2, Section 1.3 (Horner's rule for evaluating polynomials), so that step counts are introduced into the function. Express the total count as an equation.

2. Redo Exercise 3, Section 1.3 (truth tables), so that steps counts are introduced into the function. Express the total count as an equation.

3. Redo Exercise 4, Section 1.3 so that step counts are introduced into the function. Express the total count as an equation.

4. (a) Rewrite Program 1.19 so that step counts are introduced into the function.

    (b) Simplify the resulting function by eliminating statements.

    (c) Determine the value of *count* when the function ends.

    (d) Write the step count table for the function.

5. Repeat Exercise 4 with Program 1.20.

6. Repeat Exercise 4 with Program 1.21

7. Repeat Exercise 4 with Program 1.22

```
void printMatrix(int matrix[][MAX_SIZE], int rows,
                                        int cols)
{
   int i, j;
   for (i = 0; i < rows; i++) {
      for (j = 0; j < cols; j++)
         printf("%d",matrix[i][j]);
      printf("\n");
   }
}
```

Program 1.19: Printing out a matrix

```
void mult(int a[][MAX_SIZE], int b[][MAX_SIZE],
                             int c[][MAX_SIZE])
{
   int i, j, k;
   for (i = 0; i < MAX_SIZE; i++)
      for (j = 0; j < MAX_SIZE; j++) {
         c[i][j] = 0;
         for (k = 0; k < MAX_SIZE; k++)
            c[i][j] += a[i][k] * b[k][j];
      }
}
```

Program 1.20: Matrix multiplication function

1.5.3 Asymptotic Notation (O, Ω, Θ)

Our motivation to determine step counts is to be able to compare the time complexities of two programs that compute the same function and also to predict the growth in run time as the instance characteristics change.

Determining the exact step count (either worst case or average) of a program can prove to be an exceedingly difficult task. Expending immense effort to determine the step count exactly isn't a very worthwhile endeavor as the notion of a step is itself inexact. (Both the instructions $x = y$ and $x = y + z + (x/y) + (x*y*z-x/z)$ count as one step.) Because of the inexactness of what a step stands for, the exact step count isn't very

```
void prod(int a[][MAX_SIZE], int b[][MAX_SIZE],
     int c[][MAX_SIZE], int rowsa, int colsb, int colsa)
{
   int i, j, k;
   for (i = 0; i < rowsa; i++)
     for (j = 0; j < colsb; j++) {
        c[i][j] = 0;
        for (k = 0; k < colsa; k++)
           c[i][j] += a[i][k] * b[k][j];
     }
}
```

Program 1.21: Matrix product function

```
void transpose(int a[][MAX_SIZE])
{
   int i, j, temp;
   for (i = 0; i < MAX_SIZE-1; i++)
     for (j = i+1; j < MAX_SIZE; j++)
        SWAP(a[i][j], a[j][i], temp);
}
```

Program 1.22: Matrix transposition function

useful for comparative purposes. An exception to this is when the difference in the step counts of two programs is very large as in $3n+3$ versus $100n+10$. We might feel quite safe in predicting that the program with step count $3n+3$ will run in less time than the one with step count $100n+10$. But even in this case, it isn't necessary to know that the exact step count is $100n+10$. Something like, "it's about $80n$, or $85n$, or $75n$," is adequate to arrive at the same conclusion.

For most situations, it is adequate to be able to make a statement like $c_1n^2 \leq T_P(n) \leq c_2n^2$ or $T_Q(n,m) = c_1n + c_2m$ where c_1 and c_2 are nonnegative constants. This is so because if we have two programs with a complexity of $c_1n^2 + c_2n$ and c_3n, respectively, then we know that the one with complexity c_3n will be faster than the one with complexity $c_1n^2 + c_2n$ for sufficiently large values of n. For small values of n, either program could be faster (depending on c_1, c_2, and c_3). If $c_1 = 1, c_2 = 2$, and $c_3 = 100$ then $c_1n^2 + c_2n \leq c_3n$ for $n \leq 98$ and $c_1n^2 + c_2n > c_3n$ for $n > 98$. If $c_1 = 1, c_2 = 2$, and $c_3 = 1000$, then $c_1 n^2 + c_2 n \le c_3 n$ for $n \le 998$.

No matter what the values of c_1, c_2, and c_3, there will be an n beyond which the program with complexity $c_3 n$ will be faster than the one with complexity $c_1 n^2 + c_2 n$. This value of n will be called the *break even point*. If the break even point is 0 then the program with complexity $c_3 n$ is always faster (or at least as fast). The exact break even point cannot be determined analytically. The programs have to be run on a computer in order to determine the break even point. To know that there is a break even point it is adequate to know that one program has complexity $c_1 n^2 + c_2 n$ and the other $c_3 n$ for some constants c_1, c_2, and c_3. There is little advantage in determining the exact values of c_1, c_2, and c_3.

With the previous discussion as motivation, we introduce some terminology that will enable us to make meaningful (but inexact) statements about the time and space complexities of a program. In the remainder of this chapter, the functions f and g are nonnegative functions.

Definition: [Big "oh"] $f(n) = O(g(n))$ (read as "f of n is big oh of g of n") iff (if and only if) there exist positive constants c and n_0 such that $f(n) \le cg(n)$ for all n, $n \ge n_0$. $\square$

Example 1.15: $3n + 2 = O(n)$ as $3n + 2 \le 4n$ for all $n \ge 2$. $3n + 3 = O(n)$ as $3n + 3 \le 4n$ for all $n \ge 3$. $100n + 6 = O(n)$ as $100n + 6 \le 101n$ for $n \ge 10$. $10n^2 + 4n + 2 = O(n^2)$ as $10n^2 + 4n + 2 \le 11n^2$ for $n \ge 5$. $1000n^2 + 100n - 6 = O(n^2)$ as $1000n^2 + 100n - 6 \le 1001n^2$ for $n \ge 100$. $6*2^n + n^2 = O(2^n)$ as $6*2^n + n^2 \le 7*2^n$ for $n \ge 4$. $3n + 3 = O(n^2)$ as $3n + 3 \le 3n^2$ for $n \ge 2$. $10n^2 + 4n + 2 = O(n^4)$ as $10n^2 + 4n + 2 \le 10n^4$ for $n \ge 2$. $3n + 2 \ne O(1)$ as $3n + 2$ is not less than or equal to c for any constant c and all n, $n \ge n_0$. $10n^2 + 4n + 2 \ne O(n)$. $\square$

We write $O(1)$ to mean a computing time which is a constant. $O(n)$ is called linear, $O(n^2)$ is called quadratic, $O(n^3)$ is called cubic, and $O(2^n)$ is called exponential. If an algorithm takes time $O(\log n)$ it is faster, for sufficiently large n, than if it had taken $O(n)$. Similarly, $O(n \log n)$ is better than $O(n^2)$ but not as good as $O(n)$. These seven computing times, $O(1)$, $O(\log n)$, $O(n)$, $O(n \log n)$, $O(n^2)$, $O(n^3)$, and $O(2^n)$ are the ones we will see most often in this book.

As illustrated by the previous example, the statement $f(n) = O(g(n))$ only states that $g(n)$ is an upper bound on the value of $f(n)$ for all n, $n \ge n_0$. It doesn't say anything about how good this bound is. Notice that $n = O(n^2)$, $n = O(n^{2.5})$, $n = O(n^3)$, $n = O(2^n)$, etc. In order for the statement $f(n) = O(g(n))$ to be informative, $g(n)$ should be as small a function of n as one can come up with for which $f(n) = O(g(n))$. So, while we shall often say $3n + 3 = O(n)$, we shall almost never say $3n + 3 = O(n^2)$ even though this latter statement is correct.

From the definition of O, it should be clear that $f(n) = O(g(n))$ is not the same as $O(g(n)) = f(n)$. In fact, it is meaningless to say that $O(g(n)) = f(n)$. The use of the symbol "=" is unfortunate as this symbol commonly denotes the "equals" relation. Some of the confusion that results from the use of this symbol (which is standard terminology) can be avoided by reading the symbol "=" as "is" and not as "equals."

Theorem 1.2 obtains a very useful result concerning the order of $f(n)$ (i.e., the $g(n)$ in $f(n) = O(g(n))$) when $f(n)$ is a polynomial in n.

Theorem 1.2: If $f(n) = a_m n^m + \ldots + a_1 n + a_0$, then $f(n) = O(n^m)$.

Proof: $f(n) \leq \sum_{i=0}^{m} |a_i| n^i$

$$\leq n^m \sum_{0}^{m} |a_i| n^{i-m}$$

$$\leq n^m \sum_{0}^{m} |a_i|, \text{ for } n \geq 1$$

So, $f(n) = O(n^m)$. $\square$

Definition: [Omega] $f(n) = \Omega(g(n))$ (read as "f of n is omega of g of n") iff there exist positive constants c and n_0 such that $f(n) \geq cg(n)$ for all $n, n \geq n_0$. $\square$

Example 1.16: $3n + 2 = \Omega(n)$ as $3n + 2 \geq 3n$ for $n \geq 1$ (actually the inequality holds for $n \geq 0$ but the definition of Ω requires an $n_0 > 0$). $3n + 3 = \Omega(n)$ as $3n + 3 \geq 3n$ for $n \geq 1$. $100n + 6 = \Omega(n)$ as $100n + 6 \geq 100n$ for $n \geq 1$. $10n^2 + 4n + 2 = \Omega(n^2)$ as $10n^2 + 4n + 2 \geq n^2$ for $n \geq 1$. $6*2^n + n^2 = \Omega(2^n)$ as $6*2^n + n^2 \geq 2^n$ for $n \geq 1$. Observe also that $3n + 3 = \Omega(1)$; $10n^2 + 4n + 2 = \Omega(n)$; $10n^2 + 4n + 2 = \Omega(1)$; $6*2^n + n^2 = \Omega(n^{100})$; $6*2^n + n^2 = \Omega(n^{50.2})$; $6*2^n + n^2 = \Omega(n^2)$; $6*2^n + n^2 = \Omega(n)$; and $6*2^n + n^2 = \Omega(1)$. $\square$

As in the case of the "big oh" notation, there are several functions $g(n)$ for which $f(n) = \Omega(g(n))$. $g(n)$ is only a lower bound on $f(n)$. For the statement $f(n) = \Omega(g(n))$ to be informative, $g(n)$ should be as large a function of n as possible for which the statement $f(n) = \Omega(g(n))$ is true. So, while we shall say that $3n + 3 = \Omega(n)$ and that $6*2^n + n^2 = \Omega(2^n)$, we shall almost never say that $3n + 3 = \Omega(1)$ or that $6*2^n + n^2 = \Omega(1)$ even though both these statements are correct.

Theorem 1.3 is the analogue of Theorem 1.2 for the omega notation.

Theorem 1.3: If $f(n) = a_m n^m + \ldots + a_1 n + a_0$ and $a_m > 0$, then $f(n) = \Omega(n^m)$.

Proof: Left as an exercise. $\square$

Definition: [Theta] $f(n) = \Theta(g(n))$ (read as "f of n is theta of g of n") iff there exist positive constants c_1, c_2, and n_0 such that $c_1 g(n) \leq f(n) \leq c_2 g(n)$ for all $n, n \geq n_0$. $\square$

Example 1.17: $3n + 2 = \Theta(n)$ as $3n + 2 \geq 3n$ for all $n \geq 2$ and $3n + 2 \leq 4n$ for all $n \geq 2$, so c_1 3, $c_2 = 4$, and $n_0 = 2$. $3n + 3 = \Theta(n)$; $10n^2 + 4n + 2 = \Theta(n^2)$; $6*2^n + n^2 = \Theta(2^n)$; and $10*\log n + 4 = \Theta(\log n)$. $3n + 2 \neq \Theta(1)$; $3n + 3 \neq \Theta(n^2)$; $10n^2 + 4n + 2 \neq \Theta(n)$; $10n^2 + 4n + 2 \neq \Theta(1)$; $6*2^n + n^2 \neq \Theta(n^2)$; $6*2^n + n^2 \neq \Theta(n^{100})$; and $6*2^n + n^2 \neq \Theta(1)$. $\square$

The theta notation is more precise than both the "big oh" and omega notations. $f(n) = \Theta(g(n))$ iff $g(n)$ is both an upper and lower bound on $f(n)$.

Notice that the coefficients in all of the $g(n)$'s used in the preceding three examples has been 1. This is in accordance with practice. We shall almost never find ourselves saying that $3n + 3 = O(3n)$, or that $10 = O(100)$, or that $10n^2 + 4n + 2 = \Omega(4n^2)$, or that $6*2^n + n^2 = \Omega(6*2^n)$, or that $6*2^n + n^2 = \Theta(4*2^n)$, even though each of these statements is true.

Theorem 1.4: If $f(n) = a_m n^m + \ldots + a_1 n + a_0$ and $a_m > 0$, then $f(n) = \Theta(n^m)$.

Proof: Left as an exercise. $\square$

Let us reexamine the time complexity analyses of the previous section. For function *sum* (Program 1.12) we had determined that $T_{sum}(n) = 2n + 3$. So, $T_{sum}(n) = \Theta(n)$. $T_{rsum}(n) = 2n + 2 = \Theta(n)$ and $T_{add}(rows, cols) = 2rows.cols + 2rows + 1 = \Theta(rows.cols)$.

While we might all see that the O, Ω, and Θ notations have been used correctly in the preceding paragraphs, we are still left with the question: "Of what use are these notations if one has to first determine the step count exactly?" The answer to this question is that the asymptotic complexity (i.e., the complexity in terms of O, Ω, and Θ) can be determined quite easily without determining the exact step count. This is usually done by first determining the asymptotic complexity of each statement (or group of statements) in the program and then adding up these complexities.

Example 1.18 [*Complexity of matrix addition*]: Using a tabular approach, we construct the table of Figure 1.5. This is quite similar to Figure 1.4. However, instead of putting in exact step counts, we put in asymptotic ones. For nonexecutable statements, we enter a step count of 0. Constructing a table such as the one in Figure 1.5 is actually easier than constructing the one is Figure 1.4. For example, it is harder to obtain the exact step count of $rows.(cols +1)$ for line 5 than it is to see that line 5 has an asymptotic complexity that is $\Theta(rows.cols)$. To obtain the asymptotic complexity of the function, we can add the asymptotic complexities of the individual program lines. Alternately, since the number of lines is a constant (i.e., is independent of the instance characteristics), we may simply take the maximum of the line complexities. Using either approach, we obtain $\Theta(rows.cols)$ as the asymptotic complexity. $\square$

Example 1.19 [*Binary search*]: Let us obtain the time complexity of the binary search function *binsearch* (Program 1.7). The instance characteristic we shall use is the number

Statement	Asymptotic complexity
void add(int a[][MAX–SIZE] $\cdots$)	0
{	0
int i, j;	0
for (i=0; i<rows; i++)	$\Theta(rows)$
for (j = 0; j < cols; j++)	$\Theta(rows.cols)$
c[i][j] = a[i][j] + b[i][j];	$\Theta(rows.cols)$
}	0
Total	$\Theta(rows.cols)$

Figure 1.5: Time complexity of matrix addition

n of elements in the list. Each iteration of the **while** loop takes $\Theta(1)$ time. We can show that the **while** loop is iterated at most $\lceil \log_2(n+1) \rceil$ times. Since an asymptotic analysis is being performed, we don't need such an accurate count of the worst-case number of iterations. Each iteration except for the last results in a decrease in the size of the segment of *list* that has to be searched by a factor of about 2. That is, the value of *right − left* + 1 reduces by a factor of about 2 on each iteration. So, this loop is iterated $\Theta(\log n)$ times in the worst case. As each iteration takes $\Theta(1)$ time, the overall worst-case complexity of *binsearch* is $\Theta(\log n)$. Notice that the best case complexity is $\Theta(1)$ as in the best case *searchnum* is found in the first iteration of the **while** loop. □

Example 1.20 [*Permutations*]: Consider function *perm* (Program 1.9). When $i = n$, the time taken is $\Theta(n)$. When $i < n$, the **else** clause is entered. The **for** loop of this clause is entered $n - i + 1$ times. Each iteration of this loop takes $\Theta(n + T_{perm}(i + 1, n))$ time. So, $T_{perm}(i, n) = \Theta((n - i + 1)(n + T_{perm}(i + 1, n)))$ when $i < n$. Since, $T_{perm}(i + 1, n)$, is at least n when $i + 1 \leq n$, we get $T_{perm}(i, n) = \Theta((n - i + 1)T_{perm}(i + 1, n))$ for $i < n$. Solving this recurrence, we obtain $T_{perm}(1,n) = \Theta(n(n!)), n \geq 1$. □

Example 1.21 [*Magic square*]: As our last example of complexity analysis, we use a problem from recreational mathematics, the creation of a magic square. A *magic square* is an $n \times n$ matrix of the integers from 1 to n^2 such that the sum of each row and column and the two major diagonals is the same. Figure 1.6 shows a magic square for the case $n = 5$. In this example, the common sum is 65.

Coxeter has given the following rule for generating a magic square when n is odd:

Put a one in the middle box of the top row. Go up and left assigning numbers in increasing order to empty boxes. If your move causes you to jump off the square (that is,

15	8	1	24	17
16	14	7	5	23
22	20	13	6	4
3	21	19	12	10
9	2	25	18	11

Figure 1.6: Magic square for $n = 5$

you go beyond the square's boundaries), figure out where you would be if you landed on a box on the opposite side of the square. Continue with this box. If a box is occupied, go down instead of up and continue.

We created Figure 1.6 using Coxeter's rule. Program 1.23 contains the coded algorithm. Let n denote the size of the magic square (i.e., the value of the variable *size* in Program 1.23. The **if** statements that check for errors in the value of n take $\Theta(1)$ time. The two nested **for** loops have a complexity $\Theta(n^2)$. Each iteration of the next **for** loop takes $\Theta(1)$ time. This loop is iterated $\Theta(n^2)$ time. So, its complexity is $\Theta(n^2)$. The nested **for** loops that output the magic square also take $\Theta(n^2)$ time. So, the asymptotic complexity of Program 1.23 is $\Theta(n^2)$. □

```
#include <stdio.h>
#define MAX_SIZE  15 /* maximum size of square */
void main(void)
{/* construct a magic square, iteratively */
   int square[MAX_SIZE][MAX_SIZE];
   int i, j, row, column;     /* indexes */
   int count;                 /* counter */
   int size;                  /* square size */

   printf("Enter the size of the square: ");
   scanf("%d", &size);
   /* check for input errors */
   if (size < 1 || size > MAX_SIZE + 1) {
      fprintf(stderr, "Error!  Size is out of range\n");
      exit(EXIT_FAILURE);
```

```
   }
   if (!(size % 2)) {
      fprintf(stderr, "Error!  Size is even\n");
      exit(EXIT_FAILURE);
   }
   for (i = 0; i < size; i++)
      for (j = 0; j < size; j++)
         square[i][j] = 0;
   square[0][(size-1) / 2] = 1; /* middle of first row */
   /* i and j are current position */
   i = 0;
   j = (size - 1) / 2;
   for (count = 2; count <= size * size; count++) {
      row = (i-1 < 0) ? (size - 1) : (i - 1); /*up*/
      column = (j-1 < 0) ? (size - 1) : (j - 1); /*left*/
      if (square[row][column])   /*down*/
         i = (++i) % size;
      else {                            /* square is unoccupied */
         i = row;
         j = (j-1 < 0) ? (size - 1) : --j;
      }
      square[i][j] = count;
   }
   /* output the magic square */
   printf(" Magic Square of size %d : \n\n",size);
   for (i = 0; i < size; i++) {
      for (j = 0; j < size; j++)
         printf("%5d", square[i][j]);
      printf("\n");
   }
   printf("\n\n");
}
```

Program 1.23: Magic square program

When we analyze programs in the following chapters, we will normally confine ourselves to providing an upper bound on the complexity of the program. That is, we will normally use only the big oh notation. We do this because this is the current trend in practice. In many of our analyses the theta notation could have been used in place of the big oh notation as the complexity bound obtained is both an upper and a lower bound for the program.

EXERCISES

1. Show that the following statements are correct:
   (a) $5n^2 - 6n = \Theta(n^2)$
   (b) $n! = O(n^n)$
   (c) $2n^2 + n \log n = \Theta(n^2)$
   (d) $\sum_{i=0}^{n} i^2 = \Theta(n^3)$
   (e) $\sum_{i=0}^{n} i^3 = \Theta(n^4)$
   (f) $n^{2^n} + 6 \cdot 2^n = \Theta(n^{2^n})$
   (g) $n^3 + 10^6 n^2 = \Theta(n^3)$
   (h) $6n^3 / (\log n + 1) = O(n^3)$
   (i) $n^{1.001} + n \log n = \Theta(n^{1.001})$
   (j) $n^k + n + n^k \log n = \Theta(n^k \log n)$ for all $k \geq 1$.
   (k) $10n^3 + 15n^4 + 100n^2 2^n = O(n^2 2^n)$

2. Show that the following statements are incorrect:
   (a) $10n^2 + 9 = O(n)$
   (b) $n^2 \log n = \Theta(n^2)$
   (c) $n^2 / \log n = \Theta(n^2)$
   (d) $n^3 2^n + 6n^2 3^n = O(n^2 2^n)$
   (e) $3^n = O(2^n)$

3. Prove Theorem 1.3.

4. Prove Theorem 1.4.

5. Determine the worst-case complexity of Program 1.19.

6. Determine the worst-case complexity of Program 1.22.

7. Compare the two functions n^2 and $20n + 4$ for various values of n. Determine when the second function becomes smaller than the first.

8. Write an equivalent recursive version of the magic square program (Program 1.23).

1.5.4 Practical Complexities

We have seen that the time complexity of a program is generally some function of the instance characteristics. This function is very useful in determining how the time requirements vary as the instance characteristics change. The complexity function may also be used to compare two programs P and Q that perform the same task. Assume that program P has complexity $\Theta(n)$ and program Q is of complexity $\Theta(n^2)$. We can assert that program P is faster than program Q for "sufficiently large" n. To see the validity of this assertion, observe that the actual computing time of P is bounded from above by cn for some constant c and for all n, $n \geq n_1$, while that of Q is bounded from below by dn^2 for some constant d and all n, $n \geq n_2$. Since $cn \leq dn^2$ for $n \geq c/d$, program P is faster than program Q whenever $n \geq \max\{n_1, n_2, c/d\}$.

You should always be cautiously aware of the presence of the phrase "sufficiently large" in the assertion of the preceding discussion. When deciding which of the two programs to use, we must know whether the n we are dealing with is, in fact, "sufficiently large." If program P actually runs in $10^6 n$ milliseconds while program Q runs in n^2 milliseconds and if we always have $n \leq 10^6$, then, other factors being equal, program Q is the one to use, other factors being equal.

To get a feel for how the various functions grow with n, you are advised to study Figures 1.7 and 1.8 very closely. As you can see, the function 2^n grows very rapidly with n. In fact, if a program needs 2^n steps for execution, then when $n = 40$, the number of steps needed is approximately $1.1*10^{12}$. On a computer performing 1 billion steps per second, this would require about 18.3 minutes. If $n = 50$, the same program would run for about 13 days on this computer. When $n = 60$, about 310.56 years will be required to execute the program and when $n = 100$, about $4*10^{13}$ years will be needed. So, we may conclude that the utility of programs with exponential complexity is limited to small n (typically $n \leq 40$).

$\log n$	n	$n \log n$	n^2	n^3	2^n
0	1	0	1	1	2
1	2	2	4	8	4
2	4	8	16	64	16
3	8	24	64	512	256
4	16	64	256	4096	65,536
5	32	160	1024	32,768	4,294,967,296

Figure 1.7: Function values

Programs that have a complexity that is a polynomial of high degree are also of limited utility. For example, if a program needs n^{10} steps, then using our 1 billion steps per second computer we will need 10 seconds when $n = 10$; 3,171 years when $n = 100$; and $3.17*10^{13}$ years when $n = 1000$. If the program's complexity had been n^3 steps instead, then we would need 1 second when $n = 1000$; 110.67 minutes when $n = 10,000$; and 11.57 days when $n = 100,000$.

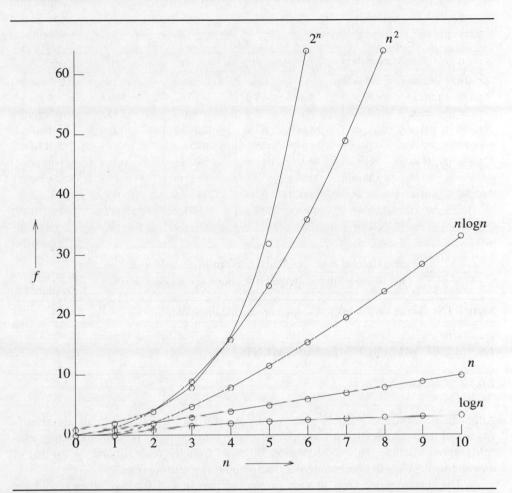

Figure 1.8 Plot of function values

Figure 1.9 gives the time needed by a 1 billion instructions per second computer to execute a program of complexity $f(n)$ instructions. You should note that currently only the fastest computers can execute about 1 billion instructions per second. From a practical standpoint, it is evident that for reasonably large n (say $n > 100$), only programs of small complexity (such as n, $n\log n$, n^2, n^3) are feasible. Further, this is the case even if one could build a computer capable of executing 10^{12} instructions per second. In this case, the computing times of Figure 1.9 would decrease by a factor of 1000. Now, when $n = 100$ it would take 3.17 years to execute n^{10} instructions, and $4*10^{10}$ years to execute 2^n instructions.

n	n	$n\log_2 n$	n^2	n^3	n^4	n^{10}	2^n
				$f(n)$			
10	.01 μs	.03 μs	.1 μs	1 μs	10 μs	10 s	1 μs
20	.02 μs	.09 μs	.4 μs	8 μs	160 μs	2.84 h	1 ms
30	.03 μ	.15 μ	.9 μ	27 μ	810 μ	6.83 d	1 s
40	.04 μs	.21 μs	1.6 μs	64 μs	2.56 ms	121 d	18 m
50	.05 μs	.28 μs	2.5 μs	125 μs	6.25 ms	3.1 y	13 d
100	.10 μs	.66 μs	10 μs	1 ms	100 ms	3171 y	$4*10^{13}$ y
10^3	1 μs	9.96 μs	1 ms	1 s	16.67 m	$3.17*10^{13}$ y	$32*10^{283}$ y
10^4	10 μs	130 μs	100 ms	16.67 m	115.7 d	$3.17*10^{23}$ y	
10^5	100 μs	1.66 ms	10 s	11.57 d	3171 y	$3.17*10^{33}$ y	
10^6	1 ms	19.92 ms	16.67 m	31.71 y	$3.17*10^7$ y	$3.17*10^{43}$ y	

μs = microsecond = 10^{-6} seconds; ms = milliseconds = 10^{-3} seconds;
s = seconds; m = minutes; h = hours; d = days; y = years

Figure 1.9: Times on a 1-billion-steps-per-second computer

1.6 PERFORMANCE MEASUREMENT

1.6.1 Clocking

Although performance analysis gives us a powerful tool for assessing an algorithm's space and time complexity, at some point we also must consider how the algorithm executes on our machine. This consideration moves us from the realm of analysis to that of measurement. We will concentrate our discussion on measuring time.

The functions we need to time events are part of C's standard library, and are accessed through the statement: *#include <time.h>*. There are actually two different methods for timing events in C. Figure 1.10 shows the major differences between these two methods.

Method 1 uses *clock* to time events. This function gives the amount of processor time that has elapsed since the program began running. To time an event we use *clock* twice, once at the start of the event and once at the end. The time is returned as a built-in type, *clock_t*. The total time required by an event is its start time subtracted from its stop time. Since this result could be any legitimate numeric type, we **type cast** it to **double**. In addition, since this result is measured as internal processor time, we must divide it by the number of clock ticks per second to obtain the result in seconds. In ANSI C, the ticks per second is held in the built-in constant, *CLOCKS_PER_SEC*. We found that

	Method 1	Method 2
Start timing	start = clock();	start = time(NULL);
Stop timing	stop = clock();	stop = time(NULL);
Type returned	clock−t	time−t
Result in seconds	duration = ((double) (stop−start)) / CLOCKS−PER−SEC;	duration = (double) difftime(stop,start);

Figure 1.10: Event timing in C

this method was far more accurate on our machine. However, the second method does not require a knowledge of the ticks per second, which is why we also present it here.

Method 2 uses *time*. This function returns the time, measured in seconds, as the built-in type *time−t*. Unlike *clock*, *time* has one parameter, which specifies a location to hold the time. Since we do not want to keep the time, we pass in a *NULL* value for this parameter. As was true of Method 1, we use *time* at the start and the end of the event we want to time. We then pass these two times into *difftime*, which returns the difference between two times measured in seconds. Since the type of this result is *time−t*, we **type cast** it to **double** before printing it out.

Example 1.22 [*Worst-case performance of selection sort*]: The worst case for selection sort occurs when the elements are in reverse order. That is, we want to sort into ascending order an array that is currently in descending order. To conduct our timing tests, we varied the size of the array from 0, 10, 20 , $\cdots$, 90, 100, 200 , $\cdots$, 1000. Program 1.24 contains the code we used to conduct the timing tests. (The code for the sort function is given in Program 1.4 and for the purposes of Program 1.24 is assumed to be in a file named *selectionSort.h*).

To conduct the timing tests, we used a **for** loop to control the size of the array. At each iteration, a new reverse ordered array of n numbers was created. We called *clock* immediately before we invoked *sort* and immediately after it returned. Surprisingly, the duration output for each n was 0! What went wrong? Although our timing program (Program 1.24) is logically correct, it fails to measure run times accurately because the events we are trying to time are too short! Since there is a measurement error of ±1 tick, Program 1.24 returns accurate results only when the sort time is much more than 1 tick. Program 1.25 is a more accurate timing program for selection sort. In this program, for each n, we do the sort as many times as needed to bring the total time up to 1 second (1000 ticks). This program has some inaccuracies of its own. For example, the reported time includes the time to initialize the array that is to be sorted. However, this

```
#include <stdio.h>
#include <time.h>
#include "selectionSort.h"
#define MAX_SIZE 1001
void main(void)
{
   int i, n, step = 10;
   int a[MAX_SIZE];
   double duration;
   clock_t start;

   /* times for n = 0, 10, ..., 100, 200, ..., 1000 */
   printf("    n      time\n");
   for (n = 0; n <= 1000; n += step)
   {/* get time for size n */

      /* initialize with worst-case data */
      for (i = 0; i < n; i++)
         a[i] = n - i;

      start = clock( );
      sort(a, n);
      duration = ((double) (clock() - start))
                              / CLOCKS_PER_SEC;
      printf("%6d    %f\n", n, duration);
      if (n == 100) step = 100;
   }
}
```

Program 1.24: First timing program for selection sort

initialization time is small compared to the actual sort time ($O(n)$ vs $O(n^2)$). In case, the initialization time is a concern, we may measure the initialization time using a separate experiment and subtract this from the time reported by Program 1.24.

The results from Program 1.24 are displayed in Figures 1.11 and 1.12. The curve of Figure 1.12 resembles the n^2 curve displayed in Figure 1.8. This agrees with our analysis of selection sort. □

```
#include <stdio.h>
#include <time.h>
#include "selectionSort.h"
#define MAX_SIZE 1001
void main(void)
{
   int i, n, step = 10;
   int a[MAX_SIZE];
   double duration;

   /* times for n = 0, 10, ..., 100, 200, ..., 1000 */
   printf("     n     repetitions      time\n");
   for (n = 0; n <= 1000; n += step)
   {
      /* get time for size n */
      long repetitions = 0;
      clock_t start = clock( );
      do
      {
         repetitions++;

         /* initialize with worst-case data */
         for (i = 0; i < n; i++)
            a[i] = n - i;

         sort(a, n);
      } while (clock( ) - start < 1000);
            /* repeat until enough time has elapsed */

      duration = ((double) (clock() - start))
                              / CLOCKS_PER_SEC;
      duration /= repetitions;
      printf("%6d  %9d   %f\n", n, repetitions, duration);
      if (n == 100) step = 100;
   }
}
```

Program 1.25: More accurate timing program for selection sort

n	repetitions	time
0	8690714	0.000000
10	2370915	0.000000
20	604948	0.000002
30	329505	0.000003
40	205605	0.000005
50	145353	0.000007
60	110206	0.000009
70	85037	0.000012
80	65751	0.000015
90	54012	0.000019
100	44058	0.000023
200	12582	0.000079
300	5780	0.000173
400	3344	0.000299
500	2096	0.000477
600	1516	0.000660
700	1106	0.000904
800	852	0.001174
900	681	0.001468
1000	550	0.001818

Figure 1.11: Worst-case performance of selection sort (seconds)

1.6.2   Generating Test Data

Generating a data set that results in the worst-case performance of a program isn't always easy. In some cases, it is necessary to use a computer program to generate the worst-case data. In other cases, even this is very difficult. In these cases, another approach to estimating worst-case performance is taken. For each set of values of the instance characteristics of interest, we generate a suitably large number of random test data. The run times for each of these test data are obtained. The maximum of these times is used as an estimate of the worst-case time for this set of values of the instance characteristics.

To measure average case times, it is usually not possible to average over all

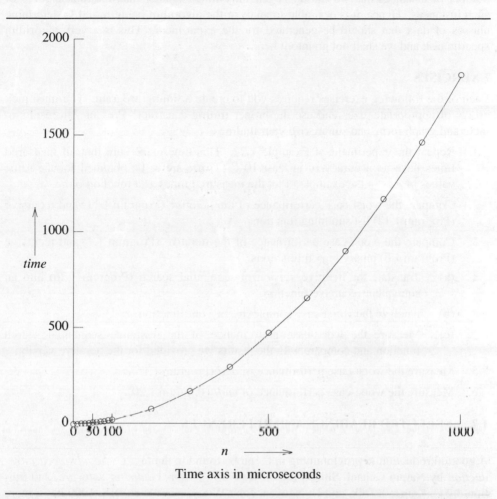

Figure 1.12: Graph of worst-case performance of selection sort

possible instances of a given characteristic. While it is possible to do this for sequential and binary search, it is not possible for a sort program. If we assume that all keys are distinct, then for any given n, $n!$ different permutations need to be used to obtain the average time.

Obtaining average case data is usually much harder than obtaining worst-case data. So, we often adopt the strategy outlined above and simply obtain an estimate of the average time.

Whether we are estimating worst-case or average time using random data, the number of instances that we can try is generally much smaller than the total number of such instances. Hence, it is desirable to analyze the algorithm being tested to determine classes of data that should be generated for the experiment. This is a very algorithm specific task and we shall not go into it here.

EXERCISES

Each of the following exercises requires you to create a timing program. You must pick arrays of appropriate sizes and use the proper timing construct. Present you results in table and graph form, and summarize your findings.

1. Repeat the experiment of Example 1.22. This time make sure that all measured times have an accuracy of at least 10%. Times are to be obtained for the same values of n as in the example. Plot the measured times as a function of n.

2. Compare the worst-case performance of the iterative (Program 1.11) and recursive (Program 1.12) list summing functions.

3. Compare the worst-case performance of the iterative (Program 1.7) and recursive (Program 1.8) binary search functions.

4. (a) Translate the iterative version of sequential search (Program 1.26) into an equivalent recursive function.

   (b) Analyze the worst-case complexity of your function.

   (c) Measure the worst-case performance of the recursive sequential search function and compare with the results we provided for the iterative version.

5. Measure the worst-case performance of *add* (Program 1.16).

6. Measure the worst-case performance of *mult* (Program 1.20).

1.7 SELECTED READINGS AND REFERENCES

A good introduction to programming in C can be found in the text *C: An advanced introduction* by Narain Gehani, Silicon Press, NJ, 1995. *Testing computer software*, 2nd Edition, by C. Kaner, J. Falk, and H. Nguyen, John Wiley, New York, NY, 1999 has a more thorough treatment of software testing and debugging techniques.

The following books provide asymptotic analyses for several programs: Handbook of data structures and applications edited by D. Mehta and S. Sahni, Chapman & Hall/CRC, Boca Raton, 2005, *Fundamentals of Computer Algorithms* by E. Horowitz, S. Sahni, and S. Rajasekaran, W. H. Freeman and Co., New York, NY, 1998; *Introduction to Algorithms*, Second Edition, by T. Cormen, C. Leiserson, and R. Rivest, McGraw-Hill, New York, NY, 2002; and *Compared to What: An Introduction to the Analysis of Algorithms* by G. Rawlins, W. H. Freeman and Co., NY, 1992.

CHAPTER 2

ARRAYS AND STRUCTURES

2.1 ARRAYS

2.1.1 The Abstract Data Type

We begin our discussion by considering an array as an ADT. This is not the usual perspective since many programmers view an array only as "a consecutive set of memory locations." This is unfortunate because it clearly shows an emphasis on implementation issues. Thus, although an array is usually implemented as a consecutive set of memory locations, this is not always the case. Intuitively an array is a set of pairs, <*index*, *value*>, such that each index that is defined has a value associated with it. In mathematical terms, we call this a *correspondence* or a *mapping*. However, when considering an ADT we are more concerned with the operations that can be performed on an array. Aside from creating a new array, most languages provide only two standard operations for arrays, one that retrieves a value, and a second that stores a value. ADT 2.1 shows a definition of the array ADT.

The *Create(j, list)* function produces a new, empty array of the appropriate size. All of the items are initially undefined. *Retrieve* accepts an *array* and an *index*. It

---

ADT *Array* is

objects: A set of pairs *<index, value>* where for each value of *index* there is a value from the set *item*. *Index* is a finite ordered set of one or more dimensions, for example, {0, ⋯ , *n*−1} for one dimension, {(0, 0), (0, 1), (0, 2), (1, 0), (1, 1), (1, 2), (2, 0), (2, 1), (2, 2)} for two dimensions, etc.

functions:

for all *A* ∈ *Array*, *i* ∈ *index*, *x* ∈ *item*, *j*, *size* ∈ integer

Array Create(*j*, *list*)	::=	**return** an array of *j* dimensions where *list* is a *j*-tuple whose *i*th element is the the size of the *i*th dimension. *Items* are undefined.
Item Retrieve(*A*, *i*)	::=	**if** (*i* ∈ *index*) **return** the item associated with index value *i* in array *A* **else return** error
Array Store(*A*,*i*,*x*)	::=	**if** (*i* in *index*) **return** an array that is identical to array *A* except the new pair *<i, x>* has been inserted **else return** error.

end *Array*

ADT 2.1: Abstract Data Type *Array*

returns the value associated with the index if the index is valid, or an error if the index is invalid. *Store* accepts an *array*, an *index*, and an *item*, and returns the original array augmented with the new *<index, value>* pair. The advantage of this ADT definition is that it clearly points out the fact that the array is a more general structure than "a consecutive set of memory locations."

2.1.2   Arrays in C

We restrict ourselves initially to one-dimensional arrays. A one-dimensional array in C is declared implicitly by appending brackets to the name of a variable. For example,

```
int list[5], *plist[5];
```

declares two arrays each containing five elements. The first array defines five integers, while the second defines five pointers to integers. In C all arrays start at index 0, so *list*[0], *list*[1], *list*[2], *list*[3], and *list*[4] (abbreviated *list* [0:4]) are the names of the five array elements, each of which contains an integer value. Similarly, *plist* [0:4] are the names of five array elements, each of which contains a pointer to an integer.

We now consider the implementation of one-dimensional arrays. When the compiler encounters an array declaration such as the one used above to create *list*, it allocates five consecutive memory locations. Each memory location is large enough to hold a single integer. The address of the first element *list*[0], is called the *base address*. If the size of an integer on your machine is denoted by *sizeof(int)*, then the memory address of *list* [i] is $\alpha + i*sizeof$ (*int*), where α is the base address. In fact, when we write *list*[i] in a C program, C interprets it as a pointer to an integer whose address is *list* [i] is $\alpha + i*sizeof$ (*int*). Observe that there is a difference between a declaration such as

```
        int *list1;
```
and
```
        int list2[5];
```

The variables *list*1 and *list*2 are both pointers to an **int**, but in the second case five memory locations for holding integers have been reserved. *list*2 is a pointer to *list*2[0] and *list*2+i is a pointer to *list*2[i]. Notice that in C, we do not multiply the offset i with the size of the type to get to the appropriate element of the array. Thus, regardless of the type of the array *list*2, it is always the case that ($list2 + i$) equals &*list*2[i]. So, *($list2 + i$) equals *list*2[i].

It is useful to consider the way C treats an array when it is a parameter to a function. All parameters of a C function must be declared within the function. However, the range of a one-dimensional array is defined only in the main program since new storage for an array is not allocated within a function. If the size of a one-dimensional array is needed, it must be either passed into the function as an argument or accessed as a global variable.

Consider Program 2.1. When *sum* is invoked, *input* = &*input* [0] is copied into a temporary location and associated with the formal parameter *list*. When *list*[i] occurs on the right-hand side of the equals sign, a dereference takes place and the value pointed at by ($list + i$) is returned. If *list*[i] appears on the left-hand side of the equals sign, then the value produced on the right-hand side is stored in the location ($list + i$). Thus in C, array parameters have their values altered, despite the fact that the parameter passing is done using *call-by-value*.

Example 2.1 [*One-dimensional array addressing*]: Assume that we have the following declaration:

```
        int one[] = {0, 1, 2, 3, 4};
```

We would like to write a function that prints out both the address of the *i*th element of this array and the value found at this address. To do this, *print*1 (Program 2.2) uses pointer arithmetic. The function is invoked as *print*1(&*one* [0],5). As you can see from the **printf** statement, the address of the *i*th element is simply *ptr* + *i*. To obtain the

```
#define MAX_SIZE 100
float sum(float [], int);
float input[MAX_SIZE], answer;
void main(void)
{
   int i;
   for (i = 0; i < MAX_SIZE; i++)
      input[i] = i;
   answer = sum(input, MAX_SIZE);
   printf("The sum is: %f\n", answer);
}
float sum(float list[], int n)
{
   int i;
   float tempsum = 0;
   for (i = 0; i < n; i++)
      tempsum += list[i];
   return tempsum;
}
```

Program 2.1: Example array program

value of the *i*th element, we use the dereferencing operator, *. Thus, *(*ptr* + *i*) indicates that we want the contents of the *ptr* + *i* position rather than the address.

```
void print1(int *ptr, int rows)
{/* print out a one-dimensional array using a pointer */
   int i;
   printf("Address Contents\n");
   for (i = 0; i < rows; i++)
      printf("%8u%5d\n", ptr + i, *(ptr + i));
   printf("\n");
}
```

Program 2.2: One-dimensional array accessed by address

Figure 2.1 shows the results we obtained when we ran *print1*. Notice that the addresses increase by four because each **int** is 4 bytes on our machine. □

Address	Contents
12244868	0
12344872	1
12344876	2
12344880	3
12344884	4

Figure 2.1: One-dimensional array addressing

2.2 DYNAMICALLY ALLOCATED ARRAYS

2.2.1 ONE-DIMENSIONAL ARRAYS

In Program 1.4, we defined the constant *MAX_SIZE* to have the value 101. As a result, the program can be used to sort a collection of up to 101 numbers. If the user wishes to sort more than 101 numbers, we have to change the definition of *MAX_SIZE* using some larger value and recompile the program. How large should this new value be? If we set *MAX_SIZE* to a very large number (say several million), we reduce the likelihood the program will fail at run time because the input value of *n* is less likely to exceed this large value of *MAX_SIZE*. However, we increase the likelihood the program may fail to compile for lack of memory for the array *list*. When writing computer programs, we often find ourselves in a situation where we cannot reliably determine how large an array to use. A good solution to this problem is to defer this decision to run time and allocate the array when we have a good estimate of the required array size. So, for example, we could change the first few lines of function *main* of Program 1.4 to:

```
int i,n,*list;
printf("Enter the number of numbers to generate: ");
scanf("%d",&n);
if( n < 1 ) {
   fprintf(stderr, "Improper value of n\n");
   exit(EXIT_FAILURE);
}
MALLOC(list, n * sizeof(int));
```

Now, the program fails only when *n*<1 or we do not have sufficient memory to hold the list of numbers that are to be sorted.

2.2.2 TWO-DIMENSIONAL ARRAYS

C uses the so-called array-of-arrays representation to represent a multidimensional array. In this representation, a two-dimensional array is represented as a one-dimensional array in which each element is, itself, a one-dimensional array. To represent the two-dimensional array

```
int x[3][5];
```

we actually create a one-dimensional array x whose length is 3; each element of x is a one-dimensional array whose length is 5. Figure 2.2 shows the memory structure. Four separate memory blocks are used. One block (the lightly shaded block) is large enough for three pointers and each of the remaining blocks is large enough for 5 **int**s.

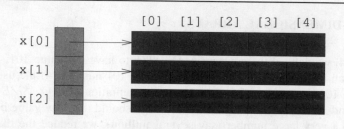

Figure 2.2: Array-of-arrays representation

C finds the element $x[i][j]$ by first accessing the pointer in $x[i]$. This pointer gives us the address, in memory, of the zeroth element of row i of the array. Then by adding $j*sizeof(int)$ to this pointer, the address of the $[j]$th element of row i (i.e., element $x[i][j]$) is determined. Program 2.3 gives a function that creates a two-dimensional array at run time.

This function may be used in the following way, for example. The second line allocates memory for a 5 by 10 two-dimensional array of integers and the third line assigns the value 6 to the [2][4] element of this array.

```
int **myArray;
myArray = make2dArray(5,10);
myArray[2][4] = 6;
```

C provides two additional memory allocation functions—*calloc* and *realloc*—that are useful in the context of dynamically allocated arrays. The function *calloc* allocates a user-specified amount of memory and initializes the allocated memory to 0 (i.e., all

```
int** make2dArray(int rows, int cols)
{/* create a two dimensional rows × cols array */
   int **x, i;

   /* get memory for row pointers */
   MALLOC(x, rows * sizeof (*x));;

   /* get memory for each row */
   for (i = 0; i < rows; i++)
     MALLOC(x[i], cols * sizeof(**x));
   return x;
}
```

Program 2.3: Dynamically create a two-dimensional array

allocated bits are set to 0); a pointer to the start of the allocated memory is returned. In case there is insufficient memory to make the allocation, the returned value is *NULL*. So, for example, the statements

```
int *x;
x = calloc(n, sizeof(int));
```

could be used to define a one-dimensional array of integers; the capacity of this array is n, and $x[0:n-1]$ are initially 0. As was the case with *malloc*, it is useful to define the macro *CALLOC* as below and use this macro to write clean robust programs.

```
#define CALLOC(p,n,s)\
        if (!((p) = calloc(n,s))) {\
            fprintf(stderr, "Insufficient memory"); \
            exit(EXIT_FAILURE);\
        }
```

The function *realloc* resizes memory previously allocated by either *malloc* or *calloc*. For example, the statement

```
                    realloc(p, s)
```

changes the size of the memory block pointed at by p to s. The contents of the first min{s, *oldSize*} bytes of the block are unchanged as a result of this resizing. When $s > oldSize$ the additional $s - oldSize$ have an unspecified value and when $s < oldSize$, the rightmost *olsSize* − *s* bytes of the old block are freed. When *realloc* is able to do the resizing, it returns a pointer to the start of the new block and when it is unable to do the resizing, the old block is unchanged and the function returns the value *NULL*.

As with *malloc* and *calloc*, it is useful to define a macro *REALLOC* as below.

```
#define REALLOC(p,s)\
        if (!((p) = realloc(p,s))) {\
                fprintf(stderr, "Insufficient memory");\
                exit(EXIT_FAILURE);\
        }
```

A three-dimensional array is represented as a one-dimensional array, each of whose elements is a two-dimensional array. Each of these two-dimensional arrays is represented as shown in Figure 2.2.

EXERCISES

1. Make the fewest number of changes to Program 2.3 so as to obtain a function that creates a two-dimensional array all of whose elements are set to 0. Test your new function.

2. Let *length* [*i*] be the desired length (size or number of elements) of row *i* of a two-dimensional array. Write a funtion similar to Program 2.3 to create a two-dimensional array such that row *i* has *length* [*i*] elements, $0 \le i < rows$. Test your code.

3. Rewrite the matrix add function of Program 1.16 using dynamically allocated arrays. The header for your function should be

    ```
    void add(int **a, int **b, int **c, int rows, int cols)
    ```

    Test your function

4. Rewrite the matrix multiplication function of Program 1.20 using dynamically allocated arrays. The header for your function should be

    ```
    void mult(int **a, int **b, int **c, int rows)
    ```

    where each matrix is a *rows* × *rows* matrix. Test your function

5. Rewrite the matrix transpose function of Program 1.22 using dynamically allocated arrays. The header for your function should be

    ```
    void transpose(int **a, int rows)
    ```

    Test your function

6. Write a matrix transpose function for matrices that may not be square. Use dynamically allocated arrays. The header for your function should be

```
void transpose(int **a, int **b, int rows, int cols)
```

where *a* is the *rows × cols* matrix that is to be transposed and *b* is the transposed matrix computed by the function. Note that the transposed matrix is a *cols × rows* matrix. Test your function

2.3   STRUCTURES AND UNIONS

2.3.1   Structures

Arrays are collections of data of the same type. In C there is an alternative way to group data that permits the data to vary in type. This mechanism is called the **struct**, short for structure. A structure (called a record in many other programming languages) is a collection of data items, where each item is identified as to its type and name. For example,

```
struct {
        char name[10];
        int age;
        float salary;
        } person;
```

creates a variable whose name is *person* and that has three fields:

*   a name that is a character array
*   an integer value representing the age of the person
*   a **float** value representing the salary of the individual

We may assign values to these fields as below. Notice the use of the . as the structure member operator. We use this operator to select a particular member of the structure.

```
strcpy(person.name,"james");
person.age = 10;
person.salary = 35000;
```

We can create our own structure data types by using the **typedef** statement as below:

```
typedef struct {
        char name[10];
        int age;                float salary;
        } humanBeing;
```

This says that *humanBeing* is the name of the type defined by the structure definition, and we may follow this definition with declarations of variables such as:

```
        humanBeing person1, person2;
```

We might have a program segment that says:

```
 if (strcmp(person1.name, person2.name))
    printf("The two people do not have the same name\n");
 else
    printf("The two people have the same name\n");
```

It would be nice if we could write `if (person1 == person2)` and have the entire structure checked for equality, or if we could write `person1 = person2` and have that mean that the value of every field of the structure of *person* 2 is assigned as the value of the corresponding field of *person* 1. ANSI C permits structure assignment, but most earlier versions of C do not. For older versions of C, we are forced to write the more detailed form:

```
        strcpy(person1.name, person2.name);
        person1.age = person2.age;
        person1.salary = person2.salary;
```

While structures cannot be directly checked for equality or inequality, we can write a function (Program 2.4) to do this. *TRUE* and *FALSE* are defined as:

```
        #define FALSE 0
        #define TRUE 1
```

A typical function call might be:

```
     if (humansEqual(person1,person2))
        printf("The two human beings are the same\n");
     else
        printf("The two human beings are not the same\n");
```

```
int humansEqual(humanBeing person1,
                humanBeing person2)
{/* return TRUE if person1 and person2 are the same human
   being otherwise return FALSE */
  if (strcmp(person1.name, person2.name))
     return FALSE;
  if (person1.age != person2.age)
     return FALSE;
  if (person1.salary != person2.salary)
     return FALSE;
  return TRUE;
}
```

Program 2.4: Function to check equality of structures

We can also embed a structure within a structure. For example, associated with our *humanBeing* structure we may wish to include the date of his or her birth. We can do this by writing:

```
typedef struct {
             int month;
             int day;
             int year;
             } date;


typedef struct {
             char name[10];
             int age;
             float salary;
             date dob;
             } humanBeing;
```

A person born on February 11, 1944, would have the values for the *date* **struct** set as:

```
person1.dob.month = 2;
person1.dob.day = 11;
person1.dob.year = 1944;
```

2.3.2 Unions

Continuing with our *humanBeing* example, it would be nice if we could distinguish between males and females. In the case of males we might ask whether they have a beard or not. In the case of females we might wish to know the number of children they have borne. This gives rise to another feature of C called a **union**. A **union** declaration is similar to a structure, but the fields of a **union** must share their memory space. This means that only one field of the **union** is "active" at any given time. For example, to add different fields for males and females we would change our definition of *humanBeing* to:

```
typedef struct {
   enum tagField {female, male} sex;
   union {
      int children;
      int beard ;
      } u;
   } sexType;
typedef struct {
   char name[10];
   int age;
   float salary;
   date dob;
   sexType sexInfo;
   } humanBeing;
humanBeing person1, person2;
```

We could assign values to *person*1 and *person*2 as:

```
person1.sexInfo.sex = male;
person1.sexInfo.u.beard = FALSE;
```
and
```
person2.sexInfo.sex = female;
person2.sexInfo.u.children = 4;
```

Notice that we first place a value in the tag field. This allows us to determine which field in the **union** is active. We then place a value in the appropriate field of the **union**. For example, if the value of *sexInfo.sex* was *male*, we would enter a *TRUE* or a *FALSE* in the *sexInfo.u.beard* field. Similarly, if the person was a *female*, we would enter an integer value in the *sexInfo.u.children* field. C does not verify that we use the appropriate field. For instance, we could place a value of *female* in the *sexInfo.sex* field, and then proceed to place a value of *TRUE* in the *sexInfo.u.beard* field. Although we know that this is not appropriate, C does not require us to use the correct fields of a **union**.

2.3.3   Internal Implementation Of Structures

In most cases you need not be concerned with exactly how the C compiler will store the
fields of a structure in memory. Generally, if you have a structure definition such as:

```
struct {int i,j; float a, b;};
```
or
```
struct {int i; int j; float a; float b; };
```

these values will be stored in the same way using increasing address locations in the
order specified in the structure definition. However, it is important to realize that holes
or padding may actually occur within a structure to permit two consecutive components
to be properly aligned within memory.

The size of an object of a **struct** or **union** type is the amount of storage necessary
to represent the largest component, including any padding that may be required. Structures must begin and end on the same type of memory boundary, for example, an even
byte boundary or an address that is a multiple of 4, 8, or 16.

2.3.4   Self-Referential Structures

A *self-referential structure* is one in which one or more of its components is a pointer to
itself. Self-referential structures usually require dynamic storage management routines
(*malloc* and *free*) to explicitly obtain and release memory. Consider as an example:

```
typedef struct {
        char data;
        struct list *link ;
        } list;
```

Each instance of the structure *list* will have two components, *data* and *link*. *data* is a single character, while *link* is a pointer to a *list* structure. The value of *link* is either the
address in memory of an instance of *list* or the null pointer. Consider these statements,
which create three structures and assign values to their respective fields:

```
list item1, item2, item3;
item1.data = 'a';
item2.data = 'b';
item3.data = 'c';
item1.link = item2.link = item3.link - NULL;
```

Structures *item* 1, *item* 2, and *item* 3 each contain the data item *a*, *b*, and *c*, respectively, and the null pointer. We can attach these structures together by replacing the null *link* field in *item* 2 with one that points to *item* 3 and by replacing the null *link* field in *item* 1 with one that points to *item* 2.

```
item1.link = &item2;
item2.link = &item3;
```

We will see more of this linking in Chapter 4.

EXERCISES

1. Develop a structure to represent the planets in the solar system. Each planet has fields for the planet's name, its distance from the sun (in miles), and the number of moons it has. Place items in each the fields for the planets: Earth and Venus.

2. Modify the *humanBeing* structure so that we can include different information based on marital status. Marital status should be an enumerated type with fields: single, married, widowed, divorced. Use a **union** to include different information based on marital status as follows:

   - *Single*. No information needed.

   - *Married*. Include a marriage date field.

   - *Widowed*. Include marriage date and death of spouse date fields.

   - *Divorced*. Include divorce date and number of divorces fields.

   Assign values to the fields for some *person* of type *humanBeing*.

3. Develop a structure to represent each of the following geometric objects: *rectangle*, *triangle*, and *circle*.

2.4 POLYNOMIALS

2.4.1 The Abstract Data Type

Arrays are not only data structures in their own right, we can also use them to implement other abstract data types. For instance, let us consider one of the simplest and most commonly found data structures: the *ordered* or *linear list*. We can find many examples of this data structure, including:

- Days of the week: (Sunday, Monday, Tuesday, Wednesday, Thursday, Friday, Saturday)

- Values in a deck of cards: (Ace, 2, 3, 4, 5, 6, 7, 8, 9, 10, Jack, Queen, King)

- Floors of a building: (basement, lobby, mezzanine, first, second)
- Years the United States fought in World War II: (1941, 1942, 1943, 1944, 1945)
- Years Switzerland fought in World War II: ( )

Notice that the years Switzerland fought in World War II is different because it contains no items. It is an example of an empty list, which we denote as ( ). The other lists all contain items that are written in the form ($item_0, item_1, \cdots, item_{n-1}$).

We can perform many operations on lists, including:

- Finding the length, n, of a list.
- Reading the items in a list from left to right (or right to left).
- Retrieving the ith item from a list, $0 \leq i < n$.
- Replacing the item in the ith position of a list, $0 \leq i < n$.
- Inserting a new item in the ith position of a list, $0 \leq i \leq n$. The items previously numbered $i, i+1, \cdots, n-1$ become items numbered $i+1, i+2, \cdots, n$.
- Deleting an item from the ith position of a list, $0 \leq i < n$. The items numbered $i+1, \cdots, n-1$ become items numbered $i, i+1, \cdots, n-2$.

Rather than state the formal specification of the ADT *list*, we want to explore briefly its implementation. Perhaps, the most common implementation is to represent an ordered list as an array where we associate the list element, $item_i$, with the array index i. We call this a sequential mapping because, assuming the standard implementation of an array, we are storing $item_i, item_{i+1}$ into consecutive slots i and $i+1$ of the array. Sequential mapping works well for most of the operations listed above. Thus, we can retrieve an item, replace an item, or find the length of a list, in constant time. We also can read the items in the list, from either direction, by simply changing subscripts in a controlled way. Only insertion and deletion pose problems since the sequential allocation forces us to move items so that the sequential mapping is preserved. It is precisely this overhead that leads us to consider nonsequential mappings of ordered lists in Chapter 4.

Let us jump right into a problem requiring ordered lists, which we will solve by using one-dimensional arrays. This problem has become the classical example for motivating the use of list processing techniques, which we will see in later chapters. Therefore, it makes sense to look at the problem and see why arrays offer only a partially adequate solution. The problem calls for building a set of functions that allow for the manipulation of symbolic polynomials. Viewed from a mathematical perspective, a polynomial is a sum of terms, where each term has a form ax^e, where x is the variable, a is the coefficient, and e is the exponent. Two example polynomials are:

$$A(x) = 3x^{20} + 2x^5 + 4 \text{ and } B(x) = x^4 + 10x^3 + 3x^2 + 1$$

The largest (or leading) exponent of a polynomial is called its *degree*. Coefficients that are zero are not displayed. The term with exponent equal to zero does not show the variable since x raised to a power of zero is 1. There are standard mathematical definitions for the sum and product of polynomials. Assume that we have two polynomials, $A(x) = \sum a_i x^i$ and $B(x) = \sum b_i x^i$ then:

$$A(x) + B(x) = \sum(a_i + b_i)x^i$$

$$A(x) \cdot B(x) = \sum(a_i x^i \cdot \sum(b_j x^j))$$

Similarly, we can define subtraction and division on polynomials, as well as many other operations.

We begin with an ADT definition of a polynomial. The particular operations in part are a reflection of what will be needed in our subsequent programs to manipulate polynomials. The definition is contained in ADT 2.2.

2.4.2 Polynomial Representation

We are now ready to make some representation decisions. A very reasonable first decision requires unique exponents arranged in decreasing order. This requirement considerably simplifies many of the operations. Using our specification and this stipulation, we can write a version of *Add* that is closer to a C function (Program 2.5), but is still representation-independent.

This algorithm works by comparing terms from the two polynomials until one or both of the polynomials becomes empty. The **switch** statement performs the comparisons and adds the proper term to the new polynomial, d. If one of the polynomials becomes empty, we copy the remaining terms from the nonempty polynomial into d. With these insights, we now consider the representation question more carefully.

One way to represent polynomials in C is to use **typedef** to create the type *polynomial* as below:

```
#define MAX_DEGREE 101 /*Max degree of polynomial+1*/
typedef struct {
    int degree;
    float coef[MAX_DEGREE];
    } polynomial;
```

Now if a is of type *polynomial* and $n < MAX\_DEGREE$, the polynomial $A(x) = \sum_{i=0}^{n} a_i x^i$ would be represented as:

$$a.degree = n$$
$$a.coef[i] = a_{n-i}, \quad 0 \le i \le n$$

ADT *Polynomial* is
    objects: $p(x) = a_1 x^{e_1} + \cdots + a_n x^{e_n}$; a set of ordered pairs of $<e_i, a_i>$ where a_i in *Coefficients* and e_i in *Exponents*, e_i are integers $>= 0$
    functions:
        for all *poly, poly*1, *poly*2 $\in$ *Polynomial*, *coef* $\in$ *Coefficients*, *expon* $\in$ *Exponents*

Polynomial Zero()	::=	**return** the polynomial, $p(x) = 0$
Boolean IsZero(*poly*)	::=	**if** (*poly*) **return** *FALSE* **else return** *TRUE*
Coefficient Coef(*poly,expon*)	::=	**if** (*expon* $\in$ *poly*) **return** its coefficient **else return** zero
Exponent LeadExp(*poly*)	::=	**return** the largest exponent in *poly*
Polynomial Attach(*poly, coef, expon*)	::=	**if** (*expon* $\in$ *poly*) **return** error **else return** the polynomial *poly* with the term *<coef, expon>* inserted
Polynomial Remove(*poly, expon*)	::=	**if** (*expon* $\in$ *poly*) **return** the polynomial *poly* with the term whose exponent is *expon* deleted **else return** error
Polynomial SingleMult(*poly, coef, expon*)	::=	**return** the polynomial $poly \cdot coef \cdot x^{expon}$
Polynomial Add(*poly*1, *poly*2)	::=	**return** the polynomial $poly1 + poly2$
Polynomial Mult(*poly*1, *poly*2)	::=	**return** the polynomial $poly1 \cdot poly2$

end *Polynomial*

ADT 2.2: Abstract data type *Polynomial*

    In this representation, we store the coefficients in order of decreasing exponents, such that $a.coef[i]$ is the coefficient of x^{n-i} provided a term with exponent $n-i$ exists; otherwise, $a.coef[i] = 0$. Although this representation leads to very simple algorithms for most of the operations, it wastes a lot of space. For instance, if $a.degree \ll MAX\_DEGREE$, (the double "less than" should be read as "is much less than"), then we will not need most of the positions in $a.coef[MAX\_DEGREE]$. The same argument

```
/* d = a + b, where a, b, and d are polynomials */
d = Zero()
while (! IsZero(a) && ! IsZero(b)) do {
   switch COMPARE(LeadExp(a), LeadExp(b)) {
      case -1: d =
         Attach(d,Coef(b,LeadExp(b)),LeadExp(b));
         b = Remove(b,LeadExp(b));
         break;
      case 0: sum = Coef( a, LeadExp(a))
                     + Coef(b, LeadExp(b));
         if (sum) {
            Attach(d,sum,LeadExp(a));
            a = Remove(a,LeadExp(a));
            b = Remove(b,LeadExp(b));
            }
         break;
      case 1: d =
         Attach(d,Coef(a,LeadExp(a)),LeadExp(a));
         a = Remove(a,LeadExp(a));
   }
}
insert any remaining terms of a or b into d
```

Program 2.5: Initial version of *padd* function

applies if the polynomial is sparse, that is, the number of terms with nonzero coefficient is small relative to the degree of the polynomial. To preserve space we devise an alternate representation that uses only one global array, *terms*, to store all our polynomials. The C declarations needed are:

```
MAX-TERMS 100 /*size of terms array*/
typedef struct {
        float coef;
        int expon;
        } polynomial;
polynomial terms[MAX-TERMS];
int avail = 0;
```

Consider the two polynomials $A(x) = 2x^{1000} + 1$ and $B(x) = x^4 + 10x^3 + 3x^2 + 1$. Figure 2.3 shows how these polynomials are stored in the array *terms*. The index of the first term of A and B is given by *startA* and *startB*, respectively, while *finishA* and *finishB* give the index of the last term of A and B. The index of the next free location in the array is given by *avail*. For our example, *startA* = 0, *finishA* = 1, *startB* = 2, *finishB* = 5, and *avail* = 6.

	startA	finishA	startB			finishB	avail
	↓	↓	↓			↓	↓
coef	2	1	1	10	3	1	
exp	1000	0	4	3	2	0	
	0	1	2	3	4	5	6

Figure 2.3: Array representation of two polynomials

This representation does not impose any limit on the number of polynomials that we can place in *terms*. The only stipulation is that the total number of nonzero terms must be no more than *MAX_TERMS*. It is worth pointing out the difference between our specification and our representation. Our specification used *poly* to refer to a polynomial, and our representation translated *poly* into a <*start*, *finish* > pair. Therefore, to use $A(x)$ we must pass in *startA* and *finishA*. Any polynomial A that has n nonzero terms has *startA* and *finishA* such that *finishA* = *startA* + n − 1.

Before proceeding, we should evaluate our current representation. Is it any better than the representation that uses an array of coefficients for each polynomial? It certainly solves the problem of many zero terms since $A(x) = 2x^{1000} + 1$ uses only six units of storage: one for *startA*, one for *finishA*, two for the coefficients, and two for the exponents. However, when all the terms are nonzero, the current representation requires about twice as much space as the first one. Unless we know before hand that each of our polynomials has few zero terms, our current representation is probably better.

2.4.3 Polynomial Addition

We would now like to write a C function that adds two polynomials, A and B, represented as above to obtain $D = A + B$. To produce $D(x)$, *padd* (Program 2.6) adds $A(x)$ and $B(x)$ term by term. Starting at position *avail*, *attach* (Program 2.7) places the terms of D into the array, *terms*. If there is not enough space in *terms* to accommodate D, an error message is printed to the standard error device and we exit the program with an error condition.

```
void padd(int startA,int finishA,int startB, int finishB,
                            int *startD,int *finishD)
{/* add A(x) and B(x) to obtain D(x) */
   float coefficient;
   *startD = avail;
   while (startA <= finishA && startB <= finishB)
      switch(COMPARE(terms[startA].expon,
                     terms[startB].expon)) {
         case -1: /* a expon < b expon */
                  attach(terms[startB].coef,terms[startB].expon);
                  startB++;
                  break;
         case 0: /* equal exponents */
                  coefficient = terms[startA].coef +
                              terms[startB].coef;
                  if (coefficient)
                     attach(coefficient,terms[startA].expon);
                  startA++;
                  startB++;
                  break;
         case 1: /* a expon > b expon */
                  attach(terms[startA].coef,terms[startA].expon);
                  startA++;
      }
   /* add in remaining terms of A(x) */
   for(; startA <= finishA; startA++)
      attach(terms[startA].coef,terms[startA].expon);
   /* add in remaining terms of B(x) */
   for( ; startB <= finishB; startB++)
      attach(terms[startB].coef, terms[startB].expon);
   *finishD = avail-1;
}
```

Program 2.6: Function to add two polynomials

Analysis of *padd*: Since the number of nonzero terms in *A* and in *B* are the most important factors in the time complexity, we will carry out the analysis using them. Therefore, let *m* and *n* be the number of nonzero terms in *A* and *B*, respectively. If $m > 0$ and $n > 0$, the **while** loop is entered. Each iteration of the loop requires O(1) time. At each iteration, we increment the value of *startA* or *startB* or both. Since the iteration terminates

```
void attach(float coefficient, int exponent)
{/* add a new term to the polynomial */
   if (avail >= MAX-TERMS) {
      fprintf(stderr,"Too many terms in the polynomial\n");
      exit(EXIT_FAILURE);
   }
   terms[avail].coef = coefficient;
   terms[avail++].expon = exponent;
}
```

Program 2.7: Function to add a new term

when either *startA* or *startB* exceeds *finishA* or *finishB*, respectively, the number of iterations is bounded by $m + n - 1$. This worst case occurs when:

$$A(x) = \sum_{i=0}^{n} x^{2i} \text{ and } B(x) = \sum_{i=0}^{n} x^{2i+1}$$

The time for the remaining two loops is bounded by $O(n + m)$ because we cannot iterate the first loop more than m times and the second more than n times. So, the asymptotic computing time of this algorithm is $O(n + m)$ □

Before proceeding let us briefly consider a few of the problems with the current representation. We have seen that, as we create polynomials, we increment *avail* until it equals *MAX TERMS*. When this occurs, must we quit? Given the current representation, we must unless there are some polynomials that we no longer need. We could write a compaction function that would remove the unnecessary polynomials and create a large, continuous available space at one end of the array. However, this requires data movement which takes time. In addition, we also must change the values of *start* and *finish* for every polynomial that is moved. In Chapter 3, we let you experiment with some "simple" compacting routines.

EXERCISES

1. Consider the type definition

```
typedef struct {
        int degree;
        int capacity;
        float* coef;
        } dpolynomial;
```

where   *coef*   is   the   dynamically   allocated   one-dimensional   array *coef* [0:*capacity* – 1]. Compare this representation for polynomials with the one using the type *polynomial*.

2. Write functions *readPoly* and *printPoly* that allow the user to create and print polynomials.

3. Write a function, *pmult*, that multiplies two polynomials. Figure out the computing time of your function.

4. Write a function, *peval*, that evaluates a polynomial at some value, x_0. Try to minimize the number of operations.

5. Let $A(x) = x^{2n} + x^{2n-2} + \cdots + x^2 + x^0$ and $B(x) = x^{2n+1} + x^{2n} + \cdots + x^3 + x$. For these polynomials, determine the exact number of times each statement of *padd* is executed.

6. The declarations that follow give us another representation of the polynomial ADT. *terms* [i][0].*expon* gives the number of nonzero terms in the ith polynomial. These terms are stored, in descending order of exponents, in positions *terms* [i][1], *terms* [i][2], $\cdots$. Create the functions *readPoly*, *printPoly*, *padd*, and *pmult* for this representation. Is this representation better or worse than the representation used in the text? (You may add declarations as necessary.)

```
#define MAX_TERMS 101 /* maximum number of terms + 1*/
#define MAX_POLYS 15 /* maximum number of
                        polynomials*/
typedef struct {
    float coef;
    int expon;
    } polynomial;
polynomial terms[MAX_POLYS][MAX_TERMS];
```

2.5   SPARSE MATRICES

2.5.1   The Abstract Data Type

We now turn our attention to a mathematical object that is used to solve many problems in the natural sciences, the matrix. As computer scientists, our interest centers not only on the specification of an appropriate ADT, but also on finding representations that let us efficiently perform the operations described in the specification.

In mathematics, a matrix contains *m* rows and *n* columns of elements as illustrated in Figure 2.4. In this figure, the elements are numbers. The first matrix has five rows and three columns; the second has six rows and six columns. In general, we write $m \times n$

(read "*m* by *n*") to designate a matrix with *m* rows and *n* columns. The total number of elements in such a matrix is *mn*. If *m* equals *n*, the matrix is square.

	col 0	col 1	col 2
row 0	-27	3	4
row 1	6	82	-2
row 2	109	-64	11
row 3	12	8	9
row 4	48	27	47

(a)

	col 0	col 1	col 2	col 3	col 4	col 5
row 0	15	0	0	22	0	-15
row 1	0	11	3	0	0	0
row 2	0	0	0	-6	0	0
row 3	0	0	0	0	0	0
row 4	91	0	0	0	0	0
row 5	0	0	28	0	0	0

(b)

Figure 2.4: Two matrices

When a matrix is represented as a two-dimensional array defined as $a[MAX\_ROWS][MAX\_COLS]$, we can locate quickly any element by writing $a[i][j]$, where i is the row index and j is the column index. However, there are some problems with this representation. For instance, if you look at the matrix of Figure 2.4(b), you notice that it contains many zero entries. We call this a *sparse matrix*. Although it is difficult to determine exactly whether a matrix is sparse or not, intuitively we can recognize a sparse matrix when we see one. In Figure 2.4(b), only 8 of 36 elements are nonzero and that certainly is sparse. When a sparse matrix is represented as a two-dimensional array, we waste space. For example, consider the space requirements necessary to store a 1000×1000 matrix that has only 2000 non-zero elements. The corresponding two-dimensional array requires space for 1,000,000 elements! We can do much better by using a representation in which only the nonzero elements are stored.

Before developing a particular representation, we first must consider the operations that we want to perform on these matrices. A minimal set of operations includes matrix creation, addition, multiplication, and transpose. ADT 2.3 contains our specification of the matrix ADT.

ADT *SparseMatrix* is

    objects: a set of triples, <*row, column, value*>, where *row* and *column* are integers and form a unique combination, and *value* comes from the set *item*.

    functions:

      for all *a, b* ∈ *SparseMatrix*, *x* ∈ *item*, *i, j, maxCol, maxRow* ∈ *index*

      SparseMatrix Create(*maxRow, maxCol*) ::=

            return a *SparseMatrix* that can hold up to *maxItems* = *maxRow* × *maxCol* and whose maximum row size is *maxRow* and whose maximum column size is *maxCol*.

      SparseMatrix Transpose(*a*) ::=

            return the matrix produced by interchanging the row and column value of every triple.

      SparseMatrix Add(*a, b*) ::=

            if the dimensions of *a* and *b* are the same
            return the matrix produced by adding corresponding items, namely those with identical *row* and *column* values.
            else return error

      SparseMatrix Multiply(*a, b*) ::=

            if number of columns in *a* equals number of rows in *b*
            return the matrix *d* produced by multiplying *a* by *b* according to the formula: $d[i][j] = \sum(a[i][k] \cdot b[k][j])$ where $d(i, j)$ is the (i, j)th element
            else return error.

ADT 2.3: Abstract data type *SparseMatrix*

2.5.2   Sparse Matrix Representation

Before implementing any of the ADT operations, we must establish the representation of the sparse matrix. By examining Figure 2.4, we know that we can characterize uniquely any element within a matrix by using the triple <*row, col, value*>. This means that we can use an array of triples to represent a sparse matrix. Since we want our transpose operation to work efficiently, we should organize the triples so that the row indices are in ascending order. We can go one step further by also requiring that all the triples for any row be stored so that the column indices are in ascending order. In addition, to ensure that the operations terminate, we must know the number of rows and columns, and the number of nonzero elements in the matrix. Putting all this information together suggests that we implement the *Create* operation as below:

SparseMatrix Create(*maxRow*, *maxCol*) ::=

```
#define MAX_TERMS 101 /* maximum number of terms +1*/
typedef struct {
        int col;
        int row;
        int value;
        } term;
term a[MAX_TERMS];
```

Since *MAX_TERMS* is greater than eight, these statements can be used to represent the second sparse matrix from Figure 2.4. Figure 2.5(a) shows how this matrix is represented in the array *a*. Thus, *a* [0].*row* contains the number of rows; *a* [0].*col* contains the number of columns; and *a* [0].*value* contains the total number of nonzero entries. Positions 1 through 8 store the triples representing the nonzero entries. The row index is in the field *row*; the column index is in the field *col*; and the value is in the field *value*. The triples are ordered by row and within rows by columns.

	row	col	value		row	col	value
a[0]	6	6	8	b[0]	6	6	8
[1]	0	0	15	[1]	0	0	15
[2]	0	3	22	[2]	0	4	91
[3]	0	5	-15	[3]	1	1	11
[4]	1	1	11	[4]	2	1	3
[5]	1	2	3	[5]	2	5	28
[6]	2	3	-6	[6]	3	0	22
[7]	4	0	91	[7]	3	2	-6
[8]	5	2	28	[8]	5	0	-15
	(a)				(b)		

Figure 2.5: Sparse matrix and its transpose stored as triples

2.5.3 Transposing A Matrix

Figure 2.5(b) shows the transpose of the sample matrix. To transpose a matrix we must interchange the rows and columns. This means that each element $a[i][j]$ in the original matrix becomes element $b[j][i]$ in the transpose matrix. Since we have organized the original matrix by rows, we might think that the following is a good algorithm for transposing a matrix:

```
for each row i
   take element <i, j, value> and store it
   as element <j, i, value> of the transpose;
```

Unfortunately, if we process the original matrix by the row indices we will not know exactly where to place element $<j, i, value>$ in the transpose matrix until we have processed all the elements that precede it. For instance, in Figure 2.5, we have:

(0, 0, 15),	which becomes	(0, 0, 15)
(0, 3, 22),	which becomes	(3, 0, 22)
(0, 5, −15),	which becomes	(5, 0, −15)

If we place these triples consecutively in the transpose matrix, then, as we insert new triples, we must move elements to maintain the correct order. We can avoid this data movement by using the column indices to determine the placement of elements in the transpose matrix. This suggests the following algorithm:

```
for all elements in column j
   place element <i, j, value> in
   element <j, i, value>
```

The algorithm indicates that we should "find all the elements in column 0 and store them in row 0 of the transpose matrix, find all the elements in column 1 and store them in row 1, etc." Since the original matrix ordered the rows, the columns within each row of the transpose matrix will be arranged in ascending order as well. This algorithm is incorporated in *transpose* (Program 2.8). The first array, a, is the original array, while the second array, b, holds the transpose.

It is not too difficult to see that the function works correctly. The variable, *currentb*, holds the position in b that will contain the next transposed term. We generate the terms in b by rows, but since the rows in b correspond to the columns in a, we collect the nonzero terms for row i of b by collecting the nonzero terms from column i of a.

```
void transpose(term a[], term b[])
{/* b is set to the transpose of a */
   int n,i,j, currentb;
   n = a[0].value;          /* total number of elements */
   b[0].row = a[0].col; /* rows in b = columns in a */
   b[0].col = a[0].row; /* columns in b = rows in a */
   b[0].value = n;
   if (n > 0 )   { /* non zero matrix */
      currentb = 1;
      for (i = 0; i < a[0].col; i++)
      /* transpose by the columns in a */
         for (j = 1; j <= n; j++)
         /* find elements from the current column */
            if (a[j].col == i) {
            /* element is in current column, add it to b */
               b[currentb].row - a[j].col;
               b[currentb].col = a[j].row;
               b[currentb].value = a[j].value;
               currentb++;
            }
   }
}
```

Program 2.8: Transpose of a sparse matrix

Analysis of *transpose*: Determining the computing time of this algorithm is easy since the nested **for** loops are the decisive factor. The remaining statements (two **if** statements and several assignment statements) require only constant time. We can see that the outer **for** loop is iterated $a[0].col$ times, where $a[0].col$ holds the number of columns in the original matrix. In addition, one iteration of the inner **for** loop requires $a[0].value$ time, where $a[0].value$ holds the number of elements in the original matrix. Therefore, the total time for the nested **for** loops is *columns · elements*. Hence, the asymptotic time complexity is O(*columns · elements*). □

We now have a matrix transpose algorithm with a computing time of O(*columns · elements*). This time is a little disturbing since we know that if we represented our matrices as two-dimensional arrays of size *rows × columns*, we could obtain the transpose in O(*rows · columns*) time. The algorithm to accomplish this has the simple form:

```
for (j = 0; j < columns; j++)
    for (i = 0; i < rows; i++)
        b[j][i] = a[i][j];
```

The O(*columns · elements*) time for our transpose function becomes O(*columns*^{2} · *rows*) when the number of elements is of the order *columns · rows*. Perhaps, to conserve space, we have traded away too much time. Actually, we can create a much better algorithm by using a little more storage. In fact, we can transpose a matrix represented as a sequence of triples in O(*columns* + *elements*) time. This algorithm, *fastTranspose* (Program 2.9), proceeds by first determining the number of elements in each column of the original matrix. This gives us the number of elements in each row of the transpose matrix. From this information, we can determine the starting position of each row in the transpose matrix. We now can move the elements in the original matrix one by one into their correct position in the transpose matrix. We assume that the number of columns in the original matrix never exceeds *MAX_COL*.

```
void fastTranspose(term a[], term b[])
{/* the transpose of a is placed in b */
   int rowTerms[MAX_COL], startingPos[MAX_COL];
   int i,j, numCols = a[0].col, numTerms = a[0].value;
   b[0].row = numCols;   b[0].col = a[0].row;
   b[0].value = numTerms;
   if (numTerms > 0) { /* nonzero matrix */
      for (i = 0; i < numCols; i++)
         rowTerms[i] = 0;
      for (i = 1; i <= numTerms; i++)
         rowTerms[a[i].col]++;
      startingPos[0] = 1;
      for (i = 1; i < numCols; i++)
         startingPos[i] =
                     startingPos[i-1] + rowTerms[i-1];
      for (i = 1; i <= numTerms; i++) {
         j = startingPos[a[i].col]++;
         b[j].row = a[i].col;   b[j].col = a[i].row;
         b[j].value = a[i].value;
      }
   }
}
```

Program 2.9: Fast transpose of a sparse matrix

Analysis of *fastTranspose*: We can verify that *fastTranspose* works correctly from the preceding discussion and the observation that the starting point of row i, $i > 1$ of the transpose matrix is $rowTerms[i-1] + startingPos[i-1]$, where $rowTerms[i-1]$ is the number of elements in row $i-1$ and $startingPos[i-1]$ is the starting point of row $i-1$. The first two **for** loops compute the values for *rowTerms*, the third **for** loop carries out the computation of *startingPos*, and the last **for** loop places the triples into the transpose matrix. These four loops determine the computing time of *fastTranspose*. The bodies of the loops are executed *numCols*, *numTerms*, *numCols* – 1, and *numTerms* times, respectively. Since the statements within the loops require only constant time, the computing time for the algorithm is O(*columns* + *elements*). The time becomes O(*columns* · *rows*) when the number of elements is of the order *columns* · *rows*. This time equals that of the two-dimensional array representation, although *fastTranspose* has a larger constant factor. However, when the number of elements is sufficiently small compared to the maximum of *columns* · *rows*, *fastTranspose* is much faster. Thus, in this representation we save both time and space. This was not true of *transpose* since the number of elements is usually greater than max{*columns, rows*} and *columns* · *elements* is always at least *columns* · *rows*. In addition, the constant factor for *transpose* is bigger than that found in the two-dimensional array representation. However, *transpose* requires less space than *fastTranspose* since the latter function must allocate space for the *rowTerms* and *startingPos* arrays. We can reduce this space to one array if we put the starting positions into the space used by the row terms as we calculate each starting position. □

If we try the algorithm on the sparse matrix of Figure 2.5(a), then after the execution of the third **for** loop, the values of *rowTerms* and *startingPos* are:

	[0]	[1]	[2]	[3]	[4]	[5]
rowTerms =	2	1	2	2	0	1
startingPos =	1	3	4	6	8	8

The number of entries in row i of the transpose is contained in $rowTerms[i]$. The starting position for row i of the transpose is held by $startingPos[i]$.

2.5.4 Matrix Multiplication

A second operation that arises frequently is matrix multiplication, which is defined below.

Definition: Given A and B where A is $m \times n$ and B is $n \times p$, the product matrix D has dimension $m \times p$. Its $<i, j>$ element is :

$$d_{ij} = \sum_{k=0}^{n-1} a_{ik}\, b_{kj}$$

for $0 \le i < m$ and $0 \le j < p$. □

The product of two sparse matrices may no longer be sparse, as Figure 2.6 shows.

$$\begin{bmatrix} 1 & 0 & 0 \\ 1 & 0 & 0 \\ 1 & 0 & 0 \end{bmatrix} \cdot \begin{bmatrix} 1 & 1 & 1 \\ 0 & 0 & 0 \\ 0 & 0 & 0 \end{bmatrix} = \begin{bmatrix} 1 & 1 & 1 \\ 1 & 1 & 1 \\ 1 & 1 & 1 \end{bmatrix}$$

Figure 2.6: Multiplication of two sparse matrices

We would like to multiply two sparse matrices represented as an ordered list (Figure 2.5). We need to compute the elements of D by rows so that we can store them in their proper place without moving previously computed elements. To do this we pick a row of A and find all elements in column j of B for $j = 0, 1, \cdots , colsB - 1$. Normally, we would have to scan all of B to find all the elements in column j. However, we can avoid this by first computing the transpose of B. This puts all column elements in consecutive order. Once we have located the elements of row i of A and column j of B we just do a merge operation similar to that used in the polynomial addition of Section 2.2. (We explore an alternate approach in the exercises at the end of this section.)

To obtain the product matrix D, *mmult* (Program 2.10) multiplies matrices A and B using the strategy outlined above. We store the matrices A, B, and D in the arrays a, b, and d, respectively. To place a triple in d and to reset *sum* to 0, *mmult* uses *storeSum* (Program 2.11). In addition, *mmult* uses several local variables that we will describe briefly. The variable *row* is the row of A that we are currently multiplying with the columns in B. The variable *rowBegin* is the position in a of the first element of the current row, and the variable *column* is the column of B that we are currently multiplying with a row in A. The variable *totalD* is the current number of elements in the product matrix D. The variables i and j are used to examine successively elements from a row of A and a column of B. Finally, the variable *newB* is the sparse matrix that is the transpose of b. Notice that we have introduced an additional term into both a ($a[totalA+1].row = rowsA;$) and *newB* ($newB[totalB+1].row = colsB;$). These dummy terms serve as sentinels that enable us to obtain an elegant algorithm.

```
void mmult(term a[], term b[], term d[])
{/* multiply two sparse matrices */
   int i, j, column, totalB = b[0].value, totalD = 0;
   int rowsA = a[0].row, colsA = a[0].col,
   totalA = a[0].value; int  colsB = b[0].col,
   int rowBegin = 1, row = a[1].row, sum = 0;
   int newB[MAX_TERMS][3];
   if (colsA != b[0].row) {
      fprintf(stderr,"Incompatible matrices\n");
      exit(EXIT_FAILURE);
   }
   fastTranspose(b,newB);
   /* set boundary condition */
   a[totalA+1].row = rowsA;
   newB[totalB+1].row = colsB;
   newB[totalB+1].col = 0;
   for (i = 1; i <= totalA; ) {
      column = newB[1].row;
      for (j = 1; j <= totalB+1;) {
      /* multiply row of a by column of b */
         if (a[i].row != row) {
            storeSum(d, &totalD, row, column, &sum);
            i = rowBegin;
            for (; newB[j].row == column; j++)
               ;
            column = newB[j].row;
         }
         else if (newB[j].row != column) {
            storeSum(d, &totalD, row, column, &sum);
            i = rowBegin;
            column = newB[j].row;
         }
         else switch (COMPARE(a[i].col, newB[j].col)) {
            case -1: /* go to next term in a */
                     i++;  break;
            case 0: /* add terms, go to next term in a and b*/
                     sum += ( a[i++].value * newB[j++].value);
                     break;
            case 1 : /* advance to next term in b */
                     j++;
         }
```

```
      }   /* end of for j <= totalB+1 */
      for (; a[i].row == row; i++)
         ;
      rowBegin = i; row = a[i].row;
   } /* end of for i<=totalA */
   d[0].row = rowsA;
   d[0].col = colsB; d[0].value =  totalD;
}
```

Program 2.10: Sparse matrix multiplication

```
void storeSum(term d[], int *totalD, int row, int column,
                                       int *sum)
{/* if *sum != 0, then it along with its row and column
    position is stored as the *totalD+1 entry in d */
  if (*sum)
     if (*totalD < MAX—TERMS) {
        d[++*totalD].row = row;
        d[*totalD].col = column;
        d[*totalD].value = *sum;
        *sum = 0;
     }
     else {
        fprintf(stderr,"Numbers of terms in product
                             exceeds %d\n",MAX—TERMS);
        exit(EXIT_FAILURE);
     }
}
```

Program 2.11: *storeSum* function

Analysis of *mmult*: We leave the correctness proof of *mmult* as an exercise and consider only its complexity. Besides the space needed for *a*, *b*, *d*, and a few simple variables, we also need space to store the transpose matrix *newB*. We also must include the additional space required by *fastTranspose*. The exercises explore a strategy for *mmult* that does not explicitly compute *newB*.

We can see that the lines before the first **for** loop require only O(*colsB* + *totalB*) time, which is the time needed to transpose *b*. The outer **for** loop is executed *totalA* times. At each iteration either *i* or *j* or both increase by 1, or *i* and *column* are reset. The maximum total increment in *j* over the entire loop is *totalB* + 1. If *termsRow* is the total number of terms in the current row of A, then i can increase at most *termsRow* times before i moves to the next row of A. When this happens, we reset i to *rowBegin*, and, at the same time, advance *column* to the next column. Thus, this resetting takes place at most *colsB* time, and the total maximum increment in i is *colsB*termsRow*. Therefore, the maximum number of iterations of the outer **for** loop is *colsB* + *colsB*termsRow* + *totalB*. The time for the inner loop during the multiplication of the current row is $O(colsB*termsRow + totalB)$, and the time to advance to the next row is $O(termsRow)$. Thus, the time for one iteration of the outer **for** loop is $O(colsB*termsRow + totalB)$. The overall time for this loop is:

$$O\left(\sum_{row}(colsB \cdot termsRow + totalB)\right) = O(colsB \cdot totalA + rowsA \cdot totalB) \quad \square$$

Once again we can compare this time with the computing time required to multiply matrices using the standard array representation. The classic multiplication algorithm is:

```
for (i = 0; i < rowsA; i++)
    for (j = 0; j < colsB; j++) {
        sum = 0;
        for (k = 0; k < colsA; k++)
            sum += (a[i][k] * b[k][j]);
        d[i][j] = sum;
    }
```

This algorithm takes $O(rowsA \cdot colsA \cdot colsB)$ time. Since $totalA \leq colsA \cdot rowsA$ and $totalB \leq colsA \cdot colsB$, the time for *mmult* is $O(rowsA \cdot colsA \cdot colsB)$. However, its constant factor is greater than that of the classic algorithm. In the worst case, when $totalA = colsA \cdot rowsA$ or $totalB = colsA \cdot colsB$, *mmult* is slower by a constant factor. However, when *totalA* and *totalB* are sufficiently smaller than their maximum value, that is, A and B are sparse, *mmult* outperforms the classic algorithm. The analysis of *mmult* is not trivial. It introduces some new concepts in algorithm analysis and you should make sure that you understand the analysis.

This representation of sparse matrices permits us to perform operations such as addition, transpose, and multiplication efficiently. However, there are other considerations that make this representation undesirable in certain applications. Since the number of terms in a sparse matrix is variable, we would like to represent all our sparse matrices in one array as we did for polynomials in Section 2.2. This would enable us to make efficient utilization of space. However, when this is done we run into difficulties in allocating space from the array to any individual matrix. These difficulties also occur with the polynomial representation and will become even more obvious when we study a similar representation for multiple stacks and queues in Section 3.4.

EXERCISES

1. Write C functions *readMatrix*, *printMatrix*, and *search* that read triples into a new sparse matrix, print out the terms in a sparse matrix, and search for a value in a sparse matrix. Analyze the computing time of each of these functions.

2. Rewrite *fastTranspose* so that it uses only one array rather than the two arrays required to hold *rowTerms* and *startingPos*.

3. Develop a correctness proof for the *mmult* function.

4. Analyze the time and space requirements of *fastTranspose*. What can you say about the existence of a faster algorithm?

5. Use the concept of an array of starting positions found in *fastTranspose* to rewrite *mmult* so that it multiplies sparse matrices A and B without transposing B. What is the computing time of your function?

6. As an alternate sparse matrix representation we keep only the nonzero terms in a one-dimensional array, *value*, in the order described in the text. In addition, we also maintain a two-dimensional array, *bits* [*rows*][*columns*], such that $bits[i][j] = 0$ if $a[i][j] = 0$ and $bits[i][j] = 1$ if $a[i][j] \neq 0$. Figure 2.7 illustrates the representation for the sparse matrix of Figure 2.5(b).

$$
\begin{bmatrix}
1 & 0 & 0 & 1 & 0 & 1 \\
0 & 1 & 1 & 0 & 0 & 0 \\
0 & 0 & 0 & 1 & 0 & 0 \\
0 & 0 & 0 & 0 & 0 & 0 \\
1 & 0 & 0 & 0 & 0 & 0 \\
0 & 0 & 1 & 0 & 0 & 0
\end{bmatrix}
\qquad
\begin{bmatrix}
15 \\
22 \\
-15 \\
11 \\
3 \\
-6 \\
91 \\
28
\end{bmatrix}
$$

Figure 2.7: Alternate representation of a sparse matrix

(a) On a computer with w bits per word, how much storage is needed to represent a sparse matrix, A, with t nonzero terms?

(b) Write a C function to add two sparse matrices A and B represented as in Figure 2.7 to obtain $D = A + B$. How much time does your algorithm take?

(c) Discuss the merits of this representation versus the one used in the text. Consider the space and time requirements for such operations as random access, add, multiply, and transpose. Note that we can improve the random access time by keeping another array, *ra*, such that $ra[i]$ = number of nonzero terms in rows 0 through $i - 1$.

2.6 REPRESENTATION OF MULTIDIMENSIONAL ARRAYS

In C, multidimensional arrays are represented using the array-of-arrays representation (Section 2.2.2). An alternative to the array-of-arrays representation is to map all elements of a multidimensional array into an ordered or linear list. The linear list is then stored in consecutuve memory just as we store a one-dimensional array. This mapping of a multidimensional array to memory requires a more complex addressing formula that required by the mapping of a one-dimensional array to memory. If an array is declared $a[upper_0][upper_1] \cdots [upper_{n-1}]$, then it is easy to see that the number of elements in the array is:

$$\prod_{i=0}^{n-1} upper_i$$

where Π is the product of the $upper_i$'s. For instance, if we declare a as $a[10][10][10]$, then we require $10 \cdot 10 \cdot 10 = 1000$ units of storage to hold the array. There are two common ways to represent multidimensional arrays: *row major order* and *column major order*. We consider only row major order here, leaving column major order for the exercises.

As its name implies, row major order stores multidimensional arrays by rows. For instance, we interpret the two-dimensional array $A[upper_0][upper_1]$ as $upper_0$ rows, $row_0, row_1, \cdots, row_{upper_0-1}$, each row containing $upper_1$ elements.

If we assume that α is the address of $A[0][0]$, then the address of $A[i][0]$ is $\alpha + i \cdot upper_1$ because there are i rows, each of size $upper_1$, preceding the first element in the ith row. Notice that we haven't multiplied by the element size. This follows C convention in which the size of the elements is automatically accounted for. The address of an arbitrary element, $a[i][j]$, is $\alpha + i \cdot upper_1 + j$.

To represent a three-dimensional array, $A[upper_0][upper_1][upper_2]$, we interpret the array as $upper_0$ two-dimensional arrays of dimension $upper_1 \times upper_2$. To locate $a[i][j][k]$, we first obtain $\alpha + i \cdot upper1 \cdot upper2$ as the address of $a[i][0][0]$ because there are i two-dimensional arrays of size $upper_1 \cdot upper_2$ preceding this element. Combining this formula with the formula for addressing a two-dimensional array, we obtain:

$$\alpha + i \cdot upper_1 \cdot upper_2 + j \cdot upper_2 + k$$

as the address of $a[i][j][k]$.

Generalizing on the preceding discussion, we can obtain the addressing formula for any element $A[i_0][i_1] \ldots [i_{n-1}]$ in an n-dimensional array declared as:

$$A[upper_0][upper_1] \ldots [upper_{n-1}]$$

If α is the address for $A[0][0] \ldots [0]$ then the address of $a[i_0][0][0] \ldots [0]$ is:

$$\alpha + i_0 \; upper_1 \; upper_2 \ldots upper \; n-1$$

The address of $a[i_0][i_1][0]\ldots[0]$ is:

$$\alpha + i_0 \; upper_1 \; upper_2 \ldots upper_{n-1} + i_1 \; upper_2 \; upper_3 \ldots upper_{n-1}$$

Repeating in this way the address for $A[i_0][i_1]\ldots[i_{n-1}]$ is:

$$\alpha + i_0 upper_1 upper_2 \ldots upper_{n-1}$$
$$+ i_1 upper_2 upper_3 \ldots upper_{n-1}$$
$$+ i_2 upper_3 upper_4 \ldots upper_{n-1}$$
$$\cdot$$
$$\cdot$$
$$\cdot$$
$$+ i_{n-2} upper_{n-1}$$
$$+ i_{n-1}$$

$$= \alpha + \sum_{j=0}^{n-1} i_j a_j \text{ where: } \begin{cases} a_j = \displaystyle\prod_{k=j+1}^{n-1} upper_k \quad 0 \le j < n-1 \\ a_{n-1} = 1 \end{cases}$$

Notice that a_j may be computed from $a_{j+1}, 0 \le j < n-1$, using only one multiplication as $a_j = upper_{j+1} \cdot a_{j+1}$. Thus, a compiler will initially take the declared bounds $upper_0, \ldots, upper_{n-1}$ and use them to compute the constants $a_0 \ldots a_{n-2}$ using $n-2$ multiplications. The address of $a[i_0]\ldots a[i_{n-1}]$ can be computed using the formula, requiring $n-1$ more multiplications and n additions and n subtractions.

EXERCISES

1. Assume that we have a one-dimensional array, $a[MAX\_SIZE]$. Normally, the subscripts for this array vary from 0 to $MAX\_SIZE - 1$. However, by using pointer arithmetic we can create arrays with arbitrary bounds. Indicate how to create an array, and obtain subscripts for an array, that has bounds between -10 to 10. That is, we view the subscripts as having the values $-10, -9, -8, \cdots, 8, 9, 10$.

2. Extend the results from Exercise 1 to create a two-dimensional array where row and column subscripts each range from -10 to 10.

3. Obtain an addressing formula for the element $a[i_0][i_1]\ldots[i_{n-1}]$ in an array declared as $a[upper_0]\ldots a[upper_{n-1}]$. Assume a column major representation of the array with one word per element and α the address of $a[0][0]\ldots[0]$. In column major order, the entries are stored by columns first. For example, the array $a[3][3]$ would be stored as $a[0][0]$, $a[1][0]$, $a[2][0]$, $a[0][1]$, $a[1][1]$, $a[2][1]$, $a[0][2]$, $a[1][2]$, $a[2][2]$.

2.7 STRINGS

2.7.1 The Abstract Data Type

Thus far, we have considered only ADTs whose component elements were numeric. For example, we created a sparse matrix ADT and represented it as an array of triples <*row*, *col*, *value* >. In this section, we turn our attention to a data type, the string, whose component elements are characters. As an ADT, we define a string to have the form, $S = s_0, \ldots, s_{n-1}$, where s_i are characters taken from the character set of the programming language. If $n = 0$, then S is an empty or null string.

There are several useful operations we could specify for strings. Some of these operations are similar to those required for other ADTs: creating a new empty string, reading a string or printing it out, appending two strings together (called *concatenation*), or copying a string. However, there are other operations that are unique to our new ADT, including comparing strings, inserting a substring into a string, removing a substring from a string, or finding a pattern in a string. We have listed the essential operations in ADT 2.4, which contains our specification of the string ADT. Actually there are many more operations on strings, as we shall see when we look at part of C's string library in Figure 2.8.

2.7.2 Strings in C

In C, we represent strings as character arrays terminated with the null character \0. For instance, suppose we had the strings:

```
#define MAX_SIZE 100 /*maximum size of string */
char s[MAX_SIZE] = {"dog"};
char t[MAX_SIZE] = {"house"};
```

Figure 2.9 shows how these strings would be represented internally in memory. Notice that we have included array bounds for the two strings. Technically, we could have declared the arrays with the statements:

```
char s[] = {"dog"};
char t[] = {"house"}
```

Using these declarations, the C compiler would have allocated just enough space to hold each word including the null character. Now suppose we want to concatenate these strings together to produce the new string, "doghouse." To do this we use the C function *strcat* (See Figure 2.8). Two strings are joined together by *strcat* (*s*, *t*), which stores the result in *s*. Although *s* has increased in length by five, we have no additional space in *s* to store the extra five characters. Our compiler handled this problem inelegantly: it

---

ADT *String* is
    objects: a finite set of zero or more characters.
    functions:
        for all $s, t \in$ *String*, $i, j, m \in$ non-negative integers

String Null(m)	::=	**return** a string whose maximum length is m characters, but is initially set to *NULL* We write *NULL* as "".
Integer Compare(s, t)	::=	**if** s equals t **return** 0 **else if** s precedes t **return** -1 **else return** +1
Boolean IsNull(s)	::=	**if** (Compare(s, *NULL*)) **return** *FALSE* **else return** *TRUE*
Integer Length(s)	::=	**if** (Compare(s, *NULL*)) **return** the number of characters in s **else return** 0.
String Concat(s, t)	::=	**if** (Compare(t, *NULL*)) **return** a string whose elements are those of s followed by those of t **else return** s.
String Substr(s, i, j)	::=	**if** (($j > 0$) && ($i+j-1$) < Length(s)) **return** the string containing the characters of s at positions $i, i + 1, \cdots , i+j-1$. **else return** *NULL*.

ADT 2.4: Abstract data type *String*

simply overwrote the memory to fit in the extra five characters. Since we declared t immediately after s, this meant that part of the word "house" disappeared.

We have already seen that C provides a built-in function to perform concatenation. In addition to this function, C provides several other string functions which we access through the statement *#include <string.h>*. Figure 2.8 contains a brief summary of these functions (we have excluded string conversion functions such as *atoi*). For each function, we have provided a generic function declaration and a brief description. Rather than discussing each function separately, we next look at an example that uses several of them.

Example 2.2 [*String insertion*]: Assume that we have two strings, say *string* 1 and *string* 2, and that we want to insert *string* 2 into *string* 1 starting at the *i*th position of *string* 1. We begin with the declarations:

Function	Description
char *strcat(char *dest, char *src)	concatenate *dest* and *src* strings; return result in *dest*
char *strncat(char *dest, char *src, int n)	concatenate *dest* and *n* characters from *src*; return result in *dest*
char *strcmp(char *str1, char *str2)	compare two strings; return < 0 if *str1* < *str2*; 0 if *str1* = *str2*; > 0 if *str1* > *str2*
char *strncmp(char *str1, char *str2, int n)	compare first *n* characters return < 0 if *str1* < *str2*; 0 if *str1* = *str2*; > 1 if *str1* > *str2*
char *strcpy(char *dest, char *src)	copy *src* into *dest*; return *dest*
char *strncpy(char *dest, char *src, int n)	copy *n* characters from *src* string into *dest*; return *dest*;
size−t strlen(char *s)	return the length of a *s*
char *strchr(char *s, int c)	return pointer to the first occurrence of *c* in *s*; return *NULL* if not present
char *strrchr(char *s, int c)	return pointer to last occurrence of *c* in *s*; return *NULL* if not present
char *strtok(char *s, char *delimiters)	return a token from *s*, token is surrounded by *delimiters*
char *strstr(char *s, char *pat)	return pointer to start of *pat* in *s*
size−t strspn(char *s, char *spanset)	scan *s* for characters in *spanset*; return length of span
size−t strcspn(char *s, char *spanset)	scan *s* for characters not in *spanset*; return length of span
char *strpbrk(char *s, char *spanset)	scan *s* for characters in *spanset*; return pointer to first occurrence of a character from *spanset*

Figure 2.8: C string functions

$s[0]s[1]s[2]s[3]$	$t[0]t[1]t[2]t[3]t[4]t[5]$

d	o	g	\0

h	o	u	s	e	\0

Figure 2.9: String representation in C

```
#include <string.h>
#define MAX_SIZE 100 /*size of largest string*/
char string1[MAX_SIZE], *s = string1;
char string2[MAX_SIZE],  *t = string2;
```

In addition to creating the two strings, we also have created a pointer for each string.

Now suppose that the first string contains "amobile" and the second contains "uto" (Figure 2.10). We want to insert "uto" starting at position 1 of the first string, thereby producing the word "automobile." We can accomplish this using only three function calls, as Figure 2.10 illustrates. Thus, in Figure 2.10(a), we assume that we have an empty string that is pointed to by *temp*. We use *strncpy* to copy the first i characters from s into *temp*. Since $i = 1$, this produces the string "a." In Figure 2.10(b), we concatenate *temp* and t to produce the string "auto." Finally, we append the remainder of s to *temp*. Since *strncat* copied the first i characters, the remainder of the string is at address $(s + i)$. The final result is shown in Figure 2.10(c).

Program 2.12 inserts one string into another. This particular function is not normally found in *<string.h>*. Since either of the strings could be empty, we also include statements that check for these conditions. It is worth pointing out that the call *strnins* $(s, t, 0)$ is equivalent to *strcat* (t, s). Program 2.12 is presented as an example of manipulating strings. It should never be used in practice as it is wasteful in its use of time and space. Try to revise it so the string *temp* is not required. □

2.7.3 Pattern Matching

Now let us develop an algorithm for a more sophisticated application of strings. Assume that we have two strings, *string* and *pat*, where *pat* is a pattern to be searched for in *string*. The easiest way to determine if *pat* is in *string* is to use the built-in function *strstr*. If we have the following declarations:

```
char pat[MAX_SIZE], string[MAX_SIZE], *t;
```

then we use the following statements to determine if *pat* is in *string*:

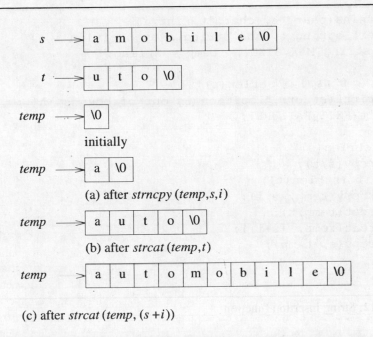

Figure 2.10: String insertion example

```
if (t = strstr(string,pat))
    printf("The string from strstr is: %s\n",t);
else
    printf("The pattern was not found with strstr\n");
```

The call ($t = strstr(string,pat)$) returns a null pointer if *pat* is not in *string*. If *pat* is in *string*, *t* holds a pointer to the start of *pat* in *string*. The entire string beginning at position *t* is printed out.

Although *strstr* seems ideally suited to pattern matching, we may want to develop our own pattern matching function because there are several different methods for implementing a pattern matching function. The easiest but least efficient method sequentially examines each character of the string until it finds the pattern or it reaches the end of the string. (We explore this approach in the Exercises.) If *pat* is not in *string*, this method has a computing time of $O(n \cdot m)$ where n is the length of *pat* and m is the length of *string*. We can do much better than this, if we create our own pattern matching function.

We can improve on an exhaustive pattern matching technique by quitting when

```
void strnins(char *s, char *t, int i)
{/* insert string t into string s at position i */
   char string[MAX-SIZE], *temp = string;

   if (i < 0 && i > strlen(s)) {
      fprintf(stderr,"Position is out of bounds \n");
      exit(EXIT_FAILURE);
   }
   if (!strlen(s))
      strcpy(s,t);
   else if (strlen(t)) {
      strncpy(temp, s,i);
      strcat(temp,t);
      strcat(temp, (s+i));
      strcpy(s, temp);
   }
}
```

Program 2.12: String insertion function

strlen (pat) is greater than the number of remaining characters in the string. Checking the first and last characters of *pat* and *string* before we check the remaining characters is a second improvement. These changes are incorporated in *nfind* (Program 2.13).

Example 2.3 [*Simulation of nfind*]: Suppose *pat* = "aab" and *string* = "ababbaabaa." Figure 2.11 shows how *nfind* compares the characters from *pat* with those of *string*. The end of the *string* and *pat* arrays are held by *lasts* and *lastp*, respectively. First *nfind* compares *string* [*endmatch*] and *pat* [*lastp*]. If they match, *nfind* uses *i* and *j* to move through the two strings until a mismatch occurs or until all of *pat* has been matched. The variable *start* is used to reset *i* if a mismatch occurs. □

Analysis of *nfind*: If we apply *nfind* to *string* = "aa · · · a" and *pat* = "a · · · ab", then the computing time for these strings is linear in the length of the string O(*m*), which is certainly far better than the sequential method. Although the improvements we made over the sequential method speed up processing on the average, the worst case computing time is still O(*n · m*). □

Ideally, we would like an algorithm that works in O(*strlen (string)* + *strlen (pat)*) time. This is optimal for this problem as in the worst case it is necessary to look at all characters in the pattern and string at least once. We want to search the string for the pattern without moving backwards in the string. That is, if a mismatch occurs we want

```
int nfind(char *string, char *pat)
{/* match the last character of pattern first, and
    then match from the beginning */
  int i,j,start = 0;
  int lasts = strlen(string)-1;
  int lastp = strlen(pat)-1;
  int endmatch = lastp;

  for (i = 0; endmatch <= lasts; endmatch++, start++) {
    if (string[endmatch] == pat[lastp])
      for (j = 0, i = start; j < lastp &&
                    string[i] == pat[j]; i++,j++)
        ;
    if (j == lastp)
      return start; /* successful */
  }
  return -1;
}
```

Program 2.13: Pattern matching by checking end indices first

to use our knowledge of the characters in the pattern and the position in the pattern where the mismatch occurred to determine where we should continue the search. Knuth, Morris, and Pratt have developed a pattern matching algorithm that works in this way and has linear complexity. Using their example, suppose

$$pat = \text{`}a\,b\,c\,a\,b\,c\,a\,c\,a\,b\text{'}$$

Let $s = s_0\,s_2\,\cdots\,s_{m-1}$ be the string and assume that we are currently determining whether or not there is a match beginning at s_i. If $s_i \neq a$ then, clearly, we may proceed by comparing s_{i+1} and a. Similarly if $s_i = a$ and $s_{i+1} \neq b$ then we may proceed by comparing s_{i+1} and a. If $s_i s_{i+1} = ab$ and $s_{i+2} \neq c$ then we have the situation:

$$
\begin{array}{ccccccccccc}
s = & \text{`-} & a & b & ? & ? & ? & . & . & . & . & ?\text{'} \\
pat = & & \text{`}a & b & c & a & b & c & a & c & a & b\text{'}
\end{array}
$$

The ? implies that we do not know what the character in s is. The first ? in s represents s_{i+2} and $s_{i+2} \neq c$. At this point we know that we may continue the search for a match by comparing the first character in pat with s_{i+2}. There is no need to compare this character

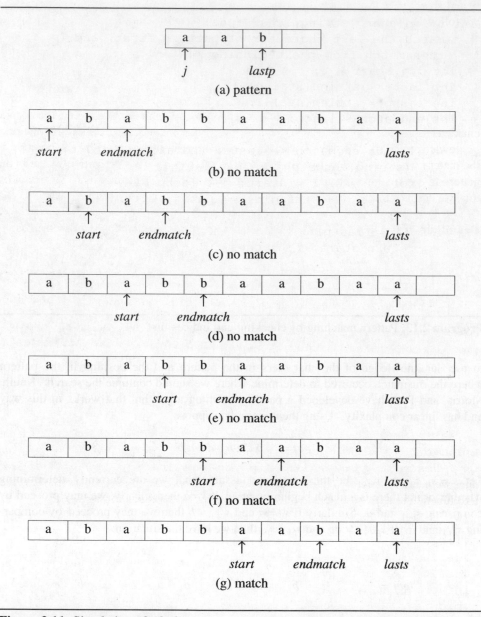

Figure 2.11: Simulation of *nfind*

of *pat* with s_{i+1} as we already know that s_{i+1} is the same as the second character of *pat*, *b*, and so $s_{i+1} \neq a$. Let us try this again assuming a match of the first four characters in *pat* followed by a nonmatch, i.e., $s_{i+4} \neq b$. We now have the situation:

$$
\begin{array}{cccccccccccc}
s = & \text{`-} & a & b & c & a & ? & ? & . & . & . & ?\text{'} \\
pat = & \text{`}a & b & c & a & b & c & a & c & a & b\text{'}
\end{array}
$$

We observe that the search for a match can proceed by comparing s_{i+4} and the second character in *pat*, *b*. This is the first place a partial match can occur by sliding the pattern *pat* towards the right. Thus, by knowing the characters in the pattern and the position in the pattern where a mismatch occurs with a character in *s* we can determine where in the pattern to continue the search for a match without moving backwards in *s*. To formalize this, we define a failure function for a pattern.

Definition: If $p = p_0 p_1 \cdots p_{n-1}$ is a pattern, then its *failure function, f*, is defined as:

$$
f(j) = \begin{cases} \text{largest } i < j \text{ such that } p_0 p_1 \cdots p_i = p_{j-i} p_{j-i+2} \cdots p_j \text{ if such an } i \geq 0 \text{ exists} \\ -1 \qquad\qquad\qquad\qquad\qquad\qquad\qquad\qquad\qquad\qquad\qquad \text{otherwise} \end{cases} \quad \Box
$$

For the example pattern, *pat = abcabcacab*, we have:

j	0	1	2	3	4	5	6	7	8	9
pat	a	b	c	a	b	c	a	c	a	b
f	-1	-1	-1	0	1	2	3	-1	0	1

From the definition of the failure function, we arrive at the following rule for pattern matching: *If a partial match is found such that $s_{i-j} \cdots s_{i-1} = p_0 p_1 \cdots p_{j-1}$ and $s_i \neq p_j$ then matching may be resumed by comparing s_i and $p_{f(j-1)+1}$ if $j \neq 0$. If $j = 0$, then we may continue by comparing s_{i+1} and p_0.* This pattern matching rule translates into function *pmatch* (Program 2.14). The following declarations are assumed:

```
#include <stdio.h>
#include <string.h>
#define max_string_size 100
#define max_pattern_size 100
int pmatch();
void fail();
int failure[max_pattern_size];
char string[max_string_size];
char pat[max_pattern_size];
```

```
int pmatch(char *string, char *pat)
{/* Knuth, Morris, Pratt string matching algorithm */
    int i = 0, j = 0;
    int lens = strlen(string);
    int lenp = strlen(pat);
    while ( i < lens && j < lenp ) {
        if (string[i] == pat[j]) {
            i++; j++; }
        else if (j == 0) i++;
            else j = failure[j-1]+1;
    }
    return ( (j == lenp) ? (i-lenp) : -1);
}
```

Program 2.14: Knuth, Morris, Pratt pattern matching algorithm

Note that we do not keep a pointer to the start of the pattern in the string. Instead we use the statement:

```
return ( (j == lenp) ? (i - lenp) : -1);
```

This statement checks to see whether or not we found the pattern. If we didn't find the pattern, the pattern index index j is not equal to the length of the pattern and we return -1. If we found the pattern, then the starting position is $i -$ the length of the pattern.

Analysis of *pmatch*: The **while** loop is iterated until the end of either the string or the pattern is reached. Since i is never decreased, the lines that increase i cannot be executed more than $m = strlen(string)$ times. The resetting of j to $failure[j-1]+1$ decreases the value of j. So, this cannot be done more times than j is incremented by the statement $j++$ as otherwise, j falls off the pattern. Each time the statement $j++$ is executed, i is also incremented. So, j cannot be incremented more than m times. Consequently, no statement of Program 2.14 is executed more than m times. Hence the complexity of function *pmatch* is $O(m) = O(strlen(string))$. $\square$

From the analysis of *pmatch*, it follows that if we can compute the failure function in $O(strlen(pat))$ time, then the entire pattern matching process will have a computing time proportional to the sum of the lengths of the string and pattern. Fortunately, there is a fast way to compute the failure function. This is based upon the following restatement of the failure function:

$$f(j) = \begin{cases} -1 & \text{if } j = 0 \\ f^m(j-1) + 1 & \text{where } m \text{ is the least integer } k \text{ for which } p_{f^k(j-1)+1} = p_j \\ -1 & \text{if there is no } k \text{ satisfying the above} \end{cases}$$

(note that $f^1(j) = f(j)$ and $f^m(j) = f(f^{m-1}(j))$).

This definition yields the function in Program 2.15 for computing the failure function of a pattern.

```
void fail(char *pat)
{/* compute the pattern's failure function */
    int n = strlen(pat);
    failure[0] = -1;
    for (j=1; j < n; j++) {
        i = failure[j-1];
        while ((pat[j] != pat[i+1]) && (i >= 0))
            i = failure[i];
        if (pat[j] == pat[i+1])
            failure[j] = i+1;
        else failure[j] = -1;
    }
}
```

Program 2.15: Computing the failure function

Analysis of *fail*: In each iteration of the **while** loop the value of i decreases (by the definition of f). The variable i is reset at the beginning of each iteration of the **for** loop. However, it is either reset to -1 (initially or when the previous iteration of the **for** loop goes through the last **else** clause) or it is reset to a value 1 greater than its terminal value on the previous iteration (i.e., when the statement *failure*$[j] = i+1$ is executed). Since the **for** loop is iterated only $n-1$ (n is the length of the pattern) times, the value of i has a total increment of at most $n-1$. Hence it cannot be decremented more than $n-1$ times. Consequently the **while** loop is iterated at most $n-1$ times over the whole algorithm and the computing time of *fail* is $O(n) = O(strlen(pat))$. □

Note that when the failure function is not known in advance, the time to first compute this function and then perform a pattern match is $O(strlen(pat) + strlen(string))$.

EXERCISES

1. Write a function that accepts as input a *string* and determines the frequency of occurrence of each of the distinct characters in *string*. Test your function using suitable data.

2. Write a function, *strndel*, that accepts a *string* and two integers, *start* and *length*. Return a new string that is equivalent to the original string, except that *length* characters beginning at *start* have been removed.

3. Write a function, *strdel*, that accepts a *string* and a *character*. The function returns *string* with the first occurrence of *character* removed.

4. Write a function, *strpos*1, that accepts a *string* and a *character*. The function returns an integer that represents the position of the first occurrence of *character* in *string*. If *character* is not in *string*, it returns −1. You may not use the function *strpos* which is part of the traditional <*string.h*> library, but not the ANSI C one.

5. Write a function, *strchr*1, that does the same thing as *strpos*1 except that it returns a pointer to *character*. If *character* is not in the list it returns *NULL*. You may not use the built-in function *strchr*.

6. Modify Program 2.12 so that it does not use a temporary string *temp*. Compare the complexity of your new function with that of the old one.

7. Write a function, *strsearch*, that uses the sequential method for pattern matching. That is, assuming we have a *string* and a *pattern*, *strsearch* examines each character in *string* until it either finds the *pattern* or it reaches the end of the *string*.

8. Show that the computing time for *nfind* is $O(n \cdot m)$ where n and m are, respectively, the lengths of the string and the pattern. Find a string and a pattern for which this is true.

9. Compute the failure function for each of the following patterns:

    (a)   *a a a a b*

    (b)   *a b a b a a*

    (c)   *a b a a b a a b*

10. Show the equivalence of the two definitions for the failure function.

2.8   REFERENCES AND SELECTED READINGS

The Knuth, Morris, Pratt pattern-matching algorithm can be found in "Fast pattern matching in strings," *SIAM Journal on Computing*, 6:2, 1977, pp. 323-350. A discussion of the Knuth Morris Pratt algorithm, along with other string matching algorithms, may be found in *Introduction to Algorithms* Second Edition, by T. Cormen, C. Leiserson, R. Rivest and C. Stein, McGraw Hill, New York, 2002.

2.9 ADDITIONAL EXERCISES

1. Given an array $a[n]$ produce the array $z[n]$ such that $z[0] = a[n-1], z[1] = a[n-2], \cdots, z[n-2] = a[1], z[n-1] = a[0]$. Use a minimal amount of storage.

2. An $m \times n$ matrix is said to have a saddle point if some entry $a[i][j]$ is the smallest value in row i and the largest value in column j. Write a C function that determines the location of a saddle point if one exists. What is the computing time of your method?

Exercises 3 through 8 explore the representation of various types of matrices that are frequently used in the solution of problems in the natural sciences.

3. A *triangular matrix* is one in which either all the elements above the main diagonal or all the elements below the main diagonal of a square matrix are zero. Figure 2.12 shows a lower and an upper triangular matrix. In a lower triangular matrix, a, with n rows, the maximum number of nonzero terms in row i is $i+1$. Thus, the total number of nonzero terms is

$$d = \sum_{i=0}^{n-1} (i+1) = n(n+1)/2.$$

Since storing a triangular matrix as a two dimensional array wastes space, we would like to find a way to store only the nonzero terms in the triangular matrix. Find an addressing formula for the elements a_{ij} so that they can be stored by rows in an array $b[n(n+1)/2-1]$, with $a[0][0]$ being stored in $b[0]$.

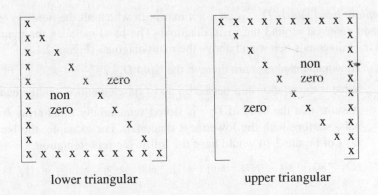

lower triangular   upper triangular

Figure 2.12: Lower and upper triangular matrices

4. Let a and b be two lower triangular matrices, each with n rows. The total number of elements in the lower triangles is $n(n+1)$. Devise a scheme to represent both triangles in an array $d[n-1][n]$. [Hint: Represent the triangle of a in the lower triangle of d and the transpose b in the upper triangle of d.] Write algorithms to determine the values of $a[i][j]$, $b[i][j]$, $0 \le i,\ j < n$.

5. A *tridiagonal matrix* is a square matrix in which all elements that are not on the major diagonal and the two diagonals adjacent to it are zero (Figure 2.13). The elements in the band formed by these three diagonals are represented by rows in an array, b, with $a[0][0]$ being stored in $b[0]$. Obtain an algorithm to determine the value of $a[i][j]$, $0 \le i,\ j < n$ from the array b.

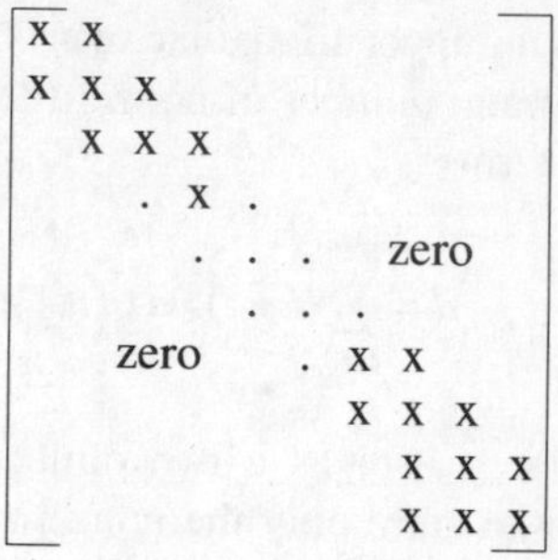

Figure 2.13: Tridiagonal matrix

6. A *square band matrix* $D_{n,a}$ is an $n \times n$ matrix in which all the nonzero terms lie in a band centered around the main diagonal. The band includes the main diagonal and $a-1$ diagonals below and above the main diagonal (Figure 2.14).

    (a) How many elements are there in the band $D_{n,a}$?

    (b) What is the relationship between i and j for elements $d_{i,j}$ in the band $D_{n,a}$?

    (c) Assume that the band of $D_{n,a}$ is stored sequentially in an array b by diagonals, starting with the lowermost diagonal. For example, the band matrix, $D_{4,3}$ of Figure 2.14 would have the following representation.

b[0]	b[1]	b[2]	b[3]	b[4]	b[5]	b[6]	b[7]	b[8]	b[9]	b[10]	b[11]	b[12]	b[13]
9	7	8	3	6	6	0	2	8	7	4	9	8	4

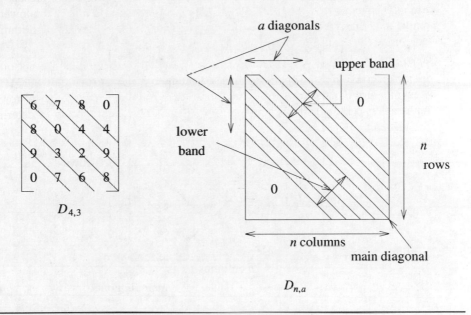

Figure 2.14: Square band matrix

d_{20} d_{31} d_{10} d_{21} d_{32} d_{00} d_{11} d_{22} d_{33} d_{01} d_{12} d_{23} d_{02} d_{13}

Obtain an addressing formula for the location of an element, $d_{i,j}$, in the lower band of $D_{n,a}$ (location(d_{10}) = 2 in the example above).

7. A *generalized band matrix* $D_{n,a,b}$ is an $n \times n$ matrix in which all the nonzero terms lie in a band made up of $a-1$ diagonals below the main diagonal, the main diagonal, and $b-1$ bands above the main diagonal (Figure 2.15).

   (a) How many elements are there in the band of $D_{n,a,b}$?

   (b) What is the relationship between i and j for the elements d_{ij} in the band of $D_{n,a,b}$?

   (c) Obtain a sequential representation of the band $D_{n,a,b}$ in the one dimensional array e. For this representation, write a C function *value* (n, a, b, i, j, e) that determines the value of element d_{ij} in the matrix $D_{n,a,b}$. The band of $D_{n,a,b}$ is represented in the array e.

8. A complex-valued matrix X is represented by a pair of matrices $<a, b>$, where a and b contain real values. Write a function that computes the product of two complex-valued matrices $<a, b>$ and $<d, e>$, where $<a, b> * <d, e> = (a + ib)$

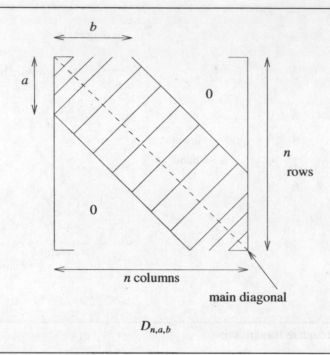

$$D_{n,a,b}$$

Figure 2.15: Generalized band matrix

* $(d + ie) = (ad - be) + i(ae + bd)$. Determine the number of additions and multiplications if the matrices are all $n \times n$.

9. § [*Programming project*] There are a number of problems, known collectively as "random walk" problems, that have been of longstanding interest to the mathematical community. All but the most simple of these are extremely difficult to solve, and, for the most part, they remain largely unsolved. One such problem may be stated as:

A (drunken) cockroach is placed on a given square in the middle of a tile floor in a rectangular room of size $n \times m$ tiles. The bug wanders (possibly in search of an aspirin) randomly from tile to tile throughout the room. Assuming that he may move from his present tile to any of the eight tiles surrounding him (unless he is against a wall) with equal probability, how long will it take him to touch every tile on the floor at least once?

Hard as this problem may be to solve by pure probability techniques, it is quite

easy to solve using a computer. The technique for doing so is called "simulation."
This technique is widely used in industry to predict traffic flow, inventory control,
and so forth. The problem may be simulated using the following method:

An $n \times m$ array *count* is used to represent the number of times our cockroach has
reached each tile on the floor. All the cells of this array are initialized to zero.
The position of the bug on the floor is represented by the coordinates (*ibug*, *jbug*).
The eight possible moves of the bug are represented by the tiles located at
(*ibug* + *imove* [*k*], *jbug* + *jmove* [*k*]), where $0 \leq k \leq 7$, and

$$imove[0] = -1 \qquad jmove[0] = 1$$
$$imove[1] = 0 \qquad jmove[1] = 1$$
$$imove[2] = 1 \qquad jmove[2] = 1$$
$$imove[3] = 1 \qquad jmove[3] = 0$$
$$imove[4] = 1 \qquad jmove[4] = -1$$
$$imove[5] = 0 \qquad jmove[5] = -1$$
$$imove[6] = -1 \qquad jmove[6] = -1$$
$$imove[7] = -1 \qquad jmove[7] = 0$$

A random walk to any one of the eight neighbor squares is simulated by generating a random value for k, lying between 0 and 7. Of course, the bug cannot move
outside the room, so that coordinates that lead up a wall must be ignored, and a
new random combination formed. Each time a square is entered, the count for that
square is incremented so that a nonzero entry shows the number of times the bug
has landed on that square. When every square has been entered at least once, the
experiment is complete.

Write a program to perform the specified simulation experiment. Your program
MUST:

(a) handle all values of n and m, $2 < n \leq 40$, $2 \leq m \leq 20$;

(b) perform the experiment for (1) $n = 15$, $m = 15$, starting point (10, 10), and
(2) $n = 39$, $m = 19$, starting point (1, 1);

(c) have an iteration limit, that is, a maximum number of squares that the bug
may enter during the experiment. This ensures that your program will terminate. A maximum of 50,000 is appropriate for this exercise.

For each experiment, print (1) the total number of legal moves that the cockroach
makes and (2) the final count array. This will show the "density" of the walk, that
is, the number of times each tile on the floor was touched during the experiment.
This exercise was contributed by Olson.

10. § [*Programming project*] Chess provides the setting for many fascinating diversions that are quite independent of the game itself. Many of these are based on the strange "L-shaped" move of the knight. A classic example is the problem of the "knight's tour," which has captured the attention of mathematicians and puzzle enthusiasts since the beginning of the eighteenth century. Briefly stated, the problem requires us to move the knight, beginning from any given square on the chessboard, successively to all 64 squares, touching each square once and only once. Usually we represent a solution by placing the numbers 0, 1, $\cdots$, 63 in the squares of the chess board to indicate the order in which the squares are reached. One of the more ingenious methods for solving the problem of the knight's tour was given by J. C. Warnsdorff in 1823. His rule stated that the knight must always move to one of the squares from which there are the fewest exits to squares not already traversed.

The goal of this programming project is to implement Warnsdorff's rule. The ensuing discussion will be easier to follow, however, if you try to construct a solution to the problem by hand, before reading any further.

The crucial decision in solving this problem concerns the data representation. Figure 2.16 shows the chess board represented as a two-dimensional array.

The eight possible moves of a knight on square (4, 2) are also shown in this figure. In general, a knight may move to one of the squares $(i-2, j+1)$, $(i-1, j+2)$, $(i+1, j+2)$, $(i+2, j+1)$, $(i+2, j-1)$, $(i+1, j-2)$, $(i-1, j-2)$, $(i-2, j-1)$. However, notice that if (i, j) is located near one of the board's edges, some of these possibilities could move the knight off the board, and, of course, this is not permitted. We can represent easily the eight possible knight moves by two arrays *ktmove* 1 and *ktmove* 2 as:

	0	1	2	3	4	5	6	7
0								
1								
2		7		0				
3	6				1			
4			K					
5	5				2			
6		4		3				
7								

Figure 2.16: Legal moves for a knight

ktmove 1	ktmove 2
−2	1
1	2
1	2
2	1
2	−1
1	−2
−1	−2
−2	−1

Then a knight at (i, j) may move to $(i + ktmove[k], j + ktmove\,2[k])$, where k is some value between 0 and 7, provided that the new square lies on the chess board. Below is a description of an algorithm for solving the knight's tour problem using Warnsdorff's rule. The data representation discussed in the previous section is assumed.

(a)   [*Initialize chessboard*] For $0 \le i, j \le 7$ set *board*[i][j] to 0.

(b) [*Set starting position*] Read and print (i, j) and then set *board*$[i][j]$ to 0.

(c) [*Loop*] For $1 \le m \le 63$, do steps (d) through (g).

(d) [*Form a set of possible next squares*] Test each of the eight squares one knight's move away from (i, j) and form a list of the possibilities for the next square (*nexti*$[l]$, *nextj*$[l]$). Let *npos* be the number of possibilities. (That is, after performing this step we have *nexti*$[l] = i + ktmove\ 1[k]$ and *nextj*$[l] = j + ktmove\ 2[k]$, for certain values of k between 0 and 7. Some of the squares $(i + ktmove\ 1[k], j + ktmove\ 2[k])$ may be impossible because they lie off the chessboard or because they have been occupied previously by the knight, that is, they contain a nonzero number. In every case we will have $0 \le npos \le 8$.)

(e) [*Test special cases*] If *npos* = 0, the knight's tour has come to a premature end; report failure and go to step (h). If *npos* = 1, there is only one next move; set *min* to 1 and go to step (g).

(f) [*Find next square with minimum number of exits*] For $1 \le l \le npos$, set *exits*$[l]$ to the number of exits from square (*nexti*$[l]$, *nextj*$[l]$). That is, for each of the values of l, examine each of the next squares (*nexti*$[l]$ + *ktmove*$1[k]$, *nextj*$[l]$ + *ktmove*$2[k]$) to see if it is an exit from (*nexti*$[l]$, *nextj*$[l]$), and count the number of such exits in *exits*$[l]$. (Recall that a square is an exit if it lies on the chessboard and has not been occupied previously by the knight.) Finally, set *min* to the location of the minimum value of *exits*. (If there is more than one occurrence of the minimum value, let *min* denote the first such occurrence. Although this does not guarantee a solution, the chances of completing the tour are very good.)

(g) [*Move knight*] Set $i = nexti[min]$, $j = nextj[min]$, and *board*$[i][j] = m$. Thus, (i, j) denotes the new position of the knight, and *board*$[i][j]$ records the move in proper sequence.

(h) [*Print*] Print out the board showing the solution to the knight's tour, and then terminate the algorithm.

Write a C program that corresponds to the algorithm. This exercise was contributed by Legenhausen and Rebman.

CHAPTER 3

STACKS AND QUEUES

3.1 STACKS

In this chapter we look at two data types that are frequently found in computer science. These data types, the stack and the queue, are special cases of the more general data type, *ordered list*, that we discussed in Chapter 2. Recall that $A = a_0, a_1, \cdots, a_{n-1}$ is an ordered list of $n \geq 0$ elements. We refer to the a_i as *atoms* or *elements* that are taken from some set. The null or empty list, denoted by ( ), has $n = 0$ elements. In this section we begin by defining the ADT *Stack* and follow with its implementation. Then, we look at the queue.

A *stack* is an ordered list in which insertions (also called pushes and adds) and deletions (also called pops and removes) are made at one end called the *top*. Given a stack $S = (a_0, \cdots, a_{n-1})$, we say that a_0 is the bottom element, a_{n-1} is the top element, and a_i is on top of element a_{i-1}, $0 < i < n$. The restrictions on the stack imply that if we add the elements A, B, C, D, E to the stack, in that order, then E is the first element we delete from the stack. Figure 3.1 illustrates this sequence of operations. Since the last element inserted into a stack is the first element removed, a stack is also known as a *Last-In-First-Out (LIFO)* list.

107

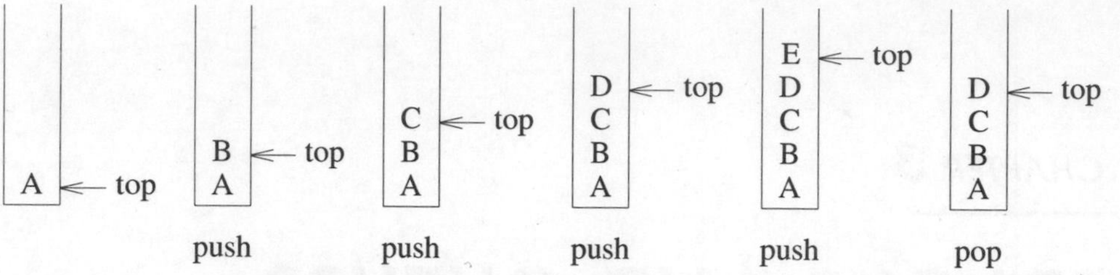

Figure 3.1: Inserting and deleting elements in a stack

Example 3.1 [*System stack*]: Before we discuss the stack ADT, we look at a special stack, called the system stack, that is used by a program at run-time to process function calls. Whenever a function is invoked, the program creates a structure, referred to as an *activation record* or a *stack frame*, and places it on top of the system stack. Initially, the activation record for the invoked function contains only a pointer to the previous stack frame and a return address. The previous stack frame pointer points to the stack frame of the invoking function, while the return address contains the location of the statement to be executed after the function terminates. Since only one function executes at any given time, the function whose stack frame is on top of the system stack is chosen. If this function invokes another function, the local variables, except those declared static, and the parameters of the invoking function are added to its stack frame. A new stack frame is then created for the invoked function and placed on top of the system stack. When this function terminates, its stack frame is removed and the processing of the invoking function, which is again on top of the stack, continues. A simple example illustrates this process.

Assume that we have a main function that invokes function *a1*. Figure 3.2(a) shows the system stack before *a1* is invoked; Figure 3.2(b) shows the system stack after *a1* has been invoked. Frame pointer *fp* is a pointer to the current stack frame. The system also maintains separately a stack pointer, *sp*, which we have not illustrated.

Since all functions are stored similarly in the system stack, it makes no difference if the invoking function calls itself. That is, a recursive call requires no special strategy; the run-time program simply creates a new stack frame for each recursive call. However, recursion can consume a significant portion of the memory allocated to the system stack; it could consume the entire available memory. □

Our discussion of the system stack suggests several operations that we include in the ADT specification (ADT 3.1).

The easiest way to implement this ADT is by using a one-dimensional array, say,

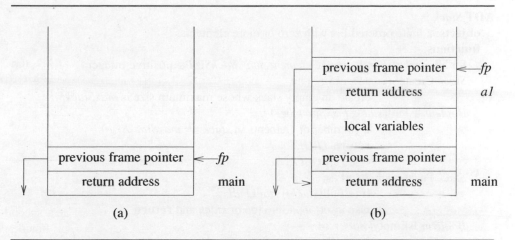

Figure 3.2: System stack after function call

stack [*MAX_STACK_SIZE*], where *MAX_STACK_SIZE* is the maximum number of entries. The first, or bottom, element of the stack is stored in *stack* [0], the second in *stack* [1], and the *i*th in *stack* [*i* −1]. Associated with the array is a variable, *top*, which points to the top element in the stack. Initially, *top* is set to −1 to denote an empty stack. Given this representation, we can implement the operations in ADT 3.1 as follows. Notice that we have specified that *element* is a structure that consists of only a *key* field. Ordinarily, we would not create a structure with a single field. However, we use *element* in this and subsequent chapters as a template whose fields we may add to or modify to meet the requirements of our application.

Stack CreateS(*maxStackSize*) ::=
```
#define MAX_STACK_SIZE 100 /* maximum stack size */
typedef struct {
        int key;
        /* other fields */
        } element;
element stack[MAX_STACK_SIZE];
int top = -1;
```

Boolean IsEmpty(Stack) ::= `top < 0;`

Boolean IsFull(Stack) ::= `top >= MAX_STACK_SIZE-1;`

ADT *Stack* is
  objects: a finite ordered list with zero or more elements.
  functions:
    for all *stack* ∈ *Stack*, *item* ∈ *element*, *maxStackSize* ∈ positive integer
    Stack CreateS(*maxStackSize*) ::=
                create an empty stack whose maximum size is *maxStackSize*
    Boolean IsFull(*stack*, *maxStackSize*) ::=
             if (number of elements in *stack* == *maxStackSize*)
             return *TRUE*
             else return *FALSE*
    Stack Push(*stack*, *item*) ::=
             if (IsFull(*stack*)) *stackFull*
             else insert *item* into top of *stack* and **return**
    Boolean IsEmpty(*stack*) ::=
             if (*stack* == CreateS(*maxStackSize*))
              return *TRUE*
             else return *FALSE*
    Element Pop(*stack*) ::=
             if (IsEmpty(*stack*)) **return**
             else remove and return the element at the top of the stack.

ADT 3.1: Abstract data type *Stack*

The *IsEmpty* and *IsFull* operations are simple, and we will implement them directly in the *push* (Program 3.1) and *pop* (Program 3.2) functions. Each of these functions assumes that the variables *stack* and *top* are global. The functions are short and require little explanation. Function *push* checks to see if the stack is full. If it is, it calls *stackFull* (Program 3.3), which prints an error message and terminates execution. When the stack is not full, we increment *top* and assign *item* to *stack* [*top*]. Implementation of the pop operation parallels that of the push operation. The code of Program 3.2 assumes that the *stackEmpty* function prints an error message and returns an item of type *element* with a *key* field that contains an error code. Typical function calls would be *push* (*item*); and *item* = *pop* ();.

EXERCISES

1. Implement the *stackEmpty* function.
2. Using Figures 3.1 and 3.2 as examples, show the status of the system stack after each function call for the iterative and recursive functions to compute binomial coefficients (Exercise 9, Section 1.2). You do not need to show the stack frame

```
void push(element item)
{/* add an item to the global stack */
   if (top >= MAX_STACK_SIZE-1)
      stackFull();
   stack[++top] = item;
}
```

Program 3.1: Add an item to a stack

```
element pop()
{/* delete and return the top element from the stack */
   if (top == -1)
      return stackEmpty(); /* returns an error key */
   return stack[top--];
}
```

Program 3.2: Delete from a stack

```
void stackFull()
{
    fprintf(stderr, "Stack is full, cannot add element");
    exit(EXIT_FAILURE);
}
```

Program 3.3: Stack full

itself for each function call. Simply add the name of the function to the stack to show its invocation and remove the name from the stack to show its termination.

3. The Fibonacci sequence 0, 1, 1, 2, 3, 5, 8, 13, 21, 34, $\cdots$, is defined as $F_0 = 0$, $F_1 = 1$, and $F_i = F_{i-1} + F_{i-2}$, $i \geq 2$. Write a recursive function, *fibon* (n), that returns the nth fibonacci number. Show the status of the system stack for the call *fibon* (4) (see Exercise 2). What can you say about the efficiency of this function?

4. Consider the railroad switching network given in Figure 3.3. Railroad cars numbered 0, 1, $\cdots$, $n-1$ are at the right. Each car is brought into the stack and removed at any time. For instance, if $n = 3$, we could move in 0, move in 1, move in 2, and then take the cars out, producing the new order 2, 1, 0. For $n = 3$ and $n = 4$, what are the possible permutations of the cars that can be obtained? Are any permutations not possible?

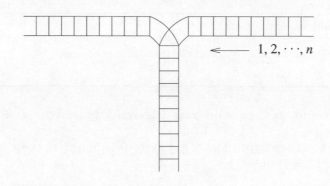

$\longleftarrow$ 1, 2, $\cdots$, n

Figure 3.3: Railroad switching network

3.2 STACKS USING DYNAMIC ARRAYS

A shortcoming of the stack implementation of the preceding section is the need to know, at compile time, a good bound (*MAX_STACK_SIZE*) on how large the stack will become. We can overcome this shortcoming by using a dynamically allocated array for the elements and then increasing the size of this array as needed. The following implementation of *CreateS*, *IsEmpty*, and *IsFull* uses a dynamically allocated array *stack* whose initial capacity (i.e., maximum number of stack elements that may be stored in the array) is 1. Specific applications may dictate other choices for the initial capacity.

Stack CreateS() ::=
```
                 typedef struct {
                    int key;
                    /* other fields */
                    } element;
              element *stack;
              MALLOC(stack, sizeof(*stack));
              int capacity = 1;
              int top = -1;
```

Boolean IsEmpty(Stack) ::= `top < 0;`

Boolean IsFull(Stack) ::= `top >= capacity-1;`

While we must alter the code for the *push* function (Program 3.1) to use the new test for a full stack (replace *MAX_STACK_SIZE* with *capacity*), the code for the *pop* function (Program 3.2) is unchanged. Additionally, the code for *stackFull* is changed. The new code for *stackFull* attempts to increase the capacity of the array *stack* so that we can add an additional element to the stack. Before we can increase the capacity of an array, we must decide what the new capacity should be. In *array doubling*, we double array capacity whenever it becomes necessary to increase the capacity of an array. Program 3.4 gives the code for *stackFull* when array doubling is used.

```
void stackFull()
{
    REALLOC(stack, 2 * capacity * sizeof(*stack))
    capacity *= 2;
}
```

Program 3.4: Stack full with array doubling

Although it may appear that a lot of time is spent doubling the capacity of *stack*, this is actually not the case. In the worst case, the *realloc* function needs to allocate $2*capacity*sizeof(*stack)$ bytes of memory and copy $capacity*sizeof(*stack))$ bytes of memory from the old array into the new one. Under the assumptions that memory may be allocated in $O(1)$ time and that a stack element can be copied in $O(1)$ time, the time required by array doubling is $O(capacity)$. Initially, *capacity* is 1. Suppose that when we are done with all the stack pushes we wish to perform, *capacity* is 2^k for some k, $k>0$. The total time spent over all array doublings is $O(\sum_{i=1}^{k} 2^i) = O(2^{k+1}) = O(2^k)$. Since the total number of pushes is more than 2^{k-1} (otherwise the array capacity would not have been doubled from 2^{k-1} to 2^k), the total time spend in array doubling is $O(n)$, where n is the total number of pushes. Hence, even with the time spent on array doubling added in, the total run time of *push* over all n pushes is $O(n)$. Notice that this conclusion remains valid whenever *stackFull* resizes the stack array by a factor $c>1$ ($c=2$ in Program 3.4).

EXERCISES

1. Let S be a stack whose initial capacity is 1 and that array doubling is used to increase the stack's capacity whenever an elemenet is added to a full stack. Let $n=2^k+1$, where k is a positive integer, be the maximum number of elements on S

during the execution of some program. How much memory is needed for this program to run successfully (consider only the memory needed for the stack and the array doubling operation)? How much memory is needed when using the representation of Section 3.1 (assume we can determine k without running the program)?

2. Prove that whenever *stackFull* resizes the stack array by a factor $c>1$, the total time for all invocastions of *push* (Program 3.1) is $O(n)$, where n is the number of pushes to the stack. In the initial configuration, te stack is empty and *capacity* $=1$.

3. Suppose that we modify Program 3.4 so that the size of *stack* is increased by an additive amount $c*sizeof$ (*stack*). Show that the time for n pushes is $O(n^2)$ when the initial configuration is an empty stack and *capacity* $=1$.

3.3 QUEUES

A *queue* is an ordered list in which insertions (also called additions, puts, and pushes) and deletions (also called removals and pops) take place at different ends. The end at which new elements are added is called the *rear*, and that from which old elements are deleted is called the *front*. The restrictions on a queue imply that if we insert A, B, C, D, and E in that order, then A is the first element deleted from the queue. Figure 3.4 illustrates this sequence of events. Since the first element inserted into a queue is the first element removed, queues are also known as *First-In-First-Out (FIFO)* lists. The ADT specification of the queue appears in ADT 3.2.

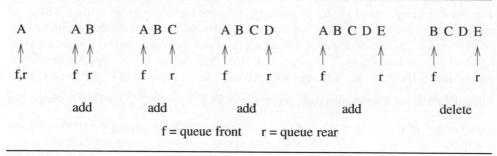

Figure 3.4: Inserting and deleting elements in a queue

The representation of a queue in sequential locations is more difficult than that of the stack. The simplest scheme employs a one-dimensional array and two variables, *front* and *rear*. Given this representation, we can define the queue operations in ADT 3.2 as:

ADT *Queue* is
    objects: a finite ordered list with zero or more elements.
    functions:
        for all *queue* $\in$ *Queue*, *item* $\in$ *element*, *maxQueueSize* $\in$ positive integer
        Queue CreateQ(*maxQueueSize*) ::=
                create an empty queue whose maximum size is *maxQueueSize*
        Boolean IsFullQ(*queue*, *maxQueueSize*) ::=
                if (number of elements in *queue* == *maxQueueSize*)
                return *TRUE*
                else return *FALSE*
        Queue AddQ(*queue*, *item*) ::=
                if (IsFullQ(*queue*)) *queueFull*
                else insert *item* at rear of *queue* and return *queue*
        Boolean IsEmptyQ(*queue*) ::=
                if (*queue* == CreateQ(*maxQueueSize*))
                return *TRUE*
                else return *FALSE*
        Element DeletcQ(*queue*) ::=
                if (IsEmptyQ(*queue*)) **return**
                else remove and return the *item* at front of queue.

ADT 3.2: Abstract data type *Queue*

Queue CreateQ(*maxQueueSize*) ::=
```
       #define MAX-QUEUE-SIZE 100 /* maximum queue size */
       typedef struct {
               int key;
               /* other fields */
               } element;
       element queue[MAX-QUEUE-SIZE];
       int rear = -1;
       int front = -1;
```
Boolean IsEmptyQ(*queue*) ::= `front == rear`

Boolean IsFullQ(*queue*) ::= `rear == MAX-QUEUE-SIZE-1`

    Since the *IsEmptyQ* and *IsFullQ* operations are quite simple, we again implement them directly in the *addq* (Program 3.5) and *deleteq* (Program 3.6) functions. The implementation of *queueFull* is similar to that of *stackFull* (Program 3.3). Functions *addq* and *deleteq* are structurally similar to *push* and *pop* on stacks. While the stack uses the variable *top* in both *push* and *pop*, the queue increments *rear* in *addq* and *front* in *deleteq*. Typical function calls would be *addq* (*item*); and *item* = *deleteq* ();.

```
void addq(element item)
{/* add an item to the queue */
   if (rear == MAX_QUEUE_SIZE-1)
     queueFull();
   queue[++rear] = item;
}
```

Program 3.5: Add to a queue

```
element deleteq()
{/* remove element at the front of the queue */
   if (front == rear)
     return queueEmpty(); /* return an error key */
   return queue[++front];
}
```

Program 3.6: Delete from a queue

This sequential representation of a queue has pitfalls that are best illustrated by an example.

Example 3.2 [*Job scheduling*]: Queues are frequently used in computer programming, and a typical example is the creation of a job queue by an operating system. If the operating system does not use priorities, then the jobs are processed in the order they enter the system. Figure 3.5 illustrates how an operating system might process jobs if it used a sequential representation for its queue.

It should be obvious that as jobs enter and leave the system, the queue gradually shifts to the right. This means that eventually the rear index equals *MAX_QUEUE_SIZE* − 1, suggesting that the queue is full. In this case, *queueFull* should move the entire queue to the left so that the first element is again at *queue* [0] and *front* is at − 1. It should also recalculate *rear* so that it is correctly positioned. Shifting an array is very time-consuming, particularly when there are many elements in it. In fact, *queueFull* has a worst case complexity of O(*MAX_QUEUE_SIZE*). □

We can obtain a more efficient queue representation if we we permit the queue to wrap around the end of the array. At this time it is convenient to think of the array

front	rear	Q[0]	Q[1]	Q[2]	Q[3]	Comments
−1	−1					queue is empty
−1	0	J1				Job 1 is added
−1	1	J1	J2			Job 2 is added
−1	2	J1	J2	J3		Job 3 is added
0	2		J2	J3		Job 1 is deleted
1	2			J3		Job 2 is deleted

Figure 3.5: Insertion and deletion from a sequential queue

positions as arranged in a circle (Figure 3.6) rather than in a straight line (Figure 3.4). In Figure 3.6, we have changed the convention for the variable *front*. This variable now points one position counterclockwise from the location of the front element in the queue. The convention for *rear* is unchanged. This change simplifies the codes slightly.

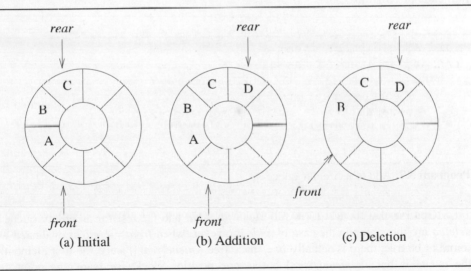

Figure 3.6: Circular queue

When the array is viewed as a circle, each array position has a next and a previous position. The position next to position $MAX\_QUEUE\_SIZE - 1$ is 0, and the position that precedes 0 is $MAX\_QUEUE\_SIZE - 1$. When the queue rear is at $MAX\_QUEUE\_SIZE - 1$, the next element is put into position 0. To work with a circular queue, we must be able to move the variables *front* and *rear* from their current position to the next position (clockwise). This may be done using code such as

```
if (rear == MAX_QUEUE_SIZE - 1) rear = 0;
else rear++;
```

Using the modulus operator, which computes remainders, this code is equivalent to (*rear+1*) % *MAX_QUEUE_SIZE*. With our conventions for *front* and *rear*, we see that the front element of the queue is located one position clockwise from *front* and the rear element is at position *rear*.

To determine a suitable test for an empty queue, we experiment with the queues of Figure 3.6. To delete an element, we advance *front* one position clockwise and to add an element, we advance *rear* one position clockwise and insert at the new position. If we perform 3 deletions from the queue of Figure 3.6(c) in this fashion, we will see that the queue becomes empty and that *front* = *rear*. When we do 5 additions to the queue of Figure 3.6(b), the queue becomes full and *front* = *rear*. So, we cannot distinguish between an empty and a full queue. To avoid the resulting confusion, we shall increase the capacity of a queue just before it becomes full. Consequently, *front* == *rear* iff the queue is empty. The initial value for both *front* and *rear* is 0. Progrms 3.7 and 3.8, respectively, given the codes to add and delete. The code for *queueFull* is similar to that of the *stackFull* code of Program 3.3.

```
void addq(element item)
{/* add an item to the queue */
   rear = (rear+1) % MAX_QUEUE_SIZE;
   if (front == rear)
      queueFull(); /* print error and exit */
   queue[rear] = item;
}
```

Program 3.7: Add to a circular queue

Observe that the test for a full queue in *addq* and the test for an empty queue in *deleteq* are the same. In the case of *addq*, however, when *front* = *rear* is evaluated and found to be true, there is actually one space free (*queue*[*rear*]) since the first element in the queue is not at *queue*[*front*] but is one position clockwise from this point. As remarked earlier, if we insert an item here, then we will not be able to distinguish between the cases of full and empty, since the insertion would leave *front* equal to *rear*. To avoid this we signal *queueFull*, thus permitting a maximum of *MAX_QUEUE_SIZE* − 1 rather than *MAX_QUEUE_SIZE* elements in the queue at any time. We leave the implementation of *queueFull* as an exercise.

```
element deleteq()
{/* remove front element from the queue */
   element item;
      if (front == rear)
         return queueEmpty(); /* return an error key */
      front = (front+1) % MAX_QUEUE_SIZE;
      return queue[front];
}
```

Program 3.8: Delete from a circular queue

EXERCISES

1. Implement the *queueFull* and *queueEmpty* functions for the noncircular queue.

2. Implement the *queueFull* and *queueEmpty* functions for the circular queue.

3. Using the noncircular queue implementation, produce a series of adds and deletes that requires O(*MAX_QUEUE_SIZE*) for each add. (Hint: Start with a full queue.)

4. A *double-ended queue (deque)* is a linear list in which additions and deletions may be made at either end. Obtain a data representation mapping a deque into a one-dimensional array. Write functions that add and delete elements from either end of the deque.

5. We can maintain a linear list circularly in an array, *circle* [*MAX_SIZE*]. We set up *front* and *rear* indices similar to those used for a circular queue.

   (a) Obtain a formula in terms of *front*, *rear*, and *MAX _ SIZE* for the number of elements in the list.

   (b) Write a function that deletes the *k*th element in the list.

   (c) Write a function that inserts an element, *item*, immediately after the *k*th element.

   (d) What is the time complexity of your functions for (b) and (c)?

3.4 CIRCULAR QUEUES USING DYNAMICALLY ALLOCATED ARRAYS

Suppose that a dynamically allocated array is used to hold the queue elements. Let *capacity* be the number of positions in the array *queue*. To add an element to a full queue, we must first increase the size of this array using a function such as *realloc*. As with dynamically allocated stacks, we use array doubling. However, it isn't sufficient to simply double array size using *realloc*. Consider the full queue of Figure 3.7(a). This figure shows a queue with seven elements in an array whose capacity is 8. To visualize array doubling when a circular queue is used, it is better to flatten out the array as in Figure 3.7(b). Figure 3.7(c) shows the array after array doubling by *realloc*.

To get a proper circular queue configuration, we must slide the elements in the right segment (i.e., elements *A* and *B*) to the right end of the array as in Figure 3.7(d). The array doubling and the slide to the right together copy at most $2*capacity - 2$ elements. The number of elements copied can be limited to $capacity - 1$ by customizing the array doubling code so as to obtain the configuration of Figure 3.7(e). This configuration may be obtained as follows:

(1) Create a new array *newQueue* of twice the capacity.

(2) Copy the second segment (i.e., the elements *queue*[*front*+1] through *queue*[*capacity*−1]) to positions in *newQueue* beginning at 0.

(3) Copy the first segment (i.e., the elements *queue*[0] through *queue*[*rear*]) to positions in *newQueue* beginning at *capacity*−*front*−1.

Program 3.9 gives the code to add to a circular queue using a dynamically allocated array. Program 3.10 gives the code for *queueFull*. The function *copy*(*a,b,c*) copies elements from locations *a* through *b*−1 to locations beginning at *c*. Program 3.10 obtains the configuration of Figure 3.7(e).

EXERCISES

1. Write and test code that implements the function *copy* used in Program 3.10. Your code should work correctly even when there is some overlap between the memory being copied from and that being copied to.

2. Write and test code for all of the queue functions specified in the queue ADT (ADT 3.2). In addition, include code for the function *queueFront*() that returns the element at the front of the queue but does not delete this element from the queue. In case the queue is empty, your function should print an error message and terminate. You should use array doubling whenever an attempt is made to add an element to a full queue.

3.5   A MAZING PROBLEM

Mazes have been an intriguing subject for many years. Experimental psychologists train rats to search mazes for food, and many a mystery novelist has used an English country garden maze as the setting for a murder. We also are interested in mazes since they present a nice application of stacks. In this section, we develop a program that runs a maze. Although this program takes many false paths before it finds a correct one, once found it can correctly rerun the maze without taking any false paths.

In creating this program the first issue that confronts us is the representation of the

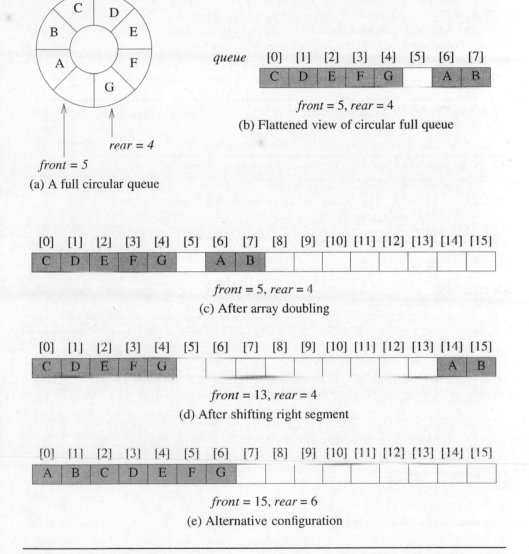

queue

	[0]	[1]	[2]	[3]	[4]	[5]	[6]	[7]
	C	D	E	F	G		A	B

front = 5, rear = 4

(b) Flattened view of circular full queue

rear = 4

front = 5

(a) A full circular queue

[0]	[1]	[2]	[3]	[4]	[5]	[6]	[7]	[8]	[9]	[10]	[11]	[12]	[13]	[14]	[15]
C	D	E	F	G		A	B								

front = 5, rear = 4

(c) After array doubling

[0]	[1]	[2]	[3]	[4]	[5]	[6]	[7]	[8]	[9]	[10]	[11]	[12]	[13]	[14]	[15]
C	D	E	F	G										A	B

front = 13, rear = 4

(d) After shifting right segment

[0]	[1]	[2]	[3]	[4]	[5]	[6]	[7]	[8]	[9]	[10]	[11]	[12]	[13]	[14]	[15]
A	B	C	D	E	F	G									

front = 15, rear = 6

(e) Alternative configuration

Figure 3.7: Doubling queue capacity

```
void addq(element item)
{/* add an item to the queue */
   rear = (rear+1) % capacity;
   if (front == rear)
     queueFull(); /* double capacity */
   queue[rear] = item;
}
```

Program 3.9: Add to a circular queue

```
void queueFull()
{
   /* allocate an array with twice the capacity */
   element* newQueue;
   MALLOC(newQueue, 2 * capacity * sizeof(*queue));

   /* copy from queue to newQueue */
   int start = (front+1) % capacity;
   if (start < 2)
      /* no wrap around */
      copy(queue+start, queue+start+capacity-1, newQueue);
   else
   {/* queue wraps around */
      copy(queue+start, queue+capacity, newQueue);
      copy(queue, queue+rear+1, newQueue+capacity-start);
   }

   /* switch to newQueue */
   front = 2 * capacity - 1;
   rear = capacity - 2;
   capacity *= 2;
   free(queue);
   queue = newQueue;
}
```

Program 3.10: Doubling queue capacity

maze. The most obvious choice is a two dimensional array in which zeros represent the open paths and ones the barriers. Figure 3.8 shows a simple maze. We assume that the rat starts at the top left and is to exit at the bottom right. With the maze represented as a two-dimensional array, the location of the rat in the maze can at any time be described by the row and column position. If X marks the spot of our current location, *maze*[*row*][*col*], then Figure 3.9 shows the possible moves from this position. We use compass points to specify the eight directions of movement: north, northeast, east, southeast, south, southwest, west, and northwest, or N, NE, E, SE, S, SW, W, NW.

entrance															
0	1	0	0	0	1	1	0	0	0	1	1	1	1	1	
1	0	0	0	1	1	0	1	1	1	0	0	1	1	1	
0	1	1	0	0	0	0	1	1	1	1	0	0	1	1	
1	1	0	1	1	1	1	0	1	1	0	1	1	0	0	
1	1	0	1	0	0	1	0	1	1	1	1	1	1	1	
0	0	1	1	0	1	1	1	0	1	0	0	1	0	1	
0	0	1	1	0	1	1	1	0	1	0	0	1	0	1	
0	1	1	1	1	0	0	1	1	1	1	1	1	1	1	
0	0	1	1	0	1	1	0	1	1	1	1	1	0	1	
1	1	0	0	0	1	1	0	1	1	0	0	0	0	0	
0	0	1	1	1	1	1	0	0	0	1	1	1	1	0	
0	1	0	0	1	1	1	1	1	0	1	1	1	1	0	exit

Figure 3.8: An example maze (can you find a path?)

We must be careful here because not every position has eight neighbors. If [*row,col*] is on a border then less than eight, and possibly only three, neighbors exist. To avoid checking for these border conditions we can surround the maze by a border of ones. Thus an $m \times p$ maze will require an $(m+2) \times (p+2)$ array. The entrance is at position [1][1] and the exit at [*m*][*p*].

Another device that will simplify the problem is to predefine the possible directions to move in an array, *move*, as in Figure 3.10. This is obtained from Figure 3.9. We represent the eight possible directions of movement by the numbers from 0 to 7. For each direction, we indicate the vertical and horizontal offset. The C declarations needed to create this table are:

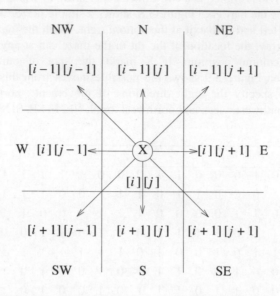

Figure 3.9: Allowable moves

Name	Dir	*move[dir].vert*	*move[dir].horiz*
N	0	−1	0
NE	1	−1	1
E	2	0	1
SE	3	1	1
S	4	1	0
SW	5	1	−1
W	6	0	−1
NW	7	−1	−1

Figure 3.10: Table of moves

```
typedef struct {
        short int vert;
        short int horiz;
        } offsets;
offsets move[8]; /* array of moves for each direction */
```

We assume that *move* is initialized according to the data provided in Figure 3.10. This means that if we are at position, *maze*[*row*][*col*], and we wish to find the position of the next move, *maze*[*nextRow*][*nextCol*], we set:

```
nextRow = row + move[dir].vert;
nextCol = col + move[dir].horiz;
```

As we move through the maze, we may have the choice of several directions of movement. Since we do not know which choice is best, we save our current position and arbitrarily pick a possible move. By saving our current position, we can return to it and try another path if we take a hopeless path. We examine the possible moves starting from the north and moving clockwise. Since we do not want to return to a previously tried path, we maintain a second two-dimensional array, *mark*, to record the maze positions already checked. We initialize this array's entries to zero. When we visit a position, *maze*[*row*][*col*], we change *mark*[*row*][*col*] to one. Program 3.11 is our initial attempt at a maze traversal algorithm. *EXIT_ROW* and *EXIT_COL* give the coordinates of the maze exit.

Although this algorithm describes the essential processing, we must still resolve several issues. Our first concern is with the representation of the stack. Examining Program 3.11, we see that the stack functions created in Sections 3.1 and 3.2 will work if we redefine *element* as:

```
typedef struct {
        short int row;
        short int col;
        short int dir;
        } element;
```

If we use the stack implementation of Sction 3.1, we also need to determine a reasonable bound for the stack size. While such a bound is not required when array doubling is used as in Section 3.2, we will need more memory on our computer to guarantee successful completion of the program (see Exercise 1 of Section 3.2). Since each position in the maze is visited no more than once, the stack need have only as many positions as there are zeroes in the maze. The maze of Figure 3.11 has only one entrance to exit path. When searching this maze for an entrance to exit path, all positions (except the exit) with value zero will be on the stack when the exit is reached. Since, an $m \times p$ maze, can have at most mp zeroes, it is sufficient for the stack to have this capacity.

Program 3.12 contains the maze search algorithm. We assume that the arrays, *maze*, *mark*, *move*, and *stack*, along with the constants *EXIT_ROW*, *EXIT_COL*, *TRUE*, and *FALSE*, and the variable, *top*, are declared as global. Notice that *path* uses a variable *found* that is initially set to zero (i.e., *FALSE*). If we find a path through the maze, we set this variable to *TRUE*, thereby allowing us to exit both **while** loops gracefully.

```
initialize a stack to the maze's entrance coordinates and
direction to north;
while (stack is not empty) {
    /* move to position at top of stack */
    <row,col,dir> = delete from top of stack;
    while (there are more moves from current position) {
        <nextRow, nextCol> = coordinates of next move;
        dir = direction of move;
        if ((nextRow == EXIT_ROW) && (nextCol == EXIT_COL))
            success;
        if (maze[nextRow][nextCol] == 0 &&
                    mark[nextRow][nextCol] == 0) {
        /* legal move and haven't been there */
            mark[nextRow][nextCol] = 1;
            /* save current position and direction */
            add <row,col,dir> to the top of the stack;
            row = nextRow;
            col = nextCol;
            dir = north;
        }
    }
}
printf("No path found\n");
```

Program 3.11: Initial maze algorithm

Analysis of *path*: The size of the maze determines the computing time of *path*. Since each position within the maze is visited no more than once, the worst case complexity of the algorithm is $O(mp)$ where m and p are, respectively, the number of rows and columns of the maze. □

EXERCISES

1. Describe how you could model a maze with horizontal and vertical walls by a matrix whose entries are zeroes and ones. What moves are permitted in your matrix model? Provide an example maze together with its matrix model.

2. Do the previous exercise for the case of mazes that have walls that are at 45 and 135 degrees in addition to horizontal and vertical ones.

$$\begin{bmatrix} 0 & 0 & 0 & 0 & 0 & 1 \\ 1 & 1 & 1 & 1 & 1 & 0 \\ 1 & 0 & 0 & 0 & 0 & 1 \\ 0 & 1 & 1 & 1 & 1 & 1 \\ 1 & 0 & 0 & 0 & 0 & 1 \\ 1 & 1 & 1 & 1 & 1 & 0 \\ 1 & 0 & 0 & 0 & 0 & 1 \\ 0 & 1 & 1 & 1 & 1 & 1 \\ 1 & 0 & 0 & 0 & 0 & 0 \end{bmatrix}$$

Figure 3.11: Simple maze with a long path

3. What is the maximum path length from start to finish for any maze of dimensions *rows* × *columns*?

4. (a) Find a path through the maze of Figure 3.8.

   (b) Trace the action of function path on the maze of Figure 3.8. Compare this to your own attempt in (a).

5. § [***Programming project***] Using the information provided in the text, write a complete program to search a maze. Print out the entrance to exit path if successful.

3.6 EVALUATION OF EXPRESSIONS

3.6.1 Expressions

The representation and evaluation of expressions is of great interest to computer scientists. As programmers, we write complex expressions such as:

$$((rear+1==front) \; || \; ((rear==MAX\_QUEUE\_SIZE - 1) \; \&\& \; !\,front)) \qquad (3.1)$$

or complex assignment statements such as:

$$x=a/b-c+d*e-a*c \qquad (3.2)$$

If we examine expression (3.1), we notice that it contains operators (==, +, −, ||, &&, !), operands (*rear, front, MAX_QUEUE_SIZE*), and parentheses. The same is true of the statement (3.2), although the operands and operators have changed, and there are no parentheses.

The first problem with understanding the meaning of these or any other expressions and statements is figuring out the order in which the operations are performed. For instance, assume that $a = 4$, $b = c = 2$, $d = e = 3$ in statement (3.2). We want to find the value of x. Is it

```
void path(void)
{/* output a path through the maze if such a path exists */
   int i, row, col, nextRow, nextCol, dir, found = FALSE;
   element position;
   mark[1][1] = 1; top = 0;
   stack[0].row = 1;  stack[0].col = 1;  stack[0].dir = 1;
   while (top > -1 && !found) {
      position = pop();
      row = position.row;  col = position.col;
      dir = position.dir;
      while (dir <  8 && !found) {
         /* move in direction dir */
         nextRow = row + move[dir].vert;
         nextCol = col + move[dir].horiz;
         if (nextRow == EXIT_ROW && nextCol == EXIT_COL)
            found = TRUE;
         else if ( !maze[nextRow][nextCol] &&
         ! mark[nextRow][nextCol]) {
            mark[nextRow][nextCol] = 1;
            position.row = row; position.col = col;
            position.dir = ++dir;
            push(position);
            row = nextRow; col = nextCol; dir = 0;
         }
         else ++dir;
      }
   }
   if (found) {
      printf("The path is:\n");
      printf("row  col\n");
      for (i = 0; i <= top; i++)
         printf("%2d%5d",stack[i].row, stack[i].col);
      printf("%2d%5d\n",row,col);
      printf("%2d%5d\n",EXIT_ROW,EXIT_COL);
   }
   else printf("The maze does not have a path\n");
}
```

Program 3.12: Maze search function

$$((4/2) - 2) + (3 * 3) - (4 * 2)$$
$$= 0 + 9 - 8$$
$$= 1$$

or

$$(4/(2 - 2 + 3)) * (3 - 4) * 2$$
$$= (4/3) * (-1) * 2$$
$$= -2.66666 \cdots$$

Most of us would pick the first answer because we know that division is carried out before subtraction, and multiplication before addition. If we wanted the second answer, we would have written (3.2) differently, using parentheses to change the order of evaluation:

$$x = ((a/(b - c + d)) * (e - a) * c \qquad (3.3)$$

Within any programming language, there is a precedence hierarchy that determines the order in which we evaluate operators. Figure 3.12 contains the precedence hierarchy for C. We have arranged the operators from highest precedence to lowest. Operators with the same precedence appear in the same box. For instance, the highest precedence operators are function calls, array elements, and structure or union members, while the comma operator has the lowest precedence. Operators with highest precedence are evaluated first. The associativity column indicates how we evaluate operators with the same precedence. For instance, the multiplicative operators have left-to-right associativity. This means that the expression $a*b/c\%d/e$ is equivalent to $((((a*b)/c)\%d)/e)$. In other words, we evaluate the operator that is furthest to the left first. With right associative operators of the same precedence, we evaluate the operator furthest to the right first. Parentheses are used to override precedence, and expressions are always evaluated from the innermost parenthesized expression first.

3.6.2   Evaluating Postfix Expressions

The standard way of writing expressions is known as infix notation because in it we place a binary operator in-between its two operands. We have used this notation for all of the expressions written thus far. Although infix notation is the most common way of writing expressions, it is not the one used by compilers to evaluate expressions. Instead compilers typically use a parenthesis-free notation referred to as postfix. In this notation, each operator appears after its operands. Figure 3.13 contains several infix expressions and their postfix equivalents.

Before writing a function that translates expressions from infix to postfix, we tackle the easier task of evaluating postfix expressions. This evaluation process is much simpler than the evaluation of infix expressions because there are no parentheses to consider. To evaluate an expression we make a single left-to-right scan of it. We place the operands on a stack until we find an operator. We then remove, from the stack, the

Token	Operator	Precedence[1]	Associativity
() [] → .	function call array element struct or union member	17	left-to-right
−− ++	increment, decrement[2]	16	left-to-right
−− ++ ! ~ − + & * sizeof	decrement, increment[3] logical not one's complement unary minus or plus address or indirection size (in bytes)	15	right-to-left
(type)	type cast	14	right-to-left
* / %	multiplicative	13	left-to-right
+ −	binary add or subtract	12	left-to-right
<< >>	shift	11	left-to-right
> >= < <=	relational	10	left-to-right
== !=	equality	9	left-to-right
&	bitwise and	8	left-to-right
^	bitwise exclusive or	7	left-to-right
		bitwise or	6	left-to-right
&&	logical and	5	left-to-right
||	logical or	4	left-to-right
?:	conditional	3	right-to-left
= += −= /= *= %= <<= >>= &= ^= |=	assignment	2	right-to-left
,	comma	1	left-to-right

1. The precedence column is taken from Harbison and Steele.
2. Postfix form
3. Prefix form

Figure 3.12: Precedence hierarchy for C

correct number of operands for the operator, perform the operation, and place the result back on the stack. We continue in this fashion until we reach the end of the expression. We then remove the answer from the top of the stack. Figure 3.14 shows this processing when the input is the nine character string 6 2/3−4 2*+.

Infix	Postfix
2+3*4	2 3 4*+
$a*b+5$	$ab*5+$
(1+2)*7	1 2+7*
$a*b/c$	$ab*c/$
$((a/(b-c+d))*(e-a)*c$	$abc-d+/ea-*c*$
$a/b-c+d*e-a*c$	$ab/c-de*+ac*-$

Figure 3.13: Infix and postfix notation

Token	Stack			Top
	[0]	[1]	[2]	
6	6			0
2	6	2		1
/	6/2			0
3	6/2	3		1
−	6/2−3			0
4	6/2−3	4		1
2	6/2−3	4	2	2
*	6/2 3	4*2		1
+	6/2−3+4*2			0

Figure 3.14: Postfix evaluation

We now consider the representation of both the stack and the expression. To simplify our task we assume that the expression contains only the binary operators +, −, *, /, and % and that the operands in the expression are single digit integers as in Figure 3.14. This permits us to represent the expression as a character array. The operands are stored on a stack of type **int** until they arc needed. We may use either of the representations of Sections 3.1 and 3.2. It is convenient to define the enumerated type *precedence*, which lists the operators by mnemonics, as below:

```
typedef enum {lparen, rparen, plus, minus, times, divide,
                    mod, eos, operand} precedence;
```

Although we will use it to process tokens (operators, operands, and parentheses) in this example, its real importance becomes evident when we translate infix expressions into postfix ones. Besides the usual operators, the enumerated type also includes an end-of-string (*eos*) operator.

The function *eval* (Program 3.13) contains the code to evaluate a postfix expression. Since an operand (*symbol*) is initially a character, we must convert it into a single digit integer. We use the statement, *symbol* − '0', to accomplish this task. The statement takes the ASCII value of *symbol* and subtracts the ASCII value of '0', which is 48, from it. For example, suppose *symbol* = '1'. The character, '1', has an ASCII value of 49. Therefore, the statement *symbol* − '0' produces as result the number 1.

We use an auxiliary function, *getToken* (Program 3.14), to obtain tokens from the expression string. If the token is an operand, we convert it to a number and add it to the stack. Otherwise, we remove two operands from the stack, perform the specified operation, and place the result back on the stack. When we have reached the end of expression, we remove the result from the stack.

3.6.3   Infix to Postfix

We can describe an algorithm for producing a postfix expression from an infix one as follows:

(1)   Fully parenthesize the expression.

(2)   Move all binary operators so that they replace their corresponding right parentheses.

(3)   Delete all parentheses.

For example, $a/b - c + d*e - a*c$ when fully parenthesized becomes:

$$((((a/b) - c) + (d*e)) - a*c))$$

Performing steps 2 and 3 gives:

$$ab/c - de* + ac* -$$

Although this algorithm works well when done by hand, it is inefficient on a computer because it requires two passes. The first pass reads the expression and parenthesizes it, while the second moves the operators. Since the order of operands is the same in infix and postfix, we can form the postfix equivalent by scanning the infix expression left-to-right. During this scan, operands are passed to the output expression as they are encountered. However, the order in which the operators are output depends

```
int eval(void)
{/* evaluate a postfix expression, expr, maintained as a
    global variable. '\0' is the the end of the expression.
    The stack and top of the stack are global variables.
    getToken is used to return the token type and
    the character symbol. Operands are assumed to be single
    character digits */
  precedence token;
  char symbol;
  int op1, op2;
  int n = 0; /* counter for the expression string */
  int top = -1;
  token = getToken(&symbol, &n);
  while (token != eos) {
    if (token == operand)
      push(symbol-'0'); /* stack insert */
    else {
      /* pop two operands, perform operation, and
         push result to the stack */
      op2 = pop(); /* stack delete */
      op1 = pop();
      switch(token) {
        case plus: push(op1+op2);
                   break;
        case minus: push(op1-op2);
                    break;
        case times: push(op1*op2);
                    break;
        case divide: push(op1/op2);
                     break;
        case mod: push(op1%op2);
      }
    }
    token = getToken(&symbol, &n);
  }
  return pop(); /* return result */
}
```

Program 3.13: Function to evaluate a postfix expression

```
precedence getToken(char *symbol, int *n)
{/* get the next token, symbol is the character
    representation, which is returned, the token is
    represented by its enumerated value, which
    is returned in the function name */
  *symbol = expr[(*n)++];
  switch (*symbol) {
     case '(' : return lparen;
     case ')' : return rparen;
     case '+' : return plus;
     case '-' : return minus;
     case '/' : return divide;
     case '*' : return times;
     case '%' : return mod;
     case ' ' : return eos;
     default  : return operand; /* no error checking,
                                   default is operand */
  }
}
```

Program 3.14: Function to get a token from the input string

on their precedence. Since we must output the higher precedence operators first, we save operators until we know their correct placement. A stack is one way of doing this, but removing operators correctly is problematic. Two examples illustrate the problem.

Example 3.3 [*Simple expression*]: Suppose we have the simple expression $a+b*c$, which yields $abc*+$ in postfix. As Figure 3.15 illustrates, the operands are output immediately, but the two operators need to be reversed. In general, operators with higher precedence must be output before those with lower precedence. Therefore, we stack operators as long as the precedence of the operator at the top of the stack is less than the precedence of the incoming operator. In this particular example, the unstacking occurs only when we reach the end of the expression. At this point, the two operators are removed. Since the operator with the higher precedence is on top of the stack, it is removed first. □

Example 3.4 [*Parenthesized expression*]: Parentheses make the translation process more difficult because the equivalent postfix expression will be parenthesis-free. We use as our example the expression $a*(b+c)*d$, which yields $abc+*d*$ in postfix. Figure 3.16 shows the translation process. Notice that we stack operators until we reach the

Token	Stack			Top	Output
	[0]	[1]	[2]		
a				−1	a
+	+			0	a
b	+			0	ab
*	+	*		1	ab
c	+	*		1	abc
eos				−1	abc*+

Figure 3.15: Translation of $a+b*c$ to postfix

right parenthesis. At this point we unstack until we reach the corresponding left parenthesis. We then delete the left parenthesis from the stack. (The right parenthesis is never put on the stack.) This leaves us with only the $*d$ remaining in the infix expression. Since the two multiplications have equal precedences, one is output before the d, the second is placed on the stack and removed after the d is output. □

Token	Stack			Top	Output
	[0]	[1]	[2]		
a				−1	a
*	*			0	a
(	*	(		1	u
b	*	(		1	ab
+	*	(	+	2	ab
c	*	(	+	2	abc
)	*			0	abc +
*	*			0	abc +*
d	*			0	abc +*d
eos	*			0	abc +*d*

Figure 3.16: Translation of $a*(b+c)*d$ to postfix

The analysis of the two examples suggests a precedence-based scheme for stacking and unstacking operators. The left parenthesis complicates matters because it behaves like a low-precedence operator when it is on the stack, and a high-precedence one when it is not. It is placed in the stack whenever it is found in the expression, but it is unstacked only when its matching right parenthesis is found. Thus, we have two types of precedence, an *in-stack precedence* (*isp*) and an *incoming precedence* (*icp*). The declarations that establish these precedences are:

```
/* isp and icp arrays -- index is value of precedence
   lparen, rparen, plus, minus, times, divide, mod, eos */
int isp[] = {0,19,12,12,13,13,13,0};
int icp[] = {20,19,12,12,13,13,13,0};
```

Notice that we are now using the stack to store the mnemonic for the token. That is, the data type of the stack elements is *precedence*. Since the value of a variable of an enumerated type is simply the integer corresponding to the position of the value in the enumerated type, we can use the mnemonic as an index into the two arrays. For example, *isp* [*plus*] is translated into *isp* [2], which gives us an in-stack precedence of 12. The precedences are taken from Figure 3.12, but we have added precedences for the left and right parentheses and the *eos* marker. We give the right parenthesis an in-stack and incoming precedence (19) that is greater than the precedence of any operator in Figure 3.12. We give the left parenthesis an instack precedence of zero, and an incoming precedence (20) greater than that of the right parenthesis. In addition, because we want unstacking to occur when we reach the end of the string, we give the *eos* token a low precedence (0). These precedences suggest that we remove an operator from the stack only if its instack precedence is greater than or equal to the incoming precedence of the new operator.

The function *postfix* (Program 3.15) converts an infix expression into a postfix one using the process just discussed. This function invokes a function, *print–token*, to print out the character associated with the enumerated type. That is, *print–token* reverses the process used in *get–token*.

Analysis of *postfix*: Let n be the number of tokens in the expression. $\Theta(n)$ time is spent extracting tokens and outputting them. Besides this, time is spent in the two **while** loops. The total time spent here is $\Theta(n)$ as the number of tokens that get stacked and unstacked is linear in n. So, the complexity of function *postfix* is $\Theta(n)$. $\square$

EXERCISES

1. Write the postfix form of the following expressions:

   (a) $a * b * c$

   (b) $-a + b - c + d$

   (c) $a * - b + c$

   (d) $(a + b) * d + e / (f + a * d) + c$

```
void postfix(void)
{/* output the postfix of the expression. The expression
    string, the stack, and top are global */
   char symbol;
   precedence token;
   int n = 0;
   int top = 0;   /* place eos on stack */
   stack[0] = eos;
   for (token = getToken(&symbol, &n); token != eos;
                        token = getToken(&symbol,&n)) {
      if (token == operand)
         printf("%c", symbol);
      else if (token == rparen) {
         /* unstack tokens until left parenthesis */
         while (stack[top] != lparen)
            printToken(pop());
         pop();  /* discard the left parenthesis */
      }
      else {
         /* remove and print symbols whose isp is greater
             than or equal to the current token's icp */
         while(isp[stack[top]] >= icp[token])
            printToken(pop());
         push(token);
      }
   }
   while ( (token = pop()) != eos)
      printToken(token);
   printf("\n");
}
```

Program 3.15: Function to convert from infix to postfix

(e) a && b || c || ! $(e > f)$ (assuming C precedence)

(f)   !(a && !(($b < c$) || ($c > d$))) || ($c < e$)

2. Write the *print–token* function used in *postfix* (Program 3.15).

3. Use the precedences of Figure 3.12 together with those for '(', ')', and \0 to answer the following:

    (a)   In the postfix function, what is the maximum number of elements that can be on the stack at any time if the input expression, *expr*, has *n* operators and an unlimited number of nested parentheses?

(b)   What is the answer to (a) if *expr* has *n* operators and the depth of the nesting of parentheses is at most six?

4. Rewrite the *eval* function so that it evaluates the unary operators + and −.

5. § Rewrite the *postfix* function so that it works with the following operators, besides those used in the text: &&, !!, <<, >>, <=, !=, <, >, <=, and >=. (Hint: Write the equation so that the operators, operands, and parentheses are separated with a space, for example, $a + b > c$. Then review the functions in *<string.h>*.)

6. Another expression form that is easy to evaluate and is parenthesis-free is known as prefix. In prefix notation, the operators precede their operands. Figure 3.17 shows several infix expressions and their prefix equivalents. Notice that the order of operands is the same in infix and prefix.

Infix	Prefix
$a*b/c$	$/*abc$
$a/b-c+d*e-a*c$	$-+-/abc*de*ac$
$a*(b+c)/d-g$	$-/*a+bcdg$

Figure 3.17: Infix and postfix expressions

(a)   Write the prefix form of the expressions in Exercise 1.

(b)   Write a C function that evaluates a prefix expression, *expr*. (Hint: Scan *expr* from right to left.)

(c)   Write a C function that transforms an infix expression, *expr*, into its prefix equivalent.

What is the time complexity of your functions for (b) and (c)? How much space is needed by each of these functions?

7. Write a C function that transforms a prefix expression into a postfix one. Carefully state any assumptions you make regarding the input. How much time and space does your function take?

8. Write a C function that transforms a postfix expression into a prefix one. How much time and space does your function take?

9. Write a C function that transforms a postfix expression into a fully parenthesized infix expression. A fully parenthesized expression is one in which all the subexpressions are surrounded by parentheses. For example, $a+b+c$ becomes

$((a+b)+c)$. Analyze the time and space complexity of your function.

10. Write a C function that transforms a prefix expression into a fully parenthesized infix expression. Analyze the time and space complexity of your function.

11. § Repeat Exercise 5, but this time transform the infix expression into prefix.

3.7 MULTIPLE STACKS AND QUEUES

Until now we have been concerned only with the representations of a single stack or a single queue. In both cases, we have seen that it is possible to obtain efficient sequential representations. We would now like to examine the case of multiple stacks. (We leave the consideration of multiple queues as an exercise.) We again examine only sequential mappings of stacks into an array, *memory[MEMORY_SIZE]*. If we have only two stacks to represent, the solution is simple. We use *memory* [0] for the bottom element of the first stack, and *memory[MEMORY_SIZE − 1]* for the bottom element of the second stack. The first stack grows toward *memory[MEMORY_SIZE − 1]* and the second grows toward *memory* [0]. With this representation, we can efficiently use all the available space.

Representing more than two stacks within the same array poses problems since we no longer have an obvious point for the bottom element of each stack. Assuming that we have *n* stacks, we can divide the available memory into *n* segments. This initial division may be done in proportion to the expected sizes of the various stacks, if this is known. Otherwise, we may divide the memory into equal segments.

Assume that *l* refers to the stack number of one of the *n* stacks. To establish this stack, we must create indices for both the bottom and top positions of this stack. The convention we use is that *boundary* [i], $0 \le i < MAX\_STACKS$, points to the position immediately to the left of the bottom element of stack i, while *top*[i], $0 \le i < MAX\_STACKS$ points to the top element. Stack i is empty iff *boundary*[i] = *top*[i]. The relevant declarations are:

```
#define MEMORY_SIZE 100 /* size of memory */
#define MAX_STACKS 10 /* max number of stacks plus 1 */
/* global memory declaration */
element memory[MEMORY_SIZE];
int top[MAX_STACKS];
int boundary[MAX_STACKS];
int n;  /* number of stacks entered by the user */
```

To divide the array into roughly equal segments we use the following code:

```
top[0] = boundary[0] = -1;
for (j = 1; j < n; j++)
   top[j] = boundary[j] = (MEMORY_SIZE/n)*j;
boundary[n] = MEMORY_SIZE-1;
```

Figure 3.18 shows this initial configuration. In the figure, n is the number of stacks entered by the user, $n < MAX\_STACKS$, and $m = MEMORY\_SIZE$. Stack i can grow from $boundary[i] + 1$ to $boundary[i + 1]$ before it is full. Since we need a boundary for the last stack, we set $boundary[n]$ to $MEMORY\_SIZE- 1$. Programs 3.16 and 3.17 implement the add and delete operations for this representation.

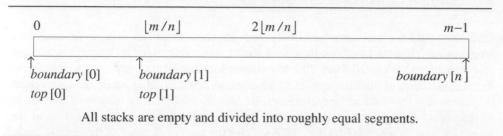

All stacks are empty and divided into roughly equal segments.

Figure 3.18: Initial configuration for n stacks in *memory* [m].

```
void push(int i, element item)
{/* add an item to the ith stack */
   if (top[i] == boundary[i+1])
      stackFull(i);
   memory[++top[i]] = item;
}
```

Program 3.16: Add an item to the *i*th stack

The *push* (Program 3.16) and *pop* (Program 3.17) functions for multiple stacks appear to be as simple as those we used for the representation of a single stack. However, this is not really the case because the *top*[*i*] == *boundary*[*i*+1] condition in *push* implies only that a particular stack ran out of memory, not that the entire memory is full. In fact, there may be a lot of unused space between other stacks in array *memory* (see Figure 3.19). Therefore, we create an error recovery function, *stackFull*, which determines if there is any free space in memory. If there is space available, it should shift the stacks so that space is allocated to the full stack.

There are several ways that we can design *stackFull* so that we can add elements to this stack until the array is full. We outline one method here. Other methods are discussed in the exercises. We can guarantee that *stackFull* adds elements as long as there is free space in array *memory* if we:

(1)   Determine the least, j, $i < j < n$, such that there is free space between stacks j and j

```
element pop(int i)
{/* remove top element from the ith stack */
   if (top[i] == boundary[i])
      return stackEmpty(i);
   return memory[top[i]--];
}
```

Program 3.17: Delete an item from the *i*th stack

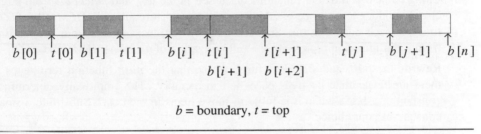

b = boundary, t = top

Figure 3.19: Configuration when stack i meets stack $i + 1$, but the memory is not full

+ 1. That is, $top[j] < boundary[j+1]$. If there is such a j, then move stacks $i+1$, $i+2$, $\cdots$, j one position to the right (treating $memory[0]$ as leftmost and $memory[MEMORY\_SIZE - 1]$ as rightmost). This creates a space between stacks i and $i+1$.

(2)   If there is no j as in (1), then look to the left of stack i. Find the largest j such that $0 \leq j < i$ and there is space between stacks j and $j+1$. That is, $top[j] < boundary[j+1]$. If there is such a j, then move stacks $j+1$, $j+2$, $\cdots$, i one space to the left. This also creates a space between stacks i and $i+1$.

(3)   If there is no j satisfying either condition (1) or condition (2), then all $MEMORY\_SIZE$ spaces of memory are utilized and there is no free space. In this case *stackFull* terminates with an error message.

We leave the implementation of *stackFull* as an exercise. However, it should be clear that the worst case performance of this representation for the n stacks together will be poor. In fact, in the worst case, the function has a time complexity of $O(MEMORY\_SIZE)$.

EXERCISES

1. We must represent two stacks in an array, *memory*[*MEMORY_SIZE*]. Write C functions that add and delete an item from stack $i, 0 \le i < n$. Your functions should be able to add elements to the stacks as long as the total number of elements in both stacks is less than *MEMORY_SIZE* − *1*.

2. Obtain a data representation that maps a stack and a queue into a single array, *memory*[*MEMORY_SIZE*]. Write C functions that add and delete elements from these two data objects. What can you say about the suitability of your data representation?

3. Write a C function that implements the *stackFull* strategy discussed in the text.

4. Using the add and delete functions discussed in the text and *stackFull* from Exercise 3, produce a sequence of additions/deletions that requires O(*MEMORY_SIZE*) time for each add. Assume that you have two stacks and that your are starting from a configuration representing a full utilization of *memory*[*MEMORY_SIZE*].

5. Rewrite the *push* and *stackFull* functions so that the *push* function terminates if there are fewer than c_1 free spaces left in memory. The empirically determined constant, c_1 shows when it is futile to move items in memory. Substitute a small constant of your choice.

6. Design a data representation that sequentially maps *n* queues into an array *memory*[*MEMORY_SIZE*]. Represent each queue as a circular queue within memory. Write functions *addq*, *deleteq*, and *queueFull* for this representation.

3.8 ADDITIONAL EXERCISES

1. § [*Programming project*] [Landweber] People have spent so much time playing solitaire that the gambling casinos are now capitalizing on this human weakness. A form of solitaire is described below. You must write a C program that plays this game, thus freeing hours of time for people to return to more useful endeavors.

To begin the game, 28 cards are dealt into seven piles. The leftmost pile has one card, the next pile has two cards, and so forth, up to seven cards in the rightmost pile. Only the uppermost card of each of the seven piles is turned face-up. The cards are dealt left-to-right, one card to each pile, dealing one less pile each time, and turning the first card in each round face-up. You may build descending sequences of red on black or black on red from the top face-up card of each pile. For example, you may place either the eight of diamonds or the eight of hearts on the nine of spades or the nine of clubs. All face-up cards on a pile are moved as a unit and may be placed on another pile according to the bottom face-up card. For example, the seven of clubs on the eight of hearts may be moved as a unit onto the nine of clubs or the nine of spades.

Whenever a face-down card is uncovered, it is turned face-up. If one pile is removed completely, a face-up king may be moved from a pile (together with all cards above it) or the top of the waste pile (see below) into the vacated space. There are four output piles, one for each suite, and the object of the game is to get as many cards as possible into the output piles. Each time an ace appears at the top of a pile or the top of the stack it is moved into the appropriate output pile. Cards are added to the output piles in sequence, the suit for each pile being determined by the ace on the bottom.

From the rest of the deck, called the stock, cards are turned up one by one and placed face-up on a waste pile. You may always play cards off the top of the waste pile, but only one at a time. Begin by moving a card from the stock to the top of the waste pile. If you can ever make more than one possible play, make them in the following order:

(a)   Move a card from the top of a playing pile or from the top of the waste pile to an output pile. If the waste pile becomes empty, move a card from the stock to the waste pile.

(b)   Move a card from the top of the waste pile to the leftmost playing pile to which it can be moved. If the waste pile becomes empty, move a card from the stock to the waste pile.

(c)   Find the leftmost playing pile that can be moved and place it on top of the leftmost playing pile to which it can be moved.

(d)   Try (a), (b), and (c) in sequence, restarting with (a) whenever a move is made.

(e)   If no move is made via (a) through (d), move a card from the stock to the waste pile and retry (a).

Only the top card of the playing piles or the waste pile may be played to an output pile. Once placed on an output pile, a card may not be withdrawn to help elsewhere. The game is over when either all the cards have been played to the output piles, or the stock pile has been exhausted and no more cards can be moved.

When played for money, the player pays the house $52 at the beginning, and wins $5 for every card played to the output piles. Write your program so that it will play several games and determine your net winnings. Use a random number generator to shuffle the deck. Output a complete record of two games in easily understandable form. Include as output the number of games played and the net winnings (+ or −).

2.   § [*Programming project*] [Landweber] We want to simulate an airport landing and takeoff pattern. The airport has three runways, runway 0, runway 1, and runway 2. There are four landing holding patterns, two for each of the first two runways.

Arriving planes enter one of the holding pattern queues, where the queues are to be as close in size as possible. When a plane enters a holding queue, it is assigned an integer identification number and an integer giving the number of time units the plane can remain in the queue before it must land (because of low fuel level). There is also a queue for takeoffs for each of the three runways. Planes arriving in a takeoff queue are assigned an integer identification number. The takeoff queues should be kept approximately the same size.

For each time period, no more than three planes may arrive at the landing queues and no more than three planes may enter the takeoff queues. Each runway can handle one takeoff or landing at each time slot. Runway 2 is used for takeoffs except when a plane is low on fuel. During each time period, planes in either landing queue whose air time has reached zero must be given priority over other landings and takeoffs. If only one plane is in this category, runway 2 is used. If there is more than one plane, then the other runways are also used.

Use successive even(odd) integers for identification numbers of the planes arriving at takeoff (landing) queues. At each time unit assume that arriving planes are entered into queues before takeoffs or landings occur. Try to design your algorithm so that neither landing nor takeoff queues grow excessively. However, arriving planes must be placed at the ends of queues and the queues cannot be reordered.

Your output should label clearly what occurs during each time unit. Periodically you should also output:
(a)   the contents of each queue
(b)   the average takeoff waiting time
(c)   the average landing waiting time
(d)   the number of planes that have crashed (run out of fuel and there was no open runway) since the last time period.

CHAPTER 4

Linked Lists

4.1 SINGLY LINKED LISTS AND CHAINS

In the previous chapters, we studied the representation of simple data structures using an array and a sequential mapping. These representations had the property that successive nodes of the data object were stored a fixed distance apart. Thus, (1) if the element a_{ij} of a table was stored at location L_{ij}, then $a_{i,j+1}$ was at the location $L_{ij} + 1$; (2) if the ith element in a queue was at location L_i, then the $(i + 1)$th element was at location $(L_i + 1)$ % n for the circular representation; (3) if the topmost node of a stack was at location L_T, then the node beneath it was at location $L_T - 1$, and so on. These sequential storage schemes proved adequate for the tasks we wished to perform (accessing an arbitrary node in a table, insertion or deletion of stack and queue elements). However, when a sequential mapping is used for ordered lists, operations such as insertion and deletion of arbitrary elements become expensive. For example, consider the following list of three-letter English words ending in AT:

(BAT, CAT, EAT, FAT, HAT, JAT, LAT, MAT, OAT, PAT, RAT, SAT, VAT, WAT)

To make this list more complete we naturally want to add the word GAT, which means

145

gun or revolver. If we are using an array and a sequential mapping to keep this list, then the insertion of GAT will require us to move elements already in the list either one location higher or lower. We must move either HAT, JAT, LAT, $\cdots$, WAT or BAT, CAT, EAT, and FAT. If we have to do many such insertions into the middle, neither alternative is attractive because of the amount of data movement. Excessive data movement also is required for deletions. Suppose we decide to remove the word LAT, which refers to the Latvian monetary unit. Then again, we have to move many elements so as to maintain the sequential representation of the list.

An elegant solution to this problem of data movement in *sequential* representations is achieved by using *linked* representations. Unlike a sequential representation, in which successive items of a list are located a fixed distance apart, in a linked representation these items may be placed anywhere in memory. In other words, in a sequential representation the order of elements is the same as in the ordered list, whereas in a linked representation these two sequences need not be the same. To access list elements in the correct order, with each element we store the address or location of the next element in that list. Thus, associated with each data item in a linked representation is a pointer or link to the next item. In general, a linked list is comprised of nodes; each node has zero or more data fields and one or more link or pointer fields.

Figure 4.1 shows how some of the elements in our list of three-letter words may be represented in memory by using pointers. The elements of the list are stored in a one-dimensional array called *data*, but the elements no longer occur in sequential order, BAT before CAT before EAT, and so on. Instead we relax this restriction and allow them to appear anywhere in the array and in any order. To remind us of the real order, a second array, *link*, is added. The values in this array are pointers to elements in the *data* array. For any i, *data* [i] and *link* [i] together comprise a node. Since the list starts at *data*[8] = BAT, let us set a variable *first* = 8. *link*[8] has the value 3, which means it points to *data*[3], which contains CAT. Since *link* [3] = 4, the next element, EAT, in the list is in *data* [4]. The element after EAT is in *data* [*link* [4]]. By continuing in this way we can list all the words in the proper order. We recognize that we have come to the end of our ordered list when *link* equals zero. To ensure that a *link* of zero always signifies the end of a list, we do not use position zero of *data* to store a list element.

It is customary to draw linked lists as an ordered sequence of nodes with links being represented by arrows, as in Figure 4.2. Notice that we do not explicitly put in the values of the pointers but simply draw arrows to indicate they are there. The arrows reinforce in our own mind the facts that (1) the nodes do not actually reside in sequential locations and (2) the actual locations of nodes are immaterial. Therefore, when we write a program that works with lists, we do not look for a specific address except when we test for zero. The linked structures of Figures 4.1 and 4.2 are called singly linked lists or chains. In a *singly linked list*, each node has exactly one pointer field. A *chain* is a singly linked list that is comprised of zero or more nodes. When the number of nodes is zero, the chain is empty. The nodes of a non-empty chain are ordered so that the first node links to the second node; the second to the third; and so on. The last node of a chain has

	data	link
1	HAT	15
2		
3	CAT	4
4	EAT	9
5		
6		
7	WAT	0
8	BAT	3
9	FAT	1
10		
11	VAT	7
.	.	.
.	.	.
.	.	.

Figure 4.1: Nonsequential list-representation

a 0 link.

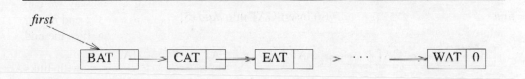

first

Figure 4.2: Usual way to draw a linked list

Let us now see why it is easier to make insertions and deletions at arbitrary positions using a linked list rather than a sequential list. To insert the data item GAT between FAT and HAT, the following steps are adequate:

(1) Get a node *a* that is currently unused.

(2) Set the *data* field of *a* to GAT.

(3)   Set the *link* field of *a* to point to the node after FAT, which contains HAT.

(4)   Set the *link* field of the node containing FAT to *a*.

Figure 4.3(a) shows how the arrays *data* and *link* will be changed after we insert GAT. Figure 4.3(b) shows how we can draw the insertion using our arrow notation. Dashed arrows are new ones. The important thing to notice is that when we insert GAT, we do not have to move any elements that are already in the list. We have overcome the need to move data at the expense of the storage needed for the field *link*. Usually, this penalty is not too severe. When each list element is large, significant time is saved by not having to move elements during an insert or delete.

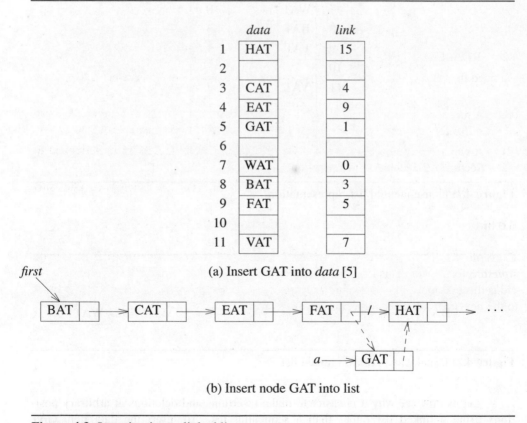

(a) Insert GAT into *data* [5]

(b) Insert node GAT into list

Figure 4.3: Inserting into a linked list

Now suppose we want to delete GAT from the list. All we need to do is find the element that immediately precedes GAT, which is FAT, and set *link*[9] to the position of HAT which is 1. Again, there is no need to move the data around. Even though the link of GAT still contains a pointer to HAT, GAT is no longer in the list as it cannot be reached by starting at the first element of list and following links (see Figure 4.4).

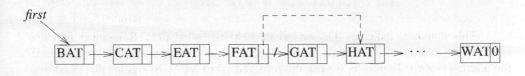

Figure 4.4: Delete GAT

4.2 REPRESENTING CHAINS IN C

We need the following capabilities to make linked representations possible:

(1) A mechanism for defining a node's structure, that is, the fields it contains. We use *self-referential structures*, discussed in Section 2.3.4, to do this.

(2) A way to create new nodes when we need them. The *MALLOC* macros defined in Section 1.2.2 handles this operation.

(3) A way to remove nodes that we no longer need. The *free* function handles this operation.

We will present several small examples to show how to create and use linked lists in C.

Example 4.1 [*List of words*]: To create a linked list of words, we first define a node structure for the list. This structure specifies the type of each of the fields. From our previous discussion we know that our structure must contain a character array and a pointer to the next node. The necessary declarations are:

```
typedef struct listNode *listPointer;
typedef struct {
        char data[4];
        listPointer link;
        } listNode;
```

These declarations contain an example of a *self-referential structure*. Notice that we have defined the pointer (*listPointer*) to the **struct** before we defined the **struct** (*listNode*). C allows us to create a pointer to a type that does not yet exist because otherwise we would face a paradox: we cannot define a pointer to a nonexistent type, but to define

the new type we must include a pointer to the type.

After defining the node's structure, we create a new empty list. This is accomplished by the statement:

```
listPointer first = NULL;
```

This statement indicates that we have a new list called *first*. Remember that *first* contains the address of the start of the list. Since the new list is initially empty, its starting address is zero. Therefore, we use the reserved word *NULL* to signify this condition. We also can use an *IS_EMPTY* macro to test for an empty list:

```
#define IS_EMPTY(first) (!(first))
```

To create new nodes for our list we use the *MALLOC* macro of Section 1.2.2. We would apply this macro as follows to obtain a new node for our list:

```
MALLOC(first, sizeof(*first));
```

We are now ready to assign values to the fields of the node. This introduces a new operator, →. If *e* is a pointer to a structure that contains the field *name*, then *e→name* is a shorthand way of writing the expression (*e).name*. The → operator is referred to as the *structure member* operator, and its use is preferred when one has a pointer to a **struct** rather than the * and dot notation.

To place the word BAT into our list we use the statements:

```
strcpy(first→data,"BAT");
first→link = NULL;
```

These statements create the list illustrated in Figure 4.5. Notice that the node has a null link field because there is no next node in the list. □

Example 4.2 [*Two-node linked list*]: We want to create a linked list of integers. The node structure is defined as:

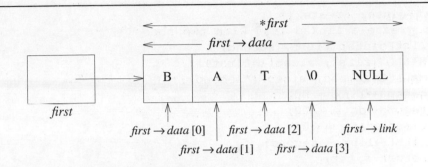

Figure 4.5: Referencing the fields of a node

```
typedef struct listNode *listPointer;
typedef struct {
        int data;
        listPointer link;
        } listNode;
```

A linked list with two nodes is created by function *create2* (Program 4.1). We set the data field of the first node to 10 and that of the second to 20. The variable *first* is a pointer to the first node; *second* is a pointer to the second node. Notice that the link field of the first node is set to point to the second node, while the link field of the second node is *NULL*. The variable *first*, which is the pointer to the start of the list, is returned by *create2*. Figure 4.6 shows the resulting list structure. □

Example 4.3 [*List insertion*]: Let *first* be a pointer to a linked list as in Example 4.2. Assume that we want to insert a node with a data field of 50 after some arbitrary node *x*. Function *Insert* (Program 4.2) accomplishes this task. In this function, we pass in two pointer variables. The variable, *first*, is the pointer to the first node in the list. If this variable contains a null address (i.e., there are no nodes in the list), we want to change *first* so that it points to the node with 50 in its data field. This means that we must pass in the address of *first*. This is why we use the declaration *listPointer *first*. Since the value of the second pointer, *x*, does not change, we do not need to pass in its address as a parameter. A typical function call would be *insert* (&*first*, *x*); where *first* points to the start of the list and *x* points to the node after which the insertion is to take place.

The function *insert* uses an **if · · · else** statement to distinguish between empty and nonempty lists. For an empty list, we set *temp*'s link field to *NULL* and change the value of *first* to the address of *temp*. For a nonempty list, we insert the *temp* node between *x*

```
listPointer create2()
{/* create a linked list with two nodes */
   listPointer first, second;
   MALLOC(first, sizeof(*first));
   MALLOC(second, sizeof(*second));
   second→link = NULL;
   second→data = 20;
   first→data = 10;
   first→link = second;
   return first;
}
```

Program 4.1: Create a two-node list

Figure 4.6: A two-node list

and the node pointed to by its link field. Figure 4.7 shows the two cases.

Example 4.4 [*List deletion*]: Deleting an arbitrary node from a list is slightly more complicated than insertion because deletion depends on the location of the node. Assume that we have three pointers: *first* points to the start of the list, *x* points to the node that we wish to delete, and *trail* points to the node that precedes *x*. Figures 4.8 and 4.9 show two examples. In Figure 4.8, the node to be deleted is the first node in the list. This means that we must change the value of *first*. In Figure 4.9, since *x* is not the first node, we simply change the link field in *trail* to point to the link field in *x*.

An arbitrary node is deleted from a linked list by function *delete* (Program 4.3). In addition to changing the link fields, or the value of **first*, *delete* also returns the space that was allocated to the deleted node to the system memory. To accomplish this task, we use *free*. □

Example 4.5 [*Printing out a list*]: Program 4.4 prints the data fields of the nodes in a list. To do this we first print out the contents of *first*'s data field, then we replace *first* with the address in its *link* field. We continue printing out the *data* field and moving to

```
void insert(listPointer *first, listPointer x)
{/* insert a new node with data = 50 into the chain
    first after node x */
  listPointer temp;
  MALLOC(temp, sizeof(*temp));
  temp→data = 50;
  if (*first) {
      temp→link = x→link;
      x→link = temp;
  }
  else {
      temp→link = NULL;
      *first = temp;
  }
}
```

Program 4.2: Simple insert into front of list

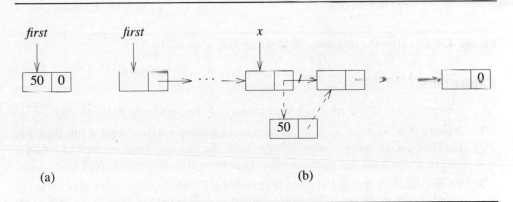

(a)   (b)

Figure 4.7: Inserting into an empty and nonempty list

the next node until we reach the end of the list. □

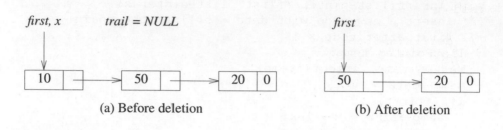

(a) Before deletion   (b) After deletion

Figure 4.8: List before and after the function call *delete(&first, NULL, first);*

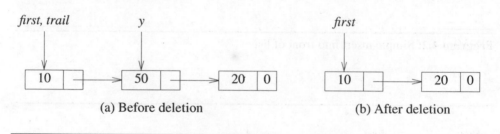

(a) Before deletion   (b) After deletion

Figure 4.9: List after the function call *delete(&first, y, y→link);*

EXERCISES

1. Rewrite *delete* (Program 4.3) so that it uses only two pointers, *first* and *trail*.

2. Assume that we have a list of integers as in Example 4.2. Create a function that searches for an integer, *num*. If *num* is in the list, the function should return a pointer to the node that contains *num*. Otherwise it should return *NULL*.

3. Write a function that deletes a node containing a number, *num*, from a list. Use the search function (Exercise 2) to determine if *num* is in the list.

4. Write a function, *length*, that returns the number of nodes in a list.

5. Let p be a pointer to the first node in a singly linked list. Write a procedure to delete every other node beginning with node p (i.e., the first, third, fifth, etc. nodes of the list are deleted). What is the time complexity of your algorithm?

6. Let $x = (x_1, x_2, \ldots, x_n)$ and $y = (y_1, y_2, \ldots, y_m)$ be two linked lists. Assume that in each list, the nodes are in nondecreasing order of their data field values. Write an algorithm to merge the two lists together to obtain a new linked list z in which

```
void delete(listPointer *first, listPointer trail,
                                listPointer x)
{/* delete x from the list, trail is the preceding node
    and *first is the front of the list */
    if (trail)
        trail→link = x→link;
    else
        *first = (*first)→link;
    free(x);
}
```

Program 4.3: Deletion from a list

```
void printList(listPointer first)
{
    printf("The list contains: ");
    for (; first; first = first→link)
        printf("%4d",first→data);
    printf("\n");
}
```

Program 4.4: Printing a list

the nodes are also in this order. Following the merge, x and y do not exist as individual lists. Each node initially in x or y is now in z. No additional nodes may be used. What is the time complexity of your algorithm?

7. Let $list_1 = (x_1, x_2, \cdots, x_n)$ and $list_2 = (y_1, y_2, \cdots, y_m)$. Write a function to merge the two lists together to obtain the linked list, $list_3 = (x_1, y_1, x_2, y_2, \cdots, x_m, y_m, x_{m+1}, \cdots, x_n)$ if $m \leq n$; and $list_3 = (x_1, y_1, x_2, y_2, \cdots, x_n, y_n, x_{n+1}, \cdots, x_m)$ if $m > n$.

8. § It is possible to traverse a linked list in both directions (i.e., left to right and restricted right-to-left) by reversing the links during the left-to-right traversal. A possible configuration for the list under this scheme is given in Figure 4.10. The variable r points to the node currently being examined and l to the node on its left. Note that all nodes to the left of r have their links reversed.

   (a) Write a function to move r to the right n nodes from a given position (l, r).

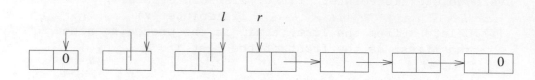

Figure 4.10: Possible configuration for a chain traversed in both directions

(b)   Write a function to move *r* to the left *n* nodes from any given position *(l, r)*.

4.3   LINKED STACKS AND QUEUES

Previously we represented stacks and queues sequentially. Such a representation proved efficient if we had only one stack or one queue. However, when several stacks and queues coexisted, there was no efficient way to represent them sequentially. Figure 4.10 shows a linked stack and a linked queue. Notice that the direction of links for both the stack and the queue facilitate easy insertion and deletion of nodes. In the case of Figure 4.10(a), we can easily add or delete a node from the top of the stack. In the case of Figure 4.11(b), we can easily add a node to the rear of the queue and add or delete a node at the front, although we normally will not add items to the front of a queue.

If we wish to represent $n \leq MAX\_STACKS$ stacks simultaneously, we begin with the declarations:

```
#define MAX_STACKS 10 /* maximum number of stacks */
typedef struct {
        int key;
        /* other fields */
        } element;
typedef struct stack *stackPointer;
typedef struct {
        element data;
        stackPointer link;
        } stack;
stackPointer top[MAX_STACKS];
```

We assume that the initial condition for the stacks is:

$$top[i] = NULL, \ 0 \leq i < MAX\_STACKS$$

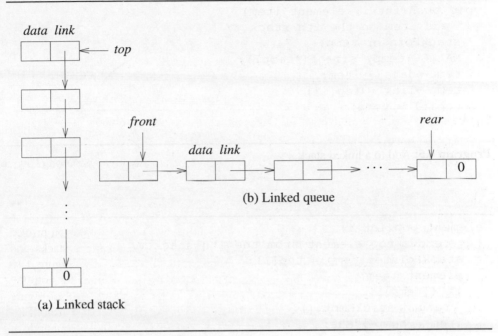

(b) Linked queue

(a) Linked stack

Figure 4.11: Linked stack and queue

and the boundary condition is:

$$top\,[i\,] = NULL \text{ iff the } i\text{th stack is empty}$$

Functions *push* (Program 4.5) and *pop* (Program 4.6) add and delete items to/from a stack. The code for each is straightforward. Function *push* creates a new node, *temp*, and places *item* in the data field and *top* in the link field. The variable *top* is then changed to point to *temp*. A typical function call to add an element to the *i*th stack would be *push* (*i*,*item*). Function *pop* returns the top element and changes *top* to point to the address contained in its link field. The removed node is then returned to system memory. A typical function call to delete an element from the *i*th stack would be *item = pop* (*i*);

To represent $m \leq MAX\_QUEUES$ queues simultaneously, we begin with the declarations:

```
void push(int i, element item)
{/* add item to the ith stack */
   stackPointer temp;
   MALLOC(temp, sizeof(*temp));
   temp→data = item;
   temp→link = top[i];
   top[i] = temp;
}
```

Program 4.5: Add to a linked stack

```
element pop(int i)
{/* remove top element from the ith stack */
   stackPointer temp = top[i];
   element item;
   if (!temp)
     return stackEmpty();
   item = temp→data;
   top[i] = temp→link;
   free(temp);
   return item;
}
```

Program 4.6: Delete from a linked stack

```
#define MAX_QUEUES 10 /* maximum number of queues */
typedef struct queue *queuePointer;
typedef struct {
        element data;
        queuePointer link;
        } queue;
queuePointer front[MAX_QUEUES], rear[MAX_QUEUES];
```

We assume that the initial condition for the queues is:

$$front[i] = NULL, 0 \le i < MAX\_QUEUES$$

and the boundary condition is:

$$front[i] = \text{NULL iff the } i\text{th queue is empty}$$

Functions *addq* (Program 4.7) and *deleteq* (Program 4.8) implement the add and delete operations for multiple queues. Function *addq* is more complex than *push* because we must check for an empty queue. If the queue is empty, we change *front* to point to the new node; otherwise we change *rear*'s link field to point to the new node. In either case, we then change *rear* to point to the new node. Function *deleteq* is similar to *pop* since we are removing the node that is currently at the start of the list. Typical function calls would be *addq* (*i,item*); and *item* = *deleteq* (*i*);.

```
void addq(i, item)
{/* add item to the rear of queue i */
   queuePointer temp;
   MALLOC(temp, sizeof(*temp));
   temp→data = item;
   temp→link = NULL;
   if (front[i])
      rear[i]→link = temp;
   else
      front[i] = temp;
   rear[i] = temp;
}
```

Program 4.7: Add to the rear of a linked queue

The solution presented above to the *n*-stack, *m*-queue problem is both computationally and conceptually simple. We no longer need to shift stacks or queues to make space. Computation can proceed as long as there is memory available. Although we need additional space for the link field, the use of linked lists makes sense because the overhead incurred by the storage of the links is overridden by (1) the ability to represent lists in a simple way, and (2) the reduced computing time required by linked representations.

EXERCISES

1. A palindrome is a word or phrase that is the same when spelled from the front or the back. For example, "reviver" and "Able was I ere I saw Elba" are both palindromes. We can determine if a word or phrase is a palindrome by using a stack. Write a C function that returns *TRUE* if a word or phrase is a palindrome and

```
element deleteq(int i)
{/* delete an element from queue i */
   queuePointer temp = front[i];
   element item;
   if (!temp)
      return queueEmpty();
   item = temp→data;
   front[i]= temp→link;
   free(temp);
   return item;
}
```

Program 4.8: Delete from the front of a linked queue

   FALSE if it is not.

2. We can use a stack to determine if the parentheses in an expression are properly nested. Write a C function that does this.

3. Consider the hypothetical data type $X2$. $X2$ is a linear list with the restriction that while additions to the list may be made at either end, deletions can be made at one end only. Design a linked list representation for $X2$. Write addition and deletion functions for $X2$. Specify initial and boundary conditions for your representation.

4.4   POLYNOMIALS

4.4.1   Polynomial Representation

Let us tackle a reasonably complex problem using linked lists. This problem, the manipulation of symbolic polynomials, has become a classic example of list processing. As in Chapter 2, we wish to be able to represent any number of different polynomials as long as memory is available. In general, we want to represent the polynomial:

$$A(x) = a_{m-1}x^{e_{m-1}} + \cdots + a_0x^{e_0}$$

where the a_i are nonzero coefficients and the e_i are nonnegative integer exponents such that $e_{m-1} > e_{m-2} > \cdots > e_1 > e_0 \geq 0$. We represent each term as a node containing coefficient and exponent fields, as well as a pointer to the next term. Assuming that the coefficients are integers, the type declarations are:

```
typedef struct polyNode *polyPointer;
typedef struct {
        int coef;
        int expon;
        polyPointer link;
        } polyNode;
polyPointer a,b;
```

We draw *polyNode*s as:

| coef | expon | link |

Figure 4.12 shows how we would store the polynomials

$$a = 3x^{14} + 2x^8 + 1$$

and

$$b = 8x^{14} - 3x^{10} + 10x^6$$

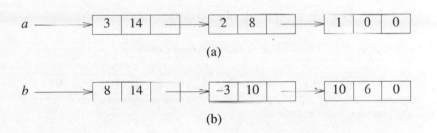

(a)

(b)

Figure 4.12: Representation of $3x^{14}+2x^8+1$ and $8x^{14}-3x^{10}+10x^6$

4.4.2 Adding Polynomials

To add two polynomials, we examine their terms starting at the nodes pointed to by a and b. If the exponents of the two terms are equal, we add the two coefficients and create a new term for the result. We also move the pointers to the next nodes in a and b. If the exponent of the current term in a is less than the exponent of the current term in b, then we create a duplicate term of b, attach this term to the result, called c, and advance the pointer to the next term in b. We take a similar action on a if $a{\rightarrow}expon > b{\rightarrow}expon$. Figure 4.13 illustrates this process for the polynomials represented in Figure 4.12.

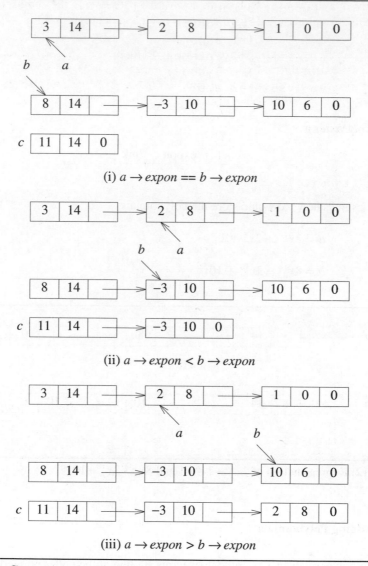

Figure 4.13: Generating the first three terms of $c = a + b$

Each time we generate a new node, we set its *coef* and *expon* fields and append it to the end of c. To avoid having to search for the last node in c each time we add a new node, we keep a pointer, *rear*, which points to the current last node in c. The complete addition algorithm is specified by *padd* (Program 4.9). To create a new node and append it to the end of *c*, *padd* uses *attach* (Program 4.10). To make things work out neatly, initially we give *c* a single node with no values, which we delete at the end of the function. Although this is somewhat inelegant, it avoids more computation.

```
polyPointer padd(polyPointer a, polyPointer b)
{/* return a polynomial which is the sum of a and b */
   polyPointer c, rear, temp;
   int sum;
   MALLOC(rear, sizeof(*rear));
   c = rear;
   while (a && b)
      switch (COMPARE(a→expon,b→expon)) {
         case -1: /* a→expon < b→expon */
                 attach(b→coef,b→expon,&rear);
                 b = b→link;
                 break;
         case 0: /* a→expon = b→expon */
                 sum = a→coef + b→coef;
                 if (sum) attach(sum,a→expon,&rear);
                 a = a→link;  b = b→link; break;
         case 1: /* a→expon > b→expon */
                 attach(a→coef,a→expon,&rear);
                 a = a→link;
      }
   /* copy rest of list a and then list b */
   for (; a; a = a→link) attach(a→coef,a→expon,&rear);
   for (; b; b = b→link) attach(b→coef,b→expon,&rear);
   rear→link = NULL;
   /* delete extra initial node */
   temp = c; c = c→link;  free(temp);
   return c;
}
```

Program 4.9: Add two polynomials

This is our first complete example of list processing, so you should study it carefully. The basic algorithm is straightforward, using a streaming process that moves along the two polynomials, either copying terms or adding them to the result. Thus, the **while** loop has three cases depending on whether the next pair of exponents are =, <, or >. Notice that there are five places where we create a new term, justifying our use of function *attach*.

```
void attach(float coefficient, int exponent,
              polyPointer *ptr)
{/* create a new node with coef = coefficient and expon =
    exponent, attach it to the node pointed to by ptr.
    ptr is updated to point to this new node */
  polyPointer temp;
  MALLOC(temp, sizeof(*temp));
  temp->coef = coefficient;
  temp->expon = exponent;
  (*ptr)->link = temp;
  *ptr = temp;
}
```

Program 4.10: Attach a node to the end of a list

Analysis of *padd*: To determine the computing time of *padd*, we first determine which operations contribute to the cost. For this algorithm, there are three cost measures:

(1)   coefficient additions

(2)   exponent comparisons

(3)   creation of new nodes for c

If we assume that each of these operations takes a single unit of time if done once, then the number of times that we perform these operations determines the total time taken by *padd*. This number clearly depends on how many terms are present in the polynomials a and b. Assume that a and b have m and n terms, respectively:

$$A(x) = a_{m-1}x^{e_{m-1}} + \cdots + a_0 x^{e_0}$$

$$B(x) = b_{n-1}x^{f_{n-1}} + \cdots + b_0 x^{f_0}$$

where $a_i, b_i \neq 0$ and $e_{m-1} > \cdots > e_0 \geq 0, f_{n-1} > \cdots > f_0 \geq 0$. Then clearly the number of coefficient additions varies as:

$$0 \leq \text{number of coefficient additions} \leq \min\{m,n\}$$

The lower bound is achieved when none of the exponents are equal, while the upper is achieved when the exponents of one polynomial are a subset of the exponents of the other.

As for the exponent comparisons, we make one comparison on each iteration of the **while** loop. On each iteration, either a or b or both move to the next term. Since the total number of terms is $m + n$, the number of iterations and hence the number of exponent comparisons is bounded by $m + n$. You can easily construct a case when $m + n - 1$ comparisons will be necessary, for example, $m = n$ and

$$e_{m-1} > f_{m-1} > e_{m-2} > f_{m-2} > \cdots > e_1 > f_1 > e_0 > f_0$$

The maximum number of terms in c is $m + n$, and so no more than $m + n$ new terms are created (this excludes the additional node that is attached to the front of d and later removed).

In summary, the maximum number of executions of any statement in *padd* is bounded above by $m + n$. Therefore, the computing time is $O(m + n)$. This means that if we implement and run the algorithm on a computer, the time it takes will be $c_1 m + c_2 n + c_3$, where c_1, c_2, c_3 are constants. Since any algorithm that adds two polynomials must look at each nonzero term at least once, *padd* is optimal to within a constant factor. $\square$

4.4.3 Erasing Polynomials

The use of linked lists is well suited to polynomial operations. We can easily imagine writing a collection of functions for input, output, addition, subtraction, and multiplication of polynomials using linked lists as the means of representation. A hypothetical user who wishes to read in polynomials $a(x)$, $b(x)$, and $d(x)$ and then compute $e(x) = a(x) * b(x) + d(x)$ would write his or her main function as:

```
polyPointer a, b, d, e
   .
   .
   .
a = readPoly();
b = readPoly();
d = readPoly();
temp = pmult(a,b);
e = padd(temp,d);
printPoly(e);
```

If our user wishes to compute more polynomials, it would be useful to reclaim the nodes that are being used to represent *temp*(x) since we created *temp*(x) only to hold a partial result for $d(x)$. By returning the nodes of *temp*(x), we may use them to hold other polynomials. One by one, *erase* (Program 4.11) frees the nodes in *temp*.

```
void erase(polyPointer *ptr)
{/* erase the polynomial pointed to by ptr */
    polyPointer temp;
    while (*ptr) {
        temp = *ptr;
        *ptr = (*ptr)→link;
        free(temp);
    }
}
```

Program 4.11: Erasing a polynomial

4.4.4   Circular List Representation of Polynomials

We can free all the nodes of a polynomial more efficiently if we modify our list structure
so that the link field of the last node points to the first node in the list (see Figure 4.14).
We call this a *circular list*. A singly linked list in which the last node has a null link is
called a *chain*.

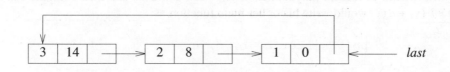

Figure 4.14: Circular representation of $3x^{14} + 2x^8 + 1$

As we indicated earlier, we free nodes that are no longer in use so that we may
reuse these nodes later. We can meet this objective, and obtain an efficient erase algorithm for circular lists, by maintaining our own list (as a chain) of nodes that have been
"freed." When we need a new node, we examine this list. If the list is not empty, then
we may use one of its nodes. Only when the list is empty do we need to use *malloc* to
create a new node.

Let *avail* be a variable of type *polyPointer* that points to the first node in our list of
freed nodes. Henceforth, we call this list the available space list or *avail* list. Initially,
we set *avail* to *NULL*. Instead of using *malloc* and *free*, we now use *getNode* (Program
4.12) and *retNode* (Program 4.13).

We may erase a circular list in a fixed amount of time independent of the number

```
polyPointer getNode(void)
{/* provide a node for use */
   polyPointer node;
   if (avail) {
      node = avail;
      avail = avail→link;
   }
   else
      MALLOC(node, sizeof(*node));
   return node;
}
```

Program 4.12: *getNode* function

```
void retNode(polyPointer node)
{/* return a node to the available list */
   node→link = avail;
   avail = node;
}
```

Program 4.13: *retNode* function

of nodes in the list using *cerase* (Program 4.14).

A direct changeover to the structure of Figure 4.14 creates problems when we implement the other polynomial operations since we must handle the zero polynomial as a special case. To avoid this special case, we introduce a *header node* into each polynomial, that is, each polynomial, zero or nonzero, contains one additional node. The *expon* and *coef* fields of this node are irrelevant. Thus, the zero polynomial has the representation of Figure 4.15(a), while $a(x) = 3x^{14} + 2x^8 + 1$ has the representation of Figure 4.15(b).

To simplify the addition algorithm for polynomials represented as circular lists, we set the *expon* field of the header node to -1. Program 4.15 gives the function to add polynomials represented in this way.

```
void cerase(polyPointer *ptr)
{/* erase the circular list pointed to by ptr */
   polyPointer temp;
   if (*ptr) {
      temp = (*ptr)→link;
      (*ptr)→link = avail;
      avail = temp;
      *ptr = NULL;
   }
}
```

Program 4.14: Erasing a circular list

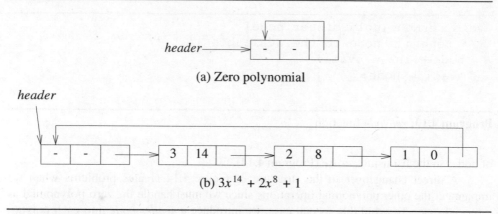

(a) Zero polynomial

(b) $3x^{14} + 2x^8 + 1$

Figure 4.15: Example polynomials with header nodes

4.4.5 Summary

Let us review what we have done so far. We have introduced the concepts of a singly linked list, a chain, and a singly linked circular list. Each node on one of these lists consists of exactly one link field and at least one other field.

In dealing with polynomials, we found it convenient to use circular lists. Another concept we introduced was an available space list. This list consisted of all nodes that had been used at least once and were not currently in use. By using the available space list and *getNode*, *retNode*, and *cerase*, it became possible to erase circular lists in

```
polyPointer cpadd(polyPointer a, polyPointer b)
{/* polynomials a and b are singly linked circular lists
    with a header node. Return a polynomial which is
    the sum of a and b */
  polyPointer startA, c, lastC;
  int sum, done = FALSE;
  startA = a;                  /* record start of a */
  a = a→link;                  /* skip header node for a and b*/
  b = b→link;
  c = getNode();               /* get a header node for sum */
  c→expon = -1; lastC = c;
  do {
     switch (COMPARE(a→expon, b→expon)) {
        case -1: /* a→expon < b→expon */
                attach(b→coef,b→expon,&lastC);
                b = b→link;
                break;
        case 0:  /* a→expon = b→expon */
                if (startA == a)  done = TRUE;
                else {
                    sum = a→coef + b→coef;
                    if (sum) attach(sum,a→expon,&lastC);
                    a = a→link; b = b→link;
                }
                break;
        case 1:  /* a→expon > b→expon */
                attach(a→coef,a→expon,&lastC);
                a = a→link;
     }
  } while (!done);
  lastC→link = c;
  return c;
}
```

Program 4.15: Adding two polynomials represented as circular lists with header nodes

constant time, and also to reuse all nodes not currently in use. As we continue, we shall see more problems that call for variations in node structure and list representation because of the operations we wish to perform.

EXERCISES

1. Write a function, *pread*, that reads in n pairs of coefficients and exponents, ($coef_i$, $expon_i$), $0 \le i < n$ of a polynomial, x. Assume that $expon_{i+1} > expon_i$, $0 \le i < n-2$, and that $coef_i \ne 0$, $0 \le i < n$. Show that this operation can be performed in $O(n)$ time.

2. Let a and b be pointers to two polynomials. Write a function to compute the product polynomial $d = a*b$. Your function should leave a and b unaltered and create d as a new list. Show that if n and m are the number of terms in a and b, respectively, then this multiplication can be carried out in $O(nm^2)$ or $O(n^2m)$ time.

3. Let a be a pointer to a polynomial. Write a function, *peval*, to evaluate the polynomial a at point x, where x is some floating point number.

4. Rewrite Exercise 1 using a circular representation for the polynomial.

5. Rewrite Exercise 2 using a circular representation for the polynomial.

6. Rewrite Exercise 3 using a circular representation for the polynomial.

7. § [*Programming project*] Design and build a linked allocation system to represent and manipulate polynomials. You should use circularly linked lists with header nodes. Each term of the polynomial will be represented as a node, using the following structure:

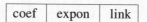

| coef | expon | link |

In order to erase polynomials efficiently, use the available space list and associated functions discussed in this section.

Write and test the following functions:

(a) *pread*. Read in a polynomial and convert it to its circular representation. Return a pointer to the header node of this polynomial.

(b) *pwrite*. Output the polynomial using a form that clearly displays it.

(c) *padd*. Compute $c = a + b$. Do not change either a or b.

(d) *psub*. Compute $c = a - b$. Do not change either a or b.

(e) *pmult*. Compute $c = a*b$. Do not change either a or b.

(f) *eval*. Evaluate a polynomial at some point, a, where a is a floating point constant. Return the result as a floating point.

(g) *perase*. Return the polynomial represented as a circular list to the available space list.

4.5   ADDITIONAL LIST OPERATIONS

4.5.1   Operations For Chains

It is often necessary, and desirable, to build a variety of functions for manipulating singly linked lists. Some that we have seen already are *getNode* and *retNode*, which get and return nodes to the available space list. Inverting (or reversing) a chain (Program 4.16) is another useful operation. This routine is especially interesting because we can do it "in place" if we use three pointers. We use the following declarations:

```
typedef struct listNode *listPointer;
typedef struct {
        char data;
        listPointer link;
        } listNode;
```

Try out this function with at least three examples, an empty list and lists of one and two nodes, so that you understand how it works. For a list of *length* ≥ 1 nodes, the **while** loop is executed *length* times and so the computing time is linear or O(*length*).

Another useful function is one that concatenates two chains, *ptr*1 and *ptr*2 (Program 4.17). The complexity of this function is O(length of list *ptr*1). Since this function does not allocate additional storage for the new list, *ptr*1 also contains the concatenated list. (The exercises explore a concatenation function that does not alter *ptr*1.)

```
listPointer invert(listPointer lead)
{/* invert the list pointed to by lead */
   listPointer middle,trail;
   middle = NULL;
   while (lead) {
      trail = middle;
      middle = lead;
      lead = lead→link;
      middle→link = trail;
   }
   return middle;
}
```

Program 4.16: Inverting a singly linked list

```
listPointer concatenate(listPointer ptr1, listPointer ptr2)
{/* produce a new list that contains the list
    ptr1 followed by the list ptr2. The
    list pointed to by ptr1 is changed permanently */
  listPointer temp;
  /* check for empty lists */
  if (!ptr1) return ptr2;
  if (!ptr2) return ptr1;

  /* neither list is empty, find end of first list */
  for (temp = ptr1; temp→link; temp = temp→link) ;

  /* link end of first to start of second */
  temp→link = ptr2;
}
```

Program 4.17: Concatenating singly linked lists

4.5.2 Operations For Circularly Linked Lists

Now let us take another look at circular lists like the one in Figure 4.14. By keeping a pointer *last* to the last node in the list rather than to the first, we are able to insert an element at both the front and end with ease. Had we kept a pointer to the first node instead of the last node, inserting at the front would require us to must move down the entire length of the list until we find the last node so that we can change the pointer in the last node to point to the new first node. Program 4.18 gives the code at insert a node at the front of a circular list. To insert at the rear, we only need to add the additional statement *last = node* to the **else** clause of *insertFront* (Program 4.18).

As another example of a simple function for circular lists, we write a function (Program 4.19) that determines the length of such a list.

EXERCISES

1. Create a function that searches for an integer, *num*, in a circularly linked list. The function should return a pointer to the node that contains *num* if *num* is in the list and *NULL* otherwise.

2. Write a function that deletes a node containing a number, *num*, from a circularly linked list. Your function should first search for *num*.

```
void insertFront(listPointer *last, listPointer node)
{/* insert node at the front of the circular list whose
    last node is last */
    if (!(*last)) {
    /* list is empty, change last to point to new entry */
        *last = node;
        node->link = node;
    }
    else {
    /* list is not empty, add new entry at front */
        node->link = (*last)->link;
        (*last)->link = node;
    }
}
```

Program 4.18: Inserting at the front of a list

```
int length(listPointer last)
{/* find the length of the circular list last */
    listPointer temp;
    int count = 0;
    if (last) {
        temp = last;
        do {
            count++;
            temp = temp->link;
        } while (temp != last);
    }
    return count;
}
```

Program 4.19: Finding the length of a circular list

3. Write a function to concatenate two circular lists together. Assume that the pointer to each such list points to the last node. Your function should return a pointer to the last node of the concatenated circular list. Following the concatenation, the input lists do not exist independently. What is the time complexity of

your function?

4. Write a function to reverse the direction of pointers in a circular list.

4.6 EQUIVALENCE CLASSES

Let us put together some of the concepts on linked and sequential representations to solve a problem that arises in the design and manufacture of very large-scale integrated (VLSI) circuits. One of the steps in the manufacture of a VLSI circuit involves exposing a silicon wafer using a series of masks. Each mask consists of several polygons. Polygons that overlap electrically are equivalent and electrical equivalence specifies a relationship among mask polygons. This relation has several properties that it shares with other equivalence relations, such as the standard mathematical equals. Suppose that we denote an arbitrary equivalence relation by the symbol $\equiv$ and that:

(1) For any polygon x, $x \equiv x$, that is, x is electrically equivalent to itself. Thus, $\equiv$ is reflexive.

(2) For any two polygons, x and y, if $x \equiv y$ then $y \equiv x$. Thus, the relation $\equiv$ is symmetric.

(3) For any three polygons, x, y, and z, if $x \equiv y$ and $y \equiv z$ then $x \equiv z$. For example, if x and y are electrically equivalent and y and z are also equivalent, then x and z are also electrically equivalent. Thus, the relation $\equiv$ is transitive.

Definition: A relation, $\equiv$, over a set, S, is said to be an *equivalence relation* over S *iff* it is symmetric, reflexive, and transitive over S. $\square$

Examples of equivalence relations are numerous. For example, the "equal to" (=) relationship is an equivalence relation since

(1) $x = x$

(2) $x = y$ implies $y = x$

(3) $x = y$ and $y = z$ implies that $x = z$

We can use an equivalence relation to partition a set S into equivalence classes such that two members x and y of S are in the same equivalence class *iff* $x \equiv y$. For example, if we have twelve polygons numbered 0 through 11 and the following pairs overlap:

$$0 \equiv 4, \ 3 \equiv 1, \ 6 \equiv 10, \ 8 \equiv 9, \ 7 \equiv 4, \ 6 \equiv 8, \ 3 \equiv 5, \ 2 \equiv 11, \ 11 \equiv 0$$

then, as a result of the reflexivity, symmetry, and transitivity of the relation $\equiv$, we can partition the twelve polygons into the following equivalence classes:

$$\{0, 2, 4, 7, 11\}; \{1, 3, 5\}; \{6, 8, 9, 10\}$$

These equivalence classes are important because they define a signal net that we can use to verify the correctness of the masks.

The algorithm to determine equivalence works in two phases. In the first phase, we read in and store the equivalence pairs $<i, j>$. In the second phase we begin at 0 and find all pairs of the form $<0, j>$, where 0 and j are in the same equivalence class. By transitivity, all pairs of the form $<j, k>$ imply that k is in the same equivalence class as 0. We continue in this way until we have found, marked, and printed the entire equivalence class containing 0. Then we continue on.

Our first design attempt appears in Program 4.20. Let m and n represent the number of related pairs and the number of objects, respectively. We first must figure out which data structure we should use to hold these pairs. To determine this, we examine the operations that are required. The pair $<i, j>$ is essentially two random integers in the range 0 to $n-1$. Easy random access would dictate an array, say $pairs[n][m]$. The ith row would contain the elements, j, that are paired directly to i in the input. However, this could waste a lot of space since very few of the array elements would be used. It also might require considerable time to insert a new pair, $<i, k>$, into row i since we would have to scan the row for the next free location or use more storage.

```
void equivalence()
{
    initialize;
    while (there are more pairs) {
        read the next pair <i,j>;
        process this pair;
    }
    initialize the output;
    do
        output a new equivalence class;
    while (not done);
}
```

Program 4.20: First pass at equivalence algorithm

These considerations lead us to a linked list representation for each row. Our node structure requires only a data and a link field. However, since we still need random access to the ith row, we use a one-dimensional array, $seq[n]$, to hold the header nodes of the n lists. For the second phase of the algorithm, we need a mechanism that tells us whether or not the object, i, has been printed. We use the array $out[n]$ and the constants *TRUE* and *FALSE* for this purpose. Our next refinement appears in Program 4.21.

```
void equivalence()
{
    initialize seq to NULL and out to TRUE;
    while (there are more pairs) {
        read the next pair, <i,j>;
        put j on the seq[i] list;
        put i on the seq[j] list;
    }
    for (i = 0; i < n; i++)
        if (out[i]) {
            out[i] = FALSE;
            output this equivalence class;
        }
}
```

Program 4.21: A more detailed version of the equivalence algorithm

Let us simulate this algorithm, as we have developed it thus far, using the previous data set. After the **while** loop is completed the lists resemble those appearing in Figure 4.16. For each relation $i \equiv j$, we use two nodes. The variable $seq[i]$ points to the list of nodes that contains every number that is directly equivalent to i by an input relation.

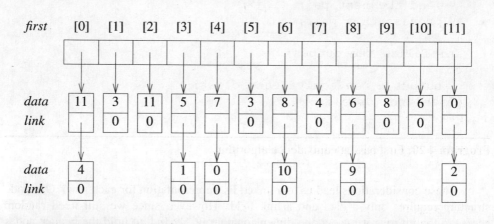

Figure 4.16: Lists after pairs have been input

In phase two, we scan the *seq* array for the first *i*, $0 \le i < n$, such that *out* [*i*] = *TRUE*. Each element in the list *seq* [*i*] is printed. To process the remaining lists which, by transitivity, belong in the same class as *i*, we create a stack of their nodes. We do this by changing the link fields so that they point in the reverse direction. Program 4.22 contains the complete equivalence algorithm.

```c
#include <stdio.h>
#include <alloc.h>
#define MAX_SIZE 24
#define FALSE 0
#define TRUE 1
typedef struct node *nodePointer;
typedef struct {
        int data;
        nodePointer link;
        } node;
void main(void)
{
    short int out[MAX_SIZE];
    nodePointer seq[MAX_SIZE];
    nodePointer x,y,top;
    int i,j,n;

    printf("Enter the size (<= %d) ",MAX_SIZE);
    scanf("%d",&n);
    for (i = 0; i < n; i++) {
    /* initialize seq and out */
        out[i] = TRUE;    seq[i] = NULL;
    }

    /* Phase 1: Input the equivalence pairs: */
    printf("Enter a pair of numbers (-1 -1 to quit): ");
    scanf("%d%d",&i,&j);
    while (i >= 0) {
        MALLOC(x, sizeof(*x));
        x→data = j;   x→link = seq[i];   seq[i] = x;
        MALLOC(x, sizeof(*x));
        x→data = i;   x→link = seq[j];   seq[j] = x;
        printf("Enter a pair of numbers (-1 -1 to quit): ");
        scanf("%d%d",&i,&j);
    }
```

```
/* Phase 2: output the equivalence classes */
for (i = 0; i < n; i++)
   if (out[i]) {
      printf("\nNew class: %5d",i);
      out[i] = FALSE;    /* set class to false */
      x = seq[i];  top = NULL; /* initialize stack */
      for (;;) {       /* find rest of class */
         while (x) {   /* process list */
            j = x→data;
            if (out[j]) {
               printf("%5d",j);  out[j] = FALSE;
               y = x→link; x→link = top; top = x; x = y;
            }
            else x = x→link;
         }
         if (!top) break;
         x = seq[top→data]; top = top→link;
                                    /* unstack */
      }
   }
}
```

Program 4.22: Program to find equivalence classes

Analysis of the equivalence program: The initialization of *seq* and *out* takes $O(n)$ time. Inputting the equivalence pairs in phase 1 takes a constant amount of time per pair. Hence, the total time for this phase is $O(m+n)$ where m is the number of pairs input. In phase 2, we put each node onto the linked stack at most once. Since there are only $2m$ nodes, and we execute the **for** loop n times, the time for this phase is $O(m + n)$. Thus, the overall computing time is $O(m + n)$. Any algorithm that processes equivalence relations must look at all m equivalence pairs and at all n polygons at least once. Thus, there is no algorithm with a computing time less than $O(m+n)$. This means that the equivalence algorithm is optimal to within a constant factor. Unfortunately, the space required by the algorithm is also $O(m + n)$. In Chapter 5, we look at an alternative solution to this problem that requires only $O(n)$ space. $\square$

4.7 SPARSE MATRICES

4.7.1 Sparse Matrix Representation

In Chapter 2, we saw that we could save space and computing time by retaining only the nonzero terms of sparse matrices. When the nonzero terms did not form a "nice" pattern, such as a triangle or a band, we devised a sequential scheme in which we represented each nonzero term by a node with three fields: *row, column,* and *value*. We organized these nodes sequentially. However, we found that when we performed matrix operations such as addition, subtraction, or multiplication, the number of nonzero terms varied. Matrices representing partial computations, as in the case of polynomials, were created and later destroyed to make space for further matrices. Thus, the sequential representation of sparse matrices suffered from the same inadequacies as the similar representation of polynomials. In this section, we study a linked list representation for sparse matrices. As we have seen previously, linked lists allow us to efficiently represent structures that vary in size, a benefit that also applies to sparse matrices.

In our data representation, we represent each column of a sparse matrix as a circularly linked list with a header node. We use a similar representation for each row of a sparse matrix. Each node has a tag field, which we use to distinguish between header nodes and entry nodes. Each header node has three additional fields: *down, right,* and *next* (Figure 4.17(a)). We use the *down* field to link into a column list and the *right* field to link into a row list. The *next* field links the header nodes together. The header node for row i is also the header node for column i, and the total number of header nodes is max {number of rows, number of columns}.

Each entry node has five fields in addition to the tag field: *row, col, down, right, value* (Figure 4.17(b)). We use the *down* field to link to the next nonzero term in the same column and the *right* field to link to the next nonzero term in the same row. Thus, if $a_{ij} \neq 0$, there is a node with tag field = *entry*, *value* = a_{ij}, *row* = i, and *col* = j (Figure 4.17(c)). We link this node into the circular linked lists for row i and column j. Hence, it is simultaneously linked into two different lists.

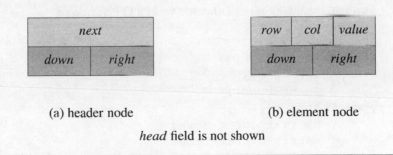

(a) header node   (b) element node

head field is not shown

Figure 4.17: Node structure for sparse matrices

As noted earlier, each header node is in three lists: a list of rows, a list of columns, and a list of header nodes. The list of header nodes also has a header node that has the same structure as an entry node (Figure 4.17(b)). We use the *row* and *col* fields of this node to store the matrix dimensions.

Consider the sparse matrix, *a*, shown in Figure 4.18. Figure 4.19 shows the linked representation of this matrix. Although we have not shown the value of the tag fields, we can easily determine these values from the node structure. For each nonzero term of *a*, we have one entry node that is in exactly one row list and one column list. The header nodes are marked $H0$-$H3$. As the figure shows, we use the *right* field of the header node list header to link into the list of header nodes. Notice also that we may reference the entire matrix through the header node, *a*, of the list of header nodes.

$$\begin{bmatrix} 2 & 0 & 0 & 0 \\ 4 & 0 & 0 & 3 \\ 0 & 0 & 0 & 0 \\ 8 & 0 & 0 & 1 \\ 0 & 0 & 6 & 0 \end{bmatrix}$$

Figure 4.18: 4×4 sparse matrix *a*

If we wish to represent a *numRows* × *numCols* matrix with *numTerms* nonzero terms, then we need max {*numRows, numCols*} + *numTerms* + 1 nodes. While each node may require several words of memory, the total storage will be less than *numRows* × *numCols* when *numTerms* is sufficiently small.

Since we have two different types of nodes in our representation, we use a **union** to create the appropriate data structure. The necessary C declarations are as follows:

```
#define MAX_SIZE 50 /*size of largest matrix*/
typedef enum {head,entry} tagfield;
typedef struct matrixNode *matrixPointer;
typedef struct {
        int row;
        int col;
        int value;
        } entryNode;
typedef struct {
        matrixPointer down;
        matrixPointer right;
        tagfield tag;
        union {
            matrixPointer next;
            entryNode entry;
            } u;
        } matrixNode;
matrixPointer hdnode[MAX_SIZE];
```

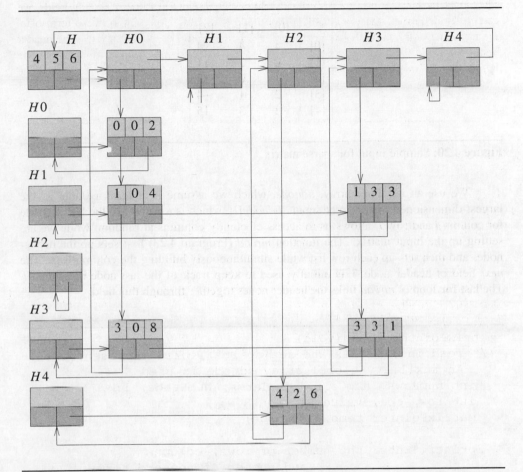

Figure 4.19: Linked representation of the sparse matrix of Figure 4.18 (the *head* field of a node is not shown)

4.7.2   Sparse Matrix Input

The first operation we implement is that of reading in a sparse matrix and obtaining its linked representation. We assume that the first input line consists of the number of rows (*numRows*), the number of columns (*numCols*), and the number of nonzero terms (*numTerms*). This line is followed by *numTerms* lines of input, each of which is of the form: *row*, *col*, *value*. We assume that these lines are ordered by rows and within rows by columns. For example, Figure 4.20 shows the input for the 4×4 matrix of Figure 4.18.

182 Linked Lists

	[0]	[1]	[2]
[0]	4	4	4
[1]	0	2	11
[2]	1	0	12
[3]	2	1	−4
[4]	3	3	−15

Figure 4.20: Sample input for sparse matrix

We use an auxiliary array, *hdnode*, which we assume is at least as large as the largest-dimensioned matrix to be input. *hdnode*[i], which is a pointer to the header node for column *i* and row *i*, allows us to access efficiently columns at random, while we are setting up the input matrix. The function *mread* (Program 4.23) first sets up the header nodes and then sets up each row list while simultaneously building the column lists. The *next* field of header node, *i*, is initially used to keep track of the last node in column *i*. The last **for** loop of *mread* links the header nodes together through this field.

```
matrixPointer mread(void)
{/* read in a matrix and set up its linked representation.
   An auxiliary global array hdnode is used */
   int numRows, numCols,  numTerms, numHeads, i;
   int row, col, value, currentRow;
   matrixPointer temp,last,node;

   printf("Enter the number of rows, columns
                     and number of nonzero terms: ");
   scanf("%d%d%d",&numRows, &numCols, &numTerms);
   numHeads = (numCols > numRows) ? numCols : numRows;
   /* set up header node for the list of header nodes */
   node = newNode(); node→tag = entry;
   node→u.entry.row = numRows;
   node→u.entry.col = numCols;

   if (!numHeads) node→right = node;
   else { /* initialize the header nodes */
      for (i = 0; i < numHeads; i++) {
         temp = newNode;
```

```
        hdnode[i] = temp; hdnode[i]→tag = head;
        hdnode[i]→right = temp;  hdnode[i]→u.next = temp;
    }
    currentRow = 0;
    last = hdnode[0]; /* last node in current row */
    for (i = 0; i < numTerms; i++) {
        printf("Enter row, column and value: ");
        scanf("%d%d%d",&row,&col,&value);
        if (row > currentRow) {/* close current row */
            last→right = hdnode[currentRow];
            currentRow = row; last = hdnode[row];
        }
        MALLOC(temp, sizeof(*temp));
        temp→tag = entry;  temp→u.entry.row = row;
        temp→u.entry.col = col;
        temp→u.entry.value = value;
        last→right = temp; /* link into row list */
        last = temp;
        /* link into column list */
        hdnode[col]→u.next→down = temp;
        hdnode[col]→u.next = temp;
    }
    /*close last row */
    last→right = hdnode[currentRow];
    /* close all column lists */
    for (i = 0; i < numCols; i++)
        hdnode[i]→u.next→down = hdnode[i];
    /* link all header nodes together */
    for (i = 0; i < numHeads-1; i++)
        hdnode[i]→u.next = hdnode[i+1];
    hdnode[numHeads-1]→u.next = node;
    node→right = hdnode[0];
    }
    return node;
}
```

Program 4.23: Read in a sparse matrix

Analysis of *mread*: Since *MALLOC* works in a constant amount of time, we can set up all of the header nodes in O(max {*numRows,numlCols*}) time. We can also set up each nonzero term in a constant amount of time because we use the variable *last* to keep track of the current row, while *next* keeps track of the current column. Thus, the **for** loop that inputs and links the entry nodes requires only O(*numTerms*) time. The remainder of the function takes O(max {*numRows,numCols*}) time. Therefore, the total time is:

$$O(\max \{numRows, numCols\} + numTerms)$$

$$= O(numRows + numCols + numTerms).$$

Notice that this is asymptotically better than the input time of O(*numRows* × *numCols*) for a *numRows* × *numCols* matrix using a two-dimensional array. However it is slightly worse than the sequential method used in Section 2.5. □

4.7.3 Sparse Matrix Output

We would now like to print out the contents of a sparse matrix in a form that resembles that found in Figure 4.20. The function *mwrite* (Program 4.24) implements this operation.

```
void mwrite(matrixPointer node)
{/* print out the matrix in row major form */
   int i;
   matrixPointer temp, head = node→right;
   /* matrix dimensions */
   printf(" \n numRows = %d, numCols = %d \n",
                  node→u.entry.row, node→u.entry.col);
   printf(" The matrix by row, column, and value: \n\n");
   for (i = 0; i < node→u.entry.row; i++) {
   /* print out the entries in each row */
      for (temp = head→right; temp != head;
                                    temp = temp→right)
         printf("%5d%5d%5d \n",temp→u.entry.row,
               temp→u.entry.col, temp→u.entry.value);
      head = head→u.next; /* next row */
   }
}
```

Program 4.24: Write out a sparse matrix

Analysis of *mwrite*: The function *mwrite* uses two **for** loops. The number of iterations of the outer **for** loop is *numRows*. For any row, *i*, the number of iterations of the inner **for** loop is equal to the number of entries for row *i*. Therefore, the computing time of the *mwrite* function is O(*numRows* + *numTerms*). □

4.7.4 Erasing a Sparse Matrix

Before closing this section we want to look at an algorithm that returns all nodes of a sparse matrix to the system memory. We return the nodes one at a time using *free*, although we could develop a faster algorithm using an available space list (see Section 4.4). The function *merase* (Program 4.25) implements the erase operation.

```
void merase(matrixPointer *node)
{/* erase the matrix, return the nodes to the heap */
   matrixPointer x,y, head = (*node)→right;
   int i;
   /* free the entry and header nodes by row */
   for (i = 0; i < (*node)→u.entry.row; i++) {
      y = head→right;
      while (y != head) {
         x = y; y = y→right; free(x);
      }
      x = head; head = head→u.next; free(x);
   }
   /* free remaining header nodes*/
   y = head;
   while (y != *node) {
      x = y; y = y→u.next; free(x);
   }
   free(*node); *node - NULL;
}
```

Program 4.25: Erase a sparse matrix

Analysis of *merase*: First, *merase* returns the entry nodes and the row header nodes to the system memory using a nested loop structure that resembles the structure found in *mwrite*. Thus, the computing time for the nested loops is O(*numRows* + *numTerms*). The time to erase the remaining header nodes is O(*numRows* + *numCols*). Hence, the computing time for *merase* is O(*numRows* + *numCols* + *numTerms*). □

EXERCISES

1. Let a and b be two sparse matrices. Write a function, *madd*, to create the matrix d = $a + b$. Your function should leave matrices a and b unchanged, and set up d as a new matrix. Show that if a and b are *numRows* × *numCols* matrices with *numterms*$_a$ and *numTerms*$_b$ nonzero terms, then we can perform this addition in

$O(numRows + numCols + numTerms_a + numTerms_b)$ time.

2. Let a and b be two sparse matrices. Write a function, *mmult*, to create the matrix $d = a*b$. Show that if a is a $numRows_a \times numCols_a$ matrix with $numTerms_a$ nonzero terms and b is a $numCols_a \times numCols_b$ matrix with $numTerms_b$ nonzero terms, then we can compute d in $O(numCols_b \times numTerms_a + numRows_a \times numTerms_b)$ time. Can you think of a way to compute d in $O(\min\{numCols_b \times numTerms_a, numRows_a \times numTerms_b\})$ time?

3. (a) Rewrite *merase* so that it places the erased list into an available space list rather than returning it to system memory.

   (b) Rewrite *mread* so that it first attempts to obtain a new node from the available space list rather than the system memory.

4. Write a function, *mtranspose*, to compute the matrix $b = a^T$, the transpose of the sparse matrix a. What is the computing time of your function?

5. Design a function that copies a sparse matrix. What is the computing time of your function?

6. § [***Programming project***] We want to implement a complete linked list system to perform arithmetic on sparse matrices using our linked list representation. Create a user-friendly, menu-driven system that performs the following operations. (The matrix names are used only for illustrative purposes. The functions are specified as templates to which you must add the appropriate parameters.)

   (a) *mread*. Read in a sparse matrix.

   (b) *mwrite*. Write out the contents of a sparse matrix.

   (c) *merase*. Erase a sparse matrix.

   (d) *madd*. Create the sparse matrix $d = a + b$

   (e) *mmult*. Create the sparse matrix $d = a*b$.

   (f) *mtranspose*. Create the sparse matrix $b = a^T$.

4.8   DOUBLY LINKED LISTS

So far we have been working chiefly with chains and singly linked circular lists. For some problems these would be too restrictive. One difficulty with these lists is that if we are pointing to a specific node, say p, then we can move only in the direction of the links. The only way to find the node that precedes p is to start at the beginning of the list. The same problem arises when one wishes to delete an arbitrary node from a singly linked list. As can be seen from Example 4.4, easy deletion of an arbitrary node requires knowing the preceding node. If we have a problem in which it is necessary to move in either direction or in which we must delete arbitrary nodes, then it is useful to have doubly linked lists. Each node now has two link fields, one linking in the forward direction and the other linking in the backward direction.

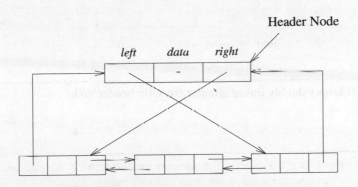

Header Node

left   *data*   *right*

Figure 4.21: Doubly linked circular list with header node

A node in a doubly linked list has at least three fields, a left link field (*llink*), a data field (*data*), and a right link field (*rlink*). The necessary declarations are:

```
typedef struct node *nodePointer;
typedef struct {
    nodePointer llink;
    element data;
    nodePointer rlink;
    } node;
```

A doubly linked list may or may not be circular. A sample doubly linked circular list with three nodes is given in Figure 4.21. Besides these three nodes, we have added a header node. As was true in previous sections, a header node allows us to implement our operations more easily. The data field of the header node usually contains no information. If *ptr* points to any node in a doubly linked list, then:

$$ptr = ptr \rightarrow llink \rightarrow rlink = ptr \rightarrow rlink \rightarrow llink$$

This formula reflects the essential virtue of this structure, namely, that we can go back and forth with equal ease. An empty list is not really empty since it always has a header node whose structure is illustrated in Figure 4.22.

To use doubly linked lists we must be able to insert and delete nodes. Insertion into a doubly linked list is fairly easy. Assume that we have two nodes, *node* and *newnode*, *node* may be either a header node or an interior node in a list. The function *dinsert* (Program 4.26) performs the insertion operation in constant time.

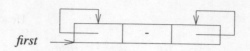

first $\longrightarrow$

Figure 4.22: Empty doubly linked circular list with header node

```
void dinsert(nodePointer node, nodePointer newnode)
{/* insert newnode to the right of node */
   newnode→llink = node;
   newnode→rlink = node→rlink;
   node→rlink→llink = newnode;
   node→rlink = newnode;
}
```

Program 4.26: Insertion into a doubly linked circular list

Deletion from a doubly linked list is equally easy. The function *ddelete* (Program 4.27) deletes the node *deleted* from the list pointed to by node. To accomplish this deletion, we only need to change the link fields of the nodes that precede (*deleted→llink→rlink*) and follow (*deleted→rlink→llink*) the node we want to delete. Figure 4.23 shows the deletion in a doubly linked list with a single node.

EXERCISES

1. Assume that we have a doubly linked list, as represented in Figure 4.21, and that we want to add a new node between the second and third nodes in the list. Redraw the figure so that it shows the insertion. Label the fields of the affected nodes so that you show how each statement in the *dinsert* function is executed. For example, label *newnode→llink*, *newnode→rlink*, and *node→rlink→llink*.

2. Repeat Exercise 1, but delete the second node from the list.

3. Devise a linked representation for a list in which insertions and deletions can be made at either end in O(1) time. Such a structure is called a *deque*. Write functions to insert and delete at either end.

```
void ddelete(nodePointer node, nodePointer deleted)
{/* delete from the doubly linked list */
   if (node == deleted)
      printf("Deletion of header node not permitted.\n");
   else {
      deleted→llink→rlink = deleted→rlink;
      deleted→rlink→llink = deleted→llink;
      free(deleted);
   }
}
```

Program 4.27: Deletion from a doubly linked circular list

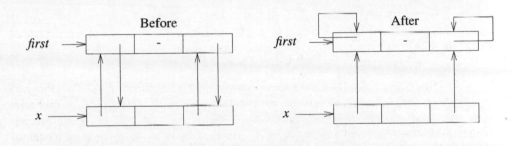

Figure 4.23: Deletion from a doubly linked circular list

4. Consider the operation XOR (exclusive OR, also written as ⊕) defined as follows (for i, j binary):

$$i \oplus j = \begin{cases} 0 & \text{if } i \text{ and } j \text{ are identical} \\ 1 & \text{otherwise} \end{cases}$$

This definition differs from the usual OR of logic, which is defined as

$$i \text{ OR } j = \begin{cases} 0 & \text{if } i = j = 0 \\ 1 & \text{otherwise} \end{cases}$$

The definition can be extended to the case in which i and j are binary strings (i.e., take the XOR of corresponding bits of i and j). So, for example, if $i = 10110$ and $j = 01100$, then i XOR $j = i \oplus j = 11010$. Note that

$$a \oplus (a \oplus b) = (a \oplus a) \oplus b = b$$

and

$$(a \oplus b) \oplus b = a \oplus (b \oplus b) = a$$

This notation gives us a space-saving device for storing the right and left links of a doubly linked list. The nodes will now have only two data members: *data* and *link*. If l is to the left of node x and r to its right, then $x \rightarrow link = l \oplus r$ If x is the leftmost node of a non-circular list, $l = 0$, and if x is the rightmost node, $r = 0$. For a new doubly linked list class in which the link field of each node is the exclusive or of the addresses of the nodes to its left and right, do the following.

(a)   Write a function to traverse the doubly linked list from left to right, printing out the contents of the *data* field of each node.

(b)   Write a function to traverse the list from right to left, printing out the contents of the *data* field of each node.

CHAPTER 5

Trees

5.1 INTRODUCTION

5.1.1 Terminology

In this chapter we shall study a very important data object, the tree. Intuitively, a tree structure means that the data are organized in a hierarchical manner. One very common place where such a structure arises is in the investigation of genealogies. There are two types of genealogical charts that are used to present such data: the *pedigree* and the *lineal* chart. Figure 5.1 gives an example of each.

The pedigree chart of Figure 5.1(a) shows someone's ancestors, in this case those of Dusty, whose two parents are Honey Bear and Brandy. Brandy's parents are Coyote and Nugget, who are Dusty's grandparents on her father's side. The chart continues one more generation back to the great-grandparents. By the nature of things, we know that the pedigree chart is normally two-way branching, though this does not allow for inbreeding. When inbreeding occurs, we no longer have a tree structure unless we insist that each occurrence of breeding is separately listed. Inbreeding may occur frequently when describing family histories of flowers or animals.

191

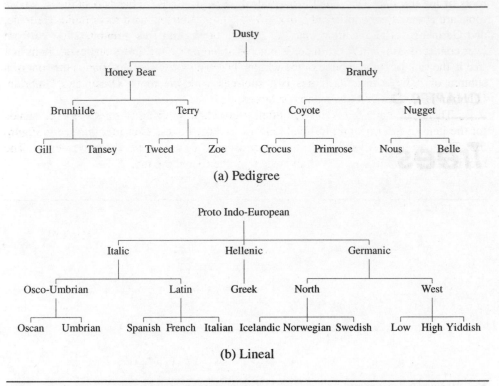

(a) Pedigree

(b) Lineal

Figure 5.1: Two types of genealogical charts

The lineal chart of Figure 5.1(b), though it has nothing to do with people, is still a genealogy. It describes, in somewhat abbreviated form, the ancestry of the modern European languages. Thus, this is a chart of descendants rather than ancestors, and each item can produce several others. Latin, for instance, is the forebear of Spanish, French, and Italian. Proto Indo-European is a prehistoric language presumed to have existed in the fifth millenium B.C. This tree does not have the regular structure of the pedigree chart, but it is a tree structure nevertheless.

With these two examples as motivation, let us define formally what we mean by a tree.

Definition: A *tree* is a finite set of one or more nodes such that

(1) There is a specially designated node called the *root*.

(2) The remaining nodes are partitioned into $n \geq 0$ disjoint sets $T_1, \cdots, T_n$, where each of these sets is a tree. $T_1, \cdots, T_n$ are called the *subtrees* of the root. □

Notice that this is a recursive definition. If we return to Figure 5.1, we see that the roots of the trees are Dusty and Proto Indo-European. Tree (a) has two subtrees, whose roots are Honey Bear and Brandy; tree (b) has three subtrees, with roots Italic, Hellenic, and Germanic. The condition that $T_1, \cdots, T_n$ be disjoint sets prohibits subtrees from ever connecting together (i.e., there is no cross-breeding). It follows that every item in a tree is the root of some subtree of the whole. For instance, Osco-Umbrian is the root of a subtree of Italic, which itself has two subtrees with the roots Oscan and Umbrian. Umbrian is the root of a tree with no subtrees.

There are many terms that are often used when referring to trees. A *node* stands for the item of information plus the branches to other nodes. Consider the tree in Figure 5.2. This tree has 13 nodes, each item of data being a single letter for convenience. The root is A, and we will normally draw trees with the root at the top.

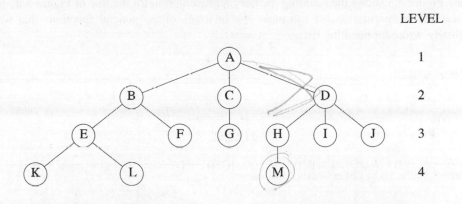

Figure 5.2: A sample tree

The number of subtrees of a node is called its *degree*. The degree of A is 3, of C is 1, and of F is zero. Nodes that have degree zero are called *leaf* or *terminal* nodes. $\{K,L,F,G,M,I,J\}$ is the set of leaf nodes. Consequently, the other nodes are referred to as *nonterminals*. The roots of the subtrees of a node X are the *children* of X. X is the *parent* of its children. Thus, the children of D are H, I, and J; the parent of D is A. Children of the same parent are said to be *siblings*. H, I, and J are siblings. We can extend this terminology if we need to so that we can ask for the grandparent of M, which is D, and so on. The *degree of a tree* is the maximum of the degree of the nodes in the tree. The tree of Figure 5.2 has degree 3. The *ancestors* of a node are all the nodes along the path from the root to that node. The ancestors of M are A, D, and H.

The *level* of a node is defined by letting the root be at level one[+]. If a node is at

[+]Note that some authors define the level of the root to be 0.

level l, then its children are at level $l + 1$. Figure 5.2 shows the levels of all nodes in that tree. The *height* or *depth* of a tree is defined to be the maximum level of any node in the tree. Thus, the depth of the tree in Figure 5.2 is 4.

5.1.2 Representation of Trees

5.1.2.1 List Representation

There are several ways to draw a tree besides the one presented in Figure 5.2. One useful way is as a list. The tree of Figure 5.2 could be written as the list

$$(A\,(B\,(E\,(K,L),F),C\,(G),D\,(H\,(M),I,J)))$$

The information in the root node comes first, followed by a list of the subtrees of that node. Figure 5.3 shows the resulting memory representation for the tree of Figure 5.2. If we use this representation, we can make use of many of the general functions that we originally wrote for handling lists.

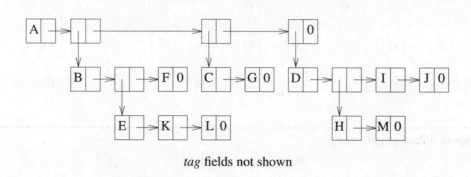

tag fields not shown

Figure 5.3: List representation of the tree of Figure 5.2

For several applications it is desirable to have a representation that is specialized to trees. One possibility is to represent each tree node by a memory node that has fields for the data and pointers to the tree node's children. Since the degree of each tree node may be different, we may be tempted to use memory nodes with a varying number of pointer fields. However, as it is often easier to write algorithms for a data representation when the node size is fixed, in practice one uses only nodes of a fixed size to represent tree nodes. For a tree of degree k, we could use the node structure of Figure 5.4. Each child field is used to point to a subtree. Lemma 5.1 shows that using this node structure is very wasteful of space.

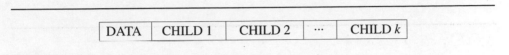

| DATA | CHILD 1 | CHILD 2 | ... | CHILD k |

Figure 5.4: Possible node structure for a tree of degree k

Lemma 5.1: If T is a k-ary tree (i.e., a tree of degree k) with n nodes, each having a fixed size as in Figure 5.4, then $n(k-1)+1$ of the nk child fields are 0, $n \geq 1$.

Proof: Since each non-zero child field points to a node and there is exactly one pointer to each node other than the root, the number of non-zero child fields in an n-node tree is exactly $n-1$. The total number of child fields in a k-ary tree with n nodes is nk. Hence, the number of zero fields is $nk - (n-1) = n(k-1)+1$. $\square$

We shall develop two specialized fixed-node-size representations for trees. Both of these require exactly two link, or pointer, fields per node.

5.1.2.2 Left Child-Right Sibling Representation

Figure 5.5 shows the node structure used in the left child–right sibling representation.

data	
left child	right sibling

Figure 5.5: Left child-right sibling node structure

To convert the tree of Figure 5.2 into this representation, we first note that every node has at most one leftmost child and at most one closest right sibling. For example, in Figure 5.2, the leftmost child of A is B, and the leftmost child of D is H. The closest right sibling of B is C, and the closest right sibling of H is I. Strictly speaking, since the order of children in a tree is not important, any of the children of a node could be the leftmost child, and any of its siblings could be the closest right sibling. For the sake of definiteness, we choose the nodes based on how the tree is drawn. The *left child* field of each node points to its leftmost child (if any), and the *right sibling* field points to its closest right sibling (if any). Figure 5.6 shows the tree of Figure 5.2 redrawn using the left child-right sibling representation.

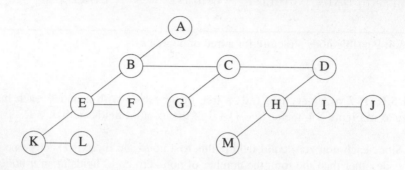

Figure 5.6: Left child-right sibling representation of tree of Figure 5.2

5.1.2.3 Representation as a Degree-Two Tree

To obtain the degree-two tree representation of a tree, we simply rotate the right-sibling pointers in a left child-right sibling tree clockwise by 45 degrees. This gives us the degree-two tree displayed in Figure 5.7. In the degree-two representation, we refer to the two children of a node as the left and right children. Notice that the right child of the root node of the tree is empty. This is always the case since the root of the tree we are transforming can never have a sibling. Figure 5.8 shows two additional examples of trees represented as left child-right sibling trees and as left child-right child (or degree-two) trees. Left child-right child trees are also known as *binary trees*.

EXERCISES

1. Write a function to input a tree given as a generalized list (e.g., $(A (B (E (K,L),F),C (G),D (H (M),I,J))))$ and create its internal representation using nodes with three fields: *tag*, *data*, and *link*.

2. Write a function that reverses the process in Exercise 1 and takes a pointer to a tree and outputs it as a generalized list.

3. [*Programming Project*] Write the Write the following C functions.

   (a) [read]: accept a tree represented as a parenthesized list as input and create the generalized list representation of the tree (see Figure 5.3)

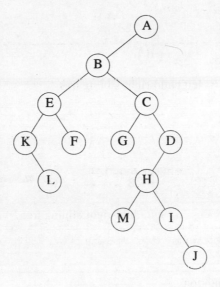

Figure 5.7: Left child-right child tree representation of tree of Figure 5.2

(b)   [copy]: make a copy of a tree represented as a generalized list

(c)   [isequal]: test for equality between two trees represented as generalized lists

(d)   [clear]: delete a tree represented as a generalized list

(e)   [write]: output a tree in its parenthesized list notation

Test the correctness of your functions using suitable test data.

5.2   BINARY TREES

5.2.1   The Abstract Data Type

We have seen that we can represent any tree as a binary tree. In fact, binary trees are an important type of tree structure that occurs very often. The chief characteristic of a binary tree is the stipulation that the degree of any given node must not exceed two. For binary trees, we also distinguish between the left subtree and the right subtree, while for trees the order of the subtrees is irrelevant. In addition, a binary tree may have zero nodes. Thus, a binary tree is really a different object than a tree.

Definition: A *binary tree* is a finite set of nodes that is either empty or consists of a root

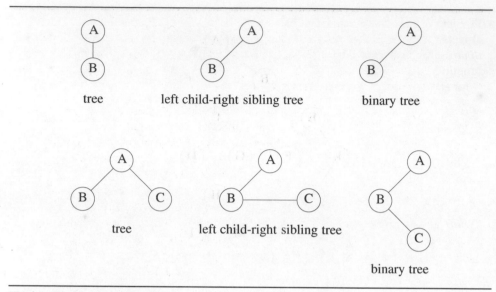

Figure 5.8: Tree representations

and two disjoint binary trees called the left subtree and the right subtree. □

ADT 5.1 contains the specification for the binary tree ADT. This structure defines only a minimal set of operations on binary trees which we use as a foundation on which to build additional operations.

Let us carefully review the distinctions between a binary tree and a tree. First, there is no tree having zero nodes, but there is an empty binary tree. Second, in a binary tree we distinguish between the order of the children while in a tree we do not. Thus, the two binary trees of Figure 5.9 are different since the first binary tree has an empty right subtree, while the second has an empty left subtree. Viewed as trees, however, they are the same, despite the fact that they are drawn slightly differently.

Figure 5.10 shows two special kinds of binary trees. The first is a *skewed* tree, skewed to the left, and there is a corresponding tree that skews to the right. The tree of Figure 5.10(b) is called a *complete* binary tree. This kind of binary tree will be defined formally later. Notice that all leaf nodes are on adjacent levels. The terms that we introduced for trees such as degree, level, height, leaf, parent, and child all apply to binary trees in the natural way.

ADT *Binary_Tree* (abbreviated *BinTree*) is
    objects: a finite set of nodes either empty or consisting of a root node, left *Binary_Tree*, and right *Binary_Tree*.
    functions:
        for all $bt,bt1,bt2 \in BinTree, item \in element$

BinTree Create()	::=	creates an empty binary tree
Boolean IsEmpty(*bt*)	::=	**if** (*bt* == empty binary tree) **return** *TRUE* **else return** *FALSE*
BinTree MakeBT(*bt*1, *item*, *bt*2)	::=	**return** a binary tree whose left subtree is *bt*1, whose right subtree is *bt*2, and whose root node contains the data *item*.
BinTree Lchild(*bt*)	::=	**if** (IsEmpty(*bt*)) **return** error **else return** the left subtree of *bt*.
element Data(*bt*)	::=	**if** (IsEmpty(*bt*)) **return** error **else return** the data in the root node of *bt*.
BinTree Rchild(*bt*)	::=	**if** (IsEmpty(*bt*)) **return** error **else return** the right subtree of *bt*.

ADT 5.1: Abstract data type *Binary_Tree*

Figure 5.9: Two different binary trees

5.2.2 Properties of Binary Trees

Before examining data representations for binary trees, let us make some observations about such trees. In particular, we want to determine the maximum number of nodes in a binary tree of depth k and the relationship between the number of leaf nodes and the number of degree-two nodes in a binary tree.

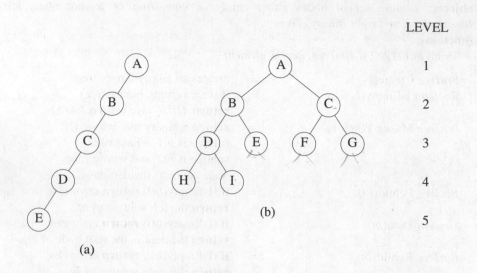

Figure 5.10: Skewed and complete binary trees

$$2^{i-1} \, \& \, 2^k - 1$$

Lemma 5.2 [*Maximum number of nodes*]:

(1)   The maximum number of nodes on level i of a binary tree is 2^{i-1}, $i \geq 1$.
(2)   The maximum number of nodes in a binary tree of depth k is $2^k - 1$, $k \geq 1$.

Proof:

(1) The proof is by induction on i.

Induction Base: The root is the only node on level $i = 1$. Hence, the maximum number of nodes on level $i = 1$ is $2^{i-1} = 2^0 = 1$.

Induction Hypothesis: Let i be an arbitrary positive integer greater than 1. Assume that the maximum number of nodes on level $i - 1$ is 2^{i-2}.

Induction Step: The maximum number of nodes on level $i - 1$ is 2^{i-2} by the induction hypothesis. Since each node in a binary tree has a maximum degree of 2, the maximum number of nodes on level i is two times the maximum number of nodes on level $i-1$, or 2^{i-1}.

(2) The maximum number of nodes in a binary tree of depth k is

$$\sum_{i=1}^{k} (\text{maximum number of nodes on level } i) = \sum_{i=1}^{k} 2^{i-1} = 2^k - 1 \quad \square$$

Lemma 5.3 [*Relation between number of leaf nodes and degree-2 nodes*]: For any nonempty binary tree, T, if n_0 is the number of leaf nodes and n_2 the number of nodes of degree 2, then $n_0 = n_2 + 1$.

Proof: Let n_1 be the number of nodes of degree one and n the total number of nodes. Since all nodes in T are at most of degree two, we have

$$n = n_0 + n_1 + n_2 \tag{5.1}$$

If we count the number of branches in a binary tree, we see that every node except the root has a branch leading into it. If B is the number of branches, then $n = B+1$. All branches stem from a node of degree one or two. Thus, $B = n_1 + 2n_2$. Hence, we obtain

$$n = B + 1 = n_1 + 2n_2 + 1 \tag{5.2}$$

Subtracting Eq. (5.2) from Eq. (5.1) and rearranging terms, we get

$$n_0 = n_2 + 1 \quad \square$$

In Figure 5.10(a), $n_0 = 1$ and $n_2 = 0$; in Figure 5.10(b), $n_0 = 5$ and $n_2 = 4$.

We are now ready to define full and complete binary trees.

Definition: A *full binary tree* of depth k is a binary tree of depth k having $2^k - 1$ nodes, $k \geq 0$. $\square$

By Lemma 5.2, $2^k - 1$ is the maximum number of nodes in a binary tree of depth k. Figure 5.11 shows a full binary tree of depth 4. Suppose we number the nodes in a full binary tree starting with the root on level 1, continuing with the nodes on level 2, and so on. Nodes on any level are numbered from left to right. This numbering scheme gives us the definition of a complete binary tree.

Definition: A binary tree with n nodes and depth k is *complete* iff its nodes correspond to the nodes numbered from 1 to n in the full binary tree of depth k. $\square$

From Lemma 5.2, it follows that the height of a complete binary tree with n nodes is $\lceil \log_2(n + 1) \rceil$. (Note that $\lceil x \rceil$ is the smallest integer $\geq x$.)

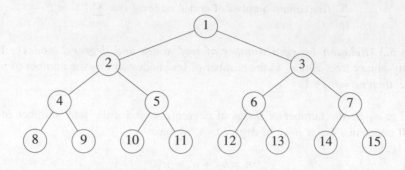

Figure 5.11: Full binary tree of depth 4 with sequential node numbers

5.2.3   Binary Tree Representations

5.2.3.1   Array Representation

The numbering scheme used in Figure 5.11 suggests our first representation of a binary tree in memory. Since the nodes are numbered from 1 to n, we can use a one-dimensional array to store the nodes. Position 0 of this array is left empty and the node numbered i in Figure Figure 5.11 is mapped to position i of the array. Using Lemma 5.4 we can easily determine the locations of the parent, left child, and right child of any node, i, in the binary tree.

Lemma 5.4: If a complete binary tree with n nodes is represented sequentially, then for any node with index i, $1 \le i \le n$, we have

(1)   *parent* (i) is at $\lfloor i / 2 \rfloor$ if $i \ne 1$. If $i = 1$, i is at the root and has no parent.

(2)   *leftChild* (i) is at $2i$ if $2i \le n$. If $2i > n$, then i has no left child.

(3)   *rightChild* (i) is at $2i + 1$ if $2i + 1 \le n$. If $2i + 1 > n$, then i has no right child.

Proof: We prove (2). (3) is an immediate consequence of (2) and the numbering of nodes on the same level from left to right. (1) follows from (2) and (3). We prove (2) by induction on i. For $i = 1$, clearly the left child is at 2 unless $2 > n$, in which case i has no left child. Now assume that for all j, $1 \le j \le i$, *leftChild* (j) is at $2j$. Then the two nodes immediately preceding *leftChild* $(i+1)$ are the right and left children of i. The left child is at $2i$. Hence, the left child of $i + 1$ is at $2i + 2 = 2(i + 1)$ unless $2(i + 1) > n$, in which case $i + 1$ has no left child. $\square$

This representation can clearly be used for all binary trees, though in most cases there will be a lot of unutilized space. Figure 5.12 shows the array representation for both trees of Figure 5.10. For complete binary trees such as the one in Figure 5.10(b), the representation is ideal, as no space is wasted. For the skewed tree of Figure 5.10(a), however, less than half the array is utilized. In the worst case a skewed tree of depth k will require 2^k-1 spaces. Of these, only k will be used.

	tree		tree
[0]	–		–
[1]	A		A
[2]	B		B
[3]	–		C
[4]	C		D
[5]	–		E
[6]	–		F
[7]	–		G
[8]	D		H
[9]	–		I
.	.		(b) Tree of Figure 5.10(b)
.	.		
.	.		
[16]	E		

(a) Tree of Figure 5.10(a)

Figure 5.12: Array representation of the binary trees of Figure 5.10

5.2.3.2 Linked Representation

Although the array representation is good for complete binary trees, it is wasteful for many other binary trees. In addition, the representation suffers from the general inadequacies of sequential representations. Insertion and deletion of nodes from the middle of a tree require the movement of potentially many nodes to reflect the change in level number of these nodes. These problems can be overcome easily through the use of a linked representation. Each node has three fields, *leftChild*, *data*, and *rightChild*, and is defined in C as:

```
typedef struct node *treePointer;
typedef struct {
        int data;
        treePointer leftChild, rightChild;
        } node;
```

We shall draw a tree node using either of the representations of Figure 5.13.

Figure 5.13: Node representations

Although with this node structure it is difficult to determine the parent of a node, we shall see that for most applications, this node structure is adequate. If it is necessary to be able to determine the parent of random nodes, then a fourth field, *parent*, may be included in the class *TreeNode*. The representation of the binary trees of Figure 5.10 using this node structure is given in Figure 5.14. The root of the tree is stored in the data member *root* of *Tree*. This data member serves as the access pointer to the tree.

EXERCISES

1. For the binary tree of Figure 5.15, list the leaf nodes, the nonleaf nodes, and the level of each node.

2. What is the maximum number of nodes in a k-ary tree of height h? Prove your answer.

3. Draw the internal memory representation of the binary tree of Figure 5.15 using (a) sequential and (b) linked representations.

4. Extend the array representation of a complete binary tree to the case of complete trees whose degree is d, $d>1$. Develop formulas for the parent and children of the node stored in position i of the array.

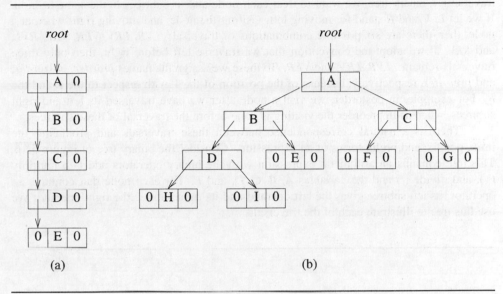

Figure 5.14: Linked representation for the binary trees of Figure 5.10

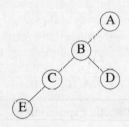

Figure 5.15: Binary tree for Exercise 1

5.3   BINARY TREE TRAVERSALS

There are many operations that we often want to perform on trees. One notion that arises frequently is the idea of traversing a tree or visiting each node in the tree exactly once. When a node is visited, some operation (such as outputting its *data* field) is performed on it. A full traversal produces a linear order for the nodes in a tree. This linear order, given by the order in which the nodes are visited, may be familiar and useful. When traversing a binary tree, we want to treat each node and its subtrees in the same fashion. If we let *L*, *V*, and *R* stand for moving left, visiting the node, and moving right when at a node, then there are six possible combinations of traversal: *LVR, LRV, VLR, VRL, RVL,* and *RLV.* If we adopt the convention that we traverse left before right, then only three traversals remain: *LVR, LRV,* and *VLR.* To these we assign the names *inorder, postorder,* and *preorder,* respectively, because of the position of the *V* with respect to the *L* and the *R.* For example, in postorder, we visit a node after we have traversed its left and right subtrees, whereas in preorder the visiting is done before the traversal of these subtrees.

There is a natural correspondence between these traversals and producing the infix, postfix, and prefix forms of an expression. Consider the binary tree of Figure 5.16. This tree contains an arithmetic expression with the binary operators add (+), multiply (*), and divide (/) and the variables *A, B, C, D,* and *E.* For each node that contains an operator, its left subtree gives the left operand and its right subtree the right operand. We use this tree to illustrate each of the traversals.

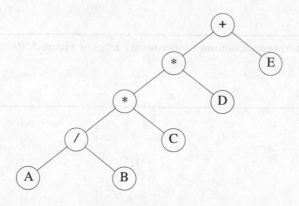

Figure 5.16: Binary tree with arithmetic expression

5.3.1   Inorder Traversal

Informally, *inorder traversal* calls for moving down the tree toward the left until you can go no farther. Then you "visit" the node, move one node to the right and continue. If you cannot move to the right, go back one more node. A precise way of describing this traversal is by using recursion as in Program 5.1.

Recursion is an elegant device for describing this traversal. Figure 5.17 is a trace

```
void inorder(treePointer ptr)
{/* inorder tree traversal */
   if (ptr) {
      inorder(ptr→leftChild);
      printf("%d",ptr→data);
      inorder(ptr→rightChild);
   }
}
```

Program 5.1: Inorder traversal of a binary tree

of *inorder* using the tree of Figure 5.16. Each step of the trace shows the call of *inorder*, the value in the root, and whether or not the **printf** function is invoked. The first three columns show the first 13 steps of the traversal. The second three columns show the remaining 14 steps. The numbers in columns 1 and 4 correspond to the node numbers displayed in Figure 5.16 and are used to show the location of the node in the tree.

Call of *inorder*	Value in *root*	Action	*inorder*	Value in *root*	Action
1	+		11	C	
2	*		12	NULL	
3	*		11	C	**printf**
4	/		13	NULL	
5	A		2	*	**printf**
6	NULL		14	D	
5	A	**printf**	15	NULL	
7	NULL		14	D	**printf**
4	/	**printf**	16	NULL	
8	B		1	+	**printf**
9	NULL		17	E	
8	B	**printf**	18	NULL	
10	NULL		17	E	**printf**
3	*	**printf**	19	NULL	

Figure 5.17: Trace of Program 5.1

Since there are 19 nodes in the tree, *inorder* is invoked 19 times for the complete traversal. The data fields are output in the order:

$$A / B * C * D + E$$

which corresponds to the infix form of the expression.

5.3.2 Preorder Traversal

The code for the second form of traversal, *preorder*, is given in Program 5.2. In words, we would say "visit a node, traverse left, and continue. When you cannot continue, move right and begin again or move back until you can move right and resume." The nodes of Figure 5.16 would be output in *preorder* as

$$+ * * / A\ B\ C\ D\ E$$

which we recognize as the *prefix* form of the expression.

```
void preorder(treePointer ptr)
{/* preorder tree traversal */
   if (ptr) {
      printf("%d",ptr→data);
      preorder(ptr→leftChild);
      preorder(ptr→rightChild);
   }
}
```

Program 5.2: Preorder traversal of a binary tree

5.3.3 Postorder Traversal

The code for *postorder* traversal is given in Program 5.3. On the tree of Figure 5.16, this function produces the following output:

$$A\ B / C * D * E +$$

which is the *postfix* form of our expression.

```
void postorder(treePointer ptr)
{/* postorder tree traversal */
   if (ptr) {
      postorder(ptr→leftChild);
      postorder(ptr→rightChild);
      printf("%d",ptr→data);
   }
}
```

Program 5.3: Postorder traversal of a binary tree

5.3.4   Iterative Inorder Traversal

Although we have written the inorder, preorder, and postorder traversal functions recursively, we can develop equivalent iterative functions. Let us take inorder traversal as an example. To simulate the recursion, we must create our own stack. We add nodes to and remove nodes from our stack in the same manner that the recursive version manipulates the system stack. This helps us to understand fully the operation of the recursive version. Figure 5.17 implicitly shows this stacking and unstacking. A node that has no action indicates that the node is added to the stack, while a node that has a *printf* action indicates that the node is removed from the stack. Notice that the left nodes are stacked until a null node is reached, the node is then removed from the stack, and the node's right child is stacked. The traversal then continues with the left child. The traversal is complete when the stack is empty. Function *iterInorder* (Program 5.4) stems directly from this discussion. The stack function *push* differs from that defined in Chapter 3 only in that the type of the elements in the stack is different. Similarly, the *pop* function returns a value of type *treePointer* rather than of type *element*. It returns *NULL* in case the stack is empty.

Analysis of *iterInorder*: Let n be the number of nodes in the tree. If we consider the action of *iterInorder*, we note that every node of the tree is placed on and removed from the stack exactly once. So, if the number of nodes in the tree is n, the time complexity is $O(n)$. The space requirement is equal to the depth of the tree which is $O(n)$. $\square$

5.3.5   Level-Order Traversal

Whether written iteratively or recursively, the inorder, preorder, and postorder traversals all require a stack. We now turn to a traversal that requires a queue. This traversal, called *level-order traversal*, visits the nodes using the ordering suggested by the node

```
void iterInorder(treePointer node)
{
    int top = -1; /* initialize stack */
    treePointer stack[MAX_STACK_SIZE];
    for (;;) {
        for(; node; node = node→leftChild)
            push(node); /* add to stack */
        node = pop(); /* delete from stack */
        if (!node) break; /* empty stack */
        printf("%d", node→data);
        node = node→rightChild;
    }
}
```

Program 5.4: Iterative inorder traversal

numbering scheme of Figure 5.11. Thus, we visit the root first, then the root's left child, followed by the root's right child. We continue in this manner, visiting the nodes at each new level from the leftmost node to the rightmost node.

The code for this traversal is contained in *levelOrder* (Program 5.5). This assumes a circular queue as in Chapter 3. Function *addq* differs from the corresponding function of Chapter 3 only in that the data type of the elements in the queue is different. Similarly, the function *deleteq* used in Program 5.5 returns a value of type *treePointer* rather than of type element. It returns *NULL* in case the queue is empty.

We begin by adding the root to the queue. The function operates by deleting the node at the front of the queue, printing out the node's data field, and adding the node's left and right children to the queue. Since a node's children are at the next lower level, and we add the left child before the right child, the function prints out the nodes using the ordering scheme found in Figure 5.11. The level order traversal of the tree in Figure 5.16 is:

$$+ * E * D / C A B$$

5.3.6 Traversal without a Stack

Before we leave the topic of tree traversal, we shall consider one final question. Is binary tree traversal possible without the use of extra space for a stack? (Note that a recursive tree traversal algorithm also implicitly uses a stack.) One simple solution is to add a *parent* field to each node. Then we can trace our way back up to any root and

```
void levelOrder(treePointer ptr)
{/* level order tree traversal */
   int front = rear = 0;
   treePointer queue[MAX_QUEUE_SIZE];
   if (!ptr) return; /* empty tree */
   addq(ptr);
   for (;;) {
      ptr = deleteq();
      if (ptr) {
         printf("%d",ptr→data);
         if(ptr→leftChild)
            addq(ptr→leftChild);
         if (ptr→rightChild)
            addq(ptr→rightChild);
      }
      else break;
   }
}
```

Program 5.5: Level-order traversal of a binary tree

down again. Another solution, which requires two bits per node, represents binary trees as threaded binary trees. We study this in Section 5.5. If the allocation of this extra space is too costly, then we can use the *leftChild* and *rightChild* fields to maintain the paths back to the root. The stack of addresses is stored in the leaf nodes.

EXERCISES

1. Write out the inorder, preorder, postorder, and level-order traversals for the binary trees of Figure 5.10.

2. Do Exercise 1 for the binary tree of Figure 5.11.

3. Do Exercise 1 for the binary tree of Figure 5.15.

4. Write a nonrecursive version of function *preorder* (Program 5.2).

5. Write a nonrecursive version of function *postorder* (Program 5.3).

6. Rework *iterInorder* (Program 5.4) so that it is as fast as possible. (Hint: Minimize the stacking and the testing within the loop.)

5.4 ADDITIONAL BINARY TREE OPERATIONS

5.4.1 Copying Binary Trees

By using the definition of a binary tree and the recursive versions of inorder, preorder, and postorder traversals, we can easily create C functions for other binary tree operations. One practical operation is copying a binary tree. The code for this operation is containted in *copy* (Program 5.6). Notice that this function is only a slightly modified version of *postorder* (Program 5.3).

```
treePointer copy(treePointer original)
{/* this function returns a treePointer to an exact copy
    of the original tree */
  treePointer temp;
  if (original) {
    MALLOC(temp, sizeof(*temp));
    temp→leftChild = copy(original→leftChild);
    temp→rightChild = copy(original→rightChild);
    temp→data = original→data;
    return temp;
  }
  return NULL;
}
```

Program 5.6: Copying a binary tree

5.4.2 Testing Equality

Another useful operation is determining the equivalence of two binary trees. Equivalent binary trees have the same structure and the same information in the corresponding nodes. By the same structure we mean that every branch in one tree corresponds to a branch in the second tree, that is, the branching of the two trees is identical. The function *equal* (Program 5.7) uses a modification of preorder traversal to test for equality. This function returns *TRUE* if the two trees are equivalent and *FALSE* if they are not.

```
int equal(treePointer first, treePointer second)
{/* function returns FALSE if the binary trees first and
     second are not equal, Otherwise it returns TRUE */
    return ((!first && !second) || (first && second &&
            (first→data == second→data) &&
            equal(first→leftChild,second→leftChild) &&
            equal(first→rightChild, second→rightChild))
}
```

Program 5.7: Testing for equality of binary trees

5.4.3   The Satisfiability Problem

Consider the set of formulas that we can construct by taking variables $x_1, x_2, \cdots, x_n$ and operators $\wedge$ (*and*), $\vee$ (*or*), and $\neg$ (*not*). The variables can hold only one of two possible values, *true* or *false*. The set of expressions that we can form using these variables and operators is defined by the following rules:

(1)   A variable is an expression.

(2)   If x and y are expressions, then $\neg x, x \wedge y , x \vee y$ are expressions.

(3)   Parentheses can be used to alter the normal order of evaluation, which is $\neg$ before $\wedge$ before $\vee$.

These rules comprise the formulas in the propositional calculus since other operations, such as implication, can be expressed using $\neg$, $\vee$, and $\wedge$.

The expression:

$$x_1 \vee (x_2 \wedge \neg x_3)$$

is a formula (read as "x_1 *or* x_2 *and not* x_3"). If x_1 and x_3 are *false* and x_2 is *true*, then the value of the expression is:

$$\begin{aligned} &\textit{false} \vee (\textit{true} \wedge \neg \textit{false}) \\ &= \textit{false} \vee \textit{true} \\ &= \textit{true} \end{aligned}$$

The satisfiability problem for formulas of the propositional calculus asks if there is an assignment of values to the variables that causes the value of the expression to be true. This problem was originally used by Newell, Shaw, and Simon in the late 1950s to show the viability of heuristic programming (The Logic Theorist) and is still of keen interest to computer scientists.

Again, let us assume that our formula is already in a binary tree, say

$$(x_1 \wedge \neg x_2) \vee (\neg x_1 \wedge x_3) \vee \neg x_3$$

in the tree of Figure 5.18. The inorder traversal of this tree is

$$x_1 \wedge \neg x_2 \vee \neg x_1 \wedge x_3 \vee \neg x_3$$

which is the infix form of the expression. The most obvious algorithm to determine satisfiability is to let (x_1, x_2, x_3) take on all possible combinations of *true* and *false* values and to check the formula for each combination. For n variables there are 2^n possible combinations of *true* $= t$ and *false* $= f$. For example, for $n = 3$, the eight combinations are: (t,t,t), (t,t,f), (t,f,t), (t,f,f), (f,t,t), (f,t,f), (f,f,t), (f,f,f). The algorithm will take $O(g\, 2^n)$, or exponential time, where g is the time to substitute values for $x_1, x_2, \cdots, x_n$ and evaluate the expression.

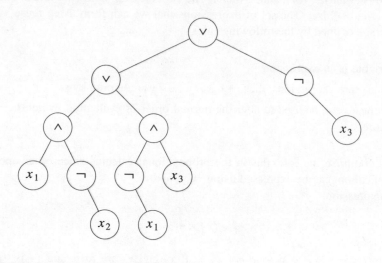

Figure 5.18: Propositional formula in a binary tree

To evaluate an expression, we traverse its tree in postorder. When visiting a node p, we compute the value of the expression represented by the subtree rooted at p. Recall that, in postorder, the left and right subtrees of a node are traversed before we visit that node. In other words, when we visit the node p, the subexpressions represented by its left and right subtrees have been computed. So, when we reach the $\vee$ node on level 2, the values of $x_1 \wedge \neg x_2$ and $\neg x_1 \wedge x_3$ will already be available to us, and we can apply the rule for **or**. Notice that a node containing ¬ has only a right branch, since ¬ is a unary operator.

The node structure for this problem is found in Figure 5.19. The *leftChild* and *rightChild* fields are similar to those used previously. The field *data* holds either the value of a variable or a propositional calculus operator, while *value* holds either a value of *TRUE* or *FALSE*.

leftChild	data	value	rightChild

Figure 5.19: Node structure for the satisfiability problem

We define this node structure in C as:

```
typedef enum {not,and,or,true,false} logical;
typedef struct node *treePointer;
typedef struct {
        treePointer leftChild;
        logical      data;
        short int    value;
        treePointer rightChild;
        } node;
```

We assume that for leaf nodes, *node* → *data* contains the current value of the variable represented at this node. For example, we assume that the tree of Figure 5.18 contains either *TRUE* or *FALSE* in the data field of x_1, x_2, and x_3. We also assume that an expression tree with n variables is pointed at by *root*. With these assumptions we can write our first version of a satisfiability algorithm (Program 5.8).

The C function that evaluates the tree is easily obtained by modifying the original, recursive postorder traversal. The function *postOrderEval* (Program 5.9) shows the C code that implements this portion of the satisfiability algorithm.

EXERCISES

1. Write a C function that counts the number of leaf nodes in a binary tree. Determine the computing time of the function.

2. Write a C function *swapTree* that takes a binary tree and swaps the left and right children of every node. An example is given in Figure 5.20.

```
for (all 2ⁿ possible combinations) {
   generate the next combination;
   replace the variables by their values;
   evaluate root by traversing it in postorder;
   if (root→value) {
      printf(<combination>);
      return;
   }
}
printf("No satisfiable combination\n");
```

Program 5.8: First version of satisfiability algorithm

3. What is the computing time of *postOrderEval*?

4. Devise an external representation for the formulas in propositional calculus. Write a function that reads such a formula and creates its binary tree representation. What is the complexity of your function?

5. § [***Programming project***] Devise a representation for formulas in the propositional calculus. Write a C function that inputs such a formula and creates a binary tree representation of it. Determine the computing time of your function.

5.5   THREADED BINARY TREES

5.5.1   Threads

If we look carefully at the linked representation of any binary tree, we notice that there are more null links than actual pointers. Specifically, there are $n + 1$ null links out of $2n$ total links. A. J. Perlis and C. Thornton have devised a clever way to make use of these null links. They replace the null links by pointers, called *threads*, to other nodes in the tree. To construct the threads we use the following rules (assume that *ptr* represents a node):

(1)   If *ptr* → *leftChild* is null, replace *ptr* → *leftChild* with a pointer to the node that would be visited before *ptr* in an inorder traversal. That is we replace the null link with a pointer to the *inorder predecessor* of *ptr*.

(2)   If *ptr* → *rightChild* is null, replace *ptr* → *rightChild* with a pointer to the node that would be visited after *ptr* in an inorder traversal. That is we replace the null link with a pointer to the *inorder successor* of *ptr*.

```
void postOrderEval(treePointer node)
{/* modified post order traversal to evaluate a
    propositional calculus tree */
  if (node) {
    postOrderEval(node→leftChild);
    postOrderEval(node→rightChild);
    switch(node→data) {
      case not:   node→value =
                  !node→rightChild→value;
                  break;
      case and:   node→value =
                  node→rightChild→value &&
                  node→leftChild→value;
                  break;
      case or:    node→value =
                  node→rightChild→value ||
                  node→leftChild→value;
                  break;
      case true:  node→value = TRUE;
                  break;
      case false: node→value = FALSE;
    }
  }
}
```

Program 5.9: Postorder evaluation function

Figure 5.21 shows the binary tree of Figure 5.10(b) with its new threads drawn in as broken lines. This tree has 9 nodes and 10 0-links, which have been replaced by threads. If we traverse the tree in inorder, the nodes will be visited in the order *H, D, I, B, E, A, F, C, G*. For example, node *E* has a predecessor thread that points to *B* and a successor thread that points to *A*.

When we represent the tree in memory, we must be able to distinguish between threads and normal pointers. This is done by adding two additional fields to the node structure, *leftThread* and *rightThread*. Assume that *ptr* is an arbitrary node in a threaded tree. If *ptr* → *leftThread* = *TRUE*, then *ptr* → *leftChild* contains a thread; otherwise it contains a pointer to the left child. Similarly, if *ptr* → *rightThread* = *TRUE*, then *ptr* → *rightChild* contains a thread; otherwise it contains a pointer to the right child.

This node structure is given by the following C declarations:

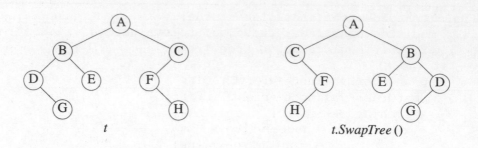

Figure 5.20: A swap tree example

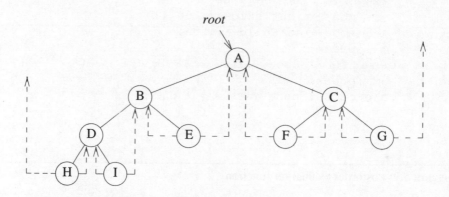

Figure 5.21: Threaded tree corresponding to Figure 5.10(b)

```
typedef struct threadedTree *threadedPointer;
typedef struct {
        short int leftThread;
        threadedPointer leftChild;
        char data;
        threadedPointer rightChild;
        short int rightThread;
        } threadedTree;
```

In Figure 5.21 two threads have been left dangling: one in the left child of *H*, the other in the right child of *G*. In order that we leave no loose threads, we will assume a header node for all threaded binary trees. The original tree is the left subtree of the header node. An empty binary tree is represented by its header node as in Figure 5.22. The complete memory representation for the tree of Figure 5.21 is shown in Figure 5.23.

leftThread	leftChild	data	rightChild	rightThread
true				false

Figure 5.22: An empty threaded binary tree

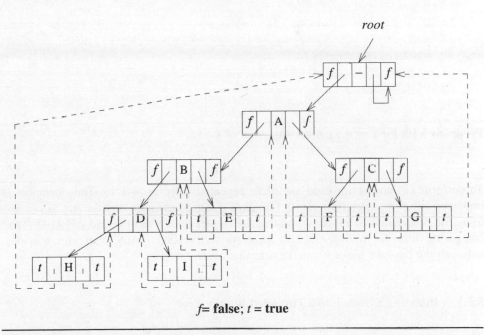

f= **false**; *t* = **true**

Figure 5.23: Memory representation of threaded tree

The variable *root* points to the header node of the tree, while *root* → *leftChild* points to the start of the first node of the actual tree. This is true for all threaded trees. Notice that we have handled the problem of the loose threads by having them point to the head node, *root*.

5.5.2 Inorder Traversal of a Threaded Binary Tree

By using the threads, we can perform an inorder traversal without making use of a stack. Observe that for any node, *ptr*, in a threaded binary tree, if $ptr \rightarrow rightThread = TRUE$, the inorder successor of *ptr* is $ptr \rightarrow rightChild$ by definition of the threads. Otherwise we obtain the inorder successor of *ptr* by following a path of left-child links from the right-child of *ptr* until we reach a node with $leftThread = TRUE$. The function *insucc* (Program 5.10) finds the inorder successor of any node in a threaded tree without using a stack.

```
threadedPointer insucc(threadedPointer tree)
{/* find the inorder sucessor of tree in a threaded binary
    tree */
   threadedPointer temp;
   temp = tree→rightChild;
   if (!tree→rightThread)
      while (!temp→leftThread)
         temp = temp→leftChild;
   return temp;
}
```

Program 5.10: Finding the inorder successor of a node

To perform an inorder traversal we make repeated calls to *insucc*. The operation is implemented in *tinorder* (Program 5.11). This function assumes that the tree is pointed to by the header node's left child and that the header node's right thread is *FALSE*. The computing time for *tinorder* is still $O(n)$ for a threaded binary tree with *n* nodes, although the constant factor is smaller than that of *iterInorder*.

5.5.3 Inserting a Node into a Threaded Binary Tree

We now examine how to make insertions into a threaded tree. This will give us a function for growing threaded trees. We shall study only the case of inserting *r* as the right child of a node *s*. The case of insertion of a left child is given as an exercise. The cases

```
void tinorder(threadedPointer tree)
{/* traverse the threaded binary tree inorder */
   threadedPointer temp = tree;
   for (;;) {
      temp = insucc(temp);
      if (temp == tree) break;
      printf("%3c", temp→data);
   }
}
```

Program 5.11: Inorder traversal of a threaded binary tree

for insertion are

(1)   If s has an empty right subtree, then the insertion is simple and diagrammed in Figure 5.24(a).

(2)   If the right subtree of s is not empty, then this right subtree is made the right subtree of r after insertion. When this is done, r becomes the inorder predecessor of a node that has a *leftThread* == **true** field, and consequently there is a thread which has to be updated to point to r. The node containing this thread was previously the inorder successor of s. Figure 5.24(b) illustrates the insertion for this case. The function *insertRight* (Program 5.12) contains the C code which handles both cases.

EXERCISES

1.   Draw the binary tree of Figure 5.15, showing its threaded representation.

2.   Write a function, *insertLeft*, that inserts a new node, *child*, as the left child of node *parent* in a threaded binary tree. The left child pointer of *parent* becomes the left child pointer of *child*.

3.   Write a function that traverses a threaded binary tree in postorder. What are the time and space requirements of your method?

4.   Write a function that traverses a threaded binary tree in preorder. What are the time and space requirements of your method?

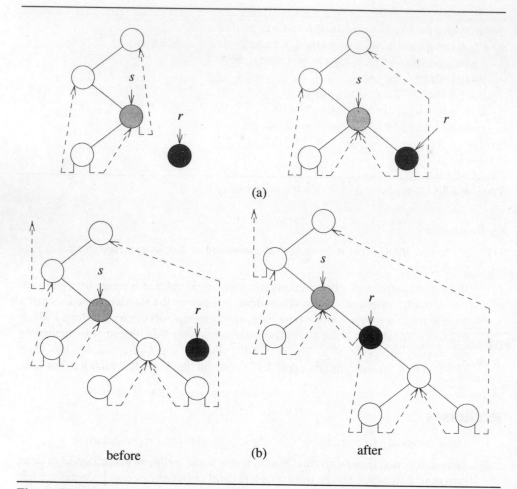

(a)

before   (b)   after

Figure 5.24: Insertion of *r* as a right child of *s* in a threaded binary tree

5.6   HEAPS

5.6.1   Priority Queues

Heaps are frequently used to implement *priority queues*. In this kind of queue, the element to be deleted is the one with highest (or lowest) priority. At any time, an element with arbitrary priority can be inserted into the queue. ADT 5.2 specifies a max priority queue.

```
void insertRight(threadedPointer s, threadedPointer r)
{/* insert r as the right child of s */
   threadedPointer temp;
   r→rightChild = parent→rightChild;
   r→rightThread = parent→rightThread;
   r→leftChild = parent;
   r→leftThread = TRUE;
   s→rightChild = child;
   s→rightThread = FALSE;
   if (!r→rightThread) {
      temp = insucc(r);
      temp→leftChild = r;
   }
}
```

Program 5.12: Right insertion in a threaded binary tree

ADT *MaxPriorityQueue* is
   objects: a collection of $n > 0$ elements, each element has a key
   functions:
     for all $q \in$ *MaxPriorityQueue*, *item* $\in$ *Element*, $n \in$ integer

MaxPriorityQueue create(*max_size*)	::=	create an empty priority queue.
Boolean isEmpty(q, n)	::=	**if** ($n > 0$) **return** *TRUE* **else return** *FALSE*
Element top(q, n)	::=	**if** (!isEmpty(q, n)) **return** an instance of the largest element in q **else return** error.
Element pop(q, n)	::=	**if** (!isEmpty(q, n)) **return** an instance of the largest element in q and remove it from the heap **else return** error.
MaxPriorityQueue push($q, item, n$)	::=	insert *item* into *pq* and return the resulting priority queue.

ADT 5.2: Abstract data type *MaxPriorityQueue*

Example 5.1: Suppose that we are selling the services of a machine. Each user pays a fixed amount per use. However, the time needed by each user is different. We wish to maximize the returns from this machine under the assumption that the machine is not to be kept idle unless no user is available. This can be done by maintaining a priority queue of all persons waiting to use the machine. Whenever the machine becomes available, the user with the smallest time requirement is selected. Hence, a min priority queue is required. When a new user requests the machine, his/her request is put into the priority queue.

If each user needs the same amount of time on the machine but people are willing to pay different amounts for the service, then a priority queue based on the amount of payment can be maintained. Whenever the machine becomes available, the user paying the most is selected. This requires a max priority queue. □

Example 5.2: Suppose that we are simulating a large factory. This factory has many machines and many jobs that require processing on some of the machines. An *event* is said to occur whenever a machine completes the processing of a job. When an event occurs, the job has to be moved to the queue for the next machine (if any) that it needs. If this queue is empty, the job can be assigned to the machine immediately. Also, a new job can be scheduled on the machine that has become idle (provided that its queue is not empty).

To determine the occurrence of events, a priority queue is used. This queue contains the finish time of all jobs that are presently being worked on. The next event occurs at the least time in the priority queue. So, a min priority queue can be used in this application. □

The simplest way to represent a priority queue is as an unordered linear list. Regardless of whether this list is represented sequentially or as a chain, the *isEmpty* function takes $O(1)$ time; the *top* () function takes $\Theta(n)$ time, where n is the number of elements in the priority queue; a push can be done in $O(1)$ time as it doesn't matter where in the list the new element is inserted; and a *pop* takes $\Theta(n)$ time as me must first find the element with max priority and then delete it. As we shall see shortly, when a max heap is used, the complexity of *isEmpty* and *top* is $O(1)$ and that of *push* and *pop* is $O(\log n)$.

5.6.2 Definition of a Max Heap

In Section 5.2.2, we defined a complete binary tree. In this section we present a special form of a complete binary tree that is useful in many applications.

Definition: A *max (min) tree* is a tree in which the key value in each node is no smaller (larger) than the key values in its children (if any). A *max heap* is a complete binary tree that is also a max tree. A *min heap* is a complete binary tree that is also a min tree. □

Some examples of max heaps and min heaps are shown in Figures 5.25 and 5.26, respectively.

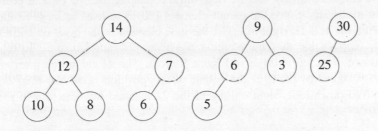

Figure 5.25: Max heaps

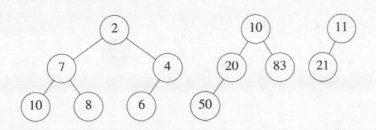

Figure 5.26: Min heaps

From the definitions, it follows that the key in the root of a min tree is the smallest key in the tree, whereas that in the root of a max tree is the largest. When viewed as an ADT, a max heap is very simple. The basic operations are the same as those for a max priority queue (ADT 5.2). Since a max heap is a complete binary tree, we represent it using an array *heap*.

5.6.3 Insertion into a Max Heap

A max heap with five elements is shown in Figure 5.27(a). When an element is added to this heap, the resulting six-element heap must have the structure shown in Figure 5.27(b), because a heap is a complete binary tree. To determine the correct place for the element that is being inserted, we use a *bubbling up* process that begins at the new node of the tree and moves toward the root. The element to be inserted bubbles up as far as is necessary to ensure a max heap following the insertion. If the element to be inserted has key value 1, it may be inserted as the left child of 2 (i.e., in the new node). If instead, the key value of the new element is 5, then this cannot be inserted as the left child of 2 (as otherwise, we will not have a max heap following the insertion). So, the 2 is moved down to its left child (Figure 5.27(c)), and we determine if placing the 5 at the old position of 2 results in a max heap. Since the parent element (20) is at least as large as the element being inserted (5), it is all right to insert the new element at the position shown in the figure. Next, suppose that the new element has value 21 rather than 5. In this case, the 2 moves down to its left child as in Figure 5.27(c). The 21 cannot be inserted into the old position occupied by the 2, as the parent of this position is smaller than 21. Hence, the 20 is moved down to its right child and the 21 inserted into the root of the heap (Figure 5.27(d)).

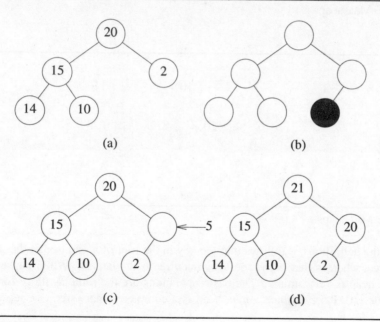

Figure 5.27: Insertion into a max heap

To implement the insertion strategy just described, we need to go from an element to its parent. Lemma 5.4 enables us to locate the parent of any element easily. Program 5.13 performs an insertion into a max heap. We assume that the heap is created using the following C declarations:

```
#define MAX_ELEMENTS 200 /* maximum heap size+1 */
#define HEAP_FULL(n) (n == MAX_ELEMENTS-1)
```

```
#define HEAP_EMPTY(n) (!n)
typedef struct {
        int key;
        /* other fields */
        } element;
element heap[MAX_ELEMENTS];
int n = 0;
```

An alternative representation using a dynamically allocated array whose initial capacity is 1 and doubling array capacity whenever we wish to insert into a full heap is considered in the exercises.

```
void push(element item, int *n)
{/* insert item into a max heap of current size *n */
   int i;
   if (HEAP_FULL(*n)){
      fprintf(stderr, "The heap is full. \n");
      exit(EXIT_FAILURE);
   }
   i = ++(*n);
   while ((i != 1) && (item.key > heap[i/2].key)) {
      heap[i] = heap[i/2];
      i /= 2;
   }
   heap[i] = item;
}
```

Program 5.13: Insertion into a max heap

Analysis of *push*: The function *push* first checks for a full heap. If the heap is not full, we set i to the size of the new heap $(n + 1)$. We must now determine the correct position of *item* in the heap. We use the **while** loop to accomplish this task. This follows a path from the new leaf of the max heap to the root until it either reaches the root or reaches a position i such that the value in the parent position $i/2$ is at least as large as the value to be inserted. Since a heap is a complete binary tree with n elements, it has a height of $\lceil \log_2(n + 1) \rceil$. This means that the **while** loop is iterated $O(\log_2 n)$ times. Hence, the complexity of the insertion function is $O(\log_2 n)$. $\square$

5.6.4 Deletion from a Max Heap

When an element is to be deleted from a max heap, it is taken from the root of the heap. For instance, a deletion from the heap of Figure 5.27(d) results in the removal of the element 21. Since the resulting heap has only five elements in it, the binary tree of Figure 5.27(d) needs to be restructured to correspond to a complete binary tree with five elements. To do this, we remove the element in position 6 (i.e., the element 2). Now we have the right structure (Figure 5.28(a)), but the root is vacant and the element 2 is not in the heap. If the 2 is inserted into the root, the resulting binary tree is not a max heap. The element at the root should be the largest from among the 2 and the elements in the left and right children of the root. This element is 20. It is moved into the root, thereby creating a vacancy in position 3. Since this position has no children, the 2 may be inserted here. The resulting heap is shown in Figure 5.27(a).

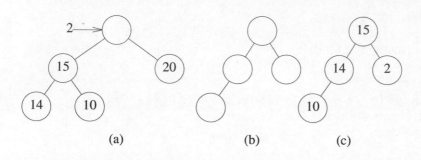

(a)   (b)   (c)

Figure 5.28: Deletion from a heap

Now, suppose we wish to perform another deletion. The 20 is to be deleted. Following the deletion, the heap has the binary tree structure shown in Figure 5.28(b). To get this structure, the 10 is removed from position 5. It cannot be inserted into the root, as it is not large enough. The 15 moves to the root, and we attempt to insert the 10 into position 2. This is, however, smaller than the 14 below it. So, the 14 is moved up and the 10 inserted into position 4. The resulting heap is shown in Figure 5.28(c).

Program 5.14 implements this *trickle down* strategy to delete from a heap.

Analysis of *pop*: The function *pop* operates by moving down the heap, comparing and exchanging parent and child nodes until the heap definition is re-established. Since the height of a heap with n elements is $\lceil \log_2(n + 1) \rceil$, the **while** loop of *pop* is iterated $O(\log_2 n)$ times. Hence, the complexity of a deletion is $O(\log_2 n)$. □

```
element pop(int *n)
{/* delete element with the highest key from the heap */
   int parent, child;
   element item, temp;
   if (HEAP_EMPTY(*n)) {
      fprintf(stderr, "The heap is empty\n");
      exit(EXIT_FAILURE);
   }
   /* save value of the element with the highest key */
   item = heap[1];
   /* use last element in heap to adjust heap */
   temp = heap[(*n)--];
   parent = 1;
   child = 2;
   while (child <= *n) {
      /* find the larger child of the current parent */
      if     (child   <    *n)    &&    (heap[child].key    <
   heap[child+1].key)
         child++;
      if (temp.key >= heap[child].key) break;
      /* move to the next lower level */
      heap[parent] = heap[child];
      parent = child;
      child *= 2;
   }
   heap[parent] = temp;
   return item;
}
```

Program 5.14: Deletion from a max heap

EXERCISES

1. Suppose that we have the following key values: 7, 16, 49, 82, 5, 31, 6, 2, 44.

    (a) Write out the max heap after each value is inserted into the heap.

    (b) Write out the min heap after each value is inserted into the heap.

2. Write a structure specification similar to ADT 5.2 for the ADT *MinPQ*, which defines a min priority queue.

3. Compare the run-time performance of max heaps with that of unordered and ordered linear lists as a representation for priority queues. For this comparison, program the max heap push and pop algorithms, as well as algorithms to perform these tasks on unordered and ordered linear lists that are maintained as sequential lists in a one-dimensional array. Generate a random sequence of n values and insert these into the priority queue. Next, perform a random sequence of m inserts and deletes starting with the initial queue of n values. This sequence is to be generated so that the next operation in the sequence has an equal chance of being either an insert or a delete. Care should be taken so that the sequence does not cause the priority queue to become empty at any time. Measure the time taken for the sequence of m operations using both a max heap and an unordered list. Divide the total time by m and plot the times as a function of n. Make some qualitative statements about the relative performance of the two representations for a max priority queue.

4. The worst-case number of comparisons performed during an insertion into a max heap can be reduced to $O(\log\log n)$ by performing a binary search on the path from the new leaf to the root. This does not affect the number of data moves though. Write an insertion algorithm that uses this strategy. Redo Exercise 1 using this insertion algorithm. Based on your experiments, what can you say about the value of this strategy over the one used in Program 5.13?

5. Write a C function that changes the priority of an arbitrary element in a max heap. The resulting heap must satisfy the max heap definition. What is the computing time of your function?

6. Write a C function that deletes an arbitrary element from a max heap (the deleted element may be anywhere in the heap). The resulting heap must satisfy the max heap definition. What is the computing time of your function? (Hint: Change the priority of the element to one greater than that of the root, use the change priority function of Exercise 3, and then *pop*.)

7. Write a C function that searches for an arbitrary element in a max heap. What is the computing time of your function?

8. Write insertion and deletion functions for a max heap represented as a linked binary tree. Assume that each node has a parent field as well as the usual left child, right child, and data fields.

9. § [*Programming project*] Write a user-friendly, menu-driven program that allows the user to perform the following operations on min heaps.

   (a) create a min heap

   (b) remove the key with the lowest value

   (c) change the priority of an arbitrary element

   (d) insert an element into the heap.

10. Develop C functions to insert and delete into/from a max heap under the assumptions that a dynamically allocate array is used, the initil capacity of this array is 1, and array doubling is done whenever we are to insert into a max heap that is full. Test your functions.

5.7 BINARY SEARCH TREES

5.7.1 Definition

A *dictionary* is a collection of pairs, each pair has a key and an associated item. Although naturally occurring dictionaries have several pairs that have the same key, we make the assumption here that no two pairs have the same key. The data structure, binary search tree, that we study in this section is easily extended to accommodate dictionaries in which several pairs have the same key. ADT 5.3 gives the specification of a dictionary.

ADT *Dictionary* is
    objects: a collection of $n > 0$ pairs, each pair has a key and an associated item
    functions:
        for all $d \in Dictionary, item \in Item, k \in Key, n \in$ integer

Dictionary Create(*max_size*)	::=	create an empty dictionary.
Boolean IsEmpty(*d, n*)	::=	**if** $(n > 0)$ **return** *TRUE*
		else return *FALSE*
Element Search(*d, k*)	::=	**return** item with key k,
		return NULL if no such element.
Element Delete(*d, k*)	::=	delete and return item (if any) with key k;
void Insert(*d, item, k*)	::=	insert *item* with key k into d.

ADT 5.3: Abstract data type *dictionary*

A binary search tree has a better performance than any of the data structures studied so far when the functions to be performed are search, insert, and delete. In fact, with a binary search tree, these functions can be performed both by key value and by rank (i.e., find the item with key k; find the fifth smallest item; delete the item with key k; delete the fifth smallest item; insert an item and determine its rank; and so on).

Definition: A *binary search tree* is a binary tree. It may be empty. If it is not empty then it satisfies the following properties:

(1)   Each node has exactly one key and the keys in the tree are distinct.

(2)   The keys (if any) in the left subtree are smaller than the key in the root.

(3)   The keys (if any) in the right subtree are larger than the key in the root.

(4)   The left and right subtrees are also binary search trees. □

There is some redundancy in this definition. Properties (2), (3), and (4) together imply that the keys must be distinct. So, property (1) can be replaced by the property: The root has a key.

Some examples of binary trees in which the nodes have distinct keys are shown in Figure 5.29. In this figure, only the key component of each dictionary pair is shown. The tree of Figure 5.29(a) is not a binary search tree, despite the fact that it satisfies properties (1), (2), and (3). The right subtree fails to satisfy property (4). This subtree is not a binary search tree, as its right subtree has a key value (22) that is smaller than that in the subtree's root (25). The binary trees of Figures 5.29(b) and (c) are binary search trees.

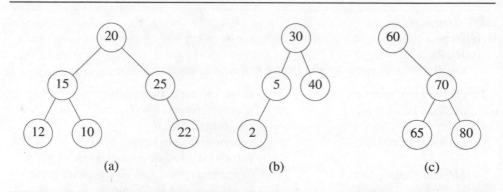

Figure 5.29: Binary trees

5.7.2   Searching a Binary Search Tree

Since the definition of a binary search tree is recursive, it is easiest to describe a recursive search method. Suppose we wish to search for a node whose key is k. We begin at the root of the binary search tree. If the root is *NULL*, the search tree contains no nodes and the search is unsuccessful. Otherwise, we compare k with the key in root. If k equals the root's key, then the search terminates successfully. If k is less than root's key, then no element in the right subtree can have a key value equal to k. Therefore, we search the left subtree of the root. If k is larger than root's key value, we search the right subtree of the root. The function *search* (Program 5.15) recursively searches the subtrees. We assume that the *data* field of a node is of type *element* and that the type *element* has two components *key* and *item* whose types are **int** and *iType*, respectively.

```
element* search(treePointer root, int key)
{/* return a pointer to the element whose key is k, if
   there is no such element, return NULL. */
  if (!root) return NULL;
  if (k == root→data.key) return &(root→data);
  if (k < root→data.key)
    return search(root→leftChild, k);
  return search(root→rightChild, k);
}
```

Program 5.15: Recursive search of a binary search tree

We can easily replace the recursive search function with a comparable iterative one. The function *iterSearch* (Program 5.16) accomplishes this by replacing the recursion with a **while** loop.

```
element* iterSearch(treePointer tree, int k)
{/* return a pointer to the element whose key is k, if
   there is no such element, return NULL. */
  while (tree) {
    if (k == tree→data.key) return &(tree→data);
    if (k < tree→data.key)
      tree = tree→leftChild;
    else
      tree = tree→rightChild;
  }
  return NULL;
}
```

Program 5.16: Iterative search of a binary search tree

Analysis of *search* and *iterSearch*: If h is the height of the binary search tree, then we can perform the search using either *search* or *iterSearch* in $O(h)$. However, *search* has an additional stack space requirement which is O(*h*). □

5.7.3   Inserting into a Binary Search Tree

To insert a dictionary pair whose key is *k*, we must first verify that the key is different from those of existing pairs. To do this we search the tree. If the search is unsuccessful, then we insert the pair at the point the search terminated. For instance, to insert a pair with key 80 into the tree of Figure 5.29(b) (only keys are shown), we first search the tree for 80. This search terminates unsuccessfully, and the last node examined has key 40. We insert the new pair as the right child of this node. The resulting search tree is shown in Figure 5.29(a). Figure 5.30(b) shows the result of inserting the key 35 into the search tree of Figure 5.30(a). This strategy is implemented by *insert* (Program 5.17). This function uses the function *modifiedSearch* which is a slightly modified version of function *iterSearch* (Program 5.16), which searches the binary search tree **node* for the key *k*. If the tree is empty or if *k* is present, it returns *NULL*. Otherwise, it returns a pointer to the last node of the tree that was encountered during the search. The new pair is to be inserted as a child of this node.

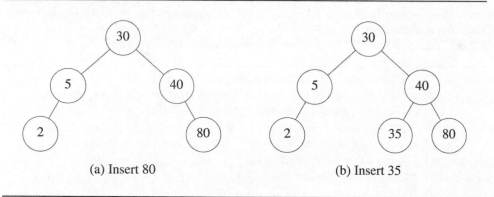

(a) Insert 80   (b) Insert 35

Figure 5.30: Inserting into a binary search tree

Analysis of *insert*: The time required to search the tree for *k* is O(*h*) where *h* is its height. The remainder of the algorithm takes Θ(1) time. So, the overall time needed by *insert* is O(*h*). □

```
void insert(treePointer *node, int k, iType theItem)
{/* if k is in the tree pointed at by node do nothing;
    otherwise add a new node with data = (k, theItem) */
   treePointer ptr, temp = modifiedSearch(*node, k);
   if (temp || !(*node)) {
      /* k is not in the tree */
      MALLOC(ptr, sizeof(*ptr));
      ptr→data.key = k;
      ptr→data.item = theItem;
      ptr→leftChild = ptr→rightChild = NULL;
      if (*node) /* insert as child of temp */
         if (k < temp→data.key) temp→leftChild = ptr;
         else temp→rightChild = ptr;
      else *node = ptr;
   }
}
```

Program 5.17: Inserting a dictionary pair into a binary search tree

5.7.4 Deletion from a Binary Search Tree

Deletion of a leaf is quite easy. For example, to delete 35 from the tree of Figure 5.30(b), the left-child field of its parent is set to 0 (*NULL*) and the node freed. This gives us the tree of Figure 5.30(a). To delete the 80 from this tree, the right-child field of 40 is set to 0, obtaining the tree of Figure 5.29(b), and the node containing 80 is freed.

The deletion of a nonleaf that has only one child is also easy. The node containing the dictionary pair to be deleted is freed, and its single-child takes the place of the freed node. So, to delete the 5 from the tree of Figure 5.30(a), we simply change the pointer from the parent node (i.e., the node containing 30) to the single-child node (i.e., the node containing 2).

When the pair to be deleted is in a nonleaf node that has two children, the pair to be deleted is replaced by either the largest pair in its left subtree or the smallest one in its right subtree. Then we proceed to delete this replacing pair from the subtree from which it was taken. For instance, if we wish to delete the pair with key 30 from the tree of Figure 5.30(a), then we replace it by either the largest pair, the one with key 5, in its left subtree or the smallest pair, the one with key 40, in its right subtree. Suppose we opt for the largest pair in the left subtree. The pair with key 5 is moved into the root, and the tree of Figure 5.31(a) is obtained. Now we must delete the second 5. Since the node with the second 5 has only one child, the pointer from its parent is changed to point to this child. The tree of Figure 5.31(b) is obtained. One may verify that regardless of whether the replacing pair is the largest in the left subtree or the smallest in the right subtree, it is originally in a node with a degree of at most one. So, deleting it from this node is quite easy. We leave the writing of the deletion function as an exercise. It should be evident that a deletion can be performed in O(h) time if the search tree has a height of h.

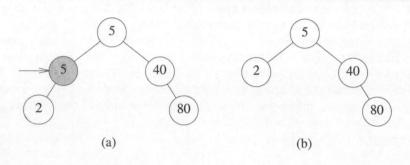

(a)   (b)

Figure 5.31: Deletion from a binary search tree

5.7.5 Joining and Splitting Binary Trees

Although search, insert, and delete are the operations most frequently performed on a binary search tree, the following additional operations are useful in certain applications:

(a) *threeWayJoin* (*small,mid,big*): This creates a binary search tree consisting of the pairs initially in the binary search trees *small* and *big*, as well as the pair *mid*. It is assumed that each key in *small* is smaller than *mid . key* and that each key in *big* is greater than *mid . key*. Following the join, both *small* and *big* are empty.

(b) *twoWayJoin* (*small,big*): This joins the two binary search trees *small* and *big* to obtain a single binary search tree that contains all the pairs originally in *small* and *big*. It is assumed that all keys of *small* are smaller than all keys of *big* and that following the join both *small* and *big* are empty.

(c) *split* (*theTree,k,small,mid,big*): The binary search tree *theTree* is split into three parts: *small* is a binary search tree that contains all pairs of *theTree* that have key less than k; *mid* is the pair (if any) in *theTree* whose key is k; and *big* is a binary search tree that contains all pairs of *theTree* that have key larger than k. Following the split operation *theTree* is empty. When *theTree* has no pair whose key is k, *mid.key* is set to -1 (this assumes that -1 is not a valid key for a dictionary pair).

A three-way join operation is particularly easy to perform. We simply obtain a new node and set its data field to *mid*, its left-child pointer to *small*, and its right-child pointer to *big*. This new node is the root of the binary search tree that was to be created. Finally, *small* and *big* are set to NULL. The time taken for this operation is O(1), and the height of the new tree is max{*height* (*small*), *height* (*big*)} + 1.

Consider the two-way join operation. If either *small* or *big* is empty, the result is the other tree. When neither is empty, we may first delete from *small* the pair *mid* with the largest key. Let the resulting binary search tree be *small'*. To complete the operation, we perform the three-way join operation *threeWayJoin* (*small'*,*mid*,*big*). The overall time required to perform the two-way join operation is O(*height* (*small*)), and the height of the resulting tree is max{*height* (*small'*), *height* (*big*)} + 1. The run time can be made O(min{*height* (*small*), *height* (*big*)}) if we retain with each tree its height. Then we delete the pair with the largest key from *small* if the height of *small* is no more than that of *big*; otherwise, we delete from *big* the pair with the smallest key. This is followed by a three-way join operation.

To perform a split, we first make the following observation about splitting at the root (i.e., when *k* = *theTree* →*data* . *key*). In this case, *small* is the left subtree of *theTree*, *mid* is the pair in the root, and *big* is the right subtree of *theTree*. If *k* is smaller than the key at the root, then the root together with its right subtree is to be in *big*. When *k* is larger than the key at the root, the root together with its left subtree is to be in *small*. Using these observations, we can perform a split by moving down the search tree *theTree* searching for a pair with key *k*. As we move down, we construct the two search trees *small* and *big*. The function to split *theTree* given in Program 5.18. To simplify the code, we begin with two header nodes *sHead* and *bHead* for *small* and *big*, respectively. *small* is grown as the right subtree of *sHead*; *big* is grown as the left subtree of *bHead*. *s* (*b*) points to the node of *sHead* (*bHead*) at which further subtrees of *theTree* that are to be part of *small* (*big*) may be attached. Attaching a subtree to *small* (*big*) is done as the right (left) child of *s* (*b*).

Analysis of *split*: The **while** loop maintains the invariant that all keys in the subtree with root *currentNode* are larger than those in the tree rooted at *sHead* and smaller than those in the tree rooted at *bHead*. The correctness of the function is easy to establish, and its complexity is seen to be O(*height* (*theTree*)). One may verify that neither *small* nor *big* has a height larger than that of *theTree*. □

5.7.6   Height of a Binary Search Tree

Unless care is taken, the height of a binary search tree with *n* elements can become as large as *n*. This is the case, for instance, when Program 5.17 is used to insert the keys [1, 2, 3, . . ., *n*], in this order, into an initially empty binary search tree. It can, however, be shown that when insertions and deletions are made at random using the functions given here, the height of the binary search tree is O(log *n*) on the average.

```
void split(nodePointer *theTree, int k, nodePointer *small,
           element *mid, nodePointer *big)
{/* split the binary search tree with respect to key k */
    if (!theTree) {*small = *big = 0;
                    (*mid).key = -1; return;} /* empty tree */
    nodePointer sHead, bHead, s, b, currentNode;
    /* create header nodes for small and big */
    MALLOC(sHead, sizeof(*sHead));
    MALLOC(bHead, sizeof(*bHead));
    s = sHead; b = bHead;

    /* do the split */
    currentNode = *theTree;
    while (currentNode)
        if (k < currentNode→data.key) {/* add to big */
            b→leftChild = currentNode;
            b = currentNode; currentNode = currentNode→leftChild;
        }
        else if (k > currentNode→data.key) {/* add to small */
            s→rightChild = currentNode;
            s = currentNode; currentNode = currentNode→rightChild;
        }
        else {/* split at currentNode */
            s→rightChild = currentNode→leftChild;
            b→leftChild = currentNode→rightChild;
            *small = sHead→rightChild; free(sHead);
            *big = bHead→leftChild; free(bHead);
            (*mid).item = currentNode→data.item;
            (*mid).key = currentNode→data.key;
            free(currentNode);
            return;
        }
    /* no pair with key k */
    s→rightChild = b→leftChild = 0;
    *small = sHead→rightChild; free(sHead);
    *big = bHead→leftChild; free(bHead);
    (*mid).key = -1;
    return;
}
```

Program 5.18 Splitting a binary search tree

Search trees with a worst-case height of O(log n) are called *balanced search trees*. Balanced search trees that permit searches, inserts, and deletes to be performed in O(h) time exist. Most notable among these are AVL, red/black, 2-3, 2-3-4, B, and B$^+$ trees. These are discussed in Chapters 10 and 11.

EXERCISES

1. Write a C function to delete the element with key k from a binary search tree. What is the time complexity of your function?

2. Write a program to start with an initially empty binary search tree and make n random insertions. Use a uniform random number generator to obtain the values to be inserted. Measure the height of the resulting binary search tree and divide this height by $\log_2 n$. Do this for $n = 100, 500, 1000, 2000, 3000, \cdots, 10,000$. Plot the ratio *height* $/\log_2 n$ as a function of n. The ratio should be approximately constant (around 2). Verify that this is so.

3. Suppose that each node in a binary search tree also has the field *leftSize* as described in the text. Write a function to insert a pair into such a binary search tree. The complexity of your function should be O(h), where h is the height of the search tree. Show that this is the case.

4. Do Exercise 3, but this time write a function to delete the pair with the kth smallest key in the binary search tree.

5. Write a C function that implements the three-way join operation in O(1) time.

6. Write a C function that implements the two-way join operation in O(h) time, where h is the height of one of the two trees being joined.

7. Any algorithm that merges together two sorted lists of size n and m, respectively, must make at least $n + m - 1$ comparisons in the worst case. What implications does this result have on the time complexity of any comparison-based algorithm that combines two binary search trees that have n and m pairs, respectively?

8. In Chapter 7, we shall see that every comparison-based algorithm to sort n elements must make O($n \log n$) comparisons in the worst case. What implications does this result have on the complexity of initializing a binary search tree with n pairs?

9. Notice that a binary search tree can be used to implement a priority queue.

   (a) Write a C functions for a max priority queue that represents the priority queue as a binary search tree. Your codes for *top*, *pop* and *push* should have complexity O(h), where h is the height of the search tree. Since h is O(log n) on average, we can perform each these priority queue operations in average time O(log n).

   (b) Compare the actual performance of heaps and binary search trees as data structures for priority queues. For this comparison, generate random sequences of delete max and insert operations and measure the total time taken for each sequence by each of these data structures.

10. Assume that we change the definition of a binary search tree so that equal keys are permitted and that we add a count field to the node structure.

   (a) Rewrite *insertNode* so that it increments the count field when a plural key is found. Otherwise, a new node is created.

   (b) Rewrite *delete* so that it decrements the count field when the key is found. The node is eliminated only if its count is 0.

11. Write the C code for the function *modifiedSearch* that is used in Program 5.17.

12. Obtain a recursive version of *insertNode*. Which of the two versions is more efficient? Why?

13. Write a recursive C function to delete a key from a binary search tree. What is the time and space complexity of your function?

14. Obtain an iterative C function to delete a key from a binary search tree. The space complexity of your function should be O(1). Show that this is the case. What is the time complexity of your function?

15. Assume that a binary search tree is represented as a threaded binary search tree. Write functions to search, insert, and delete.

5.8 SELECTION TREES

5.8.1 Introduction

Suppose we have k ordered sequences, called *runs*, that are to be merged into a single ordered sequence. Each run consists of some records and is in nondecreasing order of a designated field called the *key*. Let n be the number of records in all k runs together. The merging task can be accomplished by repeatedly outputting the record with the smallest key. The smallest has to be found from k possibilities, and it could be the leading record in any of the k runs. The most direct way to merge k runs is to make $k - 1$ comparisons to determine the next record to output. For $k > 2$, we can achieve a reduction in the number of comparisons needed to find the next smallest element by using the *selection tree* data structure. There are two kinds of selection trees: *winner trees* and *loser trees*.

5.8.2 Winner Trees

A *winner tree* is a complete binary tree in which each node represents the smaller of its two children. Thus, the root node represents the smallest node in the tree. Figure 5.32 illustrates a winner tree for the case $k = 8$.

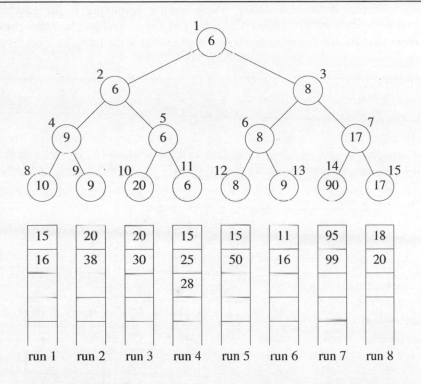

Figure 5.32: Winner tree for $k = 8$, showing the first three keys in each of the eight runs

The construction of this winner tree may be compared to the playing of a tournament in which the winner is the record with the smaller key. Then, each nonleaf node in the tree represents the winner of a tournament, and the root node represents the overall winner, or the smallest key. Each leaf node represents the first record in the corresponding run. Since the records being merged are generally large, each node will contain only a pointer to the record it represents. Thus, the root node contains a pointer to the first record in run 4.

A winner tree may be represented using the sequential allocation scheme for binary trees that results from Lemma 5.4. The number above each node in Figure 5.32 is the address of the node in this sequential representation. The record pointed to by the root has the smallest key and so may be output. Now, the next record from run 4 enters the winner tree. It has a key value of 15. To restructure the tree, the tournament has to be replayed only along the path from node 11 to the root. Thus, the winner from nodes 10 and 11 is again node 11 (15 < 20). The winner from nodes 4 and 5 is node 4 (9 < 15). The winner from 2 and 3 is node 3 (8 < 9). The new tree is shown in Figure 5.33. The tournament is played between sibling nodes and the result put in the parent node. Lemma 5.4 may be used to compute the address of sibling and parent nodes efficiently. Each new comparison takes place at the next higher level in the tree.

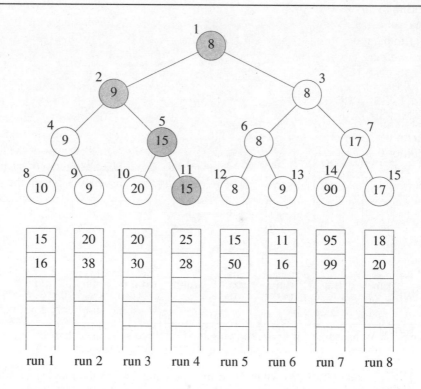

Figure 5.33: Winner tree of Figure 5.32 after one record has been output and the tree restructured (nodes that were changed are shaded)

Analysis of merging runs using winner trees: The number of levels in the tree is $\lceil \log_2(k + 1) \rceil$. So, the time to restructure the tree is $O(\log_2 k)$. The tree has to be restructured each time a record is merged into the output file. Hence, the time required to merge all n records is $O(n \log_2 k)$. The time required to set up the selection tree the first time is $O(k)$. Thus, the total time needed to merge the k runs is $O(n \log_2 k)$. □

5.8.3   Loser Trees

After the record with the smallest key value is output, the winner tree of Figure 5.32 is to be restructured. Since the record with the smallest key value is in run 4, this restructuring involves inserting the next record from this run into the tree. The next record has key value 15. Tournaments are played between sibling nodes along the path from node 11 to the root. Since these sibling nodes represent the losers of tournaments played earlier, we can simplify the restructuring process by placing in each nonleaf node a pointer to the record that loses the tournament rather than to the winner of the tournament. A selection tree in which each nonleaf node retains a pointer to the loser is called a *loser tree*. Figure 5.34 shows the loser tree that corresponds to the winner tree of Figure 5.32. For convenience, each node contains the key value of a record rather than a pointer to the record represented. The leaf nodes represent the first record in each run. An additional node, node 0, has been added to represent the overall winner of the tournament. Following the output of the overall winner, the tree is restructured by playing tournaments along the path from node 11 to node 1. The records with which these tournaments are to be played are readily available from the parent nodes. As a result, sibling nodes along the path from 11 to 1 are not accessed.

EXERCISES

1. Write abstract data type specifications for winner and loser trees.

2. Write a function to construct a winner tree for k records. Assume that k is a power of 2. Each node at which a tournament is played should store only a pointer to the winner. Show that this construction can be carried out in time $O(k)$.

3. Do Exercise 2 for the case when k is not restricted to being a power of 2.

4. Write a function to construct a loser tree for k records. Use position 0 of your loser-tree array to store a pointer to the overall winner. Show that this construction can be carried out in time $O(k)$. Assume that k is a power of 2.

5. Do Exercise 4 for the case when k is not restricted to being a power of 2.

6. Write a function, using a tree of losers, to carry out a k-way merge of k runs, $k \geq 2$. Assume the existence of a function to initialize a loser tree in linear time. Show that if there are $n > k$ records in all k runs together, then the computing time is $O(n \log_2 k)$.

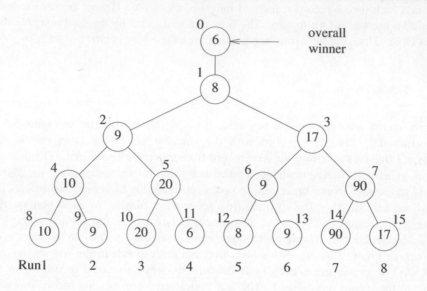

Figure 5.34: Loser tree corresponding to winner tree of Figure 5.32

7. Do the previous exercise for the case in which a tree of winners is used. Assume the existence of a function to initialize a winner tree in linear time.

8. Compare the performance of your functions for the preceding two exercises for the case $k = 8$. Generate eight runs of data, each having 100 records. Use a random number generator for this (the keys obtained from the random number generator will need to be sorted before the merge can begin). Measure and compare the time taken to merge the eight runs using the two strategies.

5.9 FORESTS

Definition: A *forest* is a set of $n \geq 0$ disjoint trees. □

A three-tree forest is shown in Figure 5.35. The concept of a forest is very close to that of a tree because if we remove the root of a tree, we obtain a forest. For example, removing the root of any binary tree produces a forest of two trees. In this section, we briefly consider several forest operations, including transforming a forest into a binary tree and forest traversals. In the next section, we use forests to represent disjoint sets.

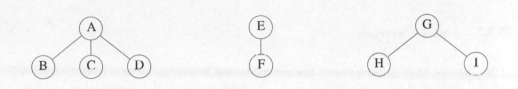

Figure 5.35: Three-tree forest

5.9.1 Transforming a Forest into a Binary Tree

To transform a forest into a single binary tree, we first obtain the binary tree representation of each of the trees in the forest and then link these binary trees together through the *rightChild* field of the root nodes. Using this transformation, the forest of Figure 5.35 becomes the binary tree of Figure 5.36.

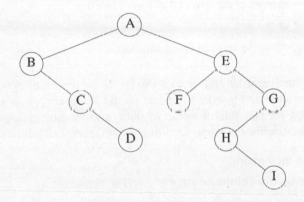

Figure 5.36: Binary tree representation of forest of Figure 5.35

We can define this transformation in a formal way as follows:

Definition: If $T_1, \cdots, T_n$ is a forest of trees, then the binary tree corresponding to this forest, denoted by $B(T_1, \cdots, T_n)$,

(1) is empty if $n = 0$

(2) has root equal to root (T_1); has left subtree equal to $B(T_{11}, T_{12}, \cdots, T_{1m})$, where

$T_{11}, \cdots, T_{1m}$ are the subtrees of root(T_1); and has right subtree $B(T_2, \cdots, T_n)$.
□

5.9.2   Forest Traversals

Preorder and inorder traversals of the corresponding binary tree T of a forest F have a natural correspondence to traversals on F. Preorder traversal of T is equivalent to visiting the nodes of F in *forest preorder*, which is defined as follows:

(1)   If F is empty then return.

(2)   Visit the root of the first tree of F.

(3)   Traverse the subtrees of the first tree in forest preorder.

(4)   Traverse the remaining trees of F in forest preorder.

Inorder traversal of T is equivalent to visiting the nodes of F in *forest inorder*, which is defined as follows:

(1)   If F is empty then return.

(2)   Traverse the subtrees of the first tree in forest inorder.

(3)   Visit the root of the first tree.

(4)   Traverse the remaining trees in forest inorder.

The proofs that preorder and inorder traversals on the corresponding binary tree are the same as preorder and inorder traversals on the forest are left as exercises. There is no natural analog for postorder traversal of the corresponding binary tree of a forest. Nevertheless, we can define the *postorder traversal of a forest* as follows:

(1)   If F is empty then return.

(2)   Traverse the subtrees of the first tree of F in forest postorder.

(3)   Traverse the remaining trees of F in forest postorder.

(4)   Visit the root of the first tree of F.

In a *level-order traversal of a forest*, nodes are visited by level, beginning with the roots of each tree in the forest. Within each level, nodes are visited from left to right. One may verify that the level-order traversal of a forest and that of its associated binary tree do not necessarily yield the same result.

EXERCISES

1. Define the inverse transformation of the one that creates the associated binary tree from a forest. Are these transformations unique?

2. Prove that the preorder traversal of a forest and the preorder traversal of its associated binary tree give the same result.

3. Prove that the inorder traversal of a forest and the inorder traversal of its associated binary tree give the same result.

4. Prove that the postorder traversal of a forest and that of its corresponding binary tree do not necessarily yield the same result.

5. Prove that the level-order traversal of a forest and that of its corresponding binary tree do not necessarily yield the same result.

6. Write a nonrecursive function to traverse the associated binary tree of a forest in forest postorder. What are the time and space complexities of your function?

7. Do the preceding exercise for the case of forest level-order traversal.

5.10 REPRESENTATION OF DISJOINT SETS

5.10.1 Introduction

In this section, we study the use of trees in the representation of sets. For simplicity, we assume that the elements of the sets are the numbers $0, 1, 2, \cdots, n-1$. In practice, these numbers might be indices into a symbol table that stores the actual names of the elements. We also assume that the sets being represented are pairwise disjoint, that is, if S_i and S_j are two sets and $i \neq j$, then there is no element that is in both S_i and S_j. For example, if we have 10 elements numbered 0 through 9, we may partition them into three disjoint sets, $S_1 = \{0, 6, 7, 8\}$, $S_2 = \{1, 4, 9\}$, and $S_3 = \{2, 3, 5\}$. Figure 5.37 shows one possible representation for these sets. Notice that for each set we have linked the nodes from the children to the parent, rather than our usual method of linking from the parent to the children. The reason for this change in linkage will become apparent when we discuss the implementation of set operations.

The minimal operations that we wish to perform on these sets are:

(1) *Disjoint set union.* If S_i and S_j are two disjoint sets, then their union $S_i \cup S_j = \{$all elements, x, such that x is in S_i or $S_j\}$. Thus, $S_1 \cup S_2 = \{0, 6, 7, 8, 1, 4, 9\}$. Since we have assumed that all sets are disjoint, following the union of S_i and S_j we can assume that the sets S_i and S_j no longer exist independently. That is, we replace them by $S_i \cup S_j$.

(2) *Find(i).* Find the set containing the element, i. For example, 3 is in set S_3 and 8 is in set S_1.

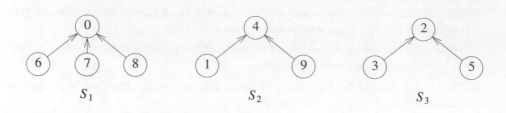

Figure 5.37: Possible tree representation of sets

5.10.2   Union And Find Operations

Let us consider the union operation first. Suppose that we wish to obtain the union of S_1 and S_2. Since we have linked the nodes from children to parent, we simply make one of the trees a subtree of the other. $S_1 \cup S_2$ could have either of the representations of Figure 5.38.

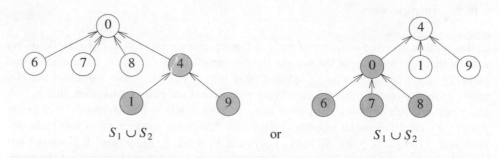

Figure 5.38: Possible representation of $S_1 \cup S_2$

To implement the set union operation, we simply set the parent field of one of the roots to the other root. We can accomplish this easily if, with each set name, we keep a pointer to the root of the tree representing that set. If, in addition, each root has a pointer to the set name, we can find which set an element is in by following the parent links to the root of its tree and then returning the pointer to the set name. Figure 5.39 shows this representation of S_1, S_2, and S_3.

To simplify the discussion of the union and find algorithms, we will ignore the set names and identify the sets by the roots of the trees representing them. For example, rather than using the set name S_1 we refer to this set as 0. The transition to set names is easy. We assume that a table, *name* [ ], holds the set names. If i is an element in a tree

Set
Name Pointer

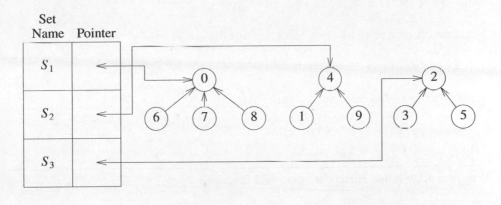

Figure 5.39: Data representation of S_1, S_2, and S_3

with root j, and j has a pointer to entry k in the set name table, then the set name is just $name[k]$.

Since the nodes in the trees are numbered 0 through $n - 1$ we can use the node's number as an index. This means that each node needs only one field, the index of its parent, to link to its parent. Thus, the only data structure that we need is an array, *int parent*[*MAX_ELEMENTS*], where *MAX_ELEMENTS* is the maximum number of elements. Figure 5.40 shows this representation of the sets, S_1, S_2, and S_3. Notice that root nodes have a parent of -1.

i	[0]	[1]	[2]	[3]	[4]	[5]	[6]	[7]	[8]	[9]
parent	-1	4	-1	2	-1	2	0	0	0	4

Figure 5.40: Array representation of S_1, S_2, and S_3

We can now find element i by simply following the parent values starting at i and continuing until we reach a negative parent parent value. For example, to find 5, we start at 5, and then move to 5's parent, 2. Since this node has a negative parent value we have reached the root. The operation $union(i,j)$ is equally simple. We pass in two trees with roots i and j. Assuming that we adopt the convention that the first tree becomes a subtree of the second, the statement *parent* $[i] = j$ accomplishes the union. Program 5.19 implements the simple union and find operations as just discussed.

```
int simpleFind(int i)
{
   for(; parent[i] >= 0; i = parent[i])
     ;
   return i;
}
void simpleUnion(int i, int j)
{
   parent[i] = j;
}
```

Program 5.19: Initial attempt at union-find functions

Analysis of *simpleUnion*1 and *simpleFind*1: Although *simpleUnion* and *simpleFind* are easy to implement, their performance characteristics are not very good. For instance, if we start with p elements, each in a set of its own, that is, $S_i = \{i\}$, $0 \le i < p$, then the initial configuration is a forest with p nodes and $parent[i] = -1$, $0 \le i < p$. Now let us process the following sequence of union-find operations:

$$union(0, 1), find(0)$$
$$union(1, 2), find(0)$$

$$\cdot$$
$$\cdot$$
$$\cdot$$

$$union(n{-}2, n{-}1), find(0)$$

This sequence produces the degenerate tree of Figure 5.41. Since the time taken for a union is constant, we can process all the $n - 1$ unions in time $O(n)$. However, for each *find*, we must follow a chain of parent links from 0 to the root. If the element is at level i, then the time required to find its root is $O(i)$. Hence, the total time needed to process the $n - 1$ finds is:

$$\sum_{i=2}^{n} i = O(n^2) \; \square$$

By avoiding the creation of degenerate trees, we can attain far more efficient implementations of the union and find operations. We accomplish this by adopting the following *Weighting rule* for *union(i, j)*.

Definition: *Weighting rule for union(i, j).* If the number of nodes in tree i is less than the number in tree j then make j the parent of i; otherwise make i the parent of j. $\square$

Figure 5.41: Degenerate tree

When we use this rule on the sequence of set unions described above, we obtain the trees of Figure 5.42. To implement the weighting rule, we need to know how many nodes there are in every tree. To do this easily, we maintain a count field in the root of every tree. If i is a root node, then $count[i]$ equals the number of nodes in that tree. Since all nodes but the roots of trees have a nonnegative number in the parent field, we can maintain the count in the parent field of the roots as a negative number. When we incorporate the weighting rule, the union operation takes the form given in *weightedUnion* (Program 5.20). Remember that the arguments passed into *weightedUnion* must be roots of trees.

Lemma 5.5: Let T be a tree with n nodes created as a result of *weightedUnion*. No node in T has level greater than $\lfloor \log_2 n \rfloor + 1$.

Proof: The lemma is clearly true for $n = 1$. Assume that it is true for all trees with i nodes, $i \leq n - 1$. We show that it is also true for $i = n$. Let T be a tree with n nodes created by *weightedUnion*. Consider the last union operation performed, $union(k,j)$. Let m be the number of nodes in tree j and $n-m$, the number of nodes in k. Without loss of generality, we may assume that $1 \leq m \leq n / 2$. Then the maximum level of any node in T is either the same as k or is one more than in j. If the former is the case, then the maximum level in T is $\leq \lfloor \log_2(n-m) \rfloor + 1 \leq \lfloor \log_2 n \rfloor + 1$. If the latter is the case, then the maximum level is $\leq \lfloor \log_2 m \rfloor + 2 \leq \lfloor \log_2 n/2 \rfloor + 2 \leq \lfloor \log_2 n \rfloor + 1$. $\square$

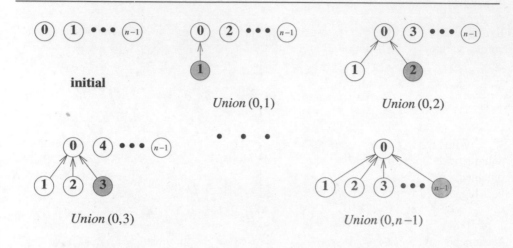

Figure 5.42: Trees obtained using the weighting rule

```
void weightedUnion(int i, int j)
{/* union the sets with roots i and j, i != j, using
    the weighting rule. parent[i] = -count[i] and
    parent[j] = -count[j] */
  int temp = parent[i] + parent[j];
  if (parent[i] > parent[j]) {
     parent[i] = j; /* make j the new root */
     parent[j] = temp;
  }
  else {
     parent[j] = i; /*make i the new root */
     parent[i] = temp;
  }
}
```

Program 5.20: Union function using weighting rule

Example 5.3 shows that the bound of Lemma 5.5 is achievable for some sequence of unions.

Example 5.3: Consider the behavior of *weightedUnion* on the following sequence of unions starting from the initial configuration of *parent* $[i] = -count[i] = -1, 0 \le i < n = 2^3$:

$$union(0, 1) \quad union(2, 3) \quad union(4, 5) \quad union(6, 7)$$
$$union(0, 2) \quad union(4, 6) \quad union(0, 4)$$

When the sequence of unions is performed by columns (i.e., top to bottom within a column with column 1 first, column 2 next, and so on), the trees of Figure 5.43 are obtained. As is evident from this example, in the general case, the maximum level can be $\lfloor \log_2 m \rfloor + 1$ if the tree has m nodes. $\square$

From Lemma 5.5, it follows that the time to process a find is $O(\log m)$ if there are m elements in a tree. If an intermixed sequence of $u - 1$ union and f find operations is to be processed, the time becomes $O(u + f \log u)$, as no tree has more than u nodes in it. Of course, we need $O(n)$ additional time to initialize the n-tree forest.

Surprisingly, further improvement is possible. This time the modification will be made in the find algorithm using the *collapsing rule*.

Definition [*Collapsing rule*]: If j is a node on the path from i to its root and *parent* $[i] \ne$ *root* (i), then set *parent* $\lfloor j \rfloor$ to *root* (i). $\square$

Function *collapsingFind* (Program 5.21) incorporates the collapsing rule.

Example 5.4: Consider the tree created by function *weightedUnion* on the sequence of unions of Example 5.5. Now process the following eight finds:

$$find(7), find(7), \cdots, find(7)$$

If *simpleFind* is used, each *find*(7) requires going up three parent link fields for a total of 24 moves to process all eight finds. When *collapsingFind* is used, the first *find*(7) requires going up three links and then resetting two links. Note that even though only two parent links need to be reset, function *collapsingFind* will actually reset three (the parent of 4 is reset to 0). Each of the remaining seven finds requires going up only one link field. The total cost is now only 13 moves. $\square$

Analysis of *weightedUnion* and *collapsingFind*: Use of the collapsing rule roughly doubles the time for an individual find. However, it reduces the worst-case time over a sequence of finds. The worst-case complexity of processing a sequence of unions and finds using *weightedUnion* and *collapsingFind* is stated in Lemma 5.6. This lemma

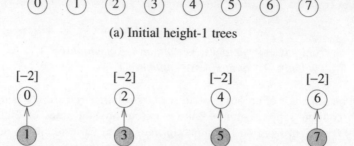

(a) Initial height-1 trees

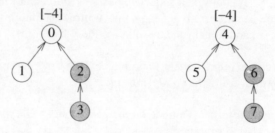

(b) Height-2 trees following *Union* (0,1), (2,3), (4,5), and (6,7)

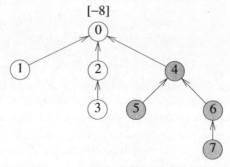

(c) Height-3 trees following *Union* (0,2) and (4,6)

(d) Height-4 tree following *Union* (0,4)

Figure 5.43: Trees achieving worst case bound

```
int collapsingFind(int i)
{/* find the root of the tree containing element i. Use the
    collapsing rule to collapse all nodes from i to root */
    int root, trail, lead;
    for (root = i; parent[root] >= 0; root = parent[root])
      ;
    for (trail = i; trail != root; trail = lead) {
       lead = parent[trail];
       parent[trail] = root;
    }
    return root;
}
```

Program 5.21: Collapsing rule

makes use of a function $\alpha(p,q)$ that is related to a functional inverse of Ackermann's function $A(i,j)$. These functions are defined as follows:

$$A(1,j) = 2^j, \quad \text{for } j \geq 1$$
$$A(i,1) = A(i-1,2) \quad \text{for } i \geq 2$$
$$A(i,j) = A(i-1,A(i,j-1)) \quad \text{for } i,j \geq 2$$

$$\alpha(p,q) = \min\{z \geq 1 \mid A(z,\lfloor p/q \rfloor) > \log_2 q\}, \; p \geq q \geq 1$$

The function $A(i,j)$ is a very rapidly growing function. Consequently, α grows very slowly as p and q are increased. In fact, since $A(3,1) = 16$, $\alpha(p,q) \leq 3$ for $q < 2^{16} = 65,536$ and $p \geq q$. Since $A(4,1)$ is a very large number and in our application q will be the number, n, of set elements and p will be $n + f$ (f is the number of finds), $\alpha(p,q) \leq 4$ for all practical purposes. □

Lemma 5.6 [*Tarjan and Van Leeuwen*]: Assume that we start with a forest of trees, each having one node. Let $T(f,u)$ be the maximum time required to process any inter-mixed sequence of f finds and u unions. Assume that $u \geq n/2$. Then

$$k_1(n + f\,\alpha(f + n,n)) \leq T(f,u) \leq k_2(n + f\,\alpha(f + n,n))$$

for some positive constants k_1 and k_2. □

The requirement that $u \geq n/2$ in Lemma 5.6, is really not significant, as when $u < n/2$, some elements are involved in no union operation. These elements remain in singleton sets throughout the sequence of union and find operations and can be eliminated from consideration, as find operations that involve these can be done in O(1) time each. Even though the function $\alpha(f, u)$ is a very slowly growing function, the complexity of our solution to the set representation problem is not linear in the number of unions and finds. The space requirements are one node for each element.

In the exercises, we explore alternatives to the weight rule and the collapsing rule that preserve the time bounds of Lemma 5.6.

5.10.3   Application to Equivalence Classes

Consider the equivalence pairs processing problem of Section 4.6. The equivalence classes to be generated may be regarded as sets. These sets are disjoint, as no polygon can be in two equivalence classes. Initially, all n polygons are in an equivalence class of their own; thus $parent [i] = -1, 0 \le i < n$. If an equivalence pair, $i \equiv j$, is to be processed, we must first determine the sets containing i and j. If these are different, then the two sets are to be replaced by their union. If the two sets are the same, then nothing is to be done, as the relation $i \equiv j$ is redundant; i and j are already in the same equivalence class. To process each equivalence pair we need to perform two finds and at most one union. Thus, if we have n polygons and m equivalence pairs, we need to spend O(n) time to set up the initial n-tree forest, and then we need to process $2m$ finds and at most min$\{n - 1, m\}$ unions. (Note that after $n - 1$ unions, all n polygons will be in the same equivalence class and no more unions can be performed.) If we use *weightedUnion* and *collapsingFind*, the total time to process the equivalence relations is O($n + m\alpha(2m, \min\{n-1, m\})$). Although this is slightly worse than the algorithm of Section 4.9, it needs less space and is on line. By "on line," we mean that as each equivalence is processed, we can tell which equivalence class each polygon is in.

Example 5.6: Consider the equivalence pairs example of Section 4.6. Initially, there are 12 trees, one for each variable. $parent[i] = -1, 0 \le i < 12$. The tree configuration following the processing of each equivalence pair is shown in Figure 5.44. Each tree represents an equivalence class. It is possible to determine if two elements are currently in the same equivalence class at each stage of the processing simply by making two finds. □

EXERCISES

1. Suppose we start with n sets, each containing a distinct element.

    (a) Show that if u unions are performed, then no set contains more than $u + 1$ elements.

    (b) Show that at most $n - 1$ unions can be performed before the number of sets becomes 1.

    (c) Show that if fewer than $\lceil n/2 \rceil$ unions are performed, then at least one set

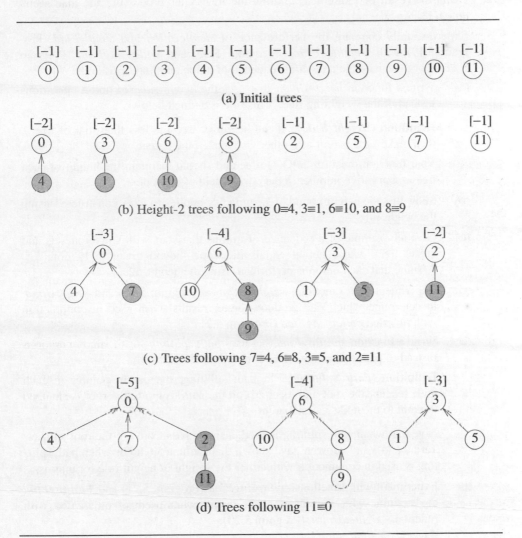

(a) Initial trees

(b) Height-2 trees following 0≡4, 3≡1, 6≡10, and 8≡9

(c) Trees following 7≡4, 6≡8, 3≡5, and 2≡11

(d) Trees following 11≡0

Figure 5.44: Trees for Example 5.6

with a single element in it remains.

(d) Show that if u unions are performed, then at least $\max\{n - 2u, 0\}$ singleton sets remain.

2. Using the result of Example 5.6, draw the trees after processing the instruction *union*(11,9).

3. Experimentally compare the performance of *simpleUnion* and *simpleFind* (Program 5.19) with *weightedUnion* (Program 5.20) and *collapsingFind* (Program 5.21). For this, generate a random sequence of union and find operations.

4. (a) Write a function *heightUnion* that uses the *height rule* for union operations instead of the weighting rule. This rule is defined below:

   Definition [*Height Rule*]: If the height of tree *i* is less than that of tree *j*, then make *j* the parent of *i*, otherwise make *i* the parent of *j*. □

   Your function must run in O(1) time and should maintain the height of each tree as a negative number in the *parent* field of the root.

   (b) Show that the height bound of Lemma 5.5 applies to trees constructed using the height rule.

   (c) Give an example of a sequence of unions that start with singleton sets and create trees whose height equals the upper bound given in Lemma 5.5. Assume that each union is performed using the height rule.

   (d) Experiment with functions *weightedUnion* (Program 5.20) and *heightUnion* to determine which one produces better results when used in conjunction with function *collapsingFind* (Program 5.21).

5. (a) Write a function *splittingFind* that uses *path splitting* for the find operations instead of path collapsing. This is defined below:

   Definition [*Path Splitting*]: In path splitting, the parent pointer in each node (except the root and its child) on the path from *i* to the root is changed to point to the node's grandparent. □

   Note that when path splitting is used, a single pass from *i* to the root suffices. Tarjan and Van Leeuwen have shown that Lemma 5.6 holds when path splitting is used in conjunction with either the weight or height rule for unions.

   (b) Experiment with functions *collapsingFind* (Program 5.21) and *splittingFind* to determine which produces better results when used in conjunction with function *weightedUnion* (Program 5.20).

6. (a) Write a function *halvingFind* that uses *path halving* for the find operations instead of path collapsing. This is defined below:

   Definition [*Path Halving*]: In path halving, the parent pointer of every other node (except the root and its child) on the path from *i* to the root is changed to point to the node's grandparent. □

   Note that path halving, like path splitting (Exercise 5) can be implemented with a single pass from *i* to the root. However, in path halving, only half as many pointers are changed as in path splitting. Tarjan and Van Leeuwen have shown that Lemma 5.6 holds when path halving is used in conjunction with either the weight or height rule for unions.

(b)   Experiment with functions *collapsingFind* and *halvingFind* to determine which one produces better results when used in conjunction with function *weightedUnion*.

5.11   COUNTING BINARY TREES

As a conclusion to our chapter on trees, we consider three disparate problems that amazingly have the same solution. We wish to determine the number of distinct binary trees having n nodes, the number of distinct permutations of the numbers from 1 through n obtainable by a stack, and the number of distinct ways of multiplying $n + 1$ matrices. Let us begin with a quick look at these problems.

5.11.1   Distinct Binary Trees

We know that if $n = 0$ or $n = 1$, there is only one binary tree. If $n = 2$, then there are two distinct trees (Figure 5.45), and if $n = 3$, there are five such trees (Figure 5.46). How many distinct trees are there with n nodes? Before deriving a solution, we will examine the two remaining problems. You might attempt to sketch out a solution of your own before reading further.

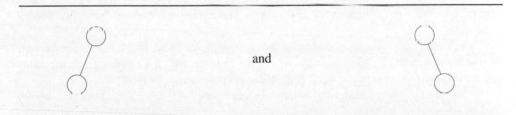

and

Figure 5.45: Distinct binary trees with $n = 2$

5.11.2   Stack Permutations

In Section 5.3, we introduced preorder, inorder, and postorder traversals and indicated that each traversal requires a stack. Suppose we have the preorder sequence *A B C D E F G H I* and the inorder sequence *B C A E D G H F I* of the same binary tree. Does such a pair of sequences uniquely define a binary tree? Put another way, can this pair of sequences come from more than one binary tree?

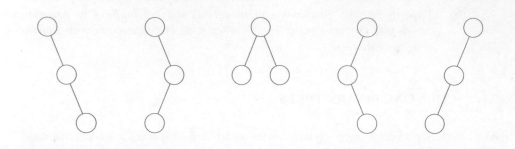

Figure 5.46: Distinct binary trees with $n = 3$

To construct the binary tree from these sequences, we look at the first letter in the preorder sequence, A. This letter must be the root of the tree by definition of the preorder traversal (VLR). We also know by definition of the inorder traversal (LVR) that all nodes preceding A in the inorder sequence ($B\ C$) are in the left subtree, and the remaining nodes ($E\ D\ G\ H\ F\ I$) are in the right subtree. Figure 5.47(a) is our first approximation to the correct tree.

Moving right in the preorder sequence, we find B as the next root. Since no node precedes B in the inorder sequence, B has an empty left subtree, which means that C is in its right subtree. Figure 5.47(b) is the next approximation. Continuing in this way, we arrive at the binary tree of Figure 5.48(a). By formalizing this argument (see the exercises), we can verify that every binary tree has a unique pair of preorder/inorder sequences.

Let the nodes of an n-node binary tree be numbered from 1 through n. The inorder permutation defined by such a binary tree is the order in which its nodes are visited during an inorder traversal of the tree. A preorder permutation is similarly defined.

As an example, consider the binary tree of Figure 5.48(a) with the node numbering of Figure 5.48(b). Its preorder permutation is $1, 2, \cdots, 9$, and its inorder permutation is $2, 3, 1, 5, 4, 7, 8, 6, 9$.

If the nodes of the tree are numbered such that its preorder permutation is $1, 2, \cdots, n$, then from our earlier discussion it follows that distinct binary trees define distinct inorder permutations. Thus, the number of distinct binary trees is equal to the number of distinct inorder permutations obtainable from binary trees having the preorder permutation, $1, 2, \cdots, n$.

Using the concept of an inorder permutation, we can show that the number of distinct permutations obtainable by passing the numbers 1 through n through a stack and deleting in all possible ways is equal to the number of distinct binary trees with n nodes (see the exercises). If we start with the numbers 1, 2, and 3, then the possible permutations obtainable by a stack are

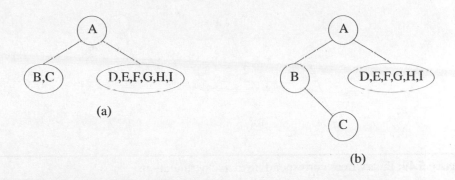

Figure 5.47: Constructing a binary tree from its inorder and preorder sequences

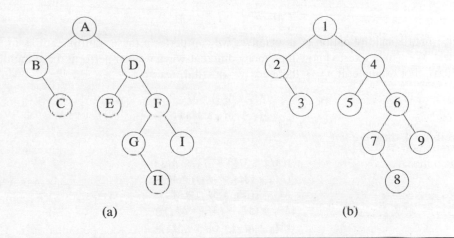

Figure 5.48: Binary tree constructed from its inorder and preorder sequences

$$(1, 2, 3) \ (1, 3, 2) \ (2, 1, 3) \ (2, 3, 1) \ (3, 2, 1)$$

Obtaining (3, 1, 2) is impossible. Each of these five permutations corresponds to one of the five distinct binary trees with three nodes (Figure 5.49).

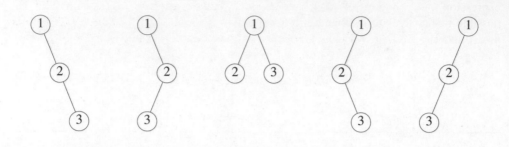

Figure 5.49: Binary trees corresponding to five permutations

5.11.3 Matrix Multiplication

Another problem that surprisingly has a connection with the previous two involves the product of n matrices. Suppose that we wish to compute the product of n matrices:

$$M_1 * M_2 * \cdots * M_n$$

Since matrix multiplication is associative, we can perform these multiplications in any order. We would like to know how many different ways we can perform these multiplications. For example, if $n = 3$, there are two possibilities:

$$(M_1 * M_2) * M_3$$
$$M_1 * (M_2 * M_3)$$

and if $n = 4$, there are five:

$$((M_1 * M_2) * M_3) * M_4$$
$$(M_1 * (M_2 * M_3)) * M_4$$
$$M_1 * ((M_2 * M_3) * M_4)$$
$$(M_1 * (M_2 * (M_3 * M_4)))$$
$$((M_1 * M_2) * (M_3 * M_4))$$

Let b_n be the number of different ways to compute the product of n matrices. Then $b_2 = 1$, $b_3 = 2$, and $b_4 = 5$. Let M_{ij}, $i \leq j$, be the product $M_i * M_{i+1} * \cdots * M_j$. The product we wish to compute is M_{1n}. We may compute M_{1n} by computing any one of the products $M_{1i} * M_{i+1,n}$, $1 \leq i \leq n$. The number of distinct ways to obtain M_{1i} and $M_{i+1,n}$ are b_i and b_{n-i}, respectively. Therefore, letting $b_1 = 1$, we have

$$b_n = \sum_{i=1}^{n-1} b_i\, b_{n-i}, n > 1$$

If we can determine the expression for b_n only in terms of n, then we have a solution to our problem.

Now instead let b_n be the number of distinct binary trees with n nodes. Again an expression for b_n in terms of n is what we want. Then we see that b_n is the sum of all the possible binary trees formed in the following way: a root and two subtrees with b_i and b_{n-i-1} nodes, for $0 \le i < n$ (Figure 5.50). This explanation says that

$$b_n = \sum_{i=0}^{n-1} b_i \, b_{n-i-1} \ , \ n \ge 1 \ , \text{ and } b_0 = 1 \tag{5.3}$$

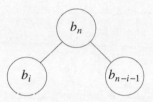

Figure 5.50: Decomposing b_n

This formula and the previous one are essentially the same. Therefore, the number of binary trees with n nodes, the number of permutations of 1 to n obtainable with a stack, and the number of ways to multiply $n + 1$ matrices are all equal.

5.11.4   Number of Distinct Binary Trees

To obtain the number of distinct binary trees with n nodes, we must solve the recurrence of Eq. (5.3). To begin we let

$$B(x) = \sum_{i \ge 0} b_i x^i \tag{5.4}$$

which is the generating function for the number of binary trees. Next observe that by the recurrence relation we get the identity

$$xB^2(x) = B(x) - 1$$

Using the formula to solve quadratics and the fact that $B(0) = b_0 = 1$ (Eq.(5.3)), we get

$$B(x) = \frac{1 - \sqrt{1-4x}}{2x}$$

We can use the binomial theorem to expand $(1 - 4x)^{1/2}$ to obtain

$$B(x) = \frac{1}{2x} \left[1 - \sum_{n \geq 0} \begin{bmatrix} 1/2 \\ n \end{bmatrix} (-4x)^n \right] = \sum_{m \geq 0} \begin{bmatrix} 1/2 \\ m+1 \end{bmatrix} (-1)^m 2^{2m+1} x^m \qquad (5.5)$$

Comparing Eqs. (5.4) and (5.5), we see that b_n, which is the coefficient of x^n in $B(x)$, is

$$\begin{bmatrix} 1/2 \\ n+1 \end{bmatrix} (-1)^n 2^{2n+1}$$

Some simplification yields the more compact form

$$b_n = \frac{1}{n+1} \begin{bmatrix} 2n \\ n \end{bmatrix} \sim O(4^n/n^{3/2})$$

EXERCISES

1. Prove that every binary tree is uniquely defined by its preorder and inorder sequences.

2. Do the inorder and postorder sequences of a binary tree uniquely define the binary tree? Prove your answer.

3. Do the inorder and preorder sequences of a binary tree uniquely define the binary tree? Prove your answer.

4. Do the inorder and level-order sequences of a binary tree uniquely define the binary tree? Prove your answer.

5. Write an algorithm to construct the binary tree with given preorder and inorder sequences.

6. Repeat Exercise 5 with the inorder and postorder sequences.

7. Prove that the number of distinct permutations of $1, 2, \cdots, n$ obtainable by a stack is equal to the number of distinct binary trees with n nodes. (Hint: Use the concept of an inorder permutation of a tree with preorder permutation $1, 2, \cdots, n$).

5.12   REFERENCES AND SELECTED READINGS

For more on trees, see *The Art of Computer Programming: Fundamental Algorithms*, Third Edition, by D. Knuth, Addison-Wesley, Reading, MA, 1998 and "Handbook of data structures and applications," edited by D. Mehta and S. Sahni, Chapman & Hall/CRC, Boca Raton, 2005.

CHAPTER *6*

GRAPHS

6.1 THE GRAPH ABSTRACT DATA TYPE

6.1.1 Introduction

The first recorded evidence of the use of graphs dates back to 1736, when Leonhard Euler used them to solve the now classical Königsberg bridge problem. In the town of Königsberg (now Kaliningrad) the river Pregel (Pregolya) flows around the island Kneiphof and then divides into two. There are, therefore, four land areas that have this river on its borders (see Figure 6.1(a)). These land areas are interconnected by seven bridges labeled $a-g$. The land areas themselves are labeled $A-D$. The Königsberg bridge problem is to determine whether, starting at one land area, it is possible to walk across all the bridges exactly once in returning to the starting land area. One possible walk is

- start from land area B
- walk across bridge a to island A
- take bridge e to area D

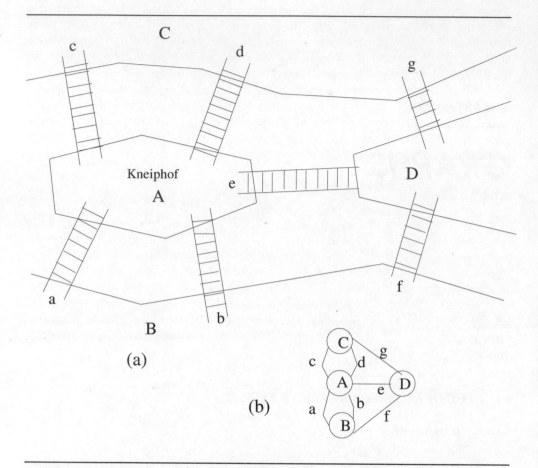

Figure 6.1: (a) Section of the river Pregel in Königsberg; (b) Euler's graph

- take bridge *g* to *C*
- take bridge *d* to *A*
- take bridge *b* to *B*
- take bridge *f* to *D*

This walk does not go across all bridges exactly once, nor does it return to the starting land area *B*. Euler answered the Königsberg bridge problem in the negative: The people of Königsberg will not be able to walk across each bridge exactly once and return to the starting point. He solved the problem by representing the land areas as vertices and the bridges as edges in a graph (actually a multigraph) as in Figure 6.1(b). His solution is elegant and applies to all graphs. Defining the *degree* of a vertex to be the number of edges incident to it, Euler showed that there is a walk starting at any vertex, going through each edge exactly once and terminating at the start vertex iff the degree of each vertex is even. A walk that does this is called *Eulerian*. There is no Eulerian walk for the Königsberg bridge problem, as all four vertices are of odd degree.

Since this first application, graphs have been used in a wide variety of applications. Some of these applications are: analysis of electrical circuits, finding shortest routes, project planning, identification of chemical compounds, statistical mechanics, genetics, cybernetics, linguistics, social sciences, and so on. Indeed, it might well be said that of all mathematical structures, graphs are the most widely used.

6.1.2   Definitions

A graph, G, consists of two sets, V and E. V is a finite, nonempty set of *vertices*. E is a set of pairs of vertices; these pairs are called *edges*. $V(G)$ and $E(G)$ will represent the sets of vertices and edges, respectively, of graph G. We will also write $G = (V,E)$ to represent a graph. In an *undirected graph* the pair of vertices representing any edge is unordered. Thus, the pairs (u,v) and (v,u) represent the same edge. In a *directed graph* each edge is represented by a directed pair $<u,v>$; u is the *tail* and v the *head* of the edge[+]. Therefore, $<v,u>$ and $<u,v>$ represent two different edges. Figure 6.2 shows three graphs: G_1, G_2, and G_3. The graphs G_1 and G_2 are undirected. G_3 is a directed graph.

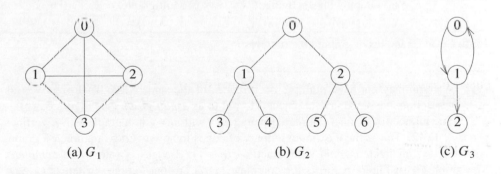

(a) G_1 (b) G_2 (c) G_3

Figure 6.2: Three sample graphs

[+]Often, both the undirected edge (i,j) and the directed edge $<i,j>$ are written as (i,j). Which is meant is deduced from the context. In this book, we refrain from this practice.

The set representation of each of these graphs is

$V(G_1) = \{0,1,2,3\}; \quad E(G_1) = \{(0,1),(0,2),(0,3),(1,2),(1,3),(2,3)\}$
$V(G_2) = \{0,1,2,3,4,5,6\}; \quad E(G_2) = \{(0,1),(0,2),(1,3),(1,4),(2,5),(2,6)\}$
$V(G_3) = \{0,1,2\}; \quad E(G_3) = \{<0,1>,<1,0>,<1,2>\}.$

Notice that the edges of a directed graph are drawn with an arrow from the tail to the head. The graph G_2 is a tree; the graphs G_1 and G_3 are not.

Since we define the edges and vertices of a graph as sets, we impose the following restrictions on graphs:

(1)   A graph may not have an edge from a vertex, v, back to itself. That is, edges of the form (v, v) and $<v, v>$ are not legal. Such edges are known as *self edges* or *self loops*. If we permit self edges, we obtain a data object referred to as a *graph with self edges*. An example is shown in Figure 6.3(a).

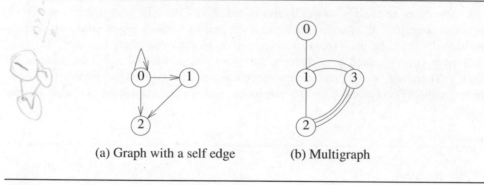

(a) Graph with a self edge   (b) Multigraph

Figure 6.3: Examples of graphlike structures

(2)   A graph may not have multiple occurrences of the same edge. If we remove this restriction, we obtain a data object referred to as a *multigraph* (see Figure 6.3(b)). The number of distinct unordered pairs (u,v) with $u \neq v$ in a graph with n vertices is $n(n-1)/2$. This is the maximum number of edges in any n-vertex, undirected graph. An n-vertex, undirected graph with exactly $n(n-1)/2$ edges is said to be *complete*. The graph G_1 of Figure 6.2(a) is the complete graph on four vertices, whereas G_2 and G_3 are not complete graphs. In the case of a directed graph on n vertices, the maximum number of edges is $n(n-1)$.

If (u,v) is an edge in $E(G)$, then we shall say the vertices u and v are *adjacent* and that the edge (u,v) is *incident* on vertices u and v. The vertices adjacent to vertex 1 in G_2 are 3, 4, and 0. The edges incident on vertex 2 in G_2 are (0,2), (2,5), and (2,6). If $<u,v>$ is a directed edge, then vertex u is *adjacent to* v, and v is *adjacent from* u. The edge $<u,v>$ is incident to u and v. In G_3, the edges incident to vertex 1 are $<0,1>$, $<1,0>$, and $<1,2>$.

A *subgraph* of G is a graph G' such that $V(G') \subseteq V(G)$ and $E(G') \subseteq E(G)$. Figure 6.4 shows some of the subgraphs of G_1 and G_3.

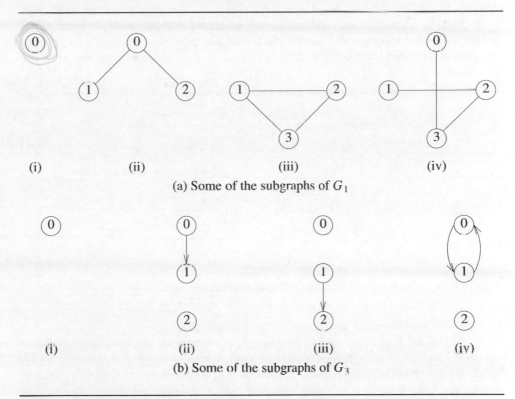

(i)   (ii)   (iii)   (iv)

(a) Some of the subgraphs of G_1

(i)   (ii)   (iii)   (iv)

(b) Some of the subgraphs of G_3

Figure 6.4: Some subgraphs

A *path* from vertex u to vertex v in graph G is a sequence of vertices $u, i_1, i_2, \cdots, i_k, v$ such that $(u, i_1), (i_1, i_2), \cdots, (i_k, v)$ are edges in $E(G)$. If G' is directed, then the path consists of $<u, i_1>, <i_1, i_2>, \cdots, <i_k, v>$ edges in $E(G')$. The *length* of a path is the number of edges on it. A *simple path* is a path in which all vertices except possibly the first and last are distinct. A path such as $(0,1), (1,3), (3,2)$, is also written as $0,1,3,2$. Paths $0,1,3,2$ and $0,1,3,1$ of G_1 are both of length 3. The first is a simple path; the second is not. $0,1,2$ is a simple directed path in G_3. $0,1,2,1$ is not a path in G_3, as the edge $<2,1>$ is not in $E(G_3)$.

A *cycle* is a simple path in which the first and last vertices are the same. $0,1,2,0$ is a cycle in G_1. $0,1,0$ is a cycle in G_3. For the case of directed graphs we normally add the prefix "directed" to the terms cycle and path.

In an undirected graph, G, two vertices u and v are said to be *connected* iff there is a path in G from u to v (since G is undirected, this means there must also be a path from v to u). An undirected graph is said to be connected iff for every pair of distinct vertices u and v in $V(G)$ there is a path from u to v in G. Graphs G_1 and G_2 are connected, whereas G_4 of Figure 6.5 is not. A *connected component* (or simply a component), H, of an undirected graph is a *maximal* connected subgraph. By maximal, we mean that G contains no other subgraph that is both connected and properly contains H. G_4 has two components, H_1 and H_2 (see Figure 6.5).

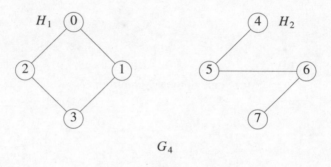

G_4

Figure 6.5: A graph with two connected components

A *tree* is a connected acyclic (i.e., has no cycles) graph.

A directed graph G is said to be *strongly connected* iff for every pair of distinct vertices u and v in $V(G)$, there is a directed path from u to v and also from v to u. The graph G_3 is not strongly connected, as there is no path from vertex 2 to 1. A *strongly connected component* is a maximal subgraph that is strongly connected. G_3 has two strongly connected components (see Figure 6.6).

Figure 6.6: Strongly connected components of G_3

The degree of a vertex is the number of edges incident to that vertex. The degree of vertex 0 in G_1 is 3. If G is a directed graph, we define the *in-degree* of a vertex v to be the number of edges for which v is the head. The *out-degree* is defined to be the number of edges for which v is the tail. Vertex 1 of G_3 has in-degree 1, out-degree 2, and degree 3. If d_i is the degree of vertex i in a graph G with n vertices and e edges, then the number of edges is

$$e = (\sum_{i=0}^{n-1} d_i)/2$$

In the remainder of this chapter, we shall refer to a directed graph as a *digraph*. When we use the term *graph*, we assume that it is an undirected graph. Now that we have defined all the terminology we will need, let us consider the graph as an ADT. The resulting specification is given in ADT 6.1.

ADT *Graph* is
    objects: a nonempty set of vertices and a set of undirected edges, where each edge is a pair of vertices.
    functions:
        for all *graph* $\in$ *Graph*, v, v_1, and $v_2 \in$ *Vertices*

Graph Create()	::=	**return** an empty graph.
Graph InsertVertex(*graph, v*)	::=	**return** a graph with v inserted. v has no incident edges.
Graph InsertEdge(*graph*, v_1, v_2)	::=	**return** a graph with a new edge between v_1 and v_2.
Graph DeleteVertex(*graph, v*)	::=	**return** a graph in which v and all edges incident to it are removed.
Graph DeleteEdge(*graph*, v_1, v_2)	::=	**return** a graph in which the edge (v_1, v_2) is removed. Leave the incident nodes in the graph.
Boolean IsEmpty(*graph*)	::=	**if** (*graph* == empty graph) **return** *TRUE* **else return** *FALSE*.
List Adjacent(*graph, v*)	::=	**return** a list of all vertices that are adjacent to v.

ADT 6.1: Abstract data type *Graph*

The operations in ADT 6.1 are a basic set in that they allow us to create any arbitrary graph and do some elementary tests. In the later sections of this chapter we shall see functions that traverse a graph (depth first or breadth first search) and that determine if a graph has special properties (connected, biconnected, planar).

6.1.3 Graph Representations

Although several representations for graphs are possible, we shall study only the three most commonly used: adjacency matrices, adjacency lists, and adjacency multilists. Once again, the choice of a particular representation will depend upon the application one has in mind and the functions one expects to perform on the graph.

6.1.3.1 Adjacency Matrix

Let $G = (V, E)$ be a graph with n vertices, $n \geq 1$. The adjacency matrix of G is a two-dimensional $n \times n$ array, say a, with the property that $a[i][j] = 1$ iff the edge (i, j) ($<i, j>$ for a directed graph) is in $E(G)$. $a[i][j] = 0$ if there is no such edge in G. The adjacency matrices for the graphs G_1, G_3, and G_4 are shown in Figure 6.7. The adjacency matrix for an undirected graph is symmetric, as the edge (i, j) is in $E(G)$ iff the edge (j, i) is also in $E(G)$. The adjacency matrix for a directed graph may not be symmetric (as is the case for G_3). The space needed to represent a graph using its adjacency matrix is n^2 bits. About half this space can be saved in the case of undirected graphs by storing only the upper or lower triangle of the matrix.

	0	1	2	3	4	5	6	7
0	0	1	1	0	0	0	0	0
1	1	0	0	1	0	0	0	0
2	1	0	0	1	0	0	0	0
3	0	1	1	0	0	0	0	0
4	0	0	0	0	0	1	0	0
5	0	0	0	0	1	0	1	0
6	0	0	0	0	0	1	0	1
7	0	0	0	0	0	0	1	0

	0	1	2	3
0	0	1	1	1
1	1	0	1	1
2	1	1	0	1
3	1	1	1	0

(a) G_1

	0	1	2
0	0	1	0
1	1	0	1
2	0	0	0

(b) G_3

(c) G_4

Figure 6.7: Adjacency matrices

From the adjacency matrix, one may readily determine if there is an edge connecting any two vertices i and j. For an undirected graph the degree of any vertex i is its row sum:

$$\sum_{j=0}^{n-1} a[i][j]$$

For a directed graph the row sum is the out-degree, and the column sum is the in-degree.

Suppose we want to answer a nontrivial question about graphs, such as, How many edges are there in G? or, Is G connected? Adjacency matrices will require at least $O(n^2)$ time, as $n^2 - n$ entries of the matrix (diagonal entries are zero) have to be examined. When graphs are sparse (i.e., most of the terms in the adjacency matrix are zero) one would expect that the former question could be answered in significantly less time, say $O(e + n)$, where e is the number of edges in G, and $e << n^2/2$. Such a speed-up can be made possible through the use of a representation in which only the edges that are in G are explicitly stored. This leads to the next representation for graphs, adjacency lists.

6.1.3.2 Adjacency Lists

In this representation of graphs, the n rows of the adjacency matrix are represented as n chains (though sequential lists could be used just as well). There is one chain for each vertex in G. The nodes in chain i represent the vertices that are adjacent from vertex i. The *data* field of a chain node stores the index of an adjacent vertex. The adjacency lists for G_1, G_3, and G_4 are shown in Figure 6.8. Notice that the vertices in each chain are not required to be ordered. An array *adjLists* is used so that we can access the adjacency list for any vertex in $O(1)$ time. *adjLists*[i] is a pointer to the first node in the adjacency list for vertex i.

For an undirected graph with n vertices and e edges, the linked adjacency lists representation requires an array of size n and $2e$ chain nodes. Each chain node has two fields. In terms of the number of bits of storage needed, the node count should be multiplied by $\log n$ for the array positions and $\log n + \log e$ for the chain nodes, as it takes $O(\log m)$ bits to represent a number of value m. If instead of chains, we use sequential lists, the adjacency lists may be packed into an integer array *node*[$n + 2e + 1$]. In one possible sequential mapping , *node*[i] gives the starting point of the list for vertex i, $0 \le i < n$, and *node*[n] is set to $n + 2e + 1$. The vertices adjacent from vertex i are stored in *node*[i], $\cdots$, *node*[$i + 1$] $- 1$, $0 \le i < n$. Figure 6.9 shows the representation for the graph G_4 of Figure 6.5.

The degree of any vertex in an undirected graph may be determined by just counting the number of nodes in its adjacency list.

For a digraph, the number of list nodes is only e. The out-degree of any vertex may be determined by counting the number of nodes on its adjacency list. Determining the in-degree of a vertex is a little more complex. If there is a need to access repeatedly all vertices adjacent to another vertex, then it may be worth the effort to keep another set

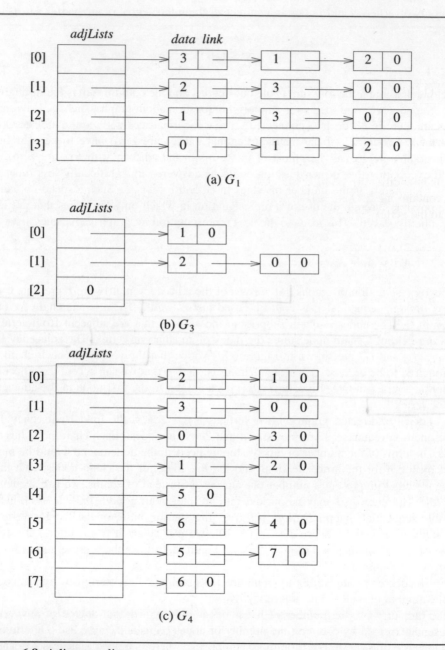

Figure 6.8: Adjacency lists

int *nodes* [*n* + 2*e* + 1];

0	1	2	3	4	5	6	7	8	9	10	11	12	13	14	15	16	17	18	19	20	21	22
9	11	13	15	17	18	20	22	23	2	1	3	0	0	3	1	2	5	6	4	5	7	6

Figure 6.9: Sequential representation of graph G_4

of lists in addition to the adjacency lists. This set of lists, called *inverse adjacency lists*, will contain one list for each vertex. Each list will contain a node for each vertex adjacent to the vertex it represents (see Figure 6.10).

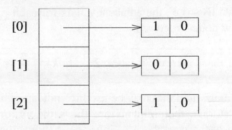

Figure 6.10: Inverse adjacency lists for $\overline{G}_3$ (Figure 6.2(c))

Alternatively, one can adopt a simplified version of the list structure used for sparse matrix representation in Chapter 4. Figure 6.11 shows the resulting structure for the graph G_3 of Figure 6.2(c). The header nodes are stored sequentially. The first two fields in each node give the head and tail of the edge represented by the node, the remaining two fields are links for row and column chains.

6.1.3.3 Adjacency Multilists

In the adjacency-list representation of an undirected graph, each edge (u,v) is represented by two entries, one on the list for u and the other on the list for v. As we shall see, in some situations it is necessary to be able to determine the second entry for a particular edge and mark that edge as having been examined. This can be accomplished easily if the adjacency lists are actually maintained as multilists (i.e., lists in which nodes

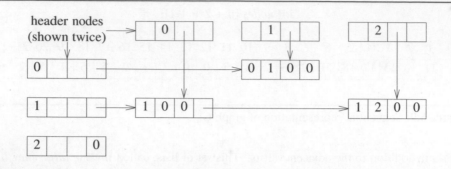

Figure 6.11: Orthogonal list representation for G_3 of Figure 6.2(c)

may be shared among several lists). For each edge there will be exactly one node, but this node will be in two lists (i.e., the adjacency lists for each of the two nodes to which it is incident). The new node structure is

m	$vertex1$	$vertex2$	$link1$	$link2$

where m is a Boolean mark field that may be used to indicate whether or not the edge has been examined. The storage requirements are the same as for normal adjacency lists, except for the addition of the mark bit m. Figure 6.12 shows the adjacency multilists for G_1 of Figure 6.2(a).

6.1.3.4 Weighted Edges

In many applications, the edges of a graph have weights assigned to them. These weights may represent the distance from one vertex to another or the cost of going from one vertex to an adjacent vertex. In these applications, the adjacency matrix entries $a[i][j]$ would keep this information too. When adjacency lists are used, the weight information may be kept in the list nodes by including an additional field, *weight*. A graph with weighted edges is called a *network*.

EXERCISES

1. Does the multigraph of Figure 6.13 have an Eulerian walk? If so, find one.

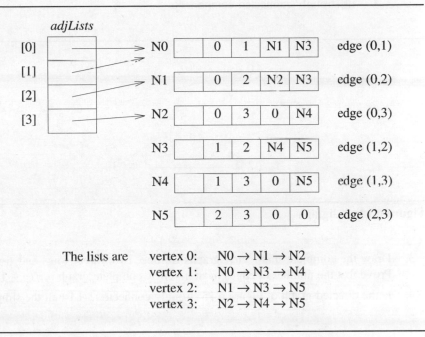

The lists are   vertex 0:   N0 → N1 → N2
                  vertex 1:   N0 → N3 → N4
                  vertex 2:   N1 → N3 → N5
                  vertex 3:   N2 → N4 → N5

Figure 6.12: Adjacency multilists for G_1 of Figure 6.2(a)

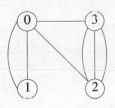

Figure 6.13: A multigraph

2. For the digraph of Figure 6.14 obtain
    (a)   the in-degree and out-degree of each vertex
    (b)   its adjacency-matrix
    (c)   its adjacency-list representation

(d)   its adjacency-multilist representation

(e)   its strongly connected components

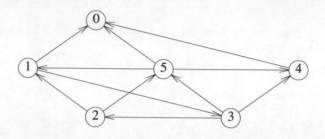

Figure 6.14: A digraph

3. Draw the complete undirected graphs on one, two, three, four, and five vertices. Prove that the number of edges in an n-vertex complete graph is $n(n-1)/2$.

4. Is the directed graph of Figure 6.15 strongly connected? List all the simple paths.

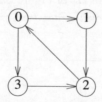

Figure 6.15: A directed graph

5. Obtain the adjacency-matrix, adjacency-list, and adjacency-multilist representations of the graph of Figure 6.15.

6. Show that the sum of the degrees of the vertices of an undirected graph is twice the number of edges.

7. (a)   Let G be a connected, undirected graph on n vertices. Show that G must have at least $n-1$ edges and that all connected, undirected graphs with $n-1$ edges are trees.

    (b)   What is the minimum number of edges in a strongly connected digraph on n

vertices? What form do such digraphs have?

8. For an undirected graph G with n vertices, prove that the following are equivalent:

   (a) G is a tree

   (b) G is connected, but if any edge is removed the resulting graph is not connected

   (c) For any two distinct vertices $u \in V(G)$ and $v \in V(G)$, there is exactly one simple path from u to v

   (d) G contains no cycles and has $n - 1$ edges

9. Write a C function to input the number of vertices and edges in an undirected graph. Next, input the edges one by one and to set up the linked adjacency-list representation of the graph. You may assume that no edge is input twice. What is the run time of your function as a function of the number of vertices and the number of edges?

10. Do the preceding exercise but this time set up the multilist representation.

11. Let G be an undirected, connected graph with at least one vertex of odd degree. Show that G contains no Eulerian walk.

6.2 ELEMENTARY GRAPH OPERATIONS

When we discussed binary trees in Chapter 5, we indicated that tree traversals were among the most frequently used tree operations. Thus, we defined and implemented preorder, inorder, postorder, and level order tree traversals. An analogous situation occurs in the case of graphs. Given an undirected graph, $G = (V, E)$, and a vertex, v, in $V(G)$ we wish to visit all vertices in G that are reachable from v, that is, all vertices that are connected to v. We shall look at two ways of doing this: *depth first search* and *breadth first search*. Depth first search is similar to a preorder tree traversal, while breadth first search resembles a level order tree traversal. In our discussion of depth first search and breadth first search, we shall assume that the linked adjacency list representation for graphs is used. The exercises explore the use of other representations.

6.2.1 Depth First Search

We begin the search by visiting the start vertex, v. In this simple application, visiting consists of printing the node's vertex field. Next, we select an unvisited vertex, w, from v's adjacency list and carry out a depth first search on w. We preserve our current position in v's adjacency list by placing it on a stack. Eventually our search reaches a vertex, u, that has no unvisited vertices on its adjacency list. At this point, we remove a vertex from the stack and continue processing its adjacency list. Previously visited vertices are discarded; unvisited vertices are visited and placed on the stack. The search terminates when the stack is empty. Although this sounds like a complicated function, it is easy to implement recursively. As indicated previously, it is similar to a preorder tree traversal since we visit a vertex and then continue with the next unvisited descendant. The recursive implementation of depth first search is presented in *dfs* (Program 6.1). This function uses a global array, *visited*[*MAX_VERTICES*], that is initialized to *FALSE*. When we visit a vertex, *i*, we change *visited[i]* to *TRUE*. The declarations are:

```
#define FALSE 0
#define TRUE 1
short int visited[MAX_VERTICES];
```

```
void dfs(int v)
{/* depth first search of a graph beginning at v */
   nodePointer w;
   visited[v] = TRUE;
   printf("%5d",v);
   for (w = graph[v]; w; w = w→link)
     if (!visited[w→vertex])
        dfs(w→vertex);
}
```

Program 6.1: Depth first search

Example 6.1: We wish to carry out a depth first search of graph G of Figure 6.16(a). Figure 6.16(b) shows the adjacency lists for this graph. If we initiate this search from vertex v_0, then the vertices of G are visited in the following order: $v_0, v_1, v_3, v_7, v_4, v_5, v_2, v_6$.

By examining Figures 6.16(a) and (b), we can verify that *dfs* (v_0) visits all vertices connected to v_0. This means that all the vertices visited, together with all edges in G incident to these vertices, form a connected component of G. □

Analysis of *dfs*: If we represent G by its adjacency lists, then we can determine the vertices adjacent to v by following a chain of links. Since *dfs* examines each node in the adjacency lists at most once, the time to complete the search is O(e). If we represent G by its adjacency matrix, then determining all vertices adjacent to v requires O(n) time. Since we visit at most n vertices, the total time is O(n^2). □

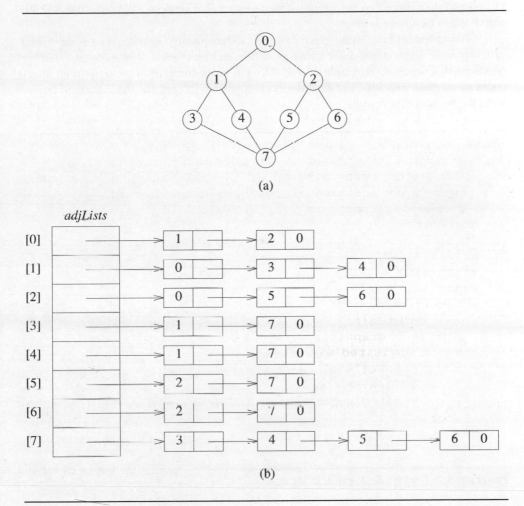

Figure 6.16: Graph *G* and its adjacency lists

6.2.2 Breadth First Search

Breadth first search starts at vertex *v* and marks it as visited. It then visits each of the vertices on *v*'s adjacency list. When we have visited all the vertices on *v*'s adjacency list, we visit all the unvisited vertices that are adjacent to the first vertex on *v*'s adjacency list. To implement this scheme, as we visit each vertex we place the vertex in a queue. When we have exhausted an adjacency list, we remove a vertex from the queue and proceed by examining each of the vertices on its adjacency list. Unvisited vertices are visited and then placed on the queue; visited vertices are ignored. We have finished the search when the queue is empty.

To implement breadth first search, we use a dynamically linked queue as described in Chapter 4. Each queue node contains vertex and link fields. The *addq* and *deleteq* functions of Chapter 4 (Programs 4.7 and 4.8) will work correctly if we replace all references to *element* with **int**. The function *bfs* (Program 6.2) contains the C code to implement the breadth first search.

```
void bfs(int v)
{/* breadth first traversal of a graph, starting at v
    the global array visited is initialized to 0, the queue
    operations are similar to those described in
    Chapter 4, front and rear are global */
  nodePointer w;
  front = rear = NULL; /* initialize queue */
  printf("%5d",v);
  visited[v] = TRUE;
  addq(v);
  while (front) {
    v = deleteq();
    for (w = graph[v]; w; w = w→link)
      if (!visited[w→vertex]) {
        printf("%5d", w→vertex);
        addq(w→vertex);
        visited[w→vertex] = TRUE;
      }
  }
}
```

Program 6.2: Breadth first search of a graph

The queue definition and the function prototypes used by *bfs* are:

```
typedef struct queue *queuePointer;
typedef struct {
        int vertex;
        queuePointer link;
        } queue;
queuePointer front, rear;
void addq(int);
int deleteq();
```

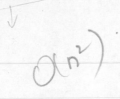

Analysis of *bfs*: Since each vertex is placed on the queue exactly once, the **while** loop is iterated at most n times. For the adjacency list representation, this loop has a total cost of $d_0 + \cdots + d_{n-1} = O(e)$, where $d_i = degree\,(v_i)$. For the adjacency matrix representation, the **while** loop takes $O(n)$ time for each vertex visited. Therefore, the total time is $O(n^2)$. As was true of *dfs*, all vertices visited, together with all edges incident to them, form a connected component of G. $\square$

6.2.3 Connected Components

We can use the two elementary graph searches to create additional, more interesting, graph operations. For illustrative purposes, let us look at the problem of determining whether or not an undirected graph is connected. We can implement this operation by simply calling either *dfs* (0) or *bfs* (0) and then determining if there are any unvisited vertices. For example, the call *dfs* (0) applied to graph G_4 of Figure 6.5 terminates without visiting vertices 4, 5, 6, and 7. Therefore, we can conclude that graph G_4 is not connected. The computing time for this operation is $O(n + e)$ if adjacency lists are used.

A closely related problem is that of listing the connected components of a graph. This is easily accomplished by making repeated calls to either *dfs* (v) or *bfs* (v) where v is an unvisited vertex. The function *connected* (Program 6.3) carries out this operation. Although we have used *dfs*, *bfs* may be used with no change in the time complexity.

```
void connected(void)
{/* determine the connected components of a graph */
int i;
for (i = 0; i < n; i++)
   if(!visited[i]) {
      dfs(i);
      printf("\n");
   }
}
```

Program 6.3: Connected components

Analysis of *connected*: If G is represented by its adjacency lists, then the total time taken by *dfs* is $O(e)$. Since the **for** loop takes $O(n)$ time, the total time needed to generate all the connected components is $O(n + e)$.

If G is represented by its adjacency matrix, then the time needed to determine the connected components is $O(n^2)$. $\square$

6.2.4 Spanning Trees

When graph G is connected, a depth first or breadth first search starting at any vertex visits all the vertices in G. The search implicitly partitions the edges in G into two sets: T (for tree edges) and N (for nontree edges). T is the set of edges used or traversed during the search and N is the set of remaining edges. We can determine the set of tree edges by adding a statement to the **if** clause of either *dfs* or *bfs* that inserts the edge (v, w) into a linked list of edges. (T represents the head of this linked list.) The edges in T form a tree that includes all vertices of G. A *spanning tree* is any tree that consists solely of edges in G and that includes all the vertices in G. Figure 6.17 shows a graph and three of its spanning trees.

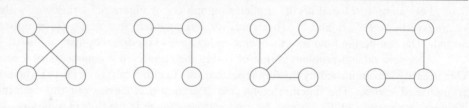

Figure 6.17: A complete graph and three of its spanning trees

As we just indicated, we may use either *dfs* or *bfs* to create a spanning tree. When *dfs* is used, the resulting spanning tree is known as a *depth first spanning tree*. When *bfs* is used, the resulting spanning tree is called a *breadth first spanning tree*. Figure 6.18 shows the spanning trees that result from a depth first and breadth first search starting at vertex v_0 in the graph of Figure 6.16.

Now suppose we add a nontree edge, (v, w), into any spanning tree, T. The result is a cycle that consists of the edge (v, w) and all the edges on the path from w to v in T. For example, if we add the nontree edge $(7, 6)$ to the *dfs* spanning tree of Figure 6.18(a), the resulting cycle is 7, 6, 2, 5, 7. We can use this property of spanning trees to obtain an independent set of circuit equations for an electrical network.

Example 6.2 [*Creation of circuit equations*]: To obtain the circuit equations, we must first obtain a spanning tree for the electrical network. Then we introduce the nontree edges into the spanning tree one at a time. The introduction of each such edge produces a cycle. Next we use Kirchoff's second law on this cycle to obtain a circuit equation. The cycles obtained in this way are independent (we cannot obtain any of these cycles by taking a linear combination of the remaining cycles) since each contains a nontree edge that is not contained in any other cycle. Thus, the circuit equations are also independent. In fact, we can show that the cycles obtained by introducing the nontree edges one at a time into the spanning tree form a cycle basis. This means that we can

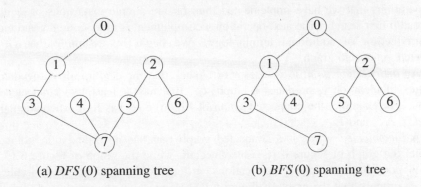

(a) *DFS* (0) spanning tree   (b) *BFS* (0) spanning tree

Figure 6.18: Depth-first and breadth-first spanning trees for graph of Figure 6.16

construct all other cycles in the graph by taking a linear combination of the cycles in the basis. (For further details, see the Harary text cited in the References and Selected Readings.) □

Let us examine a second property of spanning trees. A spanning tree is a *minimal subgraph*, G', of G such that $V(G') = V(G)$ and G' is connected. We define a minimal subgraph as one with the fewest number of edges. Any connected graph with n vertices must have at least $n - 1$ edges, and all connected graphs with $n - 1$ edges are trees. Therefore, we conclude that a spanning tree has $n - 1$ edges. (The exercises explore this property more fully.)

Constructing minimal subgraphs finds frequent application in the design of communication networks. Suppose that the vertices of a graph, G, represent cities and the edges represent communication links between cities. The minimum number of links needed to connect n cities is $n - 1$. Constructing the spanning trees of G gives us all feasible choices. However, we know that the cost of constructing communication links between cities is rarely the same. Therefore, in practical applications, we assign weights to the edges. These weights might represent the cost of constructing the communication link or the length of the link. Given such a weighted graph, we would like to select the spanning tree that represents either the lowest total cost or the lowest overall length. We assume that the cost of a spanning tree is the sum of the costs of the edges of that tree. Algorithms to obtain minimum cost spanning trees are studied in a later section.

6.2.5 Biconnected Components

The operations that we have implemented thus far are simple extensions of depth first and breadth first search. The next operation we implement is more complex and requires the introduction of additional terminology. We begin by assuming that G is an undirected connected graph.

An *articulation point* is a vertex v of G such that the deletion of v, together with all edges incident on v, produces a graph, G', that has at least two connected components. For example, the connected graph of Figure 6.19 has four articulation points, vertices 1, 3, 5, and 7.

A *biconnected graph* is a connected graph that has no articulation points. For example, the graph of Figure 6.16 is biconnected, while the graph of Figure 6.19 obviously is not. In many graph applications, articulation points are undesirable. For instance, suppose that the graph of Figure 6.19(a) represents a communication network. In such graphs, the vertices represent communication stations and the edges represent communication links. Now suppose that one of the stations that is an articulation point fails. The result is a loss of communication not just to and from that single station, but also between certain other pairs of stations.

A *biconnected component* of a connected undirected graph is a *maximal biconnected subgraph, H,* of *G*. By maximal, we mean that G contains no other subgraph that is both biconnected and properly contains H. For example, the graph of Figure 6.19(a) contains the six biconnected components shown in Figure 6.19(b). The biconnected graph of Figure 6.16, however, contains just one biconnected component: the whole graph. It is easy to verify that two biconnected components of the same graph have no more than one vertex in common. This means that no edge can be in two or more biconnected components of a graph. Hence, the biconnected components of G partition the edges of G.

We can find the biconnected components of a connected undirected graph, G, by using any depth first spanning tree of G. For example, the function call *dfs* (3) applied to the graph of Figure 6.19(a) produces the spanning tree of Figure 6.20(a). We have redrawn the tree in Figure 6.20(b) to better reveal its tree structure. The numbers outside the vertices in either figure give the sequence in which the vertices are visited during the depth first search. We call this number the *depth first number*, or *dfn*, of the vertex. For example, $dfn(3) = 0$, $dfn(0) = 4$, and $dfn(9) = 8$. Notice that vertex 3, which is an ancestor of both vertices 0 and 9, has a lower *dfn* than either of these vertices. Generally, if u and v are two vertices, and u is an ancestor of v in the depth first spanning tree, then $dfn(u) < dfn(v)$.

The broken lines in Figure 6.20(b) represent nontree edges. A nontree edge (u, v) is a *back edge iff* either u is an ancestor of v or v is an ancestor of u. From the definition of depth first search, it follows that all nontree edges are back edges. This means that the root of a depth first spanning tree is an articulation point *iff* it has at least two children. In addition, any other vertex u is an articulation point *iff* it has at least one child w such

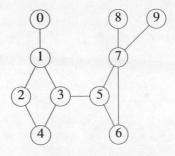

(a) Connected graph

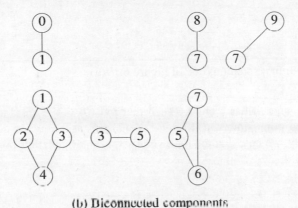

(b) Biconnected components

Figure 6.19: A connected graph and its biconnected components

that we cannot reach an ancestor of u using a path that consists of only w, descendants of w, and a single back edge. These observations lead us to define a value, *low*, for each vertex of G such that $low(u)$ is the lowest depth first number that we can reach from u using a path of descendants followed by at most one back edge:

$$low(u) = \min\{dfn(u), \min\{low(w) \mid w \text{ is a child of } u\},$$
$$\min\{dfn(w) \mid (u, w) \text{ is a back edge}\}\}$$

Therefore, we can say that u is an articulation point *iff* u is either the root of the spanning tree and has two or more children, or u is not the root and u has a child w such that $low(w) \geq dfn(u)$. Figure 6.21 shows the *dfn* and low values for each vertex of the spanning tree of Figure 6.20(b). From this table we can conclude that vertex 1 is an

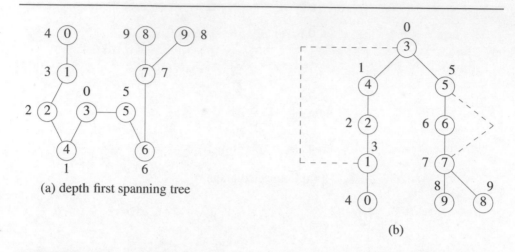

(a) depth first spanning tree

(b)

Figure 6.20: Depth first spanning tree of Figure 6.19(a)

articulation point since it has a child 0 such that $low(0) = 4 \geq dfn(1) = 3$. Vertex 7 is also an articulation point since $low(8) = 9 \geq dfn(7) = 7$, as is vertex 5 since $low(6) = 5 \geq dfn(5) = 5$. Finally, we note that the root, vertex 3, is an articulation point because it has more than one child.

Vertex	0	1	2	3	4	5	6	7	8	9
dfn	4	3	2	0	1	5	6	7	9	8
low	4	3	0	0	0	5	5	7	9	8

Figure 6.21: *dfn* and *low* values for *dfs* spanning tree with *root* = 3

We can easily modify *dfs* to compute *dfn* and *low* for each vertex of a connected undirected graph. The result is *dfnlow* (Program 6.4).

We invoke the function with the call *dfnlow(x, −1)*, where *x* is the starting vertex for the depth first search. The function uses a *MIN2* macro that returns the smaller of its two parameters. The results are returned as two global variables, *dfn* and *low*. We also use a global variable, *num*, to increment *dfn* and *low*. The function *init* (Program 6.5) contains the code to correctly initialize *dfn*, *low*, and *num*. The global declarations are:

```
void dfnlow(int u, int v)
{/* compute dfn and low while performing a dfs search
    beginning at vertex u, v is the parent of u (if any) */
  nodePointer ptr;
  int w;
  dfn[u] = low[u] = num++;
  for (ptr = graph[u]; ptr; ptr = ptr→link) {
    w = ptr→vertex;
    if (dfn[w] < 0) { /* w is an unvisited vertex */
      dfnlow(w,u);
      low[u] = MIN2(low[u],low[w]);
    }
    else if (w != v)
      low[u] = MIN2(low[u],dfn[w]);
  }
}
```

Program 6.4: Determining *dfn* and *low*

```
#define MIN2(x,y) ((x) < (y) ? (x) : (y))
short int dfn[MAX_VERTICES];
short int low[MAX_VERTICES];
int num;
```

```
void init(void)
{
  int i;
  for (i = 0; i < n; i++) {
    visited[i] = FALSE;
    dfn[i] = low[i] = -1;
  }
  num = 0;
}
```

Program 6.5: Initialization of *dfn* and *low*

We can partition the edges of the connected graph into their biconnected components by adding some code to *dfnlow*. We know that *low[w]* has been computed following the return from the function call *dfnlow* (*w*, *u*). If *low* [*w*] ≥ *dfn* [*u*], then we have identified a new biconnected component. We can output all edges in a biconnected component if we use a stack to save the edges when we first encounter them. The function *bicon* (Program 6.6) contains the code. The same initialization function (Program 6.5) is used. The function call is *bicon* (*x*, −1), where *x* is the root of the spanning tree. Note that the parameters for the stack operations *push* and *pop* are slightly different from those used in Chapter 3.

```
void bicon(int u, int v)
{/* compute dfn and low, and output the edges of G by their
   biconnected components, v is the parent (if any) of u
   in the resulting spanning tree. It is assumed that all
   entries of dfn[] have been initialized to -1, num is
   initially to 0, and the stack is initially empty */
nodePointer ptr;
int w,x,y;
dfn[u] = low[u] = num++;
for (ptr = graph[u]; ptr; ptr = ptr→link) {
   w = ptr→vertex;
   if (v != w && dfn[w] < dfn[u])
      push(u,w); /* add edge to stack */
      if (dfn[w] <0) { /* w has not been visited */
         bicon(w,u);
         low[u] = MIN2(low[u],low[w]);
         if (low[w] >= dfn[u]) {
            printf("New biconnected component: ");
            do { /* delete edge from stack */
               pop(&x, &y);
               printf(" <%d,%d>",x,y);
            } while (!((x == u) && (y == w)));
            printf("\n");
         }
      }
      else if (w != v) low[u] = MIN2(low[u],dfn[w]);
   }
}
```

Program 6.6: Biconnected components of a graph

Analysis of *bicon*: The function *bicon* assumes that the connected graph has at least two vertices. Technically, a graph with one vertex and no edges is biconnected, but, our implementation does not handle this special case. The complexity of *bicon* is $O(n + e)$. We leave the proof of its correctness as an exercise. □

EXERCISES

1. Rewrite *dfs* so that it uses an adjacency matrix representation of graphs.

2. Rewrite *bfs* so that it uses an adjacency matrix representation.

3. Let G be a connected undirected graph. Show that no edge of G can be in two or more biconnected components of G. Can a vertex of G be in more than one biconnected component?

4. Let G be a connected graph and let T be any of its depth first spanning trees. Show that every edge of G that is not in T is a back edge relative to T.

5. Write the stack operations necessary to fully implement the *bicon* function. Use a dynamically linked representation for the stack.

6. Prove that function *bicon* correctly partitions the edges of a connected graph into the biconnected components of the graph.

7. A *bipartite graph*, $G = (V, E)$, is an undirected graph whose vertices can be partitioned into two disjoint sets V_1 and $V_2 = V - V_1$ with the properties:

   - no two vertices in V_1 are adjacent in G
   - no two vertices in V_2 are adjacent in G

   The graph G_4 of Figure 6.5 is bipartite. A possible partitioning of V is $V_1 = \{0, 3, 4, 6\}$ and $V_2 = \{1, 2, 5, 7\}$. Write a function to determine whether a graph is bipartite. If the graph is bipartite your function should obtain a partitioning of the vertices into two disjoint sets, V_1 and V_2, satisfying the two properties listed. Show that if G is represented by its adjacency lists, then this function has a computing time of $O(n + e)$, where $n = |V(G)|$ and $e = |E(G)|$ ($|\ |$ is the cardinality of the set, that is, the number of elements in it).

8. Show that every tree is a bipartite graph.

9. Prove that a graph is bipartite *iff* it contains no cycles of odd length.

10. Apply depth first and breadth first searches to the complete graph on four vertices. List the vertices in the order that they are visited.

11. Show how to modify *dfs* as it is used in *connected* to produce a list of all newly visited vertices.

12. Prove that when *dfs* is applied to a connected graph the edges of T form a tree.

13. Prove that when *bfs* is applied to a connected graph the edges of T form a tree.

14. An edge, (u, v), of a connected graph, G, is a *bridge iff* its deletion from G produces a graph that is no longer connected. In the graph of Figure 6.19, the edges $(0, 1)$, $(3, 5)$, $(7, 8)$, and $(7, 9)$ are bridges. Write a function that finds the bridges in a graph. Your function should have a time complexity of $O(n + e)$. (Hint: use *bicon* as a starting point.)

15. Using a complete graph with n vertices, show that the number of spanning trees is at least $2^{n-1} - 1$.

6.3 MINIMUM COST SPANNING TREES

The *cost* of a spanning tree of a weighted undirected graph is the sum of the costs (weights) of the edges in the spanning tree. A *minimum cost spanning tree* is a spanning tree of least cost. Three different algorithms can be used to obtain a minimum cost spanning tree of a connected undirected graph. All three use an algorithm design strategy called the *greedy method*. We shall refer to the three algorithms as Kruskal's, Prim's, and Sollin's algorithms, respectively.

In the greedy method, we construct an optimal solution in stages. At each stage, we make a decision that is the best decision (using some criterion) at this time. Since we cannot change this decision later, we make sure that the decision will result in a feasible solution. The greedy method can be applied to a wide variety of programming problems. Typically, the selection of an item at each stage is based on either a least cost or a highest profit criterion. A feasible solution is one which works within the constraints specified by the problem.

For spanning trees, we use a least cost criterion. Our solution must satisfy the following constraints:

(1) we must use only edges within the graph

(2) we must use exactly $n - 1$ edges

(3) we may not use edges that would produce a cycle.

6.3.1 Kruskal's Algorithm

Kruskal's algorithm builds a minimum cost spanning tree T by adding edges to T one at a time. The algorithm selects the edges for inclusion in T in nondecreasing order of their cost. An edge is added to T if it does not form a cycle with the edges that are already in T. Since G is connected and has $n > 0$ vertices, exactly $n - 1$ edges will be selected for inclusion in T.

Example 6.3: We will construct a minimum cost spanning tree of the graph of Figure 6.22(a). Figure 6.23 shows the order in which the edges are considered for inclusion, as well as the result and the changes (if any) in the spanning tree. For example, edge (0, 5) is the first considered for inclusion. Since it obviously cannot create a cycle, it is added to the tree. The result is the tree of Figure 6.22(c). Similarly, edge (2, 3) is considered next. It is also added to the tree, and the result is shown in Figure 6.22(d). This process continues until the spanning tree has $n-1$ edges (Figure 6.22(h)). The cost of the spanning tree is 99. □

Program 6.7 presents a formal description of Kruskal's algorithm. (We leave writing the C function as an exercise.) We assume that initially E is the set of all edges in G. To implement Kruskal's algorithm, we must be able to determine an edge with minimum cost and delete that edge. We can handle both of these operations efficiently if we maintain the edges in E as a sorted sequential list. As we shall see in Chapter 7, we can sort the edges in E in $O(e \log e)$ time. Actually, it is not necessary to sort the edges in E as long as we are able to find the next least cost edge quickly. Obviously a min heap is ideally suited for this task since we can determine and delete the next least cost edge in $O(\log e)$ time. Construction of the heap itself requires $O(e)$ time.

To check that the new edge, (v, w), does not form a cycle in T and to add such an edge to T, we may use the union-find operations discussed in Section 5.9. This means that we view each connected component in T as a set containing the vertices in that component. Initially, T is empty and each vertex of G is in a different set (see Figure 6.22(b)). Before we add an edge, (v, w), we use the find operation to determine if v and w are in the same set. If they are, the two vertices are already connected and adding the edge (v, w) would cause a cycle. For example, when we consider the edge (3, 2), the sets would be $\{0\}$, $\{1, 2, 3\}$, $\{5\}$, $\{6\}$. Since vertices 3 and 2 are already in the same set, the edge (3, 2) is rejected. The next edge examined is (1, 5). Since vertices 1 and 5 are in different sets, the edge is accepted. This edge connects the two components $\{1, 2, 3\}$ and $\{5\}$. Therefore, we perform a union on these sets to obtain the set $\{1, 2, 3, 5\}$.

Since the union-find operations require less time than choosing and deleting an edge (lines 3 and 4), the latter operations determine the total computing time of Kruskal's algorithm. Thus, the total computing time is $O(e \log e)$. Theorem 6.1 proves that Program 6.7 produces a minimum spanning tree of G.

Theorem 6.1: Let G be an undirected connected graph. Kruskal's algorithm generates a minimum cost spanning tree.

Proof: We shall show that:

(a) Kruskal's method produces a spanning tree whenever a spanning tree exists.

(b) The spanning tree generated is of minimum cost.

For (a), we note that Kruskal's algorithm only discards edges that produce cycles. We know that the deletion of a single edge from a cycle in a connected graph produces a

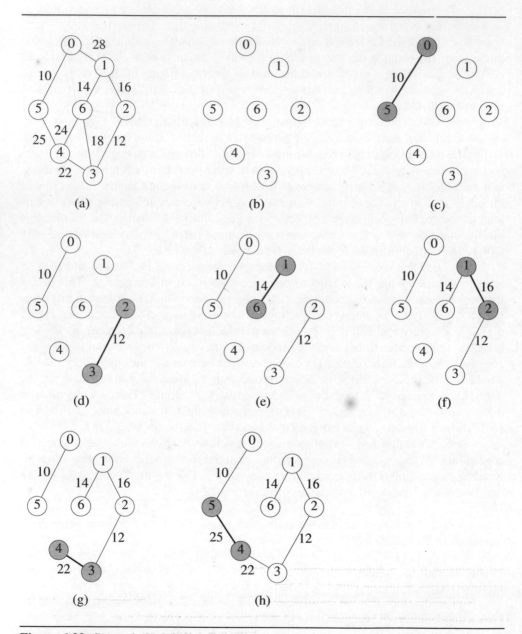

Figure 6.22: Stages in Kruskal's algorithm

Edge	Weight	Result	Figure
----	---	initial	Figure 6.22(b)
(0,5)	10	added to tree	Figure 6.22(c)
(2,3)	12	added	Figure 6.22(d)
(1,6)	14	added	Figure 6.22(e)
(1,2)	16	added	Figure 6.22(f)
(3,6)	18	discarded	
(3,4)	22	added	Figure 6.22(g)
(4,6)	24	discarded	
(4,5)	25	added	Figure 6.22(h)
(0,1)	28	not considered	

Figure 6.23: Summary of Kruskal's algorithm applied to Figure 6.22(a)

```
T = {};
while (T contains less than n-1 edges && E is not empty) {
    choose a least cost edge (v,w) from E;
    delete (v,w) from E;
    if ((v,w) does not create a cycle in T)
        add (v,w) to T;
    else
        discard (v,w);
}
if (T contains fewer than n-1 edges)
    printf("No spanning tree\n");
```

Program 6.7: Kruskal's algorithm

graph that is also connected. Therefore, if G is initially connected, the set of edges in T and E always form a connected graph. Consequently, if G is initially connected, the algorithm cannot terminate with $E = \{\}$ and $|T| < n - 1$.

Now let us show that the constructed spanning tree, T, is of minimum cost. Since G has a finite number of spanning trees, it must have at least one that is of minimum cost. Let U be such a tree. Both T and U have exactly $n - 1$ edges. If $T = U$, then T is of minimum cost and we have nothing to prove. So, assume that $T \neq U$. Let k, $k > 0$, be the number of edges in T that are not in U (k is also the number of edges in U that are not in

T).

We shall show that T and U have the same cost by transforming U into T. This transformation is done in k steps. At each step, the number of edges in T that are not in U is reduced by exactly 1. Furthermore, the cost of U is not changed as a result of the transformation. As a result, U after k transformation steps has the same cost as the initial U and contains exactly those edges that are in T. This implies that T is of minimum cost.

For each transformation step, we add one edge, e, from T to U and remove one edge, f, from U. We select the edges e and f in the following way:

(1) Let e be the least cost edge in T that is not in U. Such an edge must exist because $k > 0$.

(2) When we add e to U, we create a unique cycle. Let f be any edge on this cycle that is not in T. We know that at least one of the edges on this cycle is not in T because T contains no cycles.

Given the way e and f are selected, it follows that $V = U + \{e\} - \{f\}$ is a spanning tree and that T has exactly $k - 1$ edges that are not in V. We need to show that the cost of V is the same as the cost of U. Clearly, the cost of V is the cost of U plus the cost of the edge e minus the cost of the edge f. The cost of e cannot be less than the cost of f since this would mean that the spanning tree V has a lower cost than the tree U. This is impossible. If e has a higher cost than f, then f is considered before e by Kruskal's algorithm. Since it is not in T, Kruskal's algorithm must have discarded this edge at this time. Therefore, f together with the edges in T having a cost less than or equal to the cost of f must form a cycle. By the choice of e, all these edges are also in U. Thus, U must contain a cycle. However, since U is a spanning tree it cannot contain a cycle. So the assumption that e is of higher cost than f leads to a contradiction. This means that e and f must have the same cost. Hence, V has the same cost as U. □

6.3.2 Prim's Algorithm

Prim's algorithm, like Kruskal's, constructs the minimum cost spanning tree one edge at a time. However, at each stage of the algorithm, the set of selected edges forms a tree. By contrast, the set of selected edges in Kruskal's algorithm forms a forest at each stage. Prim's algorithm begins with a tree, T, that contains a single vertex. This may be any of the vertices in the original graph. Next, we add a least cost edge (u, v) to T such that $T \cup \{(u, v)\}$ is also a tree. We repeat this edge addition step until T contains $n - 1$ edges. To make sure that the added edge does not form a cycle, at each step we choose the edge (u, v) such that exactly one of u or v is in T. Program 6.8 contains a formal description of Prim's algorithm. T is the set of tree edges, and TV is the set of tree vertices, that is, vertices that are currently in the tree. Figure 6.24 shows the progress of Prim's algorithm on the graph of Figure 6.22(a).

```
T = {};
TV = {0}; /* start with vertex 0 and no edges */
while (T contains fewer than n-1 edges) {
   let (u, v) be a least cost edge such that u ∈ TV and
   v ∉ TV;
   if (there is no such edge)
      break;
   add v to TV;
   add (u, v) to T;
}
if (T contains fewer than n-1 edges)
   printf("No spanning tree\n");
```

Program 6.8: Prim's algorithm

To implement Prim's algorithm, we assume that each vertex v that is not in TV has a companion vertex, $near(v)$, such that $near(v) \in TV$ and $cost(near(v), v)$ is minimum over all such choices for $near(v)$. (We assume that $cost(v, w) = \infty$ if $(v, w) \notin E$). At each stage we select v so that $cost(near(v), v)$ is minimum and $v \notin TV$. Using this strategy we can implement Prim's algorithm in $O(n^2)$, where n is the number of vertices in G. Asymptotically faster implementations are also possible. One of these results from the use of Fibonacci heaps which we examine in Chapter 9.

6.3.3   Sollin's Algorithm

Unlike Kruskal's and Prim's algorithms, Sollin's algorithm selects several edges for inclusion in T at each stage. At the start of a stage, the selected edges, together with all n graph vertices, form a spanning forest. During a stage we select one edge for each tree in the forest. This edge is a minimum cost edge that has exactly one vertex in the tree. Since two trees in the forest could select the same edge, we need to eliminate multiple copies of edges. At the start of the first stage the set of selected edges is empty. The algorithm terminates when there is only one tree at the end of a stage or no edges remain for selection.

Figure 6.25 shows Sollin's algorithm applied to the graph of Figure 6.22(a). The initial configuration of zero selected edges is the same as that shown in Figure 6.22(b). Each tree in this forest is a a single vertex. At the next stage, we select edges for each of the vertices. The edges selected are (0, 5), (1, 6), (2, 3), (3, 2), (4, 3), (5, 0), (6, 1). After eliminating the duplicate edges, we are left with edges (0, 5), (1, 6), (2, 3), and (4, 3). We add these edges to the set of selected edges, thereby producing the forest of Figure

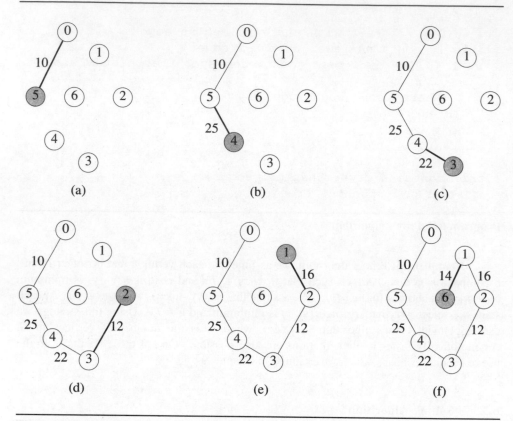

Figure 6.24: Stages in Prim's algorithm

6.25(a). In the next stage, the tree with vertex set {0, 5} selects edge (5, 4), and the two remaining trees select edge (1, 2). After these two edges are added, the spanning tree is complete, as shown in Figure 6.25(b). We leave the development of Sollin's algorithm into a C function and its correctness proof as exercises.

EXERCISES

1. Prove that Prim's algorithm finds a minimum cost spanning tree for every undirected connected graph.

2. Refine Prim's algorithm (Program 6.8) into a C function that finds a minimum cost spanning tree. The complexity of your function should be $O(n^2)$, where n is the number of vertices in the graph. Show that this is the case.

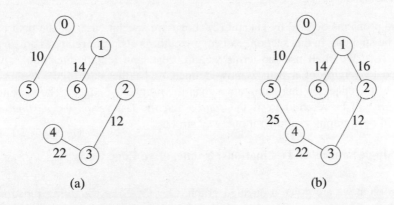

Figure 6.25: Stages in Sollin's algorithm

3. Prove that Sollin's algorithm finds a minimum cost spanning tree for every connected undirected graph.

4. What is the maximum number of stages in Sollin's algorithm? Give this as a function of the number of vertices, n, in the graph.

5. Write a C function that finds a minimum cost spanning tree using Sollin's algorithm. What is the complexity of your function?

6. Write a C function that finds a minimum cost spanning tree using Kruskal's algorithm. You may use the *union* and *find* functions from Chapter 5 and the *sort* function from Chapter 1 or the min heap functions from Chapter 5.

7. Show that if T is a spanning tree for an undirected graph G, then the addition of an edge $e, e \notin E(T)$ and $e \in E(G)$, to T creates a unique cycle.

6.4 SHORTEST PATHS AND TRANSITIVE CLOSURE

MapQuest, Google Maps, Yahoo! Maps, and MapNation are a few of the many Web systems that find a path between any two specified locations in the country. Path finding systemes generally use a graph to represent the highway system of a state or a country. In this graph, the vertices represent cities and the edges represent sections of the highway. Each edge has a weight representing the distance between the two cities connected by the edge. Alternatively, the weight could be an estimate of the time it takes to travel between the two cities. A motorist wishing to drive from city A to city B would be interested in answers to the following questions:

(1)   Is there a path from A to B?

(2)   If there is more than one path from A to B, which path is the shortest?

The problems defined by (1) and (2) above are special cases of the path problems we shall be studying in this section. An edge weight is also referred to as an edge length or edge cost. We shall use the terms weight, cost, and length interchangeably. The length (cost, weight) of a path is now defined to be the sum of the lengths (costs, weights) of the edges on that path, rather than the number of edges. The starting vertex of the path will be referred to as the *source* and the last vertex the *destination*. The graphs will be digraphs to allow for one-way streets.

6.4.1   Single Source/All Destinations: Nonnegative Edge Costs

In this problem we are given a directed graph, $G = (V, E)$, a weighting function, $w(e)$, $w(e) > 0$, for the edges of G, and a source vertex, v_0. We wish to determine a shortest path from v_0 to each of the remaining vertices of G. As an example, consider the graph of Figure 6.26(a). If v_0 is the source vertex, then the shortest path from v_0 to v_1 is v_0, v_2, v_3, v_1. The length of this path is $10 + 15 + 20 = 45$. Although there are three edges on this path, it is shorter than the path $v_0 v_1$, which has a length of 50. Figure 6.26(b) lists the shortest paths from v_0 to v_1, v_2, v_3, and v_4 in nondecreasing order of path length. There is no path from v_0 to v_5.

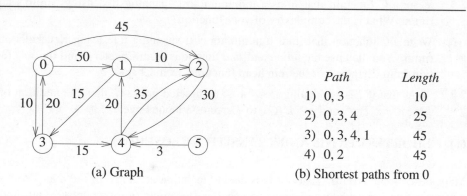

Path	Length
1) 0, 3	10
2) 0, 3, 4	25
3) 0, 3, 4, 1	45
4) 0, 2	45

(a) Graph   (b) Shortest paths from 0

Figure 6.26: Graph and shortest paths from vertex 0 to all destinations

We may use a greedy algorithm to generate the shortest paths in the order indicated in Figure 6.26(b). Let S denote the set of vertices, including v_0, whose shortest paths have been found. For w not in S, let *distance*[w] be the length of the shortest path starting from v_0, going through vertices only in S, and ending in w. Generating the paths in nondecreasing order of length leads to the following observations:

(1)   If the next shortest path is to vertex u, then the path from v_0 to u goes through only those vertices that are in S. To prove this we must show that all intermediate vertices on the shortest path from v_0 to u are already in S. Assume that there is a vertex w on this path that is not in S. Then, the path from v_0 to u also contains a path from v_0 to w which has a length that is less than the length of the path from v_0 to u. Since we assume that the shortest paths are generated in nondecreasing order of path length, we must have previously generated the path from v_0 to w. This is obviously a contradiction. Therefore, there cannot be any intermediate vertex that is not in S.

(2)   Vertex u is chosen so that it has the minimum distance, $distance[u]$, among all the vertices not in S. This follows from the definition of $distance$ and observation (1). If there are several vertices not in S with the same distance, then we may select any one of them.

(3)   Once we have selected u and generated the shortest path from v_0 to u, u becomes a member of S. Adding u to S can change the distance of shortest paths starting at v_0, going through vertices only in S, and ending at a vertex, w, that is not currently in S. If the distance changes, we have found a shorter such path from v_0 to w. This path goes through u. The intermediate vertices on this path are in S and its subpath from u to w can be chosen so as to have no intermediate vertices. The length of the shorter path is $distance[u] + length(<u, w>)$.

We attribute these observations, along with the algorithm to determine the shortest paths from v_0 to all other vertices in G to Edsger Dijkstra. To implement Dijkstra's algorithm, we assume that the n vertices are numbered from 0 to $n - 1$. We maintain the set S as an array, $found$, with $found[i] = FALSE$ if vertex i is not in S and $found[i] = TRUE$ if vertex i is in S. We represent the graph by its cost adjacency matrix, with $cost[i][j]$ being the weight of edge $<i, j>$. If the edge $<i, j>$ is not in G, we set $cost[i][j]$ to some large number. The choice of this number is arbitrary, although we make two stipulations regarding its value:

(1)   The number must be larger than any of the values in the cost matrix.

(2)   The number must be chosen so that the statement $distance[u] + cost[u][w]$ does not produce an overflow into the sign bit.

Restriction (2) makes INT_MAX (defined in $<limits.h>$) a poor choice for nonexistent edges. For $i = j$, we may set $cost[i][j]$ to any nonnegative number without affecting the outcome. For the digraph of Figure 6.26(a), we may set the cost of a nonexistent edge with $i \neq j$ to 1000, for example. The function $shortestPath$ (Program 6.9) contains our implementation of Dijkstra's algorithm. This function uses $choose$ (Program 6.10) to return a vertex, u, such that u has the minimum distance from the start vertex, v.

```
void shortestPath(int v, int cost[][MAX_VERTICES],
                  int distance[], int n, short int found[])
{/* distance[i] represents the shortest path from vertex v
   to i, found[i] is 0 if the shortest path from i
   has not been found and a 1 if it has, cost is the
   adjacency matrix */
   int i,u,w;
   for (i = 0; i < n; i++) {
     found[i] = FALSE;
     distance[i] = cost[v][i];
   }
   found[v] = TRUE;
   distance[v] = 0;
   for (i = 0; i < n-2; i++) {
     u = choose(distance,n,found);
     found[u] = TRUE;
     for (w = 0; w < n; w++)
       if (!found[w])
          if (distance[u] + cost[u][w] < distance[w])
             distance[w] = distance[u] + cost[u][w];
   }
}
```

Program 6.9: Single source shortest paths

Analysis of *shortestpath*: The time taken by the algorithm on a graph with n vertices is $O(n^2)$. To see this, note that the first **for** loop takes $O(n)$ time. The second **for** loop is executed $n - 2$ times. Each execution of this loop requires $O(n)$ time to select the next vertex and also to update *dist*. So the total time for this loop is $O(n^2)$. Any shortest path algorithm must examine each edge in the graph at least once since any of the edges could be in a shortest path. Hence, the minimum possible time for such an algorithm is $O(e)$. Since we represented the graph as a cost adjacency matrix, it takes $O(n^2)$ time just to determine the edges that are in G. Therefore, any shortest path algorithm using this representation has a time complexity of $O(n^2)$. The exercises explore several variations that speed up the algorithm, but the asymptotic time complexity remains $O(n^2)$. For the case of graphs with few edges, the use of Fibonacci heaps together with an adjacency list representation produces a more efficient implementation of the greedy algorithm for the single-source all-destinations problem. We discuss this in Chapter 9. □

Example 6.4: Consider the eight-vertex digraph of Figure 6.27(a) with length-

```
int choose(int distance[], int n, short int found[])
{/* find the smallest distance not yet checked */
   int i, min, minpos;
   min = INT_MAX;
   minpos = -1;
   for (i = 0; i < n; i++)
      if (distance[i] < min && !found[i]) {
         min = distance[i];
         minpos = i;
      }
   return minpos;
}
```

Program 6.10: Choosing the least cost edge

adjacency matrix as in Figure 6.27(b). Suppose that the source vertex is Boston. The values of *dist* and the vertex *u* selected in each iteration of the outer **for** loop of Program 6.9 are shown in Figure 6.28. We use ∞ to denote the value *LARGE*. Note that the algorithm terminates after only 6 iterations of the **for** loop. By the definition of *dist*, the distance of the last vertex, in this case Los Angeles, is correct, as the shortest path from Boston to Los Angeles can go through only the remaining six vertices. □

6.4.2 Single Source/All Destinations: General Weights

We now consider the general case when some or all of the edges of the directed graph *G* may have negative length. To see that function *shortestpath* (Program 6.9) does not necessarily give the correct results on such graphs, consider the graph of Figure 6.29. Let $v - 0$ be the source vertex. Since $n = 3$, the loop of lines 7 to 14 is iterated just once; $u = 2$ in line 8, and no changes are made to *dist*. The function terminates with *dist* [1] = 7 and *dist* [2] = 5. The shortest path from 0 to 2 is 0, 1, 2. This path has length 2, which is less than the computed value of *dist* [2].

When negative edge lengths are permitted, we require that the graph have no cycles of negative length. This is necessary so as to ensure that shortest paths consist of a finite number of edges. For example, consider the graph of Figure 6.30. The length of the shortest path from vertex 0 to vertex 2 is $-\infty$, as the length of the path

$$0, 1, 0, 1, 0, 1, \cdots, 0, 1, 2$$

can be made arbitrarily small. This is so because of the presence of the cycle 0, 1, 0, which has a length of -1.

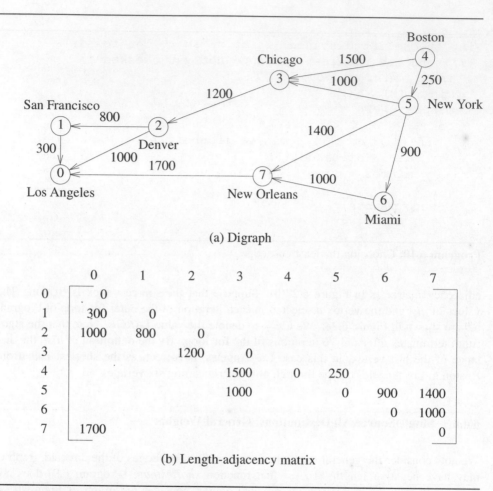

(a) Digraph

	0	1	2	3	4	5	6	7
0	0							
1	300	0						
2	1000	800	0					
3			1200	0				
4				1500	0	250		
5				1000		0	900	1400
6							0	1000
7	1700							0

(b) Length-adjacency matrix

Figure 6.27: Digraph for Example 6.4

When there are no cycles of negative length, there is a shortest path between any two vertices of an n-vertex graph that has at most $n-1$ edges on it. To see this, observe that a path that has more than $n-1$ edges must repeat at least one vertex and hence must contain a cycle. Elimination of the cycles from the path results in another path with the same source and destination. This path is cycle-free and has a length that is no more than that of the original path, as the length of the eliminated cycles was at least zero. We can use this observation on the maximum number of edges on a cycle-free shortest path to obtain an algorithm to determine a shortest path from a source vertex to all remaining vertices in the graph. As in the case of function *shortestPath* (Program 6.9), we shall compute only the length, $dist[u]$, of the shortest path from the source vertex v to u. An exercise examines the extension needed to construct the shortest paths.

Iteration	Vertex selected	Distance							
		LA [0]	SF [1]	DEN [2]	CHI [3]	BOST [4]	NY [5]	MIA [6]	NO [7]
Initial	----	∞	∞	∞	1500	0	250	∞	∞
1	5	∞	∞	∞	1250	0	250	1150	1650
2	6	∞	∞	∞	1250	0	250	1150	1650
3	3	∞	∞	2450	1250	0	250	1150	1650
4	7	3350	∞	2450	1250	0	250	1150	1650
5	2	3350	3250	2450	1250	0	250	1150	1650
6	1	3350	3250	2450	1250	0	250	1150	1650

Figure 6.28: Action of *shortestPath* on digraph of Figure 6.27

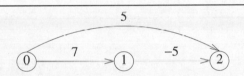

Figure 6.29: Directed graph with a negative-length edge

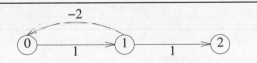

Figure 6.30: Directed graph with a cycle of negative length

Let $dist^l[u]$ be the length of a shortest path from the source vertex v to vertex u under the constraint that the shortest path contains at most l edges. Then, $dist^1[u] = length[v][u]$, $0 \leq u < n$. As noted earlier, when there are no cycles of negative length, we can limit our search for shortest paths to paths with at most $n-1$ edges. Hence, $dist^{n-1}[u]$ is the length of an unrestricted shortest path from v to u.

Our goal then is to compute $dist^{n-1}[u]$ for all u. This can be done using the dynamic programming methodology. First, we make the following observations:

(1)   If the shortest path from v to u with at most k, $k > 1$, edges has no more than $k - 1$ edges, then $dist^k[u] = dist^{k-1}[u]$.

(2)   If the shortest path from v to u with at most k, $k > 1$, edges has exactly k edges, then it is comprised of a shortest path from v to some vertex j followed by the edge $<j,u>$. The path from v to j has $k - 1$ edges, and its length is $dist^{k-1}[j]$. All vertices i such that the edge $<i,u>$ is in the graph are candidates for j. Since we are interested in a shortest path, the i that minimizes $dist^{k-1}[i] + length[i][u]$ is the correct value for j.

These observations result in the following recurrence for $dist$:

$$dist^k[u] = \min\{dist^{k-1}[u], \min_i\{dist^{k-1}[i] + length[i][u]\}\}$$

This recurrence may be used to compute $dist^k$ from $dist^{k-1}$, for $k = 2, 3, \cdots, n-1$.

Example 6.5: Figure 6.31 gives a seven-vertex graph, together with the arrays $dist^k$, $k = 1, \cdots, 6$. These arrays were computed using the equation just given. □

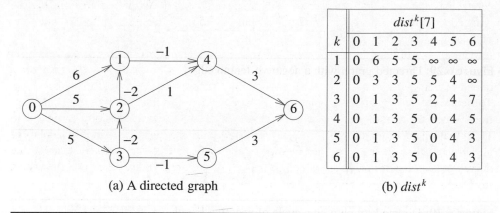

				$dist^k[7]$			
k	0	1	2	3	4	5	6
1	0	6	5	5	∞	∞	∞
2	0	3	3	5	5	4	∞
3	0	1	3	5	2	4	7
4	0	1	3	5	0	4	5
5	0	1	3	5	0	4	3
6	0	1	3	5	0	4	3

(a) A directed graph   (b) $dist^k$

Figure 6.31: Shortest paths with negative edge lengths

An exercise shows that if we use the same memory location $dist[u]$ for $dist^k[u]$, $k = 1, \cdots, n - 1$, then the final value of $dist[u]$ is still $dist^{n-1}[u]$. Using this fact and the recurrence for $dist$ shown above, we arrive at the algorithm of Program 6.11 to compute the length of the shortest path from vertex v to each other vertex of the graph. This algorithm is referred to as the Bellman and Ford algorithm.

```
1  void BellmanFord(int n, int v)
2  {/* Single source all destination shortest paths
3     with negative edge lengths. */
4     for (int i = 0; i < n; i++)
5        dist[i] = length[v][i]; /* initialize dist */

6     for (int k = 2; k <= n-1; k++)
7        for (each u such that u != v and u
8           has at least one incoming edge)
9           for (each <i, u> in the graph)
10             if (dist[u] > dist[i] + length[i][u])
11                dist[u] = dist[i] + length[i][u];
12 }
```

Program 6.11: Bellman and Ford algorithm to compute shortest paths

Analysis of *BellmanFord*: Each iteration of the **for** loop of lines 6 to 11 takes $O(n^2)$ time if adjacency matrices are used and $O(e)$ time if adjacency lists are used. The overall complexity is $O(n^3)$ when adjacency matrices are used and $O(ne)$ when adjacency lists are used. The observed complexity of the shortest-path algorithm can be reduced by noting that if none of the *dist* values change on one iteration of the **for** loop of lines 6 to 11, then none will change on successive iterations. So, this loop may be rewritten to terminate either after $n - 1$ iterations or after the first iteration in which no *dist* values are changed, whichever occurs first. Another possibility is to maintain a queue of vertices i whose *dist* value changed on the previous iteration of the **for** loop. These are the only values for i that need to be considered in line 9 during the next iteration. When a queue of these values is maintained, we can rewrite the loop of lines 6 to 11 so that on each iteration, a vertex i is removed from the queue, and the *dist* values of all vertices adjacent from i are updated as in lines 10 and 11. Vertices whose *dist* value decreases as a result of this are added to the end of the queue unless they are already on it. The loop terminates when the queue becomes empty. □

6.4.3 All Pairs Shortest Paths

In the all-pairs-shortest-path problem we must find the shortest paths between all pairs of vertices, $v_i, v_j, i \neq j$. We could solve this problem using *shortestpath* with each of the vertices in $V(G)$ as the source. Since G has n vertices and *shortestpath* has a time complexity of $O(n^2)$, the total time required would be $O(n^3)$. However, we can obtain a conceptually simpler algorithm that works correctly even if some edges in G have negative weights. (We do require that G has no cycles with a negative length.) Although this algorithm still has a computing time of $O(n^3)$, it has a smaller constant factor. This new algorithm uses the dynamic programming method.

We represent the graph G by its cost adjacency matrix with $cost[i][j] = 0$, $i = j$. If the edge $<i, j>$, $i \neq j$ is not in G, we set $cost[i][j]$ to some sufficiently large number using the same restrictions discussed in the single source problem. Let $A^k[i][j]$ be the cost of the shortest path from i to j, using only those intermediate vertices with an index $\leq k$. The cost of the shortest path from i to j is $A^{n-1}[i][j]$ as no vertex in G has an index greater than $n-1$. Further, $A^{-1}[i][j] = cost[i][j]$ since the only i to j paths allowed have no intermediate vertices on them.

The basic idea in the all pairs algorithm is to begin with the matrix A^{-1} and successively generate the matrices $A^0, A^1, A^2, \cdots, A^{n-1}$. If we have already generated A^{k-1}, then we may generate A^k by realizing that for any pair of vertices i, j one of the two rules below applies.

(1) The shortest path from i to j going through no vertex with index greater than k does not go through the vertex with index k and so its cost is $A^{k-1}[i][j]$.

(2) The shortest such path does go through vertex k. Such a path consists of a path from i to k followed by one from k to j. Neither of these goes through a vertex with index greater than $k-1$. Hence, their costs are $A^{k-1}[i][k]$ and $A^{k-1}[k][j]$.

These rules yield the following formulas for $A^k[i][j]$:

$$A^k[i][j] = \min\{A^{k-1}[i][j], A^{k-1}[i][k] + A^{k-1}[k][j]\}, k \geq 0$$

and

$$A^{-1}[i][j] = cost[i][j]$$

Example 6.6: Figure 6.32 shows a digraph together with its A^{-1} matrix. For this graph $A^1[0][2] \neq \min\{A^1[0][2], A^0[0][1] + A^0[1][2]\} = 2$. Instead, $A^1[0][2] = -\infty$ because the length of the path:

$$0, 1, 0, 1, 0, 1, \cdots, 0, 1, 2$$

can be made arbitrarily small. This situation occurs because we have a cycle, 0, 1, 0, that has a negative length (-1). $\square$

The function *allCosts* (Program 6.12) computes $A^{n-1}[i][j]$. The computations are done in place using the array *distance*, which we define as:

```
int distance[MAX_VERTICES][MAX_VERTICES];
```

The reason this computation can be carried out in place is that $A^k[i,k] = A^{k-1}[i,k]$ and $A^k[k,j] = A^{k-1}[k,j]$ and so the in place computation does not alter the outcome.

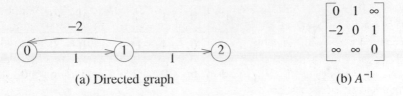

(a) Directed graph

$$A^{-1} = \begin{bmatrix} 0 & 1 & \infty \\ -2 & 0 & 1 \\ \infty & \infty & 0 \end{bmatrix}$$

(b) A^{-1}

Figure 6.32: Graph with negative cycle

```
void allCosts(int cost[][MAX_VERTICES],
                int distance[][MAX_VERTICES], int n)
{/* compute the shortest distance from each vertex
    to every other, cost is the adjacency matrix,
    distance is the matrix of computed  distances */
  int i,j,k;
  for (i = 0; i < n; i++)
      for (j = 0; j < n; j++)
        distance[i][j] = cost[i][j];
  for (k = 0; k < n; k++)
      for (i = 0; i < n; i++)
        for (j = 0; j < n; j++)
            if (distance[i][k] + distance[k][j] <
                                    distance[i][j])
              distance[i][j] =
              distance[i][k] + distance[k][j];
}
```

Program 6.12: All pairs, shortest paths function

Analysis of *allCosts*: This algorithm is especially easy to analyze because the looping is independent of the data in the distance matrix. The total time for *allCosts* is $O(n^3)$. An exercise examines the extensions needed to generate the $<i, j>$ paths with these lengths. We can speed up the algorithm by using our knowledge of the fact that the innermost **for** loop is executed only when *distance*$[i][k]$ and *distance*$[k][j]$ are not equal to ∞. □

Example 6.7: For the digraph of Figure 6.33(a), the initial a matrix, A^{-1}, plus its value after each of three iterations, A^0, A^1, and A^2, is also given in Figure 6.33. □

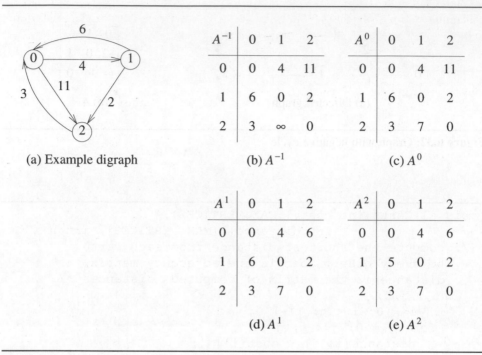

(a) Example digraph

A^{-1}	0	1	2
0	0	4	11
1	6	0	2
2	3	∞	0

(b) A^{-1}

A^0	0	1	2
0	0	4	11
1	6	0	2
2	3	7	0

(c) A^0

A^1	0	1	2
0	0	4	6
1	6	0	2
2	3	7	0

(d) A^1

A^2	0	1	2
0	0	4	6
1	5	0	2
2	3	7	0

(e) A^2

Figure 6.33: Example for all-pairs shortest-paths problem

6.4.4 Transitive Closure

We end this section by studying a problem that is closely related to the all pairs, shortest path problem. Assume that we have a directed graph G with unweighted edges. We want to determine if there is a path from i to j for all values of i and j. Two cases are of interest. The first case requires positive path lengths, while the second requires only nonnegative path lengths. These cases are known as the *transitive closure* and *reflexive transitive closure* of a graph, respectively. We define them as follows:

Definition: The *transitive closure matrix*, denoted A^+, of a directed graph, G, is a matrix such that $A^+[i][j] = 1$ if there is a path of length > 0 from i to j; otherwise, $A^+[i][j] = 0$.
□

Definition: The *reflexive transitive closure matrix*, denoted A^*, of a directed graph, G, is a matrix such that $A^*[i][j] = 1$ if there is a path of length ≥ 0 from i to j; otherwise, $A^*[i][j] = 0$. □

Figure 6.34 shows A^+ and A^* for a digraph. Clearly, the only difference between A^* and A^+ is in the terms on the diagonal. $A^+[i][i] = 1$ iff there is a cycle of length >1 containing vertex i, whereas $A^*[i][i]$ is always one, as there is a path of length 0 from i to i.

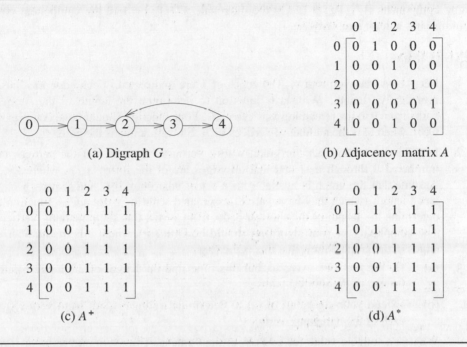

	0	1	2	3	4
0	0	1	0	0	0
1	0	0	1	0	0
2	0	0	0	1	0
3	0	0	0	0	1
4	0	0	1	0	0

(a) Digraph G (b) Adjacency matrix A

	0	1	2	3	4
0	0	1	1	1	1
1	0	0	1	1	1
2	0	0	1	1	1
3	0	0	1	1	1
4	0	0	1	1	1

	0	1	2	3	4
0	1	1	1	1	1
1	0	1	1	1	1
2	0	0	1	1	1
3	0	0	1	1	1
4	0	0	1	1	1

(c) A^+ (d) A^*

Figure 6.34: Graph G and its adjacency matrix A, A^+, and A^*

We can use *allCosts* to compute A^+. We begin with $cost[i][j] = 1$ if $<i, j>$ is an edge in G and $cost[i][j] = +\infty$ if $<i, j>$ is not in G. When *allCosts* terminates, we obtain A^+ from *distance* by letting $A^+[i][j] = 1$ *iff distance[i][j]* $< +\infty$. We then obtain A^* by setting all the diagonal elements in A^+ to 1. The total time is $O(n^3)$. We can simplify the algorithm by changing the **if** statement in the nested **for** loops to:

```
distance[i][j] = distance[i][j] || distance[i][k] &&
                     distance[k][j]
```

and initializing *distance* to be the adjacency matrix of the graph. With this modification, *distance* will be equivalent to A^+ when *allCosts* terminates.

The transitive closure of an undirected graph G can be found more easily from its connected components. From the definition of a connected component, it follows that there is a path between every pair of vertices in the component and there is no path in G between two vertices that are in different components. Hence, if A is the adjacency matrix of an undirected graph (i.e., A is symmetric) then its transitive closure A^+ may be determined in $O(n^2)$ time by first determining the connected components of the graph. $A^+[i][j] = 1$ iff there is a path from vertex i to j. For every pair of distinct vertices in the same component, $A^+[i][j] = 1$. On the diagonal, $A^+[i][i] = 1$ iff the component containing i has at least two vertices.

EXERCISES

1. Let T be a tree with root v. The edges of T are undirected. Each edge in T has a nonnegative length. Write a C function to determine the length of the shortest paths from v to the remaining vertices of T. Your function should have complexity $O(n)$, where n is the number of vertices in T. Show that this is the case.

2. Let G be a directed, acyclic graph with n vertices. Assume that the vertices are numbered 0 through $n-1$ and that all edges are of the form $<i,j>$, where $i < j$. Assume that the graph is available as a set of adjacency lists and that each edge has a length (which may be negative) associated with it. Write a C++ function to determine the length of the shortest paths from vertex 0 to the remaining vertices. The complexity of your algorithm should be $O(n + e)$, where e is the number of edges in the graph. Show that this is the case.

3. (a) Do the previous exercise, but this time find the length of the longest paths instead of the shortest paths.

   (b) Extend your algorithm of (a) to determine a longest path from vertex 0 to each of the remaining vertices.

4. What is a suitable value for *LARGE* in the context of function *shortestpath* (Program 6.9)? Provide this as a function of the largest edge length *maxL* and the number of vertices n.

5. Using the idea of *shortestpath* (Program 6.9), write a C++ function to find a minimum-cost spanning tree whose worst-case time is $O(n^2)$.

6. Use *shortestpath* (Program 6.9) to obtain, in nondecreasing order, the lengths of the shortest paths from vertex 0 to all remaining vertices in the digraph of Figure 6.35.

7. Rewrite *shortestpath* (Program 6.9) under the following assumptions:

   (a) G is represented by its adjacency lists, where each node has three fields: *vertex*, *length*, and *link*. *length* is the length of the corresponding edge and n the number of vertices in G.

   (b) Instead of S (the set of vertices to which the shortest paths have already been found), the set $T = V(G) - S$ is represented using a linked list.

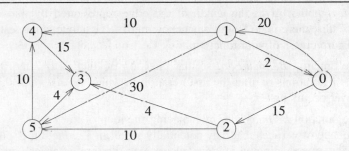

Figure 6.35: A digraph

What can you say about the computing time of your new function relative to that of *shortestpath*?

8. Modify *shortestpath* (Program 6.9) so that it obtains the shortest paths, in addition to the lengths of these paths. What is the computing time of your modified function?

9. Using the directed graph of Figure 6.36, explain why *shortestpath* will not work properly. What is the shortest path between vertices 0 and 6?

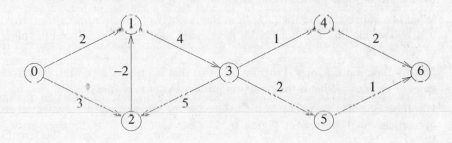

Figure 6.36: Directed graph on which *ShortestPath* does not work properly

10. Prove the correctness of function *BellmanFord* (Program 6.11). Note that this function does not faithfully implement the computation of the recurrence for $dist^k$. In fact, for $k < n - 1$, the *dist* values following iteration k of the **for** loop of lines 4 to 7 may not be $dist^k$.

11. Transform function *BellmanFord* into a complete C function. Assume that graphs are represented using adjacency lists in which each node has an additional field called *length* that gives the length of the edge represented by that node. As a result of this, there is no length-adjacency matrix. Generate some test graphs and test the correctness of your function.

12. Rewrite function *BellmanFord* so that the loop of lines 4 to 7 terminates either after $n - 1$ iterations or after the first iteration in which no *dist* values are changed, whichever occurs first.

13. Rewrite function *BellmanFord* by replacing the loop of lines 4 to 7 with code that uses a queue of vertices that may potentially result in a reduction of other *dist* vertices. This queue initially contains all vertices that are adjacent from the source vertex v. On each successive iteration of the new loop, a vertex i is removed from the queue (unless the queue is empty), and the *dist* values to vertices adjacent from i are updated as in line 7 of Program 6.11. When the *dist* value of a vertex is reduced because of this, it is added to the queue unless it is already on the queue.

    (a) Prove that the new function produces the same results as the original one.

    (b) Show that the complexity of the new function is no more than that of the original one.

14. Compare the run-time performance of the Bellman and Ford functions of the preceding two exercises and that of Program 6.11. For this, generate test graphs that will expose the relative performance of the three functions.

15. Modify function *BellmanFord* so that it obtains the shortest paths, in addition to the lengths of these paths. What is the computing time of your function?

16. What is a suitable value for *LARGE* in the context of function *allCosts* (Program 6.12)? Provide this as a function of the largest edge length *maxL* and the number of vertices n.

17. Modify function *allCosts* (Program 6.12) so that it obtains a shortest path for all pairs of vertices. What is the computing time of your new function?

18. Use function *allCosts* to obtain the lengths of the shortest paths between all pairs of vertices in the graph of Figure 6.35. Does *allCosts* give the right answers? Why?

19. By considering the complete graph with n vertices, show that the maximum number of simple paths between two vertices is $O((n - 1)!)$.

20. Show that $A^+ = A^* \times A$, where matrix multiplication of the two matrices is defined as $a_{ij}^+ = \vee_{k=1}^{n} a_{ik}^* \wedge a_{kj}$. $\vee$ is the logical **or** operation, and $\wedge$ is the logical **and** operation.

21. Obtain the matrices A^+ and A^* for the digraph of Figure 6.15.

22. What is a suitable value for *LARGE* when *allCosts* (Program 6.12) is used to compute the transitive closure of a directed graph? Provide this as a function of the number of vertices *n*.

6.5 ACTIVITY NETWORKS

6.5.1 Activity-on-Vertex (AOV) Networks

All but the simplest of projects can be subdivided into several subprojects called activities. The successful completion of these activities results in the completion of the entire project. A student working toward a degree in computer science must complete several courses successfully. The project in this case is to complete the major, and the activities are the individual courses that have to be taken. Figure 6.37 lists the courses needed for a computer science major at a hypothetical university. Some of these courses may be taken independently of others; other courses have prerequisites and can be taken only if all the prerequisites have already been taken. The data structures course cannot be started until certain programming and math courses have been completed. Thus, prerequisites define precedence relations between courses. The relationships defined may be more clearly represented using a directed graph in which the vertices represent courses and the directed edges represent prerequisites.

Definition: A directed graph *G* in which the vertices represent tasks or activities and the edges represent precedence relations between tasks is an *activity-on-vertex network* or AOV network. □

Figure 6.37(b) is the AOV network corresponding to the courses of Figure 6.37(a). Each edge <*i*, *j*> implies that course *i* is a prerequisite of course *j*.

Definition: Vertex *i* in an AOV network *G* is a *predecessor* of vertex *j* iff there is a directed path from vertex *i* to vertex *j*. *i* is an *immediate predecessor* of *j* iff <*i*,*j*> is an edge in *G*. If *i* is a predecessor of *j*, then *j* is a *successor* of *i*. If *i* is an immediate predecessor of *j*, then *j* is an *immediate successor* of *i*. □

C3 and C6 are immediate predecessors of C7. C9, C10, C12, and C13 are immediate successors of C7. C14 is a successor, but not an immediate successor, of C3.

Definition: A relation · is *transitive* iff it is the case that for all triples *i*,*j*,*k*, *i*·*j* and *j*·*k* ⟹ *i*·*k*. A relation · is *irreflexive* on a set *S* if for no element *x* in *S* is it the case that *x*·*x*. A precedence relation that is both transitive and irreflexive is a *partial order*. □

Notice that the precedence relation defined by course prerequisites is transitive.

Course number	Course name	Prerequisites
C1	Programming I	None
C2	Discrete Mathematics	None
C3	Data Structures	C1, C2
C4	Calculus I	None
C5	Calculus II	C4
C6	Linear Algebra	C5
C7	Analysis of Algorithms	C3, C6
C8	Assembly Language	C3
C9	Operating Systems	C7, C8
C10	Programming Languages	C7
C11	Compiler Design	C10
C12	Artificial Intelligence	C7
C13	Computational Theory	C7
C14	Parallel Algorithms	C13
C15	Numerical Analysis	C5

(a) Courses needed for a computer science degree at a hypothetical university

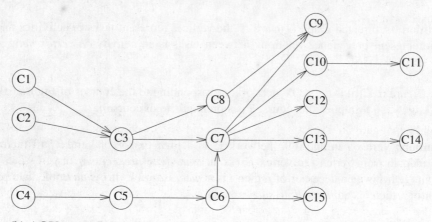

(b) AOV network representing courses as vertices and prerequisites as edges

Figure 6.37: An activity-on-vertex (AOV) network

That is, if course i must be taken before course j (as i is a prerequiste of j), and if j must be taken before k, then i must be taken before k. This fact is not obvious from the AOV network. For example, <C4, C5> and <C5, C6> are edges in the AOV network of Figure 6.37(b). However, <C4, C6> is not. Generally, AOV networks are incompletely specified, and the edges needed to make the precedence relation transitive are implied.

If the precedence relation defined by the edges of an AOV network is not irreflexive, then there is an activity that is a predecessor of itself and so must be completed before it can be started. This is clearly impossible. When there are no inconsistencies of this type, the project is feasible. Given an AOV network, one of our concerns would be to determine whether or not the precedence relation defined by its edges is irreflexive. This is identical to determining whether or not the network contains any directed cycles. A directed graph with no directed cycles is an *acyclic* graph. Our algorithm to test an AOV network for feasibility will also generate a linear ordering, $v_0, v_1, \cdots, v_{n-1}$, of the vertices (activities). This linear ordering will have the property that if vertex i is a predecessor of j in the network, then i precedes j in the linear ordering. A linear ordering with this property is called a *topological order*.

Definition: A *topological order* is a linear ordering of the vertices of a graph such that, for any two vertices i and j, if i is a predecessor of j in the network, then i precedes j in the linear ordering. □

There are several possible topological orders for the network of Figure 6.37(b). Two of these are

C1, C2, C4, C5, C3, C6, C8, C7, C10, C13, C12, C14, C15, C11, C9

and

C4, C5, C2, C1, C6, C3, C8, C15, C7, C9, C10, C11, C12, C13, C14

If a student were taking just one course per term, then she or he would have to take them in topological order. If the AOV network represented the different tasks involved in assembling an automobile, then these tasks would be carried out in topological order on an assembly line. The algorithm to sort the tasks into topological order is straightforward and proceeds by listing a vertex in the network that has no predecessor. Then, this vertex together with all edges leading out from it is deleted from the network. These two steps are repeated until all vertices have been listed or all remaining vertices in the network have predecessors, and so none can be removed. In this case there is a cycle in the network, and the project is infeasible. The algorithm is stated more formally in Program 6.13.

Example 6.8: Let us try out our topological sorting algorithm on the network of Figure 6.38(a). The first vertex to be picked in line 6 is 0, as it is the only one with no predecessors. Vertex 0 and the edges <0, 1>, <0, 2>, and <0, 3> are deleted. In the resulting network (Figure 6.38(b)), vertices 1, 2, and 3 have no predecessor. Any of these can be the next vertex in the topological order. Assume that 3 is picked. Deletion of vertex 3 and

```
1  Input the AOV network.  Let n be the number of vertices.
2  for (i = 0; i < n; i++) /* output the vertices */
3  {
4    if (every vertex has a predecessor) return;
5      /* network has a cycle and is infeasible */
6    pick a vertex v that has no predecessors;
7    output v;
8    delete v and all edges leading out of v;
9  }
```

Program 6.13: Design of an algorithm for topological sorting

the edges <3, 5> and <3, 4> results in the network of Figure 6.38(c). Either 1 or 2 may be picked next. Figure 6.38 shows the progress of the algorithm on the network. □

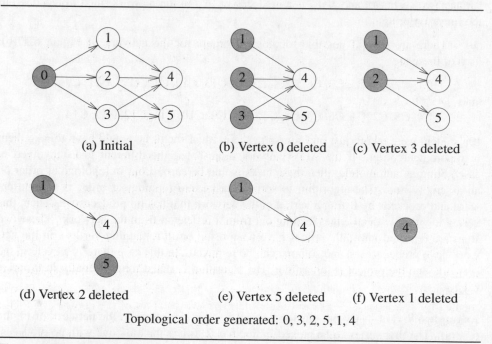

(a) Initial   (b) Vertex 0 deleted   (c) Vertex 3 deleted

(d) Vertex 2 deleted   (e) Vertex 5 deleted   (f) Vertex 1 deleted

Topological order generated: 0, 3, 2, 5, 1, 4

Figure 6.38: Action of Program 6.13 on an AOV network (shaded vertices represent candidates for deletion)

To obtain a complete algorithm that can be easily translated into a computer program, it is necessary to specify the data representation for the AOV network. The choice of a data representation, as always, depends on the functions you wish to perform. In this problem, the functions are

(1)   decide whether a vertex has any predecessors (line 4)

(2)   delete a vertex together with all its incident edges (line 8)

To perform the first task efficiently, we maintain a count of the number of immediate predecessors each vertex has. The second task is easily implemented if the network is represented by its adjacency lists. Then the deletion of all edges leading out of vertex v can be carried out by decreasing the predecessor count of all vertices on its adjacency list. Whenever the count of a vertex drops to zero, that vertex can be placed onto a list of vertices with a zero count. Then the selection in line 6 just requires removal of a vertex from this list.

As a result of the preceding analysis, we represent the AOV network using adjacency lists. The complete C function for performing a topological sort on a network is *topSort* (Program 6.14). This function assumes that the network is represented by its adjacency lists. The header nodes of these lists now contain count and link fields.

The declarations used in *topSort* are:

```
typedef struct node *nodePointer;
typedef struct {
        int vertex;
        nodePointer link;
        } node;
typedef struct {
        int count;
        nodePointer link;
        } hdnodes;
hdnodes graph[MAX_VERTICES];
```

The *count* field contains the in-degree of that vertex and *link* is a pointer to the first node on the adjacency list. Each node has two fields, *vertex* and *link*. This can be done easily at the time of input. When edge $<i,j>$ is input, the count of vertex j is incremented by 1. Figure 6.39(a) shows the internal representation of the network of Figure 6.38(a).

Inserting these details into Program 6.13, we obtain the C function *topSort* (Program 6.14). The list of vertices with zero count is maintained as a custom stack. A queue could have been used instead, but a stack is slightly simpler. The stack is linked through the *count* field of the header nodes, since this field is of no use after a vertex's

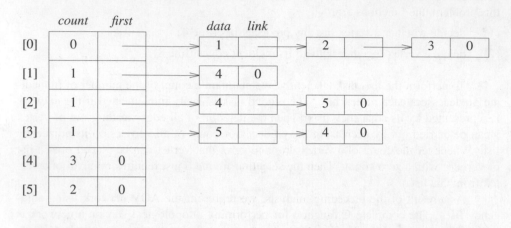

Figure 6.39: Internal representation used by topological sorting algorithm

count has become zero.

Analysis of *topSort*: As a result of a judicious choice of data structures, *topSort* is very efficient. The first **for** loop takes $O(n)$ time, on a network with n vertices and e edges. The second **for** loop is iterated n times. The **if** clause is executed in constant time; the **for** loop within the **else** clause takes time $O(d_i)$, where d_i is the out-degree of vertex i. Since this loop is encountered once for each vertex that is printed, the total time for this part of the algorithm is:

$$O((\sum_{i=0}^{n-1} d_i) + n) = O(e + n)$$

Thus, the asymptotic computing time of the algorithm is $O(e + n)$. It is linear in the size of the problem! □

6.5.2 Activity-on-Edge (AOE) Networks

An activity network closely related to the AOV network is the *activity-on-edge*, or *AOE, network*. The tasks to be performed on a project are represented by directed edges. Vertices in the network represent events. Events signal the completion of certain activities. Activities represented by edges leaving a vertex cannot be started until the event at that vertex has occurred. An event occurs only when all activities entering it have been

```
void topSort(hdnodes graph[], int n)
{
   int i,j,k,top;
   nodePointer ptr;
   /* create a stack of vertices with no predecessors */
   top = -1;
   for (i = 0; i < n; i++)
     if (!graph[i].count) {
        graph[i].count = top;
        top = i;
   }
   for (i = 0; i < n; i++)
     if (top == -1) {
        fprintf(stderr,
           "\nNetwork has a cycle. Sort terminated. \n");
        exit(EXIT_FAILURE);
   }
     else {
        j = top;    /* unstack a vertex */
        top = graph[top].count;
        printf("v%d, ",j);
        for (ptr = graph[j].link; ptr; ptr = ptr->link) {
        /* decrease the count of the successor vertices
           of j */
          k = ptr->vertex;
          graph[k].count--;
          if (!graph[k].count) {
          /* add vertex k to the stack */
            graph[k].count = top;
            top = k;
        }
      }
    }
  }
}
```

Program 6.14: Topological sort

completed. Figure 6.40(a) is an AOE network for a hypothetical project with 11 tasks or activities: $a_1, \cdots, a_{11}$. There are nine events: 0, 1, $\cdots$, 8. The events 0 and 8 may be interpreted as "start project" and "finish project," respectively. Figure 6.40(b) gives interpretations for some of the nine events. The number associated with each activity is the time needed to perform that activity. Thus, activity a_1 requires 6 days, whereas a_{11} requires 4 days. Usually, these times are only estimates. Activities a_1, a_2, and a_3 may be carried out concurrently after the start of the project. Activities a_4, a_5, and a_6 cannot be started until events 1, 2, and 3, respectively, occur. Activities a_7 and a_8 can be carried out concurrently after the occurrence of event 4 (i.e., after a_4 and a_5 have been completed). If additional ordering constraints are to be put on the activities, dummy activities whose time is zero may be introduced. Thus, if we desire that activities a_7 and a_8 not start until both events 4 and 5 have occurred, a dummy activity a_{12} represented by an edge <5,4> may be introduced.

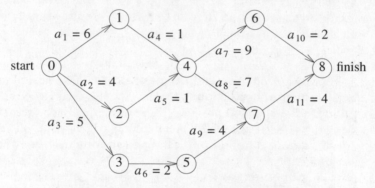

(a) Activity network of a hypothetical project

event	interpretation
0	start of project
1	completion of activity a_1
4	completion of activities a_4 and a_5
7	completion of activities a_8 and a_9
8	completion of project

(b) Interpretation of some of the events in the network of (a)

Figure 6.40: An AOE network

Activity networks of the AOE type have proved very useful in the performance evaluation of several types of projects. This evaluation includes determining such facts about the project as what is the least amount of time in which the project may be completed (assuming there are no cycles in the network), which activities should be speeded to reduce project length, and so on.

Since the activities in an AOE network can be carried out in parallel, the minimum time to complete the project is the length of the longest path from the start vertex to the finish vertex (the length of a path is the sum of the times of activities on this path). A path of longest length is a *critical path*. The path 0, 1, 4, 6, 8 is a critical path in the network of Figure 6.40(a). The length of this critical path is 18. A network may have more than one critical path (the path 0, 1, 4, 7, 8 is also critical).

The *earliest time* that an event i can occur is the length of the longest path from the start vertex 0 to the vertex i. The earliest time that event v_4 can occur is 7. The earliest time an event can occur determines the *earliest start time* for all activities represented by edges leaving that vertex. Denote this time by $e(i)$ for activity a_i. For example, $e(7)=e(8)=7$.

For every activity a_i, we may also define the *latest time*, $l(i)$, that an activity may start without increasing the project duration (i.e., length of the longest path from start to finish). In Figure 6.40(a) we have $e(6)=5$ and $l(6)=8$, $e(8)=7$ and $l(8)=7$.

All activities for which $e(i)=l(i)$ are called *critical activities*. The difference $l(i)-e(i)$ is a measure of the criticality of an activity. It gives the time by which an activity may be delayed or slowed without increasing the total time needed to finish the project. If activity a_6 is slowed down to take 2 extra days, this will not affect the project finish time. Clearly, all activities on a critical path are strategic, and speeding up non-critical activities will not reduce the project duration.

The purpose of critical-path analysis is to identify critical activities so that resources may be concentrated on these activities in an attempt to reduce project finish time. Speeding a critical activity will not result in a reduced project length unless that activity is on all critical paths. In Figure 6.40(a) the activity a_{11} is critical, but speeding it up so that it takes only 3 days instead of 4 does not reduce the finish time to 17 days. This is so because there is another critical path (0, 1, 4, 6, 8) that does not contain this activity. The activities a_1 and a_4 are on all critical paths. Speeding a_1 by 2 days reduces the critical path length to 16 days. Critical-path methods have proved very valuable in evaluating project performance and identifying bottlenecks.

Critical-path analysis can also be carried out with AOV networks. The length of a path would now be the sum of the activity times of the vertices on that path. By analogy, for each activity or vertex we could define the quantities $e(i)$ and $l(i)$. Since the activity times are only estimates, it is necessary to reevaluate the project during several stages of its completion as more accurate estimates of activity times become available. These changes in activity times could make previously noncritical activities critical, and vice versa.

Before ending our discussion on activity networks, let us design an algorithm to calculate $e(i)$ and $l(i)$ for all activities in an AOE network. Once these quantities are known, then the critical activities may easily be identified. Deleting all noncritical activities from the AOE network, all critical paths may be found by just generating all paths from the start-to-finish vertex (all such paths will include only critical activities and so must be critical, and since no noncritical activity can be on a critical path, the network with noncritical activities removed contains all critical paths present in the original network).

6.5.2.1 Calculation of Early Activity Times

When computing the early and late activity times, it is easiest first to obtain the earliest event time, $ee[j]$, and latest event time, $le[j]$, for all events, j, in the network. Thus if activity a_i is represented by edge $<k,l>$, we can compute $e(i)$ and $l(i)$ from the following formulas:

$$e(i)=ee[k]$$

and   (6.1)

$$l(i)=le[l]-\text{duration of activity } a_i$$

The times $ee[j]$ and $le[j]$ are computed in two stages: a forward stage and a backward stage. During the forward stage we start with $ee[0]=0$ and compute the remaining early start times, using the formula

$$ee[j]= \max_{i \in P(j)} \{ee[i] + \text{duration of} <i,j> \} \qquad (6.2)$$

where $P(j)$ is the set of all vertices adjacent to vertex j. If this computation is carried out in topological order, the early start times of all predecessors of j would have been computed prior to the computation of $ee[j]$. So, if we modify *topSort* (Program 6.14) so that it returns the vertices in topological order (rather than outputs them in this order), then we may use this topological order and Eq. 6.2 to compute the early event times. To use Eq. 6.2, however, we must have easy access to the vertex set $P(j)$. Since the adjacency list representation does not provide easy access to $P(j)$, we make a more major modification to Program 6.14. We begin with the *ee* array initialized to zero and insert the code

```
if (earliest[k] < earliest[j] + ptr→duration)
        earliest[k] = earliest[j] + ptr→duration;
```

just after the line

```
k = ptr→vertex;
```

This modification results in the evaluation of Eq. (6.2) in parallel with the generation of a topological order. $ee(k)$ is updated each time the $ee()$ of one of its predecessors is known (i.e., when j is ready for output).

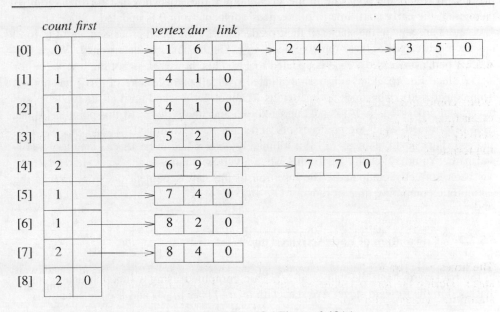

(a) Adjacency lists for Figure 6.40(a)

ee	[0]	[1]	[2]	[3]	[4]	[5]	[6]	[7]	[8]	Stack
initial	0	0	0	0	0	0	0	0	0	[0]
output 0	0	6	4	5	0	0	0	0	0	[3, 2, 1]
output 3	0	6	4	5	0	7	0	0	0	[5, 2, 1]
output 5	0	6	4	5	0	7	0	11	0	[2, 1]
output 2	0	6	4	5	5	7	0	11	0	[1]
output 1	0	6	4	5	7	7	0	11	0	[4]
output 4	0	6	4	5	7	7	16	14	0	[7, 6]
output 7	0	6	4	5	7	7	16	14	18	[6]
output 6	0	6	4	5	7	7	16	14	18	[8]
output 8										

(b) Computation of ee

Figure 6.41: Computing ee using modified *topSort* (Program 6.14)

To illustrate the working of the modified *topSort* algorithm, let us try it out on the network of Figure 6.40(a). The adjacency lists for the network are shown in Figure 6.41(a). The order of nodes on these lists determines the order in which vertices will be considered by the algorithm. At the outset, the early start time for all vertices is 0, and the start vertex is the only one in the stack. When the adjacency list for this vertex is processed, the early start time of all vertices adjacent from 0 is updated. Since vertices 1, 2, and 3 are now in the stack, all their predecessors have been processed, and Eq. (6.2) has been evaluated for these three vertices. *ee* [5] is the next one determined. When vertex 5 is being processed, *ee* [7] is updated to 11. This, however, is not the true value for *ee* [7], since Eq. (6.2) has not been evaluated over all predecessors of 7 (v_4 has not yet been considered). This does not matter, as 7 cannot get stacked until all its predecessors have been processed. *ee* [4] is next updated to 5 and finally to 7. At this point *ee* [4] has been determined, as all the predecessors of 4 have been examined. The values of *ee* [6] and *ee* [7] are next obtained. *ee* [8] is ultimately determined to be 18, the length of a critical path. You may readily verify that when a vertex is put into the stack, its early time has been correctly computed. The insertion of the new statement does not change the asymptotic computing time; it remains O($e + n$).

6.5.2.2 Calculation of Late Activity Times

In the backward stage the values of *le* [i] are computed using a function analogous to that used in the forward stage. We start with *le* [$n-1$]=*ee* [$n-1$] and use the equation

$$le [j] = \min_{i \in S(j)} \{ le [i] - \text{duration of} <j,i> \} \tag{6.3}$$

where $S(j)$ is the set of vertices adjacent from vertex j. The initial values for *le* [i] may be set to *ee* [$n-1$]. Basically, Eq. (6.3) says that if $<j,i>$ is an activity and the latest start time for event i is *le* [i], then event j must occur no later than *le* [i] − duration of $<j,i>$. Before *le* [j] can be computed for some event j, the latest event time for all successor events (i.e., events adjacent from j) must be computed. Once we have obtained the topological order and *ee* [$n-1$] from the modified version of Program 6.14, we may compute the late event times in reverse toplogical order using the adjacency list of vertex j to access the vertices in $S(j)$. This computation is shown below for our example of Figure 6.40(a).

le [8] = *ee* [8] = 18
le [6] = min{*le* [8] − 2} = 16
le [7] = min{*le* [8] − 4} = 14
le [4] = min{*le* [6] − 9, *le* [7] − 7} = 7
le [1] = min{*le* [4] − 1} = 6
le [2] = min{*le* [4] − 1} = 6

$le\,[5] = \min\{le\,[7] - 4\} = 10$
$le\,[3] = \min\{le\,[5] - 2\} = 8$
$le\,[0] = \min\{le\,[1] - 6,\ le\,[2] - 4,\ le\,[3] - 5\} = 0$

If the forward stage has already been carried out and a topological ordering of the vertices obtained, then the values of $le\,[i\,]$ can be computed directly, using Eq. (6.3), by performing the computations in the reverse topological order. The topological order generated in Figure 6.41(b) is 0, 3, 5, 2, 1, 4, 7, 6, 8. We may compute the values of $le\,[i\,]$ in the order 8, 6, 7, 4, 1, 2, 5, 3, 0, as all successors of an event precede that event in this order. In practice, one would usually compute both ee and le. The procedure would then be to compute ee first, using algorithm $topSort$, modified as discussed for the forward stage, and then to compute le directly from Eq. (6.3) in reverse topological order.

Using the values of ee (Figure 6.41) and of le (above), and Eq. (6.1), we may compute the early and late times $e\,(i)$ and $l\,(i)$ and the degree of criticality (also called slack) of each task. Figure 6.42 gives the values. The critical activities are a_1, a_4, a_7, a_8, a_{10}, and a_{11}. Deleting all noncritical activities from the network, we get the directed graph or critical network of Figure 6.43. All paths from 0 to 8 in this graph are critical paths, and there are no critical paths in the original network that are not paths in this graph.

activity	early time e	late time l	slack $l - e$	critical $l - e = 0$
a_1	0	0	0	Yes
a_2	0	2	2	No
a_3	0	3	3	No
a_4	6	6	0	Yes
a_5	4	6	2	No
a_6	5	8	3	No
a_7	7	7	0	Yes
a_8	7	7	0	Yes
a_9	7	10	3	No
a_{10}	16	16	0	Yes
a_{11}	14	14	0	Yes

Figure 6.42: Early, late, and criticality values

As a final remark on activity networks, we note that the function $topSort$ detects only directed cycles in the network. There may be other flaws, such as vertices not reachable from the start vertex (Figure 6.44). When a critical-path analysis is carried out on such networks, there will be several vertices with $ee\,[i\,] = 0$. Since all activity times are assumed > 0, only the start vertex can have $ee\,[i\,] = 0$. Hence, critical-path analysis

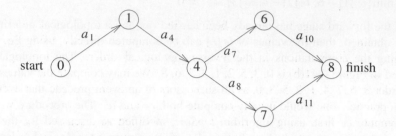

Figure 6.43: Graph obtained after deleting all noncritical activities

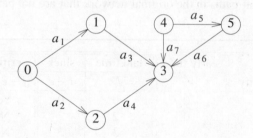

Figure 6.44: AOE network with some nonreachable activities

can also be used to detect this kind of fault in project planning.

EXERCISES

1. Does the following set of precedence relations (<) define a partial order on the elements 0 through 4? Explain your answer.

$$0 < 1; \; 1 < 4; \; 1 < 2; \; 2 < 3; \; 2 < 4; \; 4 < 0$$

2. (a) For the AOE network of Figure 6.46, obtain the *early* and *late* starting times for each activity. Use the forward-backward approach.

   (b) What is the earliest time the project can finish?

   (c) Which activities are critical?

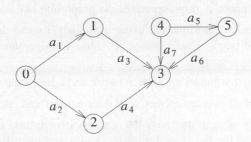

Figure 6.45: AOE network with unreachable activities

(d)   Is there a single activity whose speed up would result in a reduction of the project length?

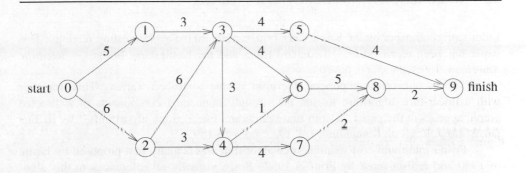

Figure 6.46: An AOE network

3.   § [*Programming project*] Write a C program that allows the user to input an AOE network. The program should calculate and output the *early(i)* and *late(i)* times and the degree of criticality for each activity. If the project is not feasible, it should indicate this. If the project is feasible it should print out the critical activities in an appropriate format.

4.   Define a critical AOE network to be an AOE network in which all activities are critical. Let *G* be the undirected graph obtained by removing the directions and weights from the edges of the network.

(a)   Show that the project length can be decreased by speeding up exactly one activity if there is an edge in G that lies on every path from the start vertex to the finish vertex. Such an edge is called a bridge. Deletion of a bridge from a connected graph separates the graph into two connected components.

(b) Write an $O(n + e)$ function using adjacency lists to determine whether the connected graph G has a bridge. If G has a bridge, your function should output one such bridge.

5. Write a program that inputs an AOE network and outputs the following:

(a) A table of all events together with their earliest and latest times.

(b) A table of all activities together with their early and late times. This table should also list the slack for each activity and identify all critical activities (see Figure 6.42).

(c) The critical network.

(d) Whether or not the project length can be reduced by speeding a single activity. If so, then by how much?

6.6 REFERENCES AND SELECTED READINGS

Euler's original paper on the Königsberg bridge problem makes interesting reading. This paper has been reprinted in: "Leonhard Euler and the Königsberg bridges," *Scientific American*, 189:1, 1953, pp. 66-70.

The biconnected-component algorithm is due to Robert Tarjan. This, together with a linear-time algorithm to find the strongly connected components of a directed graph, appears in the paper "Depth-first search and linear graph algorithms," by R. Tarjan, *SIAM Journal on Computing*, 1:2, 1972, pp. 146-159.

Prim's minimum-cost spanning tree algorithm was actually first proposed by Jarnik in 1930 and rediscovered by Prim in 1957. Since virtually all references to this algorithm give credit to Prim, we continue to refer to it as Prim's algorithm. Similarly, the algorithm we refer to as Sollin's algorithm was first proposed by Boruvka in 1926 and rediscovered by Sollin several years later. For an interesting discussion of the history of the minimum spanning tree problem, see "On the history of the minimum spanning tree problem," by R. Graham and P. Hell, *Annals of the History of Computing*, 7:1, 1985, pp. 43-57.

Further algorithms on graphs may be found in *Graphs: Theory and applications*, by K. Thulasiraman and M. Swamy, Wiley Interscience, 1992.

6.7 ADDITIONAL EXERCISES

1. A *bipartite graph* $G = (V, E)$ is an undirected graph whose vertices can be partitioned into two disjoint sets, A and $B = V - A$, with the following properties: (1) No two vertices in A are adjacent in G, and (2) no two vertices in B are adjacent in G. The graph G_4 of Figure 6.5 is bipartite. A possible partitioning of V is $A = \{0,3,4,6\}$ and $B = \{1,2,5,7\}$. Write an algorithm to determine whether a graph G is bipartite. If G is bipartite your algorithm should obtain a partitioning of the vertices into two disjoint sets, A and B, satisfying properties (1) and (2) above. Show that if G is represented by its adjacency lists, then this algorithm can be made to work in time $O(n + e)$, where $n = |V|$ and $e = |E|$.

2. Show that every tree is a bipartite graph.

3. Prove that a graph G is bipartite iff it contains no cycles of odd length.

4. The *radius* of a tree is the maximum distance from the root to a leaf. Given a connected, undirected graph, write a function to find a spanning tree of minimum radius. (Hint: Use breadth-first search.) Prove that your algorithm is correct.

5. The *diameter* of a tree is the maximum distance between any two vertices. Given a connected, undirected graph, write an algorithm for finding a spanning tree of minimum diameter. Prove the correctness of your algorithm.

6. Let $G[n][n]$ be a wiring grid. $G[i][j] > 0$ represents a grid position that is blocked; $G[i][j] = 0$ represents an unblocked position. Assume that positions $[a][b]$ and $[c][d]$ are blocked positions. A path from $[a][b]$ to $[b][c]$ is a sequence of grid positions such that

   (a) $[a][b]$ and $[c][d]$ are, respectively, the first and last positions on the path

   (b)   successive positions of the sequence are vertically or horizontally adjacent in the grid

   (c)   all positions of the sequence other than the first and last are unblocked positions

   The length of a path is the number of grid positions on the path. We wish to connect positions $[a][b]$ and $[c][d]$ by a wire of shortest length. The wire path is a shortest grid path between these two vertices. Lee's algorithm for this works in the following steps:

   (a)   [Forward step] Start a breadth-first search from position $[a][b]$, labeling unblocked positions by their shortest distance from $[a][b]$. To avoid conflicts with existing labels, use negative labels. The labeling stops when the position $[c][d]$ is reached.

   (b)   [Backtrace] Use the labels of (a) to label the shortest path between $[a][b]$ and $[c][d]$, using the unique label $w > 0$ for the wire. For this, start at position $[c][d]$.

   (c)   [Clean-up] Change the remaining negative labels to 0.

Write algorithms for each of the three steps of Lee's algorithm. What is the complexity of each step?

7. Another way to represent a graph is by its incidence matrix, INC. There is one row for each vertex and one column for each edge. Then $INC[i][j] = 1$ if edge j is incident to vertex i. The incidence matrix for the graph of Figure 6.16(a) is given in Figure 6.47.

$$
\begin{array}{c}
\;0\;1\;2\;3\;4\;5\;6\;7\;8\;9 \\
\begin{array}{c}
0 \\ 1 \\ 2 \\ 3 \\ 4 \\ 5 \\ 6 \\ 7
\end{array}
\left[
\begin{array}{cccccccccc}
1 & 1 & 0 & 0 & 0 & 0 & 0 & 0 & 0 & 0 \\
1 & 0 & 1 & 1 & 0 & 0 & 0 & 0 & 0 & 0 \\
0 & 1 & 0 & 0 & 1 & 1 & 0 & 0 & 0 & 0 \\
0 & 0 & 1 & 0 & 0 & 0 & 1 & 0 & 0 & 0 \\
0 & 0 & 0 & 1 & 0 & 0 & 0 & 1 & 0 & 0 \\
0 & 0 & 0 & 0 & 1 & 0 & 0 & 0 & 1 & 0 \\
0 & 0 & 0 & 0 & 0 & 1 & 0 & 0 & 0 & 1 \\
0 & 0 & 0 & 0 & 0 & 0 & 1 & 1 & 1 & 1
\end{array}
\right]
\end{array}
$$

Figure 6.47: Incidence matrix of graph of Figure 6.16(a)

The edges of Figure 6.16(a) have been numbered from left to right and top to bottom. Rewrite function *DFS* (Program 6.15) so that it works on a graph represented by its incidence matrix.

8. If ADJ is the adjacency matrix of a graph $G = (V,E)$, and INC is the incidence matrix, under what conditions will $ADJ = INC \times INC^T - I$, where INC^T is the transpose of matrix INC? I is the identity matrix, and the matrix product $C = A \times B$, where all matrices are $n \times n$, is defined as $c_{ij} = \vee_{k=0}^{n-1} a_{ik} \wedge b_{kj}$. $\vee$ is the || operation, and $\wedge$ is the && operation.

9. An edge (u, v) of a connected, undirected graph G is a *bridge* iff its deletion from G results in a graph that is not connected. In the graph of Figure 6.48, the edges $(0, 1)$, $(3, 5)$, $(7, 8)$, and $(7, 9)$ are bridges. Write an algorithm that runs in $O(n + e)$ time to find the bridges of G. n and e are, respectively, the number of vertices and edges of G. (Hint: Use the ideas in function *Biconnected* (Program 6.16).)

CHAPTER 7

Sorting

7.1 MOTIVATION

In this chapter, we use the term *list* to mean a collection of records, each record having one or more fields. The fields used to distinguish among the records are known as *keys*. Since the same list may be used for several different applications, the key fields for record identification depend on the particular application. For instance, we may regard a telephone directory as a list, each record having three fields: name, address, and phone number. The key is usually the person's name. However, we may wish to locate the record corresponding to a given number, in which case the phone number field would be the key. In yet another application we may desire the phone number at a particular address, so the address field could also be the key.

One way to search for a record with the specified key is to examine the list of records in left-to-right or right-to-left order. Such a search is known as a sequential search. We assume that the list of records is stored in positions 1 through n of an array. We use array indexes 1 through n for our records rather than 0 through $n-1$ because one of the sort methods we develop, heap sort, employs the the array representation of a heap. This representation (see Section 5.6), begins at position 1 of an array. However,

333

all the sort methods and examples of this chapter are adapted easily to work with record indexes that begin at 0. The datatype of each record is *element* and each record is assumed to have an integer field *key*. Program 7.1 gives a sequential search function that examines the records in the list $a[1:n]$ in left-to-right order.

```
int seqSearch(element a[], int k, int n)
{/* search a[1:n]; return the least i such that
    a[i].key = k; return 0, if k is not in the array */
   int i;
   for (i = 1; i <= n && a[i].key != k; i++)
      ;
   if (i > n) return 0;
   return i;
}
```

Program 7.1 Sequential search

If $a[1:n]$ does not contain a record with key k, the search is *unsuccessful*. Program 7.1 makes n key comparisons when the search is unsuccessful. For a successful search, the number of key comparisons depends on the position of the search key in the array a. When all keys are distinct and $a[i]$ is being searched for, i key comparisons are made. So, the average number of comparisons for a successful search is

$$(\sum_{1 \le i \le n} i)/n = (n + 1)/2.$$

It is possible to do much better than this when looking up phone numbers. The fact that the entries in the list (i.e., the telephone directory) are in lexicographic order (on the name key) enables one to look up a number while examining only a very few entries in the list. Binary search (see Chapter 1) is one of the better-known methods for searching an ordered, sequential list. A binary search takes only $O(\log n)$ time to search a list with n records. This is considerably better than the $O(n)$ time required by a sequential search. We note that when a sequential search is performed on an ordered list, the conditional of the **for** loop of *seqSearch* can be changed to $i <= n \ \&\& \ a[i].key < k$. This change must be accompanied by a change of the conditional $i > n$ to $i > n \ || \ a[i].key != k$. These changes improve the performance of Program 7.1 for unsuccessful searches.

Getting back to our example of the telephone directory, we notice that neither a sequential nor a binary search strategy corresponds to the search method actually employed by humans. If we are looking for a name that begins with the letter W, we start the search toward the end of the directory rather than at the middle. A search method based on this interpolation scheme would begin by comparing k with $a[i].key$, where

$i = ((k - a[1].key)/(a[n].key - a[1].key)) * n$, and $a[1].key$ and $a[n].key$ are the smallest and largest keys in the list. An interpolation search can be used only when the list is ordered. The behavior of such a search depends on the distribution of the keys in the list.

Let us now look at another example in which the use of ordered lists greatly reduces the computational effort. The problem we are now concerned with is that of comparing two lists of records containing data that are essentially the same but have been obtained from two different sources. Such a problem could arise, for instance, in the case of the United States Internal Revenue Service (IRS), which might receive millions of forms from various employers stating how much they paid their employees and then another set of forms from individual employees stating how much they received. So we have two lists of records, and we wish to verify that there is no discrepancy between the two. Since the forms arrive at the IRS in a random order, we may assume a random arrangement of the records in the lists. The keys here are the social security numbers of the employees.

Let *list1* be the employer list and *list2* the employee list. Let *list1*[i].*key* and *list2*[i].*key*, respectively, denote the key of the ith record in *list*1 and *list*2. We make the following assumptions about the required verification:

(1)   If there is no record in the employee list corresponding to a key in the employer list, a message is to be sent to the employee.

(2)   If the reverse is true, then a message is to be sent to the employer.

(3)   If there is a discrepancy between two records with the same key, a message to this effect is to be output.

Function *verify*1 (Program 7.2) solves the verification problem by directly comparing the two unsorted lists. The data type of the records in each list is *element* and we assume that the keys are integer. The complexity of *verify*1 is O(mn), where n amd m are, respectively, the number of records in the employer and employee lists. On the other hand, if we first sort the two lists and then do the comparison, we can carry out the verification task in time O($t_{Sort}(n) + t_{Sort}(m) + n + m$), where $t_{Sort}(n)$ is the time needed to sort a list of n records. As we shall see, it is possible to sort n records in O($n \log n$) time, so the computing time becomes O(max$\{n \log n, m \log m\}$). Function *verify*2 (Program 7.3) achieves this time.

We have seen two important uses of sorting: (1) as an aid in searching and (2) as a means for matching entries in lists. Sorting also finds application in the solution of many other more complex problems from areas such as optimization, graph theory and job scheduling. Consequently, the problem of sorting has great relevance in the study of computing. Unfortunately, no one sorting method is the best for all applications. We shall therefore study several methods, indicating when one is superior to the others.

First let us formally state the problem we are about to consider. We are given a list of records $(R_1, R_2, \cdots, R_n)$. Each record, R_i, has key value K_i. In addition, we assume an ordering relation (<) on the keys so that for any two key values x and y, $x = y$

```
void verify1(element list1[], element list2[], int n, int m)
{/* compare two unordered lists list1[1:n] and list2[1:m] */
  int i,j, marked[MAX_SIZE];

  for (i = 1; i <= m; i++)
    marked[i] = FALSE;
  for (i = 1; i <= n; i++)
    if ((j = seqSearch(list2,m,list1[i].key)) == 0)
      printf("%d is not in list 2\n",list1[i].key);
    else
    /* check each of the other fields from list1[i] and
       list2[j], and print out any discrepancies */
      marked[j] = TRUE;
  for (i = 1; i <= m; i++)
    if (!marked[i])
      printf("%d is not in list 1\n",list2[i].key);
}
```

Program 7.2: Verifying two unsorted lists using a sequential search

or $x < y$ or $y < x$. The ordering relation ($<$) is assumed to be transitive (i.e., for any three values x, y, and z, $x < y$ and $y < z$ implies $x < z$). The sorting problem then is that of finding a permutation, σ, such that $K_{\sigma(i)} \leq K_{\sigma(i+1)}$, $1 \leq i \leq n - 1$. The desired ordering is $(R_{\sigma(1)}, R_{\sigma(2)}, \cdots, R_{\sigma(n)})$.

Note that when the list has several key values that are identical, the permutation, σ, is not unique. We shall distinguish one permutation, σ_s, from the others that also order the list. Let σ_s be the permutation with the following properties:

(1) $K_{\sigma_s(i)} \leq K_{\sigma_s(i+1)}$, $1 \leq i \leq n - 1$.

(2)   If $i < j$ and $K_i == K_j$ in the input list, then R_i precedes R_j in the sorted list.

A sorting method that generates the permutation σ_s is *stable*.

We characterize sorting methods into two broad categories: (1) internal methods (i.e., methods to be used when the list to be sorted is small enough so that the entire sort can be carried out in main memory) and (2) external methods (i.e., methods to be used on larger lists). The following internal sorting methods will be developed: insertion sort, quick sort, merge sort, heap sort, and radix sort. This development will be followed by a discussion of external sorting. Throughout, we assume that relational operators have been overloaded so that record comparison is done by comparing their keys.

```
void verify2(element list1[], element list2[], int n, int m)
{/* same as verify1, but we sort list1 and list2 first */
   int i,j;
   sort(list1,n); sort(list2,m);
   i = j = 1;
   while (i <= n && j <= m)
      if (list1[i].key < list2[j].key) {
         printf("%d is not in list 2\n",list1[i].key);
         i++;
      }
      else if (list1[i].key == list2[j].key) {
      /* compare list1[i] and list2[j] on each of the other
         fields and report any discrepancies */
         i++; j++;
      }
      else {
         printf("%d is not in list 1\n", list2[j].key);
         j++;
      }
   for(; i <= n; i++)
      printf("%d is not in list 2\n",list1[i].key);
   for (; j <= m; j++)
      printf("%d is not in list 1\n",list2[j].key);
}
```

Program 7.3: Fast verification of two sorted lists

7.2 INSERTION SORT

The basic step in this method is to insert a new record into a sorted sequence of i records in such a way that the resulting sequence of size $i + 1$ is also ordered. Function *insert* (Program 7.4) accomplishes this insertion.

The use of $a[0]$ enables us to simplify the **while** loop, avoiding a test for end of list (i.e., $i < 1$). In insertion sort, we begin with the ordered sequence $a[1]$ and successively insert the records $a[2], a[3], \cdots, a[n]$. Since each insertion leaves the resultant sequence ordered, the list with n records can be ordered making $n - 1$ insertions. The details are given in function *insertionSort* (Program 7.5).

```
void insert(element e, element a[], int i)
{/* insert e into the ordered list a[1:i] such that the
    resulting list a[1:i+1] is also ordered, the array a
    must have space allocated for at least i+2 elements */
    a[0] = e;
    while (e.key < a[i].key)
    {
        a[i+1] = a[i];
        i--;
    }
    a[i+1] = e;
}
```

Program 7.4: Insertion into a sorted list

```
void insertionSort(element a[], int n)
{/* sort a[1:n] into nondecreasing order */
    int j;
    for (j = 2; j <= n; j++) {
        element temp = a[j];
        insert(temp, a, j-1);
    }
}
```

Program 7.5: Insertion sort

Analysis of *insertionSort*: In the worst case *insert* (e, a, i) makes $i + 1$ comparisons before making the insertion. Hence the complexity of *Insert* is $O(i)$. Function *insertionSort* invokes *insert* for $i = j - 1 = 1, 2, \cdots, n - 1$. So, the complexity of *insertionSort* is

$$O(\sum_{i=1}^{n-1} (i+1)) = O(n^2).$$

We can also obtain an estimate of the computing time of insertion sort based on the relative disorder in the input list. Record R_i is *left out of order* (LOO) iff $R_i < \max_{1 \le j < i}\{R_j\}$. The insertion step has to be carried out only for those records that are LOO. If k is the number of LOO records, the computing time is $O((k + 1)n) = O(kn)$. We can show that the average time for *insertionSort* is $O(n^2)$ as well. $\square$

Example 7.1: Assume that $n = 5$ and the input key sequence is 5, 4, 3, 2, 1. After each insertion we have

j	[1]	[2]	[3]	[4]	[5]
—	**5**	4	3	2	1
2	**4**	**5**	3	2	1
3	**3**	**4**	**5**	2	1
4	**2**	**3**	**4**	**5**	1
5	**1**	**2**	**3**	**4**	**5**

For convenience, only the key field of each record is displayed, and the sorted part of the list is shown in bold. Since the input list is in reverse order, as each new record is inserted into the sorted part of the list, the entire sorted part is shifted right by one position. Thus, this input sequence exhibits the worst-case behavior of insertion sort. □

Example 7.2: Assume that $n = 5$ and the input key sequence is 2, 3, 4, 5, 1. After each iteration we have

j	[1]	[2]	[3]	[4]	[5]
—	**2**	**3**	**4**	**5**	1
2	**2**	**3**	**4**	**5**	1
3	**2**	**3**	**4**	**5**	1
4	**2**	**3**	**4**	**5**	1
5	**1**	**2**	**3**	**4**	**5**

In this example, only record 5 is LOO, and the time for each $j = 2$, 3, and 4 is $O(1)$, whereas for $j = 5$ it is $O(n)$. □

It should be fairly obvious that *insertionSort* is stable. The fact that the computing time is $O(kn)$ makes this method very desirable in sorting sequences in which only a very few records are LOO (i.e., $k << n$). The simplicity of this scheme makes it about the fastest sorting method for small n (say, $n \le 30$).

Variations

1. *Binary Insertion Sort:* We can reduce the number of comparisons made in an insertion sort by replacing the sequential searching technique used in *insert* (Program 7.4) with binary search. The number of record moves remains unchanged.

2. *Linked Insertion Sort:* The elements of the list are represented as a linked list rather than as an array. The number of record moves becomes zero because only the link fields

require adjustment. However, we must retain the sequential search used in *insert*.

EXERCISES

1. Write the status of the list (12, 2, 16, 30, 8, 28, 4, 10, 20, 6, 18) at the end of each iteration of the **for** loop of *insertionSort* (Program 7.5).

2. Write a function that implements binary insertion sort. What is the worst-case number of comparisons made by your sort function? What is the worst-case number of record moves made? How do these compare with the corresponding numbers for Program 7.5?

3. Write a function that implements linked insertion sort. What is the worst-case number of comparisons made by your sort function? What is the worst-case number of record moves made? How do these compare with the corresponding numbers for Program 7.5?

7.3 QUICK SORT

We now turn our attention to a sorting scheme with very good average behavior. The quick sort scheme developed by C. A. R. Hoare has the best average behavior among the sorting methods we shall be studying. In quick sort, we select a pivot record from among the records to be sorted. Next, the records to be sorted are reordered so that the keys of records to the left of the pivot are less than or equal to that of the pivot and those of the records to the right of the pivot are greater than or equal to that of the pivot. Finally, the records to the left of the pivot and those to its right are sorted independently (using the quick sort method recursively).

Program 7.6 gives the resulting quick sort function. To sort $a[1:n]$, the function invocation is *quickSort* $(a, 1, n)$. Function *quickSort* assumes that $a[n + 1]$ has been set to have a key at least as large as the remaining keys.

Example 7.3: Suppose we are to sort a list of 10 records with keys (26, 5, 37, 1, 61, 11, 59, 15, 48, 19). Figure 7.1 gives the status of the list at each call of *quickSort*. Square brackets indicate sublists yet to be sorted. □

Analysis of *quickSort*: The worst-case behavior of *quickSort* is examined in Exercise 2 and shown to be $O(n^2)$. However, if we are lucky, then each time a record is correctly positioned, the sublist to its left will be of the same size as that to its right. This would leave us with the sorting of two sublists, each of size roughly $n/2$. The time required to position a record in a list of size n is $O(n)$. If $T(n)$ is the time taken to sort a list of n records, then when the list splits roughly into two equal parts each time a record is positioned correctly, we have

```
void quickSort(element a[], int left, int right)
{/* sort a[left:right] into nondecreasing order
    on the key field; a[left].key is arbitrarily
    chosen as the pivot key;   it is assumed that
    a[left].key <= a[right+1].key */
  int pivot,i,j;
  element temp;
  if (left < right) {
     i = left; j = right + 1;
     pivot = a[left].key;
     do {/* search for keys from the left and right
             sublists, swapping out-of-order elements until
             the left and right boundaries cross or meet */
         do i++; while (a[i].key < pivot);
         do j--; while (a[j].key > pivot);
         if (i < j) SWAP(a[i],a[j],temp);
     } while (i < j);
     SWAP(a[left],a[j],temp);
     quickSort(a,left,j-1);
     quickSort(a,j+1,right);
  }
}
```

Program 7.6: Quick sort

$$T(n) \leq cn + 2T(n/2), \text{ for some constant } c$$

$$\leq cn + 2(cn/2 + 2T(n/4))$$

$$\leq 2cn + 4T(n/4)$$

.

.

.

$$\leq cn \log_2 n + nT(1) = O(n \log n)$$

Lemma 7.1 shows that the average computing time for function *quickSort* is $O(n \log n)$. Moreover, experimental results show that as far as average computing time is concerned, Quick sort is the best of the internal sorting methods we shall be studying.

R_1	R_2	R_3	R_4	R_5	R_6	R_7	R_8	R_9	R_{10}	left	right
[26	5	37	1	61	11	59	15	48	19]	1	10
[11	5	19	1	15]	26	[59	61	48	37]	1	5
[1	5]	11	[19	15]	26	[59	61	48	37	1	2
1	5	11	[19	15]	26	[59	61	48	37]	4	5
1	5	11	15	19	26	[59	61	48	37]	7	10
1	5	11	15	19	26	[48	37]	59	[61]	7	8
1	5	11	15	19	26	37	48	59	[61]	10	10
1	5	11	15	19	26	37	48	59	61		

Figure 7.1: Quick sort example

Lemma 7.1: Let $T_{avg}(n)$ be the expected time for function *quickSort* to sort a list with n records. Then there exists a constant k such that $T_{avg}(n) \leq kn\log_e n$ for $n \geq 2$.

Proof: In the call to *quickSort* $(list, 1, n)$, the pivot gets placed at position j. This leaves us with the problem of sorting two sublists of size $j - 1$ and $n - j$. The expected time for this is $T_{avg}(j - 1) + T_{avg}(n - j)$. The remainder of the function clearly takes at most cn time for some constant c. Since j may take on any of the values 1 to n with equal probability, we have

$$T_{avg}(n) \leq cn + \frac{1}{n}\sum_{j=1}^{n}(T_{avg}(j - 1) + T_{avg}(n - j)) = cn + \frac{2}{n}\sum_{j=0}^{n-1}T_{avg}(j) \qquad (7.1)$$

for $n \geq 2$. We may assume $T_{avg}(0) \leq b$ and $T_{avg}(1) \leq b$ for some constant b. We shall now show $T_{avg}(n) \leq kn\log_e n$ for $n \geq 2$ and $k = 2(b + c)$. The proof is by induction on n.

Induction base: For $n = 2$, Eq. (7.1) yields $T_{avg}(2) \leq 2c + 2b \leq kn\log_e 2$.

Induction hypothesis: Assume $T_{avg}(n) \leq kn\log_e n$ for $1 \leq n < m$.

Induction step: From Eq. (7.1) and the induction hypothesis we have

$$T_{avg}(m) \leq cm + \frac{4b}{m} + \frac{2}{m}\sum_{j=2}^{m-1}T_{avg}(j) \leq cm + \frac{4b}{m} + \frac{2k}{m}\sum_{j=2}^{m-1}j\log_e j \qquad (7.2)$$

Since $j\log_e j$ is an increasing function of j, Eq. (7.2) yields

$$T_{avg}(m) \leq cm + \frac{4b}{m} + \frac{2k}{m}\int_{2}^{m}x\log_e x\, dx = cm + \frac{4b}{m} + \frac{2k}{m}\left[\frac{m^2\log_e m}{2} - \frac{m^2}{4}\right]$$

$$= cm + \frac{4b}{m} + km\log_e m - \frac{km}{2} \leq km\log_e m, \text{ for } m \geq 2 \ \square$$

Unlike insertion sort, where the only additional space needed was for one record, quick sort needs stack space to implement the recursion. If the lists split evenly, as in the above analysis, the maximum recursion depth would be $\log n$, requiring a stack space of $O(\log n)$. The worst case occurs when the list is split into a left sublist of size $n-1$ and a right sublist of size 0 at each level of recursion. In this case, the depth of recursion becomes n, requiring stack space of $O(n)$. The worst-case stack space can be reduced by a factor of 4 by realizing that right sublists of size less than 2 need not be stacked. An asymptotic reduction in stack space can be achieved by sorting smaller sublists first. In this case the additional stack space is at most $O(\log n)$.

Variation—Quick sort using a median-of-three: Our version of quick sort always picked the key of the first record in the current sublist as the pivot. A better choice for this pivot is the median of the first, middle, and last keys in the current sublist. Thus, $pivot = median \ \{K_l, K_{(l+r)/2}, K_r\}$. For example, $median\{10, 5, 7\} = 7$ and $median\{10, 7, 7\} = 7$.

EXERCISES

1. Draw a figure similar to Figure 7.1 starting with the list (12, 2, 16, 30, 8, 28, 4, 10, 20, 6, 18).

2. (a) Show that *quickSort* takes $O(n^2)$ time when the input list is already in sorted order.

   (b) Show that the worst-case time complexity of *quickSort* is $O(n^2)$.

   (c) Why is *list* [*left*] $\leq$ *list* [*right* + 1] required in *quickSort*?

3. (a) Write a nonrecursive version of *quickSort* incorporating the median-of-three rule to determine the pivot key.

   (b) Show that this function takes $O(n \log n)$ time on an already sorted list.

4. Show that if smaller sublists are sorted first, then the recursion in *quickSort* can be simulated by a stack of depth $O(\log n)$.

5. Quick sort is an unstable sorting method. Give an example of an input list in which the order of records with equal keys is not preserved.

7.4 HOW FAST CAN WE SORT?

Both of the sorting methods we have seen so far have a worst-case behavior of $O(n^2)$. It is natural at this point to ask the question, What is the best computing time for sorting that we can hope for? The theorem we shall prove shows that if we restrict our question to sorting algorithms in which the only operations permitted on keys are comparisons and interchanges, then O($n \log n$) is the best possible time.

The method we use is to consider a tree that describes the sorting process. Each vertex of the tree represents a key comparison, and the branches indicate the result. Such a tree is called a *decision tree*. A path through a decision tree represents a sequence of computations that an algorithm could produce.

Example 7.4: Let us look at the decision tree obtained for insertion sort working on a list with three records (Figure 7.2). The input sequence is R_1, R_2, and R_3, so the root of the tree is labeled [1, 2, 3]. Depending on the outcome of the comparison between keys K_1 and K_2, this sequence may or may not change. If $K_2 < K_1$, then the sequence becomes [2, 1, 3]; otherwise it stays [1, 2, 3]. The full tree resulting from these comparisons is given in Figure 7.2.

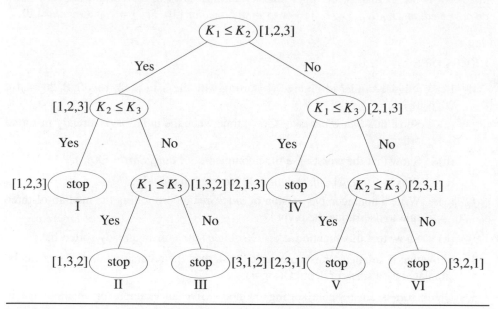

Figure 7.2: Decision tree for insertion sort

The leaf nodes are labeled I to VI. These are the only points at which the algorithm may terminate. Hence, only six permutations of the input sequence are obtainable from this algorithm. Since all six of these are different, and 3! = 6, it follows that this algorithm has enough leaves to constitute a valid sorting algorithm for three records. The maximum depth of this tree is 3. Figure 7.3 gives six different orderings of the key values 7, 9, and 10, which show that all six permutations are possible. □

leaf	permutation	sample input key values that give the permutation
I	1 2 3	[7, 9, 10]
II	1 3 2	[7, 10, 9]
III	3 1 2	[9, 10, 7]
IV	2 1 3	[9, 7, 10]
V	2 3 1	[10, 7, 9]
VI	3 2 1	[10, 9, 7]

Figure 7.3: Sample input permutations

Theorem 7.1: Any decision tree that sorts n distinct elements has a height of at least $\log_2(n!) + 1$.

Proof: When sorting n elements, there are $n!$ different possible results. Thus, every decision tree for sorting must have at least $n!$ leaves. But a decision tree is also a binary tree, which can have at most 2^{k-1} leaves if its height is k. Therefore, the height must be at least $\log_2 n! + 1$. □

Corollary: Any algorithm that sorts only by comparisons must have a worst-case computing time of $\Omega(n \log n)$.

Proof: We must show that for every decision tree with $n!$ leaves, there is a path of length $cn\log_2 n$, where c is a constant. By the theorem, there is a path of length $\log_2 n!$. Now

$$n! = n(n-1)(n-2) \cdots (3)(2)(1) \geq (n/2)^{n/2}$$

So, $\log_2 n! \geq (n/2)\log_2(n/2) = \Omega(n \log n)$. □

Using a similar argument and the fact that binary trees with 2^n leaves must have an average root-to-leaf path length of $\Omega(n \log n)$, we can show that the average complexity of comparison-based sorting methods is $\Omega(n \log n)$.

7.5   MERGE SORT

7.5.1   Merging

Before looking at the merge sort method to sort n records, let us see how one may merge two sorted lists to get a single sorted list. Program 7.7 gives the code for this. The two lists to be merged are $initList[i:m]$ and $initList[m+1:n]$. The resulting merged list is $mergedList[i:n]$.

```
void merge(element initList[], element mergedList[],
           int i, int m, int n)
{/*  the sorted lists initList[i:m] and initList[m+1:n] are
     merged to obtain the sorted list mergedList[i:n] */
  int j,k,t;
  j = m+1;         /* index for the second sublist */
  k = i;           /* index for the merged list */

  while (i <= m && j <= n) {
    if (initList[i].key <= initList[j].key)
       mergedList[k++] = initList[i++];
    else
       mergedList[k++] = initList[j++];
  }
  if (i > m)
  /* mergedList[k:n] = initList[j:n] */
     for (t = j; t <= n; t++)
        mergedList[t] = initList[t];
     else
     /* mergedList[k:n] = initList[i:m] */
        for (t = i; t <= m; t++)
           mergedList[k+t-i] = initList[t];
}
```

Program 7.7: Merging two sorted lists

Analysis of *merge*: In each iteration of the **while** loop, k increases by 1. The total increment in k is at most $n - i + 1$. Hence, the **while** loop is iterated at most $n - i + 1$ times. The **for** statements copy at most $n - i + 1$ records. The total time is therefore $O(n - i + 1)$.

If each record has a size s, then the time is $O(s(n - l + 1))$. When s is greater than

1, we can use linked lists instead of arrays and obtain a new sorted linked list containing these $n - l + 1$ records. Now, we will not need the additional space for $n - l + 1$ records as needed in *merge* for the array *mergedList*. Instead, space for $n - l + 1$ links is needed. The merge time becomes $O(n - i + 1)$ and is independent of s. Note that $n - l + 1$ is the number of records being merged. $\square$

7.5.2 Iterative Merge Sort

This version of merge sort begins by interpreting the input list as compriscd of n sorted sublists, each of size 1. In the first merge pass, these sublists are merged by pairs to obtain $n/2$ sublists, each of size 2 (if n is odd, then one sublist is of size 1). In the second merge pass, these $n/2$ sublists are then merged by pairs to obtain $n/4$ sublists. Each merge pass reduces the number of sublists by half. Merge passes are continued until we are left with only one sublist. The example below illustrates the process.

Example 7.5: The input list is (26, 5, 77, 1, 61, 11, 59, 15, 48, 19). The tree of Figure 7.4 illustrates the sublists being merged at each pass. $\square$

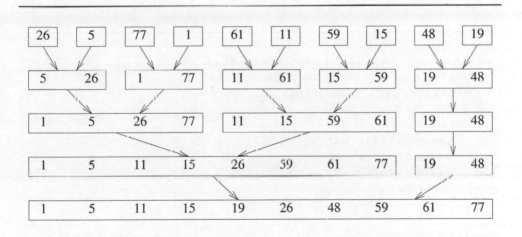

Figure 7.4: Merge tree

Since a merge sort consists of several merge passes, it is convenient first to write a function (Program 7.8) for a merge pass. Now the sort can be done by repeatedly invoking the merge-pass function as in Program 7.9.

```
void mergePass(element initList[], element mergedList[],
               int n, int s)
{/* perform one pass of the merge sort, merge adjacent
    pairs of sorted segments from initList[] into mergedList[],
    n is the number of elements in the list, s is
    the size of each sorted segment */
  int i,j;
  for (i = 1; i <= n - 2 * s + 1; i += 2 * s)
    merge(initList,mergedList,i,i + s - 1,i + 2 * s - 1);
  if (i + s - 1 < n)
    merge(initList,mergedList,i,i + s - 1,n);
  else
    for (j = i; j <= n; j++)
      mergedList[j] = initList[j];
}
```

Program 7.8: A merge pass

```
void mergeSort(element a[], int n)
{/* sort a[1:n] using the merge sort method */
  int s = 1; /* current segment size */
  element extra[MAX_SIZE];

  while (s < n) {
    mergePass(a, extra, n, s);
    s *= 2;
    mergePass(extra, a, n, s);
    s *= 2;
  }
}
```

Program 7.9: Merge sort

Analysis of *mergeSort*: A merge sort consists of several passes over the input. The first pass merges segments of size 1, the second merges segments of size 2, and the *i*th pass merges segments of size 2^{i-1}. Thus, the total number of passes is $\lceil \log_2 n \rceil$. As *merge* showed, we can merge two sorted segments in linear time, which means that each pass

takes O(n) time. Since there are $\lceil \log_2 n \rceil$ passes, the total computing time is O($n \log n$).
□

You may verify that *mergeSort* is a stable sorting function.

7.5.3   Recursive Merge Sort

In the recursive formulation we divide the list to be sorted into two roughly equal parts called the left and the right sublists. These sublists are sorted recursively, and the sorted sublists are merged.

Example 7.6: The input list (26, 5, 77, 1, 61, 11, 59, 15, 49, 19) is to be sorted using the recursive formulation of merge sort. If the sublist from *left* to *right* is currently to be sorted, then its two sublists are indexed from *left* to $\lfloor (left + right)/2 \rfloor$ and from $\lfloor (left + right)/2 \rfloor + 1$ to *right*. The sublist partitioning that takes place is described by the binary tree of Figure 7.5. Note that the sublists being merged are different from those being merged in *mergeSort*. □

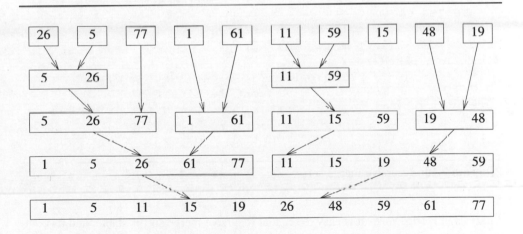

Figure 7.5: Sublist partitioning for recursive merge sort

To eliminate the record copying that takes place when *merge* (Program 7.7) is used to merge sorted sublists we associate an integer pointer with each record. For this purpose, we employ an integer array *link* [1:n] such that *link* [i] gives the record that follows record i in the sorted sublist. In case *link* [i] = 0, there is no next record. With the addition of this array of links, record copying is replaced by link changes and the runtime of our sort function becomes independent of the size s of a record. Also the additional space required is $O(n)$. By comparison, the iterative merge sort described earlier takes $O(sn\log n)$ time and $O(sn)$ additional space. On the down side, the use of an array of links yields a sorted chain of records and we must have a follow up process to physically rearrange the records into the sorted order dictated by the final chain. We describe the algorithm for this physical rearrangement in Section 7.8.

We assume that initially $link[i] = 0$, $1 \le i \le n$. Thus, each record is initially in a chain containing only itself. Let $start1$ and $start2$ be pointers to two chains of records. The records on each chain are in nondecreasing order. Let $listMerge\ (a,\ link,\ start1,\ start2)$ be a function that merges two chains $start1$ and $start2$ in array a and returns the first position of the resulting chain that is linked in nondecreasing order of key values. The recursive version of merge sort is given by function $rmergeSort$ (Program 7.10). To sort the array $a[1{:}n]$ this function is invoked as $rmergeSort\ (a,\ link,\ 1,\ n)$. The start of the chain ordered as described earlier is returned. Function $listMerge$ is given in Program 7.11.

```
int rmergeSort(element a[], int link[], int left, int right)
{/* a[left:right] is to be sorted, link[i] is initially 0
    for all i, returns the index of the first element in the
    sorted chain */
   if (left >= right) return left;
   int mid = (left + right) / 2;
   return listMerge(a, link,
                 rmergeSort(a, link, left, mid),
                        /* sort left half */
                 rmergeSort(a, link, mid + 1, right));
                        /* sort right half */
}
```

Program 7.10: Recursive merge sort

Analysis of *rmergeSort:* It is easy to see that recursive merge sort is stable, and its computing time is $O(n \log n)$. □

Variation—Natural Merge Sort: We may modify *mergeSort* to take into account the prevailing order within the input list. In this implementation we make an initial pass over the data to determine the sublists of records that are in order. Merge sort then uses these initially ordered sublists for the remainder of the passes. Figure 7.6 shows natural merge sort using the input sequence of Example 7.6.

```
int listMerge(element a[], int link[], int start1, int start2)
{/* sorted chains beginning at start1 and start2,
    respectively, are merged; link[0] is used as a
    temporary header; returns start of merged chain */
    int last1, last2, lastResult = 0;
    for (last1 = start1, last2 = start2; last1 && last2;)
        if (a[last1] <= a[last2]) {
            link[lastResult] = last1;
            lastResult = last1; last1 = link[last1];
        }
        else {
            link[lastResult] = last2;
            lastResult = last2; last2 = link[last2];
        }

    /* attach remaining records to result chain */
    if (last1 == 0) link[lastResult] = last2;
    else link[lastResult] = last1;
    return link[0];
}
```

Program 7.11: Merging sorted chains

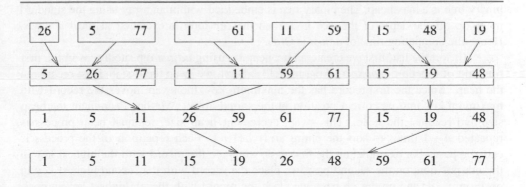

Figure 7.6: Natural merge sort

EXERCISES

1. Write the status of the list (12, 2, 16, 30, 8, 28, 4, 10, 20, 6, 18) at the end of each phase of *mergeSort* (Program 7.9).

2. Prove that *mergeSort* is stable.

3. Write an iterative natural merge sort function using arrays as in function *mergeSort*. How much time does this function take on an initially sorted list? Note that *mergeSort* takes $O(n \log n)$ on such an input list. What is the worst-case computing time of the new function? How much additional space is needed?

4. Do the previous exercise using chains.

7.6 HEAP SORT

Although the merge sort scheme discussed in the previous section has a computing time of $O(n \log n)$, both in the worst case and as average behavior, it requires additional storage proportional to the number of records to be sorted. The sorting method we are about to study, heap sort, requires only a fixed amount of additional storage and at the same time has as its worst-case and average computing time $O(n \log n)$. However, heap sort is slightly slower than merge sort.

In heap sort, we utilize the max-heap structure introduced in Chapter 5. The deletion and insertion functions associated with max heaps directly yield an $O(n \log n)$ sorting method. The n records are first inserted into an initially empty max heap. Next, the records are extracted from the max heap one at a time. It is possible to create the max heap of n records faster than by inserting the records one by one into an initially empty heap. For this, we use the function *adjust* (Program 7.12), which starts with a binary tree whose left and right subtrees are max heaps and rearranges records so that the entire binary tree is a max heap. The binary tree is embedded within an array using the standard mapping. If the depth of the tree is d, then the **for** loop is executed at most d times. Hence the computing time of *adjust* is $O(d)$.

To sort the list, first we create a max heap by using *adjust* repeatedly, as in the first **for** loop of function *heapSort* (Program 7.13). Next, we swap the first and last records in the heap. Since the first record has the maximum key, the swap moves the record with maximum key into its correct position in the sorted array. We then decrement the heap size and readjust the heap. This swap, decrement heap size, readjust heap process is repeated $n - 1$ times to sort the entire array $a[1:n]$. Each repetition of the process is called a pass. For example, on the first pass, we place the record with the highest key in the nth position; on the second pass, we place the record with the second highest key in position $n - 1$; and on the ith pass, we place the record with the ith highest key in position $n - i + 1$.

Example 7.7: The input list is (26, 5, 77, 1, 61, 11, 59, 15, 48, 19). If we interpret this list as a binary tree, we get the tree of Figure 7.7(a). Figure 7.7(b) depicts the max heap

```
void adjust(element a[], int root, int n)
{/* adjust the binary tree to establish the heap */
   int child,rootkey;
   element temp;
   temp = a[root];
   rootkey = a[root].key;
   child = 2 * root;                        /* left child */
   while (child <= n) {
      if ((child < n) &&
      (a[child].key < a[child+1].key))
         child++;
      if (rootkey > a[child].key) /* compare root and
                                     max. child */
         break;
      else {
         a[child / 2] = a[child]; /* move to parent */
         child *= 2;
      }
   }
   a[child/2] = temp;
}
```

Program 7.12: Adjusting a max heap

after the first **for** loop of *heapSort*. Figure 7.8 shows the array of records following each of the first seven iterations of the second **for** loop. The portion of the array that still represents a max heap is shown as a binary tree; the sorted part of the array is shown as an array. ☐

Analysis of *heapSort*: Suppose $2^{k-1} \leq n < 2^k$, so the tree has k levels and the number of nodes on level i is $\leq 2^{i-1}$. In the first **for** loop, *adjust* (Program 7.12) is called once for each node that has a child. Hence, the time required for this loop is the sum, over each level, of the number of nodes on a level multiplied by the maximum distance the node can move. This is no more than

$$\sum_{1 \leq i \leq k} 2^{i-1}(k-i) = \sum_{1 < i < k-1} 2^{k-i-1} i \leq n \sum_{1 \leq i \leq k-1} i/2^i < 2n = O(n)$$

In the next **for** loop, $n-1$ applications of *adjust* are made with maximum tree-depth $k = \lceil \log_2 (n + 1) \rceil$ and *SWAP* is invoked $n-1$ times. Hence, the computing time for this loop is $O(n \log n)$. Consequently, the total computing time is $O(n \log n)$. Note that apart

```
void heapSort(element a[], int n)
{/* perform a heap sort on a[1:n] */
    int i,j;
    element temp;

    for (i = n/2; i > 0; i--)
        adjust(a,i,n);
    for (i = n-1; i > 0; i--) {
        SWAP(a[1],a[i+1],temp);
        adjust(a,1,i);
    }
}
```

Program 7.13: Heap sort

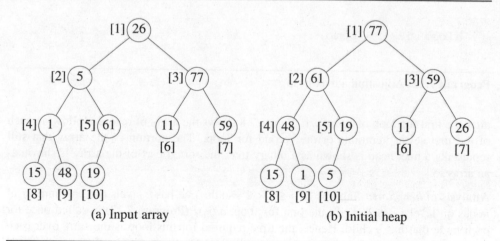

(a) Input array   (b) Initial heap

Figure 7.7: Array interpreted as a binary tree

from some simple variables, the only additional space needed is space for one record to carry out the swap in the second **for** loop. □

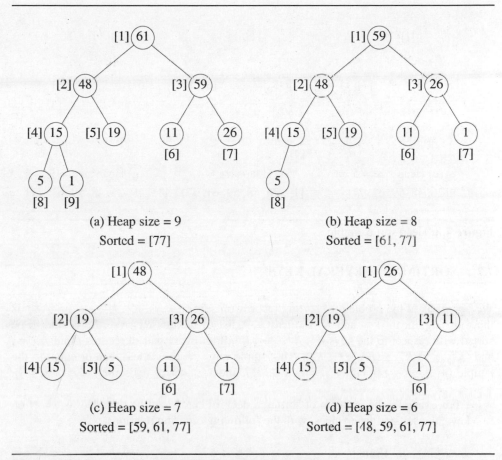

(a) Heap size = 9
Sorted = [77]

(b) Heap size = 8
Sorted = [61, 77]

(c) Heap size = 7
Sorted = [59, 61, 77]

(d) Heap size = 6
Sorted = [48, 59, 61, 77]

Figure 7.8: Heap sort example (continued on next page)

EXERCISES

1. Write the status of the list (12, 2, 16, 30, 8, 28, 4, 10, 20, 6, 18) at the end of the first **for** loop as well as at the end of each iteration of the second **for** loop of *heap-Sort* (Program 7.13).

2. Heap sort is unstable. Give an example of an input list in which the order of records with equal keys is not preserved.

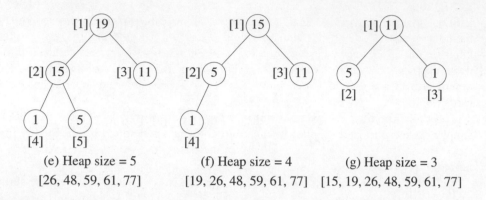

(e) Heap size = 5
[26, 48, 59, 61, 77]

(f) Heap size = 4
[19, 26, 48, 59, 61, 77]

(g) Heap size = 3
[15, 19, 26, 48, 59, 61, 77]

Figure 7.8: Heap sort example

7.7   SORTING ON SEVERAL KEYS

We now look at the problem of sorting records on several keys, $K^1, K^2, \cdots, K^r$ (K^1 is the most significant key and K^r the least). A list of records $R_1, \cdots, R_n$ is said to be sorted with respect to the keys $K^1, K^2, \cdots, K^r$ iff for every pair of records i and j, $i < j$ and $(K_i^1, \cdots, K_i^r) \le (K_j^1, \cdots, K_j^r)$. The r-tuple $(x_1, \cdots, x_r)$ is less than or equal to the r-tuple $(y_1, \cdots, y_r)$ iff either $x_i = y_i$, $1 \le i \le j$, and $x_{j+1} < y_{j+1}$ for some $j < r$, or $x_i = y_i$, $1 \le i \le r$.

For example, the problem of sorting a deck of cards may be regarded as a sort on two keys, the suit and face values, with the following ordering relations:

K^1 [Suits]:   ♣ < ♦ < ♥ < ♠

K^2 [Face values]:   2 < 3 < 4 $\cdots$ < 10 < J < Q < K < A

A sorted deck of cards therefore has the following ordering:

2♣, . . ., A♣, . . ., 2♠, . . ., A♠

There are two popular ways to sort on multiple keys. In the first, we begin by sorting on the most significant key K^1, obtaining several ''piles'' of records, each having the same value for K^1. Then each of these piles is independently sorted on the key K^2 into ''subpiles'' such that all the records in the same subpile have the same values for K^1 and K^2. The subpiles are then sorted on K^3, and so on, and the piles are combined. Using this method on our card deck example, we would first sort the 52 cards into four piles, one for each of the suit values, then sort each pile on the face value. Then we would place the piles on top of each other to obtain the desired ordering.

A sort proceeding in this fashion is referred to as a most-significant-digit-first (MSD) sort. The second way, quite naturally, is to sort on the least significant digit first (LSD). An LSD sort would mean sorting the cards first into 13 piles corresponding to their face values (key K^2). Then, we would place the 3's on top of the 2's, $\cdots$, the kings on top of the queens, the aces on top of the kings; we would turn the deck upside down and sort on the suit (K^1) using a stable sorting method to obtain four piles, each orderd on K^2; and we would combine the piles to obtain the required ordering on the cards.

Comparing the two functions outlined here (MSD and LSD), we see that LSD is simpler, as the piles and subpiles obtained do not have to be sorted independently (provided the sorting scheme used for sorting on the keys K^i, $1 \le i < r$, is stable). This in turn implies less overhead.

The terms LSD and MSD specify only the order in which the keys are to be sorted. They do not specify how each key is to be sorted. When sorting a card deck manually, we generally use an MSD sort. The sorting on suit is done by a *bin sort* (i.e., four "bins" are set up, one for each suit value and the cards are placed into their corresponding bins). Next, the cards in each bin are sorted using an algorithm similar to insertion sort. However, there is another way to do this. First use a bin sort on the face value. To do this we need 13 bins, one for each distinct face value. Then collect all the cards together as described above and perform a bin sort on the suits using four bins. Note that a bin sort requires only $O(n)$ time if the spread in key values is $O(n)$.

LSD or MSD sorting can be used to sort even when the records have only one key. For this, we interpret the key as being composed of several subkeys. For example, if the keys are numeric, then each decimal digit may be regarded as a subkey. So, if the keys are in the range $0 \le K \le 999$, we can use either the LSD or MSD sorts for three keys (K^1, K^2, K^3), where K^1 is the digit in the hundredths place, K^2 the digit in the tens place, and K^3 the digit in the units place. Since $0 \le K^i \le 9$ for each key K^i, the sort on each key can be carried out using a bin sort with 10 bins.

In a *radix sort*, we decompose the sort key using some radix r. When r is 10, we get the decimal decomposition described above. When $r = 2$, we get binary decomposition of the keys. In a Radix-r Sort, the number of bins required is r.

Assume that the records to be sorted are $R_1, \cdots, R_n$. The record keys are decomposed using a radix of r. This results in each key having d digits in the range 0 through $r - 1$. Thus, we shall need r bins. The records in each bin will be linked together into a chain with *front* [i], $0 \le i < r$, a pointer to the first record in bin i and *rear* [i], a pointer to the last record in bin i. These chains will operate as queues. Function *radixSort* (Program 7.14) formally presents the LSD radix-r method.

Analysis of *radixSort*: *radixSort* makes d passes over the data, each pass taking $O(n + r)$ time. Hence, the total computing time is $O(d(n + r))$. The value of d will depend on the choice of the radix r and also on the largest key. Different choices of r

```
int radixSort(element a[], int link[], int d, int r, int n)
{/* sort a[1:n]) using a d-digit radix-r sort, digit(a[i],j,r)
   returns the jth radix-r digit (from the left) of a[i]'s key;
   each digit is in the range is [0,r); sorting within a digit
   is done using a bin sort */
   int front[r], rear[r]; /* queue front and rear pointers */
   int i, bin, current, first, last;
   /* create initial chain of records starting at first */
   first = 1;
   for (i = 1; i < n; i++) link[i] = i + 1;
   link[n] = 0;

   for (i = d-1; i >= 0; i--)
   {/* sort on digit i */
      /* initialize bins to empty queues */
      for (bin = 0; bin < r; bin++) front[bin] = 0;

      for (current = first; current; current = link[current])
      {/* put records into queues/bins */
         bin = digit(a[current],i,r);
         if (front[bin] == 0) front[bin] = current;
         else link[rear[bin]] = current;
         rear[bin] = current;
      }
      /* find first nonempty queue/bin */
      for (bin = 0; !front[bin]; bin++);
      first = front[bin]; last = rear[bin];

      /* concatenate remaining queues */
      for (bin++; bin < r; bin++)
         if (front[bin])
            {link[last] = front[bin]; last = rear[bin];}
      link[last] = 0;
   }
   return first;
}
```

Program 7.14: LSD radix sort

will yield different computing times. □

Example 7.8: Suppose we are to sort 10 numbers in the range [0, 999]. For this example, we use $r = 10$ (though other choices are possible). Hence, $d = 3$. The input list is linked and has the form given in Figure 7.9(a). The nodes are labeled $R_1, \cdots, R_{10}$. Figure 7.9 shows the queues formed when sorting on each of the digits, as well as the lists after the queues have been collected from the 10 bins. □

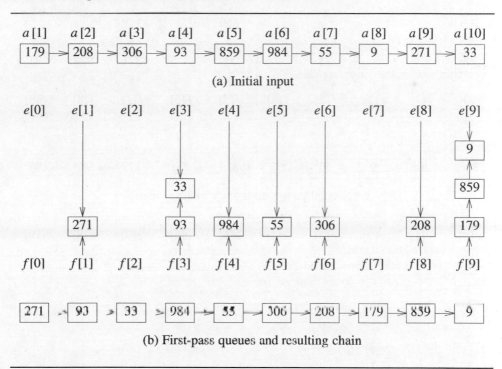

(a) Initial input

(b) First-pass queues and resulting chain

Figure 7.9: Radix sort example (continued on next page)

EXERCISES

1. Write the status of the list (12, 2, 16, 30, 8, 28, 4, 10, 20, 6, 18) at the end of each pass of *radixSort* (Program 7.14). Use $r = 10$.

2. Under what conditions would an MSD radix sort be more efficient than an LSD radix sort?

3. Does *radixSort* result in a stable sort when used to sort numbers as in Example 7.8?

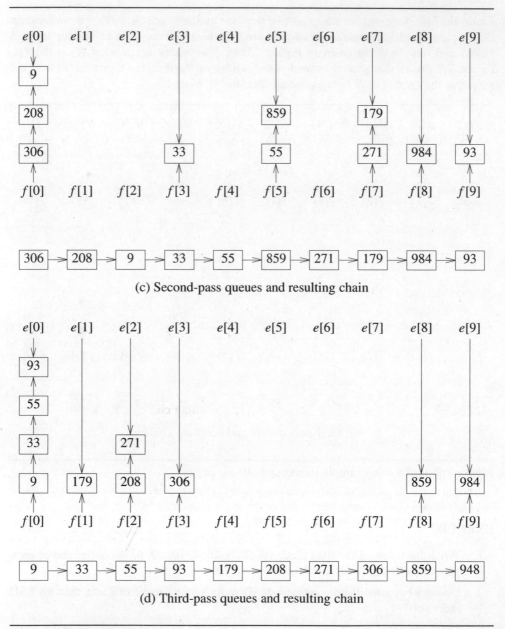

(c) Second-pass queues and resulting chain

(d) Third-pass queues and resulting chain

Figure 7.9: Radix sort example

4. Write a sort function to sort records $R_1, \cdots, R_n$ lexically on keys $(K^1, \cdots, K^r)$ for the case when the range of each key is much larger than n. In this case, the bin-sort scheme used in *radixSort* to sort within each key becomes inefficient (why?). What scheme would you use to sort within a key if we desired a function with (a) good worst-case behavior, (b) good average behavior, (c) small n, say <15?

5. If we have n records with integer keys in the range $[0, n^2)$, then they may be sorted in $O(n \log n)$ time using heap sort or merge sort. Radix sort on a single key (i.e., $d = 1$ and $r = n^2$) takes $O(n^2)$ time. Show how to interpret the keys as two subkeys so that radix sort will take only $O(n)$ time to sort n records. (Hint: Each key, K_i, may be written as $K_i = K_i^1 n + K_i^2$ with K_i^1 and K_i^2 integers in the range $[0, n)$.)

6. Generalize the method of the previous exercise to the case of integer keys in the range $(0, n^p)$ obtaining an $O(pn)$ sorting method.

7. Experiment with *radixSort* to see how it performs relative to the comparison-based sort methods discussed in earlier sections.

7.8 LIST AND TABLE SORTS

Apart from radix sort and recursive merge sort, all the sorting methods we have looked at require excessive data movement. That is, as the result of a comparison, records may be physically moved. This tends to slow down the sorting process when records are large. When sorting lists with large records, it is necessary to modify the sorting methods so as to minimize data movement. Methods such as insertion sort and our iterative merge sort can be modified to work with a linked list rather than a sequential list. In this case each record will require an additional link field. Instead of physically moving the record, we change its link field to reflect the change in the position of the record in the list. At the end of the sorting process, the records are linked together in the required order. In many applications (e.g., when we just want to sort lists and then output them record by record on some external media in the sorted order), this is sufficient. However, in some applications it is necessary to physically rearrange the records *in place* so that they are in the required order. Even in such cases, considerable savings can be achieved by first performing a linked-list sort and then physically rearranging the records according to the order specified in the list. This rearranging can be accomplished in linear time using some additional space.

If the list has been sorted so that at the end of the sort, *first* is a pointer to the first record in a linked list of records, then each record in this list will have a key that is greater than or equal to the key of the previous record (if there is a previous record). To physically rearrange these records into the order specified by the list, we begin by interchanging records R_1 and R_{first}. Now, the record in the position R_1 has the smallest key.

If *first* ≠ 1, then there is some record in the list whose link field is 1. If we could change this link field to indicate the new position of the record previously at position 1, then we would be left with records $R_2, \cdots, R_n$ linked together in nondecreasing order. Repeating the above process will, after $n - 1$ iterations, result in the desired rearrangement. The snag, however, is that in a singly linked list we do not know the predecessor of a node. To overcome this difficulty, our first rearrangement function, *listSort*1 (Program 7.15), begins by converting the singly linked list *first* into a doubly linked list and then proceeds to move records into their correct places. This function assumes that links are stored in an integer array as in the case of our radix sort and recursive merge sort functions.

```
void listSort1(element a[], int linka[], int n, int first)
{/* rearrange the sorted chain beginning at first so that
    the records a[1:n] are in sorted order */
  int linkb[MAX_SIZE]; /* array for backward links */
  int i, current, prev = 0;
  element temp;
  for (current = first; current; current = linka[current])
  {/* convert chain into a doubly linked list */
      linkb[current] = prev;
      prev = current;
  }

  for (i = 1; i < n ; i++) /* move a[first] to position i
                              while maintaining the list */
  {
      if (first != i) {
          if (linka[i]) linkb[linka[i]] = first;
          linka[linkb[i]] = first;
          SWAP(a[first], a[i], temp);
          SWAP(linka[first], linka[i], temp);
          SWAP(linkb[first], linkb[i], temp);
      }
      first = linka[i];
  }
}
```

Program 7.15: Rearranging records using a doubly linked list

Example 7.9: After a list sort on the input list (26, 5, 77, 1, 61, 11, 59, 15, 48, 19) has been made, the list is linked as in Figure 7.10(a) (only the key and link fields of each record are shown).

i	R_1	R_2	R_3	R_4	R_5	R_6	R_7	R_8	R_9	R_{10}
key	26	5	77	1	61	11	59	15	48	19
linka	9	6	0	2	3	8	5	10	7	1

(a) Linked list following a list sort, $first = 4$

i	R_1	R_2	R_3	R_4	R_5	R_6	R_7	R_8	R_9	R_{10}
key	26	5	77	1	61	11	59	15	48	19
linka	9	6	0	2	3	8	5	10	7	1
linkb	10	4	5	0	7	2	9	6	1	8

(b) Corresponding doubly linked list, $first = 4$

Figure 7.10: Sorted linked lists

Following the links starting at *first*, we obtain the logical sequence of records R_4, R_2, R_6, $R_8, R_{10}, R_1, R_9, R_7, R_5$, and R_3. This sequence corresponds to the key sequence 1, 5, 11, 15, 19, 26, 48, 59, 61, 33. Filling in the backward links, we get the doubly linked list of Figure 7.10(b). Figure 7.11 shows the list following the first four iterations of the second **for** loop of *listSort1*. The changes made in each iteration are shown in boldface. □

Analysis of *listSort1*: If there are n records in the list, then the time required to convert the chain *first* into a doubly linked list is $O(n)$. The second **for** loop is iterated $n - 1$ times. In each iteration, at most two records are interchanged. This requires three record moves. If each record is m words long, then the cost per record swap is $O(m)$. The total time is therefore $O(nm)$.

The worst case of $3(n - 1)$ record moves (note that each swap requires 3 record moves) is achievable. For example, consider the input key sequence $R_1, R_2, \cdots, R_n$, with $R_2 < R_3 < \cdots < R_n$ and $R_1 > R_n$. □

Although several modifications to *list*1 are possible, one of particular interest was given by M. D. MacLaren. This modification results in a rearrangement function, *listSort2*, in which no additional link fields are necessary. In this function (Program 7.16), after the record R_{first} is swapped with R_i, the link field of the new R_i is set to *first* to indicate that the original record was moved. This, together with the observation that *first* must always be $\geq i$, permits a correct reordering of the records.

i	$\mathbf{R_1}$	R_2	R_3	$\mathbf{R_4}$	R_5	R_6	R_7	R_8	R_9	R_{10}
key	**1**	5	77	**26**	61	11	59	15	48	19
linka	**2**	6	0	**9**	3	8	5	10	7	4
linkb	**0**	4	5	**10**	7	2	9	6	4	8

(a) Configuration after first iteration of the **for** loop of *listSort*1, *first* = 2

i	R_1	R_2	R_3	R_4	R_5	R_6	R_7	R_9	R_9	R_{10}
key	1	5	77	26	61	11	59	15	48	19
linka	2	6	0	9	3	8	5	10	7	4
linkb	0	4	5	10	7	2	9	6	4	8

(b) Configuration after second iteration, *first* = 6

i	R_1	R_2	$\mathbf{R_3}$	R_4	R_5	$\mathbf{R_6}$	R_7	R_8	R_9	R_{10}
key	1	5	**11**	26	61	**77**	59	15	48	19
linka	2	6	**8**	9	6	**0**	5	10	7	4
linkb	0	4	**2**	10	7	**5**	9	6	4	8

(c) Configuration after third iteration, *first* = 8

i	R_1	R_2	R_3	$\mathbf{R_4}$	R_5	R_6	R_7	$\mathbf{R_8}$	R_9	R_{10}
key	1	5	11	**15**	61	77	59	**26**	48	19
linka	2	6	8	**10**	6	0	5	**9**	7	8
linkb	0	4	2	**6**	7	5	9	**10**	8	8

(d) Configuration after fourth iteration, *first* = 10

Figure 7.11: Example for *listSort*1 (Program 7.15)

Example 7.10: The data are the same as in Example 7.9. After the list sort we have the configuration of Figure 7.10(a). The configuration after each of the first five iterations of the **for** loop of *listSort*2 is shown in Figure 7.12. □

Analysis of *listSort*2: The sequence of record moves for *listSort*2 is identical to that for *listSort*1. Hence, in the worst case $3(n-1)$ record moves for a total cost of O(nm) are

```
void listSort2(element a[], int link[], int n, int first)
{/* same function as list1 except that a second link array
   linkb is not required. */
{
    int i;
    element temp;
    for (i = 1; i < n; i++)
    {/* find correct record for ith position,  its index is
        ≥ i as records in positions 1, 2, ..., i - 1 are
        already correctly positioned */
        while (first < i) first = link[first];
        int q = link[first]; /* a[q] is next in sorted order */
        if (first != i)
        {/* a[first] has ith smallest key, swap with a[i] and
            set link from old position of a[i] to new one */
            SWAP(a[i], a[first], temp);
            link[first] = link[i];
            link[i] = first;
        }
        first = q;
    }
}
```

Program 7.16: Rearranging records using only one link field

made. No node is examined more than once in the **while** loop. So, the total time for the **while** loop is O(n). □

Although the asymptotic computing time for both *listSort1* and *listSort2* is the same, and the same number of record moves is made in either case, we expect *listSort2* to be slightly faster than *listSort1* because each time two records are swapped, *listSort1* does more work than *listSort2* does. *listSort1* is inferior to *listSort2* in both space and time considerations.

The list sort technique is not well suited for quick sort and heap sort. The sequential representation of the heap is essential to heap sort. For these sort methods, as well as for methods suited to list sort, one can maintain an auxiliary table, t, with one entry per record. The entries in this table serve as an indirect reference to the records.

At the start of the sort, $t[i] = i$, $1 \leq i \leq n$. If the sorting function requires a swap of $a[i]$ and $a[j]$, then only the table entries (i.e., $t[i]$ and $t[j]$) need to be swapped. At the end of the sort, the record with the smallest key is $a[t[1]]$ and that with the largest

i	R_1	R_2	R_3	R_4	R_5	R_6	R_7	R_8	R_9	R_{10}
key	1	5	77	26	61	11	59	15	48	19
link	4	6	0	9	3	8	5	10	7	1

(a) Configuration after first iteration of the **for** loop of *listSort2*, *first* = 2

i	R_1	R_2	R_3	R_4	R_5	R_6	R_7	R_8	R_9	R_{10}
key	1	5	77	26	61	11	59	15	48	19
link	4	6	0	9	3	8	5	10	7	1

(b) Configuration after second iteration, *first* = 6

i	R_1	R_2	R_3	R_4	R_5	R_6	R_7	R_8	R_9	R_{10}
key	1	5	11	26	61	77	59	15	48	19
link	4	6	6	9	3	0	5	10	7	1

(c) Configuration after third iteration, *first* = 8

i	R_1	R_2	R_3	R_4	R_5	R_6	R_7	R_8	R_9	R_{10}
key	1	5	11	15	61	77	59	26	48	19
link	4	6	6	8	3	0	5	9	7	1

(d) Configuration after fourth iteration, *first* = 10

i	R_1	R_2	R_3	R_4	R_5	R_6	R_7	R_8	R_9	R_{10}
key	1	5	11	15	19	77	59	26	48	61
link	4	6	6	8	10	0	5	9	7	3

(e) Configuration after fifth iteration, *first* = 1

Figure 7.12: Example for *listSort2* (Program 7.16)

$a[t[n]]$. The required permutation on the records is $a[t[1]]$, $a[t[2]]$, $\cdots$, $a[t[n]]$ (see Figure 7.13). This table is adequate even in situations such as binary search, where a sequentially ordered list is needed. In other situations, it may be necessary to physically rearrange the records according to the permutation specified by t.

The function to rearrange records corresponding to the permutation $t[1]$, $t[2]$, $\cdots$, $t[n]$ is a rather interesting application of a theorem from mathematics: Every

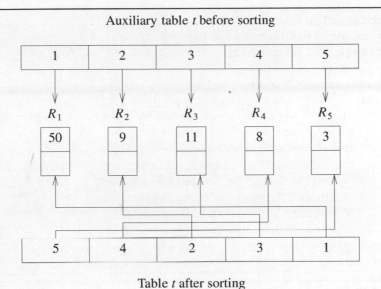

Auxiliary table t before sorting

Table t after sorting

Figure 7.13: Table sort

permutation is made up of disjoint cycles. The cycle for any element i is made up of i, $t[i]$, $t^2[i]$, $\cdots$, $t^k[i]$, where $t^j[i] = t[t^{j-1}[i]]$, $t^0[i] = i$, and $t^k[i] = i$. Thus, the permutation t of Figure 7.13 has two cycles, the first involving R_1 and R_5 and the second involving R_4, R_3, and R_2. Function *table* (Program 7.17) utilizes this cyclic decomposition of a permutation. First, the cycle containing R_1 is followed, and all records are moved to their correct positions. The cycle containing R_2 is the next one examined unless this cycle has already been examined. The cycles for R_3, R_4, $\cdots$, R_{n-1} are followed in this order. The result is a physically sorted list.

When processing a trivial cycle for R_i (i.e., $t[i] = i$), no rearrangement involving record R_i is required, since the condition $t[i] = i$ means that the record with the ith smallest key is R_i. In processing a nontrivial cycle for record R_i (i.e., $t[i] \neq i$), R_i is moved to a temporary position *temp*, then the record at $t[i]$ is moved to i; next the record at $t[t[i]]$ is moved to $t[i]$, and so on until the end of the cycle $t^k[i]$ is reached and the record at *temp* is moved to $t^{k-1}[i]$.

Example 7.11: Suppose we start with the table t of Figure 7.14(a). This figure also shows the record keys. The table configuration is that following a Table Sort. There are two nontrivial cycles in the permutation specified by t. The first is R_1, R_3, R_8, R_6, R_1. The second is R_4, R_5, R_7, R_4. During the first iteration ($i = 1$) of the **for** loop of *tableSort* (Program 7.17), the cycle R_1, $R_{t[1]}$, $R_{t^2[1]}$, $R_{t^3[1]}$, R_1 is followed. Record R_1 is moved to a temporary spot *temp*; $R_{t[1]}$ (i.e., R_3) is moved to the position R_1; $R_{t^2[1]}$ (i.e.,

```
void tableSort(element a[], int n, int t[])
{/* rearrange a[1:n] to correspond to the sequence
    a[t[1]], ... , a[t[n]] */
    int i, current, next;
    element temp;
    for (i = 1; i < n; i++)
        if (t[i] != i)  {/* nontrivial cycle starting at i */
            temp = a[i]; current = i;
            do {
                next = t[current]; a[current] = a[next];
                t[current] = current; current = next;
            } while (t[current] != i);
            a[current] = temp;
            t[current] = current;
        }
}
```

Program 7.17: Table sort

	R_1	R_2	R_3	R_4	R_5	R_6	R_7	R_8
key	35	14	12	42	26	50	31	18
t	3	2	8	5	7	1	4	6

(a) Initial configuration

key	12	14	18	42	26	35	31	50
t	1	2	3	5	7	6	4	8

(b) Configuration after rearrangement of first cycle

key	12	14	18	26	31	35	42	50
t	1	2	3	4	5	6	7	8

(c) Configuration after rearrangement of second cycle

Figure 7.14: Table sort example

R_8) is moved to R_3; R_6 is moved to R_8; and finally, the record in *temp* is moved to R_6. Thus, at the end of the first iteration we have the table configuration of Figure 7.14(b).

For $i = 2$ or 3, $t[i] = i$, indicating that these records are already in their correct positions. When $i = 4$, the next nontrivial cycle is discovered, and the records on this cycle (R_4, R_5, R_7, R_4) are moved to their correct positions. Following this we have the table configuration of Figure 7.14(c).

For the remaining values of i ($i = 5$, 6, and 7), $t[i] = i$, and no more nontrivial cycles are found. □

Analysis of *tableSort:* If each record uses m words of storage, then the additional space needed is m words for *temp* plus a few more for variables such as i, *current*, and *next*. For the computing time, we observe that the **for** loop is executed $n - 1$ times. If for some value of i, $t[i] \neq i$, then there is a nontrivial cycle including $k > 1$ distinct records $R_i, R_{t[i]}, \cdots, R_{t^{k-1}[i]}$. Rearranging these records requires $k + 1$ record moves. Following this, the records involved in this cycle are not moved again at any time in the algorithm, as $t[j] = j$ for all such records R_j. Hence, no record can be in two different nontrivial cycles. Let k_l be the number of records on a nontrivial cycle starting at R_l when $i = l$ in the **for** loop. Let $k_l = 0$ for a trivial cycle. The total number of record moves is

$$\sum_{l=0, k_l \neq 0}^{n-1} (k_l + 1)$$

Since the records on nontrivial cycles must be different, $\sum k_l \leq n$. The total number of record moves is maximum when $\sum k_l = n$ and there are $\lfloor n/2 \rfloor$ cycles. When n is even, each cycle contains two records. Otherwise, one cycle contains three and the others two each. In either case the number of record moves is $\lfloor 3n/2 \rfloor$. One record move costs $O(m)$ time. The total computing time is therefore $O(mn)$. □

Comparing *listSort2* (Program 7.16) and *tableSort*, we see that in the worst case, *listSort2* makes $3(n-1)$ record moves, whereas *tableSort* makes only $\lfloor 3n/2 \rfloor$ record moves. For larger values of m it is worthwhile to make one pass over the sorted list of records, creating a table t corresponding to a table sort. This would take $O(n)$ time. Then *tableSort* could be used to rearrange the records in the order specified by t.

EXERCISES

1. Complete Example 7.9.

2. Complete Example 7.10.

3. Write a version of selection sort (see Chapter 1) that works on a chain of records.

4. Write a table sort version of quick sort. Now during the sort, records are not physically moved. Instead, $t[i]$ is the index of the record that would have been in position i if records were physically moved around as in *quickSort* (Program 7.6). Begin with $t[i] = i$, $1 \leq i \leq n$. At the end of the sort, $t[i]$ is the index of the record

that should be in the *i*th position in the sorted list. So now function *table* may be used to rearrange the records into the sorted order specified by *t*. Note that this reduces the amount of data movement taking place when compared to *quickSort* for the case of large records.

5. Do Exercise 4 for the case of insertion sort.

6. Do Exercise 4 for the case of merge sort.

7. Do Exercise 4 for the case of heap sort.

7.9   SUMMARY OF INTERNAL SORTING

Of the several sorting methods we have studied, no one method is best under all circumstances. Some methods are good for small *n*, others for large *n*. Insertion sort is good when the list is already partially ordered. Because of the low overhead of the method, it is also the best sorting method for "small" *n*. Merge sort has the best worst-case behavior but requires more storage than heap sort. Quick sort has the best average behavior, but its worst-case behavior is $O(n^2)$. The behavior of radix sort depends on the size of the keys and the choice of *r*. Figure 7.15 summarizes the asymptotic complexity of the first four of these sort methods.

Method	Worst	Average
Insertion sort	n^2	n^2
Heap sort	$n\log n$	$n\log n$
Merge sort	$n\log n$	$n\log n$
Quick sort	n^2	$n\log n$

Figure 7.15: Comparison of sort methods

Figures 7.16 and 7.17 give the average runtimes for the four sort methods of Figure 7.15. These times were obtained on a 1.7GHz Intel Pentium 4 PC with 512 MB RAM and Microsoft Visual Studio .NET 2003. For each *n* at least 100 randomly generated integer instances were run. These random instances were constructed by making repeated calls to the C function *rand*. If the time taken to sort these instances was less than 1 second then additional random instances were sorted until the total time taken was at least this much. The times reported in Figure 7.16 include the time taken to set up the random data. For each *n* the time taken to set up the data and the time for the remaining overheads included in the reported numbers is the same for all sort methods. As a result, the data of Figure 7.16 are useful for comparative purposes.

n	Insert	Heap	Merge	Quick
0	0.000	0.000	0.000	0.000
50	0.004	0.009	0.008	0.006
100	0.011	0.019	0.017	0.013
200	0.033	0.042	0.037	0.029
300	0.067	0.066	0.059	0.045
400	0.117	0.090	0.079	0.061
500	0.179	0.116	0.100	0.079
1000	0.662	0.245	0.213	0.169
2000	2.439	0.519	0.459	0.358
3000	5.390	0.809	0.721	0.560
4000	9.530	1.105	0.972	0.761
5000	15.935	1.410	1.271	0.970

Times are in milliseconds

Figure 7.16: Average times for sort methods

As Figure 7.18 shows, quick sort outperforms the other sort methods for suitably large n. We see that the break-even point between insertion and quick sort is between 50 and 100. The exact break-even point can be found experimentally by obtaining run-time data for n between 50 and 100. Let the exact break-even point be *nBreak*. For average performance, insertion sort is the best sort method (of those tested) to use when $n < nBreak$, and quick sort is the best when $n > nBreak$. We can improve on the performance of quick sort for $n > nBreak$ by combining insertion and quick sort into a single sort function by replacing the following statement in Program 7.6

```
if (left < right) {code to partition and make recursive calls}
```

with the code

```
if (left+nBreak < right) {
    code to partition and make recursive calls
}
else {
    sort a [left:right] using insertion sort;
    return;
}
```

For worst-case behavior most implementations will show merge sort to be best for $n > c$ where c is some constant. For $n \leq c$ insertion sort has the best worst-case behavior.

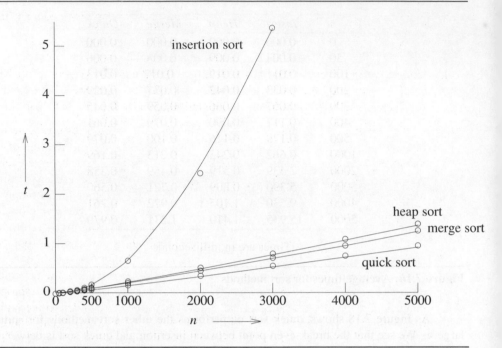

Figure 7.18: Plot of average times (milliseconds)

The performance of merge sort can be improved by combining insertion sort and merge sort in a manner similar to that described above for combining insertion sort and quick sort.

The run-time results for the sort methods point out some of the limitations of asymptotic complexity analysis. Asymptotic analysis is not a good predictor of performance for small instances—insertion sort with its $O(n^2)$ complexity is better than all of the $O(n\log n)$ methods for small instances. Programs that have the same asymptotic complexity often have different actual runtimes.

EXERCISES

1. [*Count Sort*] The simplest known sorting method arises from the observation that the position of a record in a sorted list depends on the number of records with smaller keys. Associated with each record there is a *count* field used to determine the number of records that must precede this one in the sorted list. Write a function to determine the count of each record in an unordered list. Show that if the list has *n* records, then all the counts can be determined by making at most

$n(n-1)/2$ key comparisons.

2. Write a function similar to *table* (Program 7.17) to rearrange the records of a list if, with each record, we have a count of the number of records preceding it in the sorted list (see Exercise 1).

3. Obtain Figures 7.16 and 7.18 for the worst-case runtime.

4. [*Programming Project*] The objective of this assignment is to come up with a composite sorting function that is good on the worst-time criterion. The candidate sort methods are (a) Insertion sort, (b) Quick sort, (c) Merge sort, (d) Heap sort.

To begin with, program these sort methods in C. In each case, assume that n integers are to be sorted. In the case of quick sort, use the median-of-three method. In the case of merge sort, use the iterative method (as a separate exercise, you might wish to compare the runtimes of the iterative and recursive versions of merge sort and determine what the recursion penalty is in your favorite language using your favorite compiler). Check out the correctness of the programs using some test data. Since quite detailed and working functions are given in the book, this part of the assignment should take little effort. In any case, no points are earned until after this step.

To obtain reasonably accurate runtimes, you need to know the accuracy of the clock or timer you are using. Determine this by reading the appropriate manual. Let the clock accuracy be δ. Now, run a pilot test to determine ballpark times for your four sorting functions for $n = 500, 1000, 2000, 3000, 4000$, and 5000. You will notice times of 0 for many of these values of n. The other times may not be much larger than the clock accuracy.

To time an event that is smaller than or near the clock accuracy, repeat it many times and divide the overall time by the number of repetitions. You should obtain times that are accurate to within 1%.

We need worst-case data for each of the four sort methods. The worst-case data for insertion sort are easy to generate. Just use the sequence $n, n-1, n-2$, $\cdots$, 1. Worst-case data for merge sort can be obtained by working backward. Begin with the last merge your function will perform and make this work hardest. Then look at the second-to-last merge, and so on. Use this logic to obtain a program that will generate worst-case data for merge sort for each of the above values of n.

Generating worst-case data for heap sort is the hardest, so, here we shall use a random permutation generator (one is provided in Program 7.18). We shall generate random permutations of the desired size, clock heap sort on each of these, and use the max of these times to approximate to the worst-case time. You will be able to use more random permutations for smaller values of n than for larger. For no value of n should you use fewer than 10 permutations. Use the same technique to obtain worst-case times for quick sort.

Having settled on the test data, we are ready to perform our experiment.

```
void permute(element a[], int n)
{/* random permutation generator */
    int i, j;
    element temp;
    for (i = n; i >= 2; i--)
    {
        j = rand() % i + 1;
            /* j = random integer in the range [1, i] */
        SWAP(a[j], a[i], temp);
    }
}
```

Program 7.18: Random permutation generator

Obtain the worst-case times. From these times you will get a rough idea when one function performs better than the other. Now, narrow the scope of your experiments and determine the exact value of n when one sort method outperforms another. For some methods, this value may be 0. For instance, each of the other three methods may be faster than quick sort for all values of n.

Plot your findings on a single sheet of graph paper. Do you see the n^2 behavior of insertion sort and quick sort and the $n \log n$ behavior of the other two methods for suitably large n (about $n > 20$)? If not, there is something wrong with your test or your clock or with both. For each value of n determine the sort function that is fastest (simply look at your graph). Write a composite function with the best possible performance for all n. Clock this function and plot the times on the same graph sheet you used earlier.

WHAT TO TURN IN

You are required to submit a report that states the clock accuracy, the number of random permutations tried for heap sort, the worst-case data for merge sort and how you generated it, a table of times for the above values of n, the times for the narrowed ranges, the graph, and a table of times for the composite function. In addition, your report must be accompanied by a complete listing of the program used by you (this includes the sorting functions and the main program for timing and test-data generation).

5. Repeat the previous exercise for the case of average runtimes. Average-case data are usually very difficult to create, so use random permutations. This time, however, do not repeat a permutation many times to overcome clock inaccuracies. Instead, use each permutation once and clock the overall time (for a fixed n).

6. Assume you are given a list of five-letter English words and are faced with the problem of listing these words in sequences such that the words in each sequence are anagrams (i.e., if x and y are in the same sequence, then word x is a permutation of word y). You are required to list out the fewest such sequences. With this restriction, show that no word can appear in more than one sequence. How would you go about solving this problem?

7. Assume you are working in the census department of a small town where the number of records, about 3000, is small enough to fit into the internal memory of a computer. All the people currently living in this town were born in the United States. There is one record for each person in this town. Each record contains (a) the state in which the person was born, (b) county of birth, and (c) name of person. How would you produce a list of all persons living in this town? The list is to be ordered by state. Within each state the persons are to be listed by their counties, the counties being arranged in alphabetical order. Within each county, the names are also listed in alphabetical order. Justify any assumptions you make.

8. [*Bubble Sort*] In a bubble sort several left-to-right passes are made over the array of records to be sorted. In each pass, pairs of adjacent records are compared and exchanged if necessary. The sort terminates following a pass in which no records are exchanged.

   (a) Write a C function for bubble sort.

   (b) What is the worst-case complexity of your function?

   (c) How much time does your function take on a sorted array of records?

   (d) How much time does your function take on an array of records that are in the reverse of sorted order?

9. Redo the preceding exercise beginning with an unsorted chain of records and ending with a sorted chain.

10. [*Programming Project*] The objective of this exercise is to study the effect of the size of an array element on the computational time of various sorting algorithms.

   (a) Use insertion sort, quick sort, iterative merge sort, and heap sort to sort arrays of (*i*) characters (**char**), (*ii*) integers (**int**), (*iii*) floating point numbers (**float**), and (*iv*) rectangles (Assume that a rectangle is represented by the coordinates of its bottom left point and its height and width, all of which are of type **float**. Assume, also, that rectangles are to be sorted in non-decreasing order of their areas.)

   (b) Obtain a set of runtimes for each algorithm-data type pair specified above. (There should be sixteen such pairs.) To obtain a set of runtimes of an algorithm-data type pair, you should run the algorithm on at least four arrays of different sizes containing elements of the appropriate data type. The elements in an array should be generated using a random number generator

(c)   Draw tables and graphs displaying your experimental results. What do you conclude from the experiments?

7.10   EXTERNAL SORTING

7.10.1   Introduction

In this section, we assume that the lists to be sorted are so large that an entire list cannot be contained in the internal memory of a computer, making an internal sort impossible. We shall assume that the list (or file) to be sorted resides on a disk. The term *block* refers to the unit of data that is read from or written to a disk at one time. A block generally consists of several records. For a disk, there are three factors contributing to the read/write time:

(1)   *Seek time:* time taken to position the read/write heads to the correct cylinder. This will depend on the number of cylinders across which the heads have to move.

(2)   *Latency time:* time until the right sector of the track is under the read/write head.

(3)   *Transmission time:* time to transmit the block of data to/from the disk.

The most popular method for sorting on external storage devices is merge sort. This method consists of two distinct phases. First, segments of the input list are sorted using a good internal sort method. These sorted segments, known as *runs*, are written onto external storage as they are generated. Second, the runs generated in phase one are merged together following the merge-tree pattern of Figure 7.4, until only one run is left. Because the simple merge function *merge* (Program 7.7) requires only the leading records of the two runs being merged to be present in memory at one time, it is possible to merge large runs together. It is more difficult to adapt the other internal sort methods considered in this chapter to external sorting.

Example 7.12: A list containing 4500 records is to be sorted using a computer with an internal memory capable of sorting at most 750 records. The input list is maintained on disk and has a block length of 250 records. We have available another disk that may be used as a scratch pad. The input disk is not to be written on. One way to accomplish the sort using the general function outlined above is to

(1) Internally sort three blocks at a time (i.e., 750 records) to obtain six runs R_1 to R_6. A method such as heap sort, merge sort, or quick sort could be used. These six runs are written onto the scratch disk (Figure 7.19).

(2) Set aside three blocks of internal memory, each capable of holding 250 records. Two of these blocks will be used as input buffers and the third as an output buffer. Merge runs R_1 and R_2. This merge is carried out by first reading one block of each of these runs into input buffers. Blocks of runs are merged from the input buffers

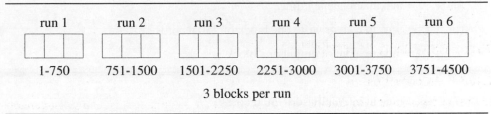

3 blocks per run

Figure 7.19: Blocked runs obtained after internal sorting

into the output buffer. When the output buffer gets full, it is written onto the disk. If an input buffer gets empty, it is refilled with another block from the same run. After runs R_1 and R_2 are merged, R_3 and R_4 and finally R_5 and R_6 are merged. The result of this pass is three runs, each containing 1500 sorted records or six blocks. Two of these runs are now merged using the input/output buffers set up as above to obtain a run of size 3000. Finally, this run is merged with the remaining run of size 1500 to obtain the desired sorted list (Figure 7.20). □

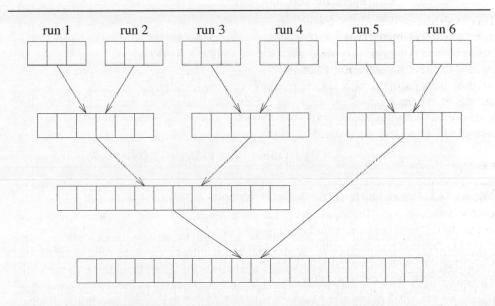

Figure 7.20: Merging the six runs

To analyze the complexity of external sort, we use the following notation:

t_s = maximum seek time

t_l = maximum latency time

t_{rw} = time to read or write one block of 250 records

t_{IO} = time to input or output one block

$= t_s + t_l + t_{rw}$

t_{IS} = time to internally sort 750 records

nt_m = time to merge n records from input buffers to the output buffer

We shall assume that each time a block is read from or written onto the disk, the maximum seek and latency times are experienced. Although this is not true in general, it will simplify the analysis. The computing times for the various operations in our 4500-record example are given in Figure 7.21.

operation	time
(1) read 18 blocks of input, $18t_{IO}$, internally sort, $6t_{IS}$, write 18 blocks, $18t_{IO}$	$36t_{IO} + 6t_{IS}$
(2) merge runs 1 to 6 in pairs	$36t_{IO} + 4500t_m$
(3) merge two runs of 1500 records each, 12 blocks	$24t_{IO} + 3000t_m$
(4) merge one run of 3000 records with one run of 1500 records	$36t_{IO} + 4500t_m$
total time	$132t_{IO} + 12{,}000t_m + 6t_{IS}$

Figure 7.21: Computing times for disk sort example

The contribution of seek time can be reduced by writing blocks on the same cylinder or on adjacent cylinders. A close look at the final computing time indicates that it depends chiefly on the number of passes made over the data. In addition to the initial input pass made over the data for the internal sort, the merging of the runs requires 2-2/3 passes over the data (one pass to merge 6 runs of length 750 records, two-thirds of a pass to merge two runs of length 1500, and one pass to merge one run of length 3000 and one of length 1500). Since one full pass covers 18 blocks, the input and output time is $2 \times (2\text{-}2/3 + 1) \times 18\, t_{IO} = 132t_{IO}$. The leading factor of 2 appears because each record that is read is also written out again. The merge time is $2\text{-}2/3 \times 4500t_m = 12,000t_m$. Because of this close relationship between the overall computing time and the number of passes made over the data, future analysis will be concerned mainly with counting the number of passes being made. Another point to note regarding the above sort is that no attempt was made to use the computer's ability to carry out input/output and CPU operation in parallel and thus overlap some of the time. In the ideal situation we would overlap almost all the input/output time with CPU processing so that the real time would be approximately $132\ t_{IO} \approx 12,000\ t_m + 6t_{IS}$.

If we have two disks, we can write on one, read from the other, and merge buffer loads already in memory in parallel. A proper choice of buffer lengths and buffer handling schemes will result in a time of almost $66t_{IO}$. This parallelism is an important consideration when sorting is being carried out in a nonmultiprogramming environment. In this situation, unless input/output and CPU processing is going on in parallel, the CPU is idle during input/output. In a multiprogramming environment, however, the need for the sorting program to carry out input/output and CPU processing in parallel may not be so critical, since the CPU can be busy working on another program (if there are other programs in the system at the time) while the sort program waits for the completion of its input/output. Indeed, in many multiprogramming environments it may not even be possible to achieve parallel input, output, and internal computing because of the structure of the operating system.

The number of merge passes over the runs can be reduced by using a higher-order merge than two-way merge. To provide for parallel input, output, and merging, we need an appropriate buffer-handling scheme. Further improvement in runtime can be obtained by generating fewer (or equivalently longer) runs than are generated by the strategy described above. This can be done using a loser tree. The loser-tree strategy to be discussed in Section 7.10.4 results in runs that are on the average almost twice as long as those obtained by the above strategy. However, the generated runs are of varying size. As a result, the order in which the runs are merged affects the time required to merge all runs into one. We consider these factors now.

7.10.2   k-Way Merging

The two-way merge function *merge* (Program 7.7) is almost identical to the merge function just described (Figure 7.20). In general, if we start with m runs, the merge tree corresponding to Figure 7.20 will have $\lceil \log_2 m \rceil + 1$ levels, for a total of $\lceil \log_2 m \rceil$ passes over the data list. The number of passes over the data can be reduced by using a higher-order merge (i.e., k-way merge for $k \geq 2$). In this case, we would simultaneously merge k runs together. Figure 7.22 illustrates a four-way merge of 16 runs. The number of passes over the data is now two, versus four passes in the case of a two-way merge. In general, a k-way merge on m runs requires $\lceil \log_k m \rceil$ passes over the data. Thus, the input/output time may be reduced by using a higher-order merge.

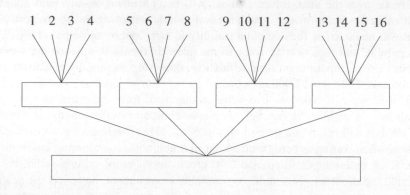

Figure 7.22: A four-way merge on 16 runs

The use of a higher-order merge, however, has some other effects on the sort. To begin with, k runs of size $s_1, s_2, s_3, \cdots, s_k$ can no longer be merged internally in $O(\sum_1^k s_i)$ time. In a k-way merge, as in a two-way merge, the next record to be output is the one with the smallest key. The smallest has now to be found from k possibilities and it could be the leading record in any of the k runs. The most direct way to merge k runs is to make $k - 1$ comparisons to determine the next record to output. The computing time for this is $O((k - 1) \sum_1^k s_i)$. Since $\log_k m$ passes are being made, the total number of key comparisons is $n(k - 1)\log_k m = n(k - 1)\log_2 m /\log_2 k$, where n is the number of records in the list. Hence, $(k - 1)/\log_2 k$ is the factor by which the number of key comparisons increases. As k increases, the reduction in input/output time will be outweighed by the resulting increase in CPU time needed to perform the k-way merge.

For large k (say, $k \geq 6$) we can achieve a significant reduction in the number of comparisons needed to find the next smallest element by using a loser tree with k leaves (see Chapter 5). In this case, the total time needed per level of the merge tree is $O(n \log_2 k)$. Since the number of levels in this tree is $O(\log_k m)$, the asymptotic internal processing time becomes $O(n \log_2 k \log_k m) = O(n\log_2 m)$. This is independent of k.

In going to a higher-order merge, we save on the amount of input/output being carried out. There is no significant loss in internal processing speed. Even though the internal processing time is relatively insensitive to the order of the merge, the decrease in input/output time is not as much as indicated by the reduction to $\log_k m$ passes. This is so because the number of input buffers needed to carry out a k-way merge increases with k. Although $k + 1$ buffers are sufficient, in the next section we shall see that the use of

$2k + 2$ buffers is more desirable. Since the internal memory available is fixed and independent of k, the buffer size must be reduced as k increases. This in turn implies a reduction in the block size on disk. With the reduced block size, each pass over the data results in a greater number of blocks being written or read. This represents a potential increase in input/output time from the increased contribution of seek and latency times involved in reading a block of data. Hence, beyond a certain k value the input/output time will increase despite the decrease in the number of passes being made. The optimal value for k depends on disk parameters and the amount of internal memory available for buffers.

7.10.3   Buffer Handling for Parallel Operation

If k runs are being merged together by a k-way merge, then we clearly need at least k input buffers and one output buffer to carry out the merge. This, however, is not enough if input, output, and internal merging are to be carried out in parallel. For instance, while the output buffer is being written out, internal merging has to be halted, since there is no place to collect the merged records. This can be overcome through the use of two output buffers. While one is being written out, records are merged into the second. If buffer sizes are chosen correctly, then the time to output one buffer will be the same as the CPU time needed to fill the second buffer. With only k input buffers, internal merging will have to be held up whenever one of these input buffers becomes empty and another block from the corresponding run is being read in. This input delay can also be avoided if we have $2k$ input buffers. These $2k$ input buffers have to be used cleverly to avoid reaching a situation in which processing has to be held up because of a lack of input records from any one run. Simply assigning two buffers per run does not solve the problem.

Example 7.13: Assume that a two-way merge is carried out using four input buffers, $in[i]$, $0 \le i \le 3$, and two output buffers, $ou[0]$ and $ou[1]$. Each buffer is capable of holding two records. The first few records of run 0 have key value 1, 3, 5, 7, 8, 9. The first few records of run 1 have key value 2, 4, 6, 15, 20, 25. Buffers $in[0]$ and $in[2]$ are assigned to run 0. The remaining two input buffers are assigned to run 1. We start the merge by reading in one buffer load from each of the two runs. At this time the buffers have the configuration of Figure 7.23(a). Now runs 0 and 1 are merged using records from $in[0]$ and $in[1]$. In parallel with this, the next buffer load from run 0 is input. If we assume that buffer lengths have been chosen such that the times to input, output, and generate an output buffer are all the same, then when $ou[0]$ is full, we have the situation of Figure 7.23(b). Next, we simultaneously output $ou[0]$, input into $in[3]$ from run 1, and merge into $ou[1]$. When $ou[1]$ is full, we have the situation of Figure 7.23(c). Continuing in this way, we reach the configuration of Figure 7.23(e). We now begin to output $ou[1]$, input from run 0 into $in[2]$, and merge into $ou[0]$. During the merge, all records from run 0 get used before $ou[0]$ gets full. Merging must now be delayed until the inputting of another buffer load from run 0 is completed. □

Example 7.13 makes it clear that if $2k$ input buffers are to suffice, then we cannot assign two buffers per run. Instead, the buffer must be floating in the sense that an individual buffer may be assigned to any run depending upon need. In the buffer assignment strategy we shall describe, there will at any time be at least one input buffer containing records from each run. The remaining buffers will be filled on a priority basis (i.e., the run for which the k-way merging algorithm will run out of records first is the one from which the next buffer will be filled). One may easily predict which run's records will be exhausted first by simply comparing the keys of the last record read from each of the k runs. The smallest such key determines this run. We shall assume that in the case of equal keys, the merge process first merges the record from the run with least index. This means that if the key of the last record read from run i is equal to the key of the last record read from run j, and $i < j$, then the records read from i will be exhausted before those from j. So, it is possible to have more than two bufferloads from a given run and only one partially full buffer from another run. All bufferloads from the same run are queued together. Before formally presenting the algorithm for buffer utilization, we make the following assumptions about the parallel processing capabilities of the computer system available:

(1)   We have two disk drives and the input/output channel is such that we can simultaneously read from one disk and write onto the other.

(2)   While data transmission is taking place between an input/output device and a block of memory, the CPU cannot make references to that same block of memory. Thus, it is not possible to start filling the front of an output buffer while it is being written out. If this were possible, then by coordinating the transmission and merging rate, only one output buffer would be needed. By the time the first record for the new output block is determined, the first record of the previous output block has been written out.

(3)   To simplify the discussion we assume that input and output buffers are of the same size.

Keeping these assumptions in mind, we provide a high-level description of the algorithm obtained using the strategy outlined earlier and then illustrate how it works through an example. Our algorithm, Program 7.19, merges k-runs, $k \geq 2$, using a k-way merge. $2k$ input buffers and two output buffers are used. Each buffer is a continuous block of memory. Input buffers are queued in k queues, one queue for each run. It is assumed that each input/output buffer is long enough to hold one block of records. Empty buffers are placed on a linked stack. The algorithm also assumes that the end of each run has a sentinel record with a very large key, say $+\infty$. It is assumed that all other records have key value less than that of the sentinel record. If block lengths, and hence buffer lengths, are chosen such that the time to merge one output buffer load equals the time to read a block, then almost all input, output, and computation will be carried out in

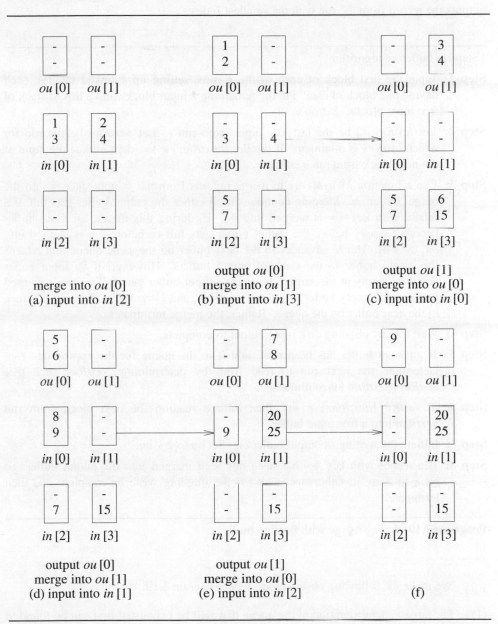

Figure 7.23: Example showing that two fixed buffers per run are not enough for continued parallel operation

parallel. It is also assumed that in the case of equal keys, the k-way merge algorithm first outputs the record from the run with the smallest index.

{Steps in buffering algorithm}

Step 1: Input the first block of each of the k runs, setting up k linked queues, each having one block of data. Put the remaining k input blocks into a linked stack of free input blocks. Set *ou* to 0.

Step 2: Let *lastKey* [i] be the last key input from run i. Let *nextRun* be the run for which *lastKey* is minimum. If *lastKey* [*nextRun*] $\neq +\infty$, then initiate the input of the next block from run *nextRun*.

Step 3: Use a function *kWayMerge* to merge records from the k input queues into the output buffer *ou*. Merging continues until either the output buffer gets full or a record with key $+\infty$ is merged into *ou*. If, during this merge, an input buffer becomes empty before the output buffer gets full or before $+\infty$ is merged into *ou*, the *kWayMerge* advances to the next buffer on the same queue and returns the empty buffer to the stack of empty buffers. However, if an input buffer becomes empty at the same time as the output buffer gets full or $+\infty$ is merged into *ou*, the empty buffer is left on the queue, and *kWayMerge* does not advance to the next buffer on the queue. Rather, the merge terminates.

Step 4: Wait for any ongoing disk input/output to complete.

Step 5: If an input buffer has been read, add it to the queue for the appropriate run. Determine the next run to read from by determining *NextRun* such that *lastKey* [*nextRun*] is minimum.

Step 6: If *lastKey* [*nextRun*] $\neq +\infty$, then initiate reading the next block from run *nextRun* into a free input buffer.

Step 7: Initiate the writing of output buffer *ou*. Set *ou* to $1 - ou$.

Step 8: If a record with key $+\infty$ has been not been merged into the output buffer, go back to Step 3. Otherwise, wait for the ongoing write to complete and then terminate.

Program 7.19: k-way merge with floating buffers

We make the following observations about Program 7.19:

(1)   For large k, determination of the queue that will be exhausted first can be found in $\log_2 k$ comparisons by setting up a loser tree for *last* [i], $0 \leq i < k$, rather than making $k - 1$ comparisons each time a buffer load is to be read in. The change in computing time will not be significant, since this queue selection represents only a

very small fraction of the total time taken by the algorithm.

(2)   For large k, function *kWayMerge* uses a tree of losers (see Chapter 5).

(3)   All input and output except for the input of the initial k blocks and the output of the last block is done concurrently with computing. Since, after k runs have been merged, we would probably begin to merge another set of k runs, the input for the next set can commence during the final merge stages of the present set of runs. That is, when *lastKey* [*nextRun*] = +∞ in Step 6, we begin reading one by one the first blocks from each of the next set of k runs to be merged. So, over the entire sorting of a file the only time that is not overlapped with the internal merging time is the time to input the first k blocks and that to output the last block.

(4)   The algorithm assumes that all blocks are of the same length. Ensuring this may require inserting a few dummy records into the last block of each run following the sentinel record with key +∞.

Example 7.14: To illustrate the algorithm of Program 7.19, let us trace through it while it performs a three-way merge on the three runs of Figure 7.24. Each run consists of four blocks of two records each; the last key in the fourth block of each of these three runs is +∞. We have six input buffers and two output buffers. Figure 7.25 shows the status of the input buffer queues, the run from which the next block is being read, and the output buffer being output at the beginning of each iteration of the loop of Steps 3 through 8 of the buffering algorithm.

Run 0	20 25	26 28	29 30	33 +∞
Run 1	23 29	34 36	38 60	70 +∞
Run 2	24 28	31 33	40 43	50 +∞

Figure 7.24: Three runs

From line 5 of Figure 7.25 it is evident that during the k-way merge, the test for "output buffer full?" should be carried out before the test "input buffer empty?", as the next input buffer for that run may not have been read in yet, so there would be no next buffer in that queue. In lines 3 and 4 all six input buffers are in use, and the stack of free buffers is empty. □

We end our discussion of buffer handling by proving that Program 7.19 is correct.

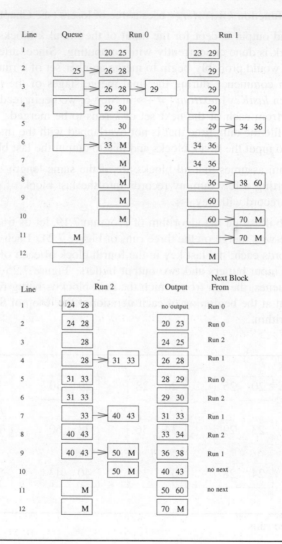

Figure 7.25: Buffering example

Theorem 7.2: The following are true for Program 7.19:

(1) In Step 6, there is always a buffer available in which to begin reading the next block.

(2) During the *k*-way merge of Step 3, the next block in the queue has been read in by the time it is needed.

Proof: (1) Each time we get to Step 6 of the algorithm, there are at most $k + 1$ buffer loads in memory, one of these being in an output buffer. For each queue there can be at most one buffer that is partially full. If no buffer is available for the next read, then the remaining k buffers must be full. This means that all the k partially full buffers are empty (as otherwise there will be more than $k+1$ buffer loads in memory). From the way the merge is set up, only one buffer can be both unavailable and empty. This may happen only if the output buffer gets full exactly when one input buffer becomes empty. But $k > 1$ contradicts this. So, there is always at least one buffer available when Step 6 is being executed.

(2) Assume this is false. Let run R_i be the one whose queue becomes empty during *kWayMerge*. We may assume that the last key merged was not $+\infty$, since otherwise *kWayMerge* would terminate the merge rather than get another buffer for R_i. This means that there are more blocks of records for run R_i on the input file, and $lastKey[i] \neq +\infty$. Consequently, up to this time whenever a block was output, another was simultaneously read in. Input and output therefore proceeded at the same rate, and the number of available blocks of data was always k. An additional block is being read in, but it does not get queued until Step 5. Since the queue for R_i has become empty first, the selection rule for choosing the next run to read from ensures that there is at most one block of records for each of the remaining $k - 1$ runs. Furthermore, the output buffer cannot be full at this time, as this condition is tested for before the input-buffer-empty condition. Thus, fewer than k blocks of data are in memory. This contradicts our earlier assertion that there must be exactly k such blocks of data. $\square$

7.10.4 Run Generation

Using conventional internal sorting methods such as those discussed earlier in this chapter, it is possible to generate runs that are only as large as the number of records that can be held in internal memory at one time. Using a tree of losers, it is possible to do better than this. In fact, the algorithm we shall present will, on the average, generate runs that are twice as long as obtainable by conventional methods. This algorithm was devised by Walters, Painter, and Zalk. In addition to being capable of generating longer runs, this algorithm will allow for parallel input, output, and internal processing.

We assume that input/output buffers have been set up appropriately for maximum overlapping of input, output, and internal processing. Wherever there is an input/output instruction in the run-generation algorithm, it is assumed that the operation takes place through the input/output buffers. The run generation algorithm uses a tree of losers. We assume that there is enough space to construct such a tree for k records, $record[i]$, $0 \leq i < k$. Each node, i, in this tree has one field $loser[i]$. $loser[i]$, $1 \leq i < k$, represents the loser of the tournament played at node i. Each of the k record positions $record[i]$ has a run number $runNum[i]$, $0 \leq i < k$. This field enables us to determine whether or not $record[i]$ can be output as part of the run currently being generated. Whenever the tournament winner is output, a new record (if there is one) is input, and the tournament is replayed as discussed in Chapter 5.

Function *runGeneration* (Program 7.20) is an implementation of the loser tree strategy just discussed. The variables used in this function have the following significance:

$$record[i], 0 \leq i < k \quad \dots \quad \text{the } k \text{ records in the tournament tree}$$

$$loser[i], 1 \leq i < k \quad \dots \quad \text{loser of the tournament played at node } i$$

$$loser[0] \quad \dots \quad \text{winner of the tournament}$$

$$runNum[i], 0 \leq i < k \quad \dots \quad \text{the run number to which } record[i] \text{ belongs}$$

$$currentRun \quad \dots \quad \text{run number of current run}$$

$$winner \quad \dots \quad \text{overall tournament winner}$$

$$winnerRun \quad \dots \quad \text{run number for } record[winner]$$

$$maxRun \quad \dots \quad \text{number of runs that will be generated}$$

$$lastKey \quad \dots \quad \text{key of last record output}$$

The loop of lines 10 to 37 repeatedly plays the tournament outputting records. The variable *lastKey* is made use of in line 21 to determine whether or not the new record input, *record*[*winner*], can be output as part of the current run. If *key*[*winner*] < *lastKey* then *record*[*winner*] cannot be output as part of the current run *currentRun*, as a record with larger key value has already been output in this run. When the tree is being readjusted (lines 27 to 36), a record with lower run number wins over one with a higher run number. When run numbers are equal, the record with lower key value wins. This ensures that records come out of the tree in nondecreasing order of their run numbers. Within the same run, records come out of the tree in nondecreasing order of their key values. *maxRun* is used to terminate the function. In line 18, when we run out of input, a record with run number *maxRun* + 1 is introduced. When this record is ready for output, the function terminates from line 13.

Analysis of *runGeneration*: When the input list is already sorted, only one run is generated. On the average, the run size is almost $2k$. The time required to generate all the runs for an n run list is $O(n \log k)$, as it takes $O(\log k)$ time to adjust the loser tree each time a record is output. $\square$

7.10.5 Optimal Merging of Runs

The runs generated by function *runs* may not be of the same size. When runs are of different size, the run merging strategy employed so far (i.e., make complete passes over the collection of runs) does not yield minimum runtimes. For example, suppose we have four runs of length 2, 4, 5, and 15, respectively. Figure 7.26 shows two ways to merge these using a series of two-way merges. The circular nodes represent a two-way merge using as input the data of the children nodes. The square nodes represent the initial runs. We shall refer to the circular nodes as *internal nodes* and the square ones as *external*

```
 1 void runGeneration(int k)
 2 {/* run generation using a k-player loser tree,
 3     variable declarations have been omitted */
 4   for (i = 0; i < k; i++) {/* input records */
 5     readRecord(record[i]); runNum[i] = 1;
 6   }
 7   initializeLoserTree();
 8   winner = loser[0]; winnerRun = 1;
 9   currentRun = 1; maxRun = 1;
10   while(1) {/* output runs */
11     if (winnerRun != currentRun) {/* end of run */
12       output end of run marker;
13       if (winnerRun > maxRun) return;
14       else currentRun = winnerRun;
15     }
16     writeRecord(record[winner]);
17     lastKey = record[winner].key;
18     if (end of input) runNum[winner] = maxRun + 1;
19     else { /* input new record into tree */
20       readRecord(record[winner]);
21       if (record[winner].key < lastKey)
22         /* new record is in next run */
23         runNum[winner] = maxRun = winnerRun + 1;
24       else runNum[winner] = currentRun;
25     }
26     winnerRun = runNum[winner];
27     /* adjust losers */
28     for (parent = (k+winner)/2; parent; parent /= 2;)
29       if ((runNum[loser[parent]] < winnerRun) ||
30           ((runNum[loser[parent]] == winnerRun)
31              && (record[loser[parent]].key <
32                  record[winner].key)))
33       {/* parent is the winner */
34         SWAP(winner, loser[parent], temp);
35         winnerRun = runNum[winner];
36       }
37   }
38 }
```

Program 7.20: Run generation using a loser tree

nodes. Each figure is a *merge tree*.

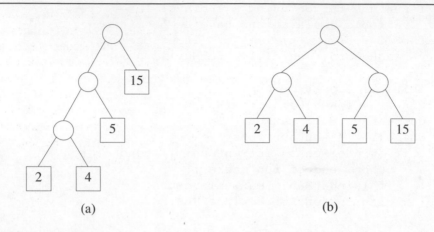

(a)   (b)

Figure 7.26: Possible two-way merges

In the first merge tree, we begin by merging the runs of size 2 and 4 to get one of size 6; next this is merged with the run of size 5 to get a run of size 11; finally this run of size 11 is merged with the run of size 15 to get the desired sorted run of size 26. When merging is done using the first merge tree, some records are involved in only one merge, and others are involved in up to three merges. In the second merge tree, each record is involved in exactly two merges. This corresponds to the strategy in which complete merge passes are repeatedly made over the data.

The number of merges that an individual record is involved in is given by the distance of the corresponding external node from the root. So, the records of the run with 15 records are involved in one merge when the first merge tree of Figure 7.26 is used and in two merges when the second tree is used. Since the time for a merge is linear in the number of records being merged, the total merge time is obtained by summing the products of the run lengths and the distance from the root of the corresponding external nodes. This sum is called the *weighted external path length*. For the two trees of Figure 7.26, the respective weighted external path lengths are

$$2 \cdot 3 + 4 \cdot 3 + 5 \cdot 2 + 15 \cdot 1 = 43$$

and

$$2 \cdot 2 + 4 \cdot 2 + 2 + 5 \cdot 2 + 15 \cdot 2 = 52$$

The cost of a k-way merge of n runs of length q_i, $1 \le i \le n$, is minimized by using a merge tree of degree k that has minimum weighted external path length. We shall consider the case $k = 2$ only. The discussion is easily generalized to the case $k > 2$ (see the exercises).

We briefly describe another application for binary trees with minimum weighted external path length. Suppose we wish to obtain an optimal set of codes for messages $M_1, \cdots, M_{n+1}$. Each code is a binary string that will be used for transmission of the corresponding message. At the receiving end the code will be decoded using a *decode tree*. A decode tree is a binary tree in which external nodes represent messages. The binary bits in the code word for a message determine the branching needed at each level of the decode tree to reach the correct external node. For example, if we interpret a zero as a left branch and a one as a right branch, then the decode tree of Figure 7.27 corresponds to codes 000, 001, 01, and 1 for messages M_1, M_2, M_3, and M_4, respectively. These codes are called Huffman codes. The cost of decoding a code word is proportional to the number of bits in the code. This number is equal to the distance of the corresponding external node from the root node. If q_i is the relative frequency with which message M_i will be transmitted, then the expected decoding time is

$$\sum_{1 \le i \le n+1} q_i d_i$$

where d_i is the distance of the external node for message M_i from the root node. The expected decoding time is minimized by choosing code words resulting in a decode tree with minimal weighted external path length.

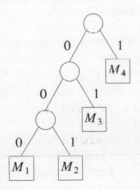

Figure 7.27: A decode tree

A very nice solution to the problem of finding a binary tree with mini~~ weighted external path length has been given by D. Huffman. We simply state his ~~rithm and leave the correctness proof as an exercise. The following type declarati~~ assumed:

```
typedef struct treeNode *tree-pointer;
typedef struct {
    treePointer leftChild;
    int         weight;
    treePointer rightChild;
    } treeNode;
```

The *huffman* function (Program 7.21) begins with n extended binary trees, each containing one node. These are in the array *heap* []. Each node in a tree has three fields: *weight*, *left_child*, and *right_child*. The single node in each of the initial extended binary trees has as weight of one of the q_i's. During the course of the algorithm, for any tree in *heap* with root node *tree* and depth greater than 1, *tree* $\rightarrow$ *weight* is the sum of the weights of all external nodes in the tree rooted at *tree*. The *huffman* function uses the min heap functions *push*, *pop*, and *initialize*; *push* adds a new element to the min heap, *pop* deletes and returns the element with minimum weight, and *initialize* initializes the min heap. As discussed in Section 7.6, a heap can be initialized in linear time.

```
void huffman(treePointer heap[], int n)
{/* heap[1:n] is a list of single-node binary trees */
   treePointer tree;
   int i;
   /* initialize min heap */
   initialize(heap, n);
   /* create a new tree by combining the trees with the
      smallest weights until one tree remains */

   for (i = 1; i < n; i++) {
      MALLOC(tree, sizeof(*tree));
      tree →leftChild = pop(&n);
      tree→rightChild = pop(&n);
      tree→weight = tree→leftChild→weight +
                          tree→rightChild→weight;
      sh(tree,&n); /* add to min heap */
```

ng a binary tree with minimum weighted external path length

have the weights $q_1 = 2$, $q_2 = 3$, $q_3 = 5$, $q_4 = 7$, $q_5 = 9$,
ce of trees we would get is given in Figure 7.28 (the

number in a circular node represents the sum of the weights of external nodes in that subtree).

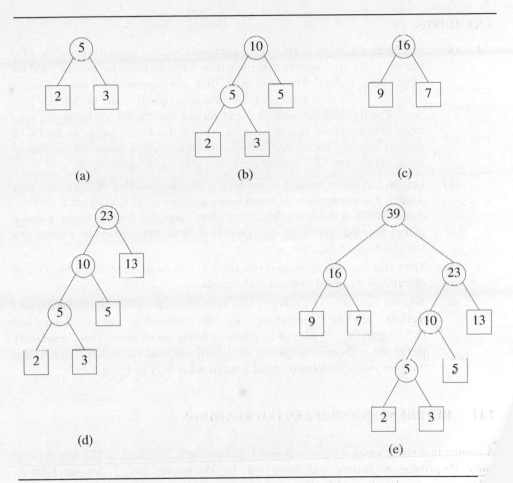

Figure 7.28: Construction of a Huffman tree

The weighted external path length of this tree is

$$2 \cdot 4 + 3 \cdot 4 + 5 \cdot 3 + 13 \cdot 2 + 7 \cdot 2 + 9 \cdot 2 = 93$$

By comparison, the best complete binary tree has weighted path length 95. ☐

Analysis of *huffman*: Heap initialization takes O(n) time. The main **for** loop is executed $n - 1$ times. Each call to *push* and *pop* requires only O(log n) time. Hence, the asymptotic computing time for the algorithm is O(n log n). □

EXERCISES

1. (a) n records are to be sorted on a computer with a memory capacity of S records ($S \ll n$). Assume that the entire S-record capacity may be used for input/output buffers. The input is on disk and consists of m runs. Assume that each time a disk access is made, the seek time is t_s and the latency time is t_l. The transmission time is t_t per record transmitted. What is the total input time for phase two of external sorting if a k-way merge is used with internal memory partitioned into input/output buffers to permit overlap of input, output, and CPU processing as in *buffering* (Program 7.19)?

   (b)   Let the CPU time needed to merge all the runs together be t_{CPU} (we may assume it is independent of k and hence constant). Let $t_s = 80$ *ms*, $t_l = 20ms$, $n = 200,000$, $m = 64$, $t_t = 10^{-3}$ sec/record, and $S = 2000$. Obtain a rough plot of the total input time, t_{input}, versus k. Will there always be a value of k for which $t_{CPU} \approx t_{input}$?

2. (a)   Show that function *huffman* (Program 7.21) correctly generates a binary tree of minimal weighted external path length.

   (b)   When n runs are to be merged together using an m-way merge, Huffman's method can be generalized to the following rule: "First add $(1 - n) \bmod (m - 1)$ runs of length zero to the set of runs. Then, repeatedly merge the m shortest remaining runs until only one run is left." Show that this rule yields an optimal merge pattern for m-way merging.

REFERENCES AND SELECTED READINGS

hensive discussion of sorting and searching may be found in *The Art of Com-*
ramming: Sorting and Searching, by D. Knuth, Vol. 3, Second Edition,
ey, Reading, MA, 1998.

CHAPTER *8*
_____

Hashing

8.1 INTRODUCTION

In this chapter, we again consider the ADT dictionary that was introduced in Chapter 5 (ADT 5.3). Examples of dictionaries are found in many applications, including the spelling checker, the thesaurus, the index for a database, and the symbol tables generated by loaders, assemblers, and compilers. When a dictionary with n entries is represented as a binary search tree as in Chapter 5, the dictionary operations *search*, *insert* and *delet* take $O(n)$ time. These dictionary operations may be performed in $O(\log n)$ time using balanced binary search tree (Chapter 10). In this chapter, we examine a techniq called hashing, that enables us to perform the dictionary operations *search*, *insert delete* in $O(1)$ expected time. We divide our discussion of hashing into two parts: *hashing* and *dynamic hashing*.

395

8.2   STATIC HASHING

8.2.1   Hash Tables

In *static hashing* the dictionary pairs are stored in a table, *ht*, called the *hash table*. The hash table is partitioned into b buckets, $ht[0], \cdots, ht[b-1]$. Each bucket is capable of holding s dictionary pairs (or pointers to this many pairs). Thus, a bucket is said to consist of s slots, each slot being large enough to hold one dictionary pair. Usually $s = 1$, and each bucket can hold exactly one pair. The address or location of a pair whose key is k is determined by a hash function, h, which maps keys into buckets. Thus, for any key k, $h(k)$ is an integer in the range 0 through $b-1$. $h(k)$ is the hash or home address of k. Under ideal conditions, dictionary pairs are stored in their home buckets.

Definition: The *key density* of a hash table is the ratio n/T, where n is the number of pairs in the table and T is the total number of possible keys. The *loading density* or *loading factor* of a hash table is $\alpha = n/(sb)$. $\square$

Suppose our keys are at most six characters long, where a character may be a decimal digit or an uppercase letter, and that the first character is a letter. Then the number of possible keys is $T = \sum_{0 \le i \le 5} 26 \times 36^i > 1.6 \times 10^9$. Any reasonable application, however, uses only a very small fraction of these. So, the key density, n/T, is usually very small. Consequently, the number of buckets, b, which is usually of the same magnitude as the number of keys, in the hash table is also much less than T. Therefore, the hash function h maps several different keys into the same bucket. Two keys, k_1, and k_2, are said to be *synonyms* with respect to h if $h(k_1) = h(k_2)$.

As indicated earlier, under ideal conditions, dictionary pairs are stored in their ⁀e buckets. Since many keys typically have the same home bucket, it is possible that ⁀me bucket for a new dictionary pair is full at the time we wish to insert this pair   dictionary. When this situation arises, we say that an *overflow* has occurred. A   ⁀ccurs when the home bucket for the new pair is not empty at the time of inser-   ⁀ach bucket has 1 slot (i.e., $s = 1$), collisions and overflows occur simultane-

⁀sider the hash table *ht* with $b = 26$ buckets and $s = 2$. We have   ⁀fiers, each representing a C library function. This table has a load-   ⁀ $= 0.19$. The hash function must map each of the possible   ⁀numbers, 0–25. We can construct a fairly simple hash func-   ⁀ers, a–z, with the numbers, 0–25, respectively, and then   ⁀(x), as the first character of x. Using this scheme, the   ⁀at, **exp**, **char**, **atan**, **ceil**, **floor**, **clock**, and **ctime** hash   ⁀2, and 2, respectively. Figure 8.1 shows the first 8 identifiers entered into the hash table.

	Slot 0	Slot 1
0	acos	atan
1		
2	char	ceil
3	define	
4	exp	
5	float	floor
6		
...		
25		

Figure 8.1: Hash table with 26 buckets and two slots per bucket

The identifiers **acos** and **atan** are synonyms, as are **float** and **floor**, and **ceil** and **char**. The next identifier, **clock**, hashes into the bucket $ht[2]$. Since this bucket is full, we have an overflow. Where in the table should we place **clock** so that we may retrieve it when necessary? We consider various solutions to the overflow problem in Section 8.2.3. □

When no overflows occur, the time required to insert, delete or search using hashing depends only on the time required to compute the hash function and the time to search one bucket. Hence, the insert, delete and search times are independent of n, the number of entries in the dictionary. Since the bucket size, s, is usually small (for internal-memory tables s is usually 1) the search within a bucket is carried out using a sequential search.

The hash function of Example 8.1 is not well suited for most practical application because of the very large number of collisions and resulting overflows that occur. This so because it is not unusual to find dictionaries in which many of the keys begin with same letter. Ideally, we would like to choose a hash function that is both easy to c pute and results in very few collisions. Since the ratio b/T is usually very small impossible to avoid collisions altogether.

In summary, hashing schemes use a hash function to map keys into ha buckets. It is desirable to use a hash function that is both easy to compute and m the number of collisions. Since the size of the key space is usually several magnitude larger than the number of buckets and since the number of slots in small, overflows necessarily occur. Hence, a mechanism to handle overflows

8.2.2 Hash Functions

A hash function maps a key into a bucket in the hash table. As mentioned earlier, the desired properties of such a function are that it be easy to compute and that it minimize the number of collisions. In addition, we would like the hash function to be such that it does not result in a biased use of the hash table for random inputs; that is, if k is a key chosen at random from the key space, then we want the probability that $h(k) = i$ to be $1/b$ for all buckets i. With this stipulation, a random key has an equal chance of hashing into any of the buckets. A hash function satisfying this property is called a *uniform hash function*.

Several kinds of uniform hash functions are in use in practice. Some of these compute the home bucket by performing arithmetic (e.g., multiplication and division) on the key. Since, in many applications, the data type of the key is not one for which arithmetic operations are defined (e.g., string), it is necessary to first convert the key into an integer (say) and then perform arithmetic on the obtained integer. In the following subsections, we describe four popular hash functions as well as ways to convert strings into integers.

8.2.2.1 Division

This hash function, which is the most widely used hash function in practice, assumes the keys are non-negative integers. The home bucket is obtained by using the modulo (%) operator. The key k is divided by some number D, and the remainder is used as the home bucket for k. More formally,

$$h(k) = k \% D$$

s function gives bucket addresses in the range 0 through $D - 1$, so the hash table must t least $b = D$ buckets. Although for most key spaces, every choice of D makes h a hash function, the number of overflows on real-world dictionaries is criticaly on the choice of D. If D is divisible by two, then odd keys are mapped to odd he remainder is odd), and even keys are mapped to even buckets. Since onaries tend to have a bias toward either odd or even keys, the use of an sults in a corresponding bias in the distribution of home buckets. In n found that for real-world dictionaries, the distribution of home never D has small prime factors such as 2, 3, 5, 7 and so on. How-decreases as the smallest prime factor of D increases. Hence, for riety of dictionaries, you should select D so that it is a prime he smallest prime factor of D is D itself. For most practical tribution of keys to buckets is seen even when we choose smaller than 20.

nctions for general use, the size of the dictionary to not known. This makes it impractical to choose D

as suggested above. So, we relax the requirement on D even further and require only that D be odd to avoid the bias caused by an even D. In addition, we set b equal to the divisor D. As the size of the dictionary grows, it will be necessary to increase the size of the hash table ht dynamically. To satisfy the relaxed requirement on D, array doubling results in increasing the number of buckets (and hence the divisor D) from b to $2b + 1$.

8.2.2.2 Mid-Square

The mid-square hash function determines the home bucket for a key by squaring the key and then using an appropriate number of bits from the middle of the square to obtain the bucket address; the key is assumed to be an integer. Since the middle bits of the square usually depend on all bits of the key, different keys are expected to result in different hash addresses with high probability, even when some of the digits are the same. The number of bits to be used to obtain the bucket address depends on the table size. If r bits are used, the range of values is 0 through 2^r-1. So the size of hash tables is chosen to be a power of two when the mid-square function is used.

8.2.2.3 Folding

In this method the key k is partitioned into several parts, all but possibly the last being of the same length. These partitions are then added together to obtain the hash address for k. There are two ways of carrying out this addition. In the first, all but the last partition are shifted to the right so that the least significant digit of each lines up with the corresponding digit of the last partition. The different partitions are now added together to get $h(k)$. This method is known as *shift folding*. In the second method, *folding at the boundaries*, the key is folded at the partition boundaries, and digits falling into the same position are added together to obtain $h(k)$. This is equivalent to reversing every other partition and then adding.

Example 8.2: Suppose that $k = 12320324111220$, and we partition it into parts that are three decimal digits long. The partitions are $P_1 = 123$, $P_2 = 203$, $P_3 = 241$, $P_4 = 112$, and $P_5 = 20$. Using shift folding, we obtain

$$h(k) = \sum_{i=1}^{5} P_i = 123 + 203 + 241 + 112 + 20 = 699$$

When folding at the boundaries is used, we first reverse P_2 and P_4 to obtain 302 and 211, respectively. Next, the five partitions are added to obtain $h(k) = 123 + 302 + 241 + 211 + 20 = 897$. □

8.2.2.4 Digit Analysis

This method is particularly useful in the case of a static file where all the keys in the table are known in advance. Each key is interpreted as a number using some radix r. The same radix is used for all the keys in the table. Using this radix, the digits of each key are examined. Digits having the most skewed distributions are deleted. Enough digits are deleted so that the number of remaining digits is small enough to give an address in the range of the hash table.

8.2.2.5 Converting Keys to Integers

To use some of the described hash functions, keys need to first be converted to nonnegative integers. Since all hash functions hash several keys into the same home bucket, it is not necessary for us to convert keys into unique nonnegative integers. It is ok for us to convert the strings *data*, *structures*, and *algorithms* into the same integer (say, 199). In this section, we consider only the conversion of strings into non-negative integers. Similar methods may be used to convert other data types into non-negative integers to which the described hash functions may be applied.

Example 8.3: *[Converting Strings to Integers]* Since it is not necessary to convert strings into unique nonnegative integers, we can map every string, no matter how long, into an integer. Programs 8.1 and 8.2 show you two ways to do this.

```
unsigned int stringToInt(char *key)
{/* simple additive approach to create a natural number
    that is within the integer range */
  int number = 0;
  while (*key)
    number += *key++;
  return number;
}
```

Program 8.1: Converting a string into a non-negative integer

Program 8.1 converts each character into a unique integer and sums these unique integers. Since each character maps to an integer in the range 0 through 255, the integer returned by the function is not much more than 8 bits long. For example, strings that are eight characters long would produce integers up to 11 bits long.

Program 8.2 shifts the integer corresponding to every other character by 8 bits and then sums. This results in a larger range for the integer returned by the function. □

```
unsigned int stringToInt(char *key)
{/* alternative additive approach to create a natural number
    that is within the integer range */
  int number = 0;
  while (*key)
  {
    number += *key++;
    if (*key) number += ((int) *key++) << 8;
  }
  return number;
}
```

Program 8.2: Alternative way to convert a string into a non-negative integer

8.2.3 Overflow Handling

8.2.3.1 Open Addressing

There are two popular ways to handle overflows: *open addressing* and *chaining*. In this section, we describe four open addressing methods—linear probing, which also is known as linear open addressing, quadratic probing, rehashing and random probing. In linear probing, when inserting a new pair whose key is k, we search the hash table buckets in the order, $ht[h(k) + i] \% b$, $0 \le i \le b - 1$, where h is the hash function and b is the number of buckets. This search terminates when we reach the first unfilled bucket and the new pair is inserted into this bucket. In case no such bucket is found, the hash table is full and it is necessary to increase the table size. In practice, to ensure good performance, table size is increased when the loading density exceeds a prespecified threshold such as 0.75 rather than when the table is full. Notice that when we resize the hash table, we must change the hash function as well. For example, when the division hash function is used, the divisor equals the number of buckets. This change in the hash function potentially changes the home bucket for each key in the hash table. So, all dictionary entries need to be remapped into the new larger table.

Example 8.4: Assume we have a 13-bucket table with one slot per bucket. As our data we use the words **for, do, while, if, else**, and **function**. Figure 8.2 shows the hash value for each word using the simplified scheme of Program 8.1 and the division hash function. Inserting the first five words into the table poses no problem since they have different hash addresses. However, the last identifier, **function**, hashes to the same bucket as **if**. Using a circular rotation, the next available bucket is at $ht[0]$, which is where we place **function** (Figure 8.3). □

Identifier	Additive Transformation	x	Hash
for	102 + 111 + 114	327	2
do	100 + 111	211	3
while	119 + 104 + 105 + 108 + 101	537	4
if	105 + 102	207	12
else	101 + 108 + 115 + 101	425	9
function	102 + 117 + 110 + 99 + 116 + 105 + 111 + 110	870	12

Figure 8.2: Additive transformation

[0]	**function**
[1]	
[2]	**for**
[3]	**do**
[4]	**while**
[5]	
[6]	
[7]	
[8]	
[9]	**else**
[10]	
[11]	
[12]	**if**

Figure 8.3: Hash table with linear probing (13 buckets, one slot per bucket)

When $s = 1$ and linear probing is used to handle overflows, a hash table search for the pair with key k proceeds as follows:

(1)   Compute $h(k)$.

(2)   Examine the hash table buckets in the order $ht[h(k)]$, $ht[(h(k) + 1) \% b]$, $\cdots$, $ht[(h(k) + j) \% b]$ until one of the following happens:

(a)   The bucket $ht[(h(k) + j) \% b]$ has a pair whose key is k; in this case, the desired pair has been found.

(b) $ht[h(k)+j]$ is empty; k is not in the table.

(c) We return to the starting position $ht[h(k)]$; the table is full and k is not in the table.

Program 8.3 is the resulting search function. This function assumes that the hash table ht stores pointers to dictionary pairs. The data type of a dictionary pair is *element* and data of this type has two componenets *item* and *key*.

```
element* search(int k)
{/* search the linear probing hash table ht (each bucket has
    exactly one slot) for k, if a pair with key k is found,
    return a pointer to this pair; otherwise, return NULL */
  int homeBucket, currentBucket;
  homeBucket = h(k);
  for (currentBucket = homeBucket; ht[currentBucket]
              && ht[currentBucket]->key != k;) {
    currentBucket = (currentBucket + 1) % b;
                    /* treat the table as circular */
    if (currentBucket == homeBuket)
      return NULL; /* back to start point */
  }
  if (ht[currentBucket]->key == k)
    return ht[currentBucket];
  return NULL;
}
```

Program 8.3: Linear probing

When linear probing is used to resolve overflows, keys tend to cluster together. Moreover, adjacent clusters tend to coalesce, thus increasing the search time. For example, suppose we enter the C built-in functions **acos, atoi, char, define, exp, ceil, cos, float, atol, floor**, and **ctime** into a 26-bucket hash table in that order. For illustrative purposes, we assume that the hash function uses the first character in each function name. Figure 8.4 shows the bucket number, the identifier contained in the bucket, and the number of comparisons required to insert the identifier. Notice that before we can insert **atol**, we must examine $ht[0], \ldots, ht[8]$, a total of nine comparisons. This is far worse than the worst case behavior of the search trees we will study in Chapter 10. If we retrieved each of the identifiers in ht exactly once, the average number of buckets examined would be $35/11 = 3.18$ per identifier.

When linear probing is used together with a uniform hash hash function, the expected average number of key comparisons to look up a key is approximately

bucket	x	buckets searched
0	acos	1
1	atoi	2
2	char	1
3	define	1
4	exp	1
5	ceil	4
6	cos	5
7	float	3
8	atol	9
9	floor	5
10	ctime	9
...		
25		

Figure 8.4: Hash table with linear probing (26 buckets, one slot per bucket)

$(2 - \alpha)/(2 - 2\alpha)$, where α is the loading density. This is the average over all possible sets of keys yielding the given loading density and using a uniform function h. In the example of Figure 8.4, $\alpha = 11/26 = .42$ and $p = 1.36$. This indicates that the expected average number of comparisons to search a table with a loading density of .42 is 1.36. Even though the average number of comparisons is small, the worst case can be quite large.

Some improvement in the growth of clusters and hence in the average number of comparisons needed for searching can be obtained by *quadratic probing*. Linear probing was characterized by searching the buckets $(h(k) + i) \% b$, $0 \le i \le b - 1$, where b is the number of buckets in the table. In quadratic probing, a quadratic function of i is used as the increment. In particular, the search is carried out by examining buckets $h(k)$, $(h(k) + i^2) \% b$, and $(h(k) - i^2) \% b$ for $1 \le i \le (b - 1)/2$. When b is a prime number of the form $4j + 3$, for j an integer, the quadratic search described above examines every bucket in the table. Figure 8.5 lists some primes of the form $4j + 3$.

An alternative method to retard the growth of clusters is to use a series of hash functions $h_1, h_2, \cdots, h_m$. This method is known as *rehashing*. Buckets $h_i(k)$, $1 \le i \le m$ are examined in that order. Yet another alternative, random probing, is explored in the exercises.

Prime	j	Prime	j
3	0	43	10
7	1	59	14
11	2	127	31
19	4	251	62
23	5	503	125
31	7	1019	254

Figure 8.5: Some primes of the form $4j + 3$

8.2.3.2 Chaining

Linear probing and its variations perform poorly because the search for a key involves comparison with keys that have different hash values. In the hash table of Figure 8.4, for instance, searching for the key **atol** involves comparisons with the buckets ht [0] through ht [8], even though only the keys in ht [0] and ht [1] had a collision with with **atol**; the remainder cannot possibly be **atol**. Many of the comparisons can be saved if we maintain lists of keys, one list per bucket, each list containing all the synonyms for that bucket. If this is done, a search involves computing the hash address $h(k)$ and examining only those keys in the list for $h(k)$. Although the list for $h(k)$ may be maintained using any data structure that supports the search, insert and delete operations (e.g., arrays, chains, search trees), chains are most frequently used. We typically use an array ht [0:b−1] with ht [i] pointing to the first node of the chain for bucket i. Program 8.4 gives the search algorithm for chained hash tables.

Figure 8.6 shows the chained hash table corresponding to the linear table found in Figure 8.4. The number of comparisons needed to search for any of the identifiers is now one each for **acos**, **char**, **define**, **exp** and **float**; two each for **atoi**, **ceil**, and **float**, three each for **atol** and **cos**; and four for **ctime**. The average number of comparisons is now $21/11 = 1.91$.

To insert a new key, k, into a chain, we must first verify that it is not currently on the chain. Following this, k may be inserted at any position of the chain. Deletion from a chained hash table can be done by removing the appropriate node from its chain.

When chaining is used along with a uniform hash function, the expected average number of key comparisons for a successful search is $\approx 1 + \alpha/2$, where α is the loading density n/b (b = number of buckets). For $\alpha = 0.5$ this number is 1.25, and for $\alpha = 1$ it is 1.5. The corresponding numbers for linear probing are 1.5 and b, the table size.

The performance results cited in this section tend to imply that provided we use a uniform hash function, performance depends only on the method used to handle

```
element* search(int k)
{/* search the chained hash table ht for k, if a pair with
    this key is found, return a pointer to this pair;
    otherwise, return NULL.
    nodePointer current;
    int homeBucket = h(k);
    /* search the chain ht[homeBucket] */
    for (current = ht[homeBucket]; current;
                                    current = current->link)
        if (current->data.key == k) return &current->data;
    return NULL;
}
```

Program 8.4: Chain search

[0] $\rightarrow$ **acos atoi atol**
[1] $\rightarrow$ *NULL*
[2] $\rightarrow$ **char ceil cos ctime**
[3] $\rightarrow$ **define**
[4] $\rightarrow$ **exp**
[5] $\rightarrow$ **float floor**
[6] $\rightarrow$ *NULL*
· · ·
[25] $\rightarrow$ *NULL*

Figure 8.6: Hash chains corresponding to Figure 8.4

overflows. Although this is true when the keys are selected at random from the key space, it is not true in practice. In practice, there is a tendency to make a biased use of keys. Hence, in practice, different hash functions result in different performance. Generally, the division hash function coupled with chaining yields best performance.

The worst-case number of comparisons needed for a successful search remains O(n) regardless of whether we use open addressing or chaining. The worst-case number of comparisons may be reduced to O(log$n$) by storing synonyms in a balanced search tree (see Chapter 10) rather than in a chain.

8.2.4   Theoretical Evaluation of Overflow Techniques

The experimental evaluation of hashing techniques indicates a very good performance over conventional techniques such as balanced trees. The worst-case performance for hashing can, however, be very bad. In the worst case, an insertion or a search in a hash table with n keys may take $O(n)$ time. In this section, we present a probabilistic analysis for the expected performance of the chaining method and state without proof the results of similar analyses for the other overflow handling methods. First, we formalize what we mean by expected performance.

Let $ht[0:b-1]$ be a hash table with b buckets, each bucket having one slot. Let h be a uniform hash function with range $[0, b-1]$. If n keys $k_1, k_2, \cdots, k_n$ are entered into the hash table, then there are b^n distinct hash sequences $h(k_1), h(k_2), \cdots, h(k_n)$. Assume that each of these is equally likely to occur. Let S_n denote the expected number of key comparisons needed to locate a randomly chosen k_i, $1 \le i \le n$. Then, S_n is the average number of comparisons needed to find the jth key k_j, averaged over $1 \le j \le n$, with each j equally likely, and averaged over all b^n hash sequences, assuming each of these also to be equally likely. Let U_n be the expected number of key comparisons when a search is made for a key not in the hash table. This hash table contains n keys. The quantity U_n may be defined in a manner analogous to that used for S_n.

Theorem 8.1: Let $\alpha = n/b$ be the loading density of a hash table using a uniform hashing function h. Then

(1)   for linear open addressing

$$U_n \approx \frac{1}{2} \left[1 + \frac{1}{(1-\alpha)^2} \right]$$

$$S_n \approx \frac{1}{2} \left[1 + \frac{1}{1-\alpha} \right]$$

(2)   for rehashing, random probing, and quadratic probing

$$U_n \approx 1/(1-\alpha)$$

$$S_n \approx - \left[\frac{1}{\alpha} \right] \log_e(1-\alpha)$$

(3) for chaining

$$U_n \approx \alpha$$

$$S_n \approx 1 + \alpha/2$$

Proof: Exact derivations of U_n and S_n are fairly involved and can be found in Knuth's book *The Art of Computer Programming: Sorting and Searching* (see the References and

Selected Readings section). Here we present a derivation of the approximate formulas for chaining. First, we must make clear our count for U_n and S_n. If the key k being sought has $h(k) = i$, and chain i has q nodes on it, then q comparisons are needed if k is not on the chain. If k is in the jth node of the chain, $1 \le j \le q$, then j comparisons are needed.

When the n keys are distributed uniformly over the b possible chains, the expected number in each chain is $n/b = \alpha$. Since U_n equals the expected number of keys on a chain, we get $U_n = \alpha$.

When the ith key, k_i, is being entered into the table, the expected number of keys on any chain is $(i-1)/b$. Hence, the expected number of comparisons needed to search for k_i after all n keys have been entered is $1 + (i-1)/b$ (this assumes that new entries will be made at the end of the chain). Thus,

$$S_n = \frac{1}{n} \sum_{i=1}^{n} \{1 + (i-1)/b\} = 1 + \frac{n-1}{2b} \approx 1 + \frac{\alpha}{2} \quad \square$$

EXERCISES

1. Show that the hash function $h(k) = k \% 17$ does not satisfy the one-way property, weak collision resistance, or strong collision resistance.

2. Consider a hash function $h(k)=k \% D$, where D is not given. We want to figure out what value of D is being used. We wish to achieve this using as few attempts as possible, where an attempt consists of supplying the function with k and observing $h(k)$. Indicate how this may be achieved in the following two cases.

   (a) D is known to be a prime number in the range [10,20].

   (b) D is of the form 2^k, where k is an integer in [1,5].

3. Write a function to delete the pair with key k from a hash table that uses linear probing. Show that simply setting the slot previously occupied by the deleted pair to empty does not solve the problem. How must *Get* (Program 8.3) be modified so that a correct search is made in the situation when deletions are permitted? Where can a new key be inserted?

4. (a) Show that if quadratic searching is carried out in the sequence $(h(k) + q^2)$, $(h(k) + (q-1)^2)$, $\cdots$, $(h(k) + 1)$, $h(k)$, $(h(k) - 1)$, $\cdots$, $(h(k) - q^2)$ with $q = (b-1)/2$, then the address difference $\% b$ between successive buckets being examined is

   $$b - 2, b - 4, b - 6, \ldots, 5, 3, 1, 1, 3, 5, \ldots, b - 6, b - 4, b - 2$$

   (b) Write a function to search a hash table ht of size b for the key k. Use h as the hash function and the quadratic probing scheme discussed in the text to resolve overflows. Use the results of part (a) to reduce the computations.

5. [*Morris 1968*] In random probing, the search for a key, k, in a hash table with b buckets is carried out by examining the buckets in the order $h(k)$, $(h(k) + s(i)) \% b$, $1 \le i \le b-1$ where $s(i)$ is a pseudo random number. The random number generator must satisfy the property that every number from 1 to $b-1$ must be generated exactly once as i ranges from 1 to $b-1$.

   (a) Show that for a table of size 2^r, the following sequence of computations generates numbers with this property:

   Initialize q to 1 each time the search routine is called.
   On successive calls for a random number do the following:
   $q *= 5$
   q = low order $r + 2$ bits of q
   $s(i) = q/4$

   (b) Write search and insert functions for a hash table using random probing and the mid-square hash function. Use the random number generator of (a).

   It can be shown that for this method, the expected value for the average number of comparisons needed to search for a dictionary pair is $-(1/\alpha)\log(1-\alpha)$ for large tables (α is the loading factor).

6. Develop a hash table implementation in which overflows are resolved using a binary search tree. Use the division hash function with an odd divisor D and array doubling whenever the loading density exceeds a prespecified amount. Recall that in this context, array doubling actually increases the size of the hash table from its current size $b = D$ to $2b + 1$.

7. Write a function to list all the keys in a hash table in lexicographic order. Assume that linear probing is used. How much time does your function take?

8. Let the binary representation of key k be $k_1 k_2$. Let $|t|$ denote the number of bits in k and let the first bit of k_1 be 1. Let $|k_1| = \lceil |k|/2 \rceil$ and $|k_2| = \lfloor |k|/2 \rfloor$. Consider the following hash function

$$h(k) = \text{middle } q \text{ bits of } (k_1 \oplus k_2)$$

where $\oplus$ is the exclusive-or operator. Is this a uniform hash function if keys are drawn at random from the space of integers? What can you say about the behavior of this hash function in actual dictionary usage?

9. [*T. Gonzalez*] Design a dictionary representation that allows you to search, insert, and delete in O(1) time. Assume that the keys are integer and in the range $[0, m)$ and that $m + n$ units of space are available, where n is the number of insertions to be made. (Hint: Use two arrays, $a[n]$ and $b[m]$, where $a[i]$ will be the $(i+1)$th pair inserted into the table. If k is the ith key inserted, then $b[k] = i$.) Write C++ functions to search, insert, and delete. Note that you cannot initialize the arrays a

and b as this would take $O(n + m)$ time.

10. [*T. Gonzalez*] Let $s = \{s_1, s_2, \cdots, s_n\}$ and $t = \{t_1, t_2, \cdots, t_r\}$ be two sets. Assume $1 \leq s_i \leq m$, $1 \leq i \leq n$, and $1 \leq t_i \leq m$, $1 \leq i \leq r$. Using the idea of Exercise 9, write a function to determine if $s \subseteq t$. Your function should work in $O(r + n)$ time. Since $s \equiv t$ iff $s \subseteq t$ and $t \subseteq s$, one can determine in linear time whether two sets are the same. How much space is needed by your function?

11. [*T. Gonzalez*] Using the idea of Exercise 9, write an $O(n + m)$ time function to carry out the task of *Verify2* (Program 7.3). How much space does your function need?

12. Using the notation of Section 8.2.4, show that when linear probing is used

$$S_n = \frac{1}{n} \sum_{i=0}^{n-1} U_i$$

Using this equation and the approximate equality

$$U_n \approx \frac{1}{2} \left[1 + \frac{1}{(1 - \alpha)^2} \right] \quad \text{where } \alpha = \frac{n}{b}$$

show that

$$S_n \approx \frac{1}{2} \left[1 + \frac{1}{(1 - \alpha)} \right]$$

8.3   DYNAMIC HASHING

8.3.1   Motivation for Dynamic Hashing

To ensure good performance, it is necessary to increase the size of a hash table whenever its loading density exceeds a prespecified threshold. So, for example, if we currently have b buckets in our hash table and are using the division hash function with divisor $D = b$, then, when an insert causes the loading density to exceed the prespecified threshold, we use array doubling to increase the number of buckets to $2b + 1$. At the same time, the hash function divisor changes to $2b + 1$. This change in divisor requires us to rebuild the hash table by collecting all dictionary pairs in the original smaller size table and reinserting these into the new larger table. We cannot simply copy dictionary entries from the smaller table into corresponding buckets of the bigger table as the home bucket for each entry has potentially changed. For very large dictionaries that must be accessible on a 24/7 basis, the required rebuild means that dictionary operations must be suspended for unacceptably long periods while the rebuild is in progress. Dynamic hashing, which also is known as extendible hashing, aims to reduce the rebuild time by ensuring that each rebuild changes the home bucket for the entries in only 1 bucket. In other words, although table doubling increases the total time for a sequence of n dictionary operations by only $O(n)$, the time required to complete an insert that triggers the doubling is excessive in the context of a large dictionary that is required to respond quickly on a per operation basis. The objective of dynamic hashing is to provide acceptable hash table performance on a per operation basis.

We consider two forms of dynamic hashing—one uses a directory and the other does not—in this section. For both forms, we use a hash function h that maps keys into non-negative integers. The range of h is assumed to be sufficiently large and we use $h(k,p)$ to denote the integer formed by the p least significant bits of $h(k)$.

For the examples of this section, we use a hash function $h(k)$ that transforms keys into 6-bit non-negative integers. Our example keys will be two characters each and h transforms letters such as A, B and C into the bit sequence 100, 101, and 110, respectively. Digits 0 through 7 are transformed into their 3-bit representation. Figure 8.7 shows 8 possible 2 character keys together with the binary representation of $h(k)$ for each. For our example hash function, $h(A0,1) = 0$, $h(A1,3) = 1$, $h(B1,4) = 1001 = 9$, and $h(C1,6) = 110\ 001 = 49$.

k	$h(k)$
A0	100 000
A1	100 001
B0	101 000
B1	101 001
C1	110 001
C2	110 010
C3	110 011
C5	110 101

Figure 8.7: An example hash function

8.3.2 Dynamic Hashing Using Directories

We employ a directory, d, of pointers to buckets. The size of the directory depends on the number of bits of $h(k)$ used to index into the directory. When indexing is done using, say, $h(k, 2)$, the directory size is $2^2 = 4$; when $h(k, 5)$ is used, the directory size is 32. The number of bits of $h(k)$ used to index the directory is called the *directory depth*. The size of the directory is 2^t, where t is the directory depth and the number of buckets is at most equal to the directory size. Figure 8.8 (a) shows a dynamic hash table that contains the keys A0, B0, A1, B1, C2, and C3. This hash table uses a directory whose depth is 2 and uses buckets that have 2 slots each. In Figure 8.8, the directory is shaded while the buckets are not. In practice, the bucket size is often chosen to match some physical characteristic of the storage media. For example, when the dictionary pairs reside on disk, a bucket may correspond to a disk track or sector.

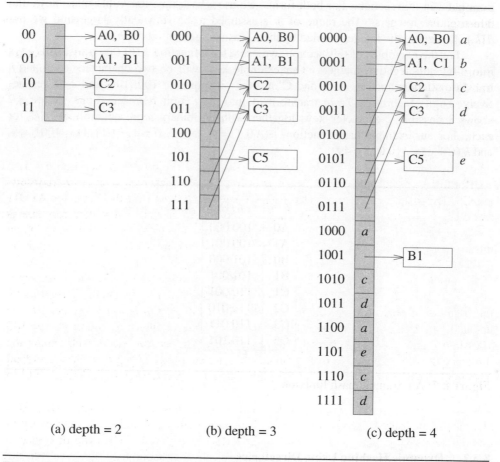

(a) depth = 2   (b) depth = 3   (c) depth = 4

Figure 8.8: Dynamic hash tables with directories

To search for a key k, we merely examine the bucket pointed to by $d[h(k,t)]$, where t is the directory depth.

Suppose we insert C5 into the hash table of Figure 8.8 (a). Since, $h(C5,2) = 01$, we follow the pointer, $d[01]$, in position 01 of the directory. This gets us to the bucket with A1 and B1. This bucket is full and we get a bucket overflow. To resolve the overflow, we determine the least u such that $h(k,u)$ is not the same for all keys in the overflowed bucket. In case the least u is greater than the directory depth, we increase the directory depth to this least u value. This requires us to increase the directory size but not the number of buckets. When the directory size doubles, the pointers in the original directory are duplicated so that the pointers in each half of the directory are the same. A quadrupling of the directory size may be handled as two doublings and so on. For our example, the least u for which $h(k,u)$ is not the same for A1, B1, and C5 is 3. So, the directory is expanded to have depth 3 and size 8. Following the expansion, $d[i] = d[i+4], 0 \le i < 4$.

Following the resizing (if any) of the directory, we split the overflowed bucket using $h(k,u)$. In our case, the overflowed bucket is split using $h(k,3)$. For A1 and B1, $h(k,3) = 001$ and for C5, $h(k,3) = 101$. So, we create a new bucket with C5 and place a pointer to this bucket in $d[101]$. Figure 8.8 (b) shows the result. Notice that each dictionary entry is in the bucket pointed at by the directory position $h(k,3)$, although, in some cases the dictionary entry is also pointed at by other buckets. For example, bucket 100 also points to A0 and B0, even though $h(A0,3) = h(B0,3) \ne 000$.

Suppose that instead of C5, we were to insert C1. The pointer in position $h(C1,2) = 01$ of the directory of Figure 8.8 (a) gets us to the same bucket as when we were inserting C5. This bucket overflows. The least u for which $h(k,u)$ isn't the same for A1, B1 and C1 is 4. So, the new directory depth is 4 and its new size is 16. The directory size is quadrupled and the pointers $d[0:3]$ are replicated 3 times to fill the new directory. When the overflowed bucket is split, A1 and C1 are placed into a bucket that is pointed at by $d[0001]$ and B1 into a bucket pointed at by $d[1001]$.

When the current directory depth is greater than or equal to u, some of the other pointers to the split bucket also must be updated to point to the new bucket. Specifically, the pointers in positions that agree with the last u bits of the new bucket need to be updated. The following example illustrates this. Consider inserting A4 ($h(A4) = 100$ 100) into Figure 8.8 (b). Bucket $d[100]$ overflows. The least u is 3, which equals the directory depth. So, the size of the directory is not changed. Using $h(k,3)$, A0 and B0 hash to 000 while A4 hashes to 100. So, we create a new bucket for A4 and set $d[100]$ to point to this new bucket.

As a final insert example, consider inserting C1 into Figure 8.8 (b). $h(C1,3) = 001$. This time, bucket $d[001]$ overflows. The minumum u is 4 and so it is necessary to double the directory size and increase the directory depth to 4. When the directory is doubled, we replicate the pointers in the first half into the second half. Next we split the overflowed bucket using $h(k,4)$. Since $h(k,4) = 0001$ for A1 and C1 and 1001 for B1, we create a new bucket with B1 and put C1 into the slot previously occupied by B1. A pointer to the new bucket is placed in $d[1001]$. Figure 8.8 (c) shows the resulting configuration. For clarity, several of the bucket pointers have been replaced by lower-case letters indicating the bucket pointed to.

Deletion from a dynamic hash table with a directory is similar to insertion. Although dynamic hashing employs array doubling, the time for this array doubling is considerably less than that for the array doubling used in static hashing. This is so because, in dynamic hashing, we need to rehash only the entries in the bucket that overflows rather than all entries in the table. Further, savings result when the directory resides in memory while the buckets are on disk. A search requires only 1 disk access; an insert makes 1 read and 2 write accesses to the disk, the array doubling requires no disk access.

8.3.3   Directoryless Dynamic Hashing

As the name suggests, in this method, which also is known as linear dynamic hashing, we dispense with the directory, d, of bucket pointers used in the method of Section 8.3.2. Instead, an array, ht, of buckets is used. We assume that this array is as large as possible and so there is no possibility of increasing its size dynamically. To avoid initializing such a large array, we use two variables q and r, $0 \leq q < 2^r$, to keep track of the *active buckets*. At any time, only buckets 0 through $2^r + q - 1$ are active. Each active bucket is the start of a chain of buckets. The remaining buckets on a chain are called *overflow buckets*. Informally, r is the number of bits of $h(k)$ used to index into the hash table and q is the bucket that will split next. More accurately, buckets 0 through $q - 1$ as well as buckets 2^r through $2^r + q - 1$ are indexed using $h(k, r + 1)$ while the remaining active buckets are indexed using $h(k, r)$. Each dictionary pair is either in an active or an overflow bucket.

Figure 8.9 (a) shows a directoryless hash table ht with $r = 2$ and $q = 0$. The hash function is that of Figure 8.7, $h(B4) = 101\ 100$, and $h(B5) = 101\ 101$. The number of active buckets is 4 (indexed 00, 01, 10, and 11). The index of an active bucket identifies its chain. Each active bucket has 2 slots and bucket 00 contains B4 and A0. There are 4 bucket chains, each chain begins at one of the 4 active buckets and comprises only that active bucket (i.e., there are no overflow buckets). In Figure 8.9 (a), all keys have been mapped into chains using $h(k, 2)$. In Figure 8.9 (b), $r = 2$ and $q = 1$; $h(k, 3)$ has been used for chains 000 and 100 while $h(k, 2)$ has been used for chains 001, 010, and 011. Chain 001 has an overflow bucket; the capacity of an overflow bucket may or may not be the same as that of an active bucket.

To search for k, we first compute $h(k, r)$. If $h(k, r) < q$, then k, if present, is in a chain indexed using $h(k, r + 1)$. Otherwise, the chain to examine is given by $h(k, r)$. Program 8.5 gives the algorithm to search a directoryless dynamic hash table.

To insert C5 into the table of Figure 8.9 (a), we use the search algorithm of Program 8.5 to determine whether or not C5 is in the table already. Chain 01 is examined and we verify that C5 is not present. Since the active bucket for the searched chain is full, we get an overflow. An overflow is handled by activating bucket $2^r + q$; reallocating the entries in the chain q between q and the newly activated bucket (or chain) $2^r + q$,

if $(h(k,r) < q)$ search the chain that begins at bucket $h(k,r+1)$;
else search the chain that begins at bucket $h(k,r)$;

Program 8.5: Searching a directoryless hash table

---

and incrementing q by 1. In case q now becomes 2^r, we increment r by 1 and reset q to 0. The reallocation is done using $h(k, r + 1)$. Finally, the new pair is inserted into the chain where it would be searched for by Program 8.5 using the new r and q values.

For our example, bucket 4 = 100 is activated and the entries in chain 00 ($q = 0$) are rehashed using $r + 1 = 3$ bits. B4 hashes to the new bucket 100 and A0 to bucket 000. Following this, $q = 1$ and $r = 2$. A search for C5 would examine chain 1 and so C5 is added to this chain using an overflow bucket (see Figure 8.9 (b)). Notice that at this time, the keys in buckets 001, 010 and 011 are hashed using $h(k, 2)$ while those in buckets 000 and 100 are hashed using $h(k, 3)$.

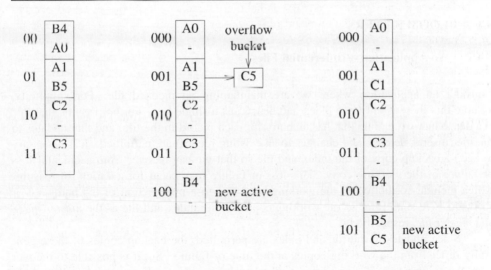

(a) $r = 2, q = 0$ (b) Insert C5, $r = 2, q = 1$ (c) Insert C1, $r = 2, q = 2$

Figure 8.9: Inserting into a directoryless dynamic hash table

Let us now insert C1 into the table of Figure 8.9 (b). Since, $h(C1,2) = 01 = q$, chain $01 = 1$ is examined by our search algorithm (Program 8.5). The search verifies that C1 is not in the dictionary. Since the active bucket 01 is full, we get an overflow. We activate bucket $2^r + q = 5 = 101$ and rehash the keys A1, B5, and C5 that are in chain q. The rehashing is done using 3 bits. A1 is hashed into bucket 001 while B5 and C5 hash into bucket 101. q is incremented by 1 and the new key C1 is inserted into bucket 001. Figure 8.9 (c) shows the result.

EXERCISES

1. Write an algorithm to insert a dictionary pair into a dynamic hash table that uses a directory.

2. Write an algorithm to delete a dictionary pair from a dynamic hash table that uses a directory.

3. Write an algorithm to insert a dictionary pair into a directoryless dynamic hash table.

4. Write an algorithm to delete a dictionary pair from a directoryless dynamic hash table.

8.4   BLOOM FILTERS

8.4.1   An Application—Differential Files

Consider an application where we are maintaining an indexed file. For simplicity, assume that there is only one index and hence just a single key. Further assume that this is a dense index (i.e., one that has an entry for each record in the file) and that updates to the file (inserts, deletes, and changes to an existing record) are permitted. It is necessary to keep a backup copy of the index and file so that we can recover from accidental loss or failure of the working copy. This loss or failure may occur for a variety of reasons, which include corruption of the working copy due to a malfunction of the hardware or software. We shall refer to the working copies of the index and file as the *master index* and *master file*, respectively.

Since updates to the file and index are permitted, the backup copies of these generally differ from the working copies at the time of failure. So, it is possible to recover from the failure only if, in addition to the backup copies, we have a log of all updates made since the backup copies were created. We shall call this log the *transaction log*. To recover from the failure, it is necessary to process the backup copies and the transaction log to reproduce an index and file that correspond to the working copies at the time of failure. The time needed to recover is therefore a function of the sizes of the backup index and file and the size of the transaction log. The recovery time can be reduced by making more frequent backups. This results in a smaller transaction log. Making sufficiently frequent backups of the master index and file is not practical when these are very large and when the update rate is very high.

When only the file (but not the index) is very large, a reduction in the recovery time may be obtained by keeping updated records in a separate file called the *differential file*. The master file is unchanged. The master index is, however, changed to reflect the position of the most current version of the record with a given key. We assume that the addresses for differential-file records and master-file records are different. As a result, by examining the address obtained from a search of the master index, we can tell whether the most current version of the record we are seeking is in the master file or in the differential file. The steps to follow when accessing a record with a given key are given in Program 8.6(b). Program 8.6(a) gives the steps when a differential file is not used.

Notice that when a differential file is used, the backup file is an exact replica of the master file. Hence, it is necessary to backup only the master index and differential file frequently. Since these are relatively small, it is feasible to do this. To recover from a failure of the master index or differential file, the transactions in the transaction log need to be processed using the backup copies of the master file, index, and differential file. The transaction log can be expected to be relatively small, as backups are done more frequently. To recover from a failure of the master file, we need merely make a new copy of its backup. When the differential file becomes too large, it is necessary to create a new version of the master file by merging the old master file and the differential file. This also results in a new index and an empty differential file. It is interesting to note that using a differential file as suggested does not affect the number of disk accesses needed to perform a file operation (see Program 8.6(a,b)).

Suppose that both the index and the file are very large. In this case the differential-file scheme discussed above does not work as well, as it is not feasible to backup the master index as frequently as is necessary to keep the transaction log sufficiently small. We can get around this difficulty by using a differential file and a differential index. The master index and master file remain unchanged as updates are performed. The differential file contains all newly inserted records and the current versions of all changed records. The differential index is an index to the differential file. This also has null address entries for deleted records. The steps needed to perform a file operation when both a differential index and file are used are given in Program 8.6(c). Comparing with Program 8.6(a), we see that additional disk accesses are frequently needed, as we will often first query the differential index and then the master index. Observe that the differential file is much smaller than the master file, so most requests are satisfied from the master file.

When a differential index and file are used, we must backup both of these with high frequency. This is possible, as both are relatively small. To recover from a loss of the differential index or file, we need to process the transactions in the transaction log using the available backup copies. To recover from a loss of the master index or master file, a copy of the appropriate backup needs to be made. When the differential index and/or file becomes too large, the master index and/or file is reorganized so that the differential index and/or file becomes empty.

Step 1: Search master index for record address.

Step 2: Access record from this master file address.

Step 3: If this is an update, then update master index, master file, and transaction log.

(a) No differential file

Step 1: Search master index for record address.

Step 2: Access record from either the master file or the differential file, depending on the address obtained in Step 1.

Step 3: If this is an update, then update master index, differential file, and transaction log.

(b) Differential file in use

Step 1: Search differential index for record address. If the search is unsuccessful, then search the master index.

Step 2: Access record from either the master file or the differential file, depending on the address obtained in Step 1.

Step 3: If this is an update, then update differential index, differential file, and transaction log.

(c) Differential index and file in use

Step 1: Query the Bloom filter. If the answer is "maybe," then search differential index for record address. If the answer is "no" or if the differential index search is unsuccessful, then search the master index.

Step 2: Access record from either the master file or the differential file, depending on the address obtained in Step 1.

Step 3: If this is an update, then update Bloom filter, differential index, differential file, and transaction log.

(d) Differential index and file and Bloom filter in use

Program 8.6: Access steps

8.4.2 Bloom Filter Design

The performance degradation that results from the use of a differential index can be considerably reduced by the use of a *Bloom filter*. This is a device that resides in internal memory and accepts queries of the following type: Is key k in the differential index? If queries of this type can be answered accurately, then there will never be a need to search both the differential and master indexes for a record address. Clearly, the only way to answer queries of this type accurately is to have a list of all keys in the differential index. This is not possible for differential indexes of reasonable size.

A Bloom filter does not answer queries of the above type accurately. Instead of returning one of "yes" and "no" as its answer, it returns one of "maybe" and "no". When the answer is "no," then we are assured that the key k is not in the differential index. In this case, only the master index is to be searched, and the number of disk accesses is the same as when a differential index is not used. If the answer is "maybe," then the differential index is searched. The master index needs to be searched only if k is not found in the differential index. Program 8.6(d) gives the steps to follow when a Bloom filter is used in conjunction with a differential index.

A *filter error* occurs whenever the answer to the Bloom filter query is "maybe" and the key is not in the differential index. Both the differential and master indexes are searched only when a filter error occurs. To obtain a performance close to that when a differential index is not in use, we must ensure that the probability of a filter error is close to zero.

Let us take a look at a Bloom filter. Typically, it consists of m bits of memory and h uniform and independent hash functions $f_1, \cdots, f_h$. Each f_i hashes a key k to an integer in the range $[1,m]$. Initially all m filter bits are zero, and the differential index and file are empty. When key k is added to the differential index, bits $f_1(k), \cdots, f_h(k)$ of the filter are set to 1. When a query of the type "Is key k in the differential index?" is made, bits $f_1(k), \cdots, f_h(k)$ are examined. The query answer is "maybe" if all these bits are 1. Otherwise, the answer is "no." One may verify that whenever the answer is "no," the key cannot be in the differential index and that when the answer is "maybe," the key may or may not be in the differential index.

We can compute the probability of a filter error in the following way. Assume that initially there are n records and that u updates are made. Assume that none of these is an insert or a delete. Hence, the number of records remains unchanged. Further, assume that the record keys are uniformly distributed over the key space and that the probability that an update request is for record i is $1/n$, $1 \le i \le n$. From these assumptions, it follows that the probability that a particular update does not modify record i is $1 - 1/n$. So, the probability that none of the u updates modifies record i is $(1 - 1/n)^u$. Hence, the expected number of unmodified records is $n(1 - 1/n)^u$, and the probability that the $(u+1)$'st update is for an unmodified record is $(1 - 1/n)^u$.

Next, consider bit i of the Bloom filter and the hash function f_j, $1 \le j \le h$. Let k be the key corresponding to one of the u updates. Since f_j is a uniform hash function, the probability that $f_j(k) \ne i$ is $1 - 1/m$. As the h hash functions are independent, the probability that $f_j(k) \ne i$ for all h hash functions is $(1 - 1/m)^h$. If this is the only update, the probability that bit i of the filter is zero is $(1 - 1/m)^h$. From the assumption on update requests, it follows that the probability that bit i is zero following the u updates is $(1 - 1/m)^{uh}$. From this, we conclude that if after u updates we make a query for an unmodified record, the probability of a filter error is $(1 - (1 - 1/m)^{uh})^h$. The probability, $P(u)$, that an arbitrary query made after u updates results in a filter error is this quantity times the probability that the query is for an unmodified record. Hence,

$$P(u) = (1 - 1/n)^u (1 - (1 - 1/m)^{uh})^h$$

Using the approximation

$$(1 - 1/x)^q \sim e^{-q/x}$$

for large x, we obtain

$$P(u) \sim e^{-u/n}(1 - e^{-uh/m})^h$$

when n and m are large.

Suppose we wish to design a Bloom filter that minimizes the probability of a filter error. This probability is highest just before the master index is reorganized and the differential index becomes empty. Let u denote the number of updates done up to this time. In most applications, m is determined by the amount of memory available, and n is fixed. So, the only variable in design is h. Differentiating $P(u)$ with respect to h and setting the result to zero yields

$$h = (\log_e 2)m/u \sim 0.693m/u$$

We may verify that this h yields a minimum for $P(u)$. Actually, since h has to be an integer, the number of hash functions to use either is $\lceil 0.693m/u \rceil$ or $\lfloor 0.693m/u \rfloor$, depending on which one results in a smaller $P(u)$.

EXERCISES

1. By differentiating $P(u)$ with respect to h, show that $P(u)$ is minimized when $h = (\log_e 2)m/u$.

2. Suppose that you are to design a Bloom filter with minimum $P(u)$ and that $n = 100,000$, $m = 5000$, and $u = 1000$.

   (a) Using any of the results obtained in the text, compute the number, h, of hash functions to use. Show your computations.

   (b) What is the probability, $P(u)$, of a filter error when h has this value?

8.5 REFERENCES AND SELECTED READINGS

For more on hashing, see *The Art of Computer Programming: Sorting and Searching*, by D. Knuth, Vol. 3, Second Edition, Addison-Wesley, Reading, MA, 1998 and "Hash tables", by P. Morin, in *Handbook of data structures and algorithms*, edited by D. Mehta and S. Sahni, Chapman & Hall/CRC, Boca Raton, 2005.

Our development of differential files and Bloom filters parallels that of Severence and Lohman in the paper "Differential files: Their application to the maintenance of large databases," by D. Severence and G. Lohman, *ACM Transactions on Database Systems*, 1:3, 1976, pp. 256-267. This paper also provides several advantages of using differential files. The assumptions of uniformity made in the filter error analysis are unrealistic, as, in practice, future accesses are more likely to be for records previously accessed. Several authors have attempted to take this into account. Two references are "A practical guide to the design of differential file architectures," by H. Aghili and D. Severance, *ACM Transactions on Database Systems*, 7:2, 1982, pp. 540-565; and "A regression approach to performance analysis for the differential file architecture," by T. Hill and A. Srinivasan, *Proceedings of the Third IEEE International Conference on Data Engineering*, 1987, pp. 157-164.

Bloom filters have found application in the solution to problems in a variety of domains. Some applications to network related problems may be found in "Space-code Bloom filter for efficient traffic flow measurement," by A. Kumar, J. Xu, L. Li and J. Wang, *ACM Internet Measurement Conference*, 2003; "Hash-based paging and location update using Bloom filters," by P. Mutaf and C. Castelluccia, *Mobile Networks and Applications*, Kluwer Academic, 9, 627-631, 2004; and "Approximate caches for packet classification," by F. Chang, W. Feng and K. Li, *IEEE INFOCOM*, 2004.

CHAPTER 9

Priority Queues

9.1 SINGLE- AND DOUBLE-ENDED PRIORITY QUEUES

A *priority queue* is a collection of elements such that each element has an associated priority. We study two varieties of priority queues—single- and double-ended—in this chapter. Single-ended priority queues, which were first studied in Section 5.6, may be further categorized as min and max priority queues. As noted in Section 5.6.1, the operations supported by a min priority queue are:

SP1: Return an element with minimum priority.

SP2: Insert an element with an arbitrary priority.

SP3: Delete an element with minimum priority.

The operations supported by a max priority queue are the same as those supported by a min priority queue except that in SP1 and SP3 we replace minimum by maximum. The heap structure of Section 5.6 is a classic data structure for the representation of a priority queue. Using a min (max) heap, the minimum (maximum) element can be found in O(1) time and each of the other two single-ended priority queue operations may be done in O(log n) time, where n is the number of elements in the priority queue. In this chapter, we consider several extensions of a single-ended priority queue. The first extension, *meldable (single-ended) priority queue*, augments the operations SP1 through SP3 with a *meld* operation that melds together two priority queues. One application for the meld operation is when the server for one priority queue shuts down. At this time, it is necessary to meld its priority queue with that of a functioning server. Two data structures for meldable priority queues—leftist trees and binomial heaps—are developed in this chapter.

A further extension of meldable priority queues includes operations to delete an arbitrary element (given its location in the data structure) and to decrease the key/priority (or to increase the key, in case of a max priority queue) of an arbitrary element (given its location in the data structure). Two data structures—Fibonacci heaps and pairing heaps—are developed for this extension. The section on Fibonacci heaps describes how Fibonacci heaps may be used to improve the run time of Dijkstra's shortest paths algorithm of Section 6.4.1.

A *double-ended priority queue* (DEPQ) is a data structure that supports the following operations on a collection of elements.

DP1: Return an element with minimum priority.

DP2: Return an element with maximum priority.

DP3: Insert an element with an arbitrary priority.

DP4: Delete an element with minimum priority.

DP5: Delete an element with maximum priority.

So, a DEPQ is a min and a max priority queue rolled into one structure.

Example 9.1: A DEPQ may be used to implement a network buffer. This buffer holds packets that are waiting their turn to be sent out over a network link; each packet has an associated priority. When the network link becomes available, a packet with the highest priority is transmitted. This corresponds to a *DeleteMax* operation. When a packet arrives at the buffer from elsewhere in the network, it is added to this buffer. This corresponds to an *Insert* operation. However, if the buffer is full, we must drop a packet with minimum priority before we can insert one. This is achieved using a *DeleteMin* operation. □

Example 9.2: In Section 7.10, we saw how to adapt merge sort to the external sorting environment. We now consider a similar adaptation of quick sort, which has the best expected run time of all known internal sorting methods. Recall that the basic idea in quick sort (Section 7.3) is to partition the elements to be sorted into three groups L, M, and R. The middle group M contains a single element called the *pivot*, all elements in the left group L are ≤ the pivot, and all elements in the right group R are ≥ the pivot.

Following this partitioning, the left and right element groups are sorted recursively.

In an external sort (Section 7.10), we have more elements than can be held in the memory of our computer. The elements to be sorted are initially on a disk and the sorted sequence is to be left on the disk. When the internal quick sort method outlined above is extended to an external quick sort, the middle group M is made as large as possible through the use of a DEPQ. The external quick sort strategy is:

(1)   Read in as many elements as will fit into an internal DEPQ. The elements in the DEPQ will eventually be the middle group of elements.

(2)   Process the remaining elements one at a time. If the next element is ≤ the smallest element in the DEPQ, output this next element as part of the left group. If the next element is ≥ the largest element in the DEPQ, output this next element as part of the right group. Otherwise, remove either the max or min element from the DEPQ (the choice may be made randomly or alternately); if the max element is removed, output it as part of the right group; otherwise, output the removed element as part of the left group; insert the newly input element into the DEPQ.

(3)   Output the elements in the DEPQ, in sorted order, as the middle group.

(4)   Sort the left and right groups recursively.   □

9.2   LEFTIST TREES

9.2.1   Height-Biased Leftist Trees

Leftist trees provide an efficient implementation of meldable priority queues. Consider the meld operation. Let n be the total number of elements in the two priority queues (throughout this section, we use the term priority queue to mean a single-ended priority queue) that are to be melded. If heaps are used to represent meldable priority queues, then the meld operation takes $O(n)$ time (this may, for example, be accomplished using the heap initialization algorithm of Section 7.6). Using a leftist tree, the meld operation as well as the insert and delete min (or delete max) operations take logarithmic time; the minimum (or maximum) element may be found in $O(1)$ time.

Leftist trees are defined using the concept of an extended binary tree. An *extended binary tree* is a binary tree in which all empty binary subtrees have been replaced by a square node. Figure 9.1 shows two examples of binary trees. Their corresponding extended binary trees are shown in Figure 9.2. The square nodes in an extended binary tree are called *external nodes*. The original (circular) nodes of the binary tree are called *internal nodes*.

There are two varieties of leftist trees—height biased (HBLT) and weight biased (WBLT). We study HBLTs in this section and WBLTs in the next. HBLTs were invented first and are generally referred to simply as leftist trees. We continue with this tradition

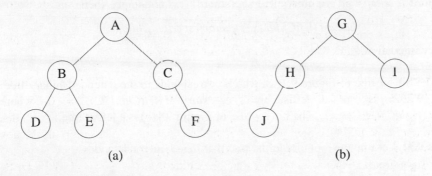

(a)   (b)

Figure 9.1: Two binary trees

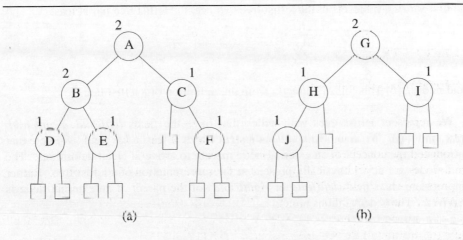

(a)   (b)

Figure 9.2: Extended binary trees corresponding to Figure 9.1

and refer to HBLTs simply as leftist trees in this section.

Let x be a node in an extended binary tree. Let $leftChild(x)$ and $rightChild(x)$, respectively, denote the left and right children of the internal node x. Define $shortest(x)$ to be the length of a shortest path from x to an external node. It is easy to see that $shortest(x)$ satisfies the following recurrence:

$$shortest(x) = \begin{cases} 0 \text{ if } x \text{ is an external node} \\ 1 + \min\{shortest(leftChild(x)), shortest(rightChild(x))\} \text{ otherwise} \end{cases}$$

The number outside each internal node x of Figure 9.2 is the value of *shortest* (x).

Definition: A *leftist tree* is a binary tree such that if it is not empty, then

$$shortest\,(leftChild\,(x)) \geq shortest\,(rightChild\,(x))$$

for every internal node x. □

The binary tree of Figure 9.1(a), which corresponds to the extended binary tree of Figure 9.2(a), is not a leftist tree, as *shortest* $(leftChild\,(C)) = 0$, whereas *shortest* $(rightChild(C)) = 1$. The binary tree of Figure 9.1(b) is a leftist tree.

Lemma 9.1: Let r be the root of a leftist tree that has n (internal) nodes.

(a) $n \geq 2^{shortest(r)} - 1$

(b) The rightmost root to external node path is the shortest root to external node path. Its length is *shortest* $(r) \leq \log_2(n+1)$.

Proof: (a) From the definition of *shortest* (r) it follows that there are no external nodes on the first *shortest* (r) levels of the leftist tree. Hence, the leftist tree has at least

$$\sum_{i=1}^{shortest(r)} 2^{i-1} = 2^{shortest(r)} - 1$$

internal nodes. (b) This follows directly from the definition of a leftist tree. □

We represent leftist trees with nodes that have the fields *leftChild*, *rightChild*, *shortest*, and *data*. We assume that *data* is a **struct** with at least a *key* field. We note that we introduced the concept of an external node merely to arrive at clean definitions. The external nodes are never physically present in the representation of a leftist tree. Rather the appropriate child field (*leftChild* or *rightChild*) of the parent of an external node is set to *NULL*. The C declarations are:

```
typedef struct {
        int key;
        /* other fields */
        } element;
typedef struct leftist *leftistTree;
        struct {
                leftistTree leftChild;
                element data;
                leftistTree rightChild;
                int shortest;
                } leftist;
```

Definition: A *min leftist tree* (*max leftist tree*) is a leftist tree in which the key value in each node is no larger (smaller) than the key values in its children (if any). In other words, a min (max) leftist tree is a leftist tree that is also a min (max) tree. □

Two min leftist trees are shown in Figure 9.3. The number inside a node x is the priority of the element in x, and the number outside x is *shortest* (x). *For convenience, all priority queue figures in this chapter show only element priority rather than the complete element.* The operations insert, delete min (delete-max), and meld can be performed in logarithmic time using a min (max) leftist tree. We shall continue our discussion using min leftist trees.

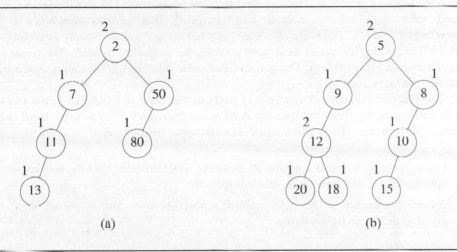

(a)   (b)

Figure 9.3: Examples of min leftist trees

The insert and delete min operations can both be performed by using the meld operation. To insert an element, x, into a min-leftist tree, a, we first create a min-leftist tree, b, that contains the single element x. Then we meld the min-leftist trees a and b. To delete the min element from a nonempty min-leftist tree, a, we meld the min-leftist trees $a \to leftChild$ and $a \to rightChild$ and delete node a.

The meld operation is itself simple. Suppose that we wish to meld the min-leftist trees a and b. First, we obtain a new binary tree containing all elements in a and b by following the rightmost paths in a and/or b. This binary tree has the property that the key in each node is no larger than the keys in its children (if any). Next, we interchange the left and right subtrees of nodes as necessary to convert this binary tree into a leftist tree.

As an example, consider melding the two min leftist trees of Figure 9.3. To obtain a binary tree that contains all the elements in each tree and that satisfies the required relationship between parent and child keys, we first compare the root keys 2 and 5. Since $2 < 5$, the new binary tree should have 2 in its root. We shall leave the left subtree of 2 unchanged and meld 2's right subtree with the entire binary tree rooted at 5. The resulting binary tree will become the new right subtree of 2. When melding the right subtree of 2 and the binary tree rooted at 5, we notice that $5 < 50$. So, 5 should be in the root of the melded tree. Now, we proceed to meld the subtrees with root 8 and 50. Since $8 < 50$ and 8 has no right subtree, we can make the subtree with root 50 the right subtree of 8. This gives us the binary tree of Figure 9.4(a). Hence, the result of melding the right subtree of 2 and the tree rooted at 5 is the tree of Figure 9.4(b). When the tree of Figure 9.4(b) is made the right subtree of 2, we get the binary tree of Figure 9.4(c). The leftist tree that is made a subtree is represented by shading its nodes, in each step. To convert the tree of Figure 9.4(c) into a leftist tree, we begin at the last modified root (i.e., 8) and trace back to the overall root, ensuring that $shortest\,(leftChild\,(\,)) \geq shortest\,(rightChild\,(\,))$. This inequality holds at 8 but not at 5 and 2. Simply interchanging the left and right subtrees at these nodes causes the inequality to hold. The result is the leftist tree of Figure 9.4(d). The pointers that were interchanged are represented by dotted lines in the figure.

The function *minMeld* (Program 9.1) contains the code to meld two leftist trees. This function uses the recursive function *minUnion* (Program 9.2) to actually meld two nonempty leftist trees. The function *minMeld* intertwines the two steps:

(1)   Create a binary tree that contains all elements while ensuring that the root of each subtree has the smallest key in that subtree.

(2)   Ensure that each node has a left subtree whose *shortest* value is greater than or equal to that of its right subtree.

Analysis of *minMeld*: Since *minUnion* moves down the rightmost paths in the two leftist trees being combined and since the lengths of these paths is at most logarithmic in the number of elements in each tree, the combining of two leftist trees with a total of n elements is done in time $O(\log n)$. $\square$

9.2.2   Weight-Biased Leftist Trees

We arrive at another variety of leftist tree by considering the number of nodes in a subtree, rather than the length of a shortest root to external node path. Define the weight $w\,(x)$ of node x to be the number of internal nodes in the subtree with root x. Notice that if x is an external node, its weight is 0. If x is an internal node, its weight is 1 more than the sum of the weights of its children. The weights of the nodes of the binary trees of Figure 9.2 appear in Figure 9.5.

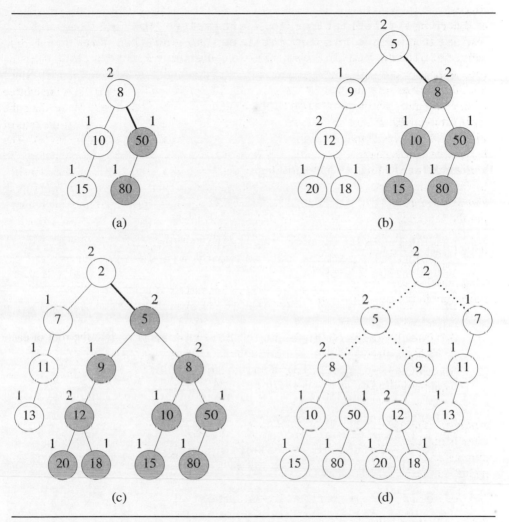

Figure 9.4: Melding the min leftist trees of Figure 9.3

Definition: A binary tree is a *weight-biased leftist tree (WBLT)* iff at every internal node the w value of the left child is greater than or equal to the w value of the right child. A max (min) WBLT is a max (min) tree that is also a WBLT. □

Note that the binary tree of Figure 9.5(a) is not a WBLT while that of Figure 9.5(b) is.

```
void minMeld(leftistTree *a, leftistTree *b)
{/* meld the two min leftist trees *a and *b.  The
    resulting min leftist tree is returned in *a, and *b
    is set to NULL */
    if (!*a) *a = *b;
    else if (*b) minUnion(a,b);
    *b = NULL;
}
```

Program 9.1: : Melding two min-leftist trees

```
void minUnion(leftistTree *a, leftistTree *b)
{/* recursively combine two nonempty min leftist trees */
    leftistTree temp;
    /* set a to be the tree with smaller root */
    if ((*a)→data.key > (*b)→data.key) SWAP(*a,*b,temp);

    /* create binary tree such that the smallest key in each
       subtree is in the root */
    if (!(*a)→rightChild) (*a)→rightChild = *b;
    else minUnion(&(*a)→rightChild, b);

    /*leftist tree property */
    if (!(*a)→leftChild) {
        (*a)→leftChild = (*a)→rightChild;
        (*a)→rightChild = NULL ;
    }
    else if ((*a)→leftChild→shortest <
             (*a)→rightChild→shortest)
        SWAP((*a)→leftChild,(*a)→rightChild, temp);
    (*a)→shortest = (!(*a)→rightChild) ? 1 :
                        (*a)→rightChild→shortest + 1;
}
```

Program 9.2: Melding two nonempty min-leftist trees

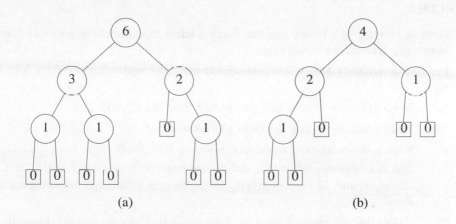

$$(a) \qquad\qquad\qquad\qquad\qquad (b)$$

Figure 9.5: Extended binary trees of Figure 9.2 with weights shown

Lemma 9.2: Let x be any internal node of a weight-biased leftist tree. The length, *rightmost* (x), of the rightmost path from x to an external node satisfies
$$rightmost\ (x) \leq \log_2(w\ (x)+1).$$

Proof: The proof is by induction on $w\ (x)$. When $w\ (x)=1$, *rightmost* $(x)=1$ and $\log_2(w\ (x)+1)=\log_2 2=1$. For the induction hypothesis, assume that *rightmost* $(x) \leq \log_2(w\ (x)+1)$ whenever $w\ (x) < n$. Let *rightChild* (x) denote the right child of x (note that this right child may be an external node). When $w\ (x)=n$, $w\ (rightChild\ (x)) \leq (n-1)/2$ and

$$
\begin{aligned}
rightmost\ (x) &= 1+rightmost\ (rightChild\ (x)) \\
&\leq 1+\log_2((n-1)/2+1) \\
&= 1+\log_2(n+1)-1 \\
&= \log_2(n+1).\ \square
\end{aligned}
$$

The insert, delete max, and initialization operations are analogous to the corresponding max HBLT operations. However, the meld operation can be done in a single top-to-bottom pass (recall that the meld operation of an HBLT performs a top-to-bottom pass as the recursion unfolds and then a bottom-to-top pass in which subtrees are possibly swapped and *shortest*-values updated). A single-pass meld is possible for WBLTs because we can determine the w values on the way down and so, on the way down, we can update w-values and swap subtrees as necessary. For HBLTs, a node's new *shortest* value cannot be determined on the way down the tree.

Experiments indicate that meldable single-ended priority queue operations are faster, by a constant factor, when we use WBLTs rather than HBLTs.

EXERCISES

1. Give an example of a binary tree that is not a leftist tree. Label the nodes of your binary tree with their *shortest* value.

2. Let t be an arbitrary binary tree represented using the node structure for a leftist tree.

    (a) Write a function to initialize the *shortest* field of each node in t.

    (b) Write a function to convert t into a leftist tree.

    (c) What is the complexity of each of these two functions?

3. (a) Into an empty min leftist tree, insert elements with priorities 20, 10, 5, 18, 6, 12, 14, 4, and 22 (in this order). Show the min leftist tree following each insert.

    (b) Delete the min element from the final min leftist tree of part (a). Show the resulting min leftist tree.

4. Compare the performance of leftist trees and min heaps under the assumption that the only operations to be performed are insert and delete min. For this, do the following:

    (a) Create a random list of n elements and a random sequence of insert and delete-min operations of length m. The latter sequence is created such that the probability of an insert or delete-min operation is approximately 0.5. Initialize a min leftist tree and a min heap to contain the n elements in the first random list. Now, measure the time to perform the m operations using the min leftist tree as well as the min heap. Divide this time by m to get the average time per operation. Do this for $n = 100, 500, 1000, 2000, \cdots$, 5000. Let m be 5000. Tabulate your computing times.

    (b) Based on your experiments, make some statements about the relative merits of the two priority-queue schemes.

5. Write a function to initialize a min leftist tree with n elements. Assume that the node structure is the same as that used in the text. Your function must run in $\Theta(n)$ time. Show that this is the case. Can you think of a way to do this initialization in $\Theta(n)$ time such that the resulting min leftist tree is also a complete binary tree?

6. Write a function to delete the element in node x of a min leftist tree. Assume that in addition to the fields stated in the text, each node has the field *parent*, which points to its parent in the leftist tree. What is the complexity of your function?

7. [*Lazy deletion*] Another way to handle the deletion of arbitrary elements from a min-leftist tree is to use a field, *deleted*, in place of the parent field of the previous exercise. When we delete an element, we set its *deleted* field to *TRUE*. However,

we do not physically delete the node. When we perform a *deleteMin* operation, we first search for the minimum element not deleted by carrying out a limited preorder search. This preorder search traverses only the upper part of the tree as needed to identify the min element. All deleted elements encountered are physically deleted, and their subtrees are melded to obtain the new min leftist tree.

(a) Write a function to delete the element in node *x* of a min leftist tree.

(b) Write another function to delete the min element from a min leftist tree from which several elements have been deleted using the former function.

(c) What is the complexity of your function of part (b)? Provide this as a function of the number of deleted elements encountered and the number of elements in the entire tree?

8. [*Skew heaps*] A *skew heap* is a min tree that supports the min leftist tree operations: insert, delete min, and meld in amortized time (see Section 9.4 for a definition of amortized time) O(log *n*) per operation. As in the case of min leftist trees, insertions and deletions are performed using the meld operation, which is carried out by following the rightmost paths in the two heaps being melded. However, unlike min leftist trees, the left and right subtrees of all nodes (except the last) on the rightmost path in the resulting heap are interchanged.

(a) Write insert, delete min, and meld functions for skewed heaps.

(b) Compare the running times of these with those for the same operations on a min leftist tree. Use random sequences of insert, delete min, and meld operations.

9. [*WBLT*] Develop a complete implementation of a weight-biased min leftist tree. You must include functions to delete and return the min element, insert an arbitrary element, and meld two min WBLTs. Your meld function should perform only a top-to-bottom pass over the WBLTs being melded. Show that the complexity of these three functions is $O(n)$. Test all functions using your own test data.

10. Give an example of an HBLT that is not a WBLT as well as one that is a WBLT but not an HBLT.

9.3 BINOMIAL HEAPS

9.3.1 Cost Amortization

A *binomial heap* is a data structure that supports the same functions (i.e., insert, delete min (or delete-max), and meld) as those supported by leftist trees. Unlike leftist trees, where an individual operation can be performed in O(log *n*) time, it is possible that certain individual operations performed on a binomial heap may take O(*n*) time. However, if we amortize (spread out) part of the cost of expensive operations over the inexpensive ones, then the amortized complexity of an individual operation is either $O(1)$ or $O(\log n)$ depending on the type of operation.

Let us examine more closely the concept of cost amortization (we shall use the terms *cost* and *complexity* interchangeably). Suppose that a sequence I1, I2, D1, I3, I4, I5, I6, D2, I7 of insert and delete-min operations is performed. Assume that the *actual cost* of each of the seven inserts is one. By this, we mean that each insert takes one unit of time. Further, suppose that the delete-min operations D1 and D2 have an actual cost of eight and ten, respectively. So, the total cost of the sequence of operations is 25.

In an amortization scheme we charge some of the actual cost of an operation to other operations. This reduces the charged cost of some operations and increases that of others. The *amortized cost* of an operation is the total cost charged to it. The cost transferring (amortization) scheme is required to be such that the sum of the amortized costs of the operations is greater than or equal to the sum of their actual costs. If we charge one unit of the cost of a delete-min operation to each of the inserts since the last delete-min operation (if any), then two units of the cost of D1 get transferred to I1 and I2 (the charged cost of each increases by one), and four units of the cost of D2 get transferred to I3 to I6. The amortized cost of each of I1 to I6 becomes two, that of I7 is equal to its actual cost (i.e., one), and that of each of D1 and D2 becomes 6. The sum of the amortized costs is 25, which is the same as the sum of the actual costs.

Now suppose we can prove that no matter what sequence of insert and delete-min operations is performed, we can charge costs in such a way that the amortized cost of each insertion is no more than two and that of each deletion is no more than six. This will enable us to make the claim that the actual cost of any insert / delete min sequence is no more than $2i + 6d$ where i and d are, respectively, the number of insert and delete min operations in the sequence. Suppose that the actual cost of a deletion is no more than ten, and that of an insertion is one. Using actual costs, we can conclude that the sequence cost is no more than $i + 10d$. Combining these two bounds, we obtain $\min\{2i + 6d, i + 10d\}$ as a bound on the sequence cost. Hence, using the notion of cost amortization, we can obtain tighter bounds on the complexity of a sequence of operations. This is useful, because in many applications, we are concerned more with the time it takes to perform a sequence of priority queue operations than we are with the time it takes to perform an individual operation. For example, when we sort using the heap sort method, we are concerned with the time it takes to complete the entire sort; not with the time it takes to remove the next element from the heap. In applications such as sorting, where we are concerned only with the overall time rather than the time per operation, it is adequate to use a data structure that has a good amortized complexity for each operation type.

We shall use the notion of cost amortization to show that although individual delete operations on a binomial heap may be expensive, the cost of any sequence of binomial heap operations is actually quite small.

9.3.2   Definition of Binomial Heaps

As in the case of heaps and leftist trees, there are two varieties of binomial heaps, min and max. A *min binomial heap* is a collection of min trees; a *max binomial heap* is a collection of max trees. We shall explicitly consider min binomial heaps only. These will be referred to as *B-heaps*. Figure 9.6 shows an example of a B-heap that is made up of three min trees.

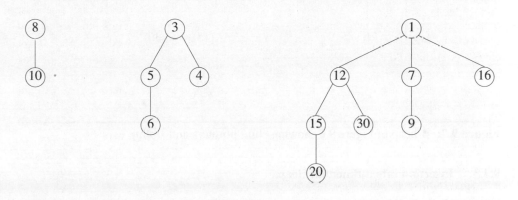

Figure 9.6: A B-heap with three min trees

Using B-heaps, we can perform an insert and a meld in O(1) actual and amortized time and a delete min in O(log n) amortized time. B-heaps are represented using nodes that have the following fields: *degree, child, link,* and *data.* The *degree* of a node is the number of children it has; the *child* data member is used to point to any one of its children (if any); the *link* data member is used to maintain singly linked circular lists of siblings. All the children of a node form a singly linked circular list, and the node points to one of these children. Additionally, the roots of the min trees that comprise a B-heap are linked to form a singly linked circular list. The B-heap is then pointed at by a single pointer *min* to the min tree root with smallest key.

Figure 9.7 shows the representation for the example of Figure 9.6. To enhance the readability of this figure, we have used bidirectional arrows to join together nodes that are in the same circular list. When such a list contains only one node, no such arrows are drawn. Each of the key sets {10}, {6}, {5,4}, {20}, {15, 30}, {9}, {12, 7, 16}, and {8, 3, 1} denotes the keys in one of the circular lists of Figure 9.7. *min* is the pointer to the B-heap. Note that an empty B-heap has a 0 pointer.

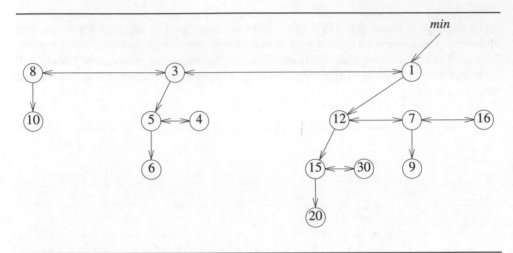

Figure 9.7: B-heap of Figure 9.6 showing child pointers and sibling lists

9.3.3   Insertion into a Binomial Heap

An element x may be inserted into a B-heap by first putting x into a new node and then inserting this node into the circular list pointed at by *min*. The pointer *min* is reset to this new node only if *min* is 0 or the key of x is smaller than the key in the node pointed at by *min*. It is evident that these insertion steps can be performed in O(1) time.

9.3.4   Melding Two Binomial Heaps

To meld two nonempty B-heaps, we meld the top circular lists of each into a single circular list. The new B-heap pointer is the *min* pointer of one of the two trees, depending on which has the smaller key. This can be determined with a single comparison. Since two circular lists can be melded into a single one in O(1) time, the total time required to meld two B-heaps is O(1).

9.3.5   Deletion of Min Element

If *min* is 0, then the B-heap is empty, and a deletion cannot be performed. Assume that *min* is not 0. *min* points to the node that contains the min element. This node is deleted from its circular list. The new B-heap consists of the remaining min trees and the sub-min trees of the deleted root. Figure 9.8 shows the situation for the example of Figure 9.6.

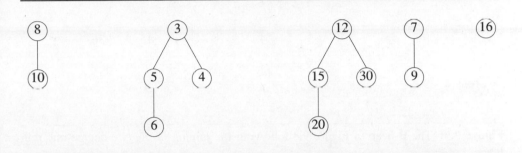

Figure 9.8: The B-heap of Figure 9.6 following the deletion of the min element

Before forming the circular list of min tree roots, we repeatedly join together pairs of min trees that have the same degree (the degree of a nonempty min tree is the degree of its root). *This min tree joining is done by making the min tree whose root has a larger key a subtree of the other (ties are broken arbitrarily).* When two min trees are joined, the degree of the resulting min tree is one larger than the original degree of each min tree, and the number of min trees decreases by one. For our example, we may first join either the min trees with roots 8 and 7 or those with roots 3 and 12. If the first pair is joined, the min tree with root 8 is made a subtree of the min tree with root 7. We now have the min tree collection of Figure 9.9. There are three min trees of degree two in this collection. If the pair with roots 7 and 3 is picked for joining, the resulting min tree collection is that of Figure 9.10. Shaded nodes in Figure 9.9 and Figure 9.10 denote the min tree that was made a subtree in the previous step. Since the min trees in this collection have different degrees, the min tree joining process terminates.

The min tree joining step is followed by a step in which the min tree roots are linked together to form a circular list and the B-heap pointer is reset to point to the min tree root with smallest key. The steps involved in a delete-min operation are summarized in Program 9.3.

Steps 1 and 2 take O(1) time. Step 3 may be implemented by using an array *tree* indexed from 0 to the maximum possible degree, *MAX $-$ DEGREE*, of a min-tree. Initially all entries in this array are *NULL*. Let s be the number of min-trees in a and y. The lists a and y created in step 2 are scanned. For each min-tree p in the lists a and y created in step 2, the code of Program 9.4 is executed. The function *joinMinTrees* makes the input tree with larger root a sub tree of the other tree. The resulting tree is returned in the first parameter. In the end, the array *tree* contains pointers to the min-trees that are to be linked together in step 4. Since each time a pair of min-trees is joined the total number of min-trees decreases by one, the number of joins is at most $s-1$. Hence, the

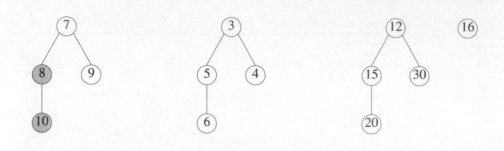

Figure 9.9: The B-heap of Figure 9.8 following the joining of the two degree-one min trees

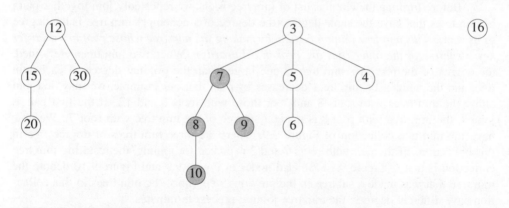

Figure 9.10: The B-heap of Figure 9.9 following the joining of two degree-two min trees

complexity of step 3 is $O(MAX\_DEGREE + s)$.

Step 4 is accomplished by scanning *tree* and linking together the min-trees found. During this scan, the min-tree with minimum key may also be determined. The complexity of step 4 is $O(MAX\_DEGREE)$.

{Delete the min element from a B-heap a, this element is returned in x}

Step 1: [Handle empty B-heap] **if** (a = NULL) *deletionError* **else** perform steps 2 - 4;

Step 2: [Deletion from nonempty B-heap] $x = a \rightarrow data$; $y = a \rightarrow child$; delete a from its doubly linked circular list; now, a points to any remaining node in the resulting list; **if** there is no such node, then a = NULL;

Step 3: [Min-tree joining] Consider the min-trees in the lists a and y; join together pairs of min-trees of the same degree until all remaining min-trees have different degree;

Step 4: [Form min-tree root list] Link the roots of the remaining min-trees (if any) together to form a doubly linked circular list; set a to point to the root (if any) with minimum key;

Program 9.3: Steps in a delete min

```
for (degree = p->degree; tree[degree]; degree++) {
    joinMinTrees(p,tree[degree]);
    tree[degree] = NULL;
}
tree[degree] = p;
```

Program 9.4. Code to handle min-tree p encountered during a scan of lists a and y

9.3.6   Analysis

Definition: The *binomial tree, B_k, of degree* k is a tree such that if $k = 0$, then the tree has exactly one node, and if $k > 0$, then the tree consists of a root whose degree is k and whose subtrees are $B_0, B_1, \cdots, B_{k-1}$. $\square$

The min trees of Figure 9.6 are B_1, B_2, and B_3, respectively. One may verify that B_k has exactly 2^k nodes. Further, if we start with a collection of empty B-heaps and perform inserts, melds, and delete mins only, then the min trees in each B-heap are binomial trees. These observations enable us to prove that when only inserts, melds, and delete mins are performed, we can amortize costs such that the amortized cost of each insert and meld is O(1), and that of each delete min is O(log n).

Lemma 9.3: Let a be a B-heap with n elements that results from a sequence of insert, meld, and delete-min operations performed on a collection of initially empty B-heaps.

Each min tree in a has degree $\leq \log_2 n$. Consequently, *maxDegree* $\leq \lfloor \log_2 n \rfloor$, and the actual cost of a delete-min operation is $O(\log n + s)$.

Proof: Since each of the min trees in a is a binomial tree with at most n nodes, none can have degree greater than $\lfloor \log_2 n \rfloor$. $\square$

Theorem 9.1: If a sequence of n insert, meld, and delete-min operations is performed on initially empty B-heaps, then we can amortize costs such that the amortized time complexity of each insert and meld is $O(1)$, and that of each delete-min operation is $O(\log n)$.

Proof: For each B-heap, define the quantities *#insert* and *LastSize* in the following way: When an initially empty B-heap is created or when a delete-min operation is performed on a B-heap, its *#insert* value is set to zero. Each time an insert is done on a B-heap, its *#insert* value is increased by one. When two B-heaps are melded, the *#insert* value of the resulting B-heap is the sum of the *#insert* values of the B-heaps melded. Hence, *#insert* counts the number of inserts performed on a B-heap or its constituent B-heaps since the last delete-min operation performed in each. When an initially empty B-heap is created, its *LastSize* value is zero. When a delete-min operation is performed on a B-heap, its *LastSize* is set to the number of min trees it contains following this delete. When two B-heaps are melded, the *LastSize* value for the resulting B-heap is the sum of the *LastSize* values in the two B-heaps that were melded. One may verify that the number of min trees in a B-heap is always equal to *#insert* + *LastSize*.

Consider any individual delete-min operation in the operation sequence. Assume this is from the B-heap a. Observe that the total number of elements in all the B-heaps is at most n, as only inserts add elements, and at most n inserts can be present in a sequence of n operations. Let $u = a.\,min \rightarrow degree \leq \log_2 n$.

From Lemma 9.3, the actual cost of this delete-min operation is $O(\log n + s)$. The log n term is due to *maxDegree* and represents the time needed to initialize the array *tree* and to complete Step 4. The s term represents the time to scan the lists *min* and y and to perform the $s - 1$ (at most) min tree joins. We see that $s = $ *#insert* + *LastSize* + $u - 1$. If we charge *#insert* units of cost to the insert operations that contribute to the count *#insert* and *LastSize* units to the delete mins that contribute to the count *LastSize* (each such delete-min operation is charged a number of cost units equal to the number of min trees it left behind), then only $u - 1$ of the s cost units remain. Since $u \leq \log_2 n$, and since the number of min trees in a B-heap immediately following a delete-min operation is $\leq \log_2 n$, the amortized cost of a delete-min operation becomes $O(\log_2 n)$.

Since this charging scheme adds at most one unit to the cost of any insert, the amortized cost of an insert becomes $O(1)$. The amortization scheme used does not charge anything extra to a meld. So, the actual and amortized costs of a meld are also $O(1)$. $\square$

From the preceding theorem and the definition of cost amortization, it follows that the actual cost of any sequence of i inserts, c melds, and dm delete-min operations is $O(i + c + dm \log i)$.

EXERCISES

1. Let S be an initially empty stack. We wish to perform two kinds of operations on S: $add(x)$ and $deleteUntil(x)$. These are defined as follows:

   (a) $add(x)$ ... add the element x to the top of the stack S. This operation takes $O(1)$ time per invocation.

   (b) $deleteUntil(x)$ ... delete elements from the top of the stack upto and including the first x encountered. If p elements are deleted, the time taken is $O(p)$.

   Consider any sequence of n stack operations ($adds$ and $deleteUntils$). Show how to amortize the cost of the add and $deleteUntil$ operations so that the amortized cost of each is $O(1)$. From this, conclude that the time needed to perform any such sequence of operations is $O(n)$.

2. Let x be an unsorted array of n elements. The function $search(x,n,i,y]$ searches x for y by examining $x[i]$, $x[i+1]$, ..., in that order, for the least j such that $x[j] = y$. In case no such j is found, j is set to $n+1$. On termination, $search$ sets i to j. Assume that the time required to examine a single element of x is $O(1)$.

   (a) What is the worst case complexity of $search$?

   (b) Suppose that a sequence of m searches is performed beginning with $i = 0$. Use a cost amortization scheme that assigns costs to both elements and search operations. Show that it is always possible to amortize costs so that the amortized cost of each element is $O(1)$ and that of each search is also $O(1)$. From this, conclude that the cost of the sequence of m searches is $O(m + n)$.

3. (a) Into an empty B-heap, insert elements with priorities 20, 10, 5, 18, 6, 12, 14, 4, and 22 (in this order). Show the final B-heap.

   (b) Delete the min element from the final B-heap of part (a). Show the resulting B-heap. Show how you arrived at this final B-heap.

4. Prove that the binomial tree B_k has 2^k nodes, $k \geq 0$.

5. Can all the functions on a B-heap be performed in the same time using singly linked circular lists rather than doubly linked circular lists? Note that we can delete from an arbitrary node x of a singly linked circular list by copy over the data from the next node and then deleting the next node rather than the node x.

6. Compare the performance of leftist trees and B-heaps under the assumption that the only permissible operations are insert and delete min. For this, do the following:

   (a) Create a random list of n elements and a random sequence of insert and delete min operations of length m. The number of delete mins and inserts should be approximately equal. Initialize a min-leftist tree and a B-heap to contain the n elements in the first random list. Now, measure the time to perform the m operations using the min-leftist tree as well as the B-heap. Divide this time by m to get the average time per operation. Do this for $n =$ 100, 500, 1000, 2000, $\cdots$, 5000. Let m be 5000. Tabulate your computing times.

(b) Based on your experiments, make some statements about the relative merits of the two data structures?

7. Is the height of every tree in a Binomial heap that has n elements $O(\log n)$? If not, what is the worst-case height as a function of n?

9.4 FIBONACCI HEAPS

9.4.1 Definition

There are two varieties of Fibonacci heaps: min and max. A *min Fibonacci heap* is a collection of min trees; a *max Fibonacci heap* is a collection of max trees. We shall explicitly consider min Fibonacci heaps only. These will be referred to as *F-heaps*. B-heaps are a special case of F-heaps. Thus, all the examples of B-heaps in the preceding section are also examples of F-heaps. As a consequence, in this section, we shall refer to these examples as F-heaps.

An F-heap is a data structure that supports the three binomial heap operations: insert, delete min or max, and meld as well as the operations:

(1) *Delete*, delete the element in a specified node. We refer to this delete operation as *arbitrary delete*.

(2) *Decrease key*, decrease the key of a specified node by a given positive amount.

When an F-heap, is used, the *delete* operation takes $O(\log n)$ amortized time and the *decrease key* takes $O(1)$ amortized time. The B-heap operations can be performed in the same asymptotic times using an F-heap as they can be using a B-heap.

To represent an F-heap, the B-heap representation is augmented by adding two fields, *parent* and *childCut* to each node. The *parent* field is used to point to the node's parent (if any). The significance of the *childCut* field will be described later. The basic operations: insert, delete min, and meld are performed exactly as for the case of B-heaps. Let us examine the remaining two operations.

9.4.2 Deletion From An F-heap

To delete an arbitrary node b from the F-heap a, we do the following:

(1)   If $a = b$, then do a delete min; otherwise do steps 2, 3, and 4 below.

(2)   Delete b from the doubly linked list it is in.

(3)   Combine the doubly linked list of b's children with the doubly linked list of a's min-tree roots to get a single doubly linked list. Trees of equal degree are not joined together as in a delete min.

(4)   Dispose of node b.

For example, if we delete the node containing 12 from the F-heap of Figure 9.6, we get the F-heap of Figure 9.11. The actual cost of an arbitrary delete is $O(1)$ unless the min element is being deleted. In this case the deletion time is the time for a delete min operation.

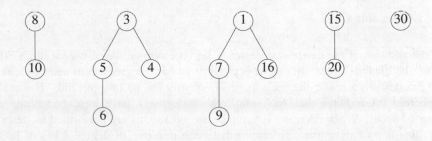

Figure 9.11: F-heap of Figure 9.6 following the deletion of 12

9.4.3   Decrease Key

To decrease the key in node b we do the following:

(1)   Reduce the key in b.

(2)   If b is not a min-tree root and its key is smaller than that in its parent, then delete b from its doubly linked list and insert it into the doubly linked list of min-tree roots.

(3)   Change a to point to b in case the key in b is smaller than that in a.

Suppose we decrease the key 15 in the F-heap of Figure 9.6 by 4. The new value for this key is 11 and the resulting F-heap is shown in Figure 9.12. The cost of performing a decrease key is $O(1)$.

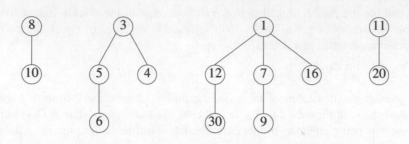

Figure 9.12: F-heap of Figure 9.6 following the reduction of 15 by 4

9.4.4   Cascading Cut

With the addition of the delete and decrease key operations, the min-trees in an F-heap need not be binomial trees. In fact, it is possible to have degree k min-trees with as few as $k+1$ nodes. As a result, the analysis of Theorem 9.1 is no longer valid. The analysis of Theorem 9.1 requires that each min-tree of degree k have an exponential (in k) number of nodes. When decrease key and delete operations are performed as described above, this is no longer true. To ensure that each min-tree of degree k has at least c^k nodes for some $c, c > 1$, each delete and decrease key operation must be followed by a *cascading cut* step. For this, we add the boolean field *childCut* to each node. The value of this field is useful only for nodes that are not a min-tree root. In this case, the *child-Cut* field of node x has the value *TRUE* iff one of the children of x was cut off (i.e., removed) after the most recent time x was made the child of its current parent. This means that each time two min-trees are joined in a delete min operation, the *childCut* field of the root with the larger key should be set to *FALSE*. Further, whenever a delete or decrease key operation deletes a node q that is not a min-tree root from its doubly linked list (step 2 of delete and decrease key), then the cascading cut step is invoked. During this, we examine the nodes on the path from the parent p of the deleted node q up to the nearest ancestor of the deleted node with *childCut* = *FALSE*. In case there is no such ancestor, then the path goes from p to the root of the min-tree containing p. All non root nodes on this path with *childCut* field *TRUE* are deleted from their respective doubly linked lists and added to the doubly linked list of min-tree root nodes of the F-heap. If the path has a node with *childCut* field *FALSE*, this field is changed to *TRUE*.

Figure 9.13 gives an example of a cascading cut. Figure 9.13(a) is the min-tree containing 14 before a decrease key operation that reduces this key by 4. The *childCut* fields are shown only for the nodes on the path from the parent of 14 to its nearest ancestor with *childCut* = *FALSE*. A *TRUE* value is indicated by T. During the decrease key operation, the min-tree with root 14 is deleted from the min-tree of Figure 9.13(a) and becomes a min-tree of the F-heap. Its root now has key 10. This is the first min-tree of Figure 9.13(b). During the cascading cut, the min-trees with roots 12, 10, 8, and 6 are cut off from the min tree with root 2. Thus the single min-tree of Figure 9.13(a) becomes six min-trees of the resulting F-heap. The *childCut* value of 4 becomes *TRUE*. All other *childCut* values are unchanged.

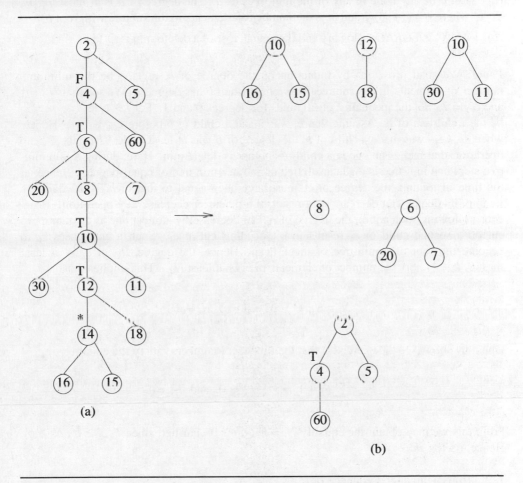

Figure 9.13: A cascading cut following a decrease of key 14 by 4

9.4.5 Analysis

Lemma 9.4: Let a be an F-heap with n elements that results from a sequence of insert, meld, delete min, delete, and decrease key operations performed on initially empty F-heaps.

(a) Let b be any node in any of the min-trees of a. The degree of b is at most $\log_\phi m$, where $\phi = (1+\sqrt{5})/2$ and m is the number of elements in the subtree with root b.

(b) $MAX\_DEGREE \le \lfloor \log_\phi n \rfloor$ and the actual cost of a delete min is $O(\log n + s)$.

Proof: We shall prove (a) by induction on the degree of b. Let N_i be the minimum number of elements in the subtree with root b when b has degree i. We see that $N_0 = 1$ and $N_1 = 2$. So, the inequality of (a) holds for degrees 0 and 1. For $i > 1$, let $c_1, \cdots, c_i$ be the i children of b. Assume that c_j was made a child of b before c_{j+1}, $j < i$. Hence, when c_k, $k \le i$ was made a child of b, the degree of b was at least $k-1$. The only F-heap operation that makes one node a child of another is delete min. Here, during a join min-tree step, one min-tree is made a sub tree of another min-tree of equal degree. Hence, at the time of joining, the degree of c_k must have been equal to that of b. Subsequent to joining, its degree can decrease as a result of a delete or decrease key operation. However, following such a join, the degree of c_k can decrease by at most one as an attempt to cut off a second child of c_k results in a cascading cut at c_k. Such a cut causes c_k to become the root of a min-tree of the F-heap. Hence, the degree, d_k, of c_k is at least $\max\{0, k-2\}$. So, the number of elements in c_k is at least N_{d_k}. This implies that

$$N_i = N_0 + \sum_{k=0}^{i-2} N_k + 1 = \sum_{k=0}^{i-2} N_k + 2$$

One may show (see the exercises) that the Fibonacci numbers satisfy the equality

$$F_h = \sum_{k=0}^{h-2} F_k + 1, h > 1, F_0 = 0, \text{ and } F_1 = 1$$

From this we may obtain the equality $N_i = F_{i+2}$, $i \ge 0$. Further, since $F_{i+2} \ge \phi^i$, $N_i \ge \phi^i$. Hence, $i \le \log_\phi m$.

(b) is a direct consequence of (a). $\square$

Theorem 9.2: If a sequence of n insert, meld, delete min, delete, and decrease key operations is performed on an initially empty F-heap, then we can amortize costs such that the amortized time complexity of each insert, meld, and decrease key operation is $O(1)$ and that of each delete min and delete is $O(\log n)$. The total time complexity of the entire sequence is the sum of the amortized complexities of the individual operations in the sequence.

Proof: The proof is similar to that of Theorem 9.1. The definition of *#insert* is unchanged. However, that of *lastSize* is augmented by requiring that following each delete and decrease key *lastSize* be changed by the net change in the number of min-trees in the F-heap (in the example of Figure 9.13 *lastSize* is increased by 5). With this modification, we see that at the time of a delete min operation s = *#insert* + *lastSize* + $u - 1$. *#insert* units of cost may me charged, one each, to the *#insert* insert operations that contribute to this count and *lastSize* units may be charged to the delete min, delete, and decrease key operations that contribute to this count. This results in an additional charge of at most $\log_\phi n$ to each contributing delete min and delete operation and of one to each contributing decrease key operation. As a result, the amortized cost of a delete min is $O(\log n)$.

Since the total number of cascading cuts is limited by the total number of deletes and decrease key operations (as these are the only operations that can set *childCut* to *TRUE*), the cost of these cuts may be amortized over the delete and decrease key operations by adding one to their amortized costs. The amortized cost of deleting an element other than the min element becomes $O(\log n)$ as its actual cost is $O(1)$ (excluding the cost of the cascading cut sequence that may be performed); at most one unit is charged to it from the amortization of all the cascading cuts; and at most $\log_\phi n$ units are charged to it from a delete min.

The amortized cost of a decrease key operation is $O(1)$ as its actual cost is $O(1)$ (excluding the cost of the ensuing cascading cut); at most one unit is charged to it from the amortization of all cascading cuts; and at most one unit is charged from a delete min.

The amortized cost of an insert is $O(1)$ as its actual cost is one and at most one cost unit is charged to it from a delete min. Since the amortization scheme transfers no charge to a meld, its actual and amortized costs are the same. This cost is $O(1)$. □

From the preceding theorem, it follows that the complexity of any sequence of F-heap operations is $O(i + c + dk + (dm + d)\log i)$ where i, c, dk, dm, and d are, respectively, the number of insert, meld, decrease key, delete min, and delete operations in the sequence.

9.4.6 Application to the Shortest-Paths Problem

We conclude this section on F-heaps by considering their application to the single-source/all-destinations algorithm of Chapter 6. Let S be the set of vertices to which a shortest path has been found and let $dist(i)$ be the length of a shortest path from the source vertex to vertex i, $i \in S$, that goes through only vertices in S. On each iteration of the shortest-path algorithm, we need to determine an i, $i \in S$, such that $dist(i)$ is minimum and add this i to S. This corresponds to a delete min operation on S. Further, the *dist* values of the remaining vertices in S may decrease. This corresponds to a decrease-key operation on each of the affected vertices. The total number of decrease-key operations is bounded by the number of edges in the graph, and the number of delete-min operations is $n - 2$. S begins with $n - 1$ vertices. If we implement S as an F-heap using *dist* as the key, then $n - 1$ inserts are needed to initialize the F-heap. Additionally, $n - 2$ delete-min operations and at most e decrease-key operations are needed. The total time for all these operations is the sum of the amortized costs for each. This is $O(n \log n + e)$. The remainder of the algorithm takes $O(n)$ time. Hence if an F-heap is used to represent S, the complexity of the shortest-path algorithm becomes $O(n \log n + e)$. This is an asymptotic improvement over the implementation discussed in Chapter 6 if the graph does not have $\Omega(n^2)$ edges. If this single-source algorithm is used n times, once with each of the n vertices in the graph as the source, then we can find a shortest path between every pair of vertices in $O(n^2 \log n + ne)$ time. Once again, this represents an asymptotic improvement over the $O(n^3)$ dynamic programming algorithm of Chapter 6 for graphs that do not have $\Omega(n^2)$ edges. It is interesting to note that $O(n \log n + e)$ is the best possible implementation of the single-source algorithm of Chapter 6, as the algorithm must examine each edge and may be used to sort n numbers (which takes $O(n \log n)$ time).

EXERCISES

1. Prove that if we start with empty F-heaps and perform only the operations insert, meld, and delete min, then all min-trees in the F-heaps are binomial trees.

2. Can all the functions on an F-heap be performed in the same time using singly linked circular lists rather than doubly linked circular lists? Note that we can delete from an arbitrary node x of a singly linked circular list by copy over the data from the next node and then deleting the next node rather than the node x.

3. Show that if we start with empty F-heaps and do not perform cascading cuts, then it is possible for a sequence of F-heap operations to result in degree k min-trees that have only $k + 1$ nodes, $k \geq 1$.

4. Is the height of every tree in a Fibonacci heap that has n elements $O(\log n)$? If not, what is the worst-case height as a function of n?

5. Suppose we change the rule for a cascading cut so that such a cut is performed only when a node loses a third child rather than when it loses a second child. For this, the *childCut* field is changed so that it can have the values 0, 1, and 2. When a node acquires a new parent, its *childCut* field is set to 1. Each time a node has a child cut off (during a delete or decrease key operation), its *childCut* field is increased by one (unless this field is already two). In case the *childCut* field is already two, a cascading cut is performed.

    (a) Obtain a recurrence equation for N_i, the minimum number of nodes in a min-tree with degree i. Assume that we start with an empty F-heap and that all operations (except cascading cut) are performed as described in the text.

Cascading cuts are performed as described above.

(b)   Solve the recurrence of part (a) to obtain a lower bound on N_i.

(c)   Does the modified rule for cascading cuts ensure that the minimum number of nodes in any min-tree of degree i is exponential in i?

(d)   For the new cascading cut rule, can you establish the same amortized complexities as for the original rule? Prove the correctness of your answer.

(e)   Answer parts (c) and (d) under the assumtion that cascading cuts are performed only after k children of a node have been cut off. Here, k is a fixed constant ($k = 2$ for the rule used in the text and $k = 3$ for the rule used earlier in this exercise).

(f)   How do you expect the performance of F-heaps to change as larger values of k (see part (e)) are used?

6.   Write C functions to do the following:

(a)   Create an empty F-heap

(b)   Insert element x into an F-heap

(c)   Perform a delete min from an F-heap. The deleted element is to be returned to the invoking function.

(d)   Delete the element in node b of an F-heap a. The deleted element is to be returned to the invoking function.

(e)   Decrease the key in the node b of an F-heap a by some positive amount c.

Note that all operations must leave behind properly structured F-heaps. Your functions for (d) and (e) must perform cascading cuts. Test the correctness of your procedures by running them on a computer using suitable test data.

7.   For the Fibonacci numbers F_k and the numbers N_i of Lemma 9.4, prove the following:

(a) $F_h = \sum_{k=0}^{h-2} F_k + 1, h > 1$

(b)   Use (a) to show that $N_i = F_{i+2}, i \geq 0$.

(c)   Use the equality $F_k = \dfrac{1}{\sqrt{5}}(\dfrac{1+\sqrt{5}}{2})^k - \dfrac{1}{\sqrt{5}}(\dfrac{1-\sqrt{5}}{2})^k, k \geq 0$ to show that F_{k+2}
$\geq \phi^k, k \geq 0$, where $\phi = (1+\sqrt{5})/2$.

8.   Implement the single source shortest path algorithm of Chapter 6 using the data structures recommended there as well as using F-heaps. However, use adjacency lists rather than an adjacency matrix. Generate 10 connected undirected graphs with different edge densities (say 10%, 20%, $\cdots$, 100% of maximum) for each of the cases $n = 100, 200, \cdots, 500$. Assign random costs to the edges (use a uniform random number generator in the range [1, 1000]). Measure the run times of the

two implementations of the shortest path algorithms. Plot the average times for each n.

9.5   PAIRING HEAPS

9.5.1   Definition

The pairing heap supports the same operations as supported by the Fibonacci heap. Pairing heaps come in two varieties—min pairing heaps and max pairing heaps. Min pairing heaps are used when we wish to represent a min priority queue, and max pairing heaps are used for max priority queues. In keeping with our discussion of Fibonacci heaps, we explicitly discuss min pairing heaps only. Max pairing heaps are analogous. Figure 9.14 compares the actual and amortized complexities of the Fibonacci and pairing heap operations.

Operation	Fibonacci Heap		Pairing Heap	
	Actual	Amortized	Actual	Amortized
getMin	$O(1)$	$O(1)$	$O(1)$	$O(1)$
insert	$O(1)$	$O(1)$	$O(1)$	$O(1)$
deleteMin	$O(n)$	$O(\log n)$	$O(n)$	$O(\log n)$
meld	$O(1)$	$O(1)$	$O(1)$	$O(\log n)$
delete	$O(n)$	$O(\log n)$	$O(n)$	$O(\log n)$
decreaseKey	$O(n)$	$O(1)$	$O(1)$	$O(\log n)$

Figure 9.14: Complexity of Fibonacci and pairing heap operations

Although the amortized complexities given in Figure 9.14 for pairing heap operations are not known to be tight (i.e., no one knows of an operation sequence whose run time actually grows logarithmically with the number of decrease key operations (say)), it is known that the amortized complexity of the decrease key operation is $\Omega(\log\log n)$ (see the section titled References and Selected Readings at the end of this chapter).

Although the amortized complexity is better when a Fibonacci heap is used rather than when a pairing heap is used, extensive experimental studies employing these structures in the implementation of Dijkstra's shortest paths algorithm (Section 6.4.1) and Prim's minimum cost spanning tree algorithm (Section 6.3.2) indicate that pairing heaps actually outperform Fibonacci heaps.

Definition: A *min pairing heap* is a min tree in which the operations are performed in a manner to be specified later.

Figure 9.15 shows four example min pairing heaps. Notice that a pairing heap is a single tree, which need not be a binary tree. The min element is in the root of this tree and hence this element may be found in $O(1)$ time.

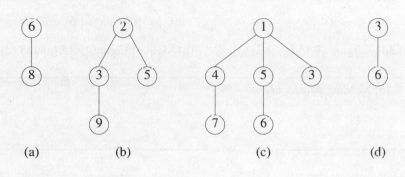

Figure 9.15: Example min pairing heaps

9.5.2   Meld and Insert

Two min pairing heaps may be melded into a single min pairing heap by performing a *compare-link* operation. In a compare-link, the roots of the two min trees are compared and the min tree that has the larger root is made the leftmost subtree of the other tree (ties are broken arbitrarily).

To meld the min trees of Figures 9.15 (a) and (b), we compare the two roots. Since tree (a) has the larger root, this tree becomes the leftmost subtree of tree (b). Figure 9.16 (a) is the resulting pairing heap. Figure 9.16 (b) shows the result of melding the pairing heaps of Figures 9.15 (c) and (d). When we meld the pairing heaps of Figures 9.16 (a) and (b), the result is the pairing heap of Figure 9.17.

To insert an element x into a pairing heap p, we first create a pairing heap q with the single element x, and then meld the two pairing heaps p and q.

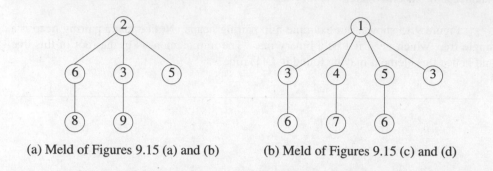

(a) Meld of Figures 9.15 (a) and (b)   (b) Meld of Figures 9.15 (c) and (d)

Figure 9.16: Melding pairing heaps

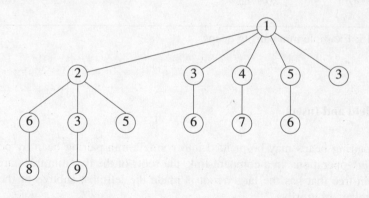

Figure 9.17: Meld of Figures 9.16 (a) and (b)

9.5.3   Decrease Key

Suppose we decrease the key/priority of the element in node N. When N is the root or when the new key in N is greater than or equal to that in its parent, no additional work is to be done. However, when the new key in N is less than that in its parent, the min tree property is violated and corrective action is to be taken. For example, if the key in the root of the tree of Figure 9.15 (c) is decreased from 1 to 0, or when the key in the left-most child of the root of Figure 9.15 (c) is decreased from 4 to 2 no additional work is necessary. When the key in the leftmost child of the root of Figure 9.15 (c) is decreased from 4 to 0 the new value is less than that in the root (see Figure 9.18 (a)) and corrective action is needed.

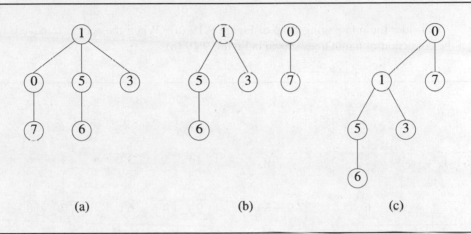

(a)   (b)   (c)

Figure 9.18: Decreasing a key

Since pairing heaps are normally not implemented with a parent pointer, it is difficult to determine whether or not corrective action is needed following a key reduction. Therefore, corrective action is taken regardless of whether or not it is needed except when N is the tree root. The corrective action consists of the following steps:

Step 1: Remove the subtree with root N from the tree. This results in two min trees.

Step 2: Meld the two min trees together.

Figure 9.18 (b) shows the two min trees following Step 1, and Figure 9.18 (c) shows the result following Step 2.

9.5.4   Delete Min

The min element is in the root of the tree. So, to delete the min element, we first delete the root node. When the root is deleted, we are left with zero or more min trees (i.e., the subtrees of the deleted root). When the number of remaining min trees is two or more, these min trees must be melded into a single min tree. In *two pass pairing heaps*, this melding is done as follows:

Step 1: Make a left to right pass over the trees, melding pairs of trees.

Step 2: Start with the rightmost tree and meld the remaining trees (right to left) into this tree one at a time.

Consider the min pairing heap of Figure 9.19 (a). When the root is removed, we get the collection of 6 min trees shown in Figure 9.19 (b).

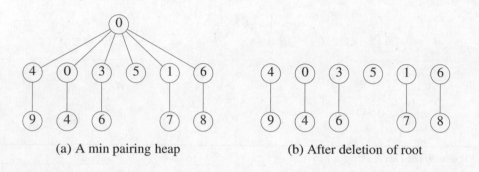

(a) A min pairing heap   (b) After deletion of root

Figure 9.19: Deleting the min element

In the left to right pass of Step 1, we first meld the trees with roots 4 and 0. Next, the trees with roots 3 and 5 are melded. Finally, the trees with roots 1 and 6 are melded. Figure 9.20 shows the resulting three min trees.

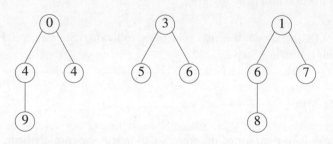

Figure 9.20: Trees following first pass

In Step 2 (which is a right to left pass), the two rightmost trees of Figure 9.20 are first melded to get the tree of Figure 9.21 (a).

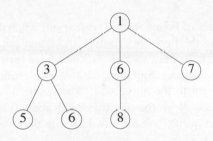

Figure 9.21: First stage of second pass

Then the tree of Figure 9.20 with root 0 is melded with the tree of Figure 9.21 to get the final min tree, which is shown in Figure 9.22.

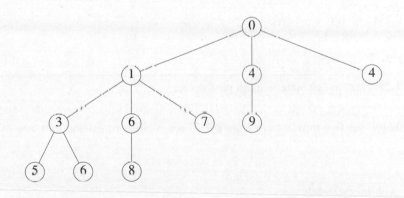

Figure 9.22: Final min pairing heaping following a delete min

Note that if the original pairing heap had 8 subtrees, then following the left to right melding pass we would be left with 4 min trees. In the right to left pass, we would first meld trees 3 and 4 to get tree 5. Then trees 2 and 5 would be melded to get tree 6. Finally, we would meld trees 1 and 6.

In *multi pass pairing heaps*, the min trees that remain following the removal of the root are melded into a single min tree as follows:

Step 1: Put the min trees onto a FIFO queue.

Step 2: Extract two trees from the front of the queue, meld them and put the resulting tree at the end of the queue. Repeat this step until only one tree remains.

Consider the six trees of Figure 9.19 (b) that result when the root of Figure 9.19 (a) is deleted. First, we meld the trees with roots 4 and 0 and put the resulting min tree at the end of the queue. Next, the trees with roots 3 and 5 are melded and the resulting min tree is put at the end of the queue. And then, the trees with roots 1 and 6 are melded and the resulting min tree added to the queue end. The queue now contains the three min trees shown in Figure 9.20. Next, the min trees with roots 0 and 3 are melded and the result put at the end of the queue. We are now left with the two min trees shown in Figure 9.23.

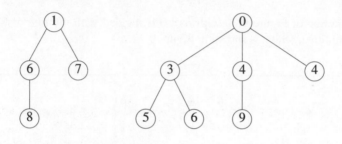

Figure 9.23: Next to last state in multi pass delete

Finally, the two min trees of Figure 9.23 are melded to get the min tree of Figure 9.24.

9.5.5 Arbitrary Delete

Deletion from an arbitrary node N is handled as a delete-min operation when N is the root of the pairing heap. When N is not the tree root, the deletion is done as follows:

Step 1: Detach the subtree with root N from the tree.

Step 2: Delete node N and meld its subtrees into a single min tree using the two pass scheme if we are implementing a two pass pairing heap or the multi pass scheme if we are implementing a multi pass pairing heap.

Step 3: Meld the min trees from Steps 1 and 2 into a single min tree.

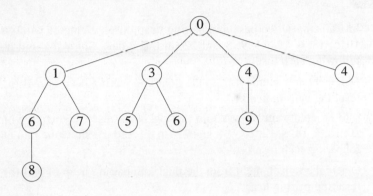

Figure 9.24: Result of multi pass delete min

9.5.6 Implementation Considerations

Although we can implement a pairing heap using nodes that have a variable number of children fields, such an implementation is expensive because of the need to dynamically increase the number of children fields as needed. An efficient implementation results when we use the binary tree representation of a tree (see Section 5.1.2.2). Siblings in the original min tree are linked together using a doubly linked list. In addition to a *data* field, each node has the three pointer fields *previous*, *next*, and *child*. The leftmost node in a doubly linked list of siblings uses its *previous* pointer to point to its parent. A leftmost child satisfies the property $x \rightarrow previous \rightarrow child = x$. The doubly linked list makes it is possible to remove an arbitrary element (as is required by the *delete* and *decrease key* operations) in $O(1)$ time.

9.5.7 Complexity

You can verify that using the described binary tree representation, all pairing heap operations (other than *delete* and *delete min* can be done in $O(1)$ time. The complexity of the *delete* and *delete min* operations is $O(n)$, because the number of subtrees that have to be melded following the removal of a node is $O(n)$.

The amortized complexity of the pairing heap operations is established in the paper by Fredman et al. cited in the References and Selected Readings section. Experimental studies conducted by Stasko and Vitter (see their paper that is cited in the References and Selected Readings section) establish the superiority of two pass pairing heaps over multipass pairing heaps.

EXERCISES

1. (a) Into an empty two pass min pairing heap, insert elements with priorities 20, 10, 5, 18, 6, 12, 14, 9, 8 and 22 (in this order). Show the min pairing heap following each insert.

    (b) Delete the min element from the final min pairing heap of part (a). Show the resulting pairing heap.

2. (a) Into an empty multi pass min pairing heap, insert elements with priorities 20, 10, 5, 18, 6, 12, 14, 9, 8 and 22 (in this order). Show the min pairing heap following each insert.

    (b) Delete the min element from the final min pairing heap of part (a). Show the resulting pairing heap.

3. Fully code and test the class *MultiPassPairingHeap*, which impements a multi pass min pairing heap. Your class must include the functions *GetMin*, *Insert*, *DeleteMin*, *Meld*, *Delete* and *DecreaseKey*. The function *Insert* should return the node into which the new element was inserted. This returned information can later be used as an input to *Delete* and *DecreaseKey*.

4. What are the worst-case height and degree of a pairing heap that has *n* elements? Show how you arrived at your answer.

5. Define a *one pass pairing heap* as an adaptation of a two pass pairing heap in which Step 1 (Make a left to right pass over the trees, melding pairs of trees.) is eliminated. Show that the amortized cost of either insert or delete min must be $\Theta(n)$.

9.6 SYMMETRIC MIN-MAX HEAPS

9.6.1 Definition and Properties

A double-ended priority queue (DEPQ) may be represented using a symmetric min-max heap (SMMH). An *SMMH* is a complete binary tree in which each node other than the root has exactly one element. The root of an SMMH is empty and the total number of nodes in the SMMH is $n+1$, where n is the number of elements. Let N be any node of the SMMH. Let *elements* (N) be the elements in the subtree rooted at N but excluding the element (if any) in N. Assume that *elements* $(N) \neq \phi$. N satisfies the following properties:

Q1: The left child of N has the minimum element in *elements* (N).

Q2: The right child of N (if any) has the maximum element in *elements* (N).

Figure 9.25 shows an example SMMH that has 12 elements. When N denotes the node with 80, *elements* (N)={6,14,30,40}; the left child of N has the minimum element 6 in *elements* (N); and the right child of N has the maximum element 40 in *elements* (N). You may verify that every node N of this SMMH satisfies properties Q1 and Q2.

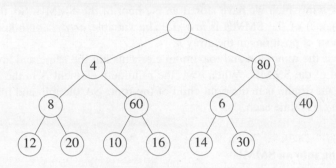

Figure 9.25: A symmetric min-max heap

It is easy to see that an $n+1$-node complete binary tree with an empty root and one element in every other node is an SMMH iff the following are true:

P1: The element in each node is less than or equal to that in its right sibling (if any).

P2: For every node N that has a grandparent, the element in the left child of the grandparent is less than or equal to that in N.

P3: For every node N that has a grandparent, the element in the right child of the grandparent is greater than or equal to that in N.

Properties P2 and P3, respectively, state that the grandchildren of each node M have elements that are greater than or equal to that in the left child of M and less than or equal to that in the right child of M. Hence, P2 and P3 follow from Q1 and Q2, respectively. Notice that if property P1 is satisfied, then at most one of P2 and P3 may be violated at any node N. Using properties P1 through P3 we arrive at simple algorithms to insert and delete elements. These algorithms are simple adaptations of the corresponding algorithms for heaps.

As we shall see, the standard DEPQ operations can be done efficiently using an SMMH.

9.6.2   SMMH Representation

Since an SMMH is a complete binary tree, it is efficiently represented as a one-dimensional array (say h) using the standard mapping of a complete binary tree into an array (Section 5.2.3.1). Position 0 of h is not used and position 1, which represents the root of the complete binary tree, is empty. We use the variable *last* to denote the right-most position of h in which we have stored an element of the SMMH. So, the size (i.e., number of elements) of the SMMH is $last-1$. The variable *arrayLength* keeps track of the current number of positions in the array h.

When $n=1$, the minimum and maximum elements are the same and are in the left child of the root of the SMMH. When $n>1$, the minimum element is in the left child of the root and the maximum is in the right child of the root. So, the min and max elements may be found in $O(1)$ time each.

9.6.3   Inserting into an SMMH

The algorithm to insert into an SMMH has three steps.

Step 1: Expand the size of the complete binary tree by 1, creating a new node E for the element x that is to be inserted. This newly created node of the complete binary tree becomes the candidate node to insert the new element x.

Step 2: Verify whether the insertion of x into E would result in a violation of property P1. Note that this violation occurs iff E is a right child of its parent and x is greater than the element in the sibling of E. In case of a P1 violation, the element in the sibling of E is moved to E and E is updated to be the now empty sibling.

Step 3: Perform a bubble-up pass from E up the tree verifying properties P2 and P3. In each round of the bubble-up pass, E moves up the tree by one level. When E is positioned so that the insertion of x into E doesn't result in a violation of either P2 or P3, insert x into E.

Suppose we wish to insert 2 into the SMMH of Figure 9.25. Since an SMMH is a complete binary tree, we must add a new node to the SMMH in the position shown in Figure 9.26; the new node is labeled E. In our example, E will denote an empty node.

If the new element 2 is placed in node E, property P2 is violated as the left child of the grandparent of E has 6. So we move the 6 down to E and move E up one level to obtain the configuration of Figure 9.27.

Now we determine if it is safe to insert the 2 into node E. We first notice that such an insertion cannot result in a violation of property P1, because the previous occupant of node E was greater than 2. For properties P2 and P3, let $N=E$. P3 cannot be violated for this value of N as the previous occupant of this node was greater than 2. So, only P2 can

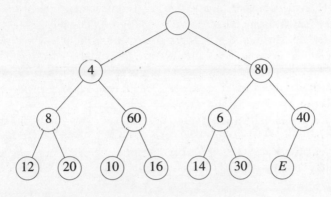

Figure 9.26: The SMMH of Figure 9.25 with a node added

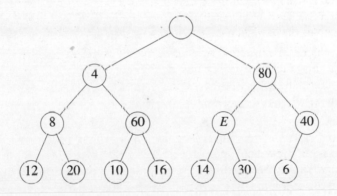

Figure 9.27: The SMMH of Figure 9.26 with 6 moved down

be violated. Checking P2 with $N=E$, we see that P2 will be violated if we insert $x=2$ into E, because the left child of the grandparent of E has the element 4. So we move the 4 down to E and move E up one level to the node that previously contained the 4. Figure 9.28 shows the resulting configuration.

For the configuration of Figure 9.28 we see that placing 2 into node E cannot violate property P1, because the previous occupant of node E was greater than 2. Also properties P2 and P3 cannot be violated, because node E has no grandparent. So we

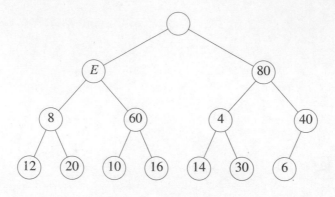

Figure 9.28: The SMMH of Figure 9.27 with 4 moved down

insert 2 into node *E* and obtain Figure 9.29.

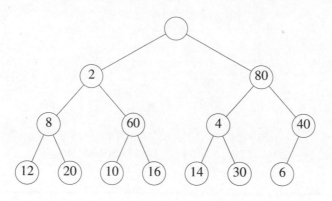

Figure 9.29: The SMMH of Figure 9.28 with 2 inserted

Let us now insert 50 into the SMMH of Figure 9.29. Since an SMMH is a complete binary tree, the new node must be positioned as in Figure 9.30.

Since *E* is the right child of its parent, we first check P1 at node *E*. If the new element (in this case 50) is smaller than that in the left sibling of *E*, we swap the new element and the element in the left sibling. In our case, no swap is done. Then we check P2 and P3. We see that placing 50 into *E* would violate P3. So the element 40 in the right

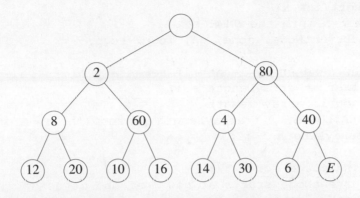

Figure 9.30: The SMMH of Figure 9.29 with a node added

child of the grandparent of E is moved down to node E. Figure 9.31 shows the resulting configuration. Placing 50 into node E of Figure 9.31 cannot create a P1 violation because the previous occupant of node E was smaller. A P2 violation isn't possible either. So only P3 needs to be checked at E. Since there is no P3 violation at E, 50 is placed into E.

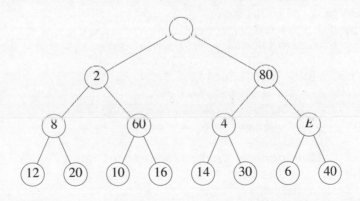

Figure 9.31: The SMMH of Figure 9.30 with 40 moved down

Program 9.5 gives the C code for the insert operation; the variable *currentNode* refers to the empty node E of our example. This code assumes that the SMMH state

```
void insert(int x)
{/* insert x into the SMMH */
    int currentNode, done, gp, lcgp, rcgp;

    /* increase array length if necessary */
    if (last == arrayLength - 1)
    {/* double array length
        REALLOC(h, 2 * arrayLength *sizeof(*h));
        arrayLength *= 2;
    }
    /* find place for x */
    /* currentNode starts at new leaf and moves up tree */
    currentNode = ++last;
    if (last % 2 == 1 && x < h[last - 1])
    {/* left sibling must be smaller, P1 */
        h[last] = h[last - 1]; currentNode--;
    }
    done = FALSE;
    while (!done && currentNode >= 4)
    {/* currentNode has a grandparent
        gp = currentNode / 4;      /* grandparent */
        lcgp = 2 * gp;             /* left child of gp */
        rcgp = lcgp + 1;           /* right child of gp */
        if (x < h[lcgp])
        {/* P2 is violated */
            h[currentNode] = h[lcgp]; currentNode = lcgp;
        }
        else if (x > h[rcgp])
            {/* P3 is violated */
                h[currentNode] = h[rcgp];
                currentNode = rcgp;
            }
            else done = TRUE; /* neither P2 nor P3 violated */
    }
    h[currentNode] = x;
}
```

Program 9.5: Insertion into a symmetric min-max heap

variables h, *arrayLength*, and *last* are global. For simplicity, we assume that the data-type of the SMMH elements is **int**. Since the height of a complete binary tree is $O(\log n)$ and Program 9.5 does $O(1)$ work at each level of the SMMH, the complexity of the insert function is $O(\log n)$.

9.6.4 Deleting from an SMMH

The algorithm to delete either the min or max element is an adaptation of the trickle-down algorithm used to delete an element from a min or a max heap. We consider only the case when the minimum element is to be deleted. If the SMMH is empty, the deletion cannot be performed. So, assume we have a non-empty SMMH. The minimum element is in $h[2]$. If *last*=2, the SMMH becomes empty following the deletion. Assume that *last*≠2. Let $x=h[last]$ and decrement *last* by 1. To complete the deletion, we must rein-sert x into an SMMH whose $h[2]$ node is empty. Let E denote the empty node. We fol-low a path from E down the tree, as in the delete algorithm for a min or max heap, veri-fying properties P1 and P2 until we reach a suitable node into which x may be inserted. In the case of a delete-min operation, the trickle-down process cannot cause a P3 viola-tion. So, we don't explicitly verify P3.

Consider the SMMH of Figure 9.31 with 50 in the node labeled E. A delete min results in the removal of 2 from the left child of the root (i.e., $h[2]$) and the removal of the last node (i.e., the one with 40) from the SMMH. So, $x=40$ and we have the configuration shown in Figure 9.32. Since $h[3]$ has the maximum element, P1 cannot be violated at E. Further, since E is the left child of its parent, no P3 violations can result from inserting x into E. So we need only concern ourselves with P2 violations. To detect such a violation, we determine the smaller of the left child of E and the left child of E's right sibling. For our example, the smaller of 8 and 4 is determined. This smaller ele-ment 4 is, by definition of an SMMH, the smallest element in the SMMH. Since $4<x=40$, inserting x into E would result in a P2 violation. To avoid this, we move the 4 into node E and the node previously occupied by 4 becomes E (see Figure 9.33). Notice that if $4 > x$, inserting x into E would result in a properly structured SMMH.

Now the new E becomes the candidate node for the insertion of x. First, we check for a possible P1 violation that may result from such an insertion. Since $x=40<50$, no P1 violation results. Then we check for a P2 violation. The left children of E and its sibling are 14 and 6. The smaller child, 6, is smaller than x. So, x cannot be inserted into E. Rather, we swap E and 6 to get the configuration of Figure 9.34.

We now check the P1 property at the new E. Since E doesn't have a right sibling, there is no P1 violation. We proceed to check the P2 property. Since E has no children, a P2 violation isn't possible either. So, x is inserted into E. Let's consider another delete-min operation. This time, we delete the minimum element from the SMMH of Figure 9.34 (recall that the node labeled E contains 40). The min element 4 is removed from $h[2]$ and the last element, 40, is removed from the SMMH and placed in x. Figure 9.35

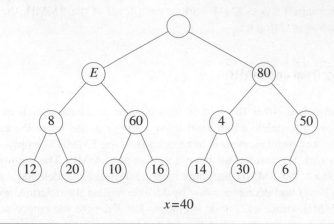

Figure 9.32: The SMMH of Figure 9.31 with 2 deleted

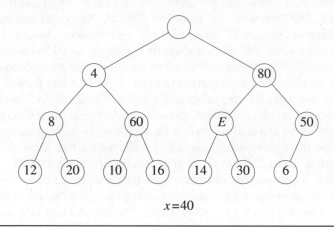

Figure 9.33: The SMMH of Figure 9.32 with E and 4 interchanged

shows the resulting configuration.

As before, a P1 violation isn't possible at $h[2]$. The smaller of the left children of E and its sibling is 6. Since $6 < x = 40$, we interchange 6 and E to get Figure 9.36.

Next, we check for a possible P1 violation at the new E. Since the sibling of E is 50 and $x = 40 \le 50$, no P1 violation is detected. The smaller left child of E and its sibling

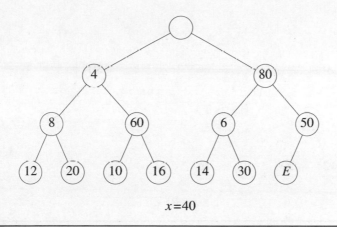

$x=40$

Figure 9.34: The SMMH of Figure 9.33 with E and 6 interchanged

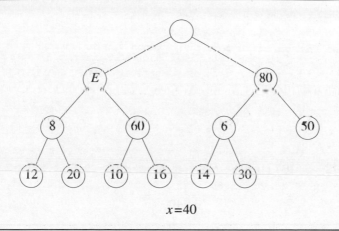

$x=40$

Figure 9.35: First step of another delete min

is 14 (actually, the sibling doesn't have a left child, so we just use the left child of E), which is $<x$. So, we swap E and 14 to get Figure 9.37.

Since there is a P1 violation at the new E, we swap x and 30 to get Figure 9.38 and proceed to check for a P2 violation at the new E. As there is no P2 violation here, $x=30$ is inserted into E.

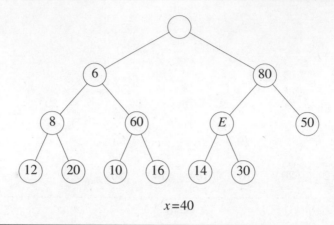

Figure 9.36: The SMMH of Figure 9.35 with E and 6 interchanged

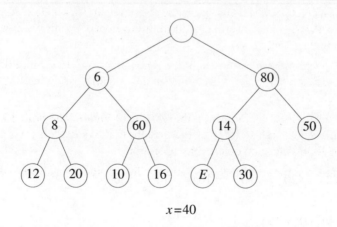

Figure 9.37: The SMMH of Figure 9.36 with E and 14 interchanged

We leave the development of the code for the delete operations as an exercise. However, you should note that these operations spend $O(1)$ time per level during the trickle-down pass. So, their complexity is $O(\log n)$.

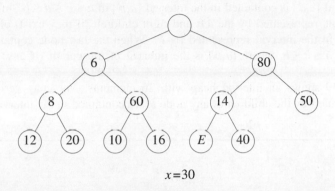

$x=30$

Figure 9.38: The SMMH of Figure 9.37 with x and 30 interchanged

EXERCISES

1. Show that every complete binary tree with an empty root and one element in every other node is an SMMH iff P1 through P3 are true.

2. Start with an empty SMMH and insert the elements 20, 10, 40, 3, 2, 7, 60, 1 and 80 (in this order) using the insertion algorithm developed in this section. Draw the SMMH following each insert.

3. Perform 3 delete-min operations on the SMMH of Figure 9.38 with 30 in the node E. Use the delete min strategy described in this section. Draw the SMMH following each delete min.

4. Perform 4 delete max operations on the SMMH of Figure 9.38 with 30 in the node E. Adapt the delete min strategy of this section to the delete max operation. Draw the SMMH following each delete max operation.

5. Develop the code for all SMMH operations. Test all functions using your own test data.

9.7 INTERVAL HEAPS

9.7.1 Definition and Properties

Like an SMMH, an interval heap is a heap inspired data structure that may be used to represent a DEPQ. An *interval heap* is a complete binary tree in which each node, except possibly the last one (the nodes of the complete binary tree are ordered using a level order traversal), contains two elements. Let the two elements in a node be a and b, where $a \leq b$. We say that the node represents the closed interval $[a,b]$. a is the left end point of the node's interval and b is its right end point.

The interval $[c,d]$ is contained in the interval $[a,b]$ iff $a \leq c \leq d \leq b$. In an interval heap, the intervals represented by the left and right children (if they exist) of each node P are contained in the interval represented by P. When the last node contains a single element c, then $a \leq c \leq b$, where $[a,b]$ is the interval of the parent (if any) of the last node.

Figure 9.39 shows an interval heap with 26 elements. You may verify that the intervals represented by the children of any node P are contained in the interval of P.

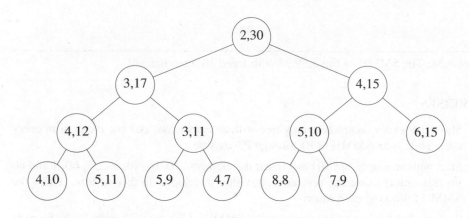

Figure 9.39: An interval heap

The following facts are immediate:

(1)   The left end points of the node intervals define a min heap, and the right end points define a max heap. In case the number of elements is odd, the last node has a single element which may be regarded as a member of either the min or max heap. Figure 9.40 shows the min and max heaps defined by the interval heap of Figure 9.39.

(2)   When the root has two elements, the left end point of the root is the minimum element in the interval heap and the right end point is the maximum. When the root has only one element, the interval heap contains just one element. This element is both the minimum and maximum element.

(3)   An interval heap can be represented compactly by mapping into an array as is done for ordinary heaps. However, now, each array position must have space for two elements.

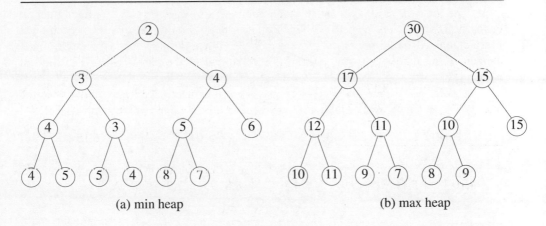

$$(a) \text{ min heap} \qquad\qquad (b) \text{ max heap}$$

Figure 9.40: Min and max heaps embedded in Figure 9.39

(4)   The height of an interval heap with n elements is $\Theta(\log n)$.

9.7.2   Inserting into an Interval Heap

Suppose we are to insert an element into the interval heap of Figure 9.39. Since this heap currently has an even number of elements, the heap following the insertion will have an additional node A as is shown in Figure 9.41.

The interval for the parent of the new node A is [6,15]. Therefore, if the new element is between 6 and 15, the new element may be inserted into node A. When the new element is less than the left end point 6 of the parent interval, the new element is inserted into the min heap embedded in the interval heap. This insertion is done using the min heap insertion procedure starting at node A. When the new element is greater than the right end point 15 of the parent interval, the new element is inserted into the max heap embedded in the interval heap. This insertion is done using the max heap insertion procedure starting at node A.

If we are to insert the element 10 into the interval heap of Figure 9.39, this element is put into the node A shown in Figure 9.41. To insert the element 3, we follow a path from node A towards the root, moving left end points down until we either pass the root or reach a node whose left end point is ≤ 3. The new element is inserted into the node that now has no left end point. Figure 9.42 shows the resulting interval heap.

To insert the element 40 into the interval heap of Figure 9.39, we follow a path from node A (see Figure 9.41) towards the root, moving right end points down until we

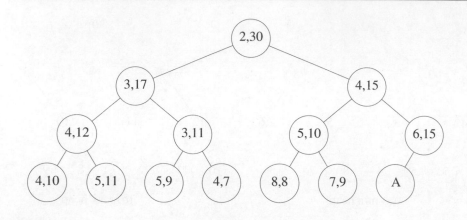

Figure 9.41: Interval heap of Figure 9.39 after one node is added

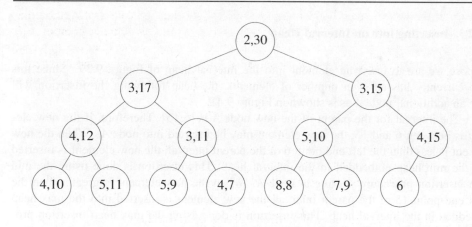

Figure 9.42: The interval heap of Figure 9.39 with 3 inserted

either pass the root or reach a node whose right end point is ≥ 40. The new element is inserted into the node that now has no right end point. Figure 9.43 shows the resulting interval heap.

Now, suppose we wish to insert an element into the interval heap of Figure 9.43. Since this interval heap has an odd number of elements, the insertion of the new element

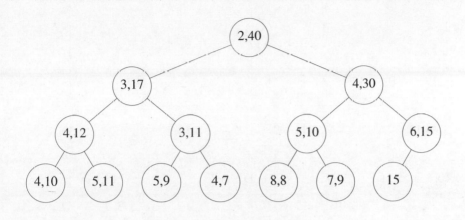

Figure 9.43: The interval heap of Figure 9.39 with 40 inserted

does not increase the number of nodes. The insertion procedure is the same as for the case when we initially have an even number of elements. Let A denote the last node in the heap. If the new element lies within the interval [6,15] of the parent of A, then the new element is inserted into node A (the new element becomes the left end point of A if it is less than the element currently in A). If the new element is less than the left end point 6 of the parent of A, then the new element is inserted into the embedded min heap; otherwise, the new element is inserted into the embedded max heap. Figure 9.44 shows the result of inserting the element 32 into the interval heap of Figure 9.43.

9.7.3   Deleting the Min Element

The removal of the minimum element is handled as several cases:

(1)   When the interval heap is empty, the *delete min* operation fails.

(2)   When the interval heap has only one element, this element is the element to be returned. We leave behind an empty interval heap.

(3)   When there is more than one element, the left end point of the root is to be returned. This point is removed from the root. If the root is the last node of the interval heap, nothing more is to be done. When the last node is not the root node, we remove the left point p from the last node. If this causes the last node to become empty, the last node is no longer part of the heap. The point p removed

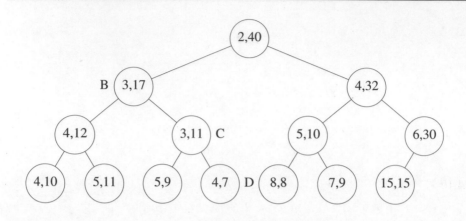

Figure 9.44: The interval heap of Figure 9.43 with 32 inserted

from the last node is reinserted into the embedded min heap by beginning at the root. As we move down, it may be necessary to swap the current p with the right end point r of the node being examined to ensure that $p \le r$. The reinsertion is done using the same strategy as used to reinsert into an ordinary heap.

Let us remove the minimum element from the interval heap of Figure 9.44. First, the element 2 is removed from the root. Next, the left end point 15 is removed from the last node and we begin the reinsertion procedure at the root. The smaller of the min heap elements that are the children of the root is 3. Since this element is smaller than 15, we move the 3 into the root (the 3 becomes the left end point of the root) and position ourselves at the left child B of the root. Since, $15 \le 17$ we do not swap the right end point of B with the current $p=15$. The smaller of the left end points of the children of B is 3. The 3 is moved from node C into node B as its left end point and we position ourselves at node C. Since $p=15>11$, we swap the two and 15 becomes the right end point of node C. The smaller of left end points of Cs children is 4. Since this is smaller than the current $p=11$, it is moved into node C as this node's left end point. We now position ourselves at node D. First, we swap $p=11$ and Ds right end point. Now, since D has no children, the current $p=7$ is inserted into node D as Ds left end point. Figure 9.45 shows the result.

The max element may be removed using an analogous procedure.

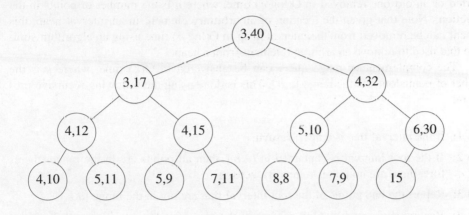

Figure 9.45: The interval heap of Figure 9.44 with minimum element removed

9.7.4 Initializing an Interval Heap

Interval heaps may be initialized using a strategy similar to that used to initialize ordinary heaps—work your way from the heap bottom to the root ensuring that each subtree is an interval heap. For each subtree, first order the elements in the root; then reinsert the left end point of this subtree's root using the reinsertion strategy used for the *DeleteMin* operation, then reinsert the right end point of this subtree's root using the strategy used for the *delete max* operation.

9.7.5 Complexity of Interval Heap Operations

The min and max elements may be found in O(1) time each; insertion as well as deletion of the min and max elements take O(log n) each; and initializing an *n* element interval heap takes $\Theta(n)$ time.

9.7.6 The Complementary Range Search Problem

In the *complementary range search* problem, we have a dynamic collection (i.e., points are added and removed from the collection as time goes on) of one-dimensional points (i.e., points have only an *x*-coordinate associated with them) and we are to answer queries of the form: what are the points outside of the interval [*a,b*]? For example, if the point collection is 3,4,5,6,8,12, the points outside the range [5,7] are 3,4,8,12.

When an interval heap is used to represent the point collection, a new point can be inserted or an old one removed in O(log n) time, where n is the number of points in the collection. Note that given the location of an arbitrary element in an interval heap, this element can be removed from the interval heap in O(log n) time using an algorithm similar to that used to remove an arbitrary element from a heap.

The complementary range query can be answered in $\Theta(k)$ time, where k is the number of points outside the range [a,b]. This is done using the following recursive procedure:

Step 1: If the interval tree is empty, **return**.

Step 2: If the root interval is contained in [a,b], then all points are in the range (therefore, there are no points to report), **return**.

Step 3: Report the end points of the root interval that are not in the range [a,b].

Step 4: Recursively search the left subtree of the root for additional points that are not in the range [a,b].

Step 5: Recursively search the right subtree of the root for additional points that are not in the range [a,b].

Step 6: return.

Let us try this procedure on the interval heap of Figure 9.44. The query interval is [4,32]. We start at the root. Since the root interval is not contained in the query interval, we reach step 3 of the procedure. Whenever step 3 is reached, we are assured that at least one of the end points of the root interval is outside the query interval. Therefore, each time step 3 is reached, at least one point is reported. In our example, both points 2 and 40 are outside the query interval and are reported. We then search the left and right subtrees of the root for additional points. When the left subtree is searched, we again determine that the root interval is not contained in the query interval. This time only one of the root interval points (i.e., 3) is outside the query range. This point is reported and we proceed to search the left and right subtrees of B for additional points outside the query range. Since the interval of the left child of B is contained in the query range, the left subtree of B contains no points outside the query range. We do not explore the left subtree of B further. When the right subtree of B is searched, we report the left end point 3 of node C and proceed to search the left and right subtrees of C. Since the intervals of the roots of each of these subtrees is contained in the query interval, these subtrees are not explored further. Finally, we examine the root of the right subtree of the overall tree root, that is the node with interval [4,32]. Since this node's interval is contained in the query interval, the right subtree of the overall tree is not searched further.

We say that a node is *visited* if its interval is examined in Step 2. With this definition of *visited*, we see that the complexity of the above six step procedure is

Θ(number of nodes visited). The nodes visited in the preceding example are the root and its two children, the two children of node B, and the two children of node C. So, 7 nodes are visited and a total of 4 points are reported.

We show that the total number of interval heap nodes visited is at most $3k+1$, where k is the number of points reported. If a visited node reports one or two points, give the node a count of one. If a visited node reports no points, give it a count of zero and add one to the count of its parent (unless the node is the root and so has no parent). The number of nodes with a nonzero count is at most k. Since no node has a count more than 3, the sum of the counts is at most $3k$. Accounting for the possibility that the root reports no point, we see that the number of nodes visited is at most $3k+1$. Therefore, the complexity of the search is $\Theta(k)$. This complexity is asymptotically optimal because every algorithm that reports k points must spend at least $\Theta(1)$ time per reported point.

In our example search, the root gets a count of 2 (1 because it is visited and reports at least one point and another 1 because its right child is visited but reports no point), node B gets a count of 2 (1 because it is visited and reports at least one point and another 1 because its left child is visited but reports no point), and node C gets a count of 3 (1 because it is visited and reports at least one point and another 2 because its left and right children are visited and neither reports a point). The count for each of the remaining nodes in the interval heap is 0.

EXERCISES

1. Start with an empty interval heap and insert the elements 20, 10, 40, 3, 2, 7, 60, 1 and 80 (in this order) using the insertion algorithm developed in this section. Draw the interval heap following each insert.

2. Perform 3 delete-min operations on the interval heap of Figure 9.45. Use the delete min strategy described in this section. Draw the interval heap following each delete min.

3. Perform 4 delete max operations on the interval heap of Figure 9.45. Adapt the delete min strategy of this section to the delete max operation. Draw the interval heap following each delete max operation.

4. Develop the code for all interval heap operations. You also must code the initialization function and a function for the complementary range search operation. Test all functions using your own test data.

5. The min-max heap is an alternative heap inspired data structure for the representation of a DEPQ. A *min-max heap* is a complete binary tree in which each node has exactly one element. Alternating levels of this tree are min levels and max levels, respectively. The root is on a min level. Let x be any node in a min-max heap. If x is on a min (max) level then the element in x has the minimum (maximum) priority from among all elements in the subtree with root x. A node on a min (max) level is called a *min* (*max*) node. Figure 9.46 shows an example 12-elements min-max heap. We use shaded circles for max nodes and unshaded circles for min

nodes.

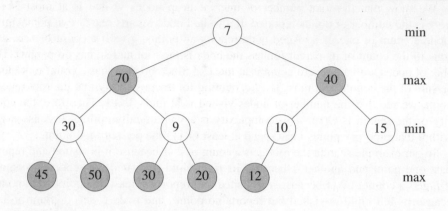

Figure 9.46: A 12-element min-max heap

Fully code and test the double-ended priority queue operations using a min-max heap that is stored using the array representation of a complete binary tree. The complexity of the functions to return the min and max elements should be O(1) and that for the remaining DEPQ functions should be O(log n).

9.8   REFERENCES AND SELECTED READINGS

Height-biased leftist trees were invented by C. Crane. See, "Linear lists and priority queues as balanced binary trees", Technical report CS-72-259, Computer Science Dept., Stanford University, Palo Alto, CA, 1972. Weight-biased leftist trees were developed in "Weight biased leftist trees and modified skip lists," S. Cho and S. Sahni, *ACM Jr. on Experimental Algorithms*, Article 2, 1998.

The exercise on lazy deletion is from "Finding minimum spanning trees," by D. Cheriton and R. Tarjan, *SIAM Journal on Computing*, 5, 1976, pp. 724-742.

B-heaps and F-heaps were invented by M. Fredman and R. Tarjan. Their work is reported in the paper "Fibonacci heaps and their uses in improved network optimization algorithms," *JACM*, 34:3, 1987, pp. 596-615. This paper also describes several variants of the basic F-heap as discussed here, as well as the application of F-heaps to the assignment problem and to the problem of finding a minimum-cost spanning tree. Their result is that using F-heaps, minimum-cost spanning trees can be found in O($e\beta(e,n)$) time, where $\beta(e,n) \le \log^* n$ when $e \ge n$. $\log^* n = \min\{i \mid \log^{(i)} n \le 1\}$, $\log^{(0)} n = n$, and $\log^{(i)} n =$

$\log(\log^{(i-1)} n)$. The complexity of finding minimum-cost spanning trees has been further reduced to $O(e \log \beta(e,n))$. The reference for this is "Efficient algorithms for finding minimum spanning trees in undirected and directed graphs," by H. Gabow, Z. Galil, T. Spencer, and R. Tarjan, *Combinatorica*, 6:2, 1986, pp. 109-122.

Pairing heaps were developed in the paper "The pairing heap: A new form of self-adjusting heap", by M. Fredman, R. Sedgewick, R. Sleator, and R. Tarjan, *Algorithmica*, 1, 1986, pp. 111-129. This paper together with "New upper bounds for pairing heaps," by J. Iacono, *Scandinavian Workshop on Algorithm Theory*, LNCS 1851, 2000, pp. 35-42 establishes the amortized complexity of the pairing heap operations. The paper "On the efficiency of pairing heaps and related data structures," by M. Fredman, *Jr. of the ACM*, 46, 1999, pp. 473-501 provides an information theoretic proof that $\Omega(\log \log n)$ is a lower bound on the amortized complexity of the decrease key operation for pairing heaps.

Experimental studies conducted by Stasko and Vitter reported in their paper "Pairing heaps: Experiments and analysis," *Communications of the ACM*, 30, 3, 1987, 234-249 establish the superiority of two pass pairing heaps over multipass pairing heaps. This paper also proposes a variant of pairing heaps (called *auxiliary two pass pairing heaps*) that performs better than two pass pairing heaps. Moret and Shapiro establish the superiority of pairing heaps over Fibonacci heaps, when implementing Prim's minimum spanning tree algorithm, in their paper "An empirical analysis of algorithms for for constructing a minimum cost spanning tree," *Second Workshop on Algorithms and Data Structures*, 1991, pp. 400-411.

A large number of data structures, inspired by the fundamental heap structure of Section 5.6, have been developed for the representation of a DEPQ. The symmetric min-max heap was developed in "Symmetric min-max heap: A simpler data structure for double-ended priority queue," by A. Arvind and C. Pandu Rangan, *Information Processing Letters*, 69, 1999, 197-199.

The twin heaps of Williams, the min-max pair heapsof Olariu et al., the interval heaps of Ding and Weiss and van Leeuwen et al., and the diamond deques of Chang and Du are virtually identical data structures. The relevant papers are: "Diamond deque: A simple data structure for priority deques," by S. Chang and M. Du, *Information Processing Letters*, 46, 231-237, 1993; "On the Complexity of Building an Interval Heap," by Y. Ding and M. Weiss, *Information Processing Letters*, 50, 143-144, 1994; "Interval heaps," by J. van Leeuwen and D. Wood, *The Computer Journal*, 36, 3, 209-216, 1993; "A mergeable double-ended priority queue," by S. Olariu, C. Overstreet, and Z. Wen, *The Computer Journal*, 34, 5, 423-427, 1991; and "Algorithm 232," by J. Williams, *Communications of the ACM*, 7, 347-348, 1964.

The min-max heap and deap are additional heap-inspired stuctures for DEPQs. These data structures were developed in "Min-max heaps and generalized priority queues," by M. Atkinson, J. Sack, N. Santoro, and T. Strothotte, *Communications of the ACM*, 29:10, 1986, pp. 996-1000 and "The deap: A double-ended heap to implement double-ended priority queues," by S. Carlsson, *Information Processing Letters*, 26,

1987, pp. 33-36, respectively.

Data structures for meldable DEPQs are developed in "The relaxed min-max heap: A mergeable double-ended priority queue," by Y. Ding and M. Weiss, *Acta Informatica*, 30, 215-231, 1993; "Fast meldable priority queues," by G. Brodal, *Workshop on Algorithms and Data Structures*, 1995 and "Mergeable double ended priority queue," by S. Cho and S. Sahni, *International Journal on Foundation of Computer Sciences*, 10, 1, 1999, 1-18.

General techniques to arrive at a data structure for a DEPQ from one for a single-ended priority queue are developed in "Correspondence based data structures for double ended priority queues," by K. Chong and S. Sahni, *ACM Jr. on Experimental Algorithmics*, Volume 5, 2000, Article 2.

For more on priority queues, see Chapters 5 through 8 of "Handbook of data structures and applications," edited by D. Mehta and S. Sahni, Chapman & Hall/CRC, Boca Raton, 2005.

CHAPTER 10

Efficient Binary Search Trees

10.1 OPTIMAL BINARY SEARCH TREES

Binary search trees were introduced in Chapter 5. In this section, we consider the construction of binary search trees for a static set of elements. That is, we make no additions to or deletions from the set. Only searches are performed.

A sorted list can be searched using a binary search. For this search, we can construct a binary search tree with the property that searching this tree using the function *iterSearch* (Program 5.17) is equivalent to performing a binary search on the sorted list. For instance, a binary search on the sorted element list (5, 10, 15) (*for convenience, all examples in this chapter show only an element's key rather than the complete element*) corresponds to using function *iterSearch* on the binary search tree of Figure 10.1. Although this tree is a full binary tree, it may not be the optimal binary search tree to use when the probabilities with which different elements are searched are different.

To find an optimal binary search tree for a given collection of elements, we must first decide on a cost measure for search trees. When searching for an element at level l,

481

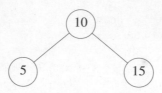

Figure 10.1: Binary search tree corresponding to a binary search on the list (5, 10, 15)

function *iterSearch* makes *l* iterations of the **while** loop. Since this **while** loop determines the cost of the search, it is reasonable to use the level number of a node as its cost.

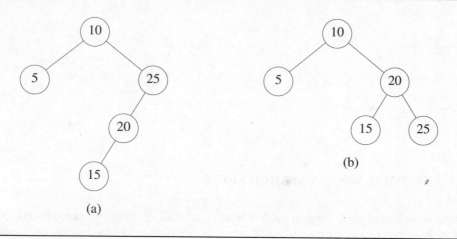

Figure 10.2: Two binary search trees

Example 10.1: Consider the two search trees of Figure 10.2. The second of these requires at most three comparisons to decide whether the element being sought is in the tree. The first binary tree may require four comparisons, since any search key k such that $10 < k < 20$ will test four nodes. Thus, as far as worst-case search time is concerned, the second binary tree is more desirable than the first. To search for a key in the first tree takes one comparison for the 10, two for each of 5 and 25, three for 20, and four for 15. Assuming that each key is searched for with equal probability, the average number of comparisons for a successful search is 2.4. For the second binary search tree this amount is 2.2. Thus, the second tree has a better average behavior, too.

Suppose that each of 5, 10, 15, 20 and 25 is searched for with probablility 0.3, 0.3, 0.05, 0.05 and 0.3, respectively. The average number of comparisons for a successful search in the trees of Figure 10.2 (a) and (b) is 1.85 and 2.05, respectively. Now, the first tree has better average behavior than the second tree! □

In evaluating binary search trees, it is useful to add a special "square" node at every null link. Doing this to the trees of Figure 10.2 yields the trees of Figure 10.3. Remember that every binary tree with n nodes has $n + 1$ null links and therefore will have $n + 1$ square nodes. We shall call these nodes *external* nodes because they are not part of the original tree. The remaining nodes will be called *internal* nodes. Each time a binary search tree is examined for an identifier that is not in the tree, the search terminates at an external node. Since all such searches are unsuccessful searches, external nodes will also be referred to as *failure nodes*. A binary tree with external nodes added is an *extended binary tree*. The concept of an extended binary tree as just defined is the same as that defined in connection with leftist trees in Chapter 9. Figure 10.3 shows the extended binary trees corresponding to the search trees of Figure 10.2.

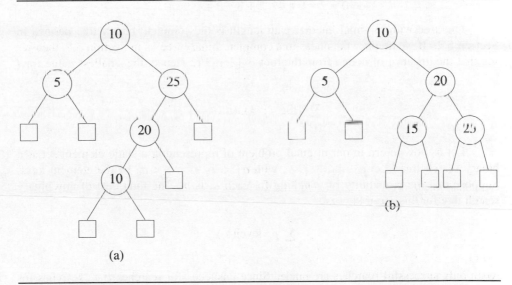

(a)

(b)

Figure 10.3: Extended binary trees corresponding to search trees of Figure 10.2

We define the *external path length* of a binary tree to be the sum over all external nodes of the lengths of the paths from the root to those nodes. Analogously, the *internal path length* is the sum over all internal nodes of the lengths of the paths from the root to those nodes. The internal path length, I, for the tree of Figure 10.3(a) is

$$I = 0 + 1 + 1 + 2 + 3 = 7$$

Its external path length, E, is

$$E = 2 + 2 + 4 + 4 + 3 + 2 = 17$$

Exercise 1 of this section shows that the internal and external path lengths of a binary tree with n internal nodes are related by the formula $E = I + 2n$. Hence, binary trees with the maximum E also have maximum I. Over all binary trees with n internal nodes, what are the maximum and minimum possible values for I? The worst case, clearly, is when the tree is skewed (i.e., when the tree has a depth of n). '.. this case,

$$I = \sum_{i=0}^{n-1} i = n(n-1)/2$$

To obtain trees with minimal I, we must have as many internal nodes as close to the root as possible. We can have at most 2 nodes at distance 1, 4 at distance 2, and in general, the smallest value for I is

$$0 + 2 * 1 + 4 * 2 + 8 * 3 + \cdots +$$

One tree with minimal internal path length is the complete binary tree defined in Section 5.2. If we number the nodes in a complete binary tree as in Section 5.2, then we see that the distance of node i from the root is $\lfloor \log_2 i \rfloor$. Hence, the smallest value for I is

$$\sum_{1 \le i \le n} \lfloor \log_2 i \rfloor = O(n \log_2 n)$$

Let us now return to our original problem of representing a static element set as a binary search tree. Let $a_1, a_2, \cdots, a_n$ with $a_1 < a_2 < \cdots < a_n$ be the element keys. Suppose that the probability of searching for each a_i is p_i. The total cost of any binary search tree for this set of keys is

$$\sum_{1 \le i \le n} p_i \cdot \text{level}(a_i)$$

when only successful searches are made. Since unsuccessful searches (i.e., searches for keys not in the table) will also be made, we should include the cost of these searches in our cost measure, too. Unsuccessful searches terminate with algorithm *iterSearch* (Program 5.17) returning a 0 pointer. Every node with an empty subtree defines a point at which such a termination can take place. Let us replace every empty subtree by a failure node. The keys not in the binary search tree may be partitioned into $n + 1$ classes E_i, $0 \le i \le n$. E_0 contains all keys X such that $X < a_1$. E_i contains all keys X such that

$a_i < X < a_{i+1}$, $1 \leq i < n$, and E_n contains all keys X, $X > a_n$. It is easy to see that for all keys in a particular class E_i, the search terminates at the same failure node, and it terminates at different failure nodes for keys in different classes. The failure nodes may be numbered 0 to n, with i being the failure node for class E_i, $0 \leq i \leq n$. If q_i is the probability that the key being sought is in E_i, then the cost of the failure nodes is

$$\sum_{0 \leq i \leq n} q_i \cdot (\text{level(failure node } i) - 1)$$

Therefore, the total cost of a binary search tree is

$$\sum_{1 \leq i \leq n} p_i \cdot \text{level}(a_i) + \sum_{0 \leq i \leq n} q_i \cdot (\text{level (failure node } i) - 1) \qquad (10.1)$$

An *optimal binary search tree* for $a_1, \cdots, a_n$ is one that minimizes Eq. (10.1) over all possible binary search trees for this set of keys. Note that since all searches must terminate either successfully or unsuccessfully, we have

$$\sum_{1 \leq i \leq n} p_i + \sum_{0 \leq i \leq n} q_i = 1$$

Example 10.2: Figure 10.4 shows the possible binary search trees for the key set $(a_1,a_2,a_3) = (5, 10, 15)$. With equal probabilities, $p_i = q_j = 1/7$ for all i and j, we have

cost (tree a) = 15/7; cost (tree b) = 13/7
cost (tree c) = 15/7; cost (tree d) = 15/7
cost (tree e) = 15/7

As expected, tree b is optimal. With $p_1 = 0.5, p_2 = 0.1, p_3 = 0.05, q_0 = 0.15, q_1 = 0.1,$ $q_2 = 0.05$, and $q_3 = 0.05$ we have

cost (tree a) = 2.65; cost (tree b) = 1.9
cost (tree c) = 1.5; cost (tree d) = 2.05
cost (tree e) = 1.6

Tree c is optimal with this assignment of p's and q's. $\square$

How does one determine the optimal binary search tree? We could proceed as in Example 10.2 and explicitly generate all possible binary search trees, then compute the cost of each tree, and determine the tree with minimum cost. Since the cost of an n-node binary search tree can be determined in $O(n)$ time, the complexity of the optimal binary search tree algorithm is $O(n\, N(n))$, where $N(n)$ is the number of distinct binary search trees with n keys. From Section 5.11 we know that $N(n) = O(4^n/n^{3/2})$. Hence, this brute-force algorithm is impractical for large n. We can find a fairly efficient algorithm by making some observations about the properties of optimal binary search trees.

Let $a_1 < a_2 < \cdots < a_n$ be the n keys to be represented in a binary search tree. Let

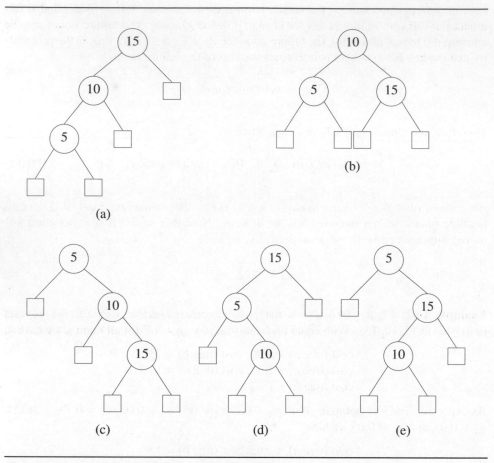

Figure 10.4: Binary search trees with three elements

T_{ij} denote an optimal binary search tree for $a_{i+1}, \cdots, a_j, i < j$. By convention T_{ii} is an empty tree for $0 \leq i \leq n$, and T_{ij} is not defined for $i > j$. Let c_{ij} be the cost of the search tree T_{ij}. By definition c_{ii} will be 0. Let r_{ij} be the root of T_{ij}, and let

$$w_{ij} = q_i + \sum_{k=i+1}^{j} (q_k + p_k)$$

be the weight of T_{ij}. By definition $r_{ii} = 0$, and $w_{ii} = q_i$, $0 \leq i \leq n$. Therefore, T_{0n} is an optimal binary search tree for $a_1, \cdots, a_n$. Its cost is c_{0n}, its weight is w_{0n}, and its root is r_{0n}.

If T_{ij} is an optimal binary search tree for $a_{i+1}, \cdots, a_j$, and $r_{ij} = k$, then k satisfies the inequality $i < k \leq j$. T_{ij} has two subtrees L and R. L is the left subtree and contains the keys $a_{i+1}, \cdots, a_{k-1}$, and R is the right subtree and contains the keys $a_{k+1}, \cdots, a_j$ (Figure 10.5). The cost c_{ij} of T_{ij} is

$$c_{ij} = p_k + \text{cost}(L) + \text{cost}(R) + \text{weight}(L) + \text{weight}(R) \qquad (10.2)$$

where weight (L) = weight $(T_{i,k-1})$ = $w_{i,k-1}$, and weight (R) = weight (T_{kj}) = w_{kj}.

Figure 10.5: An optimal binary search tree T_{ij}

From Eq. (10.2) it is clear that if c_{ij} is to be minimal, then $\text{cost}(L) = c_{i,k-1}$ and $\text{cost}(R) = c_{kj}$, as otherwise we could replace either L or R by a subtree with a lower cost, thus getting a binary search tree for $a_{i+1}, \cdots, a_j$ with a lower cost than c_{ij}. This violates the assumption that T_{ij} is optimal. Hence, Eq. (10.2) becomes

$$c_{ij} = p_k + c_{i,k-1} + c_{kj} + w_{i,k-1} + w_{kj}$$
$$= w_{ij} + c_{i,k-1} + c_{kj} \qquad (10.3)$$

Since T_{ij} is optimal, it follows from Eq. (10.3) that $r_{ij} = k$ is such that

$$w_{ij} + c_{i,k-1} + c_{kj} = \min_{i < l \leq j}\{w_{ij} + c_{i,l-1} + c_{lj}\}$$

or

$$c_{i,k-1} + c_{kj} = \min_{i < l \leq j}\{c_{i,l-1} + c_{lj}\} \qquad (10.4)$$

Equation (10.4) gives us a means of obtaining T_{0n} and c_{0n}, starting from the knowledge that $T_{ii} = \phi$ and $c_{ii} = 0$.

Example 10.3: Let $n = 4$ and $(a_1, a_2, a_3, a_4) = (10, 15, 20, 25)$. Let $(p_1, p_2, p_3, p_4) = (3, 3, 1, 1)$ and $(q_0, q_1, q_2, q_3, q_4) = (2, 3, 1, 1, 1)$. The p's and q's have been multiplied by 16 for convenience. Initially, $w_{ii} = q_i$, $c_{ii} = 0$, and $r_{ii} = 0$, $0 \leq i \leq 4$. Using Eqs. (10.3) and (10.4), we get

$$w_{01} = p_1 + w_{00} + w_{11} = p_1 + q_1 + w_{00} = 8$$

$$c_{01} = w_{01} + \min\{c_{00} + c_{11}\} = 8$$

$$r_{01} = 1$$

$$w_{12} = p_2 + w_{11} + w_{22} = p_2 + q_2 + w_{11} = 7$$

$$c_{12} = w_{12} + \min\{c_{11} + c_{22}\} = 7$$

$$r_{12} = 2$$

$$w_{23} = p_3 + w_{22} + w_{33} = p_3 + q_3 + w_{22} = 3$$

$$c_{23} = w_{23} + \min\{c_{22} + c_{33}\} = 3$$

$$r_{23} = 3$$

$$w_{34} = p_4 + w_{33} + w_{44} = p_4 + q_4 + w_{33} = 3$$

$$c_{34} = w_{34} + \min\{c_{33} + c_{44}\} = 3$$

$$r_{34} = 4$$

Knowing $w_{i,i+1}$ and $c_{i,i+1}, 0 \le i < 4$, we can use Eqs. (10.3) and (10.4) again to compute $w_{i,i+2}, c_{i,i+2}, r_{i,i+2}, 0 \le i < 3$. This process may be repeated until w_{04}, c_{04}, and r_{04} are obtained. The table of Figure 10.6 shows the results of this computation. From the table, we see that $c_{04} = 32$ is the minimal cost of a binary search tree for a_1 to a_4. The root of tree T_{04} is a_2. Hence, the left subtree is T_{01} and the right subtree T_{24}. T_{01} has root a_1 and subtrees T_{00} and T_{11}. T_{24} has root a_3; its left subtree is therefore T_{22} and right subtree T_{34}. Thus, with the data in the table it is possible to reconstruct T_{04}. Figure 10.7 shows T_{04}. □

Example 10.3 illustrates how Eq. (10.4) may be used to determine the c's and r's, as well as how to reconstruct T_{0n} knowing the r's. Let us examine the complexity of this function to evaluate the c's and r's. The evaluation function described in Example 10.3 requires us to compute c_{ij} for $(j - i) = 1, 2, \cdots, n$ in that order. When $j - i = m$, there are $n - m + 1$ c_{ij}'s to compute. The computation of each of these c_{ij}'s requires us to find the minimum of m quantities (see Eq. (10.4)). Hence, each such c_{ij} can be computed in time $O(m)$. The total time for all c_{ij}'s with $j - i = m$ is therefore $O(nm - m^2)$. The total time to evaluate all the c_{ij}'s and r_{ij}'s is

$$\sum_{1 \le m \le n} (nm - m^2) = O(n^3)$$

Actually we can do better than this using a result due to D. E. Knuth that states that the optimal l in Eq. (10.4) may be found by limiting the search to the range $r_{i,j-1} \le l \le r_{i+1,j}$. In this case, the computing time becomes $O(n^2)$ (see Exercise 3). Function *obst* (Program 10.1) uses this result to obtain in $O(n^2)$ time the values of w_{ij}, r_{ij}, and $c_{ij}, 0 \le i \le j \le n$. The actual tree T_{0n} may be constructed from the values of

	0	1	2	3	4
0	$w_{00} = 2$ $c_{00} = 0$ $r_{00} = 0$	$w_{11} = 3$ $c_{11} = 0$ $r_{11} = 0$	$w_{22} = 1$ $c_{22} = 0$ $r_{22} = 0$	$w_{33} = 1$ $c_{33} = 0$ $r_{33} = 0$	$w_{44} = 1$ $c_{44} = 0$ $r_{44} = 0$
1	$w_{01} = 8$ $c_{01} = 8$ $r_{01} = 1$	$w_{12} = 7$ $c_{12} = 7$ $r_{12} = 2$	$w_{23} = 3$ $c_{23} = 3$ $r_{23} = 3$	$w_{34} = 3$ $c_{34} = 3$ $r_{34} = 4$	
2	$w_{02} = 12$ $c_{02} = 19$ $r_{02} = 1$	$w_{13} = 9$ $c_{13} = 12$ $r_{13} = 2$	$w_{24} = 5$ $c_{24} = 8$ $r_{24} = 3$		
3	$w_{03} = 14$ $c_{03} = 25$ $r_{03} = 2$	$w_{14} = 11$ $c_{14} = 19$ $r_{14} = 2$			
4	$w_{04} = 16$ $c_{04} = 32$ $r_{04} = 2$				

Figure 10.6: Computation of c_{04} and r_{01}. The computation is carried out by row from row 0 to row 4

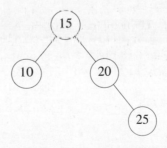

Figure 10.7: Optimal binary search tree for Example 10.3

r_{ij} in $O(n)$ time. The algorithm for this is left as an exercise.

Function *obst* (Program 10.1) computes the cost $c[i][j] = c_{ij}$ of optimal binary search trees T_{ij} for keys $a_{i+1}, \cdots, a_j$. It also computes $r[i][j] = r_{ij}$, the root of T_{ij}. $w[i][j] = w_{ij}$ is the weight of T_{ij}. The two-dimensional arrays c, r and w are global arrays of type **int**. The inputs to this function are the success and failure probability arrays, $p[\ ]$ and $q[\ ]$ and the number of keys n. The array elements $p[0]$ and $a[0]$ are not used.

```
void obst(double *p, double *q, int n)
{
    int i, j, k, m;
    for (i = 0; i < n; i++) {/* initialize */
        /* 0-node trees */
        w[i][i] = q[i]; r[i][i] = c[i][i] = 0;
        /* one-node trees */
        w[i][i+1] = q[i] + q[i+1] + p[i+1];
        r[i][i+1] = i + 1;
        c[i][i+1] = w[i][i+1];
    }
    w[n][n] = q[n]; r[n][n] = c[n][n] = 0;

    /* find optimal trees with m > 1 nodes */
    for (m = 2; m <= n; m++)
        for (i = 0; i <= n- m; i++)
        {
            j = i + m;
            w[i][j] = w[i][j-1] + p[j] + q[j];
            k = KnuthMin(i,j);
            /* KnuthMin returns a value k in the range
                [r[i][j-1], r[i+1][j]] minimizing
                c[i][k-1]+c[k][j] */
            c[i][j] = w[i][j] + c[i][k-1] + c[k][j];
                                /* Eq. (10.3) */
            r[i][j] = k;
        }
}
```

Program 10.1: Finding an optimal binary search tree

EXERCISES

1. (a) Prove by induction that if T is a binary tree with n internal nodes, I its internal path length, and E its external path length, then $E = I + 2n, n \geq 0$.

   (b) Using the result of (a), show that the average number of comparisons s in a successful search is related to the average number of comparisons, u, in an unsuccessful search by the formula

$$s = (1 + 1/n)u - 1, n \geq 1$$

2. Use function *obst* (Program 10.1), to compute w_{ij}, r_{ij}, and c_{ij}, $0 \leq i < j \leq 4$, for the key set $(a_1, a_2, a_3, a_4) = (5, 10, 15, 20)$, with $p_1 = 1/20$, $p_2 = 1/5$, $p_3 = 1/10$, $p_4 = 1/20$, $q_0 = 1/5$, $q_1 = 1/10$, $q_2 = 1/5$, $q_3 = 1/20$, and $q_4 = 1/20$. Using the r_{ij}'s, construct the optimal binary search tree.

3. (a) Complete function *obst* by providing the code for function *KnuthMin*.

   (b) Show that the computing time complexity of *obst* is $O(n^2)$.

   (c) Write a C function to construct the optimal binary search tree T_{0n} given the roots r_{ij}, $0 \leq i < j \leq n$. Show that this can be done in time $O(n)$.

4. Since, often, only the approximate values of the p's and q's are known, it is perhaps just as meaningful to find a binary search tree that is nearly optimal (i.e., its cost, Eq. (10.1), is almost minimal for the given p's and q's). This exercise explores an $O(n \log n)$ algorithm that results in nearly optimal binary search trees. The search tree heuristic we shall study is

   Choose the root a_k such that $|w_{0,k-1} - w_{k,n}|$ is as small as possible. Repeat this process to find the left and right subtrees of a_k.

   (a) Using this heuristic obtain the resulting binary search tree for the data of Exercise 2. What is its cost?

   (b) Write a C function implementing the above heuristic. The time complexity of your function should be $O(n \log n)$.

   An analysis of the performance of this heuristic may be found in the paper by Mehlhorn (see the References and Selected Readings section).

10.2 AVL TREES

Dynamic collections of elements may also be maintained as binary search trees. In Chapter 5, we saw how insertions and deletions can be performed on binary search trees. Figure 10.8 shows the binary search tree obtained by entering the months JANUARY to DECEMBER in that order into an initially empty binary search tree by using function *insert* (Program 5.21).

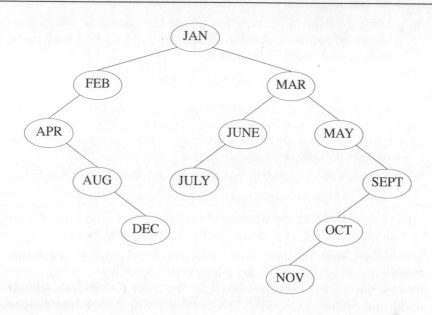

Figure 10.8: Binary search tree obtained for the months of the year

The maximum number of comparisons needed to search for any key in the tree of Figure 10.8 is six for NOVEMBER. The average number of comparisons is (1 for JANUARY + 2 each for FEBRUARY and MARCH + 3 each for APRIL, JUNE and MAY + $\cdots$ + 6 for NOVEMBER)/12 = 42/12 = 3.5. If the months are entered in the order JULY, FEBRUARY, MAY, AUGUST, DECEMBER, MARCH, OCTOBER, APRIL, JANUARY, JUNE, SEPTEMBER, NOVEMBER, then the tree of Figure 10.9 is obtained.

The tree of Figure 10.9 is well balanced and does not have any paths to a leaf node that are much longer than others. This is not true of the tree of Figure 10.8, which has six nodes on the path from the root to NOVEMBER and only two nodes on the path to APRIL. Moreover, during the construction of the tree of Figure 10.9, all intermediate trees obtained are also well balanced. The maximum number of key comparisons needed to find any key is now 4, and the average is $37/12 \approx 3.1$. If the months are entered in lexicographic order, instead, the tree degenerates to a chain as in Figure 10.10. The maximum search time is now 12 key comparisons, and the average is 6.5. Thus, in the worst case, searching a binary search tree corresponds to sequential searching in a sorted linear list. When the keys are entered in a random order, the tree tends to be balanced as in

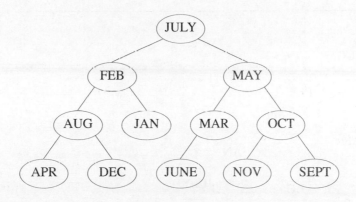

Figure 10.9: A balanced tree for the months of the year

Figure 10.9. If all permutations are equally probable, then the average search and insertion time is O(log n) for an n-node binary search tree.

From our earlier study of binary trees, we know that both the average and maximum search time will be minimized if the binary search tree is maintained as a complete
binary tree at all times. However, since we are dealing with a dynamic situation, it is
difficult to achieve this ideal without making the time required to insert a key very high.
This is so because in some cases it would be necessary to restructure the whole tree to
accommodate the new entry and at the same time have a complete binary search tree. It
is, however, possible to keep the tree balanced to ensure both an average and worst case
search time of O(log n) for a tree with n nodes. In this section, we study one method of
growing balanced binary trees. These balanced trees will have satisfactory search, insertion and deletion time properties. Other ways to maintain balanced search trees are studied in later sections.

In 1962, Adelson-Velskii and Landis introduced a binary tree structure that is balanced with respect to the heights of subtrees. As a result of the balanced nature of this
type of tree, dynamic retrievals can be performed in O(log n) time if the tree has n nodes
in it. At the same time, a new key can be entered or deleted from such a tree in time
O(log n). The resulting tree remains height-balanced. This tree structure is called an
AVL tree. As with binary trees, it is natural to define AVL trees recursively.

Definition: An empty tree is height-balanced. If T is a nonempty binary tree with T_L
and T_R as its left and right subtrees respectively, then T is *height-balanced* iff (1) T_L and
T_R are height-balanced and (2) $| h_L - h_R | \leq 1$ where h_L and h_R are the heights of T_L and
T_R, respectively. □

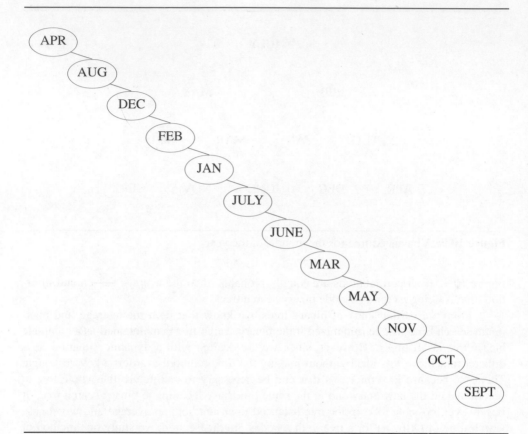

Figure 10.10: Degenerate binary search tree

The definition of a height-balanced binary tree requires that every subtree also be height-balanced. The binary tree of Figure 10.8 is not height-balanced, since the height of the left subtree of the tree with root APRIL is 0 and that of the right subtree is 2. The tree of Figure 10.9 is height-balanced while that of Figure 10.10 is not. To illustrate the processes involved in maintaining a height-balanced binary search tree, let us try to construct such a tree for the months of the year. This time let us assume that the insertions are made in the following order: MARCH, MAY, NOVEMBER, AUGUST, APRIL, JANUARY, DECEMBER, JULY, FEBRUARY, JUNE, OCTOBER, SEPTEMBER. Figure 10.11 shows the tree as it grows and the restructuring involved in keeping the tree balanced. The numbers above each node represent the difference in heights between the left and right subtrees of that node. This number is referred to as the balance factor of the node.

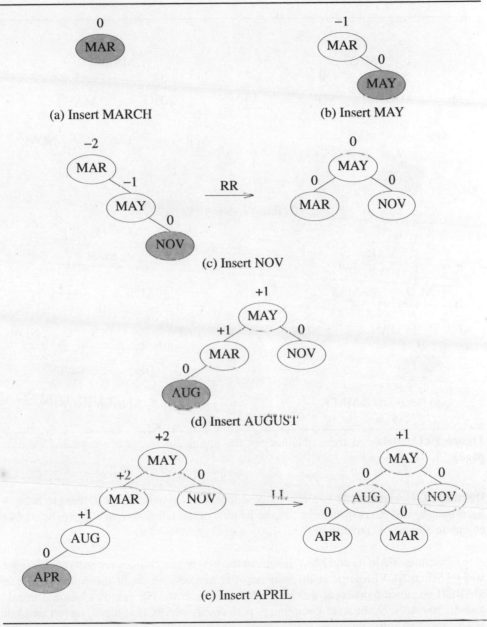

Figure 10.11: Balanced trees obtained for the months of the year (continued on next page)

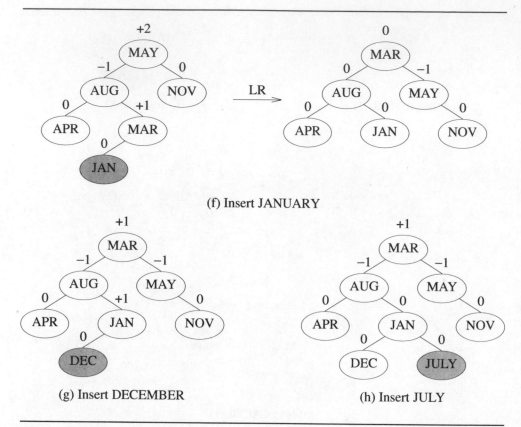

(f) Insert JANUARY

(g) Insert DECEMBER

(h) Insert JULY

Figure 10.11: Balanced trees obtained for the months of the year (continued on next page)

Definition: The *balance factor*, $BF(T)$, of a node T in a binary tree is defined to be $h_L - h_R$, where h_L and h_R, respectively, are the heights of the left and right subtrees of T. For any node T in an AVL tree, $BF(T) = -1, 0,$ or 1. □

Inserting MARCH and MAY results in the binary search trees (a) and (b) of Figure 10.11. When NOVEMBER is inserted into the tree, the height of the right subtree of MARCH becomes 2, whereas that of the left subtree is 0. The tree has become unbalanced. To rebalance the tree, a rotation is performed. MARCH is made the left child of MAY, and MAY becomes the root (Figure 10.11(c)). The introduction of AUGUST leaves the tree balanced (Figure 10.11(d)).

The next insertion, APRIL, causes the tree to become unbalanced again. To

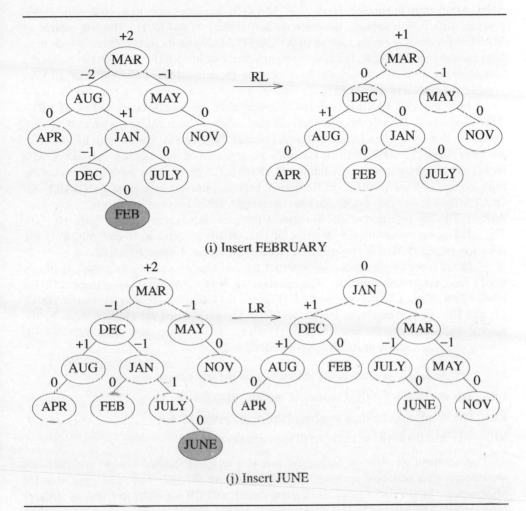

(i) Insert FEBRUARY

(j) Insert JUNE

Figure 10.11: Balanced trees obtained for the months of the year (continued on next page)

rebalance the tree, another rotation is performed. This time, it is a clockwise rotation. MARCH is made the right child of AUGUST, and AUGUST becomes the root of the subtree (Figure 10.11(e)). Note that both of the previous rotations were carried out with respect to the closest parent of the new node that had a balance factor of ±2. The insertion of JANUARY results in an unbalanced tree. This time, however, the rotation involved is somewhat more complex than in the earlier situations. The common point, however, is that the rotation is still carried out with respect to the nearest parent of JANUARY with a balance factor ±2. MARCH becomes the new root. AUGUST, together with its left subtree, becomes the left subtree of MARCH. The left subtree of MARCH becomes the right subtree of AUGUST. MAY and its right subtree, which have keys greater than MARCH, become the right subtree of MARCH. (If MARCH had had a nonempty right subtree, this could have become the left subtree of MAY, since all keys would have been less than MAY.)

Inserting DECEMBER and JULY necessitates no rebalancing. When FEBRU-ARY is inserted, the tree becomes unbalanced again. The rebalancing process is very similar to that used when JANUARY was inserted. The nearest parent with balance fac-tor ±2 is AUGUST. DECEMBER becomes the new root of that subtree. AUGUST, with its left subtree, becomes the left subtree. JANUARY, with its right subtree, becomes the right subtree of DECEMBER; FEBRUARY becomes the left subtree of JANUARY. (If DECEMBER had had a left subtree, it would have become the right subtree of AUGUST.) The insertion of JUNE requires the same rebalancing as in Figure 10.11(f). The rebalancing following the insertion of OCTOBER is identical to that following the insertion of NOVEMBER. Inserting SEPTEMBER leaves the tree balanced.

In the preceding example we saw that the addition of a node to a balanced binary search tree could unbalance it. The rebalancing was carried out using four different kinds of rotations: LL, RR, LR, and RL (Figure 10.11 (e), (c), (f), and (i), respectively). LL and RR are symmetric, as are LR and RL. These rotations are characterized by the nearest ancestor, A, of the inserted node, Y, whose balance factor becomes ±2. The fol-lowing characterization of rotation types is obtained:

LL: new node Y is inserted in the left subtree of the left subtree of A

LR: Y is inserted in the right subtree of the left subtree of A

RR: Y is inserted in the right subtree of the right subtree of A

RL: Y is inserted in the left subtree of the right subtree of A

A moment's reflection will show that if a height-balanced binary tree becomes unbalanced as a result of an insertion, then these are the only four cases possible for rebalancing. Figures 10.12 and 10.13 show the LL and LR rotations in terms of abstract binary trees. The RR and RL rotations are symmetric. The root node in each of the trees of the figures represents the nearest ancestor whose balance factor has become ±2 as a result of the insertion. In the example of Figure 10.11 and in the rotations of Figures 10.12 and 10.13, notice that the height of the subtree involved in the rotation is the same after rebalancing as it was before the insertion. This means that once the rebalancing has been carried out on the subtree in question, examining the remaining tree is unneces-sary. The only nodes whose balance factors can change are those in the subtree that is rotated.

The transformations done to remedy LL and RR imbalances are often called *single rotations*, while those done for LR and RL imbalances are called *double rotations*. The

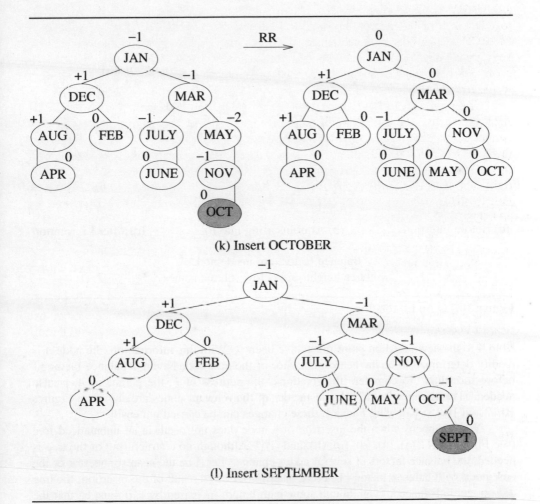

(k) Insert OCTOBER

(l) Insert SEPTEMBER

Figure 10.11: Balanced trees obtained for the months of the year

transformation for an LR imbalance can be viewed as an RR rotation followed by an LL rotation, while that for an RL imbalance can be viewed as an LL rotation followed by an RR rotation.

To carry out the rotations of Figures 10.12 and 10.13, it is necessary to locate the node A around which the rotation is to be performed. As remarked earlier, this is the nearest ancestor of the newly inserted node whose balance factor becomes ±2. For a node's balance factor to become ±2, its balance factor must have been ±1 before the insertion. Therefore, before the insertion, the balance factors of all nodes on the path

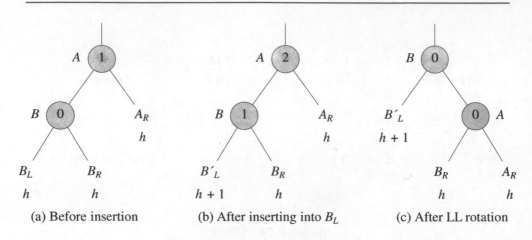

(a) Before insertion   (b) After inserting into B_L (c) After LL rotation

Balance factors are inside nodes
Subtree heights are below subtree names

Figure 10.12: An LL rotation

from A to the new insertion point must have been 0. With this information, the node A is readily determined to be the nearest ancestor of the new node having a balance factor ± 1 before insertion. To complete the rotations, the address of F, the parent of A, is also needed. The changes in the balance factors of the relevant nodes are shown in Figures 10.12 and 10.13. Knowing F and A, these changes can be carried out easily.

What happens when the insertion of a node does not result in an unbalanced tree (see Figure 10.11 (a), (b), (d), (g), (h), and (l))? Although no restructuring of the tree is needed, the balance factors of several nodes change. Let A be the nearest ancestor of the new node with balance factor ± 1 before insertion. If, as a result of the insertion, the tree did not get unbalanced, even though some path length increased by 1, it must be that the new balance factor of A is 0. If there is no ancestor A with a balance factor ± 1 (as in Figure 10.11 (a), (b), (d), (g), and (l)), let A be the root. The balance factors of nodes from A to the parent of the new node will change to ± 1 (see Figure 10.11 (h); $A =$ JANUARY). Note that in both cases, the procedure to determine A is the same as when rebalancing is needed. The remaining details of the insertion-rebalancing process are spelled out in function *avlInsert* (Program 10.2). The function *leftRotation* (Program 10.3) gives the code for the *LL* and *LR* rotations. The code for the *RR* and *RL* rotations is symmetric and we leave it as an exercise. The type definitions in use are:

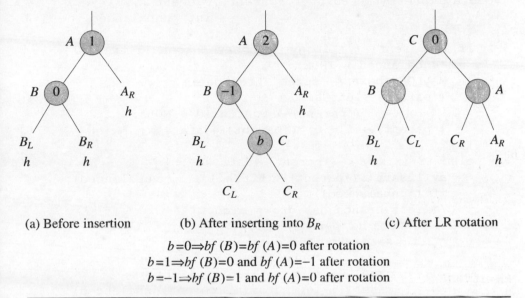

(a) Before insertion   (b) After inserting into B_R (c) After LR rotation

$$b=0 \Rightarrow bf(B)=bf(A)=0 \text{ after rotation}$$
$$b=1 \Rightarrow bf(B)=0 \text{ and } bf(A)=-1 \text{ after rotation}$$
$$b=-1 \Rightarrow bf(B)=1 \text{ and } bf(A)=0 \text{ after rotation}$$

Figure 10.13: An LR rotation

```
typedef struct {
        int key;
        } element;
typedef struct treeNode *treePointer;
        struct {
                treePointer leftChild;
                element     data;
                short int   bf;
                treePointer rightChild;
                } treeNode;
```

The pointer to the tree *root* is set to *NULL* before to the first call of *avlInsert*. We also set *unbalanced* to *FALSE* **before each call** to *avlInsert*. The function call is *avlInsert(&root, x, &unbalanced)*.

To really understand the insertion algorithm, you should apply it to the example of Figure 10.11. Once you are convinced that it keeps the tree balanced, then the next question is how much time does it take to make an insertion? An analysis of the algorithm reveals that if h is the height of the tree before insertion, then the time to insert a

```
void avlInsert(treePointer *parent, element x,
                               int *unbalanced)
{
    if (!*parent) {/* insert element into null tree */
        *unbalanced = TRUE;
        MALLOC(*parent, sizeof(treeNode));
        (*parent)→leftChild =
                    (*parent)→rightChild = NULL;
        (*parent)→bf = 0; (*parent)→data = x;
    }
    else if (x.key < (*parent)→data.key) {
        avlInsert(&(*parent)→leftChild, x, unbalanced);
        if (*unbalanced)
        /* left branch has grown higher */
            switch ((*parent)→bf) {
                case −1: (*parent)→bf = 0;
                         *unbalanced = FALSE; break;
                case  0: (*parent)→bf = 1; break;
                case  1: leftRotation(parent,unbalanced);
            }
    }
    else if (x.key > (*parent)→data.key) {
        avlInsert(&(*parent)→rightChild, x, unbalanced);
        if (*unbalanced)
            /* right branch has grown higher */
            switch((*parent)→bf) {
                case 1 : (*parent)→bf = 0;
                         *unbalanced = FALSE; break;
                case 0 : (*parent)→bf = −1; break;
                case −1: rightRotation(parent, unbalanced);
            }
    }
    else {
        *unbalanced = FALSE;
        printf("The key is already in the tree");
    }
}
```

Program 10.2: Insertion into an AVL tree

```
void leftRotation(treePointer *parent, int *unbalanced)
{
    treePointer grandChild, child;
    child = (*parent)→leftChild;
    if (child→bf == 1) {
        /* LL rotation */
        (*parent)→leftChild = child→rightChild;
        child→rightChild = *parent;
        (*parent)→bf = 0;
        (*parent) = child;
    }
    else {
        /* LR rotation */
        grandChild = child→rightChild;
        child→rightChild = grandChild→leftChild;
        grandChild→leftChild = child;
        (*parent)→leftChild = grandChild→rightChild;
        grandChild→rightChild = *parent;
        switch(grandChild→bf) {
            case 1: (*parent)→bf = -1;
                    child→bf = 0;
                    break;
            case 0: (*parent)→bf = child→bf = 0;
                    break;
            case -1: (*parent)→bf = 0;
                     child→bf = 1;
        }
        *parent = grandChild;
    }
    (*parent)→bf = 0;
    *unbalanced = FALSE;
}
```

Program 10.3: Left rotation function

new identifier is O(h). This is the same as for unbalanced binary search trees, although the overhead is significantly greater now. In the case of binary search trees, however, if there were n nodes in the tree, then h could be n (Figure 10.10) and the worst case insertion time would be O(n). In the case of AVL trees, since h is at most O(log n), the worst case insertion time is O(log n). To see this, let N_h be the minimum number of nodes in a height balanced tree of height h. In the worst case, the height of one of the subtrees is $h - 1$ and the height of the other is $h - 2$. Both these subtrees are also height balanced. Hence, $N_h = N_{h-1} + N_{h-2} + 1$ and $N_0 = 0$, $N_1 = 1$ and $N_2 = 2$. Notice the similarity between this recursive definition for N_h and the definition of the Fibonacci numbers $F_n = F_{n-1} + F_{n-2}$, $F_0 = 0$, and $F_1 = 1$. In fact, we can show (Exercise 2) that $N_h = F_{h+2} - 1$ for $h \geq 0$. From Fibonacci number theory we know that $F_h \approx \phi^h / \sqrt{5}$ where $\phi = (1 + \sqrt{5})/2$. Hence, $N_h \approx \phi^{n+2} / \sqrt{5} - 1$. This means that if there are n nodes in the tree, then its height, h, is at most $\log_\phi (\sqrt{5}(n + 1)) - 2$. Therefore, the worst case insertion time for a height balanced tree with n nodes is O($\log n$).

The exercises show that it is possible to find and delete an element with a specified key and to find and delete the element with the kth smallest key from a height-balanced tree in O($\log n$) time. Results of an empirical study of deletion in height-balanced trees may be found in the paper by Karlton et al. (see the References and Selected Readings section). Their study indicates that a random insertion requires no rebalancing, a rebalancing rotation of type LL or RR, and a rebalancing rotation of type LR and RL, with probabilities 0.5349, 0.2327, and 0.2324, respectively. Figure 10.14 compares the worst-case times of certain operations on sorted sequential lists, sorted linked lists, and AVL trees.

Operation	Sequential list	Linked list	AVL tree
Search for element with key k	O($\log n$)	O(n)	O($\log n$)
Search for jth item	O(1)	O(j)	O($\log n$)
Delete element with key k	O(n)	O(1)[1]	O($\log n$)
Delete jth element	O($n - j$)	O(j)	O($\log n$)
Insert	O(n)	O(1)[2]	O($\log n$)
Output in order	O(n)	O(n)	O(n)

1. Doubly linked list and position of k known
2. Position for insertion known

Figure 10.14: Comparison of various structures

EXERCISES

1. (a) Convince yourself that Figures 10.12 and 10.13 together with the cases for the symmetric rotations RR and RL takes care of all the possible situations that may arise when a height-balanced binary tree becomes unbalanced as a result of an insertion. Alternately, come up with an example that is not covered by any of the cases in this figure.

(b)   Draw the transformations for the rotation types RR and RL.

2. Show that the LR rotation of Figure 10.13 is equivalent to an RR rotation followed by an LL rotation and that an RL rotation is equivalent to an LL rotation followed by an RR rotation.

3. Prove by induction that the minimum number of nodes in an AVL tree of height h is $N_h = F_{h+2} - 1, h \geq 0$.

4. Complete *avlInsert* (Program 10.2) by filling in the code needed to rebalance the tree in case of a right imbalance.

5. Start with an empty AVL tree and perform the following sequence of insertions: DECEMBER, JANUARY, APRIL, MARCH, JULY, AUGUST, OCTOBER, FEBRUARY, NOVEMBER, MAY, JUNE. Use the strategy of *avlInsert* to perform each insert. Draw the AVL tree following each insertion and state the rotation type (if any) for each insert.

6. Assume that each node in an AVL tree has the data member *lsize*. For any node, a, $a \rightarrow lsize$ is the number of nodes in its left subtree plus one. Write a C function to locate the kth smallest key in the tree. Show that this can be done in $O(\log n)$ time if there are n nodes in the tree.

7. Rewrite the insertion function *avlInsert with the added assumption that each node has an lsize data member* as in Exercise 6. Show that the insertion time remains $O(\log n)$.

8. Write a C function to list the elements of an AVL tree in ascending order of key. Show that this can be done in $O(n)$ time if the tree has n nodes.

9. Write an algorithm to delete the element with key k from an AVL tree. The resulting tree should be restructured if necessary. Show that the time required for this is $O(\log n)$ when there are n nodes in the tree. [**Hint**: If k is not in a leaf, then replace k by the largest value in its left subtree or the smallest value in its right subtree. Continue until the deletion propagates to a leaf. Deletion from a leaf can be handled using the reverse of the transformations used for insertion.]

10. Do Exercise 9 for the case when each node has an *lsize* data member and the kth smallest key is to be deleted.

11. Complete Figure 10.14 by adding a column for hashing.

12. For a fixed k, $k \geq 1$, we define a height-balanced tree $HB(k)$ as below:

    Definition: An empty binary tree is an $HB(k)$ tree. If T is a nonempty binary tree with T_L and T_R as its left and right subtrees, then T is $HB(k)$ iff (a) T_L and T_R are $HB(k)$ and (b) $|h_L - h_R| \leq k$, where h_L and h_R are the heights of T_L and T_R, respectively. □

    (a)   Obtain the rebalancing transformations for $HB(2)$.

    (b)   Write an insertion algorithm for $HB(2)$ trees.

10.3 RED-BLACK TREES

10.3.1 Definition

A *red-black tree* is a binary search tree in which every node is colored either red or black. The remaining properties satisfied by a red-black tree are best stated in terms of the corresponding extended binary tree. Recall, from Section 9.2, that we obtain an extended binary tree from a regular binary tree by replacing every null pointer with an external node. The additional properties are

RB1. The root and all external nodes are colored black.

RB2. No root-to-external-node path has two consecutive red nodes.

RB3. All root-to-external-node paths have the same number of black nodes.

An equivalent definition arises from assigning colors to the pointers between a node and its children. The pointer from a parent to a black child is black and to a red child is red. Additionally,

RB1´. Pointers from an internal node to an external node are black.

RB2´. No root-to-external-node path has two consecutive red pointers.

RB3´. All root-to-external-node paths have the same number of black pointers.

Notice that if we know the pointer colors, we can deduce the node colors and vice versa. In the red-black tree of Figure 10.15, the external nodes are shaded squares, black nodes are shaded circles, red nodes are unshaded circles, black pointers are thick lines, and red pointers are thin lines. Notice that every path from the root to an external node has exactly two black pointers and three black nodes (including the root and the external node); no such path has two consecutive red nodes or pointers.

Let the *rank* of a node in a red-black tree be the number of black pointers (equivalently the number of black nodes minus 1) on any path from the node to any external node in its subtree. So the rank of an external node is 0. The rank of the root of Figure 10.15 is 2, that of its left child is 2, and of its right child is 1.

Lemma 10.1: Let the length of a root-to-external-node path be the number of pointers on the path. If P and Q are two root-to-external-node paths in a red-black tree, then $length(P) \leq 2length(Q)$.

Proof: Consider any red-black tree. Suppose that the rank of the root is r. From RB1´ the last pointer on each root-to-external-node path is black. From RB2´ no such path has two consecutive red pointers. So each red pointer is followed by a black pointer. As a

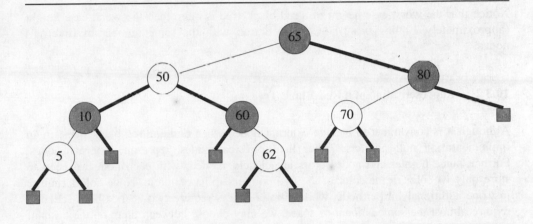

Figure 10.15: A red-black tree

result, each root-to-external-node path has between r and $2r$ pointers, so $length(P) \leq 2length(Q)$. To see that the upper bound is possible, consider the red-black tree of Figure 10.15. The path from the root to the left child of 5 has length 4, while that to the right child of 80 has length 2. □

Lemma 10.2: Let h be the height of a red-black tree (excluding the external nodes), let n be the number of internal nodes in the tree, and let r be the rank of the root.

(a) $h \leq 2r$

(b) $n \geq 2^r - 1$

(c) $h < 2\log_2(n+1)$

Proof: From the proof of Lemma 10.1, we know that no root-to-external-node path has length $> 2r$, so $h \leq 2r$. (The height of the red-black tree of Figure 10.15 with external nodes removed is $2r = 4$.)

Since the rank of the root is r, there are no external nodes at levels 1 through r, so there are $2^r - 1$ internal nodes at these levels. Consequently, the total number of internal nodes is at least this much. (In the red-black tree of Figure 10.15, levels 1 and 2 have $3 = 2^2 - 1$ internal nodes. There are additional internal nodes at levels 3 and 4.)

From (b) it follows that $r \leq \log_2(n+1)$. This inequality together with (a) yields (c). □

Since the height of a red-black tree is at most $2\log_2(n+1)$, search, insert, and delete algorithms that work in O(h) time have complexity O(log n).

Notice that the worst-case height of a red-black tree is more than the worst-case height (approximately $1.44\log_2(n+2)$) of an AVL tree with the same number of (internal) nodes.

10.3.2 Representation of a Red-Black Tree

Although it is convenient to include external nodes when defining red-black trees, in an implementation null pointers, rather than physical nodes, represent external nodes. Further, since pointer and node colors are closely related, with each node we need to store only its color or the color of the two pointers to its children. Node colors require just one additional bit per node, while pointer colors require two. Since both schemes require almost the same amount of space, we may choose between them on the basis of actual run times of the resulting red-black tree algorithms.

In our discussion of the insert and delete operations, we will explicitly state the needed color changes only for the nodes. The corresponding pointer color changes may be inferred.

10.3.3 Searching a Red-Black Tree

We can search a red-black tree with the code we used to search an ordinary binary search tree (Program 5.17). This code has complexity O(h), which is O(log n) for a red-black tree. Since we use the same code to search ordinary binary search trees, AVL trees, and red-black trees and since the worst-case height of an AVL tree is least, we expect AVL trees to show the best worst-case performance in applications where search is the dominant operation.

10.3.4 Inserting into a Red-Black Tree

Elements may be inserted using the strategy used for ordinary binary trees (Program 5.21). When the new node is attached to the red-black tree, we need to assign the node a color. If the tree was empty before the insertion, then the new node is the root and must be colored black (see property RB1). Suppose the tree was not empty prior to the insertion. If the new node is given the color black, then we will have an extra black node on paths from the root to the external nodes that are children of the new node. On the other hand, if the new node is assigned the color red, then we might have two consecutive red nodes. Making the new node black is guaranteed to cause a violation of property RB3, while making the new node red may or may not violate property RB2. We will make the new node red.

If making the new node red causes a violation of property RB2, we will say that the tree has become imbalanced. The nature of the imbalance is classified by examining the new node u, its parent pu, and the grandparent gu of u. Observe that since property RB2 has been violated, we have two consecutive red nodes. One of these red nodes is u, and the other must be its parent; therefore, pu exists. Since pu is red, it cannot be the root (as the root is black by property RB1); u must have a grandparent gu, which must be black (property RB2). When pu is the left child of gu, u is the left child of pu and the other child of gu is black (this case includes the case when the other child of gu is an external node); the imbalance is of type LLb. The other imbalance types are LLr (pu is the left child of gu, u is the left child of pu, the other child of gu is red), LRb (pu is the left child of gu, u is the right child of pu, the other child of gu is black), LRr, RRb, RRr, RLb, and RLr.

Imbalances of the type XYr (X and Y may be L or R) are handled by changing colors, while those of type XYb require a rotation. When we change a color, the RB2 violation may propagate two levels up the tree. In this case we will need to reclassify at the new level, with the new u being the former gu, and apply the transformations again. When a rotation is done, the RB2 violation is taken care of and no further work is needed.

Figure 10.16 shows the color changes performed for LLr and LRr imbalances; these color changes are identical. Black nodes are shaded, while red ones are not. In Figure 10.16(a), for example, gu is black, while pu and u are red; the pointers from gu to its left and right children are red; gu_R is the right subtree of gu; and pu_R is the right subtree of pu. Both LLr and LRr color changes require us to change the color of pu and of the right child of gu from red to black. Additionally, we change the color of gu from black to red provided gu is not the root. Since this color change is not done when gu is the root, the number of black nodes on all root-to-external-node paths increases by 1 when gu is the root of the red-black tree.

If changing the color of gu to red causes an imbalance, gu becomes the new u node, its parent becomes the new pu, its grandparent becomes the new gu, and we continue to rebalance. If gu is the root or if the color change does not cause an RB2 violation at gu, we are done.

Figure 10.17 shows the rotations performed to handle LLb and LRb imbalances. In Figures 10.17(a) and (b), u is the root of pu_L. Notice the similarity between these rotations and the LL (refer to Figure 10.12) and LR (refer to Figure 10.13) rotations used to handle an imbalance following an insertion in an AVL tree. The pointer changes are the same. In the case of an LLb rotation, for example, in addition to pointer changes we need to change the color of gu from black to red and of pu from red to black.

In examining the node (or pointer) colors after the rotations of Figure 10.17, we see that the number of black nodes (or pointers) on all root-to-external-node paths is unchanged. Further, the root of the involved subtree (gu before the rotation and pu after) is black following the rotation; therefore, two consecutive red nodes cannot exist on the

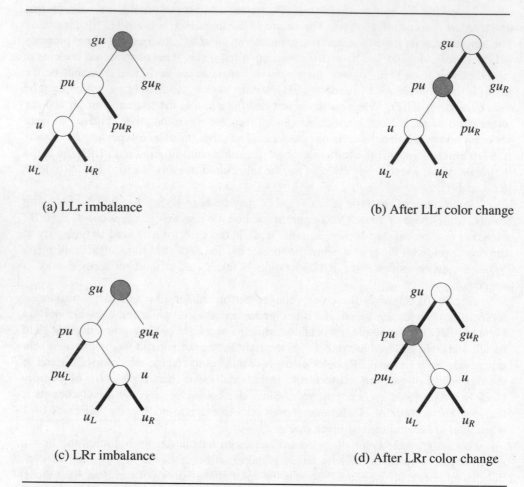

(a) LLr imbalance   (b) After LLr color change

(c) LRr imbalance   (d) After LRr color change

Figure 10.16: LLr and LRr color changes

path from the tree root to the new *pu*. Consequently, no additional rebalancing work is to be done. *A single rotation (preceded possibly by* O(log *n*) *color changes) suffices to restore balance following an insertion!*

Example 10.4: Consider the red-black tree of Figure 10.18(a). External nodes are shown for convenience. In an actual implementation, the shown black pointers to external nodes are simply null pointers and external nodes are not represented. Notice that all root-to-external-node paths have three black nodes (including the external node) and two black pointers.

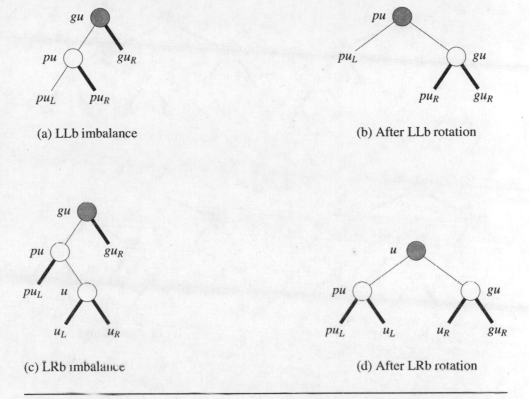

(a) LLb imbalance   (b) After LLb rotation

(c) LRb imbalance   (d) After LRb rotation

Figure 10.17: LLb and LRb rotations for red-black insertion

To insert 70 into this red-black tree, we use the algorithm of Program 5.18. The new node is added as the left child of 80. Since the insertion is done into a nonempty tree, the new node is assigned the color red. So the pointer to it from its parent (80) is also red. This insertion does not result in a violation of property RB2, and no remedial action is necessary. Notice that the number of black pointers on all root-to-external-node paths is the same as before the insertion.

Next insert 60 into the tree of Figure 10.18(b). The algorithm of Program 5.18 attaches a new node as the left child of 70, as is shown in Figure 10.18(c). The new node is red, and the pointer to it is also red. The new node is the *u* node, its parent (70) is *pu*, and its grandparent (80) is *gu*. Since *pu* and *u* are red, we have an imbalance. This imbalance is classified as an LLr imbalance (as *pu* is the left child of *gu*, *u* is the left child of *pu*, and the other child of *gu* is red). When the LLr color change of Figure 10.16(a) and (b) is performed, we get the tree of Figure 10.18(d). Now *u*, *pu*, and *gu* are

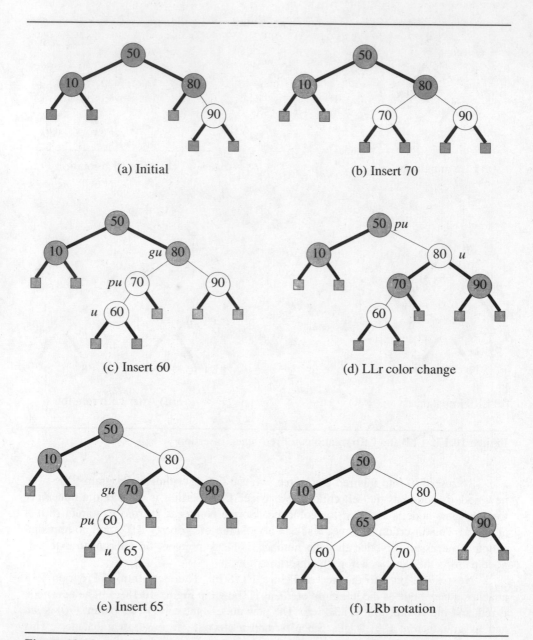

(a) Initial

(b) Insert 70

(c) Insert 60

(d) LLr color change

(e) Insert 65

(f) LRb rotation

Figure 10.18: Insertion into a red-black tree (continued on next page)

each moved two levels up the tree. The node with 80 is the new u node, the root becomes pu, and gu is **NULL**. Since there is no gu node, we cannot have an RB2 imbalance at this location and we are done. All root-to-external-node paths have exactly two black pointers.

Now insert 65 into the tree of Figure 10.18(d). The result appears in Figure 10.18(e). The new node is the u node. Its parent and grandparent are, respectively, the pu and gu nodes. We have an LRb imbalance that requires us to perform the rotation of Figures 10.17(c) and (d). The result is the tree of Figure 10.18(f).

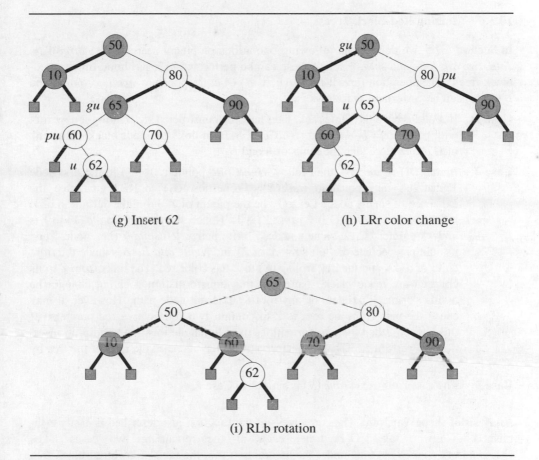

(g) Insert 62

(h) LRr color change

(i) RLb rotation

Figure 10.18: Insertion into a red-black tree

Finally, insert 62 to obtain the tree of Figure 10.18(g). We have an LRr imbalance that requires a color change. The resulting tree and the new u, pu, and gu nodes appear in Figure 10.18(h). The color change just performed has caused an RLb imbalance two levels up, so we now need to perform an RLb rotation. The rotation results in the tree of Figure 10.18(i). Following a rotation, no further work is needed, and we are done. □

10.3.5 Deletion from a Red-Black Tree

The development of the deletion transformations is left as an exercise.

10.3.6 Joining Red-Black Trees

In Section 5.7.5, we defined the following operations on binary search trees: *threeWay-Join*, *twoWayJoin*, and *split*. Each of these can be performed in logarithmic time on red-black trees. The operation *threeWayJoin* (A, x, B) (A corresponds to *small*, x to *mid*, and B to *big*) can be performed as follows.

Case 1: If A and B have the same rank, then let C be constructed by creating a new root with pair x, *leftChild* A, and *rightChild* B. Both links are made black. The rank of C is one more than the ranks of A and B.

Case 2: If $rank(A) > rank(B)$, then follow *rightChild* pointers from A to the first node Y that has rank equal to $rank(B)$. Properties RB1 to RB3 guarantee the existence of such a node. Let $p(Y)$ be the parent of Y. From the definition of Y, it follows that $rank(p(Y)) = rank(Y) + 1$. Hence, the pointer from $p(Y)$ to Y is a black pointer. Create a new node, Z, with pair x, *leftChild* Y (i.e., node Y and its subtrees become the left subtree of Z) and *rightChild* B. Z is made the right child of $p(Y)$, and the link from $p(Y)$ to Z has color red. The links from Z to its children are made black. Note that this transformation does not change the number of black pointers on any root-to-external-node path. However, it may cause the path from the root to Z to contain two consecutive red pointers. If this happens, then the transformations used to handle this in a bottom-up insertion are performed. These transformations may increase the rank of the tree by one.

Case 3: The case $rank(A) < rank(B)$ is similar to Case 2.

Analysis of threeWayJoin: The correctness of the function just described is easily established. Case 1 takes $O(1)$ time; each of the remaining two cases takes $O(|rank(A) - rank(B)|)$ time under the assumption that the rank of each red-black tree is known prior to computing the join. Hence, a three-way join can be done in $O(\log n)$ time, where n is the number of nodes in the two trees being joined. A two-way join can be performed in a similar manner. Note that there is no need to add parent data members to the nodes to perform a join, as the needed parents can be saved on a stack as we move from the root to the node Y. □

A two-way join may be done in a similar fashion.

10.3.7   Splitting a Red-Black Tree

We now turn our attention to the split operation. Assume for simplicity that the splitting key, i, is actually present in the red-black tree A. Under this assumption, the split operation $split(A, i, B, x, C)$ (see Section 5.7.5, A corresponds to *theTree*, i to k, B to *small*, x to *mid*, and C to *big*) can be performed as in Program 10.4.

Step 1:   Search A for the node P that contains the element with key i. Copy this element to the parameter *mid*. Initialize B and C to be the left and right subtrees of P, respectively.

Step 2:
```
for (Q = parent(P); Q; P = Q, Q = parent(Q))
    if (P == Q→leftChild)
        C = threeWayJoin(C, Q→data, Q→rightChild)
    else B = threeWayJoin(Q→leftChild, Q→data, B);
}
```

Program 10.4: Splitting a red-black tree

We first locate the splitting element, x, in the red-black tree. Let P be the node that contains this element. The left subtree of P contains elements with key less than i. B is initialized to be this subtree. All elements in the right subtree of P have a key larger than i, and C is initialized to be this subtree. In Step 2, we trace the path from P to the root of the red-black tree A. During this traceback, two kinds of subtrees are encountered. One of these contains elements with keys that are larger than i as well as all keys in C. This happens when the traceback moves from a left child of a node to its parent. The other kind of subtree contains elements with keys that are smaller than i, as well as smaller than all keys in B. This happens when we move from a right child to its parent. In the former case a three-way join with C is performed, and in the latter a three-way join with B is performed. One may verify that the two-step procedure outlined here does indeed implement the split operation for the case when i is the key of an element in the tree A. It is easily extended to handle the case when the tree A contains no element with key i.

Analysis of split: Call a node red if the pointer to it from its parent is red. The root and all nodes that have a black pointer from their parent are black. Let $r(X)$ be the rank of node X in the unsplit tree. First, we shall show that during a split, if P is a black node in the unsplit tree, and $Q \neq 0$, then

$$r(Q) \geq \max\{r(B), r(C)\}$$

where P, Q, B, and C are as defined at the start of an iteration of the **for** loop in Step 2.

From the definition of rank, the inequality holds at the start of the first iteration of the **for** loop regardless of the color of P. If P is red initially, then its parent, Q, exists and is black. Let q' be the parent of Q. If $q' = 0$, then there is no Q at which the inequality is violated. So, assume $q' \neq 0$. From the definition of rank and the fact that Q is black, it follows that $r(q') = r(Q) + 1$. Let B' and C' be the trees B and C following the three-way join of Step 2. Since $r(B') \leq r(B) + 1$ and $r(C') \leq r(C) + 1$, $r(q') = r(Q) + 1 \geq \max\{r(B), r(C)\} + 1 \geq \max\{r(B'), r(C')\}$. So, the inequality holds the first time Q points to a node with a black child P (i.e., at the start of the second iteration of the **for** loop, when $Q = q'$).

Having established the induction base, we can proceed to show that the inequality holds at all subsequent iterations when Q points to a node with a black child P. Suppose Q is currently pointing to a node q with a black child $P = p$. Assume that the inequality holds. We shall show that it will hold again the next time Q is at a node with a black P. For there to be such a next time, the parent q' of q must exist. If q is black, the proof is similar to that provided for a black Q and a red P in the induction base.

If q is red, then q' is black. Further, for there to be a next time when Q is at a node with a black P, q must have a grandparent q'', as when Q moves to q' and P to q, $Q = q'$ has a red child $P = q$. Let B' and C' represent the B and C trees following the iteration that begins with $P = p$ and $Q = q$. Similarly, let B'' and C'' represent these trees following the iteration that begins with $P = q$ and $Q = q'$.

Suppose that C is joined with q and its right subtree R to create C'. If $r(C) = r(R)$, then $r(C') = r(C) + 1$, and C' has two black children (recall that when the rank increases by one, the root has two black children). If $C'' = C'$, then $B = B'$ is combined with q' and its left subtree L' to form B''. Since $r(L') \leq r(q')$, $r(B'') \leq \max\{r(B), r(L')\} + 1$, and $r(q'') = r(q') + 1 = r(q) + 1$, $r(B'') \leq r(q'')$. Also, $r(C'') = r(C') = r(C) + 1 \leq r(q) + 1 \leq r(q'')$. So, the inequality holds when $Q = q''$. If $C'' \neq C'$, then C' is combined with q' and its right subtree R' to form C''. If $r(R') \geq r(C')$, then $r(C'') \leq r(R') + 1 \leq r(q') + 1 = r(q'')$. If $r(R') < r(C')$, then $r(C'') = r(C')$, as C' has two black children, and the join of C', q', and R' does not increase the rank. Once again, $r(C'') \leq r(q'')$, and the inequality holds when $Q = q''$.

If $r(C) > r(R)$ and $r(C') = r(C)$, then $r(q'') = r(q) + 1 \geq \max\{r(B), r(C)\} + 1 \geq \max\{r(B''), r(C'')\}$. If $r(C') = r(C) + 1$, then C' has two black children, and $r(C'') \leq r(q) + 1 = r(q'')$. Also, $r(B'') \leq r(q'')$. So, the inequality holds when $Q = q''$. The case $r(C) < r(R)$ is similar.

The case when B is joined with q and its left subtree L is symmetric.

Using the rank inequality just established, we can show that whenever Q points to a node with a black child, the total work done in Step 2 of the splitting algorithm from initiation to the time Q reaches this node is $O(r(B) + r(C) + r(Q))$. Here, B and C are, respectively, the current red-black trees with values smaller and larger than the splitting value. Since $r(Q) \geq \max\{r(B), r(C)\}$, the total work done in Step 2 is $O(r(Q))$. From this, it follows that the time required to perform a split is $O(\log n)$, where n is the number of nodes in the tree to be split. $\square$

EXERCISES

1. Start with an empty red-black tree and insert the following keys in the given order: 15, 14, 13, 12, 11, 10, 9, 8, 7, 6, 5, 4, 3, 2, 1. Draw figures similar to Figure 10.18 depicting your tree immediately after each insertion and following the rebalancing rotation or color change (if any). Label all nodes with their color and identify the rotation type (if any) that is done.

2. Do Exercise 1 using the insert key sequence: 1, 2, 3, 4, 5, 6, 7, 8, 9, 10, 11, 12, 13, 14, 15.

3. Do Exercise 1 using the insert key sequence: 20, 10, 5, 30, 40, 57, 3, 2, 4, 35, 25, 18, 22, 21.

4. Do Exercise 1 using the insert key sequence: 40, 50, 70, 30, 42, 15, 20, 25, 27, 26, 60, 55.

5. Draw the RRr and RLr color changes that correspond to the LLr and LRr changes of Figure 10.16.

6. Draw the RRb and RLb rotations that correspond to the LLb and LRb changes of Figure 10.17.

7. Let T be a red-black tree with rank r. Write a function to compute the rank of each node in the tree. The time complexity of your function should be linear in the number of nodes in the tree. Show that this is the case.

8. Compare the worst-case height of a red-black tree with n nodes and that of an AVL tree with the same number of nodes.

9. Develop the deletion transformations for a red-black tree. Show that a deletion from a red-black tree requires at most one rotation.

10. (a) Use the strategy described in this section to obtain a C function to compute a three-way join. Assume the existence of a function *rebalance* (X) that performs the necessary transformations if the tree pointer to node X is the second of two consecutive red pointers. The complexity of this function may be assumed to be $O(level (X))$.

    (b) Prove the correctness of your function.

    (c) What is the time complexity of your function?

11. Obtain a function to perform a two-way join on red-black trees. You may assume the existence of functions to search, insert, delete, and perform a three-way join. What is the time complexity of your two-way join function?

12. Use the strategy suggested in Program 10.4 to obtain a C function to perform the split operation in a red-black tree T. The complexity of your algorithm must be $O(height (T))$. Your function must work when the splitting key i is present in T and when it is not present in T.

13. Complete the complexity proof for the split operation by showing that whenever Q has a black child, the total work done in Step 2 of the splitting algorithm from initiation to the time that Q reaches the current node is $O(r(Q))$.

14. Program the search, insert, and delete operations for AVL trees and red-black trees.

(a) Test the correctness of your functions.

(b) Generate a random sequence of n inserts of distinct values. Use this sequence to initialize each of the data structures. Next, generate a random sequence of searches, inserts, and deletes. In this sequence, the probability of a search should be 0.5, that of an insert 0.25, and that of a delete 0.25. The sequence length is m. Measure the time needed to perform the m operations in the sequence using each of the above data structures.

(c) Do part (b) for $n = 100, 1000, 10,000$, and $100,000$ and $m = n, 2n$, and $4n$.

(d) What can you say about the relative performance of these data structures?

10.4 SPLAY TREES

We have studied balanced search trees that allow one to perform operations such as search, insert, delete, join, and split in $O(\log n)$ worst-case time per operation. In the case of priority queues, we saw that if we are interested in amortized complexity rather than worst-case complexity, simpler structures can be used. This is also true for search trees. Using a splay tree, we can perform the operations in $O(\log n)$ amortized time per operation. In this section, we develop two varieties of splay trees—bottom up and top down. Although the amortized complexity of each operation is $O(\log n)$ for both varieties, experiments indicate that top-down splay trees are faster than bottom-up splay trees by a constant factor.

10.4.1 Bottom-Up Splay Trees

A *bottom-up splay tree* is a binary search tree in which each search, insert, delete, and join operation is performed in the same way as in an ordinary binary search tree (see Chapter 5) except that each of these operations is followed by a *splay*. In a split, however, we *first* perform a splay. This makes the split very easy to perform. A splay consists of a sequence of rotations. For simplicity, we assume that each of the operations is always successful. A failure can be modeled as a different successful operation. For example, an unsuccesful search may be modeled as a search for the element in the last node encountered in the unsuccessful search, and an unsuccessful insert may be modeled as a successful search. With this assumption, the start node for a splay is obtained as follows:

(1) *search*: The splay starts at the node containing the element being sought.

(2) *insert*: The start node for the splay is the newly inserted node.

(3) *delete*: The parent of the physically deleted node is used as the start node for the splay. If this node is the root, then no splay is done.

(4) *threeWayJoin*: No splay is done.

(5) *split*: Suppose that we are splitting with respect to the key i and that key i is actually present in the tree. We first perform a splay at the node that contains i and then split the tree. As we shall see, splitting following a splay is very simple.

Splay rotations are performed along the path from the start node to the root of the binary search tree. These rotations are similar to those performed for AVL trees and red-black trees. Let q be the node at which the splay is being performed. Initially, q is the node at which the splay starts. The following steps define a splay:

(1) If q is either 0 or the root, then the splay terminates.

(2) If q has a parent, p, but no grandparent, then the rotation of Figure 10.19 is performed, and the splay terminates.

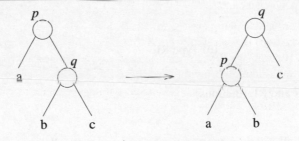

a, b, and c are subtrees

Figure 10.19: Rotation when q is a right child and has no grandparent

(3) If q has a parent, p, and a grandparent, gp, then the rotation is classified as LL (p is the left child of gp, and q is the left child of p), LR (p is the left child of gp, and q

is the right child of p), RR, or RL. The RR and RL rotations are shown in Figure 10.20. LL and LR rotations are symmetric to these. The splay is repeated at the new location of q.

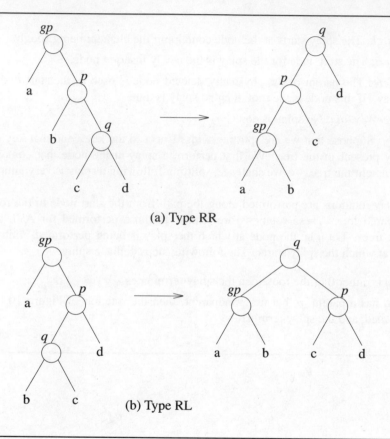

(a) Type RR

(b) Type RL

Figure 10.20: RR and RL rotations

Notice that all rotations move q up the tree and that following a splay, q becomes the new root of the search tree. As a result, splitting the tree with respect to a key, i, is done simply by performing a splay at i and then splitting at the root. Figure 10.21 shows a binary search tree before, during, and after a splay at the shaded node.

In the case of Fibonacci heaps, we obtained the amortized complexity of an operation by using an explicit cross-charging scheme. The analysis for splay trees will use a *potential* technique. Let P_0 be the initial potential of the search tree, and let P_i be its potential following the ith operation in a sequence of m operations. The amortized time

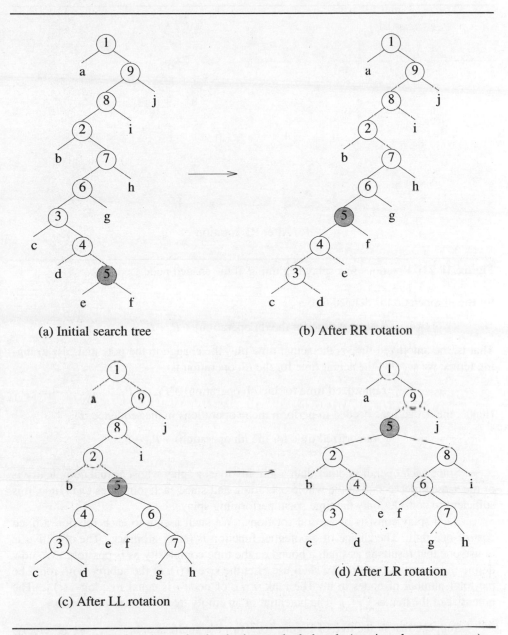

(a) Initial search tree

(b) After RR rotation

(c) After LL rotation

(d) After LR rotation

Figure 10.21: Rotations in a splay beginning at shaded node (continued on next page)

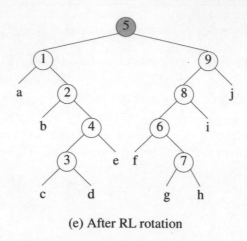

(e) After RL rotation

Figure 10.21: Rotations in a splay beginning at the shaded node

for the ith operation is defined to be

$$\text{(actual time for the } i\text{th operation)} + P_i - P_{i-1}$$

That is, the amortized time is the actual time plus the change in the potential. Rearranging terms, we see that the actual time for the ith operation is

$$\text{(amortized time for the } i\text{th operation)} + P_{i-1} - P_i$$

Hence, the actual time needed to perform the m operations in the sequence is

$$\sum_i \text{(amortized time for the } i\text{th operation)} + P_0 - P_m$$

Since each operation other than a join involves a splay whose actual complexity is of the same order as that of the whole operation, and since each join takes O(1) time, it is sufficient to consider only the time spent performing splays.

Each splay consists of several rotations. We shall assign to each rotation a fixed cost of one unit. The choice of a potential function is rather arbitrary. The objective is to use one that results in as small a bound on the time complexity as is possible. We now define the potential function we shall use. Let the size, $s(i)$, of the subtree with root i be the total number of nodes in it. The rank, $r(i)$, of node i is equal to $\lfloor \log_2 s(i) \rfloor$. The potential of the tree is $\sum_i r(i)$. The potential of an empty tree is defined to be zero.

Suppose that in the tree of Figure 10.21(a), the subtrees a, b, $\cdots$, j are all empty. Then $(s(1), \cdots, s(9)) = (9, 6, 3, 2, 1, 4, 5, 7, 8)$; $r(3) = r(4) = 1$; $r(5) = 0$; and $r(9) = 3$. In Lemma 10.3 we use r and r', respectively, to denote the rank of a node before and after a rotation.

Lemma 10.3: Consider a binary search tree that has n elements/nodes. The amortized cost of a splay operation that begins at node q is at most $3(\lfloor \log_2 n \rfloor - r(q)) + 1$.

Proof: Consider the three steps in the definition of a splay:

(1) In this case, q either is 0 or the root. This step does not alter the potential of the tree, so its amortized and actual costs are the same. This cost is 1.

(2) In this step, the rotation of Figure 10.19 (or the symmetric rotation for the case when q is the left child of p) is performed. Since only the ranks of p and q are affected, the potential change, ΔP, is $r'(p) + r'(q) - r(p) - r(q)$. Further, since $r'(p) \leq r(p)$, $\Delta P \leq r'(q) - r(q)$. The amortized cost of this step (actual cost plus potential change) is, therefore, no more than $r'(q) - r(q) + 1$.

(3) In this step only the ranks of q, p, and gp change. So, $\Delta P = r'(q) + r'(p) + r'(gp) - r(q) - r(p) - r(gp)$. Since, $r(gp) = r'(q)$,

$$\Delta P = r'(p) + r'(gp) - r(q) - r(p) \text{ -- (1)}$$

Consider an RR rotation. From Figure 10.20(a), we see that $r'(p) \leq r'(q)$, $r'(gp) \leq r'(q)$, and $r(q) \leq r(p)$. So, $\Delta P \leq 2(r'(q) - r(q))$. If $r'(q) > r(q)$, $\Delta P \leq 3(r'(q) - r(q)) - 1$. If $r'(q) = r(q)$, then $r'(q) = r(q) = r(p) = r(gp)$. Also, $s'(q) > s(q) + s'(gp)$. Consequently, $r'(gp) < r'(q)$. To see this, note that if $r'(gp) = r'(q)$, then $s'(q) > 2^{r(q)} + 2^{r'(gp)} = 2^{r(q)+1}$, which violates the definition of rank. Hence, from (1), $\Delta P \leq 2(r'(q) - r(q)) - 1 = 3(r'(q) - r(q)) - 1$. So, the amortized cost of an RR rotation is at most $1 + 3(r'(q) - r(q)) - 1 = 3(r'(q) - r(q))$.

This bound may be obtained for LL, LR, and RL rotations in a similar way.

The lemma now follows by observing that Steps 1 and 2 are mutually exclusive and can occur at most once. Step 3 occurs zero or more times. Summing up over the amortized cost of a single occurrence of Steps 1 or 2 and all occurrences of Step 3, we obtain the bound of the lemma. □

Theorem 10.1: The total time needed for a sequence of m search, insert, delete, join, and split operations performed on a collection of initially empty splay trees is $O(m \log n)$, where n, $n > 0$, is the number of inserts in the sequence.

Proof: Since none of the splay trees has more than n nodes, no node has rank more than $\lfloor \log_2 n \rfloor$. A search (excluding the splay) does not change the rank of any node and hence does not affect the potential of the splay tree involved. An insert (excluding the splay) increases, by one, the size of every node on the path from the root to the newly inserted node. This causes the ranks of the nodes with size $2^k - 1$ to change. There are at most $\lfloor \log_2 n \rfloor + 1$ such nodes on any insert path. So, each insert (excluding the splay) increases the potential by at most this much. Each join increases the total potential of all the splay trees by at most $\lfloor \log_2 n \rfloor$. Deletions do not increase the potential of the involved splay tree except for any increase that results from the splay step. The split operation (excluding the splay step) reduces the overall potential by an amount equal to the rank of the tree just before the split (but after the splay that precedes it). So, the potential increase, PI, attributable to the m operations (exclusive of that attributable to the splay steps of the operations) is O($m \log n$).

From our definition of the amortized cost of a splay operation, it follows that the time for the sequence of operations is the sum of the amortized costs of the splays, the potential change $P_0 - P_m$, and PI. From Lemma 10.3, it follows that the sum of the amortized costs is O($m \log n$). The initial potential, P_0, is 0, and the final potential, P_m, is ≥ 0. So, the total time is O($m \log n$). $\square$

10.4.2 Top-Down Splay Trees

As in the case of a bottom-up splay tree, a *threeWayJoin* is implemented the same in a top-down splay tree as in Section 5.7.5. For the remaining operations, let the splay node be as defined for a bottom-up splay tree. For each operation, we follow a path from the root to the splay node as in Section 5.7.5. However, as we follow this path, we partition the binary search tree into three components—a binary search tree *small* of elements whose key is less than that of the element in the splay node, a binary search tree *big* of elements whose key is greater than that of the element in the splay node, and the splay node. Notice that in this downward traversal of the path from the root to the splay node, we do not actually know which node is the splay node until we get to it. So, the downward traversal is done using the key k associated with the operation that is being performed.

For the partitioning, we begin with two empty binary search trees *small* and *big*. It is convenient to give these trees a header node that is deleted at the end. Let s and b, respectively, be initialized to the header nodes of *small* and *big*. The downward traversal to the splay node begins at the root. Let x denote the node we currently are at. We begin with x being the tree root. There are 7 cases to consider:

Case 0: *x is the splay node.*
Terminate the partitioning process.

Case L: *The splay node is the left child of x.*
In this case, x and its right subtree contain keys that are greater than that in the splay node. So, we make x the left child of b ($b \rightarrow leftChild = x$) and set $b = x$ and $x = x \rightarrow leftChild$. Notice that this automatically places the right subtree of x into *big*. Figure 10.22 shows a schematic for this case.

Case R: *The splay node is the right child of x.*
This case is symmetric to Case L. Now, x and its left subtree contain keys that

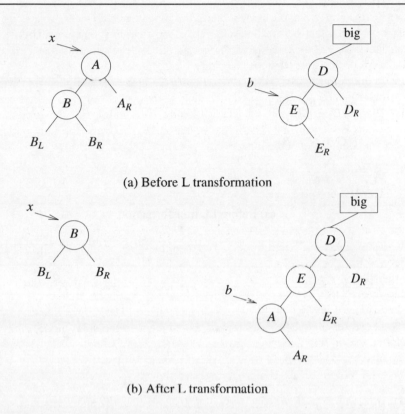

(a) Before L transformation

(b) After L transformation

Figure 10.22: Case L for a top-down splay tree

are less than that in the splay node. So, we make x the right child of s ($s \rightarrow rightChild = x$) and set $s = x$ and $x = x \rightarrow rightChild$. Notice that this automatically places the left subtree of x into *small*.

Case LR:*The splay node is in the right subtree of the left child of x.*
This case is handled as Case L followed by Case R.

Case RL:*The splay node is in the left subtree of the right child of x.*
This case is handled as Case R followed by Case L.

Case LL:*The splay node is in the left subtree of the left child of x.*
This case is *not* handled as two applications of Case L. Instead we perform an LL rotation around x. Figure 10.23 shows a schematic for this case. The shown transformation is accomplished by the following code fragment:

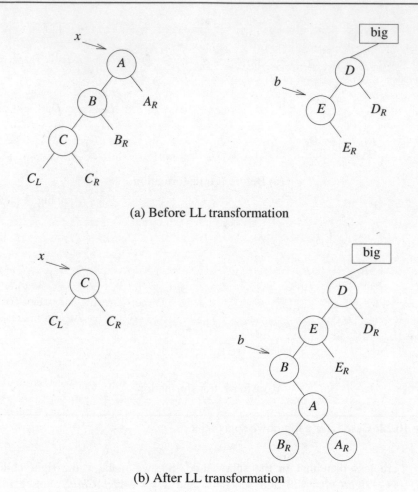

(a) Before LL transformation

(b) After LL transformation

Figure 10.23: Case LL for a top-down splay tree

```
b->leftChild  = x->leftChild;
b = b->leftChild;
x->leftChild = b->rightChild;
b->rightChild = x;
x   = b->leftChild;
```

Case RR:*The splay node is in the right subtree of the right child of x.*
     This case is symmetric to Case LL.

The above transformations are applied repeatedly until terminated by an application of Case 0. Upon termination, x is the splay node. Now, the left subtree of x is made the right subtree of s and the right subtree of x is made the left subtree of b. Finally, the header nodes of the small and big trees are deleted.

In case we were performing a split operation and x contains the split key, we return *small*, $x \rightarrow data$, and *big* as the result of the split. For a search, insert and delete, we make *small* and *big*, respectively, the left and right subtrees of x and the tree rooted at x is the new binary search tree (we assume that in the downward quest for the splay node, the remaining tasks associated with the search, insert and delete operations have been done).

Example 10.5: Suppose we are searching for the key 5 in the top-down splay tree of Figure 10.21(a). Although we don't know this at this time, the splay node is the shaded node. The path from the root to the splay node is determined by comparing the search key 5 with the key in the current node. We start with the current node pointer x at the root and two empty splay trees—*small* and *big*. These empty splay trees have a header node. The variables s and b, respectively, point to these header nodes. Since the splay node is in the left subtree of the right child of x, an RL transformation is called for. The search tree as well as the trees *small* and *big* following the RL transformation are shown in Figure 10.24(a).

Now, since the splay node is in the right subtree of the left child of the new x, an LR transformation is made and we obtain the configuration of Figure 10.24(b). Next, we make an LL transformation (Figure 10.24(c)) and an RR transformation (Figure 10.24(d)). Now, x is at the splay node. The left subtree of x is made the right subtree of s and the right subtree of x is made the left subtree of b (Figure 10.24(e)). Finally, we delete the header nodes and make the small and big trees subtrees of x as shown in Figure 10.24(f). □

EXERCISES

1. Obtain figures corresponding to Figures 10.19 and 10.20 for the symmetric bottom-up splay tree rotations.

2. What is the maximum height of a bottom-up splay tree that is created as the result of n insertions made into an initially empty splay tree? Give an example of a sequence of inserts that results in a splay tree of this height.

3. Complete the proof of Lemma 10.3 by providing the proof for the case of an RL rotation. Note that the proofs for LL and LR rotations are similar to those for RR and RL rotations, respectively, as the rotations are symmetric.

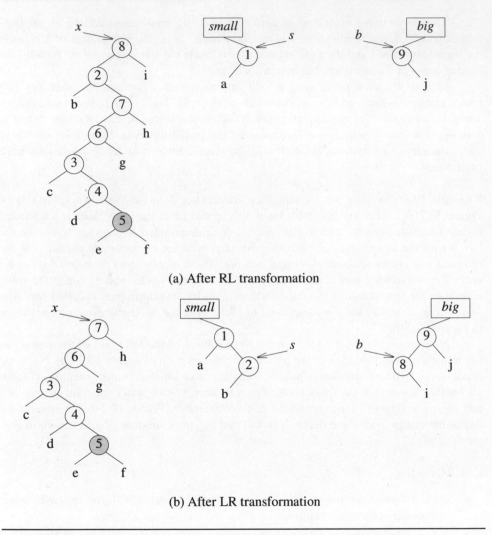

(a) After RL transformation

(b) After LR transformation

Figure 10.24: Example for top-down splay tree (continued on next page)

4. Explain how a two-way join should be performed in a bottom-up splay tree so that the amortized cost of each splay tree operation remains O(log n).

5. Explain how a split with respect to key i is to be performed when key i is not present in the bottom-up splay tree. The amortized cost of each bottom-up splay tree operation should be O(log n).

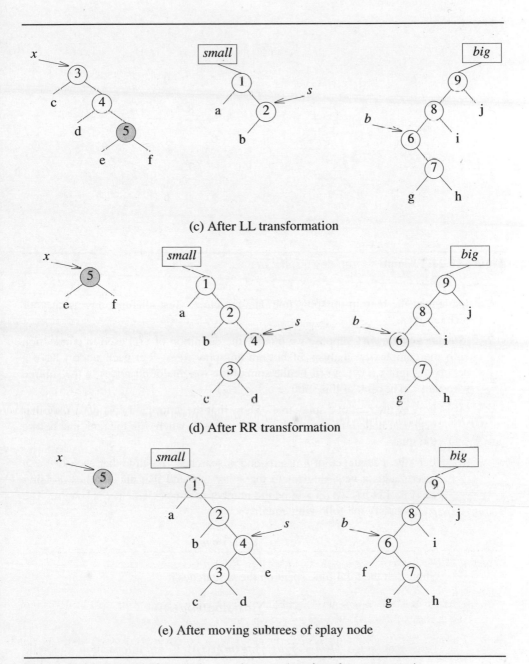

(c) After LL transformation

(d) After RR transformation

(e) After moving subtrees of splay node

Figure 10.24: Example for top-down splay tree (continued on next page)

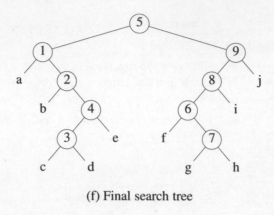

(f) Final search tree

Figure 10.24: Example for top-down splay tree

6. Implement the bottom-up splay tree data structure. Test all functions using your own test data.

7. [*Sleator and Tarjan*] Suppose we modify the definition of $s(i)$ used in connection with the complexity analysis of bottom-up splay trees. Let each node i have a positive weight $p(i)$. Let $s(i)$ be the sum of the weights of all nodes in the subtree with root i. The rank of this subtree is $\log_2 s(i)$.

(a) Let t be the root of a splay tree. Show that the amortized cost of a splay that begins at node q is at most $3(r(t) - r(q)) + 1$, where r is the rank just before the splay.

(b) Let S be a sequence of n inserts and m searches. Assume that each of the n inserts adds a new element to the splay tree and that all searches are successful. Let $p(i)$, $p(i) > 0$, be the number of times element i is sought. The $p(i)$'s satisfy the following equality:

$$\sum_{i=1}^{n} p(i) = m$$

Show that the total time spent on the m searches is

$$O(m + \sum_{i=1}^{n} p(i) \log(m/p(i)))$$

Note that since $\Omega(m + \sum_{i=1}^{n} p(i) \log(m/p(i)))$ is an information theoretic bound on the search time in a static search tree (the optimal binary search tree of Section 10.1 is an example of such a tree), bottom-up splay trees are optimal to within a constant factor for the representation of a static set of elements.

8. Obtain figures corresponding to Figures 10.22 and 10.23 for the top-down splay tree transformations R, RR, RL, and LR.

9. What is the maximum height of a top-down splay tree that is created as the result of n insertions made into an initially empty splay tree? Give an example of a sequence of inserts that results in a splay tree of this height.

10. Implement the top-down splay tree data structure. Test all functions using your own test data.

10.5 REFERENCES AND SELECTED READINGS

The $O(n^2)$ optimum binary search tree algorithm is from "Optimum binary search trees," by D. Knuth, *Acta Informatica*, 1:1, 1971, pp. 14-25. For a discussion of heuristics that obtain in $O(n \log n)$ time nearly optimal binary search trees, see "Nearly optimal binary search trees," by K. Mehlhorn, *Acta Informatica*, 5, 1975, pp. 287-295; and "Binary search trees and file organization," by J. Nievergelt, *ACM Computing Surveys*, 6:3, 1974, pp. 195-207.

The original paper on AVL trees by G. M. Adelson-Velskii and E. M. Landis appears in *Dokl. Acad. Nauk., SSR* (Soviet Math), 3, 1962, pp. 1259-1263. Additional algorithms to manipulate AVL trees may be found in "Linear lists and priority queues as balanced binary trees," by C. Crane, Technical Report STAN-CS-72-259, Computer Science Dept., Stanford University, Palo Alto, CA, 1972; and *The Art of Computer Programming: Sorting and Searching* by D. Knuth, Addison-Wesley, Reading, MA, 1973 (Section 6.2.3).

Results of an empirical study of height-balanced trees appear in "Performance of height-balanced trees," by P. L. Karlton, S. H. Fuller, R. E. Scroggs, and E. B. Koehler, *CACM*, 19:1, 1976, pp. 23-28.

Splay trees were invented by D. Sleator and R. Tarjan. Their paper "Self-adjusting binary search trees," *JACM*, 32:3, 1985, pp. 652-686, provides several other analyses of splay trees, as well as variants of the basic splaying technique discussed in the text. Our analysis is modeled after that in *Data Structures and Network Algorithms*, by R. Tarjan, SIAM Publications, Philadelphia, PA, 1983.

For more on binary search trees, see Chapters 10 through 14 of "Handbook of data structures and applications," edited by D. Mehta and S. Sahni, Chapman & Hall/CRC, Boca Raton, 2005.

CHAPTER 11

Multiway Search Trees

11.1 *m*-WAY SEARCH TREES

11.1.1 Definition and Properties

Balanced binary search trees such as AVL and red-black trees allow us to search, insert, and delete in $O(\log n)$ time, where n is the number of elements. While this may seem to be a remarkable accomplishment, we can improve the performance of search structures by capitalizing on the exhorbitant time it takes to make a memory access (whether to main memory or to disk) relative to the time it takes to perform an arithmetic or logic operation in a modern computer. An access to main memory typically takes approximately 100 times the time to do an arithmetic operation while an access to disk takes about 10,000 times the time for an arithmetic operation. Because of this significant mismatch between processor speed and memory access time, data is typically moved from main memory to cache (fast memory) in units of a cache-line size (of the order of 100 bytes) and from disk to main memory in units of a block (several kilo bytes). For uniformity with disks, we say that main memory is organized into blocks; the size of each block being equal to that of a cache line. AVL and red-black trees are unable to take advantage of this large unit (i.e., block) in which data is moved from slow memory (main or disk) to faster memory (cache or main) since the node size is typically only a few bytes. Consider an AVL tree with 1,000,000 elements. It's height may be as much as $\lfloor 1.44\log_2(n+2)\rfloor$, which is 28. To search this tree for an element with a specified key, we must access those nodes that are on the search path from the root to the node that contains the desired element. This path may contain 28 nodes and if each of these 28 nodes lies in a different memory block, a total of 28 memory accesses and 28 compares are made in the worst case. Most of the search time is spent on memory access! To improve performance, we must reduce the number of memory accesses. Notice that if halving the number of memory accesses resulted in a doubling of the number of comparisons, we would still achieve a reduction in total search time. Since the number of memory accesses is closely tied to the height of the search tree, we must reduce tree height. To break the $\log_2(n+1)$ barrier on tree height resulting from the use of binary search trees, we must use search trees whose degree is more than 2. In practice, we use the largest degree for which the tree node fits into a block (whether cache line or disk block).

Definition: An *m-way search tree* is either empty or satisfies the following properties:

(1)   The root has at most *m* subtrees and has the following structure:

$$n, A_0, (E_1, A_1), (E_2, A_2), \cdots, (E_n, A_n)$$

where the A_i, $0 \le i \le n < m$, are pointers to subtrees, and the E_i, $1 \le i \le n < m$, are elements. Each element E_i has a key $E_i.K$.

(2) $E_i.K < E_{i+1}.K$, $1 \le i < n$.

(3)   Let $E_0.K = -\infty$ and $E_{n+1}.K = \infty$. All keys in the subtree A_i are less than $E_{i+1}.K$ and greater than $E_i.K$, $0 \le i \le n$.

(4)   The subtrees A_i, $0 \le i \le n$, are also *m*-way search trees. □

We may verify that binary search trees are two-way search trees. A three-way search tree is shown in Figure 11.1. For convenience, only keys are shown in this figure as well as in all remaining figures in this chapter.

In a tree of degree *m* and height *h*, the maximum number of nodes is

$$\sum_{0 \le i \le h-1} m^i = (m^h - 1)/(m - 1)$$

Since each node has at most $m - 1$ elements, the maximum number of elements in an *m*-way tree of height *h* is $m^h - 1$. For a binary tree with $h = 3$ this quantity is 7. For a 200-way tree with $h = 3$ we have $m^h - 1 = 8 * 10^6 - 1$.

To achieve a performance close to that of the best *m*-way search trees for a given number of elements *n*, the search tree must be balanced. The particular varieties of balanced *m*-way search trees we shall consider here are known as B-trees and B$^+$-trees.

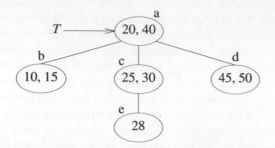

node	schematic format
a	2, b, (20, c), (40, d)
b	2, 0, (10, 0), (15, 0)
c	2, 0, (25, e), (30, 0)
d	2, 0, (45, 0), (50, 0)
e	1, 0, (28, 0)

Figure 11.1: Example of a three-way search tree

11.1.2 Searching an m-Way Search Tree

Suppose we wish to search an m-way search tree for an element whose key is x. We begin at the root of the tree. Assume that this node has the structure given in the definition of an m-way search tree. For convenience, assume that $E_0.K = -\infty$ and $E_{n+1}.K = +\infty$. By searching the keys of the root, we determine i such that $E_i.K \leq x < E_{i+1}.K$. If $x = E_i.K$, then the search is complete. If $x \neq E_i.K$, then from the definition of an m-way search tree, it follows that if x is in the tree, it must be in subtree A_i. So, we move to the root of this subtree and proceed to search it. This process continues until either we find x or we have determined that x is not in the tree (the search leads us to an empty subtree). When the number of elements in the node being searched is small, a sequential search is used. When this number is large, a binary search may be used. A high-level description of the algorithm to search an m-way search tree is given in Program 11.1.

EXERCISES

1. Draw a sample 5-way search tree.

2. What is the minimum number of elements in an m-way search tree whose height is h?

3. Write an algorithm to insert an element whose key is x into an m-way search tree. What is the complexity of your algorithm?

4. Write an algorithm to delete the element whose key is x from an m-way search tree. What is the complexity of your algorithm?

```
/* search an m-way search tree for an element with key x,
    return pointer to the element if found, return NULL otherwise */
E₀.K = - MAXKEY;
for (*p = root; p; p = Aᵢ)
{
      Let p have the format n, A₀, (E₁, A₁), · · · , (Eₙ, Aₙ);
      Eₙ₊₁.K = MAXKEY;
      Determine i such that Eᵢ.K ≤ x < Fᵢ₊₁.K;
      if ( x == Eᵢ.K) return Eᵢ;
}
/* x is not in the tree */
return NULL;
```

Program 11.1: Searching an m-way search tree

11.2 B-TREES

11.2.1 Definition and Properties

The implementation of a database management system often relies upon either B-trees or B^+-trees (Section 11.3) to facilitate quick insertion into, deletion from, and searching of a database. A knowledge of these structures is crucial to understanding how commercial database management systems function. In defining a B-tree, it is convenient to extend m-way search trees by the addition of external nodes. An external (or failure) node is added wherever we otherwise have a NULL pointer. An external node represents a node that can be reached during a search only if the element being sought is not in the tree. Nodes that are not external nodes are called *internal* nodes.

Definition: A *B-tree of order m* is an m-way search tree that either is empty or satisfies the following properties:

(1) The root node has at least two children.

(2) All nodes other than the root node and external nodes have at least $\lceil m/2 \rceil$ children.

(3) All external nodes are at the same level. □

Observe that when $m = 3$, all internal nodes of a B-tree have a degree that is either 2 or 3 and when $m = 4$, the permissible degrees for these nodes are 2, 3 and 4. For this reason, a B-tree of order 3 is known as a 2-3 tree and a B-tree of order 4 is known as a

2-3-4 tree. A B-tree of order 5 is not a 2-3-4-5 tree as a B-tree of order 5 cannot have nodes whose degree is 2 (except for the root). Also, notice that all B-trees of order 2 are full binary trees. Hence, B-trees of order 2 exist only when the number of key values is $2^k - 1$ for some k. However, for any $n \geq 0$ and any $m > 2$, there is always a B-tree of order m that contains n keys.

Figure 11.2 shows a 2-3 tree (i.e., a B-tree of order 3) and Figure 11.3 shows a 2-3-4 tree (i.e., a B-tree of order 4). Notice that each (internal) node of a 2-3 tree can hold 2 elements while each such node of a 2-3-4 tree can hold 3 elements. In the figures, only the keys are shown. Note also that although Figures 11.2 and 11.3 show external nodes, external nodes are introduced only to make it easier to define and talk about B-trees. External nodes are not physically represented inside a computer. Rather, the corresponding child pointer of the parent of each external node is set to **NULL**.

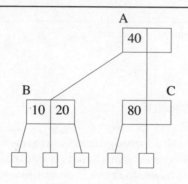

Figure 11.2: Example of a 2-3 tree

11.2.2 Number of Elements in a B-Tree

A B-tree of order m in which all external nodes are at level $l+1$ has at most $m^l - 1$ keys. What is the minimum number, N, of elements in such a B-tree? From the definition of a B-tree we know that if $l > 1$, the root node has at least two children. Hence, there are at least two nodes at level 2. Each of these nodes must have at least $\lceil m/2 \rceil$ children. Thus, there are at least $2\lceil m/2 \rceil$ nodes at level 3. At level 4 there must be at least $2\lceil m/2 \rceil^2$ nodes, and continuing this argument, we see that there are at least $2\lceil m/2 \rceil^{l-2}$ nodes at level l when $l > 1$. All of these nodes are internal nodes. If the keys in the tree are $K_1, K_2, \cdots, K_N$ and $K_i < K_{i+1}, 1 \leq i < N$, then the number of external nodes is $N + 1$. This is so because failures occur for $K_i < x < K_{i+1}, 0 \leq i \leq N$, where $K_0 = -\infty$ and $K_{N+1} = +\infty$. This results in $N + 1$ different nodes that one could reach while searching

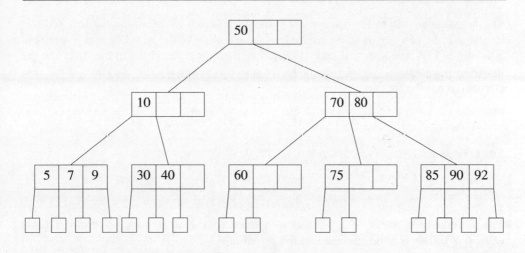

Figure 11.3: Example of a 2-3-4 tree

for a key x that is not in the B-tree. Therefore, we have

$$N + 1 = \text{number of external nodes}$$
$$= \text{number of nodes at level } (l + 1)$$
$$\geq 2\lceil m/2 \rceil^{l-1}$$

so $N \geq 2\lceil m/2 \rceil^{l-1} - 1, l \geq 1$.

This in turn implies that if there are N elements (equivalently, keys) in a B-tree of order m, then all internal nodes are at levels less than or equal to l, $l \leq \log_{\lceil m/2 \rceil}\{(N + 1)/2\} + 1$. If a B-tree node can be examined with a single memory access, the maximum number of accesses that have to be made for a search is l. Using a B-tree of order $m = 200$, which is quite practical for a disk resident B-tree, a tree with $N \leq 2 \times 10^6 - 2$ will have $l \leq \log_{100}\{(N + 1)/2\} + 1$. Since l is an integer, we obtain $l \leq 3$. For $N \leq 2 \times 10^8 - 2$ we get $l \leq 4$.

To search a B-tree with a number of memory accesses equal to the B-tree height we must be able to examine a B-tree node with a single memory access. This means that the size of a node should not exceed the size of a memory block (i.e., size of a cache line or disk block). For main-memory resident B-trees an m in the tens is practical and for disk resident B-trees an m in the hundreds is practical.

11.2.3   Insertion into a B-Tree

The insertion algorithm for B-trees first performs a search to determine the leaf node, p, into which the new key is to be inserted. If the insertion of the new key into p results in p having m keys, the node p is split. Otherwise, the new p is written to the disk, and the insertion is complete. To split the node, assume that following the insertion of the new element, p has the format

$$m, A_0, (E_1, A_1), \cdots, (E_m, A_m), \quad \text{and} \quad E_i < E_{i+1}, 1 \le i < m$$

The node is split into two nodes, p and q, with the following formats:

$$\text{node } p: \lceil m/2 \rceil - 1, A_0, (E_1 A_1), \cdots, (E_{\lceil m/2 \rceil - 1}, A_{\lceil m/2 \rceil - 1}) \quad\quad (11.5)$$

$$\text{node } q: m - \lceil m/2 \rceil, A_{\lceil m/2 \rceil}, (E_{\lceil m/2 \rceil + 1}, A_{\lceil m/2 \rceil + 1}), \cdots, (E_m, A_m)$$

The remaining element, $E_{\lceil m/2 \rceil}$, and a pointer to the new node, q, form a tuple $(E_{\lceil m/2 \rceil}, q)$. This is to be inserted into the parent of p.

Inserting into the parent may require us to split the parent, and this splitting process can propagate all the way up to the root. When the root splits, a new root with a single element is created, and the height of the B-tree increases by one. A high-level description of the insertion algorithm for a disk resident B-tree is given in Program 11.2.

Example 11.1: Consider inserting an element with key 70 into the 2-3 tree of Figure 11.2. First we search for this key. If the key is already in the tree, then the existing element with this key is replaced by the new element. Since 70 is not in our example 2-3 tree, the new element is inserted and the total number of elements in the tree increases by 1. For the insertion, we need to know the leaf node encountered during the search for 70. Note that whenever we search for a key that is not in the 2-3 tree, the search encounters a unique leaf node. The leaf node encountered during the search for 70 is the node C, with key 80. Since this node has only one element, the new element may be inserted here. The resulting 2-3 tree is shown in Figure 11.4(a).

Next, consider inserting an element with key 30. This time the search encounters the leaf node B. Since B is full, it is necessary to split B. For this, we first symbolically insert the new element into B to get the key sequence 10, 20, 30. Then the overfull node is split using Eq. 11.5. Following the split, B has the key sequence 10 and the new node, D, has 30. The middle element, whose key is 20, together with a pointer to the new node D is inserted into the parent A of B. The resulting 2-3 tree is shown in Figure 11.4(b).

Finally, consider the insertion of an element with key 60 into the 2-3 tree of Figure 11.4(b). The leaf node encountered during the search for 60 is node C. Since C is full, a new node, E, is created. Node E contains the element with the largest key (80). Node C contains the element with the smallest key (60). The element with the median key (70), together with a pointer to the new node, E, is to be inserted into the parent A of C. Again, since A is full, a new node, F, containing the element with the largest key among

---

/* insert element x into a disk resident B-tree */
Search the B-tree for an element E with key $x.K$.
if such an E is found, replace E with x and **return;**
Otherwise, let p be the leaf into which x is to be inserted;
$q = $ **NULL;**
for $(e = x; p; p = p \rightarrow parent$ ())
{/* (e, q) is to be inserted into p */
    Insert (e, q) into appropriate position in node p;
    Let the resulting node have the form: $n, A_0, (E_1, A_1), \cdots, (E_n, A_n)$;
    if ($n <= m - 1$) { /* resulting node is not too big */
        write node p to disk; **return;**
    }
    /* node p has to be split */
    Let p and q be defined as in Eq. (11.5);
    $e = E_{\lceil m/2 \rceil}$;
    write nodes p and q to the disk;
}
/* a new root is to be created */
Create a new node r with format 1, $root$, (e, q);
$root = r$;
write $root$ to disk;

Program 11.2: Insertion into a B-tree

$\{20, 40, 70\}$ is created. As before, A contains the element with the smallest key. B and D remain the left and middle children of A, respectively, and C and E become these children of F. If A had a parent, then the element with the median key 40 and a pointer to the new node, F, would be inserted into this parent node. Since A does not have a parent, we create a new root, G, for the 2-3 tree. Node G contains the element with key 40, together with child pointers to A and F. The new 2-3 tree is as shown in Figure 11.5. □

Analysis of B-tree Insertion: For convenience, assume the B-tree is disk resident. If h is the height of the B-tree, then h disk accesses are made during the top-down search. In the worst case, all h of the accessed nodes may split during the bottom-up splitting pass. When a node other than the root splits, we need to write out two nodes. When the root splits, three nodes are written out. If we assume that the h nodes read in during the top-down pass can be saved in memory so that they are not to be retrieved from disk during the bottom-up pass, then the number of disk accesses for an insertion is at most h (downward pass) + $2(h - 1)$ (nonroot splits) + 3 (root split) = $3h + 1$.

The average number of disk accesses is, however, approximately $h + 1$ for large

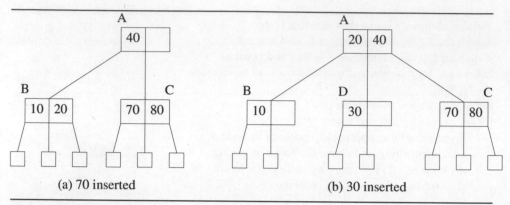

(a) 70 inserted   (b) 30 inserted

Figure 11.4: Insertion into the 2-3 tree of Figure 11.2

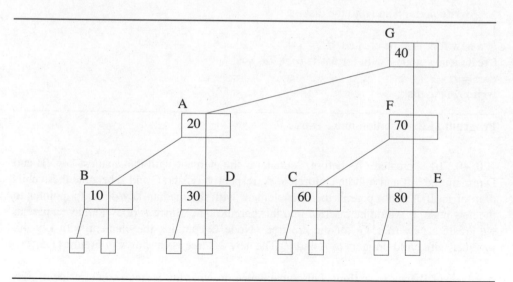

Figure 11.5: Insertion of 60 into the 2-3 tree of Figure 11.4(b)

m. To see this, suppose we start with an empty B-tree and insert N values into it. The total number of nodes split is at most $p - 2$, where p is the number of internal nodes in the final B-tree with N entries. This upper bound of $p - 2$ follows from the observation that each time a node splits, at least one additional node is created. When the root splits, two additional nodes are created. The first node created results from no splitting, and if a B-tree has more than one node, then the root must have split at least once. Figure 11.6

shows that $p - 2$ is the tightest upper bound on the number of nodes split in the creation of a p-node B-tree when $p > 2$ (note that there is no B-tree with $p = 2$). A B-tree of order m with p nodes has at least $1 + (\lceil m/2 \rceil - 1)(p - 1)$ keys, as the root has at least one key and remaining nodes have at least $\lceil m/2 \rceil - 1$ keys each. The average number of splits, s_{avg}, may now be determined as follows:

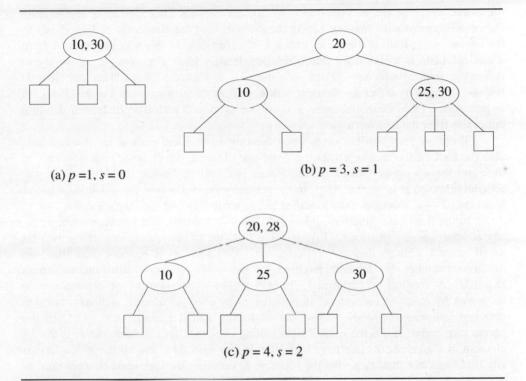

(a) $p = 1, s = 0$

(b) $p = 3, s = 1$

(c) $p = 4, s = 2$

Figure 11.6: B-trees of order 3

$$s_{avg} = (\text{total number of splits})/N$$
$$\leq (p - 2)/\{1 + (\lceil m/2 \rceil - 1)(p - 1)\}$$
$$< 1/(\lceil m/2 \rceil - 1)$$

For $m = 200$ this means that the average number of node splits is less than 1/99 per key inserted. The number of disk accesses in an insertion is $h + 2s - 1$, where s is the number of nodes that are split during the insertion. So, the average number of disk accesses is $h + 2s_{avg} + 1 < h + 101/99 \approx h + 1$. □

11.2.4 Deletion from a B-Tree

For convenience, assume we are deleting from a B-tree that resides on disk. Suppose we are to delete the element whose key is x. First, we search for this key. If x is not found, no element is to be deleted. If x is found in a node, z, that is not a leaf, then the position occupied by the corresponding element in z is filled by an element from a leaf node of the B-tree. Suppose that x is the ith key in z (i.e., $x = E_i.K$). Then E_i may be replaced by either the element with smallest key in the subtree A_i or the element with largest key in the subtree A_{i-1}. Both of these elements are in leaf nodes. In this way the deletion from a nonleaf node is transformed into a deletion from a leaf. For example, if we are to delete the element with key 20 that is in the root of Figure 11.6 (c), then this element may be replaced by either the element with key 10 or the element with key 25. Both are in leaf nodes. Once the replacement is done, we are faced with the problem of deleting either the 10 or the 25 from a leaf.

There are four possible cases when deleting from a leaf node p. In the first, p is also the root. If the root is left with at least one element, the changed root is written to disk and we are done. Otherwise, the B-tree is empty following the deletion. In the remaining cases, p is not the root. In the second case, following the deletion, p has at least $\lceil m/2 \rceil - 1$ elements. The modified leaf is written to disk, and we are done.

In the third case (rotation), p has $\lceil m/2 \rceil - 2$ elements, and its nearest sibling, q, has at least $\lceil m/2 \rceil$ elements. To determine this, we examine only one of the two (at most) nearest siblings that p may have. p is deficient, as it has one less than the minimum number of elements required. q has more elements than the minimum required. A rotation is performed. In this rotation, the number of elements in q decreases by one, and the number in p increases by one. As a result, neither p nor q is deficient following the rotation. The rotation leaves behind a valid B-tree. Let r be the parent of p and q. If q is the nearest right sibling of p, then let i be such that E_i is the ith element in r, all elements in p have a key that is less than $E_i.K$, and all those in q have a key that is greater than $E_i.K$. For the rotation, E_i becomes the rightmost element in p, E_i is replaced, in r, by the first (i.e., smallest) element in q, and the leftmost subtree of q becomes the rightmost subtree of p. The changed nodes p, q, and r are written to disk, and the deletion is complete. The case when q is the nearest left sibling of p is similar.

Figure 11.7 shows the rotation cases for a 2-3 tree. A "?" denotes a situation in which the presence or absence of an element is irrelevant. a, b, c, and d denote the children (i.e., roots of subtrees) of nodes.

In the fourth case (combine) for deletion, p has $\lceil m/2 \rceil - 2$ elements, and its nearest sibling q has $\lceil m/2 \rceil - 1$ elements. So, p is deficient, and q has the minimum number of elements required by a nonroot node. Now, nodes p and q and the in-between element E_i in the parent r are combined to form a single node. The combined node has $(\lceil m/2 \rceil - 2) + (\lceil m/2 \rceil - 1) + 1 = 2\lceil m/2 \rceil - 2 \leq m - 1$ elements, which will, at most, fill the node. The combined node is written to disk. The combining operation reduces the number of elements in the parent node, r, by one. If the parent does not become deficient

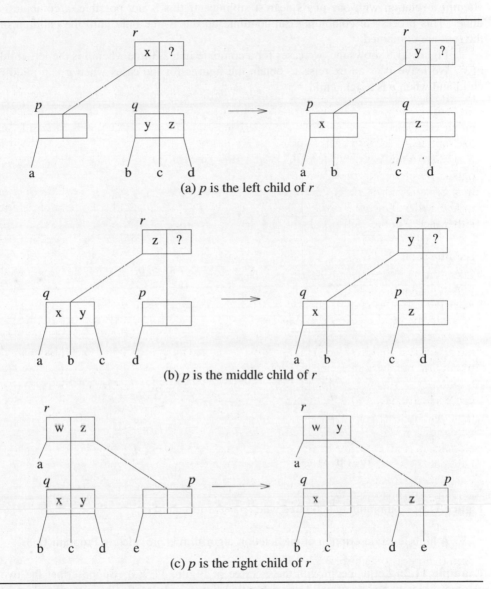

(a) *p* is the left child of *r*

(b) *p* is the middle child of *r*

(c) *p* is the right child of *r*

Figure 11.7: The three cases for rotation in a 2-3 tree

(i.e., it has at least one element if it is the root and at least $\lceil m/2 \rceil - 1$ elements if it is not the root), the changed parent is written to disk, and we are done. Otherwise, if the deficient parent is the root, it is discarded, as it has no elements. If the deficient parent is not the root, it has exactly $\lceil m/2 \rceil - 2$ elements. To remove this deficiency, we first attempt a rotation with one of r's nearest siblings. If this is not possible, a combine is done. This process of combining can continue up the B-tree only until the children of the root are combined.

Figure 11.8 shows the two cases for a combine in a 2-3 tree when p is the left child of r. We leave it as an exercise to obtain the figures for the cases when p is a middle child and when p is a right child.

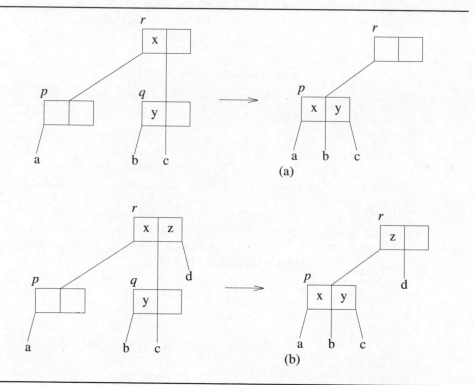

Figure 11.8: Combining in a 2-3 tree when p is the left child of r

A high-level description of the deletion algorithm is provided in Program 11.3.

Example 11.2: Let us begin with the 2-3 tree of Figure 11.9(a). Suppose that the two element fields in a node of a 2-3 tree are called *dataL* and *dataR*. To delete the element with key 70, we must merely delete this element from node C. The result is shown in Figure 11.9(b). To delete the element with key 10 from the 2-3 tree of Figure 11.9(b), we need to shift *dataR* to *dataL* in node B. This results in the 2-3 tree of Figure 11.9(c).

Next consider the deletion of the element with key 60. This leaves node C deficient. Since the right sibling, D, of C has 3 elements, we are in case 3 and a rotation

```
/* delete element with key x */
Search the B-tree for the node p that contains the element whose key is x;
if there is no such p return;   /* no element to delete */
Let p be of the form n, A₀, (E₁,A₁),  ···, (Eₙ,Aₙ) and Eᵢ.K = x;
if p is not a leaf {
        Replace Eᵢ with the element with the smallest key in subtree Aᵢ;
        Let p be the leaf of Aᵢ from which this smallest element was taken;
        Let p be of the form n, A₀, (E₁,A₁),  ···, (Eₙ,Aₙ);
        i = 1;
}
/* delete Eᵢ from node p, a leaf */
Delete (Eᵢ, Aᵢ) from p; n−−;
while ((n < ⌈m/2⌉ − 1) && p != root)
        if p has a nearest right sibling q {
                Let q : n_q, A₀^q, (E₁^q, A₁^q),  ···, (E_{n_q}^q, A_{n_q}^q);
                Let r : n_r, A₀^r, (E₁^r, A₁^r),  ···, (E_{n_r}^r, A_{n_r}^r) be the parent of p and q;
                Let A_j^r = q and A_{j−1}^r = p;
                if (n_q > = ⌈m/2⌉) {/* rotation */
                        (E_{n+1}, A_{n+1}) = (E_j^r, A₀^q); n = n + 1; /* update node p */
                        E_j^r = E₁^q; /* update node r */
                        (n_q, A₀^q, (E₁^q, A₁^q),  ···) = (n_q−1, A₁^q, (E₂^q, A₂^q),  ···);
                                        /* update node q */
                        write nodes p, q and r to disk; return;
                } /* end of rotation */
                /* combine p, E_j^r, and q */
                s = 2* ⌈m/2⌉ − 2;
                write s, A₀, (E₁, A₁),  ···, (Eₙ, Aₙ), (E_j^r, A₀^q), (E₁^q, A₁^q),  ···, (E_{n_q}^q, A_{n_q}^q)
                to disk as node p;
                /* update for next iteration */
                (n, A₀ ···) = (n_r−1, A₀^r,  ···, (E_{j−1}^r, A_{j−1}^r), (E_{j+1}^r, A_{j+1}^r) ···)
                p = r;
        } /* end of if p has a nearest right sibling */
        else {/* node p must have a left sibling */
                /* this is symmetric to the case where p has a right sibling,
                        and is left as an exercise */
        } /* end of if-else and while */
if ( n ) write p: (n, A₀,  ···, (Eₙ,Aₙ))
else root = A₀; /* new root */
```

Program 11.3: Deletion from a B-tree that resides on disk

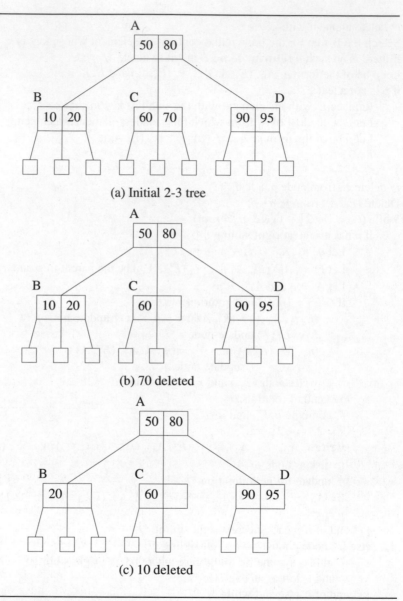

(a) Initial 2-3 tree

(b) 70 deleted

(c) 10 deleted

Figure 11.9: Deletion from a 2-3 tree (continued on next page)

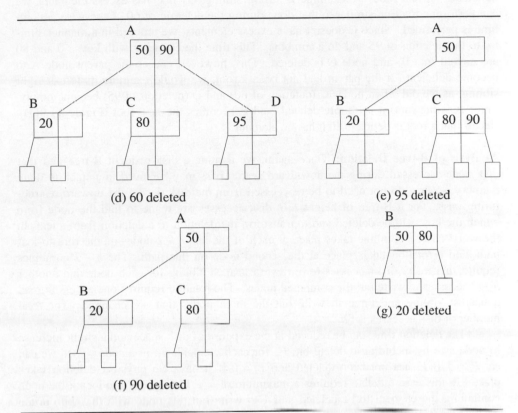

Figure 11.9: Deletion from a 2-3 tree

is performed. In this rotation, we move the the in-between element (i.e., the element whose key is 80) of the parent A of C and D to the *dataL* position of C and move the smallest element of D (i.e., the element whose key is 20) into the in-between position of the parent A of C and D (i.e., the *dataR* position of A). The resulting 2-3 tree takes the form shown in Figure 11.9(d). When the element with key 95 is deleted, node D becomes deficient. The rotation performed when the 60 was deleted is not possible now, as the left sibling, C, has the minimum number of elements required by a node in a B-tree of order 3. We now are in case 4 and must combine nodes C and D and the in-between element (90) in the parent A of C and D. For this, we move the 90 into the left sibling, C, and delete node D. Notice that in a combine, one node is deleted, whereas in a rotation, no node is deleted. The deletion of 95 results in the 2-3 tree of Figure 11.9(e). Deleting the element with key 90 from this tree results in the 2-3 tree of Figure 11.9(f). Now consider deleting the element with key 20 from this tree. Node B becomes deficient. At this time, we examine B's right sibling, C. If C has excess elements, we can perform a rotation similar to that done during the deletion of 60. Otherwise, a combine is performed. Since C doesn't have excess elements, we proceed in a manner similar to the deletion of 95 and do a combine. This time the elements with keys 50 and 80 are moved into B, and node C is deleted. This, however, causes the parent node A to become deficient. If the parent had not been a root, we would examine its left or right sibling, as we did when nodes C (deletion of 60) and D (deletion of 95) became empty. Since A is the root, it is simply deleted, and B becomes the new root (Figure 11.9(g)). Recall that a root is deficient iff it has no element. □

Analysis of B-tree Deletion: Once again, we assume a disk-resident B-tree and that disk nodes accessed during the downward search pass may be saved in a stack in main memory, so they do not need to be reaccessed from the disk during the upward restructuring pass. For a B-tree of height h, h disk accesses are made to find the node from which the key is to be deleted and to transform the deletion to a deletion from a leaf. In the worst case, a combine takes place at each of the last $h - 2$ nodes on the root-to-leaf path, and a rotation takes place at the second node on this path. The $h - 2$ combines require this many disk accesses to retrieve a nearest sibling for each node and another $h - 2$ accesses to write out the combined nodes. The rotation requires one access to read a nearest sibling and three to write out the three nodes that are changed. The total number of disk accesses is $3h$.

The deletion time can be reduced at the expense of disk space and a slight increase in node size by including a delete bit, F_i, for each element, E_i, in a node. Then we can set $F_i = 1$ if E_i has not been deleted and $F_i = 0$ if it has. No physical deletion takes place. In this case a delete requires a maximum of $h + 1$ accesses (h to locate the node containing the element to be deleted and 1 to write out this node with the appropriate delete bit set to 0). With this strategy, the number of nodes in the tree never decreases. However, the space used by deleted entries can be reused during further insertions (see Exercises). As a result, this strategy has little effect on search and insert times (the number of levels increases very slowly when m is large). The time taken to insert an item may even decrease slightly because of the ability to reuse deleted element space. Such reuses would not require us to split any nodes. □

EXERCISES

1. Show that all B-trees of order 2 are full binary trees.

2. Use the insertion algorithm of Program 11.2 to insert an element with key 40 into the 2-3 tree of Figure 11.9(a). Show the resulting 2-3 tree.

3. Use the insertion algorithm of Program 11.2 to insert elements with keys 45, 95, 96, and 97, in this order, into the 2-3-4 tree of Figure 11.3. Show the resulting 2-3-4 tree follwoing each insert.

4. Use the deletion algorithm of Program 11.3 to delete the elements with keys 90, 95, 80, 70, 60 and 50, in this order, from the 2-3 tree of Figure 11.9(a). Show the resulting 2-3 tree following each deletion.

5. Use the deletion algorithm of Program 11.3 to delete the elements with keys 85, 90, 92, 75, 60, and 70 from the 2-3-4 tree of Figure 11.3. Show the resulting 2-3-4 tree following each deletion.

6. (a) Insert elements with keys 62, 5, 85, and 75 one at a time into the order-5 B-tree of Figure 11.10. Show the new tree after each element is inserted. Do the insertion using the insertion process described in the text.

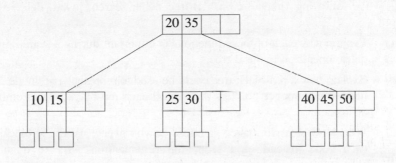

Figure 11.10: B-tree of order 5

(b) Assuming that the tree is kept on a disk and one node may be retrieved at a time, how many disk accesses are needed to make each insertion? State any assumptions you make.

(c) Delete the elements with keys 45, 40, 10, and 25 from the order-5 B-tree of Figure 11.10. Show the tree following each deletion. The deletions are to be performed using the deletion process described in the text.

(d) How many disk accesses are made for each of the deletions?

7. Complete Figure 11.8 by adding figures for the cases when p is the middle child and right child of its parent.

8. Complete the symmetric case of Program 11.3.

9. Develop 2-3 tree functions to search, insert and delete. Test your functions using your own test data.

10. Develop 2-3-4 tree functions to search, insert and delete. Test your functions using your own test data.

11. Write insertion and deletion algorithms for B-trees assuming that with each element is associated an additional data member, *deleted*, such that *deleted* = FALSE iff the corresponding element has not been deleted. Deletions should be accomplished by setting *deleted* = **FALSE**, and insertions should make use of deleted space whenever possible without restructuring the tree.

12. Write algorithms to search and delete keys from a B-tree by position; that is, *get* (k) finds the kth smallest key, and *delete* (k) deletes the kth smallest key in the tree. (**Hint**: To do this efficiently, additional information must be kept in each node. With each pair (E_i, A_i) keep $N_i = \Sigma_{j=0}^{i-1}$ (number of elements in the subtree $A_j + 1$).) What are the worst-case computing times of your algorithms?

13. The text assumed a node structure that was sequential. However, we need to perform the following functions on a B-tree node: search, insert, delete, join, and split.

    (a) Explain why each of these functions is important during a search, insert, and delete operation in the B-tree.

    (b) Explain how a red-black tree could be used to represent each node. You will need to use integer pointers and regard each red-black tree as embedded in an array.

    (c) What kind of performance gain/loss do you expect using red-black trees for each node instead of a sequential organization? Try to quantify your answer.

14. Modify Program 11.2 so that when node p has m elements, we first check to see if either the nearest left sibling or the nearest right sibling of p has fewer than $m - 1$ elements. If so, p is not split. Instead, a rotation is performed moving either the smallest or largest element in p to its parent. The corresponding element in the parent, together with a subtree, is moved to the sibling of p that has space for another element.

15. [*Bayer and McCreight*] Suppose that an insertion has been made into node p and that it has become over-full (i.e., it now contains m elements). Further, suppose that ps nearest right sibling q is full (i.e., it contains $m - 1$ elements). So, the elements in p and q together with the in-between element in the parent of p and q make $2m$ elements. These $2m$ elements may be partitioned into three nodes p, q, and r containing $\lfloor (2m - 2)/3 \rfloor, \lfloor (2m - 1)/3 \rfloor$, and $\lfloor 2m/3 \rfloor$ elements, respectively, plus two in-between elements (one for p and q and the other for q and r). So, we may split p and q into 3 nodes p, q, and r that are almost two-thirds full, replace the former in-between element for p and q with the new one, and then insert the in-between element for q and r together with a pointer to the new node r into the parent of p and q. The case when q is the nearest left sibling of p is similar.

    Rewrite Program 11.2 so that node splittings occur only as described here.

16. A *B*-tree* of order m is a search tree that either is empty or satisfies the following properties:

   (a) The root node has at least two and at most $2\lfloor(2m-2)/3\rfloor + 1$ children.

   (b) The remaining internal nodes have at most m and at least $\lceil(2m-1)/3\rceil$ children each.

   (c) All external nodes are on the same level.
   For a B*-tree of order m that contains N elements, show that if $x = \lceil(2m-1)/3\rceil$, then

   (a) the height, h, of the B*-tree satisfies $h \leq 1 + \log_x\{(N+1)/2\}$

   (b) the number of nodes p in the B*-tree satisifies $p \leq 1 + (N-1)/(x-1)$
   What is the average number of splits per insert if a B*-tree is built up starting from an empty B*-tree?

17. Using the splitting technique of Exercise 15, write an algorithm to insert a new element, x, into a B*-tree of order m. How many disk accesses are made in the worst case and on the average? Assume that the B-tree was initially of depth l and that it
   is maintained on a disk. Each access retrieves or writes one node.

18. Write an algorithm to delete the element whose key is x from a B*-tree of order m. What is the maximum number of accesses needed to delete from a B*-tree of depth l? Make the same assumptions as in Exercise 17.

11.3   B$^+$-TREES

11.3.1   Definition

A B$^+$-tree is a close cousin of the B-tree. The essential differences are:

(1) In a B$^+$-tree we have two types of nodes—index and data. The index nodes of a B$^+$-tree correspond to the internal nodes of a B-tree while the data nodes correspond to external nodes. The index nodes store keys (not elements) and pointers and the data nodes store elements (together with their keys but no pointers).

(2) The data nodes are linked together, in left to right order, to form a doubly linked list.

Figure 11.11 gives an example B$^+$-tree of order 3. The data nodes are shaded while the index nodes are not. Notice that the index nodes form a 2-3 tree whose height is 2. The capacity of a data node need not be the same as that of an index node. In Figure

11.11 each data node can hold 3 elements while each index node can hold 2 keys.

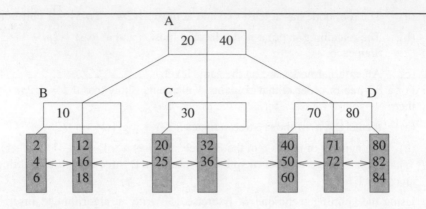

Figure 11.11: A B$^+$-tree of order 3

Definition: A *B$^+$-tree of order m* is a tree that either is empty or satisfies the following properties:

(1)   All data nodes are at the same level and are leaves. Data nodes contain elements only.

(2)   The index nodes define a B-tree of order m; each index node has keys but not elements.

(3)   Let

$$n, A_0, (K_1, A_1), (K_2, A_2), \cdots, (K_n, A_n)$$

where the A_i, $0 \leq i \leq n < m$, are pointers to subtrees, and the K_i, $1 \leq i \leq n < m$, are keys be the format of some index node. Let $K_0 = -\infty$ and $K_{n+1} = \infty$. All elements in the subtree A_i have key less than K_{i+1} and greater than or equal to K_i, $0 \leq i \leq n$.
□

11.3.2   Searching a B$^+$-Tree

B$^+$-trees support two types of searches— exact match and range. To search the tree of Figure 11.11 for the element whose key is 32, we begin at the root A, which is an index node. From the definition of a B$^+$-tree we know that all elements in the left subtree of A (i.e., the subtree whose root is B) have a key smaller than 20; those in the subtree with root C have keys ≥ 20 and < 40; and those in the subtree with root D have keys ≥ 40. So, the search moves to the index node C. Since the search key is ≥ 30, the search moves from C to the data node that contains the elements with keys 32 and 36. This data node is searched and the desired element reported. Program 11.4 gives a high-level description of the algorithm to search a B$^+$-tree.

```
/* search a B+-tree for an element with key x,
     return the element if found, return NULL otherwise */
if the tree is empty return NULL;
K0 = - MAXKEY;
for (*p = root; p is an index node; p = Ai)
{
     Let p have the format n, A0, (K1, A1), ···, (Kn, An);
     Kn+1 = MAXKEY;
     Determine i such that Ki ≤ x < Ki+1;
}
/* search the data node p */
Search p for an element E with key x;
if such an element is found return E
else return NULL;
```

Program 11.4: Searching a B$^+$-tree

To search for all elements with keys in the range [16, 70], we proceed as in an exact match search for the start, 16, of the range. This gets us to the second data node in Figure 11.11. From here, we march down (rightward) the doubly linked list of data nodes until we reach a data node that has an element whose key exceeds the end, 70, of the search range (or until we reach the end of the list). In our example, 4 additional data nodes are examined. All examined data nodes other than the first and last contain at least one element that is in the search range.

11.3.3 Insertion into a B$^+$-Tree

An important difference between inserting into a B-tree and inserting into a B$^+$-tree is how we handle the splitting of a data node. When a data node becomes overfull, half the elements (those with the largest keys) are moved into a new node; the key of the smallest element so moved together with a pointer to the newly created data node are inserted into the parent index node (if any) using the insertion procedure for a B-tree. The splitting of an index node is identical to the splitting of an internal node of a B-tree.

Consider inserting an element with key 27 into the B$^+$-tree of Figure 11.11. We first search for this key. The search gets us to the data node that is the left child of C. Since this data node contains no element with key 27 and since this data node isn't full, we insert the new element as the third element in this data node. Next, consider the insertion of an element with key 14. The search for 14 gets us to the second data node, which is full. Symbolically inserting the new element into this full node results in an overfull node with the key sequence 12, 14, 16, 18. The overfull node is split into two by moving the largest half of the elements (those with keys 16 and 18) into a new data node, which is then inserted into the doubly linked list of data nodes. The smallest key, 16, in this new data node together with a pointer to the new data node are inserted in the parent index node B to get the configuration of Figure 11.12 (a).

Finally, consider inserting an element with key 86 into the B^+-tree of Figure 11.12 (a). The search for 86 gets us to the rightmost data node, which is full. Symbolically inserting the new element into this node results in the key sequence 80, 82, 84, 86. Splitting the overfull data node creates a new data node with the elements whose keys are 84 and 86. The new data node is inserted into the doubly linked list of data nodes. Then we insert the key 84 and a pointer to the new data node into the parent index node D, which becomes overfull. The overfull D is split using Eq. 11.5. The 84 along with two of the 4 subtrees of the overfull D are moved into a new index node E and the 80 together with a pointer to E inserted into the parent A of D. This causes A to become overfull. The overfull A is split using Eq. 11.5 and we get a new index node F that has the key 80 and 2 of the 4 subtrees of the overfull A. The key 40 together with pointers to A and F form the new root of the B^+-tree (Figure 11.12 (b)).

11.3.4 Deletion from a B^+-Tree

Since elements are stored only in the leaves of a B^+-tree, we need concern ourselves only with deletion from a leaf (recall that in the case of a B-tree we had to transform a deletion from a non-leaf into a deletion from a leaf; this case doesn't arise for B^+-trees). Since the index nodes of a B^+-tree form a B-tree, a non-root index node is deficient when it has fewer than $\lceil m/2 \rceil - 1$ keys and a root index node is deficient when it has no key. When is a data node deficient? The definition of a B^+-tree doesn't specify a minimum occupancy for a data node. However, we may get some guidance from our algorithm to insert an element. Following the split of an overfull data node, the original data node as well as the new one each have at least $\lceil c/2 \rceil$ elements, where c is the capacity of a data node. So, except when a data node is the root of the B^+-tree, its occupancy is at least $\lceil c/2 \rceil$. We shall say that a non-root data node is deficient iff it has fewer than $\lceil c/2 \rceil$ elements; a root data node is deficient iff it is empty.

We illustrate the deletion process by an example. Consider the B^+-tree of Figure 11.11. The capacity c of a data node is 3. So, a non-root data node is deficient iff it has fewer than 2 elements. To delete the element whose key is 40, we first search for the element to be deleted. This element is found in the data node that is the left child of the

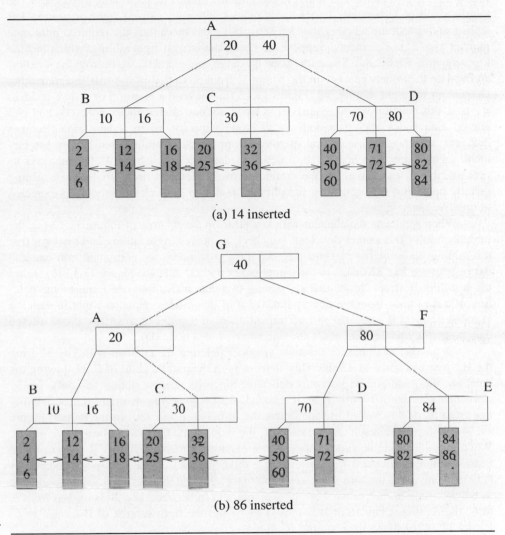

(a) 14 inserted

(b) 86 inserted

Figure 11.12: Insertion into the B$^+$-tree of Figure 11.11

index node D. Following the deletion of the element with key 40, the occupancy of this data node becomes 2. So, the data node isn't deficient and we need merely write the modified data node to disk (assuming the B$^+$-tree is disk resident) and we are done. Notice that when the deletion of an element doesn't result in a deficient data node, no index node is changed.

Next consider the deletion of the element whose key is 71 from the B$^+$-tree of

Figure 11.11. This element is found in the middle child of D. Following its deletion, the middle child of D becomes deficient. We check either its nearest right or nearest left sibling and determine whether the checked sibling has more than the required minimum number ($\lceil c/2 \rceil$) of elements. Suppose we check the nearest right sibling, which has the key sequence 80, 82, 84. Since this node has an excess element, we borrow the smallest and update the in-between key in the parent D from 80 to that of the smallest remaining element in the right sibling, 82. Figure 11.13 (a) shows the result. For a disk-resident B^+-tree, this deletion would require us to write out one altered index node (D) and two altered data nodes. For data nodes with larger capacity, when a data node becomes deficient, we may borrow several elements from a nearest sibling that has excess elements. For example, when $c=10$, a deficient data node will have 4 elements and its nearest sibling may have 10. We could borrow 3 elements from the nearest sibling thereby balancing the occupancy in both data nodes to 7. Such a balancing is expected to improve performance.

When we delete the element with key 80 from the B^+-tree of Figure 11.13 (a), the middle child of D becomes deficient. We check its nearest right sibling and discover that this sibling has only $\lceil c/2 \rceil$ elements. So, the 2 data nodes are combined into one and the in-between key 82 that is in the parent index node D deleted. Figure 11.13 (b) shows the resulting B^+-tree. Notice that combining two data nodes into one requires the deletion of a data node from the doubly linked list of data nodes. Note also that in the case of a disk resident B^+-tree, the just performed deletion requires us to write out one altered data node (the middle child of D) and one altered index node (D).

As another example for deletion, consider deleting the element with key 32 from the B^+-tree of Figure 11.12 (b). This element is in the middle child of C. Following the deletion, the middle child becomes deficient. Since its nearest sibling has only $\lceil c/2 \rceil$ elements, we cannot borrow from it. Instead, we combine the two data nodes deleting one from its doubly linked list and delete the in-between key (30) in the parent. Figure 11.14 (a) shows the result. As we can see, the index node C now has become deficient. When an index node becomes deficient, we examine a nearest sibling. If the examined nearest sibling has excess keys, we balance the occupancy of the two index nodes; this balancing involves moving some keys and associated subtrees as well as changing the in-between key in the parent. For our example, the in-between key 20 is moved from A to C, the rightmost key 16 of B is moved to A, and the right subtree of B moved to C. Figure 11.14 (b) shows the resulting B^+-tree.

As a final example, consider the deletion of the element with key 86 from the B^+-tree of Figure 11.12 (b). The middle child of E becomes deficient and is combined with its sibling; a data node is deleted from the doubly linked list of data nodes and the in-between key 84 in the parent also is deleted. This results in a deficient index node E and the configuration of Figure 11.15 (a). The deficient index node E combines with its sibling index node D and the in-between key 80 to get the configuration of Figure 11.15 (b). Finally, the deficient index node F combines with its sibling A and the in-between key 40 in its parent G. This causes the parent G, which is the root, to become deficient.

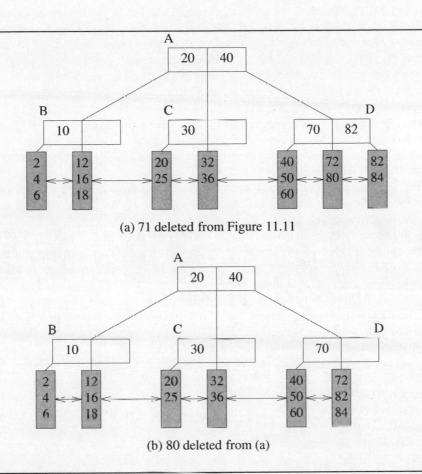

(a) 71 deleted from Figure 11.11

(b) 80 deleted from (a)

Figure 11.13: Deletion from a B$^+$-tree

The deficient root is discarded and we get the B$^+$-tree of Figure 11.12 (a). In the case of a disk resident B$^+$-tree, the deletion of 86 would require us to write to disk one altered data node and 2 altered index nodes (A and D).

EXERCISES

1. Into the B$^+$-tree of Figure 11.11 insert elements with keys 5, 38, 45, 11 and 81 (in this order). Use the insertion method described in the text. Draw the B$^+$-tree following each insert.

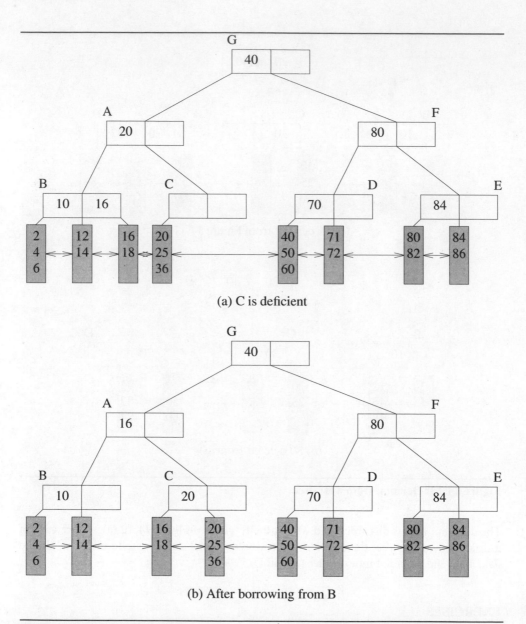

(a) C is deficient

(b) After borrowing from B

Figure 11.14: Stages in deleting 32 from the B$^+$-tree of Figure 11.12 (b)

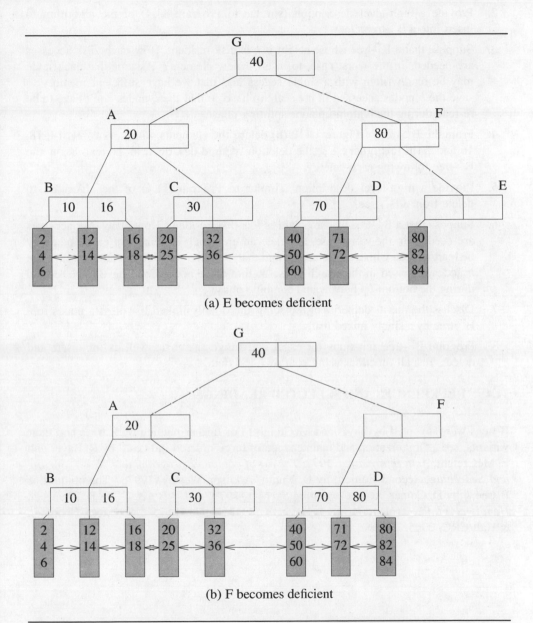

(a) E becomes deficient

(b) F becomes deficient

Figure 11.15: Stages in deleting 86 from the B+-tree of Figure 11.12 (b)

2. Provide a high-level description (similar to Program 11.4) of the algorithm to insert into a B^+-tree.

3. Suppose that a B^+-tree whose height is h is disk resident. How many disk accesses are needed, in the worst case, to insert a new element? Assume that each node may be read/written with a single access and that we have sufficient memory to save the h nodes accessed in the search phase so that these nodes don't have to be re-read during the bottom-up node splitting phase.

4. From the B^+-tree of Figure 11.12 (b) delete the elements with keys 6, 71, 14, 18, 16 and 2 (in this order). Use the deletion method described in the text. Show the B^+-tree following each delete.

5. Provide a high-level description (similar to Program 11.4) of the algorithm to delete from a B^+-tree.

6. Suppose that a B^+-tree whose height is h is disk resident. How many disk accesses are needed, in the worst case, to delete an element? Assume that each node may be read/written with a single access and that we have sufficient memory to save the h nodes accessed in the search phase so that these nodes don't have to be re-read during the bottom-up borrow and combine phase.

7. Discuss the merits/demerits of replacing the doubly linked list of data nodes in a B^+-tree by a singly linked list.

8. Program B^+-tree functions for exact and range search as well as for insert and delete. Test all functions using your own test data.

11.4 REFERENCES AND SELECTED READINGS

B-trees were invented by Bayer and McCreight. For further reading on B-trees and their variants, see "Organization and maintenance of large ordered indices," by R. Bayer and E. McCreight, *Acta Informatica*, 1972; *The art of computer programming, Vol. 3, Sorting and Searching*, Second Edition, by D. Knuth, Addison Wesley, 1997; "The ubiquitous B-tree," by D. Comer, *ACM Computing Surveys*, 1979; and " B trees," by D. Zhang, in *Handbook of data structures and applications*, D. Mehta and S. Sahni editors, Chapman & Hall/CRC, 2005.

CHAPTER 12

Digital Search Structures

12.1 DIGITAL SEARCH TREES

12.1.1 Definition

A *digital search tree* is a binary tree in which each node contains one element. The element-to-node assignment is determined by the binary representation of the element keys. Suppose that we number the bits in the binary representation of a key from left to right beginning at one. Then bit one of 1000 is 1, and bits two, three, and four are 0. All keys in the left subtree of a node at level i have bit i equal to zero whereas those in the right subtree of nodes at this level have bit $i = 1$. Figure 12.1(a) shows a digital search tree. This tree contains the keys 1000, 0010, 1001, 0001, 1100, and 0000.

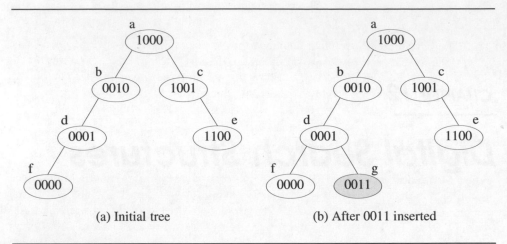

(a) Initial tree   (b) After 0011 inserted

Figure 12.1: Digital search trees

12.1.2   Search, Insert and Delete

Suppose we are to search for the key $k = 0011$ in the tree of Figure 12.1(a). k is first compared with the key in the root. Since k is different from the key in the root, and since bit one of k is 0, we move to the left child, b, of the root. Now, since k is different from the key in node b, and bit two of k is 0, we move to the left child, d, of b. Since k is different from the key in node d and since bit three of k is one, we move to the right child of d. Node d has no right child to move to. From this we conclude that $k = 0011$ is not in the search tree. If we wish to insert k into the tree, then it is to be added as the right child of d. When this is done, we get the digital search tree of Figure 12.1(b).

The digital search tree functions to search and insert are quite similar to the corresponding functions for binary search trees. The essential difference is that the sub-tree to move to is determined by a bit in the search key rather than by the result of the comparison of the search key and the key in the current node. The deletion of an item in a leaf is done by removing the leaf node. To delete from any other node, the deleted item must be replaced by a value from any leaf in its subtree and that leaf removed.

Each of these operations can be performed in $O(h)$ time, where h is the height of the digital search tree. If each key in a digital search tree has *keySize* bits, then the height of the digital search tree is at most *keySize* + 1.

EXERCISES

1. Draw a different digital search tree than Figure 12.1 (a) that has the same set of keys.

2. Write the digital search tree functions for the search, insert, and delete operations. Assume that each key has *keySize* bits and that the function *bit* (*k*, *i*) returns the *i*th (from the left) bit of the key *k*. Show that each of your functions has complexity O(*h*), where *h* is the height of the digital search tree.

12.2   BINARY TRIES AND PATRICIA

When we are dealing with very long keys, the cost of a key comparison is high. Since searching a digital search tree requires many comparisons between pairs of keys, digital search trees (and also binary and multiway search trees) are inefficient search structures when the keys are very long. We can reduce the number of key comparisons done during a search to one by using a related structure called *Patricia* (*P*ractical *a*lgorithm *t*o *r*etrieve *i*nformation *c*oded *i*n *a*lphanumeric). We shall develop this structure in three steps. First, we introduce a structure called a binary trie (pronounced try''). Then we transform binary tries into compressed binary tries. Finally, from compressed binary tries we obtain Patricia. Since binary tries and compressed binary tries are introduced only as a means of arriving at Patricia, we do not dwell much on how to manipulate these structures. A more general version of binary tries (called a trie) is considered in the next section.

12.2.1   Binary Tries

A *binary trie* is a binary tree that has two kinds of nodes: *branch nodes* and *element nodes*. A branch node has the two data members *leftChild* and *rightChild*. It has no *data* data member. An element node has the single data member *data*. Branch nodes are used to build a binary tree search structure similar to that of a digital search tree. This search structure leads to element nodes.

Figure 12.2 shows a six-element binary trie. Element nodes are shaded. To search for an element with key *k*, we use a branching pattern determined by the bits of *k*. The *i*th bit of *k* is used at level *i*. If it is zero, the search moves to the left subtree. Otherwise, it moves to the right subtree. To search for 0010 we first follow the left child, then again the left child, and finally the right child.

Observe that a successful search in a binary trie always ends at an element node. Once this element node is reached, the key in this node is compared with the key we are searching for. This is the only key comparison that takes place. An unsuccessful search may terminate either at an element node or at a 0 pointer.

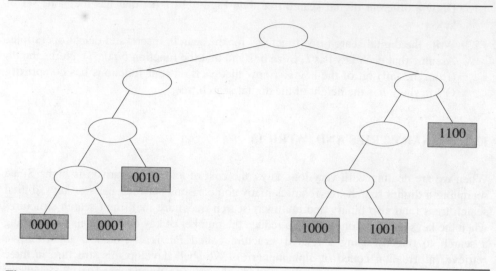

Figure 12.2: Example of a binary trie

12.2.2 Compressed Binary Tries

The binary trie of Figure 12.2 contains branch nodes whose degree is one. By adding another data member, *bitNumber*, to each branch node, we can eliminate all degree-one branch nodes from the trie. The *bitNumber* data member of a branch node gives the bit number of the key that is to be used at this node. Figure 12.3 gives the binary trie that results from the elimination of degree-one branch nodes from the binary trie of Figure 12.2. The number outside a node is its *bitNumber*. A binary trie that has been modified in this way to contain no branch nodes of degree one is called a *compressed binary trie*.

12.2.3 Patricia

Compressed binary tries may be represented using nodes of a single type. The new nodes, called *augmented branch nodes*, are the original branch nodes augmented by the data member *data*. The resulting structure is called *Patricia* and is obtained from a compressed binary trie in the following way:

(1) Replace each branch node by an augmented branch node.
(2) Eliminate the element nodes.
(3) Store the data previously in the element nodes in the *data* data members of the

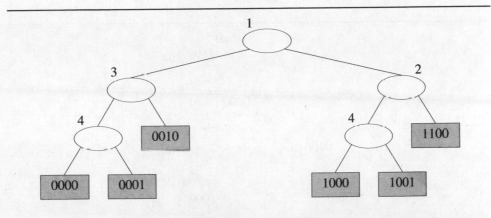

Figure 12.3: Binary trie of Figure 12.2 with degree-one nodes eliminated

augmented branch nodes. Since every nonempty compressed binary trie has one less branch node than it has element nodes, it is necessary to add one augmented branch node. This node is called the *header node*. The remaining structure is the left subtree of the header node. The header node has *bitNumber* equal to zero. Its *rightChild* data member is not used. The assignment of data to augmented branch nodes is done in such a way that the *bitNumber* in the augmented branch node is less than or equal to that in the parent of the element node that contained this data.

(4)   Replace the original pointers to element nodes by pointers to the respective augmented branch nodes.

When these transformations are performed on the compressed trie of Figure 12.3, we get the structure of Figure 12.4. Let *root* be the root of Patricia. *root* is 0 iff the Patricia is empty. A Patricia with one element is represented by a header node whose left-child data member points to itself (Figure 12.5(a)). We can distinguish between pointers that pointed originally to branch nodes and those that pointed to element nodes by noting that, in Patricia, the former pointers are directed to nodes with a greater *bitNumber* value, whereas pointers of the latter type are directed to nodes whose *bitNumber* value either is equal to or less than that in the node where the pointer originates.

12.2.3.1   Searching Patricia

To search for an element with key k, we begin at the header node and follow a path determined by the bits in k. When an element pointer is followed, the key in the node reached is compared with k. This is the only key comparison made. No comparisons are

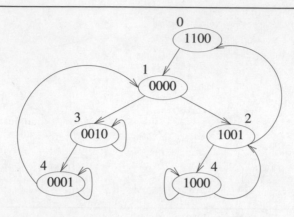

Figure 12.4: An example of Patricia

made on the way down. Suppose we wish to search for $k = 0000$ in the Patricia instance of Figure 12.4. We begin at the header node and follow the left-child pointer to the node with 0000. The bit-number data member of this node is 1. Since bit one of k is 0, we follow the left child pointer to the node with 0010. Now bit three of k is used. Since this is 0, the search moves to the node with 0001. The bit-number data member of this node is 4. The fourth bit of k is zero, so we follow the left-child pointer. This brings us to a node with bit-number data member less than that of the node we moved from. Hence, an element pointer was used. Comparing the key in this node with k, we find a match, and the search is successful.

Next, suppose that we are to search for $k = 1011$. We begin at the header node. The search moves successively to the nodes with 0000, 1001, 1000, and 1001. k is compared with 1001. Since k is not equal to 1001, we conclude that there is no element with this key.

The function to search Patricia tree t is given in Program 12.1. This function returns, a pointer to the last node encountered in the search. If the key in this node is k, the search is successful. Otherwise, t contains no element with key k. The function $bit(i,j)$ returns the jth bit (the leftmost bit is bit one) of i. The C declarations used to define a Patricia tree are:

```
typedef struct patriciaTree *patricia;
      struct {
            int bitNumber;
            element data;
            patricia leftChild, rightChild;
            } patriciaTree;
   patricia root;
```

```
patricia search(patricia t, unsigned k)
{/* search the Patricia tree t; return the last node
    encountered; if k is the key in this last node, the
    search is successful */
   patricia currentNode, nextNode;
   if (!t) return NULL; /* empty tree */
   nextNode = t→leftChild;
   currentNode = t;
   while (nextNode→bitNumber > currentNode→bitNumber) {
      currentNode = nextNode;
      nextNode = (bit(k, nextNode→bitNumber)) ?
      nextNode→rightChild : nextNode→leftChild;
   }
   return nextNode;
}
```

Program 12.1: Searching Patricia

12.2.3.2   Inserting into Patricia

Let us now examine how we can insert new elements. Suppose we begin with an empty
instance and wish to insert an element with key 1000. The result is an instance that has
only a header node (Figure 12.5(a)). Next, consider inserting an element with key $k =$
0010. First, we search for this key using function *Search* (Program 12.1). The search
terminates at the header node. Since 0010 is not equal to the key $q = 1000$ in this node,
we know that 0010 is not currently in the Patricia instance, so the element may be
inserted. For this, the keys k and q are compared to determine the first (i.e., leftmost) bit
at which they differ. This is bit one. A new node containing the element with key k is
added as the left-child of the header node. Since bit one of k is zero, the left child data
member of this new node points to itself, and its right-child data member points to the
header node. The bit-number data member is set to 1. The resulting Patricia instance is
shown in Figure 12.5(b).

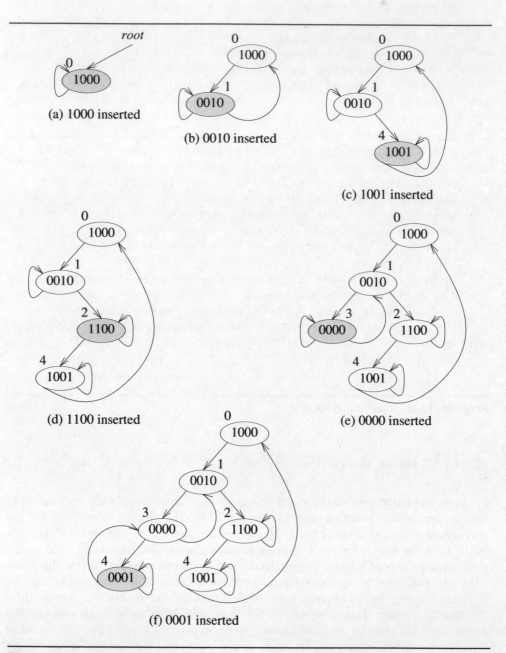

Figure 12.5: Insertion into Patricia

Suppose that the next element to be inserted has $k = 1001$. The search for this key ends at the node with $q = 1000$. The first bit at which k and q differ is bit $j = 4$. Now we search the instance of Figure 12.5(b) using only the first $j - 1 = 3$ bits of k. The last move is from the node with 0010 to that with 1000. Since this is a right-child move, a new node containing the element with key k is to be inserted as the right child of 0010. The bit-number data member of this node is set to $j = 4$. As bit four of k is 1, the right-child data member of the new node points to itself and its left-child data member points to the node with q. Figure 12.5(c) shows the resulting structure.

To insert $k = 1100$ into Figure 12.5(c), we first search for this key. Once again, $q = 1000$. The first bit at which k and q differ is $j = 2$. The search using only the first $j - 1$ bits ends at the node with 1001. The last move is a right child move from 0010. A new node containing the element with key k and bit-number data member $j = 2$ is added as the right child of 0010. Since bit j of k is one, the right-child data member of the new node points to itself. Its left-child data member points to the node with 1001 (this was previously the right child of 0010). The new Patricia instance is shown in Figure 12.5(d). Figure 12.5(e) shows the result of inserting an element with key 0000, and Figure 12.5(f) shows the Patricia instance following the insertion of 0001.

The preceding discussion leads to the insertion function *insert* of Program 12.2. Its complexity is seen to be O(h) where h is the height of t. h can be as large as min{$keySize + 1, n$} where *keySize* is the number of bits in a key and n is the number of elements. When the keys are uniformly distributed the height is O(log$n$). We leave the development of the deletion procedure as an exercise.

```
void insert(patricia *t, element theElement)
{/* insert theElement into the Patricia tree *t */
    patricia current, parent, lastNode, newNode;
    int i;
    if (!(*t)) {/* empty tree */
        MALLOC(*t, sizeof(patriciaTree));
        (*t)→bitNumber = 0; (*t)→data = theElement;
        (*t)→leftChild = *t;
    }
    lastNode = search(*t,theElement.key);
    if (theElement.key == lastNode→data.key) {
        fprintf(stderr, "The key is in the tree. Insertion
                    fails.\n");
        exit(EXIT_FAILURE);
    }
    /* find the first bit where theElement.key and
        lastNode→data.key differ */
```

```
   for (i = 1;  bit(theElement.key,i) ==
                bit(lastNode→data.key,i);  i++);

   /* search tree using the first i-1 bits */
   current = (*t)→leftChild; parent = *t;
   while (current→bitNumber > parent→bitNumber &&
                              current→bitNumber < i) {
      parent = current;
      current = (bit(theElement.key, current→bitNumber)) ?
                current→rightChild : current→leftChild;
   }

   /* insert theElement as a child of parent */
   MALLOC(newNode, sizeof(patriciaTree));
   newNode→data = theElement; newNode→bitNumber = i;
   newNode→leftChild = (bit(theElement.key,i)) ?
                       current: newNode;
   newNode→rightChild = (bit(theElement.key,i)) ?
                        newNode : current;
   if (current == parent→leftChild)
      parent→leftChild = newNode;
   else parent→rightChild = newNode;
}
```

Program 12.2: Insertion function for Patricia

EXERCISES

1. Write the binary trie functions for the search, insert, and delete operations. Assume that each key has *keySize* bits and that the function *bit* (*k*, *i*) returns the *i*th (from the left) bit of the key *k*. Show that each of your functions has complexity $O(h)$, where *h* is the height of the binary trie.

2. Write the compressed binary trie functions for the search, insert, and delete operations. Assume that each key has *keySize* bits and that the function *bit* (*k*, *i*) returns the *i*th (from the left) bit of the key *k*. Show that each of your functions has complexity $O(h)$, where *h* is the height of the compressed binary trie.

3. Write a function to delete the element with key *k* from a Patricia. The complexity of your function should be $O(h)$, where *h* is the height of the Patricia instance. Show that this is the case.

12.3   MULTIWAY TRIES

12.3.1   Definition

A multiway trie (or, simply, trie) is a structure that is particularly useful when key values are of varying size. This data structure is a generalization of the binary trie that was developed in the preceding section.

A *trie* is a tree of degree $m \geq 2$ in which the branching at any level is determined not by the entire key value, but by only a portion of it. As an example, consider the trie of Figure 12.6 in which the keys are composed of lowercase letters from the English alphabet. The trie contains two types of nodes: *element*, and *branch*. In Figure 12.6, element nodes are shaded while branch nodes are not shaded. An element node has only a *data* field; a branch node contains pointers to subtrees. In Figure 12.6, each branch node has 27 pointer fields. The extra pointer field is used for the blank character (denoted b). This character is used to terminate all keys, as a trie requires that no key be a prefix of another (see Figure 12.7).

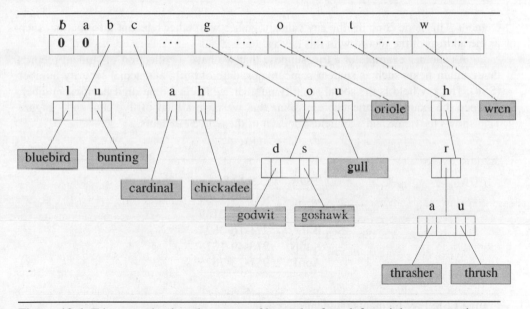

Figure 12.6: Trie created using characters of key value from left to right, one at a time

At the first level all key values are partitioned into disjoint classes depending on their first character. Thus, *root →child* [*i*] points to a subtrie containing all key values beginning with the *i*th letter. On the *j*th level the branching is determined by the *j*th character. When a subtrie contains only one key value, it is replaced by a node of type

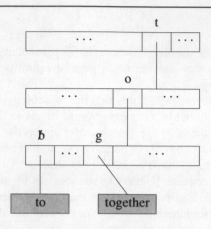

Figure 12.7: Trie showing need for a terminal character (in this case a blank)

element. This node contains the key value, together with other relevant information, such as the address of the record with this key value.

As another example of a trie, suppose that we have a collection of student records that contain fields such as student name, major, date of birth, and social security number (SS#). The key field is the social security number, which is a nine digit decimal number. To keep the example manageable, assume that we have a total of five elements. Figure 12.8 shows the name and SS# fields for each of these five elements.

Name	SS#
Jack	951-94-1654
Jill	562-44-2169
Bill	271-16-3624
Kathy	278-49-1515
April	951-23-7625

Figure 12.8: Five elements (student records)

To obtain a trie representation for these five elements, we first select a radix that will be used to decompose each key into digits. If we use the radix 10, the decomposed digits are just the decimal digits shown in Figure 12.8. We shall examine the digits of the key field (i.e., SS#) from left to right. Using the first digit of the SS#, we partition the elements into three groups—elements whose SS# begins with 2 (i.e., Bill and Kathy), those that begin with 5 (i.e., Jill), and those that begin with 9 (i.e., April and Jack). Groups with more than one element are partitioned using the next digit in the key. This partitioning process is continued until every group has exactly one element in it.

The partitioning process described above naturally results in a tree structure that has 10-way branching as is shown in Figure 12.9. The tree employs two types of nodes—*branch nodes* and *element nodes*. Each branch node has 10 children (or pointer) fields. These fields, *child*[0:9], have been labeled $0, 1, \cdots, 9$ for the root node of Figure 12.9. *root.child*[i] points to the root of a subtrie that contains all elements whose first digit is i. In Figure 12.9, nodes $A, B, D, E, F,$ and I are branch nodes. The remaining nodes, nodes $C, G, H, J,$ and K are element nodes. Each element node contains exactly one element. In Figure 12.9, only the key field of each element is shown in the element nodes.

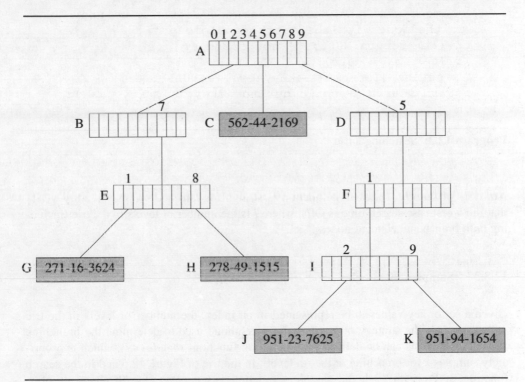

Figure 12.9: Trie for the elements of Figure 12.8

12.3.2   Searching a Trie

To search a trie for a key, x, we must break x into its constituent characters and follow the branches determined by these characters. The function *search* (Program 12.3) assumes that $p \rightarrow u$. *key* is the key represented in node p if p is an element node and that a blank has been appended to the search key before invocation. The function invocation is *search* $(t, key, 1)$. *search* uses the function *getIndex* (key, i) which performs the ith level sampling of the key. In the case of left to right single character sampling, this function extracts the ith character of the key and converts it to an integer index that tells us which pointer field of the branch node to use.

```
triePointer search(triePointer t, char *key, int i)
{/* search the trie t, return NULL if there is no
    element with this key, otherwise return a pointer
    to the node with the matching element */
  if (!t) return NULL; /* not found */
  if (t→tag == data)
      return ((strcmp(t→key,key)) ? NULL : t);
  return search(t→child[getIndex(key,i)], key, i+1);
}
```

Program 12.3: Searching a trie

Analysis of *search*: The *search* function is straightforward and we may readily verify that the worst case search time is O(l), where l is the number of levels in the trie (including both branch and element nodes). □

12.3.3   Sampling Strategies

Given a set of key values to be represented in an index, the number of levels in the trie will depend on the strategy or key sampling technique used to determine the branching at each level. This can be defined by a sampling function, *sample* (x, i), which appropriately samples x for branching at the ith level. In the trie of Figure 12.6 and in the search function of Program 12.4, the sampling function is *sample* $(x, i) = i$th character of x. Some other choices for this function are

(1)   *sample* $(x, i) = x_{n-i+1}$

(2)   *sample* $(x, i) = x_{r(x,i)}$ for $r(x, i)$ a randomization function

$$(3) \quad sample\,(x,i) = \begin{cases} x_{i/2} & \text{if } i \text{ is even} \\ x_{n-(i-1)/2} & \text{if } i \text{ is odd} \end{cases}$$

where $x = x_1 x_2 \cdots x_n$.

For each of these functions, one may easily construct key value sets for which the particular function is best (i.e., it results in a trie with the fewest number of levels). The trie of Figure 12.6 has five levels. Using function (1) on the same key values yields the trie of Figure 12.10, which has only three levels. An optimal sampling function for this data set will yield a trie that has only two levels (Figure 12.11). Choosing the optimal sampling function for any particular set of values is very difficult. In a dynamic situation, with insertion and deletion, we wish to optimize average performance. In the absence of any further information on key values, the best choice would probably be function (2).

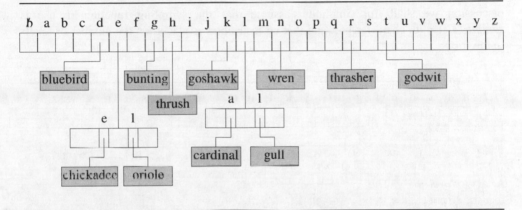

Figure 12.10: Trie constructed for data of Figure 12.6 sampling one character at a time, from right to left

Although all our examples of sampling have involved single-character sampling we need not restrict ourselves to this. The key value may be interpreted as consisting of digits using any radix we desire. Using a radix of 27^2 would result in two-character sampling. Other radixes would give different samplings.

The maximum number of levels in a trie can be kept low by adopting a different strategy for element nodes. These nodes can be designed to hold more than one key value. If the maximum number of levels allowed is l, then all key values that are synonyms up to level $l - 1$ are entered into the same element node. If the sampling function is chosen correctly, there will be only a few synonyms in each element node. The element node will therefore be small and can be processed in internal memory. Figure 12.12 shows the use of this strategy on the trie of Figure 12.6 with $l = 3$. In further

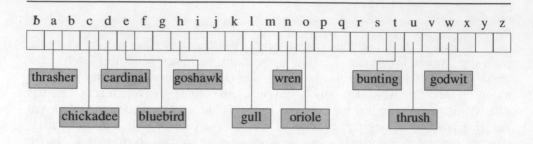

Figure 12.11: An optimal trie for the data of Figure 12.6 sampling on the first level done by using the fourth character of the key values

discussion we shall, for simplicity, assume that the sampling function in use is *sample* $(x,i) = i$th character of x and that no restriction is placed on the number of levels in the trie.

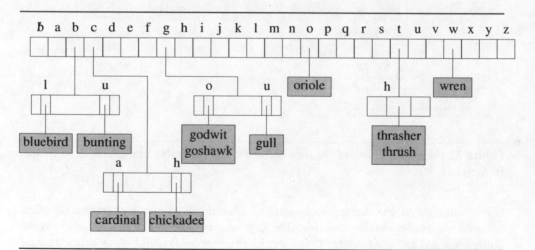

Figure 12.12: Trie obtained for data of Figure 12.6 when number of levels is limited to 3; keys have been sampled from left to right, one character at a time

12.3.4 Insertion into a Trie

Insertion into a trie is straightforward. We shall illustrate the procedure by two examples and leave the formal writing of the algorithm as an exercise. Let us consider the trie of Figure 12.6 and insert into it the keys bobwhite and bluejay. First, we have $x =$ bobwhite and we attempt to search for bobwhite. This leads us to node σ, where we discover that $\sigma.link[\text{'o'}] = 0$. Hence, x is not in the trie and may be inserted here (see Figure 12.13). Next, $x =$ bluejay, and a search of the trie leads us to the element node that contains bluebird. The keys bluebird and bluejay are sampled until the sampling results in two different values. This happens at the fifth letter. Figure 12.13 shows the trie after both insertions.

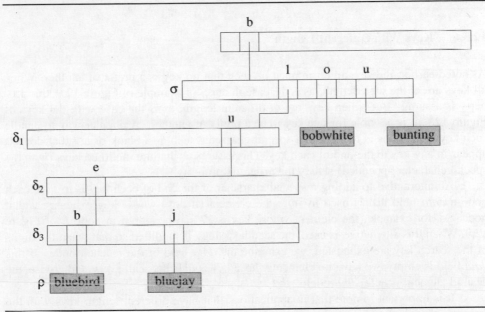

Figure 12.13: Section of trie of Figure 12.6 showing changes resulting from inserting bobwhite and bluejay

12.3.5 Deletion from a Trie

Once again, we shall not present the deletion algorithm formally but will look at two examples to illustrate some of the ideas involved in deleting entries from a trie. From the trie of Figure 12.13, let us first delete bobwhite. To do this we set $\sigma.link['o']$ equal to 0. No other changes need to be made. Next, let us delete bluejay. This deletion leaves us with only one key value in the subtrie, δ_3. This means that the node δ_3 may be deleted, and ρ can be moved up one level. The same can be done for nodes δ_1 and δ_2. Finally, the node σ is reached. The subtrie with root σ has more than one key value. Therefore, ρ cannot be moved up any more levels, and we set $\sigma.link['l']$ equal to ρ. To facilitate deletions from tries, it is useful to add a *count* data member in each branch node. This data member contains the number of children the node has.

As in the case of binary tries, we can define compressed tries in which each branch node has at least two children. In this case, each branch node is augmented to have an additional data member, *skip*, that indicates the number of levels of branching that have been eliminated (alternately, we can have a data member, *sample*, that indicates the sampling level to use).

12.3.6 Keys With Different Length

As noted earlier, the keys in a trie must be such that no key is a prefix of another. When all keys are of the same length, as is the case in our SS# example of Figure 12.9, this property is assured. But, when keys are of different length, as is the case with the keys of Figure 12.6, it is possible for one key to be a prefix of another. A popular way to handle such key collections is to append a special character such as a blank or a # that doesn't appear in any key to the end of each key. This assures us that the modified keys (with the special character appended) satisfy the no-prefix property.

An alternative to adding a special character at the end of each key is to give each node a *data* field that is used to store the element (if any) whose key exhausts at that node. So, for example, the element whose key is 27 can be stored in node E of Figure 12.9. When this alternative is used, the search strategy is modified so that when the digits of the search key are exhausted, we examine the *data* field of the reached node. If this *data* field is empty, we have no element whose key equals the search key. Otherwise, the desired element is in this *data* field.

It is important to note that in applications that have different length keys with the property that no key is a prefix of another, neither of the just-mentioned strategies is needed.

12.3.7 Height of a Trie

In the worst case, a root-node to element-node path has a branch node for every digit in a key. Therefore, the height of a trie is at most *numberofdigits* +1.

A trie for social security numbers has a height that is at most 10. If we assume that it takes the same time to move down one level of a trie as it does to move down one level of a binary search tree, then with at most 10 moves we can search a social-security trie. With this many moves, we can search a binary search tree that has at most $2^{10} - 1 = 1023$ elements. This means that, we expect searches in the social security trie to be faster than searches in a binary search tree (for student records) whenever the number of student records is more than 1023. The breakeven point will actually be less than 1023 because we will normally not be able to construct full or complete binary search trees for our element collection.

Since a SS# is nine digits, a social security trie can have up to 10^9 elements in it. An AVL tree with 10^9 elements can have a height that is as much as (approximately) $1.44\log_2(10^9+2) = 44$. Therefore, it could take us four times as much time to search for elements when we organize our collection of student records as an AVL tree rather than as a trie!

12.3.8   Space Required and Alternative Node Structures

The use of branch nodes that have as many child fields as the radix of the digits (or one more than this radix when different keys may have different length) results in a fast search algorithm. However, this node structure is often wasteful of space because many of the child fields are **NULL**. A radix r trie for d digit keys requires $O(rdn)$ child fields, where n is the number of elements in the trie. To see this, notice that in a d digit trie with n element nodes, each element node may have at most d ancestors, each of which is a branch node. Therefore, the number of branch nodes is at most dn. (Actually, we cannot have this many branch nodes, because the element nodes have common ancestors like the root node.)

We can reduce the space requirements, at the expense of increased search time, by changing the node structure. Some of the possible alternative structures for the branch node of a trie are considered below.

A chain of nodes.
Each node of the chain has the three fields *digitValue*, *child*, and *next*. Node E of Figure 12.9, for example, would be replaced by the chain shown in Figure 12.14.

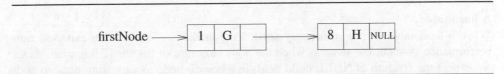

Figure 12.14: Chain for node E of Figure 12.9

The space required by a branch node changes from that required for r

children/pointer fields to that required for $2p$ pointer fields and p digit value fields, where p is the number of children fields in the branch node that are not **NULL**. Under the assumption that pointer fields and digit value fields are of the same size, a reduction in space is realized when more than two-thirds of the children fields in branch nodes are **NULL**. In the worst case, almost all the branch nodes have only 1 field that is not **NULL** and the space savings become almost $(1-3/r)*100\%$.

A (balanced) binary search tree.
Each node of the binary search tree has a digit value and a pointer to the subtrie for that digit value. Figure 12.15 shows the binary search tree for node E of Figure 12.9.

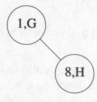

Figure 12.15: Binary search tree for node E of Figure 12.9

Under the assumption that digit values and pointers take the same amount of space, the binary search tree representation requires space for $4p$ fields per branch node, because each search tree node has fields for a digit value, a subtrie pointer, a left child pointer, and a right child pointer. The binary search tree representation of a branch node saves us space when more than three-fourths of the children fields in branch nodes are **NULL**. Note that for large r, the binary search tree is faster to search than the chain described above.

A binary trie.
Figure 12.16 shows the binary trie for node E of Figure 12.9. The space required by a branch node represented as a binary trie is at most $(2*\lceil\log_2 r\rceil+1)p$.

A hash table.
When a hash table with a sufficiently small loading density is used, the expected time performance is about the same as when the node structure of Figure 12.9 is used. Since we expect the fraction of **NULL** child fields in a branch node to vary from node to node and also to increase as we go down the trie, maximum space efficiency is obtained by consolidating all of the branch nodes into a single hash table. To accomplish this, each node in the trie is assigned a number, and each parent to child pointer is replaced by a triple of the form (*currentNode*,*digitValue*,*childNode*). The numbering scheme for

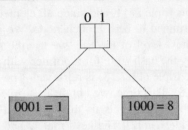

Figure 12.16: Binary trie for node E of Figure 12.9

nodes is chosen so as to easily distinguish between branch and element nodes. For example, if we expect to have at most 100 elements in the trie at any time, the numbers 0 through 99 are reserved for element nodes and the numbers 100 on up are used for branch nodes. The element nodes are themselves represented as an array *element* [100]. (An alternative scheme is to represent pointers as tuples of the form (*currentNode*,*digitValue*,*childNode*,*childNodeIsBranchNode*), where *childNodeIsBranchNode* = **true** iff the child is a branch node.)

Suppose that the nodes of the trie of Figure 12.9 are assigned numbers as given in Figure 12.17. This number assignment assumes that the trie will have no more than 10 elements.

Node	A	B	C	D	E	F	G	H	I	J	K
Number	10	11	0	12	13	14	1	2	15	3	4

Figure 12.17: Number assignment to nodes of trie of Figure 12.9

The pointers in node A are represented by the tuples $(10,2,11),(10,5,0)$, and $(10,9,12)$. The pointers in node E are represented by the tuples $(13,1,1)$ and $(13,8,2)$.

The pointer triples are stored in a hash table using the first two fields (i.e., the *currentNode* and *digitValue*) as the key. For this purpose, we may transform the two field key into an integer using the formula *currentNode* $*r+$*digitValue*, where r is the trie radix, and use the division method to hash the transformed key into a home bucket. The data presently in element node i is stored in *element* [i].

To see how all this works, suppose we have set up the trie of Figure 12.9 using the hash table scheme just described. Consider searching for an element with key 278-49-1515. We begin with the knowledge that the root node is assigned the number 10. Since the first digit of the search key is 2, we query our hash table for a pointer triple with key (10,2). The hash table search is successful and the triple (10,2,11) is retrieved. The *childNode* component of this triple is 11, and since all element nodes have a number 9 or less, the child node is determined to be a branch node. We make a move to the branch node 11. To move to the next level of the trie, we use the second digit 7 of the search key. For the move, we query the hash table for a pointer with key (11,7). Once again, the search is successful and the triple (11,7,13) is retrieved. The next query to the hash table is for a triple with key (13,8). This time, we obtain the triple (13,8,2). Since, *childNode* = 2 < 10, we know that the pointer gets us to an element node. So, we compare the search key with the key of *element* [2]. The keys match, and we have found the element we were looking for.

When searching for an element with key 322-16-8976, the first query is for a triple with key (10,3). The hash table has no triple with this key, and we conclude that the trie has no element whose key equals the search key.

The space needed for each pointer triple is about the same as that needed for each node in the chain of nodes representation of a trie node. Therefore, if we use a linear open addressed hash table with a loading density of α, the hash table scheme will take approximately $(1/\alpha-1)*100\%$ more space than required by the chain of nodes scheme. However, when the hash table scheme is used, we can retrieve a pointer in $O(1)$ expected time, whereas the time to retrieve a pointer using the chain of nodes scheme is $O(r)$. When the (balanced) binary search tree or binary trie schemes are used, it takes $O(\log r)$ time to retrieve a pointer. For large radixes, the hash table scheme provides significant space saving over the scheme of Figure 12.9 and results in a small constant factor degradation in the expected time required to perform a search.

The hash table scheme actually reduces the expected time to insert elements into a trie, because when the node structure of Figure 12.9 is used, we must spend $O(r)$ time to initialize each new branch node (see the description of the insert operation below). However, when a hash table is used, the insertion time is independent of the trie radix.

To support the removal of elements from a trie represented as a hash table, we must be able to reuse element nodes. This reuse is accomplished by setting up an available space list of element nodes that are currently not in use.

12.3.9   Prefix Search and Applications

You have probably realized that to search a trie we do not need the entire key. Most of the time, only the first few digits (i.e., a prefix) of the key is needed. For example, our search of the trie of Figure 12.9 for an element with key 951-23-7625 used only the first four digits of the key. The ability to search a trie using only the prefix of a key enables us to use tries in applications where only the prefix might be known or where we might desire the user to provide only a prefix. Some of these applications are described below.

Criminology: Suppose that you are at the scene of a crime and observe the first few characters *CRX* on the registration plate of the getaway car. If we have a trie of registration numbers, we can use the characters *CRX* to reach a subtrie that contains all registration numbers that begin with *CRX*. The elements in this subtrie can then be examined to see which cars satisfy other properties that might have been observed.

Automatic Command Completion: When using an operating system such as Unix or Windows (command prompt), we type in system commands to accomplish certain tasks. For example, the Unix and DOS command *cd* may be used to change the current directory. Figure 12.18 gives a list of commands that have the prefix *ps* (this list was obtained by executing the command *ls /usr/local/bin/ps** on a Unix system).

ps2ascii	ps2pdf	psbook	psmandup	psselect
ps2epsi	ps2pk	pscal	psmerge	pstopnm
ps2frag	ps2ps	psidtopgm	psnup	pstops
ps2gif	psbb	pslatex	psresize	pstruct

Figure 12.18: Commands that begin with "ps"

We can simplify the task of typing in commands by providing a command completion facility which automatically types in the command suffix once the user has typed in a long enough prefix to uniquely identify the command. For instance, once the letters *psi* have been entered, we know that the command must be *psidtopgm* because there is only one command that has the prefix *psi*. In this case, we replace the need to type in a 9 character command name by the need to type in just the first 3 characters of the command!

A command completion system is easily implemented when the commands are stored in a trie using ASCII characters as the digits. As the user types the command digits from left to right, we move down the trie. The command may be completed as soon as we reach an element node. If we fall off the trie in the process, the user can be informed that no command with the typed prefix exists.

Although we have described command completion in the context of operating system commands, the facilty is useful in other environments:

(1) A web browser keeps a history of the URLs of sites that you have visited. By organizing this history as a trie, the user need only type the prefix of a previously used URL and the browser can complete the URL.

(2) A word processor can maintain a collection of words and can complete words as you type the text. Words can be completed as soon as you have typed a long enough prefix to identify the word uniquely.

(3)   An automatic phone dialler can maintain a list of frequently called telephone numbers as a trie. Once you have punched in a long enough prefix to uniquely identify the phone number, the dialler can complete the call for you.

12.3.10   Compressed Tries

Take a close look at the trie of Figure 12.9. This trie has a few branch nodes (nodes *B,D*, and *F*) that do not partition the elements in their subtrie into two or more nonempty groups. We often can improve both the time and space performance metrics of a trie by eliminating all branch nodes that have only one child. The resulting trie is called a *compressed trie*.

When branch nodes with a single child are removed from a trie, we need to keep additional information so that trie operations may be performed correctly. The additional information stored in three compressed trie structures is described below.

12.3.10.1   Compressed Tries with Digit Numbers

In a *compressed trie with digit numbers*, each branch node has an additional field *digitNumber* that tells us which digit of the key is used to branch at this node. Figure 12.19 shows the compressed trie with digit numbers that corresponds to the trie of Figure 12.9. The leftmost field of each branch node of Figure 12.19 is the *digitNumber* field.

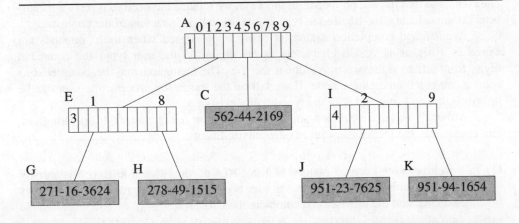

Figure 12.19: Compressed trie with digit numbers

12.3.10.2   Searching a Compressed Trie with Digit Numbers

A compressed trie with digit numbers may be searched by following a path from the root. At each branch node, the digit, of the search key, given in the branch node's *digitNumber* field is used to determine which subtrie to move to. For example, when searching the trie of Figure 12.19 for an element with key 951-23-7625, we start at the root of the trie. Since the root node is a branch node with *digitNumber* =1, we use the first digit 9 of the search key to determine which subtrie to move to. A move to node *A.child* [9]=*I* is made. Since, *I.digitNumber*=4, the fourth digit, 2, of the search key tells us which subtrie to move to. A move is now made to node *I.child* [2]=*J*. We are now at an element node, and the search key is compared with the key of the element in node *J*. Since the keys match, we have found the desired element.

Notice that a search for an element with key 913-23-7625 also terminates at node *J*. However, the search key and the element key at node *J* do not match and we conclude that the trie contains no element with key 913-23-7625.

12.3.10.3   Inserting into a Compressed Trie with Digit Numbers

To insert an element with key 987-26-1615 into the trie of Figure 12.19, we first search for an element with this key. The search ends at node *J*. Since, the search key and the key, 951-23-7625, of the element in this node do not match, we conclude that the trie has no element whose key matches the search key. To insert the new element, we find the first digit where the search key differs from the key in node *J* and create a branch node for this digit. Since, the first digit where the search key 987-26-1615 and the element key 951-23-7625 differ is the second digit, we create a branch node with *digitNumber*=2. Since, digit values increase as we go down the trie, the proper place to insert the new branch node can be determined by retracing the path from the root to node *J* and stopping as soon as either a node with digit value greater than 2 or the node *J* is reached. In the trie of Figure 12.19, this path retracing stops at node *I*. The new branch node is made the parent of node *I*, and we get the trie of Figure 12.20.

Consider inserting an element with key 958-36-4194 into the compressed trie of Figure 12.19. The search for an element with this key terminates when we fall of the trie by following the pointer *I.child* [3]=*NULL*. To complete the insertion, we must first find an element in the subtrie rooted at node *I*. This element is found by following a downward path from node *I* using (say) the first non **NULL** link in each branch node encountered. Doing this on the compressed trie of Figure 12.19, leads us to node *J*. Having reached an element node, we find the first digit where the element key and the search key differ and complete the insertion as in the previous example. Figure 12.21 shows the resulting compressed trie.

Because of the possible need to search for the first non **NULL** child pointer in each branch node, the time required to insert an element into a compressed tries with

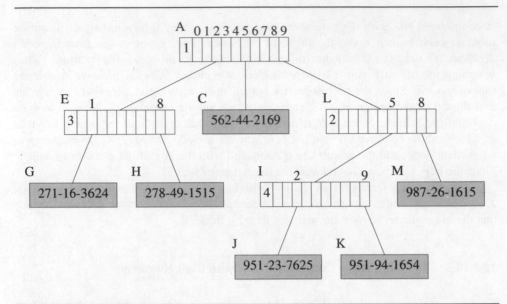

Figure 12.20: Compressed trie following the insertion of 987-26-1615 into the compressed trie of Figure 12.19

digit numbers is O(rd), where r is the trie radix and d is the maximum number of digits in any key.

12.3.10.4   Deleting an Element from a Compressed Trie with Digit Numbers

To delete an element whose key is k, we do the following:

(1)   Find the element node X that contains the element whose key is k.

(2)   Discard node X.

(3)   If the parent of X is left with only one child, discard the parent node also. When the parent of X is discarded, the sole remaining child of the parent of X becomes a child of the grandparent (if any) of X.

To remove the element with key 951-94-1654 from the compressed trie of Figure 12.21, we first locate the node K that contains the element that is to be removed. When this node is discarded, the parent I of K is left with only one child. Consequently, node I

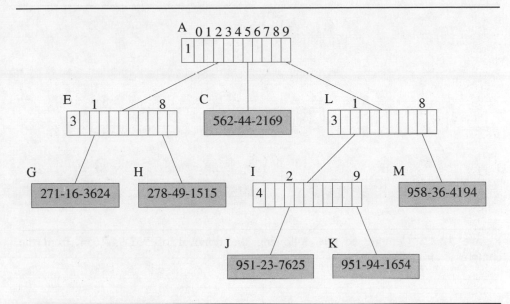

Figure 12.21: Compressed trie following the insertion of 958-36-4194 into the compressed trie of Figure 12.19

is also discarded, and the only remaining child *J* of node *I* is the made a child of the grandparent of *K*. Figure 12.22 shows the resulting compressed trie.

Because of the need to determine whether a branch node is left with two or more children, removing a d digit element from a radix r trie takes $O(d + r)$ time.

12.3.11 Compressed Tries with Skip Fields

In a *compressed trie with skip fields*, each branch node has an additional field *skip* which tells us the number of branch nodes that were originally between the current branch node and its parent. Figure 12.23 shows the compressed trie with skip fields that corresponds to the trie of Figure 12.9. The leftmost field of each branch node of Figure 12.23 is the skip field.

The algorithms to search, insert, and remove are very similar to those used for a compressed trie with digit numbers.

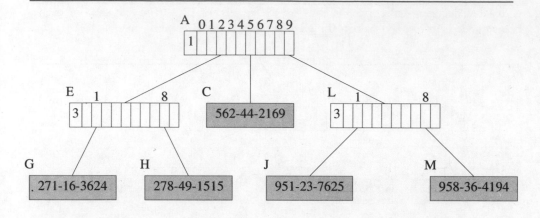

Figure 12.22: Compressed trie following the removal of 951-94-1654 from the compressed trie of Figure 12.21

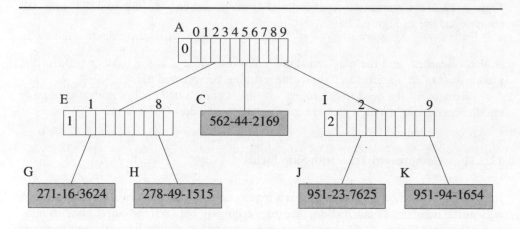

Figure 12.23: Compressed trie with skip fields

12.3.12 Compressed Tries with Labeled Edges

In a *compressed trie with labeled edges*, each branch node has the following additional information associated with it: a pointer/reference *element* to an element (or element node) in the subtrie, and an integer *skip* which equals the number of branch nodes eliminated between this branch node and its parent. Figure 12.24 shows the compressed trie with labeled edges that corresponds to the trie of Figure 12.9. The first field of each branch node is its *element* field, and the second field is the *skip* field.

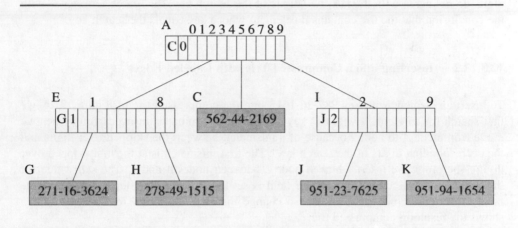

Figure 12.24: Compressed trie with labeled edges

Even though we store the "label" with branch nodes, it is convenient to think of this information as being associated with the edge that comes into the branch node from its parent (when the branch node is not the root). When moving down a trie, we follow edges, and when an edge is followed, we skip over the number of digits given by the *skip* field of the edge information. The value of the digits that are skipped over may be determined by using the *element* field.

When moving from node A to node I of the compressed trie of Figure 12.24, we use digit 1 of the key to determine which child field of A is to be used. Also, we skip over the next 2 digits, that is, digits 2 and 3, of the keys of the elements in the subtrie rooted at I. Since all elements in the subtrie I have the same value for the digits that are skipped over, we can determine the value of these skipped over digits from any of the elements in the subtrie. Using the *element* field of the edge label, we access the element node J, and determine that the digits that are skipped over are 5 and 1.

12.3.12.1 Searching a Compressed Trie with Labeled Edges

When searching a compressed trie with labeled edges, we can use the edge label to terminate unsuccessful searches (possibly) before we reach an element node or fall off the trie. As in the other compressed trie variants, the search is done by following a path from the root. Suppose we are searching the compressed trie of Figure 12.24 for an element with key 921-23-1234. Since the *skip* value for the root node is 0, we use the first digit 9 of the search key to determine which subtrie to move to. A move to node *A.child*[9]=*I* is made. By examining the edge label (stored in node *I*), we determine that, in making the move from node *A* to node *I*, the digits 5 and 1 are skipped. Since these digits do not agree with the next two digits of the search key, the search terminates with the conclusion that the trie contains no element whose key equals the search key.

12.3.12.2   Inserting into a Compressed Trie with Labeled Edges

To insert an element with key 987-26-1615 into the compressed trie of Figure 12.24, we first search for an element with this key. The search terminates unsuccessfully when we move from node *A* to node *I* because of a mismatch between the skipped over digits and the corresponding digits of the search key. The first mismatch is at the first skipped over digit. Therefore, we insert a branch node *L* between nodes *A* and *I*. The *skip* value for this branch node is 0, and its *element* field is set to reference the element node for the newly inserted element. We must also change the *skip* value of *I* to 1. Figure 12.25 shows the resulting compressed trie.

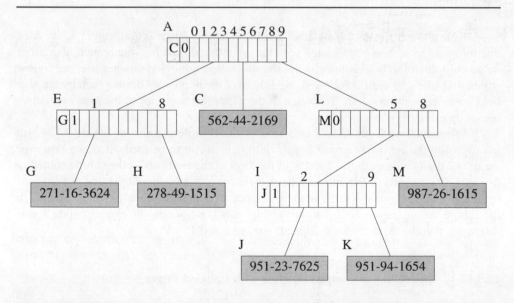

Figure 12.25: Compressed trie (with labeled edges) following the insertion of 987-26-1615 into the compressed trie of Figure 12.24

Suppose we are to insert an element with key 958-36-4194 into the compressed trie of Figure 12.25. The search for an element with this key terminates when we move to node *I* because of a mismatch between the digits that are skipped over and the corresponding digits of the search key. A new branch node is inserted between nodes *A* and *I* and we get the compressed trie that is shown in Figure 12.26.

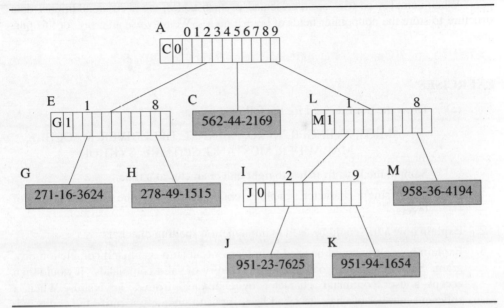

Figure 12.26: Compressed trie (with labeled edges) following the insertion of 958-36-4194 into the compressed trie of Figure 12.24

The time required to insert a d digit element into a radix r compressed trie with labeled edges is $O(r + d)$.

12.3.12.3   Deleting an Element from a Compressed Trie with Labeled Edges

This is similar to removal from a compressed trie with digit numbers except for the need to update the *element* fields of branch nodes whose *element* field references the removed element.

12.3.13 Space Required by a Compressed Trie

Since each branch node partitions the elements in its subtrie into two or more nonempty groups, an n element compressed trie has at most $n-1$ branch nodes. Therefore, the space required by each of the compressed trie variants described by us is $O(nr)$, where r is the trie radix.

When compressed tries are represented as hash tables, we need an additional data structure to store the nonpointer fields of branch nodes. We may use an array for this purpose.

EXERCISES

1. (a) Draw the trie obtained for the following data:

    AMIOT, AVENGER, AVRO, HEINKEL, HELLDIVER, MACCHI, MARAUDER, MUSTANG, SPITFIRE, SYKHOI

    Sample the keys from left to right one character at a time.

    (b) Using single-character sampling, obtain a trie with the fewest number of levels.

2. Explain how a trie could be used to implement a spelling checker.

3. Explain how a trie could be used to implement an auto-command completion program. Such a program would maintain a library of valid commands. It would then accept a user command, character by character, from a keyboard. When a sufficient number of characters had been input to uniquely identify the command, it would display the complete command on the computer monitor.

4. Write an algorithm to insert a key value x into a trie in which the keys are sampled from left to right, one character at a time.

5. Do Exercise 4 with the added assumption that the trie is to have no more than six levels. Synonyms are to be packed into the same element node.

6. Write an algorithm to delete x from a trie under the assumptions of Exercise 4. Assume that each branch node has a *count* data member equal to the number of element nodes in the subtrie for which it is the root.

7. Do Exercise 6 for the trie of Exercise 5.

8. In the trie of Figure 12.13 the nodes δ_1 and δ_2 each have only one child. Branch nodes with only one child may be eliminated from tries by maintaining a *skip* data member with each node. The value of this data member equals the number of characters to be skipped before obtaining the next character to be sampled. Thus, we can have *skip* $[\delta_3] = 2$ and delete the nodes δ_1 and δ_2. Write algorithms to search, insert, and delete from tries in which each branch node has a *skip* data

member.

9. Assume that the branch nodes of a compressed trie are represented using a hash table (one for each node). Each such hash table is augmented with a count and skip value as described above. Describe how this change to the node structure affects the time and space complexity of the trie data structure.

10. Do the previous exercise for the case when each branch node is represented by a chain in which each node has two data members: *pointer* and *link*, where *pointer* points to a subtrie and *link* points to the next node in the chain. The number of nodes in the chain for any branch node equals the number of non-0 pointers in that node. Each chain is augmented by a skip value. Draw the chain representation of the compressed version of the trie of Figure 12.6.

12.4   SUFFIX TREES

12.4.1   Have You Seen This String?

In the classical *substring search* problem, we are given a string S and a pattern P and are to report whether or not the pattern P occurs in the string S. For example, the pattern $P = cat$ appears (twice) in the string $S1 = $ *The big cat ate the small catfish.*, but does not appear in the string $S2 = $ *Dogs for sale.*.

Researchers in the human genome project, for example, are constantly searching for substrings/patterns (we use the terms substring and pattern interchangeably) in a gene databank that contains tens of thousands of genes. Each gene is represented as a sequence or string of letters drawn from the alphabet A, C, G, T. Although most of the strings in the databank are around 2000 letters long, some have tens of thousands of letters. Because of the size of the gene databank and the frequency with which substring searches are done, it is imperative that we have as fast an algorithm as possible to locate a given substring within the strings in the databank.

We can search for a pattern P in a string S using Program 2.16. The complexity of such a search is $O(|P| + |S|)$, where $|P|$ denotes the length (i.e., number of letters or digits) of P. This complexity looks pretty good when you consider that the pattern P could appear anywhere in the string S. Therefore, we must examine every letter/digit (we use the terms letter and digit interchangeably) of the string before we can conclude that the search pattern does not appear in the string. Further, before we can conclude that the search pattern appears in the string, we must examine every digit of the pattern. Hence, every pattern search algorithm must take time that is linear in the lengths of the pattern and the string being searched.

When classical pattern matching algorithms are used to search for several patterns $P_1, P_2, \cdots, P_k$ in the string S, $O(|P_1| + |P_2| + \cdots + |P_k| + k|S|)$ time is taken (because $O(|P_i| + |S|)$ time is taken to search for P_i). The suffix tree data structure that we are about to study reduces this complexity to $O(|P_1| + |P_2| + \cdots + |P_k| + |S|)$.

Of this time, O(|S|) time is spent setting up the suffix tree for the string S; an individual pattern search takes only O(|P_i|) time (after the suffix tree for S has been built). Therefore once the suffix tree for S has been created, the time needed to search for a pattern depends only on the length of the pattern.

12.4.2 The Suffix Tree Data Structure

The *suffix tree* for S is actually the compressed trie for the nonempty suffixes of the string S. Since a suffix tree is a compressed trie, we sometimes refer to the tree as a trie and to its subtrees as subtries.

The (nonempty) suffixes of the string S = *peeper* are *peeper*, *eeper*, *eper*, *per*, *er*, and *r*. Therefore, the suffix tree for the string *peeper* is the compressed trie that contains the elements (which are also the keys) *peeper*, *eeper*, *eper*, *per*, *er*, and *r*. The alphabet for the string *peeper* is *e,p,r*. Therefore, the radix of the compressed trie is 3. If necessary, we may use the mapping $e \rightarrow 0$, $p \rightarrow 1$, $r \rightarrow 2$, to convert from the letters of the string to numbers. This conversion is necessary only when we use a node structure in which each node has an array of child pointers. Figure 12.27 shows the compressed trie (with labeled edges) for the suffixes of *peeper*. This compressed trie is also the suffix tree for the string *peeper*.

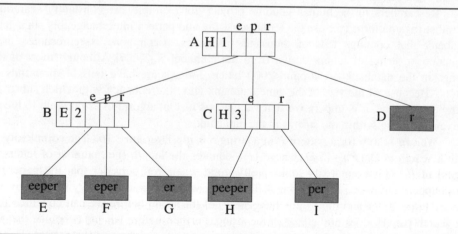

Figure 12.27: Compressed trie for the suffixes of *peeper*

Since the data in the element nodes $D-I$ are the suffixes of *peeper*, each element node need retain only the start index of the suffix it contains. When the letters in *peeper* are indexed from left to right beginning with the index 1, the element nodes $D-I$ need only retain the indexes 6, 2, 3, 5, 1, and 4, respectively. Using the index stored in an element node, we can access the suffix from the string S. Figure 12.28 shows the suffix tree of Figure 12.27 with each element node containing a suffix index.

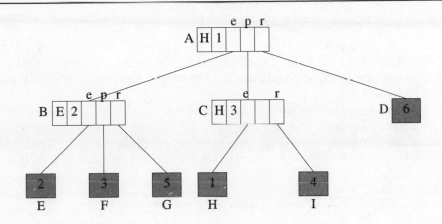

Figure 12.28: Modified compressed trie for the suffixes of *peeper*

The first component of each branch node is a reference to an element in that subtrie. We may replace the element reference by the index of the first digit of the referenced element. Figure 12.29 shows the resulting compressed trie. We shall use this modified form as the representation for the suffix tree.

When describing the search and construction algorithms for suffix trees, it is easier to deal with a drawing of the suffix tree in which the edges are labeled by the digits used in the move from a branch node to a child node. The first digit of the label is the digit used to determine which child is moved to, and the remaining digits of the label give the digits that are skipped over. Figure 12.30 shows the suffix tree of Figure 12.29 drawn in this manner.

In the more humane drawing of a suffix tree, the labels on the edges on any root to element node path spell out the suffix represented by that element node. When the digit number for the root is not 1, the humane drawing of a suffix tree includes a header node

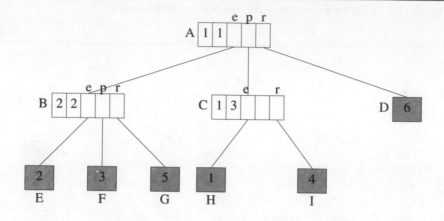

Figure 12.29: Suffix tree for *peeper*

with an edge to the former root. This edge is labeled with the digits that are skipped over.

The string *represented* by a node of a suffix tree is the string formed by the labels on the path from the root to that node. Node *A* of Figure 12.30 represents the empty string ε, node *C* represents the string *pe*, and node *F* represents the string *eper*.

Since the keys in a suffix tree are of different length, we must ensure that no key is a proper prefix of another. Whenever the last digit of string *S* appears only once in *S*, no suffix of *S* can be a proper prefix of another suffix of *S*. In the string *peeper*, the last digit is *r*, and this digit appears only once. Therefore, no suffix of *peeper* is a proper prefix of another. The last digit of *data* is *a*, and this last digit appears twice in *data*. Therefore, *data* has two suffixes *ata* and *a* that begin with *a*. The suffix *a* is a proper prefix of the suffix *ata*.

When the last digit of the string *S* appears more than once in *S* we must append a new digit (say #) to the suffixes of *S* so that no suffix is a prefix of another. Optionally, we may append the new digit to *S* to get the string *S#*, and then construct the suffix tree for *S#*. When this optional route is taken, the suffix tree has one more suffix (#) than the suffix tree obtained by appending the symbol # to the suffixes of *S*.

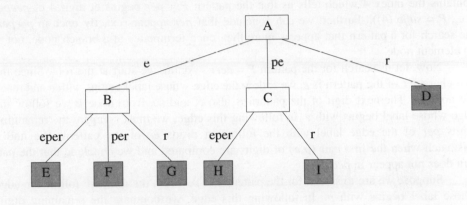

Figure 12.30 A more humane drawing of a suffix tree

12.4.3   Let's Find That Substring (Searching a Suffix Tree)

But First, Some Terminology

Let $n = |S|$ denote the length (i.e., number of digits) of the string whose suffix tree we are to build. We number the digits of S from left to right beginning with the number 1. $S[i]$ denotes the ith digit of S, and $suffix(i)$ denotes the suffix $S[i] \cdots S[n]$ that begins at digit i, $1 \le i \le n$.

On With the Search

A fundamental observation used when searching for a pattern P in a string S is that P appears in S (i.e., P is a substring of S) iff P is a prefix of some suffix of S.

Suppose that $P = P[1] \cdots P[k] = S[i] \cdots S[i+k-1]$. Then, P is a prefix of $suffix(i)$. Since $suffix(i)$ is in our compressed trie (i.e., suffix tree), we can search for P by using the strategy to search for a key prefix in a compressed trie.

Let's search for the pattern $P = per$ in the string $S = peeper$. Imagine that we have already constructed the suffix tree (Figure 12.30) for *peeper*. The search starts at the root node A. Since $P[1] = p$, we follow the edge whose label begins with the digit p. When following this edge, we compare the remaining digits of the edge label with successive digits of P. Since these remaining label digits agree with the pattern digits, we reach the branch node C. In getting to node C, we have used the first two digits of the pattern. The third digit of the pattern is r, and so, from node C we follow the edge whose label begins with r. Since this edge has no additional digits in its label, no additional digit comparisons are done and we reach the element node I. At this time, the digits in the pattern have been exhausted and we conclude that the pattern is in the string. Since an element node is reached, we conclude that the pattern is actually a suffix of the string *peeper*. In the actual suffix tree representation (rather than in the humane drawing), the element node I contains the index 4 which tells us that the pattern $P = per$ begins at digit 4 of *peeper* (i.e., $P = suffix(4)$). Further, we can conclude that *per* appears exactly once in *peeper*; the search for a pattern that appears more than once terminates at a branch node, not at an element node.

Now, let us search for the pattern $P = eeee$. Again, we start at the root. Since the first character of the pattern is e, we follow the edge whose label begins with e and reach the node B. The next digit of the pattern is also e, and so, from node B we follow the edge whose label begins with e. In following this edge, we must compare the remaining digits *per* of the edge label with the following digits *ee* of the pattern. We find a mismatch when the first pair (p,e) of digits are compared and we conclude that the pattern does not appear in *peeper*.

Suppose we are to search for the pattern $P = p$. From the root, we follow the edge whose label begins with p. In following this edge, we compare the remaining digits (only the digit e remains) of the edge label with the following digits (there aren't any) of the pattern. Since the pattern is exhausted while following this edge, we conclude that the pattern is a prefix of all keys in the subtrie rooted at node C. We can find all occurrences of the pattern by traversing the subtrie rooted at C and visiting the information nodes in this subtrie. If we want the location of just one of the occurrences of the pattern, we can use the index stored in the first component of the branch node C (see Figure 12.29). When a pattern exhausts while following the edge to node X, we say that node X has been reached; the search terminates at node X.

When searching for the pattern $P = rope$, we use the first digit r of P and reach the element node D. Since the the pattern has not been exhausted, we must check the remaining digits of the pattern against those of the key in D. This check reveals that the pattern is not a prefix of the key in D, and so the pattern does not appear in *peeper*.

The last search we are going to do is for the pattern $P = pepe$. Starting at the root of Figure 12.30, we move over the edge whose label begins with p and reach node C. The next unexamined digit of the search pattern is p. So, from node C, we wish to follow the edge whose label begins with p. Since no edge satisfies this requirement, we conclude that *pepe* does not appear in the string *peeper*.

12.4.4 Other Nifty Things You Can Do with a Suffix Tree

Once we have set up the suffix tree for a string S, we can tell whether or not S contains a pattern P in $O(|P|)$ time. This means that if we have a suffix tree for the text of Shakespeare's play "Romeo and Juliet," we can determine whether or not the phrase *wherefore art thou* appears in this play with lightning speed. In fact, the time taken will be that needed to compare up to 18 (the length of the search pattern) letters/digits. The search time is independent of the length of the play.

Some other interesting things you can do at lightning speed are described below.

Find all occurrences of a pattern *P.*

This is done by searching the suffix tree for *P*. If *P* appears at least once, the search terminates successfully either at an element node or at a branch node. When the search terminates at an element node, the pattern occurs exactly once. When we terminate at a branch node *X*, all places where the pattern occurs can be found by visiting the element nodes in the subtrie rooted at *X*. This visiting can be done in time linear in the number of occurrences of the pattern if we

(a)   Link all of the element nodes in the suffix tree into a chain, the linking is done in lexicographic order of the represented suffixes (which also is the order in which the element nodes are encountered in a left to right scan of the element nodes). The element nodes of Figure 12.30 will be linked in the order *E,F,G,H,I,D.*

(b)   In each branch node, keep a reference to the first and last element node in the subtrie of which that branch node is the root. In Figure 12.30, nodes *A, B*, and *C* keep the pairs (E,D), (E,G), and (H,I), respectively. We use the pair (*firstInformationNode,lastInformationNode*) to traverse the element node chain starting at *firstInformationNode* and ending at *lastInformationNode*. This traversal yields all occurrences of patterns that begin with the string spelled by the edge labels   from   the   root   to   the   branch   node.   Notice   that   when (*firstInformationNode,lastInformationNode*) pairs are kept in branch nodes, we can eliminate the branch node field that keeps a reference to an element node in the subtrie (i.e., the field *element*).

Find all strings that contain a pattern *P.*

Suppose we have a collection $S1, S2, \quad , Sk$ of strings and we wish to report all strings that contain a query pattern *P*. For example, the genome databank contains tens of thousands of strings, and when a researcher submits a query string, we are to report all databank strings that contain the query string. To answer queries of this type efficiently, we set up a compressed trie (we may call this a *multiple string suffix tree*) that contains the suffixes of the string $S1\$S2\$...\$Sk\#$, where $\$$ and $\#$ are two different digits that do not appear in any of the strings $S1, S2, \cdots, Sk$. In each node of the suffix tree, we keep a list of all strings *Si* that are the start point of a suffix represented by an element node in that subtrie.

Find the longest substring of *S* **that appears at least** $m>1$ **times.**

This query can be answered in $O(|S|)$ time in the following way:

(a)   Traverse the suffix tree labeling the branch nodes with the sum of the label lengths from the root and also with the number of information nodes in the subtrie.

(b)   Traverse the suffix tree visiting branch nodes with element node count $\geq m$.

Determine the visited branch node with longest label length.

Note that step (a) needs to be done only once. Following this, we can do step (b) for as many values of m as is desired. Also, note that when $m = 2$ we can avoid determining the number of element nodes in subtries. In a compressed trie, every subtrie rooted at a branch node has at least two element nodes in it.

Find the longest common substring of the strings S and T.
This can be done in time $O(|S| + |T|)$ as below:

(a) Construct a multiple string suffix tree for S and T (i.e., the suffix tree for $S\$T\#$).

(b) Traverse the suffix tree to identify the branch node for which the sum of the label lengths on the path from the root is maximum and whose subtrie has at least one information node that represents a suffix that begins in S and at least one information node that represents a suffix that begins in T.

EXERCISES

1. Draw the suffix tree for $S = ababab\#$.
2. Draw the suffix tree for $S = aaaaaa\#$.
3. Draw the multiple string suffix tree for $S1 = abba$, $S2 = bbbb$, and $S3 = aaaa$.

12.5 TRIES AND INTERNET PACKET FORWARDING

12.5.1 IP Routing

In the Internet, data packets are transported from source to destination by a series of routers. For example, a packet that originates in New York and is destined for Los Angeles will first be processed by a router in New York. This router may forward the packet to a router in Chicago, which, in turn, may foward the packet to a router in Denver. Finally, the router in Denver may forward the packet to Los Angeles. Each router moves a packet one step closer to its destination. A router does this by examining the destination address in the header of the packet to be routed. Using this destination address and a collection of forwarding rules stored in the router, the router decides where to send the packet next.

An Internet router table is a collection of rules of the form (P, NH), where where P is a prefix and NH is the next hop; NH is the next hop for packets whose destination address has the prefix P. For example, the rule $(01^*, a)$ states that the next hop for packets whose destination address (in binary) begins with 01 is a. In IPv4 (Internet Protocol version 4), destination addresses are 32 bits long. So, P may be up to 32 bits long. In IPv6, destination addresses are 128 bits long and so, P may be up to 128 bits in length.

It is not uncommon for a destination address to be matched by more than 1 rule in a commercial router table. In this case, the next hop is determined by the matching rule that has the longest prefix. So, for example, suppose that $(01*,a)$ and $(0100*,b)$ are the only two rules in our router table that match a packet whose destination address begins with the bit sequence 0100. The next hop for this packet is b. In other words, packet forwarding in the Internet is done by determining the longest matching-prefix.

Although Internet router tables are dynamic in practice (i.e., the rule set changes in time; rules are added and deleted as routers come online and go offline), data structures for Internet router tables often are optimized for the search operation—given a destination address, determine the next hop for the longest matching-prefix.

12.5.2   1-Bit Tries

A *1-bit trie* is very similar to a binary trie. It is a tree-like structure in which each node has a left child, left data, right child, and right data field. Nodes at level l of the trie store prefixes whose length is l. If the rightmost bit in a prefix whose length is l is 0, the prefix is stored in the left data field of a node that is at level l; otherwise, the prefix is stored in the right data field of a node that is at level l. At level i of a trie, branching is done by examining bit i (bits are numbered from left to right beginning with the number 1) of a prefix or destination address. When bit i is 0, we move into the left subtree; when the bit is 1, we move into the right subtree. Figure 12.31(a) gives a set of 8 prefixes, and Figure 12.31(b) shows the corresponding 1-bit trie. The height of a 1-bit trie is $O(W)$, where W is the length of the longest prefix in the router table. Note that $W \leq 32$ for IPv4 tables and $W \leq 128$ for IPv6 tables. Note also that there is no place, in a 1-bit trie, to store the prefix $*$ whose length is zero. This doesn't lead to any difficulty as this prefix matches every destination address. In case a search of a 1-bit trie fails to find a matching prefix, the next-hop associated with $*$ is used.

For any destination address d, all prefixes that match d lie on the search path determined by the bits of d. By following this search path, we may determine the longest matching-prefix in $O(W)$ time. Further, prefixes may be inserted/deleted in $O(W)$ time. The memory required by a 1-bit trie is $O(nW)$, where n is the number of rules in the router table.

Although the algorithms to search, insert and delete using a 1-bit trie are simple and of seemingly low complexity, $O(W)$, the demands of the Internet make the 1-bit trie impractical. Using trie-like structures, most of the time spent searching for the next hop goes to memory accesses. Hence, when analyzing the complexity of trie data structures for router tables, we focus on the number of memory accesses. When a 1-bit trie is used, it may take us up to W memory accesses to determine the next hop for a packet. Recall that $W \leq 32$ for IPv4 and $W \leq 128$ for IPv6. To keep the Internet operating smoothly, it

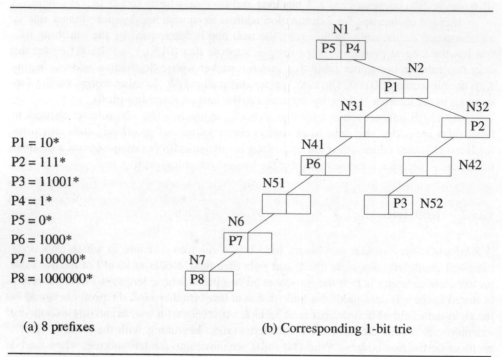

P1 = 10*
P2 = 111*
P3 = 11001*
P4 = 1*
P5 = 0*
P6 = 1000*
P7 = 100000*
P8 = 1000000*

(a) 8 prefixes   (b) Corresponding 1-bit trie

Figure 12.31: Prefixes and corresponding 1-bit trie

is necessary that the next hop for each packet be determined using far fewer memory accesses than W. In practice, we must determine the next hop using at most (say) 6 memory accesses.

12.5.3   Fixed-Stride Tries

Since the trie of Figure 12.31(b) has a height of 7, a search into this trie may make up to 7 memory accesses, one access for each node on the path from the root to a node at level 7 of the trie. The total memory required for the 1-bit trie of Figure 12.31(b) is 20 units (each node requires 2 units, one for each pair of (child, data) fields). We may reduce the height of the router-table trie at the expense of increased memory requirement by increasing the branching factor at each node, that is, we use a multiway trie. The *stride* of a node is defined to be the number of bits used at that node to determine which branch to take. A node whose stride is s has 2^s child fields (corresponding to the 2^s possible values for the s bits that are used) and 2^s data fields. Such a node requires 2^s memory units. In a *fixed-stride trie* (FST), all nodes at the same level have the same stride; nodes at different levels may have different strides.

Suppose we wish to represent the prefixes of Figure 12.31(a) using an FST that has three levels. Assume that the strides are 2, 3, and 2. The root of the trie stores prefixes whose length is 2; the level two nodes store prefixes whose length is 5 (2 + 3); and level three nodes store prefixes whose length is 7 (2 + 3 + 2). This poses a problem for the prefixes of our example, because the length of some of these prefixes is different from the storeable lengths. For instance, the length of P5 is 1. To get around this problem, a prefix with a nonpermissible length is expanded to the next permissible length. For example, P5 = 0* is expanded to P5a = 00* and P5b = 01*. If one of the newly created prefixes is a duplicate, natural dominance rules are used to eliminate all but one occurrence of the prefix. For instance, P4 = 1* is expanded to P4a = 10* and P4b = 11*. However, P1 = 10* is to be chosen over P4a = 10*, because P1 is a longer match than P4. So, P4a is eliminated. Because of the elimination of duplicate prefixes from the expanded prefix set, all prefixes are distinct. Figure 12.32(a) shows the prefixes that result when we expand the prefixes of Figure 12.31 to lengths 2, 5, and 7. Figure 12.32(b) shows the corresponding FST whose height is 3 and whose strides are 2, 3, and 2.

Since the trie of Figure 12.32(b) can be searched with at most 3 memory accesses, it represents a time performance improvement over the 1-bit trie of Figure 12.31(b), which requires up to 7 memory references to perform a search. However, the space requirements of the FST of Figure 12.32(b) are more than that of the corresponding 1-bit trie. For the root of the FST, we need 8 fields or 4 units; the two level 2 nodes require 8 units each; and the level 3 node requires 4 units. The total is 24 memory units.

We may represent the prefixes of Figure 12.31(a) using a one-level trie whose root has a stride of 7. Using such a trie, searches could be performed making a single memory access. However, the one-level trie would require $2^7 = 128$ memory units.

In the *fixed-stride trie optimization* (FSTO) problem, we are given a set P of prefixes and an integer k. We are to select the strides for a k-level FST in such a manner that the k-level FST for the given prefixes uses the smallest amount of memory.

For some P, a k-level FST may actually require more space than a $(k-1)$-level FST. For example, when $P = \{00^*, 01^*, 10^*, 11^*\}$, the unique 1-level FST for P requires 4 memory units while the unique 2-level FST (which is actually the 1-bit trie for P) requires 6 memory units. Since the search time for a $(k-1)$-level FST is less than that for a k-level tree, we would actually prefer $(k-1)$-level FSTs that take less (or even equal) memory over k-level FSTs. Therefore, in practice, we are really interested in determining the best FST that uses at most k levels (rather than exactly k levels). The *modified MSTO* problem (MFSTO) is to determine the best FST that uses at most k levels for the given prefix set P.

Let O be the 1-bit trie for the given set of prefixes, and let F be any k-level FST for this prefix set. Let $s_1, \cdots, s_k$ be the strides for F. We shall say that level j, $1 \le j \le k$, of F covers levels $a, \cdots, b$ of O, where $a = \sum_{1}^{j-1} s_q + 1$ and $b = \sum_{1}^{j} s_q$. So, level 1 of the FST of

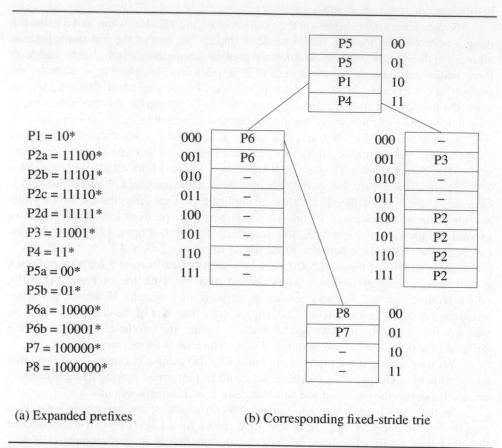

P1 = 10*	000		
P2a = 11100*	001		
P2b = 11101*	010		
P2c = 11110*	011		
P2d = 11111*	100		
P3 = 11001*	101		
P4 = 11*	110		
P5a = 00*	111		
P5b = 01*			
P6a = 10000*			
P6b = 10001*			
P7 = 100000*			
P8 = 1000000*			

(a) Expanded prefixes   (b) Corresponding fixed-stride trie

Figure 12.32: Prefix expansion and fixed-stride trie

Figure 12.32(b) covers levels 1 and 2 of the 1-bit trie of Figure 12.31(b). Level 2 of this FST covers levels 3, 4, and 5 of the 1-bit trie of Figure 12.31(b); and level 3 of this FST covers levels 6 and 7 of the 1-bit trie. We shall refer to levels $e_u = \sum_1^u s_q$, $1 \leq u \leq k$ as the *expansion levels* of O. The expansion levels defined by the FST of Figure 12.32(b) are 1, 3, and 6.

Let *nodes* (i) be the number of nodes at level i of the 1-bit trie O. For the 1-bit trie of Figure 12.31(a), *nodes* $(1:7) = [1,1,2,2,2,1,1]$. The memory required by F is $\sum_1^k nodes\,(e_q)*2^{s_q}$. For example, the memory required by the FST of Figure 12.32(b) is $nodes\,(1)*2^2 + nodes\,(3)*2^3 + nodes\,(6)*2^2 = 24$.

Let $T(j,r)$ be the best (i.e., uses least memory) FST that uses *at most* r expansion levels and covers levels 1 through j of the 1-bit trie O. Let $C(j,r)$ be the cost (i.e., memory requirement) of $T(j,r)$. So, $T(W,k)$ is the best FST for O that uses at most k expansion levels and $C(W,k)$ is the cost of this FST. We observe that the last expansion level in $T(j,r)$ covers levels $m + 1$ through j of O for some m in the range 0 through $j - 1$ and the remaining levels of this best FST define $T(m,r-1)$. So,

$$C(j,r) = \min_{0 \le m < j} \{C(m,r-1) + nodes(m+1)*2^{j-m+1}\}, j \ge 1, r > 1 \qquad (12.1)$$

$$C(0,r) = 0 \text{ and } C(j,1) = 2^j, j \ge 1 \qquad (12.2)$$

Let $M(j,r)$, $r > 1$, be the smallest m that minimizes

$$C(m,r-1) + nodes(m+1)*2^{j-m+1},$$

in Eq. 12.1. Eqs. 12.1 and 12.2 result in an algorithm to compute $C(W,k)$ in $O(kW^2)$. The $M(j,r)$s may be computed in the same amount of time while we are computing the $C(j,r)$s. Using the computed M values, the strides for the optimal FST that uses at most k expansion levels may be determined in an additional $O(k)$ time.

12.5.4 Variable-Stride Tries

In a *variable-stride trie* (VST) nodes at the same level may have different strides. Figure 12.33 shows a two-level VST for the 1-bit trie of Figure 12.31. The stride for the root is 2; that for the left child of the root is 5; and that for the root's right child is 3. The memory required by this VST is 4 (root) + 32 (left child of root) + 8 (right child of root) = 44.

Since FSTs are a special case of VSTs, the memory required by the best VST for a given prefix set P and number of expansion levels k is less than or equal to that required by the best FST for P and k.

Let r-VST be a VST that has at most r levels. Let $Opt(N,r)$ be the cost (i.e., memory requirement) of the best r-VST for a 1-bit trie whose root is N. The root of this best VST covers levels 1 through s of O for some s in the range 1 through $height(N)$ and the subtries of this root must be best $(r-1)$-VSTs for the descendents of N that are at level $s + 1$ of the subtree rooted at N. So,

$$Opt(N,r) = \min_{1 \le s \le height(N)} \{2^s + \sum_{M \in D_{s+1}(N)} Opt(M,r-1)\}, r > 1 \qquad (12.3)$$

where $D_s(N)$ is the set of all descendents of N that are at level s of N. For example,

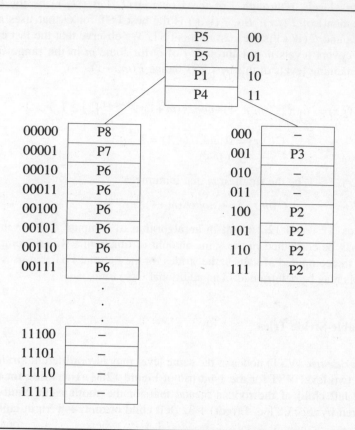

Figure 12.33: Two-level VST for prefixes of Figure 12.31(a)

$D_2(N)$ is the set of children of N and $D_3(N)$ is the set of grandchildren of N. *height* (N) is the maximum level at which the trie rooted at N has a node. For example, in Figure 12.31(b), the height of the trie rooted at N1 is 7. When $r=1$,

$$Opt(N, 1) = 2^{height(N)}. \tag{12.4}$$

Let

$$Opt(N, s, r) = \sum_{M \in D_s(N)} Opt(M, r), \; s > 1, \; r > 1,$$

and let $Opt(N, 1, r) = Opt(N, r)$. From Eqs. 12.3 and 12.4, it follows that:

$$Opt\,(N,1,r) = \min_{1\le s\le height\,(N)} \{2^s + Opt\,(N,s+1,r-1)\},\ r>1 \tag{12.5}$$

and

$$Opt\,(N,1,1) = 2^{height\,(N)}. \tag{12.6}$$

For $s>1$ and $r>1$, we get

$$Opt\,(N,s,r) = \sum_{M\in D_s(N)} Opt\,(M,r)$$

$$= Opt\,(LeftChild\,(N),s-1,r)$$

$$+\ Opt\,(RightChild\,(N),s-1,r). \tag{12.7}$$

For Eq. 12.7, we need the following initial condition:

$$Opt\,(null,*,*) = 0 \tag{12.8}$$

For an n-rule router table, the 1-bit trie O has $O(nW)$ nodes. So, the number of $Opt\,(*,*,*)$ values is $O(nW^2k)$. Each $Opt\,(*,s,*)$, $s>1$, value may be computed in $O(1)$ time using Eqs. 12.7 and 12.8 provided the Opt values are computed in postorder. The $Opt\,(*,1,*)$ values may then be computed in $O(W)$ time each using Eqs. 12.5 and 12.6. Therefore, we may compute $Opt\,(R,k) = Opt\,(R,1,k)$, where R is the root of O, in $O(nW^2k)$ time. If we keep track of the s that minimizes the right side of Eq. 12.5 for each pair (N,r), we can determine the strides of all nodes in the optimal k-VST is an additional $O(nW)$ time.

EXERCISES

1. (a) Write a C function to compute $C(j,r)$ for $0\le j\le W$ and $1\le r\le k$ using Eqs. 12.1 and 12.2. Your function should compute $M(j,r)$ as well. The complexity of your function should be $O(kW^2)$. Show that this is the case.

   (b) Write a C function that determines the strides of all levels in the best FST that has at most k levels. Your function should use the M values computed in part (a). The complexity of your function should be $O(k)$. Show that this is the case.

2. (a) Write a C function to compute $Opt(N,s,r)$ for $1 \le s \le W$, $1 \le r \le k$ and all nodes N of the 1-bit trie O. You should use Eqs. 12.5 through 12.8. Your function should compute $S(N,r)$, which is the s value that minimizes the right side of Eq. 12.5, as well. The complexity of your function should be $O(nW^2k)$, where n is the number of rules in the router table. Show that this is the case.

(b) Write a C function that determines the strides of all nodes in the best k-VST for O. Your function should use the S values computed in part (a). The complexity of your function should be $O(nW)$. Show that this is the case.

12.6 REFERENCES AND SELECTED READINGS

Digital search trees were first proposed by E. Coffman and J. Eve in *CACM*, 13, 1970, pp. 427-432. The structure Patricia was developed by D. Morrison. Digital search trees, tries, and Patricia are analyzed in the book *The Art of Computer Programming: Sorting and Searching*, Second Edition, by D. Knuth, Addison-Wesley, Reading, MA, 1998.

You can learn more about the genome project and genomic applications of pattern matching from the following Web sites: http://www.nhgri.nih.gov/HGP/ (NIH's Web site for the human genome project); http://www.ornl.gov/TechResources/Human_Genome/home.html (Department of Energy's Web site for the human genomics project); and http://merlin.mbcr.bcm.tmc.edu:8001/bcd/Curric/welcome.html; (Biocomputing Hypertext Coursebook).

Linear time algorithms to search for a single pattern in a given string can be found in most algorithm's texts. See, for example, the texts: *Computer Algorithms*, by E. Horowitz, S. Sahni, and S. Rajasekeran, Computer Science Press, New York, 1998 and *Introduction to Algorithms*, Second Edition, by T. Cormen, C. Leiserson, R. Rivest and C. Stein, McGraw-Hill Book Company, New York, 2002.

For more on suffix tree construction, see the papers: "A space economical suffix tree construction algorithm," by E. McCreight, *Journal of the ACM*, 23, 2, 1976, 262-272; "Fast string searching with suffix trees," by M. Nelson, *Dr. Dobb's Journal*, August 1996. and "Suffix trees and suffix arrays," by S. Aluru, in *Handbook of data structures and applications*, D. Mehta and S. Sahni, editors, Chapman & Hall/CRC, 2005.

You can download code to construct a suffix tree from http://www.ddj.com/ftp/1996/1996.08/suffix.zip.

The use of fixed- and variable-stride tries for IP router tables was first proposed in the paper "Faster IP lookups using controlled prefix expansion," by V. Srinivasan and G. Varghese, *ACM Transactions on Computer Systems*, Feb., 1999. Our dynamic programming formulations for fixed- and variable-stride tries are from "Efficient construction of multibit tries for IP lookup," by S. Sahni and K. Kim, *IEEE/ACM Transactions on Networking*, 2003. For more on data structures for IP router tables and packet classification, see "IP router tables," by S. Sahni, K. Kim and H. Lu and "Multi-dimensional packet classification," by P. Gupta, in *Handbook of data structures and applications*, D. Mehta and S. Sahni, editors, Chapman & Hall/CRC, 2005.

INDEX